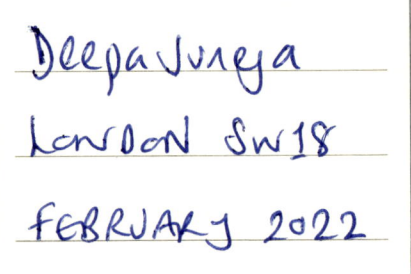

Deepa Juneja
London SW18
FEBRUARY 2022

The Law of Hedge Funds: A Global Perspective

While every care has been taken to ensure the accuracy of this work, no responsibility for loss or damage occasioned to any person acting or refraining from action as a result of any statement in it can be accepted by the authors, editors or publishers.

The Law of Hedge Funds:
A Global Perspective

Second Edition

Dale Gabbert
Partner, Simmons & Simmons

Andrew Wylie
Partner and Head of Investment Funds, DLA Piper

Members of the LexisNexis Group worldwide

United Kingdom	RELX (UK) Limited, trading as LexisNexis, 1-3 Strand, London WC2N 5JR
Australia	Reed International Books Australia Pty Ltd trading as LexisNexis, Chatswood, New South Wales
Austria	LexisNexis Verlag ARD Orac GmbH & Co KG, Vienna
Benelux	LexisNexis Benelux, Amsterdam
Canada	LexisNexis Canada, Markham, Ontario
China	LexisNexis China, Beijing and Shanghai
France	LexisNexis SA, Paris
Germany	LexisNexis GmbH, Dusseldorf
Hong Kong	LexisNexis Hong Kong, Hong Kong
India	LexisNexis India, New Delhi
Italy	Giuffrè Editore, Milan
Japan	LexisNexis Japan, Tokyo
Malaysia	Malayan Law Journal Sdn Bhd, Kuala Lumpur
New Zealand	LexisNexis New Zealand Ltd, Wellington
Poland	Wydawnictwo Prawnicze LexisNexis Sp, Warsaw
Singapore	LexisNexis Singapore, Singapore
South Africa	LexisNexis, Durban
USA	LexisNexis, Dayton, Ohio

© 2018 RELX (UK) Limited

Published by LexisNexis

All rights reserved. No part of this publication may be reproduced in any material form (including photocopying or storing it in any medium by electronic means and whether or not transiently or incidentally to some other use of this publication) without the written permission of the copyright owner except in accordance with the provisions of the Copyright, Designs and Patents Act 1988 or under the terms of a licence issued by the Copyright Licensing Agency Ltd, Saffron House, 6–10 Kirby Street, London EC1N 8TS. Applications for the copyright owner's written permission to reproduce any part of this publication should be addressed to the publisher.

Warning: The doing of an unauthorised act in relation to a copyright work may result in both a civil claim for damages and criminal prosecution.

Crown copyright material is reproduced with the permission of the Controller of HMSO and the Queen's Printer for Scotland. Parliamentary copyright material is reproduced with the permission of the Controller of Her Majesty's Stationery Office on behalf of Parliament. Any European material in this work which has been reproduced from EUR-lex, the official European Communities legislation website, is European Communities copyright.

A CIP Catalogue record for this book is available from the British Library.

ISBN 978-1-4057-5030-1

9 781405 750301

ISBN for this volume: 9781405750301

Printed and bound by CPI Group (UK) Ltd, Croydon, CR0 4YY

Visit LexisNexis at http://www.lexisnexis.co.uk

Dedication

To Camille Gabbert and Isabella Wylie

Foreword

Hedge funds are still very much shrouded in mystery so far as the general public is concerned. To the experienced investor, however, hedge funds offer a long-short geared investment strategy that is able to invest opportunistically and potentially globally, and which is capable of yielding a multiple over the returns which products which simply track indexes generate. Well, at least that was the case before the financial crisis of 2008.

Over the last seven years, global equities have witnessed something of a bull run which has taken the shine off the performance of many hedge funds. There has been a high correlation of hedge fund performance to the major equity indices, causing investors to ask why they should be paying so much more in fees to hedge fund managers.

Furthermore, as hedge funds continue to invest an ever increasing proportion of their portfolios in long equity strategies, and their business models converge with those of the wider asset management industry, there has been a blurring of the lines between hedge fund managers and traditional asset managers.

Many strategies which hedge funds pursue, such as global macro, directional and event driven strategies, are not dissimilar from the strategies which many traditional asset managers deploy. The advancement of traditional asset managers through the adoption of more sophisticated strategies such as thematic investing and quant funds will be an interesting development in the years ahead.

Many hedge funds have attracted criticism about their recent performance, and investors are questioning their value. A key issue for investors is whether hedge funds are worth the '2 and 20' fee structure which they typically charge. Warren Buffet, the renowned US billionaire investor, has expressed his view which is essentially that that fee structure is 'obscene' and 'ridiculous'. Hedge funds are accordingly being held to account to a previously unheard of extent. Whilst there will continue to be a compression of base fees, investors may be less begrudging towards hedge fund managers where performance fees are concerned.

In the past, hedge funds purported to attract extraordinary talent and to be able almost magically to generate returns of 20–25%, at a time when the concerns of investors were predominantly focused on returns. In the wake of the financial crisis, however, investors have started to analyse more deeply the risk profile of their investments and the nature of the portfolios of assets to which they are exposed. Investors want to know whether they are paying fees to hedge fund managers for resources which will generate 'alpha', such as talented people, high quality infrastructure, advanced technology and data.

Hedge fund managers face a multitude of challenges. Lower returns, increased regulation and the encroachment of artificial intelligence, machine learning and other cognitive technologies. Hedge funds businesses have merged, the size of investment funds has ballooned, and deploying funds of that magnitude

Foreword

makes it much harder to find 'alpha'. Market players are also pursuing similar strategies in a crowded space.

The challenge of technology is particularly significant. Data management and investment in technology remain critical in response to increasingly complex fund operations, heightened focus and scrutiny around cyber security as well as the ever growing number of regulatory and investor mandated reporting requirements. Artificial intelligence has arrived. Deep machine learning, pattern recognition and the automation of investment processes will become more prevalent. Indeed, it is arguable that artificial intelligence may be able to find 'alpha' more consistently than human analysts. There are already artificial intelligence funds where the investment selection is made by artificial intelligence engines.

To attract institutional capital, hedge funds have to be able to deal with managing assets at sizes much larger than before due to industry consolidation, different regulators, a higher regulatory burden and the consequently rising cost of compliance. This has potentially required hedge fund managers to hold more regulatory capital, to implement enhanced systems and controls and to make greater and more frequent disclosure to investors and regulators.

With structure, corporate governance, oversight and systems and controls coming under increasing scrutiny, the law that surrounds hedge funds requires deft navigation, and this book provides an excellent perspective on the relevant considerations.

Just as with any investment strategy, investors must look at their own specific commercial needs as a whole and decide whether hedge funds fit their commercial objectives and strategy.

With about US$3 trillion in assets in management (compared to about only US$40 billion in 1990), hedge funds have become an important market-moving force over the last two decades and a hugely significant asset class. Whilst questions remain regarding their ability to achieve 'alpha' returns, their fee charging structure, increasing regulation, and the blurring of the lines between hedge funds and traditional asset managers, hedge funds remain an important alternative asset class for many institutional investors. It will be interesting to watch events unfold in the global hedge fund industry over the next few years.

Sean Lam

Chief Executive, Walker Crips Group PLC

May 2018

Contents

Foreword vii
Table of Statutes xiii
Table of Statutory Instruments xxi
Table of European Legislation xxvii
Table of Cases xxxiii

Chapter 1   What is a Hedge Fund? 1
Chapter 2   Offshore Fund Domiciles – The Caribbean 7
A   The Cayman Islands 7
B   The British Virgin Islands 17

Chapter 3   Offshore Fund Domiciles – The Channel Islands ... 35
A   Jersey 35
B   Guernsey 51

Chapter 4   Onshore Fund Domiciles 65
A   Hong Kong 65
B   Ireland 88
C   Luxembourg 106
D   Malta 134
E   Singapore 157
F   Switzerland 167

Chapter 5   Establishment Options – Legal Form 181
A   Introduction 181
B   Companies 181
C   Partnerships 185
D   Unit trusts 188

Contents

E	Master-feeder structure	190
Chapter 6	**Service Providers – Making it Happen**	**193**
A	Introduction	193
B	Directors of the fund	194
C	The investment manager	196
D	The administrator	198
E	The prime broker	202
F	Other service providers	205
Chapter 7	**The Prime Broker**	**207**
A	Introduction	207
B	What is a prime broker?	207
C	Custody services	209
D	Clearing and settlement	209
E	Financing	210
F	Ancillary and 'value add' services	210
G	Other roles	211
H	Key documentation	211
Chapter 8	**Directors' Duties**	**213**
A	Introduction	213
B	UK common law principles	214
C	The Cayman Islands	224
Chapter 9	**Regulatory Overview – The United Kingdom**	**233**
A	Introduction	233
B	Regulated activities	233
C	Promotion of hedge funds	238
D	Market abuse	244
Chapter 10	**The Alternative Investment Fund Managers Directive**	**265**
A	Introduction	265
B	Where to find AIFMD measures	266
C	What is an AIF?	268
D	What is an AIFM?	271
E	Exemptions	273
F	Authorisation or registration of the AIFM	275

G	Organisational issues	276
H	Managing an AIF	282
I	Marketing under AIFMD	284
J	Transparency	292
K	Service providers	298
L	Conclusion and next steps	309

Chapter 11 The US Dimension ... 311

A	Introduction	311
B	Securities (SEC) regulation	312
C	Commodities (CFTC) regulation	322
D	US marketing of hedge fund interests	333
E	Other US issues affecting hedge fund managers	338

Chapter 12 UCITS ... 345

A	UCITS: The 'gold' standard	345
B	UCITS: A brief history	345
C	UCITS: Key characteristics, features and requirements	352
D	Summary of UCITS investment powers	354
E	Spreading risk and investment limits	355
F	Financial derivative instruments	357
G	Investment restrictions applicable to derivatives	360
H	Financial indices	366
I	Securities and instruments that embed derivatives	367
J	Investment management techniques	369
K	Borrowing and lending	369
L	Short selling	370
M	Fund liquidity	371
N	Future legislative changes	371

Chapter 13 Marketing – Selected Jurisdictions ... 373

A	Australia	373
B	China	379
C	France	390
D	Germany	396
E	Hong Kong	404

xi

Contents

F	Italy	411
G	Malta	421
H	Netherlands	431
I	Singapore	438
J	Spain	441
K	Switzerland	448

Chapter 14   Taxation of Hedge Funds – An Overview ... 455

A	Introduction	455
B	Structuring drivers	455
C	Typical hedge fund structures	459
D	UK taxation of the fund – tax residence considerations	461
E	UK taxation of the fund – 'trading in the UK' considerations	468
F	UK taxation of investors	474

Chapter 15   Key Fund Terms ... 479

A	Introduction	479
B	Management and performance fees	479
C	Other common terms	489

Chapter 16   Investing in Hedge Funds ... 497

A	Why invest in hedge funds?	497
B	Mainstream funds	497
C	Hedge funds	499
D	Routes to investment in hedge funds	501
E	Fund of hedge funds	503
F	Key investment and due diligence issues	504
G	Side letters	505
H	Rights as an investor	507

Index ... 509

Table of Statutes

Paragraph references printed in **bold** type indicate where legislation is set out in part or in full.

C

Companies Act 2006.... 2.63, 3.16, 8.2, 8.4, 8.6, 8.41
s 170–177 .... **8.3**
Corporation Tax Act 2009
 Pt 6, Ch 3 (ss 487–497) 14.96
Criminal Justice Act 1993 .... 9.117
 Pt V (ss 52–64) 9.58, 9.67, 9.116

F

Finance Act 2008 .... 14.68, 14.69, 14.71
Finance Act 2014 .... 14.56
Financial Services Act 2012
 Pt 7 (ss 89–95).. 9.58, 9.67, 9.103, 9.118
 s 89 .... 9.119, 9.120
 90 .... 9.122
 91 .... 9.123
 93(5) 9.120
Financial Services and Markets Act 2000
 .... 3.147, 9.4
 s 19 .... 9.3, 10.57
 21 .... 9.30, 9.37
 118 .... 9.56
  (2) 9.134, 9.137
  (3) 9.146, 9.151
 119–122 .... 9.56

Financial Services and Markets Act 2000 – cont.
 s 131 .... 9.65
 235 .... 9.5
 238 .... 9.35, 10.126
 240 .... 9.37
 401 .... 9.67
 Sch 1
  Pt 2 .... 9.120, 9.121
 Sch 6 .... 9.26

I

Insolvency Act 1986 .... 8.6, 8.17

L

Limited Partnerships Act 1907.... 5.16, 5.17
 s 7 .... **5.18**

P

Partnership Act 1890 .... 5.16, 5.18

T

Taxation (International and Other Provisions) Act 2010 .... 14.56

Other jurisdictions

Australia

Corporations Act 2001 .... 13.4

British Virgin Islands

BVI Business Companies Act, 2004
 .... 2.62, 2.63, 2.111, 2.113
 s 159 .... 2.112
Income Tax Ordinance (Cap 206)
 .... 2.130
Insolvency Act, 2003 .... 2.63
Insurance Act, 1994 .... 2.112
Insurance Act, 2008 .... 2.112
International Business Companies Act, 1984 .... 2.62
Limited Partnership Act, 2017.. 2.116, 2.117, 2.118

Mutual Funds Act, 1996 .... 2.65
Mutual Legal Assistance (Tax Matters) Act, 2003 .... 2.140
Partnership Act, 1996 .... 2.117
Proceeds of Criminal Conduct Act, 1997
 .... 2.156
Securities and Investment Business Act, 2010 ... 2.65, 2.66, 2.68, 2.69, 2.74, 2.77, 2.82, 2.86, 2.93, 2.98, 2.100, 2.107, 2.112, 2.120, 2.123, 2.126, 2.127, 2.128, 2.147, 2.155

Table of Statutes

Cayman Islands

Banks and Trust Companies Law (2018 Revision) 2.9, 2.10, 2.30
Building Societies Law (2014 Revision) 2.10
Companies Law (2018 Revision) 2.14, 2.25
Directors Registration and Licensing Law, 2014 .... 2.46, 8.89
Friendly Societies Law (1998 Revision) 2.10
Insurance Law (2010 Revision) 2.10

Limited Liability Companies Law (2018 Revision) 2.22
Mutual Funds Law (2015 Revision) 2.7, 2.11, 2.13, 2.27, 2.31, 2.34, 2.37, 2.45, 8.89
s 2 .... 2.8, 2.9, 2.30, 2.35
Proceeds of Crime Law (2018 Revision) s 2 .... 2.48
Securities Investment Business Law (2015 Revision) 2.47, 8.89

China

Company Law 1993 .... 13.26
Securities Investment Fund Law 2003 ('2003 SIF Law') 13.26, 13.36
Securities Investment Fund Law (2013 Revision) ('2013 SIF Law') 13.36, 13.37, 13.40
Securities Investment Fund Law (2015 Revision) ('2015 SIF Law') 13.36

Securities Investment Fund Law (2015 Revision) ('2015 SIF Law') – cont.
  art 91 .... 13.50
  127 .... 13.61
  133 .... 13.61
  135 .... 13.61
  137 .... 13.61
Securities Law 1998 .... 13.26

France

French Civil Code 3.15, 3.92
French Monetary and Financial Code 13.84

Germany

Capital Investment Code ('KAGB') 13.114, 13.115, 13.120, 13.127, 13.145, 13.146
  s 25 .... 13.121
  34 .... 13.124
  36 .... 13.128
  225 .... 13.119
    (2) 13.131
    (3) 13.132
  227 .... 13.126
  228 .... 13.136
  273 .... 13.122
  283 .... 13.117, 13.130
  323 .... 13.148
  329 .... 13.151

Capital Investment Code ('KAGB') – cont.
  s 330 .... 13.155
Income Tax Act ('EStG') 13.139
Investment Act ('InvG') 13.114, 13.120, 13.145, 13.146
  s 120 .... 13.127
Investment Tax Act ('InvStG 2018') 13.137, 13.144
  s 6 .... 13.139
  7 .... 13.139
    (3) 13.140
  16 .... 13.141
Investment Tax Reform Act ('InvStRefG') 13.137

Guernsey

Companies (Guernsey) Law, 2008 .... 3.108, 3.109

Financial Services Commission (Bailiwick of Guernsey) Law, 1987 .... 3.99

Table of Statutes

Income Tax (Guernsey) Law, 1975 .... 3.149, 3.152
Limited Partnerships (Guernsey) Law, 1995 .... 3.114
Protection of Investors (Bailiwick of Guernsey) Law, 1987 ('POI Law') 3.100, 3.102, 3103, 3.104, 3.106, 3.130, 3.131, 3.147

Protection of Investors (Bailiwick of Guernsey) Law, 1987 ('POI Law') – cont.
Sch 1
   cl 1 .... 3.105
Trusts (Guernsey) Law, 2007 .... 3.118

Hong Kong

Companies Ordinance (Cap 622)
   Pt 16 .... 4.39
Companies (Winding Up and Miscellaneous Provisions) Ordinance (Cap 32) ('C(WUMP)O') 13.161, 13.168, 13.175, 13.178
   Sch 17 .... 13.169, 13.176
Inland Revenue Ordinance (Cap 112) 4.4
Inland Revenue (Amendment) (No 4) Ordinance 2017 .... 4.25
Securities and Futures Ordinance (Cap 571) ('SFO') 4.1, 13.161, 13.162, 13.167, 13.168, 13.170, 13.178, 13.184, 13.185, 13.188, 13.189, 13.192, 13.193, 13.194

Securities and Futures Ordinance (Cap 571) ('SFO') – cont.
   s 103(1) 13.163, 13.164
      (2) 13.164
      (3)(k) 13.165
   115 .... 13.190
   Pt IVA 4.17, 4.21
   Sch 1 .... 13.166, 13.195
Securities and Futures (Amendment) Ordinance 2014 ('2014 Amendment Ordinance') 4.32, 4.33
Securities and Futures (Amendment) Ordinance 2016 ('2016 Amendment Ordinance') 4.17, 4.21, 4.23

Ireland

Companies Act 1990
   Pt XIII 4.130
Companies Act 2014
   Pt 24 .... 4.130

Investment Intermediaries Act 1995 .... 4.170

Italy

Italian Civil Code for Business Enterprises 13.219
Law Decree No 351 of 25 September 2001
   art 6 .... 13.240
Legislative Decree No 385 of 1 September 1993 ('Consolidated Banking Law')
   art 106 .... 13.215
Legislative Decree No 239 of 1 April 1996
   art 6 .... 13.238
Legislative Decree No 58 of 24 February 1998 ('Consolidated Law on Finance') 13.199, 13.200
   art 6
      para 2(a) no 3-bis 13.218

Legislative Decree No 58 of 24 February 1998 ('Consolidated Law on Finance') – cont.
      para 2-quinquies 13.214
          2-sexies 13.214
   art 13, 14 .... 13.220
      27, 28 .... 13.215
      41-ter 13.215
      43 .... 13.218
Legislative Decree No 44 of 4 March 2014 .... 13.199
Presidential Decree No 917 of 22 December 1986 ('Income Tax Code'). 13.235
   art 73 .... 13.234
      para 1(c) 13.240

Table of Statutes

Jersey

Collective Investment Funds (Jersey)
Law 1988............ 3.29, 3.57, 3.58
Companies (Jersey) Law 1991 ('Companies Law')...........3.16, 3.52, 3.78
Financial Services (Jersey) Law 1998
..... 3.22, 3.29, 3.42, 3.43, 3.44, 3.45
Income Tax (Jersey) Law 1961........... 3.85

Limited Liability Partnerships (Jersey)
Law 1997...................... 3.82
Limited Partnerships (Jersey) Law 1994
.............................3.16, 3.80
Partnership Law....................... 3.16
Trusts (Jersey) Law 1984.......... 3.16, 3.83

Luxembourg

Law of 10 August 1915 on Commercial
Companies....... 4.251, 4.252, 4.254,
4.315, 4.316
 art 100-2.......................... 4.305
 310-1........................... 4.305
 320-1.................... 4.248, 4.305
 710-4.......................... 4.246
 710-12(1)...................... 4.246
Law of 25 August 1983 on Undertakings
for Collective Investment........ 4.208
Law of 30 March 1988 on Undertakings
for Collective Investment....... 4.209,
4.212, 4.213
 Pt I, II........................... 4.210
Law of 19 July 1991 on Undertakings
for Collective Investment....... 4.212,
4.219, 4.221
 Pt II............................. 4.218
 art 3.............................4.289
Law of 5 April 1993 on the Financial
Sector
 art 1(5).......................... 4.289
 26-1........................... 4.268
 Annex III........................ 4.289
Law of 20 December 2002 relating to
Undertakings for Collective
Investment..............4.215, 4.219
 Pt I............................. 4.213
 II................ 4.213, 4.216, 4.218
Law of 15 June 2004 on Investment
Companies in Risk Capital
('SICAR Law')........... 4.219, 4.222
Law of 13 February 2007 on Specialised
Investment Funds ('SIF Law')... 4.221,
4.222, 4.225, 4.229, 4.242,
4.251, 4.256, 4.258, 4.293,
4.298, 4.302, 4.307, 4.311,
4.322
 Pt II............................. 4.266
 art 2............................4.288
 2bis.............................4.266
 4.......................4.227, 4.296
 10........................... 4.239
 12...................... 4.235, 4.236
 (1)...........................4.234

Law of 13 February 2007 on Specialised Investment Funds ('SIF Law') – cont.
 art 13............................ 4.232
 16...................... 4.268, 4.269
 25...................... 4.244, 4.296
 27............................. 4.250
 31............................. 4.250
 33............................ 4.268
 34............................. 4.269
 42(4)...........................4.294
 42a........................... 4.295
 42b(b), (c).......................4.294
 55(3)..........................4.276
 66............................ 4.317
 71............................ 4.255
Law of 18 December 2009 on the Audit
Profession..................... 4.275
Law of 17 December 2010 relating to
Undertakings for Collective Investment ('2010 Law')...... 4.225, 4.242,
4.251, 4.258, 4.307, 4.312
 Pt I (art 2–86)....... 4.215, 4.224, 4.229,
4.235, 4.256, 4.281, 4.308
 art 5...............................4.227
 11(1)..........................4.239
 13(1)..................... 4.234, 4.236
 (2)(a)–(i)..................... 4.235
 14(3)...........................4.232
 17............................ 4.268
 18............................ 4.269
 18bis...........................4.270
 19(1)..........................4.270
 25............................ 4.244
 27............................ 4.250
 31............................. 4.250
 33............................ 4.268
 34............................. 4.269
 34bis........................... 4.270
 35(1)..........................4.270
 41............................ 4.281
 42(3)...........................4.279
 43(1)..........................4.279
 50............................ 4.279
 52............................ 4.279
 Pt II (art 87–99)..... 4.215, 4.216, 4.217,
4.218, 4.221, 4.222, 4.229,

Table of Statutes

Law of 17 December 2010 relating to Undertakings for Collective Investment ('2010 Law') – *cont.*
    4.256, 4.265, 4.281, 4.282, 4.283, 4.284, 4.288, 4.296, 4.318, 4.322
  art 88-1.......................... 4.265
    89(1)........................... 4.281
    90...................... 4.239, 4.268
    91.............................. 4.281
    95.............................. 4.268
  Pt IV, Ch 15 (art 101–124-1)....... 4.229
  art 101-1......................... 4.230
    110............................. 4.230
  Pt IV, Ch 16 (art 125-1–126-1)..... 4.229
  art 129(1)........................ 4.308
    130............................. 4.309
    154(3).......................... 4.276
    173............................. 4.317
    181............................. 4.255

Law of 12 July 2013 relating to Alternative Investment Fund Managers
    .... 4.222, 4.265, 4.266, 4.313
  art 3(2).......................... 4.305
    18.............................. 4.230
    19.............................. 4.269
    (11), (12)..................... 4.270
    20, 21.......................... 4.303
    29.............................. 4.292

Law of 12 July 2013 relating to Alternative Investment Fund Managers – *cont.*
  art 29(1)......................... 4.301
  Annex I.......................... 4.273

Law of 27 May 2016 on the Publication of Legal Notices............... 4.236

Law of 23 July 2016 on the Audit Profession...................... 4.275

Law of 23 July 2016 relating to Reserved Alternative Investment Funds ('RAIF Law')..... 4.223, 4.225, 4.229, 4.242, 4.251, 4.258, 4.275, 4.305, 4.322
  art 1(1)(b)....................... 4.302
    2............................... 4.288
    4(1)............................ 4.265
    5............................... 4.268
    6............................... **4.227**
    12.............................. 4.239
    13(1)................... 4.234, 4.236
    (2)............................ 4.235
    23.............................. 4.244
    25.............................. 4.250
    29.............................. 4.250
    34(1)................... 4.237, 4.315
    38(1)........................... 4.303
    (4)............................ 4.303
    41.............................. 4.303
    45.............................. 4.317
    49.............................. 4.255

Malta

Companies Act (Cap 386, Laws of Malta)
    .... 4.341, 4.347
  art 194(6)........................ 4.342
    209(1)(a)....................... 4.342
    (2)(c).......................... 4.342
  Sch 10........................... 4.348
    para 5(1)(a), (b)............... 4.351
Financial Markets Act (Cap 345, Laws of Malta)........................ 4.420
Investment Services Act (Cap 370, Laws of Malta) ('IS Act')...... 4.332, 4.335, 4.337, 4.340, 4.348, 4.388, 4.400, 4.409, 13.246, 13.247, 13.248, 13.250, 13.252, 13.253, 13.254, 13.256, 13.262

Investment Services Act (Cap 370, Laws of Malta) ('IS Act') – *cont.*
  art 2............................. **4.334**
    4............................... **4.333**
    31.............................. 4.347
Securitisation Act (Cap 484, Laws of Malta)
  art 6............................. 4.337
Trusts and Trustees Act (Cap 331, Laws of Malta) ('Trusts Act')......... 4.353
  art 6(6).......................... 4.354

Netherlands

Civil Code................. 13.292, 13.305
  Book 2................. 13.295, 13.303
  Book 7A...................... 13.300

Code of Commerce.......... 13.292, 13.300
Financial Supervision Act.... 13.292, 13.302, 13.310

xvii

Table of Statutes

Singapore

Companies Act (Cap 50) 4.464
  Pt V
    Div 2
      s 145(1) 4.466
      171(1) 4.466
  Pt VI
    Div 2
      s 205(1) 4.466
Financial Advisers Act (Cap 110)
      .... 13.343, 13.345
Income Tax Act (Cap 134)
  Pt IV
      s 13CA 4.481
      13R 4.481
      13X 4.481

Limited Partnerships Act (Cap 163B)
      .... 4.470
Securities and Futures Act (Cap 289)
    . 4.452, 4.455, 4.456, 13.325, 13.326,
                13.327, 13.334, 13.346
  Pt XIII
    Div 2
      Subdiv 4
        s 305 .... 13.336, 13.338,
                        13.341, 13.342
Securities and Futures (Amendment) Act
      2017 (A4/2017) 13.334, 13.337
Trustees Act (Cap 337) 4.474, 4.475

Spain

Law 35/2003 of 4 November 2003
      on Collective Investment Schemes
      (the 'CIS Law') 13.347, 13.361

Switzerland

Federal Act of 30 March 1911 on
      the Amendment of the Swiss
      Civil Code (Part Five: The Code
      of Obligations) 4.502
Federal Act of 8 November 1934 on
      Banks and Savings Banks 4.491
Federal Act of 10 October 1997 on Combating Money Laundering and
      Terrorist Financing ('Anti-Money
      Laundering Act') 13.378
  art 2
    para 2(b^{bis}) 4.530
      3 .... 4.530
Federal Act of 23 June 2006 on Collective
      Investment Schemes ('CISA') 4.487,
                4.488, 4.499, 4.503, 4.506,
                4.508, 4.509, 4.510, 4.512,
                13.367, 13.369, 13.370,
                13.374, 13.380, 13.388
  art 8
    para 3 .... 4.492, 4.497
  art 9
    para 3 .... 4.498
      4 .... 4.504
  art 10
    para 3 .... 13.376
      3bis 13.376
      3ter 13.376
  art 13
    para 2(a) 4.491

Federal Act of 23 June 2006 on Collective
      Investment Schemes ('CISA') – *cont.*
    para 2(f) 4.494
      (c) 4.498
  art 14
    para 1(a) 4.514
      (b) 4.513
      (c) 4.519, 4.527
      (d) 4.536
      1ter 4.522
  art 15
    para 1(a) 4.492
      (b) 4.497
      (c) 4.498
      (d) 4.504
  art 18
    para 1 .... 4.518
      (c) 4.537
  art 20 .... 4.531
  26
    para 2 .... 4.492
  art 28 .... 4.490
    para 1 .... 4.491
  art 29
    para 1 .... 4.491
  art 36
    para 1(a) 4.493
      (d) 4.493
  art 51
    para 2 .... 4.494
      5 .... 4.494

Table of Statutes

Federal Act of 23 June 2006 on Collective Investment Schemes ('CISA') – *cont.*
art 102
    para 1(f)........................ 4.501
        (i)........................ 4.500
art 103
    para 2........................ 4.498
art 110............................ 4.502
126
    para 1(e)...................... 4.515

Federal Act of 12 June 2009 on Value Added Tax.................... 13.391
Federal Act on Financial Institutions (draft) ('FAFI')................ 13.386
Federal Financial Services Act (draft) ('FFSA')....... 13.386, 13.387, 13.388

United States of America

Commodity Exchange Act of 1936 ('CEA').................... 11.1, 11.4, 11.47, 11.50, 11.62
  s 1a(11) (7 United States Code ('USC') s 1a(11)).................................. 11.54
    (12)(A) (7 USC s 1a(12)(A))... 11.60
  4c.. 11.60
  4m(1) (7 USC s 6m(1))... 11.53, 11.59, **11.63**, 11.66
  14(a)(1) (7 USC s 18(a)(1))... 11.91
  19... 11.60
Dodd-Frank Wall Street Reform and Consumer Protection Act of 2010..... 4.72, 11.22, 11.48
Employee Retirement Income Security Act of 1974 ('ERISA').. 4.12, 11.1, 11.4, 11.94, 11.116,
                                                                                             11.117, 11.123
  s 2 (29 USC s 1001).. 11.113
    3(1)(A) (29 USC s 1002(1)(A)).. 11.114
    (14) (29 USC s 1002(14))... 11.119
    (21)(A) (29 USC s 1002(21)(A))... 11.113
    (32) (29 USC s 1002(32))... 11.115
    (33) (29 USC s 1002(33))... 11.115
    (42) (29 USC s 1002(42))... 11.114
    4(b)(1) (29 USC s 1003(b)(1)).. 11.115
    (2) (29 USC s 1003(b)(2)).. 11.115
    (4) (29 USC s 1003(b)(4)).. 11.115
    404(a) (29 USC s 1104(a)).. 11.118
    406(b)(1) (29 USC s 1106(b)(1))... 11.119
    409(a) (29 USC s 1109(a)).. 11.118
    408(b)(17)(A) (29 USC s 1108(b)(17)(A))....................................... 11.120
        (B) (29 USC s 1108(b)(17)(B))... 11.120
    410 (29 USC s 1110))... 11.118
Foreign Account Tax Compliance Act of 2010 ('FATCA')....... 2.54, 2.56, 2.132, 2.133, 2.134,
                                                2.136, 2.138, 2.141, 2.144, 3.159, 14.7, 14.12
Investment Advisers Act of 1940 ('Advisers Act')................ 11.1, 11.4, 11.5, 11.6, 11.20,
                                                                    11.35, 11.36, 11.37, 11.45
  s 202(a)(11) (15 USC s 80b-2(a)(11)).. 11.19
    (30).. 11.23
    203(a).. 11.19
    (b)(3) (15 USC s 80b-3(b)(3))... 11.21
    (c)(2) (15 USC s 80b-3(c)(2))... 11.34
    (e) (15 USC s 80b-3(e)).. 11.44
    (f)... 11.43
Investment Company Act of 1940 ('1940 Act')....... 11.1, 11.4, 11.5, 11.6, 11.8, 11.9, 11.12,
                                                                                  11.24, 11.94
  s 2(51)(A) (15 USC s 80a-2(51)(A))... 11.75
    3(a)(1) (15 USC s 80a-3(a)(1)).. 11.7, **11.50**
    (3) (15 USC s 80a-3(a)(3))... **11.50**
    (c)(1)............................... 11.13, 11.15, 11.16, 11.17, 11.18, 11.22, 11.41
    (7)................................. 11.14, 11.15, 11.16, 11.17, 11.18, 11.22, 11.41
    7(a), (b) (15 USC s 80a-7(a), (b))... 11.7
    (d) (15 USC s 80a-7(d))... 11.11
    8.. 11.7, 11.22
Securities Act of 1933 ('Securities Act')................. 11.1, 11.4, 11.6, 11.50, 11.92, 11.102

Table of Statutes

Securities Act of 1933 ('Securities Act') – *cont.*
  s 2(a)(1) (15 USC s 77b(a)(1)) **11.5**
    3(a)(11) (15 USC s 77c(a)(11)) **11.111**
    4(a)(2) 11.93, 11.95, 11.96
    18(b)(4)(D) (15 USC s 77r(b)(4)(D)) 11.112
Securities Exchange Act of 1934 ('Exchange Act') 11.1, 11.4, 11.5, 11.6
  s 3(a)(4) (15 USC s 78c(a)(4)) **11.99**
    15(a)(1) (15 USC s 78o(a)(1)) 11.99
    28(e) 11.123
US Constitution 11.111
  art I
    s 8
      cl 3 .... 11.19
US Internal Revenue Code of 1986
  s 871(m) 14.13, 14.14
    4975 .... 11.116
      (c)(1) (26 USC s 4975(c)(1)) 11.119
      (e)(1) (26 USC s 4975(e)(1)) 11.114
      (2) (26 USC s 4975(e)(2)) 11.119
US Tax Cuts and Jobs Act of 2017 .... 14.14

Table of Statutory Instruments

Paragraph references printed in **bold** type indicate where legislation is set out in part or in full.

A

Alternative Investment Fund Managers Order 2014, SI 2014/1292 .... 10.11
Alternative Investment Fund Managers Regulations 2013, SI 2013/1773 .... 10.11
   reg 10 .... 10.56

F

Financial Services Act 2012 (Misleading Statements and Impressions) Order 2013, SI 2013/637
   art 2 .... 9.121
Financial Services and Markets Act 2000 (Financial Promotion) Order 2005, SI 2005/1529 .... 9.34, 9.53, 9.54
Financial Services and Markets Act 2000 (Market Abuse) Regulations 2016, SI 2016/680 .... 9.56
Financial Services and Markets Act 2000 (Promotion of Collective Investment Schemes) (Exemptions) Order 2001, SI 2001/1060 ..... 9.35, 9.38, 9.54, 10.126
   art 14 .... 9.39
   15 .... 9.41
   18 .... 9.43
   19 .... 9.44
   21 .... 9.45
   22 .... 9.47
   23 .... 9.49
   23A 9.51
   Schedule
    Pt I 9.46
    II 9.52

Financial Services and Markets Act 2000 (Regulated Activities) Order 2001, SI 2001/544
   Pt II (art 4–72I) 9.4
   art 14 .... 9.6, 9.7
   18 .... 9.7
   21, 22 .... 9.8
   25 .... 9.9
   26 .... 9.10
   37 .... 9.11
   40 .... 9.12
   51ZA 9.15
   51ZB 9.16
   51ZC 9.17
   51ZD 9.18
   51ZE 9.19
   53 .... 9.13
   69 .... 9.7, 9.21
   72 .... 9.22
   Pt III (art 73–89) 9.4
   art 76, 77 .... 9.5
   78 .... 9.5
   81 .... 9.5
   83–85 .... 9.5

I

Investment Transactions (Tax) Regulations 2014, SI 2014/685 .... 14.69

O

Offshore Funds (Tax) Regulations 2009, SI 2009/3001 .... 14.89
   reg 98 .... 14.96

Other jurisdictions

British Virgin Islands

Anti-Money Laundering and Terrorist Financing Code of Practice, 2008 .... 2.155
Anti-Money Laundering Regulations, 2008 .... 2.155

Investment Business (Approved Managers) Regulations, 2012 .... 2.126
Mutual Funds Regulations, 2010 .... 2.65, 2.103
Public Funds Code, 2010 .... 2.92, 2.103

xxi

Table of Statutory Instruments

Securities and Investment Business (Incubator and Approved Funds) Regulations, 2015............ 2.65, 2.77

Securities and Investment Business (AIFMD) Regulations, 2016.. 2.150, 2.151, 2.152, 2.153, 2.154

Cayman Islands

Anti-Money Laundering Regulations, 2017 .... 2.48, 2.49, 2.50, 2.51

China

Administrative Measures for the Client Asset Management Business of Securities Companies............. 13.32
Administrative Measures on Fundraising Behaviours of Privately Offered Funds art 23–25.................. 13.59, 13.60
Foreign Exchange Administrative Regulations on Offshore Securities Investments by Qualified Domestic Institutional Investors............. 13.71
Interim Measures for the Supervision and Administration of Privately Offered Investment Funds – Decree No 105 of the China Securities Regulatory Commission (21 August 2014) ('Interim Measures'). 13.29, 13.38, 13.39, 13.40, 13.46

Interim Measures for the Supervision and Administration of Privately Offered Investment Funds – Decree No 105 of the China Securities Regulatory Commission (21 August 2014) ('Interim Measures') – cont.
art 12...................... 13.47, 13.49
13............................ 13.48
14..................... 13.51, 13.57
15..................... 13.51, 13.58
Measures for the Registration of Private Investment Fund Managers and Filing of Private Investment Funds (Trial Implementation) ('Registration and Filing Measures')........... 13.41, 13.43

Guernsey

AIFMD Rules 2013 .... 3.140
Authorised Closed-Ended Investment Schemes Rules 2013............. 3.106
Authorised Collective Investment Schemes (Class A) Rules 2008.............. 3.106
Authorised Collective Investment Schemes (Class B) Rules 2013............. 3.106
Collective Investment Schemes (Qualifying Professional Investor Funds) (Class Q) Rules 1998...................... 3.106

Guernsey Financial Services Commission Prospectus Rules 2008 ('Prospectus Rules 2008')...................... 3.106
Licensees (Conduct of Business) Rules 2016 .... 3.142
Private Investment Fund Rules 2016 .... 3.106, 3.134, 3.135
Registered Collective Investment Schemes Rules 2015............... 3.106, 3.132

Hong Kong

Securities and Futures (Financial Resources) Rules (Cap 571N).................. 4.61
Securities and Futures (Professional Investor) Rules (Cap 571D)..... 13.166, 13.167, 13.170, 13.185, 13.195

Table of Statutory Instruments

Ireland

Central Bank Reform Act (Sections 20 and 22) Regulations 2011, SI 2011/437 .... 4.117

Central Bank (Supervision and Enforcement) Act 2013 (Section 48(1)) (Undertakings for Collective Investment in Transferable Securities) Regulations 2015, SI 2015/420 ('Central Bank UCITS Regulations') 4.100, 4.101, 4.143

European Communities (Undertakings for Collective Investment in Transferable Securities) Regulations 2011, SI 2011/352 ('UCITS Regulations') 4.99, 4.124, 4.127, 4.129, 4.175, 4.176

European Union (Alternative Investment Fund Managers) Regulations 2013, SI 2013/257 ('AIFM Regulations') 4.114, 4.124, 4.175, 4.176

art 82(d) 4.153

European Union (Markets in Financial Instruments) Regulations 2017, SI 2017/375 ('MiFID Regulations') 4.190, 4.194, 4.197, 4.200

Italy

Bank of Italy and CONSOB Joint Regulation of 29 October 2007 on the organisation and procedures to be adopted by intermediaries providing investment services or collective investment management services ('Joint Regulation') 13.200, 13.226, 13.229

Bank of Italy Regulation of May 2012 (containing the Regulation on collective asset management) 13.197

Bank of Italy Regulation on collective asset management of 19 January 2015 ('Bank of Italy Regulation') 13.200, 13.211, 13.226

CONSOB Regulation No 11971 of 14 May 1999 – Regulation implementing Italian Legislative Decree No 58 of 24 February 1998, concerning the discipline of issuers ('CONSOB Regulation') 13.200

Ministerial Decree of 4 September 1996 .... 13.244

Ministry of Finance Decree No 228 of 24 May 1999 .... 13.197

Ministry of Finance Decree No 30 of 5 March 2015 ... 13.199, 13.200, 13.211

art 12 .... 13.204

14 .... 13.214

Jersey

Collective Investment Funds (Recognised Funds) (Rules) (Jersey) Order 2003 .... 3.58

Control of Borrowing (Jersey) Order 1958 ('COBO') 3.22, 3.46, 3.57

Luxembourg

Grand-Ducal Regulation of 8 February 2008 .... 4.216, 4.279

Malta

Collective Investment Schemes (Investment Income) Regulations (SL 123.51, Laws of Malta) 4.434

Continuation of Companies Regulations (SL 386.05, Laws of Malta) 4.347

Investment Services Act (Alternative Investment Fund Manager) (Third Country) Regulations 2013 (SL 370.24, Laws of Malta) 13.253

reg 8(1) 13.256

xxiii

Table of Statutory Instruments

Investment Services Act (Alternative Investment Fund Manager) (Third Country) Regulations 2013 (SL 370.24, Laws of Malta) – cont.
   reg 22(1) 13.256
Investment Services Act (Contractual Funds) Regulations (SL 370.16, Laws of Malta) 4.359
Investment Services Act (Exemption) Regulations (SL 370.02, Laws of Malta) ('Exemption Regulations')
   reg 5(1) 4.337
      (d) 4.337
      (2) 4.337
      6(1) 4.336
Investment Services Act (Fees) Regulations (SL 370.03, Laws of Malta) 13.246
Investment Services Act (Licence and Other Fees) Regulations (SL 370.03, Laws of Malta) 13.246

Investment Services Act (List of Notified AIFs) Regulations (SL 370.34, Laws of Malta) 4.337
Investment Services Act (Marketing of Alternative Investment Funds) Regulations (SL 370.21, Laws of Malta) 13.253, 13.262
   reg 4(1) 13.256
Investment Services Act (Prospectus of Collective Investment Schemes) Regulations (SL 370.04, Laws of Malta) 4.380
Investment Services Act (Recognition of Private Collective Investment Schemes) Regulations (SL 370.06, Laws of Malta)
   reg 2 .... 4.337

Spain

Circular 1/2006 of 3 May 2006 of the National Securities Market Commission 13.347
Ministerial Order EHA/1199/2006 of 25 April 2006 from the Ministry of Economy and Finance 13.347

Royal Decree 1082/2012 of 23 July 2012 (the 'CIS Regulations') 13.347
   art 73, 74 .... 13.348
Royal Decree 83/2015 of 13 February 2015 .... 13.347

Switzerland

Federal Ordinance of 22 November 2006 on Collective Investment Schemes ('CISO') 4.488, 4.502, 4.512, 13.367, 13.373, 13.374
   art 6, 6a 13.376
     10 .... 4.514
     11 .... 4.513
     12
       para 1 .... 4.514
          3 .... 4.528
     art 12a 4.522
       para 2 .... 4.524
     art 14 .... 4.537
       19 .... 4.536
       21 .... 4.536
     24
       para 1 .... 4.528
     art 29(b)
       para 2(c) 4.543
         (d) 4.544
         (f) 4.541
         4 .... 4.541
     art 31 .... 4.531

Federal Ordinance of 22 November 2006 on Collective Investment Schemes ('CISO') – cont.
   art 100
       para 2(a)–(c) 4.506
     art 121
       para 1(b) 4.498
     art 122
       para 1, 2 .... 4.505
Ordinance of the Swiss Financial Market Supervisory Authority of 27 August 2014 on Collective Investment Schemes ('CISO-FINMA') 4.488, 4.492, 4.493, 4.494, 4.495, 4.497, 4.498, 4.502, 4.504, 4.506, 4.508, 4.509, 4.512, 4.514, 4.516, 4.517, 4.530 4.532, 4.533, 4.537, 4.541, 4.542, 4.543, 4.544, 4.545
   art 66 .... 4.528
     68
       para 4 .... 4.529

Table of Statutory Instruments

United States of America

Commodities (CFTC) Regulation 11.46, 11.49, 11.55, 11.71
   Rule 1.31 (17 Code of Federal Regulations ('CFR') s 1.31)........................... 11.90
      3.33(b)(3) (17 CFR s 3.33(b)(3))...11.90
         (f) (17 CFR s 3.33(f))...11.87
         (h) (17 CFR s 3.33(h))..**11.91**
      4.7.. 11.75, 11.76, 11.77, 11.78, 11.80, 11.86
         (a)(2)(viii)(A) (17 CFR s 4.7(a)(2)(viii)(A))...................................11.56
         (b)(2)(v)..11.84
      4.13(a)(3)..11.56, 11.57
         (4)..11.56
      4.14(a)(10)..11.64, 11.65
            (ii)(C) (17 CFR s 4.14(a)(10)(ii)(C))..................................11.66
            (iii) (17 CFR s 4.14(a)(10)(iii))......................................11.66
      30.10..11.58
DOL Regulation 11.113, 11.120
SEC Regulation
   Rule 3a4-1 (17 CFR s 240.3a4-1)......................... 11.98, 11.101, 11.102, 11.103
      15a-6 (17 CFR s 240.15a-6)...11.98
         (a)(1) (17 CFR s 240.15a-6(a)(1))...11.110
         (3) (17 CFR s 240.15a-6(a)(3))...11.105
         (4)(i) (17 CFR s 240.15a-6(a)(4)(i)).......................................11.110
SEC Regulation 11.8
   Rule 2a51-1 (17 CFR s 270.2a51-1)..11.14
      3c-5 (17 CFR s 270.3c-5)...11.56
         (a)(4) (17 CFR s 270.3c-5(a)(4))...11.15
         (b) (17 CFR s 270.3c-5(b))..11.15
SEC Regulation D 11.13, 11.66, 11.97, 11.112
   Rule 501 (17 CFR s 230.501)... 11.56, 11.93
      502...11.93
      504(b)...11.96
      506..11.95
         (c)...11.93
         (d)...11.96
SEC Regulation S
   Rule 902 (17 CFR s 230.902)..11.14
         (b)...3.147
SEC Regulation S-ID 11.40
SEC Rules/Hedge Fund Advisers Rules
   Rule 203-2(c) (17 CFR s 275.203-2(c))...**11.44**
      206(4)-8...**11.42**
         (a) (17 CFR s 275.206(4)-8(a))...**11.41**

Table of European Legislation

Paragraph references printed in **bold** type indicate where legislation is set out in part or in full.

Primary legislation

Agreements and treaties

EU Treaty of Accession of 1972
    Protocol 3 .... 3.12, 3.90

Secondary legislation

Directives

Commission Directive 2007/16/EC of 19 March 2007 implementing Council Directive 85/611/EEC on the coordination of laws, regulations and administrative provisions relating to undertakings for collective investment in transferable securities (UCITS) as regards the clarification of certain definitions ('Eligible Assets Directive', 'EAD')
    ...... 4.216, 4.279, 12.53, 12.54, 12.76, 12.77, 12.121, 12.125
    art 8(2), (3) 12.75
    (4) 12.73, 12.75

Commission Directive 2010/43/EU of 1 July 2010 implementing Directive 2009/65/EC of the European Parliament and of the Council as regards organisational requirements, conflicts of interest, conduct of business, risk management and content of the agreement between a depositary and a management company ('Commission Directive') 12.89, 12.99, 12.115, 12.116, 12.118, 12.119
    art 38 .... 12.114
    40 .... 12.114
    (3), (4) 12.117
    41 .... 12.97
    42(4) 12.109
    43 .... 12.86

Council Directive 85/611/EEC of 20 December 1985 on the coordination of laws, regulations and administrative provisions relating to undertakings for collective investment in transferable securities (original 'UCITS Directive')
    .... 4.209, 4.210, 12.4, 12.5, 12.6, 12.51
    art 19(1)(g) 12.75
    53a 12.53

Council Directive 2003/48/EC of 3 June 2003 on taxation of savings income in the form of interest payments ('EU Savings Directive') 2.131, 2.132, 3.157, 3.163, 3.164

Directive 2001/107/EC of the European Parliament and of the Council of 21 January 2002 amending Council Directive 85/611/EEC on the coordination of laws, regulations and administrative provisions relating to undertakings for collective investment in transferable securities (UCITS) with a view to regulating management companies and simplified prospectuses ('Management Directive' – 'UCITS III')
    .... 4.213, 4.214, 4.227, 4.365, 12.2, 12.7, 12.8

Directive 2001/108/EC of the European Parliament and of the Council of 21 January 2002 amending Council Directive 85/611/EEC on the coordination of laws, regulations and administrative provisions relating to undertakings for collective investment in transferable securities (UCITS), with regard to investments of UCITS ('Product Directive' – 'UCITS III')
    .... 4.213, 4.214, 4.227, 4.365, 12.2, 12.7, 12.9, 12.52

Table of European Legislation

Directive 2003/6/EC of the European Parliament and of the Council of 28 January 2003 on insider dealing and market manipulation ('Market Abuse Directive', 'EU MAD') 9.56, 9.59, 9.60, 9.72, 9.74, 9.81, 9.103, 9.107, 9.110, 9.113, 9.126

Directive 2003/71/EC of the European Parliament and of the Council of 4 November 2003 on the prospectus to be published when securities are offered to the public or admitted to trading and amending Directive 2001/34/EC ('Prospectus Directive'). 4.187, 4.380, 10.127, 13.218

Directive 2004/39/EC of the European Parliament and of the Council of 21 April 2004 on markets in financial instruments amending Council Directives 85/611/EEC and 93/6/EEC and Directive 2000/12/EC of the European Parliament and of the Council and repealing Council Directive 93/22/EEC ('MiFID')..................... 9.71, 13.278

Directive 2004/109/EC of the European Parliament and of the Council of 15 December 2004 on the harmonisation of transparency requirements in relation to information about issuers whose securities are admitted to trading on a regulated market and amending Directive 2001/34/EC ('Transparency Directive') 10.166, 10.167, 13.125

Directive 2009/65/EC of the European Parliament and of the Council of 13 July 2009 on the coordination of laws, regulations and administrative provisions relating to undertakings for collective investment in transferable securities (UCITS) (recast 'UCITS Directive' – 'UCITS IV')... 4.98, 4.99, 4.215, 4.281,4.332, 4.338, 4.361, 4.508, 10.2, 10.208, 12.10, 12.11, 12.22, 12.44, 12.45, 12.47, 12.48, 12.49, 12.62, 12.68, 12.72, 12.86, 12.95, 12.118, 12.131, 12.132, 12.142, 12.145, 12.146, 12.147, 12.148, 12.149, 13.121, 13.247, 13.252, 13.385

art 1(2)................ **12.55, 12.59, 4.335**
24........................... 12.38
50(1)(e)......................... 12.69
(g).......................... 12.71
51(3).......................... 12.96
52...................... 12.79, 12.133
56............................ 12.89
111(a)......................... 12.53

Directive 2011/61/EU of the European Parliament and of the Council of 8 June 2011 on Alternative Investment Fund Managers and amending Directives 2003/41/EC and 2009/65/EC and Regulations (EC) No 1060/2009 and (EU) No 1095/2010 ('Alternative Investment Fund Managers Directive', 'AIFMD').. 1.15, 2.146, 2.147, 2.148, 3.7, 3.8, 3.9, 3.20, 3.21, 3.22, 3.138, 3.140, 3.145, 4.72, 4.73, 4.86, 4.89, 4.111, 4.112, 4.113, 4.114, 4.115, 4.222, 4.265, 4.269, 4.293, 4.305, 4.312, 4.313, 4.332, 4.338, 4.361, 4.365, 4.366, 4.369, 4.370, 4.371, 4.374, 4.379, 4.377, 4.383, 4.384, 4.400, 4.416, 4.417, 4.432, 7.3, 7.5, 10.1, 10.2, 10.3, 10.4, 10.5, 10.6, 10.9, 10.11, 10.12, 10.28,10.34, 10.35, 10.41, 10.48, 10.51, 10.52, 10.53, 10.55, 10.66, 10.71, 10.83, 10.88, 10.96, 10.103, 10.105, 10.111, 10.112, 10.114, 10.115, 10.117, 10.119, 10.120, 10.121, 10.123, 10.135, 10.143, 10.145, 10.151, 10.156, 10.158, 10.166, 10.167, 10.170, 10.185, 10.194, 10.204, 10.208, 10.216, 10.217, 10.218, 10.222, 10.223, 10.224, 10.225, 10.228, 10.229, 10.231, 10.232, 10.235, 10.236, 10.239, 10.240, 10.241, 10.243, 10.244, 10.249, 10.250, 10.263, 10.264, 10.265, 10.266, 10.268, 12.13, 12.15, 12.19, 12.20, 12.32, 12.33, 12.38, 14.55, 12.147,12.148, 13.85, 13.86, 13.87, 13.88, 13.96, 13.97, 13.101, 13.108, 13.114, 13.121, 13.127, 13.197, 13.199, 13.247, 13.250, 13.251, 13.253, 13.254, 13.255, 13.256, 13.258, 13.261, 13.262, 13.274, 13.284, 13.287, 13.293, 13.299, 13.302, 13.307, 13.308, 13.309, 13.313, 13.368

Recital 7........................... 10.29
8.................... 10.29, 10.30
art 2(3)............................10.31
3.................... 10.47, 10.190
(2).................... 4.373, 13.270
(3)(d)........................... 10.7
4(1)(a)............. **4.335**, 10.14, 10.19
(l)........................ 10.106
(v)........................ **10.80**
(x)........................ **10.118**
5(1)................ 10.36, 10.260
6(1)............................10.33
(4)............................10.45
19............................. 10.93
(10)........................... 10.97
20.................... 10.245, 10.260
(1)(c)........................ 10.248
21. 4.378, 10.113, 10.195, 10.196, 10.197, 10.234, 10.237

Directive 2011/61/EU of the European Parliament and of the Council of 8 June 2011 on Alternative Investment Fund Managers and amending Directives 2003/41/EC and 2009/65/EC and Regulations (EC) No 1060/2009 and (EU) No 1095/2010 ('Alternative Investment Fund Managers Directive', 'AIFMD') – *cont.*
art 21(7)–(9) . 10.146, 10.201, 13.153, 13.155, 13.266
(12) **10.227**
22 . . . . 10.113, 10.150, 10.161, 13.273, 13.281, 13.288
23 . 4.378, 10.150, 10.168, 13.124, 13.135, 13.149, 13.152, 13.155, 13.267, 13.273, 13.288
(1) 10.171
(a) 10.84
24 . . . . 10.150, 10.177, 13.124, 13.273, 13.281, 13.285
(1) 10.7
(2) 10.7, 10.179, 10.181, 10.182
(3)(a) 10.163
(4) 10.7
(5) 10.180, 10.186
26–30 . . . . 10.150, 13.273, 13.286
31 . . . . 10.125, 13.259
32 . . . . 10.132, 13.147, 13.148, 13.151, 13.259, 13.316
35 . . . . 10.138, 13.260
36 . 3.144, 10.125, 10.144, 10.146, 10.233, 10.238, 13.98, 13.147, 13.151, 13.156, 13.259, 13.266, 13.267, 13.270, 13.271, 13.281, 13.316
(1)(a)–(c) 13.100
37 . . . . 10.116
39 . . . . 10.154, 10.157, 13.260
40 . . . . 10.154, 10.157, 13.260
41 . . . . 10.154
42 . . 3.144, 10.149, 13.98, 13.147, 13.155, 13.259, 13.273, 13.316
(1)(a)–(c) 13.99
43 . . . . 4.368, 10.124, 10.127, 13.277
61(5) 4.373, 4.408, 4.409
67 . . . . 10.33, 10.138, 10.154
(6) 10.139, 10.142, 10.144, 10.149, 10.155
68 . . . . 10.159
69 . . . . 10.267
Annex I 10.39
point 1 . . . . 10.260
2 . . . . 10.260, **10.261**

Directive 2011/61/EU of the European Parliament and of the Council of 8 June 2011 on Alternative Investment Fund Managers and amending Directives 2003/41/EC and 2009/65/EC and Regulations (EC) No 1060/2009 and (EU) No 1095/2010 ('Alternative Investment Fund Managers Directive', 'AIFMD') – *cont.*
Annex II 13.319
III 13.124, 13.152, 13.155, 13.263
IV 13.263
Directive 2013/36/EU of the European Parliament and of the Council of 26 June 2013 on access to the activity of credit institutions and the prudential supervision of credit institutions and investment firms, amending Directive 2002/87/EC and repealing Directives 2006/48/EC and 2006/49/EC ('Capital Requirements Directive', 'CRD')
. . . . 10.249, 12.13, 12.19, 12.35
Directive 2013/50/EU of the European Parliament and of the Council of 22 October 2013 amending Directive 2004/109/EC of the European Parliament and of the Council on the harmonisation of transparency requirements in relation to information about issuers whose securities are admitted to trading on a regulated market, Directive 2003/71/EC of the European Parliament and of the Council on the prospectus to be published when securities are offered to the public or admitted to trading and Commission Directive 2007/14/EC laying down detailed rules for the implementation of certain provisions of Directive 2004/109/EC 13.125
Directive 2014/65/EU of the European Parliament and of the Council of 15 May 2014 on markets in financial instruments and amending Directive 2002/92/EC and Directive 2011/61/EU (recast 'MiFID' – 'MiFID II')
. . . . . . 4.154, 4.168, 4.189, 4.190, 4.289, 4.332, 4.365, 4.370, 4.374, 4.379, 4.416, 4.547, 9.71, 10.46, 10.249, 13.92, 13.249, 13.251, 13.252, 13.255, 13.256, 13.278
art 4(11) 4.363
Annex II 10.123

Table of European Legislation

Directive 2014/91/EU of the European Parliament and of the Council of 23 July 2014 amending Directive 2009/65/EC on the coordination of laws, regulations and administrative provisions relating to undertakings for collective investment in transferable securities (UCITS) as regards depositary functions, remuneration policies and sanctions ('UCITS V')
...... 4.215, 4.269, 4.270, 12.11, 12.12, 12.13, 12.30, 12.33, 12.35, 12.36, 12.37, 12.39, 12.42, 12.43, 12.44

Directive 2015/849/EU of the European Parliament and of the Council of 20 May 2015 on the prevention of the use of the financial system for the purposes of money laundering or terrorist financing, amending Regulation (EU) No 648/2012 of the European Parliament and of the Council, and repealing Directive 2005/60/EC of the European Parliament and of the Council and Commission Directive 2006/70/EC ('Fourth Anti-Money Laundering

Directive 2015/849/EU of the European Parliament and of the Council of 20 May 2015 on the prevention of the use of the financial system for the purposes of money laundering or terrorist financing, amending Regulation (EU) No 648/2012 of the European Parliament and of the Council, and repealing Directive 2005/60/EC of the European Parliament and of the Council and Commission Directive 2006/70/EC ('Fourth Anti-Money Laundering – cont.
Directive') 4.422

Regulations

Commission Delegated Regulation (EU) No 231/2013 of 19 December 2012 supplementing Directive 2011/61/EU of the European Parliament and of the Council with regard to exemptions, general operating conditions, depositaries, leverage, transparency and supervision ('Delegated Regulation')
.... 10.6, 10.90, 10.174, 10.177, 10.185, 10.189, 10.191, 10.195, 10.197, 10.211, 10.218, 10.231, 13.228
Recital 80 .... **10.103**
art 2 .... 10.50
    4 .... 10.50
    6 .... 10.91
    (2) 10.92
    7–11 .... 10.91
    38 .... **10.69**
    76 .... 10.246
    82 .... 10.254
    91 .... 4.270
    104–107 .... 10.164
    111 .... 10.88, 10.187, 13.118
Commission Delegated Regulation (EU) No 694/2014 of 17 December 2013 supplementing Directive 2011/61/EU of the European Parliament and of the Council with regard to regulatory technical standards determining types of alternative investment fund managers
.... 10.6

Commission Delegated Regulation (EU) 2016/438 of 17 December 2015 supplementing Directive 2009/65/EC of the European Parliament and of the Council with regard to obligations of depositaries 4.269
Commission Delegated Regulation (EU) 2016/522 of 17 December 2015 supplementing Regulation (EU) No 596/2014 of the European Parliament and of the Council as regards an exemption for certain third countries public bodies and central banks, the indicators of market manipulation, the disclosure thresholds, the competent authority for notifications of delays, the permission for trading during closed periods and types of notifiable managers' transactions 9.100
Commission Delegated Regulation (EU) 2016/958 of 9 March 2016 supplementing Regulation (EU) No 596/2014 of the European Parliament and of the Council with regard to regulatory technical standards for the technical arrangements for objective presentation of investment recommendations or other information recommending or suggesting an investment strategy and for disclosure of particular interests or indications of

Table of European Legislation

Commission Delegated Regulation (EU) 2016/958 of 9 March 2016 supplementing Regulation (EU) No 596/2014 of the European Parliament and of the Council with regard to regulatory technical standards for the technical arrangements for objective presentation of investment recommendations or other information recommending or suggesting an investment strategy and for disclosure of particular interests or indications of – *cont.*
conflicts of interest............ 9.109, 9.111
Commission Delegated Regulation (EU) 2016/960 of 17 May 2016 supplementing Regulation (EU) No 596/2014 of the European Parliament and of the Council with regard to regulatory technical standards for the appropriate arrangements, systems and procedures for disclosing market participants conducting market soundings............................. 9.93
Commission Implementing Regulation (EU) No 447/2013 of 15 May 2013 establishing the procedure for AIFMs which choose to opt in under Directive 2011/61/EU of the European Parliament and of the Council.................... 10.6
Commission Implementing Regulation (EU) No 448/2013 of 15 May 2013 establishing a procedure for determining the Member State of reference of a non-EU AIFM pursuant to Directive 2011/61/EU of the European Parliament and of the Council................. 10.116
Commission Implementing Directive (EU) 2015/2392 of 17 December 2015 on Regulation (EU) No 596/2014 of the European Parliament and of the Council as regards reporting to competent authorities of actual or potential infringements of that Regulation 9.113
Commission Implementing Regulation (EU) 2016/347 of 10 March 2016 laying down implementing technical standards with regard to the precise format of insider lists and for updating insider lists in accordance with Regulation (EU) No 596/2014 of the European Parliament and of the Council.................. 9.105

Commission Implementing Regulation (EU) 2016/959 of 17 May 2016 laying down implementing technical standards for market soundings with regard to the systems and notification templates to be used by disclosing market participants and the format of the records in accordance with Regulation (EU) No 596/2014 of the European Parliament and of the Council.................... 9.93
Regulation (EU) No 236/2012 of the European Parliament and of the Council of 14 March 2012 on short selling and certain aspects of credit default swaps ('Short Selling Regulation')......... 13.125
Regulation (EU) No 648/2012 of the European Parliament and of the Council of 4 July 2012 on OTC derivatives, central counterparties and trade repositories......................... 12.95
Regulation (EU) No 575/2013 of the European Parliament and of the Council of 26 June 2013 on prudential requirements for credit institutions and investment firms and amending Regulation (EU) No 648/2012 ('Capital Requirements Regulation')........... 12.13
Regulation (EU) No 596/2014 of the European Parliament and of the Council of 16 April 2014 on market abuse (market abuse regulation) and repealing Directive 2003/6/EC of the European Parliament and of the Council and Commission Directives 2003/124/EC, 2003/125/EC and 2004/72/EC ('EU MAR')... 9.56, 9.57, 9.59, 9.60, 9.62, 9.63, 9.72, 9.74, 9.81, 9.84, 9.94, 9.95, 9.96, 9.98, 9.103, 9.104, 9.107, 9.108, 9.112, 9.115
Recital 24, 25....................... 9.79
54........................... 9.79
art 1(34), (35)....................... 9.110
2(1)..................... 9.68, 9.69, 9.70
(2)......................... 9.69, 9.70
(3).............................. 9.70
(4).............................. 9.73
7(1)............................... 9.75
(2).............................. 9.76
(4).............................. 9.75
8.......................... 9.78, 9.86
9.............................. 9.78
(1)............................. 9.87
(2).............................. 9.88
(3).............................. 9.89

xxxi

Table of European Legislation

Regulation (EU) No 596/2014 of the European Parliament and of the Council of 16 April 2014 on market abuse (market abuse regulation) and repealing Directive 2003/6/EC of the European Parliament and of the Council and Commission Directives 2003/124/EC, 2003/125/EC and 2004/72/EC ('EU MAR') – *cont.*
art 9(4) 9.90
  (5) 9.91
  (6) 9.92
  10 .... 9.82, 9.83
  11 .... 9.93
  12 .... 9.100
    (2) 9.102
  14 .... 9.77, 9.78, 9.82, 9.86, 9.92
  15 .... 9.99
  18 .... 9.106
  20(1), (2) 9.109
    (3) 9.111
  32 .... 9.113
    (4) 9.114
  39(4) 9.71

Regulation (EU) No 600/2014 of the European Parliament and of the Council of 15 May 2014 on markets in financial instruments and amending Regulation (EU) No 648/2012 ('MiFIR') .. 4.190, 4.193, 4.547, 9.71, 10.46

Regulation (EU) No 1286/2014 of the European Parliament and of the Council of 26 November 2014 on key information documents for packaged retail and insurance-based investment products ('PRIIPs Regulation') 12.149, 12.150, 13.218

Regulation (EU) 2015/760 of the European Parliament and of the Council of 29 April 2015 on European long-term investment funds ('ELTIF') 12.146, 13.94

Regulation (EU) 2017/1131 of the European Parliament and of the Council of 14 June 2017 on money market funds 12.146

Table of Cases

B

Bairstow v Queens Moat Houses plc [2000] 1 BCLC 549, [2000] BCC 1025, [1999] Lexis Citation 4199, [1999] All ER (D) 1378, QBD; sub nom Bairstow v Queens Moat Houses plc [2001] EWCA Civ 712, [2001] 2 BCLC 531, [2002] BCC 91, [2001] All ER (D) 211 (May) 8.18
Boardman v Phipps [1967] 2 AC 46, [1966] 3 All ER 721, [1966] 3 WLR 1009, 110 Sol Jo 853, HL 8.41
Bristol and West Building Society v Mothew (t/a Stapley & Co) [1998] Ch 1, [1996] 4 All ER 698, [1997] 2 WLR 436, [1996] NLJR 1273, [1997] PNLR 11, (1996) Times, 2 August, 140 Sol Jo LB 206, CA Civ; sub nom Mothew v Bristol & West Building Society 75 P & CR 241 .... 8.25

C

City Equitable Fire Insurance Co Ltd, Re [1925] Ch 407, 94 LJ Ch 445, [1925] B & CR 109, [1924] All ER Rep 485, 133 LT 520, 40 TLR 853, CA ... 8.15, 8.17, 8.20, 8.22, 8.85

F

Foss v Harbottle (1843) 2 Hare 461, 67 ER 189, VC Ct 8.51, 8.52, 8.65
Fulham Football Club Ltd v Cabra Estates Plc [1994] 1 BCLC 363, 65 P & CR 284, [1993] 1 PLR 29, [1992] BCC 863, (1992) Times, 11 September, CA Civ 8.47

H

Hannam (Ian Charles) v Financial Conduct Authority [2014] UKUT 0233 (TCC), [2014] All ER (D) 219 (May) 9.143
Hogg v Cramphorn Ltd [1967] Ch 254, [1966] 3 All ER 420, [1966] 3 WLR 995, 110 Sol Jo 887, Ch D 8.32

L

Laerstate BV v Revenue and Customs Comrs [2009] UKFTT 209 (TC), [2009] SFTD 551, [2009] SWTI 2669 .... 14.39
Lonrho Ltd v Shell Petroleum Co Ltd [1980] 1 WLR 627, 124 Sol Jo 412, 130 NLJ 605, HL 8.6

M

Mothew v Bristol & West Building Society. See Bristol and West Building Society v Mothew (t/a Stapley & Co)

R

Regal (Hastings) Ltd v Gulliver (1942) [1967] 2 AC 134, [1942] 1 All ER 378, HL 8.35

Table of Cases

S

Scottish Co-operative Wholesale Society Ltd v Meyer [1959] AC 324, [1958] 3 All ER 66, [1958] 3 WLR 404, 102 Sol Jo 617, 1958 SC (HL) 40, HL 8.42
Securities and Futures Commission v Pacific Sun Advisors Ltd and another [2015] HKCFA 27 ...... 13.165
Smith & Fawcett Ltd, Re [1942] Ch 304, [1942] 1 All ER 542, 111 LJ Ch 265, 86 Sol Jo 147, 166 LT 279, CA 8.27

T

Thorby v Goldberg (1964) 112 CLR 597, Aus HC 8.47

W

Weavering Macro Fixed Income Fund Ltd (in liquidation) v Stefan Peterson and Hans Ekstrom (CICA 10 of 2011, 12 February 2015) [2011] 2 CILR 203, CIGC 8.53, 8.68–8.87
Wood v Holden (Inspector of Taxes) [2006] EWCA Civ 26, [2006] 1 WLR 1393, [2006] STC 443, [2006] 2 BCLC 210, 78 TC 1, 8 ITLR 468, (2006) Times, 20 February, 150 Sol Jo LB 127, [2006] SWTI 236, [2006] All ER (D) 190 (Jan), CSRC vol 29 iss 22/2 ...... 14.38

Chapter 1

WHAT IS A HEDGE FUND?

Dale Gabbert, Partner, Simmons & Simmons and Andrew Wylie, Partner and Head of Investment Funds, DLA Piper

OVERVIEW

1.1 What is a 'hedge fund'? It seems extraordinary that a trillion-dollar industry which is by turns vilified and lauded is not considered capable of precise definition by lawyers and regulators, but this is the case. Neither the Financial Conduct Authority (the 'FCA') nor the US Securities and Exchange Commission (the 'SEC') has attempted to define a hedge fund. Nevertheless, hedge funds have identifiable characteristics which are considered below.

1.2 Before examining why this is the case it is instructive to consider the issue from a broader perspective. The term 'hedge fund' implies a fund or collective investment scheme which allows several investors to participate in a common pool of assets that 'hedges', that is, it utilises the investment technique known as hedging, which seeks to offset the risk inherent in one investment by purchasing another investment the value of which is considered likely to move in the opposite direction to the initial investment. The term itself implies that a hedge fund is a fund that seeks to achieve a stable return, which is in fact not a bad definition in some respects but far too simplistic for reasons that will become evident in later chapters. Of course, if a fund were perfectly 'hedged' it would not make or lose money for investors and would therefore not be an attractive investment proposition.

1.3 It is often stated that the first 'hedge fund' was formed by Alfred Winslow Jones in the United States (the 'US') in 1949. Alfred Winslow Jones established an unregulated investment fund whose investment adviser was permitted to sell securities 'short' (that is, to sell securities it did not own hoping to profit by buying them back at a lower price to satisfy its sale obligations) as well as buying securities which it expected would appreciate in value (commonly referred to as taking a 'long' position). In this way, he hoped to be able to hedge the portfolio by making it possible to make money (or at least lose less money) if the long positions did not make profits. Alfred Winslow Jones was not doing anything new – short selling was a permitted technique – but he is credited as being the first person to make use of such a 'long-short' technique within a fund to hedge the long positions taken in the portfolio of the fund. It should be noted that not all hedge fund strategies include short selling as an investment technique.

1.4 What is a Hedge Fund?

1.4 Hedge funds exhibit some common characteristics, albeit that none of these is unique to hedge funds:

- The first characteristic is that hedge funds generally *invest the majority of their assets in financial instruments* such as securities traded on an exchange or on an 'over-the-counter' market, financial instruments related to them (known as 'derivatives' because their value derives from another asset) or in the debt obligations of companies which are insolvent (distressed debt). The significance of this is that there is generally some degree of liquidity in the underlying portfolio of the hedge fund (unlike, for instance, in the case of a private equity fund which invests in unlisted companies whose shares are not readily realisable). The degree of liquidity varies considerably between strategies (for example, distressed debt may be highly illiquid), and prior to the financial crisis hedge funds increasingly invested in alternative asset classes including private equity and real estate, which tended to reduce the liquidity of their portfolios and blurred some of the distinctions between hedge funds and other types of funds.
- The second characteristic is that the funds themselves are almost always *unregulated*. That means that they are not subject to regulation by onshore regulators such as the FCA or the SEC. The reason for this is that they are normally established in offshore jurisdictions such as Jersey, Guernsey, the Cayman Islands, the British Virgin Islands or, less commonly, Bermuda where they are also not liable to entity level taxation. Under general principles of conflict of laws, countries generally do not seek to regulate activities which occur outside their own borders. National regulators generally cannot regulate entities established outside their jurisdiction unless those entities have some qualifying nexus with their jurisdiction. That nexus can be management, trading activities or the marketing of hedge funds in that jurisdiction. Whilst all UK managers which manage third party assets are required to be authorised by the FCA and their investment personnel approved by the FCA, this is not the case in the US where smaller investment advisers may not need to be regulated by the SEC.
- The third characteristic of hedge funds is that they tend to have *much broader investment parameters* than would be the case for a retail fund (or in US parlance, a mutual fund). Most onshore jurisdictions, understandably, have rules which limit the scope of permissible investments and investment techniques in funds which are marketed to the public. In the UK, for example, there are strict limits on what 'authorised funds' (that is, funds that may be freely marketed to the general public, such as unit trusts and open-ended investment companies (known as 'OEICs')) can invest in and limits on leverage, together with requirements that the fund's portfolio is diversified, liquid and regularly priced. EU law has implemented legislation which permits qualifying funds that are established in any EU jurisdiction to be marketed in any other EU jurisdiction (the 'UCITS' Directives), and which enshrines common principles on diversification, leverage and investment techniques for funds that are to be marketed to the public on a cross-border basis within the EU.

Hedge funds seek to exploit a much broader range of investment techniques than those that are available to traditional authorised funds and indeed other types of private funds, such as private equity funds and real estate funds. The reason for this is simple – the more freedom a fund has in its investment policy, the more opportunity it has to make positive returns (and, conversely, losses).

- The fourth characteristic, which arguably is a reflection of the second and third characteristics, is that they are *not available for sale directly to the general public*. Of course, this does not mean that the general public are not exposed to them – they are, through the holdings that their pension plans have in hedge funds and as shareholders in institutions which provide services to, or trade with, hedge funds. Some jurisdictions (for example, Germany) allow the sale to the general public of funds which invest in a portfolio of hedge funds ('funds of hedge funds'). In addition, a number of large hedge funds are now listed, which provides another route for investor participation and regulation.
- The fifth characteristic of hedge funds is their ability to use *leverage or borrowing* to enhance the performance of the fund. The level of borrowing by hedge funds varies substantially and may be restricted by the rules of a stock exchange if their shares are listed on that stock exchange (for instance, the Irish Stock Exchange).
- The sixth characteristic is that they generally charge *relatively high fees*. A typical hedge fund would charge an annual management fee of between 1% and 2% and a performance fee of 20% of its gains (possibly over some target or 'hurdle'). These fees are high compared with the fees which retail funds typically charge (they generally do not have a performance fee) and very high compared with fees for managing institutional 'long only' money. This fee structure is a common feature of the vast majority of hedge funds.

1.5 None of these characteristics is unique to hedge funds. Private equity funds, for example, frequently share all of those characteristics other than the first and the sixth characteristics. However, a fund which displays all of these characteristics can legitimately be described as a hedge fund.

1.6 The hedge fund industry has seen a rapid increase in assets over the last ten years with research estimating assets under management of about US$3 trillion. Regulators across the globe have understandably become concerned about the potential impact of hedge funds on global financial markets, which in the US was reflected in a failed attempt by the SEC to regulate the managers of hedge funds.

1.7 In June 2007, the Hedge Fund Working Group (the 'HFWG') was formed with a view to formulating best practice standards for hedge fund managers. The HFWG consists of 13 European hedge fund managers and one US hedge fund manager. The HFWG consulted on proposed standards and issued its final report in January 2008. This resulted in the establishment of the Hedge Fund Standards Board (the 'HFSB') which acts as the custodian of the HFSB Best Practice Standards, which deal with best practice on a wide range of issues such as the disclosure of material side letter terms, the involvement of the manager in the valuation of the assets of the hedge fund, the adoption of a valuation policy and improved disclosure to investors. Signatory managers are

1.7 What is a Hedge Fund?

required to conform on a 'comply or explain' basis. Membership is voluntary and there is a public registry of signatory managers.

1.8 Is the increasing pressure on the hedge fund industry to self-regulate or be regulated by regulatory authorities justified?

1.9 First, whilst hedge funds themselves are strictly 'unregulated', they are still required, like anyone else, to abide by applicable securities laws and the rules of any exchanges on which they transact. Even if they have no UK nexus they will still be liable under the market abuse regime if they manipulate a security which is traded on a regulated UK market (or, indeed, a security which is priced by reference to such a UK market security).

1.10 Second, whilst hedge funds themselves are largely unregulated because they are typically established in offshore jurisdictions, this is not the case for their service providers. Press reports often omit to mention that all UK hedge fund managers are required to be regulated by the FCA and that many (but not all) US managers are registered with the SEC, the National Association of Securities Dealers and/or the US Commodity Futures Trading Commission. The overall level of regulatory oversight of the hedge funds industry is significantly broader than this because prime brokers, through whom the majority of hedge fund trades are placed, are also regulated in onshore jurisdictions.

1.11 Global regulators are aware of the need to tread carefully. If the onshore regulatory environment becomes too restrictive or onerous, hedge fund managers may move their entire operations offshore, which would adversely affect the onshore economy and remove the ability of onshore regulators directly to regulate the hedge fund manager and its employees. This would clearly have a negative effect on both the financial system and investors. The FCA has taken a measured approach by putting in place a dedicated team that liaises with the 35 largest UK hedge fund managers and separately conducts a six-monthly survey of the exposure of prime brokers to hedge funds.

1.12 The work of the Alternative Investment Management Association and other industry bodies raises legitimate issues which investors should consider. Investors should, however, be mindful that hedge funds are alternative or non-mainstream investments and are not appropriate for investors who do not know the risks involved or understand the product. This is illustrated by the additional investment, leverage and other restrictions which the FCA generally imposes on the managers of funds which are marketed to retail investors.

1.13 From a UK perspective, increased regulation and an attempt to transform offshore hedge funds into retail products is not justified or desirable.

1.14 Hopefully, once the controversy over short selling by hedge funds during and in the aftermath of the financial crisis finally subsides, the FCA will allow the robust innovation that has characterised the City of London for several hundred years to continue.

Introduction to the second edition

1.15 A lot has changed since the first edition of this book was published. In the wake of the financial crisis there has been a swing of the regulatory pendulum firmly in favour of market intervention and oversight. Most significantly, the

Alternative Investment Fund Managers Directive ('AIFMD') has been enacted, regulating funds remotely via their managers, where these are located in Europe, and imposing registration requirements on the marketing into Europe of foreign funds. AIFMD catches a far wider variety of funds than any previous legislation and is far more ambitious in its scope. In the authors' opinion it is the most profound change in the regulation of the funds industry in their working lifetime. AIFMD is explored in a new chapter.

Chapter 2

OFFSHORE FUND DOMICILES – THE CARIBBEAN

A	The Cayman Islands	2.1
B	The British Virgin Islands	2.57

A   THE CAYMAN ISLANDS

Robert Duggan, Partner, Mourant Ozannes

Introduction

2.1 The Cayman Islands is a group of three islands in the north-west Caribbean approximately 500 miles south of Florida.

2.2 As a British Overseas Territory, the Cayman Islands offers the security and stability traditionally associated with the British flag whilst having an independent legal and judicial system based on English common law, with a right of final appeal to the Privy Council in London.

2.3 With the high volume, value and sophistication of the financial transactions which are undertaken by Cayman Islands entities and which pass through the Cayman Islands, the infrastructure supporting the financial services industry is well developed and of a high quality. This infrastructure includes a number of established professional services firms (including lawyers, accountants, bankers and administrators) which have broad expertise and provide prompt advice. Additionally, the Cayman Islands provides a stable socio-political framework within which the financial services industry is permitted to thrive.

The finance industry

2.4 The Cayman Islands is the world's leading offshore hedge funds jurisdiction, with over 10,500 funds registered with the Investments Division of the Cayman Islands Monetary Authority ('CIMA')[1]. It is also home to a thriving offshore banking and trust sector, with over 300 banks and trust companies[2], including many of the financial services industry's household names.

[1] As at 16 May 2017.
[2] As at the end of March 2017, the Banking Division of CIMA had supervision of 158 banks and the Fiduciary Services Division had supervisory responsibility for 146 active trust licences.

2.5 The Cayman Islands provides a very flexible and user-friendly environment. A Cayman Islands fund may, subject to any restrictions imposed by

2.5 Offshore Fund Domiciles – The Caribbean

public policy or the doctrine of illegality or its own constitutional documents, make investments of any type anywhere in the world.

2.6 Otherwise than as described below in relation to offering shares to the public in the Cayman Islands and certain requirements relating to investment managers incorporated in the Cayman Islands, there are no governmental approvals or consents that must be obtained, nor any statutory requirements that must be complied with, in connection with the issue of shares, limited partnership interests or units by a Cayman Islands fund or in relation to the distribution of the relevant fund's offering documentation.

The funds and regulatory regime

2.7 The Cayman Islands' hedge funds regulatory regime was introduced in the form of the Mutual Funds Law on 26 July 1993 and has been consolidated and revised several times since. The Mutual Funds Law applies to all investment funds established in or operating from the Cayman Islands and which fall within the law's definition of a 'mutual fund' (discussed below). The Mutual Funds Law also applies to those who administer mutual funds in or from the Cayman Islands.

What is a mutual fund?

2.8 A mutual fund is defined[1] as a company, unit trust or partnership that issues 'equity interests', the purpose or effect of which is the pooling of investor funds with the aim of spreading investment risks and enabling investors in the mutual fund to receive profits or gains from the acquisition, holding, management or disposal of investments.

[1] Section 2 of the Mutual Funds Law.

2.9 The term 'equity interests' is defined[1] as a share, trust unit or partnership interest that carries an entitlement to participate in the profits or gains of the company, unit trust or partnership and is redeemable or repurchasable at the option of the investor, but does not include debt or alternative financial instruments as prescribed under the Banks and Trust Companies Law.

[1] Section 2 of the Mutual Funds Law.

2.10 Specifically excluded from the definition of a 'mutual fund' are persons licensed under certain financial regulatory laws of the Cayman Islands, namely the Banks and Trust Companies Law or the Insurance Law, or a person registered under the Building Societies Law or the Friendly Societies Law.

2.11 The Mutual Funds Law does not seek to cover or require the regulation of closed-ended funds, being funds in which investors do not have the right to redeem or require the repurchase of their interest. Many trusts and exempted limited partnerships are not covered by the Mutual Funds Law for this reason.

Types of fund vehicle

2.12 Mutual funds can take several different forms, including corporate entities[1], unit trusts[2] and limited partnerships[3].

[1] See paras **2.14–2.16** below.
[2] See paras **2.26–2.27** below.
[3] See paras **2.17–2.21** below.

2.13 The most appropriate form of fund vehicle will depend upon several factors, including taxation and regulatory concerns of the fund's investment manager as well as its prospective investors. Whatever legal form a fund adopts, it is subject to regulation in accordance with the terms of the Mutual Funds Law in the same way.

CORPORATE ENTITIES

2.14 The Companies Law of the Cayman Islands provides for a category of companies which are to carry on business mainly outside the Cayman Islands, which is the case for most mutual funds. Such companies – called 'exempted companies' – are extremely flexible and can adopt sophisticated structures readily and with a low administrative burden. Of significant commercial benefit when it comes to choosing to use an exempted company as a fund vehicle is the fact that such entities are entitled to a guarantee from the government of the Cayman Islands that, for up to 30 years, the company will not be subject to taxation in the Cayman Islands, notwithstanding any change to the taxation regime of the Cayman Islands.

2.15 Exempted companies can exist as companies limited by shares or by guarantee, companies without limitation on the liability of shareholders, and/or companies which are established with (or without) a limitation on their duration.

2.16 There are no residency or qualification requirements for directors or shareholders of exempted companies.

LIMITED PARTNERSHIPS

2.17 An exempted limited partnership benefits from a similar tax undertaking to that described above for corporate entities, but in this case the tax undertaking can apply for up to 50 years. An exempted limited partnership is formed by one or more general partners (whose liability for all of the debts and obligations of the partnership is, in the event that the assets of the partnership are inadequate, unlimited) and one or more limited partners (who benefit from limited liability save as stated below) entering into a partnership agreement which governs the partnership and regulates the manner of its operation.

2.18 As is the case with partnerships in many other common law jurisdictions, an exempted limited partnership is not an entity with separate legal personality and cannot therefore conduct business in its own right but rather is required by statute to be managed and operated by its general partners (who may delegate their powers). Consequently, an exempted limited partnership cannot own property in its own right, and the property of the partnership is held by

2.18 Offshore Fund Domiciles – The Caribbean

the general partners on statutory trust for the exempted limited partnership in accordance with the terms of the partnership agreement.

2.19 All letters, contracts, deeds, instruments or documents whatsoever required to be entered into by the partnership must be executed on its behalf by the general partners.

2.20 A limited partner who takes part in the conduct of the business of the partnership in its dealings with persons who are not partners will be liable, in the event of the insolvency of the partnership, for all debts and obligations of that partnership incurred during the period in which such limited partner conducted himself as a general partner (provided that the limited partner will be liable only to a person who transacts business with the partnership during that period with actual knowledge of such participation and who then reasonably believed such limited partner to be a general partner of the partnership).

2.21 There are no residency or qualification requirements for limited partners, but at least one general partner is required to be an individual who is resident in the Cayman Islands, a company incorporated or registered as a foreign company in the Cayman Islands, or a Cayman Islands exempted limited partnership.

LIMITED LIABILITY COMPANIES

2.22 The limited liability company ('LLC') is a new vehicle that was introduced in the Cayman Islands in 2016 pursuant to the Limited Liability Companies Law. This is a hybrid entity which essentially combines characteristics of an exempted company with those of an exempted limited partnership. Like an exempted company, an LLC has separate legal personality, but unlike an exempted company, it does not have share capital. Member liability is limited, capital accounts are permitted, and the members are free to determine among themselves in the LLC agreement how profits and losses are allocated and how and when distributions are made, similar to the freedoms afforded to partners of an exempted limited partnership. The LLC benefits from a similar tax undertaking to that described above for exempted companies and exempted limited partnerships, which can be granted for up to 50 years.

2.23 There are no residency or qualification requirements for members of LLCs.

2.24 As a fund vehicle, the LLC allows for simplified fund administration, and its flexibility facilitates easier tracking or calculation of a member's investment in the LLC. The LLC is also suitable to act as a private equity or other closed-ended fund vehicle as an alternative to the exempted limited partnership, which does not enjoy separate legal personality, or the exempted company, which can be constrained by share capital rules and can be cumbersome in the operation of capital call and default mechanics.

SEGREGATED PORTFOLIO COMPANIES

2.25 Under the terms of the Companies Law, an exempted company may be registered as a segregated portfolio company (an 'SPC'), whereby the company will be able to operate segregated portfolios each with the benefit of statutory segregation of the assets and liabilities which are attributable to each respective segregated portfolio. The principal advantage of an SPC over a standard exempted company is to protect the assets of each segregated portfolio from the liabilities of each other segregated portfolio; as such, the SPC is popular in the context of mutual funds as it facilitates the running of certain high risk or speculative strategies alongside others with lower associated risk.

UNIT TRUSTS

2.26 Unit trusts are trusts like any other, and all assets of a unit trust are vested in a trustee under a trust deed or declaration of trust which divides the beneficial ownership into a number of units which are usually (but not necessarily) freely transferable and redeemable, thereby going some way towards replicating the unitised interests of a company, the capital of which is divided into shares. The rights and obligations of the trustee and the unitholders, the terms of redemption and valuation rules are all set out in the trust deed.

2.27 A unit trust may be registered as a mutual fund in the same manner as companies and/or partnerships, since units in a trust fall within the definition of 'equity interests' in the Mutual Funds Law.

Types of funds

2.28 For the purposes of the Cayman Islands' regulatory regime, mutual funds fall into the following four categories, three of which require registration and therefore regulation by CIMA:

- licensed mutual funds[1];
- administered mutual funds[2];
- registered mutual funds[3]; and
- exempted mutual funds[4].

[1] See para 2.30 below.
[2] See paras 2.31–2.32 below.
[3] See paras 2.33–2.35 below.
[4] See para 2.36 below.

2.29 The most common category of mutual fund is registered mutual funds, which are the most suitable for funds which cater to sophisticated investors. Licensed and administered mutual funds are relatively uncommon and are ordinarily associated with funds with a less sophisticated investor base or where there are commercial reasons for accommodating investors with lower subscription amounts. A brief description of each of the four categories of fund is set out below.

2.30 Offshore Fund Domiciles – The Caribbean

LICENSED MUTUAL FUNDS

2.30 Licensed mutual funds are mutual funds which hold a licence under the Mutual Funds Law. They must have a registered office in the Cayman Islands or, in the case of a unit trust, a trustee which is licensed under the Banks and Trust Companies Law. In order to obtain a mutual fund licence an application must be made to CIMA in an approved form, accompanied by the prescribed application fee and the following information:

- the current offering document (or the latest draft);
- a synopsis of the offering document;
- details of the mutual fund's registered office (or, if a unit trust, its trustee);
- details of the mutual fund's administrator (if any), providing its principal office in the Cayman Islands;
- sufficient evidence to satisfy CIMA:
    - as to the sound reputation of each promoter of the mutual fund[1];
    - as to the expertise of each person undertaking the administration of the mutual fund; and
    - that the business of the mutual fund and any offering of equity interests will be carried out in a proper way;
- a letter from the mutual fund's administrator confirming its consent to act; and
- a letter from the mutual fund's auditors confirming their consent to act.

[1] 'Promoter' is defined by section 2 of the Mutual Funds Law as being any person whether within or without the Islands who causes the preparation or distribution of an offering document in respect of a mutual fund (but does not include a professional adviser acting for or on behalf of such a person).

ADMINISTERED MUTUAL FUNDS

2.31 Administered mutual funds are mutual funds which have a licensed mutual fund administrator in the Cayman Islands providing the mutual fund's principal office (as distinct from its registered office) in the Cayman Islands. Mutual funds which have a licensed mutual fund administrator as the provider of its principal office are not required to obtain a licence under the terms of the Mutual Funds Law, but the licensed mutual fund administrator is required to satisfy itself:

- as to the sound reputation of each promoter of the mutual fund;
- as to the sound reputation and expertise of the person undertaking the administration of the mutual fund; and
- that the business of the mutual fund and any offering of equity interests will be carried out in a proper way.

2.32 The licensed mutual fund administrator must give CIMA details of each mutual fund which it represents and pay the prescribed fees in respect of that mutual fund.

REGISTERED MUTUAL FUNDS

2.33 Registered mutual funds are mutual funds which have a minimum aggregate equity interest purchasable by a prospective investor of US$100,000 (or its equivalent in another currency) or the equity interests of which are listed on an approved stock exchange or over-the-counter market. Such mutual funds are not required to obtain a licence or to be represented by a licensed mutual fund administrator but they are required to register with and be regulated by CIMA.

2.34 This head of regulation is generally designed for more sophisticated or high net worth investors who have access to sufficient assets to invest in such funds (and who are therefore assumed to be better able to afford professional advice in connection with the management of their affairs), and is the most common head of registration of mutual funds under the Mutual Funds Law.

2.35 In the case of a master-feeder fund structure, both the feeder fund[1] and the master fund[2] are required to register with and be regulated by CIMA.

[1] A 'feeder fund' is defined by section 2 of the Mutual Funds Law as a mutual fund that conducts more than 51% of its investing in a master fund either directly or through an intermediary entity.
[2] Under the Mutual Funds Law, a regulated fund is a 'master fund' if it has one or more regulated feeder funds either directly or through an intermediary entity established to invest in the master fund and it holds investments and conducts trading activities for the principal purpose of implementing the overall investment strategy of the regulated feeder fund.

EXEMPTED MUTUAL FUNDS

2.36 The exception to the general requirement for mutual funds to register with CIMA are mutual funds the equity interests of which are held by not more than 15 investors, the majority of whom are capable of appointing or removing the operator of the fund (ie the board of the directors in the case of a mutual fund established as a company, the general partner in the case of a mutual fund established as an exempted limited partnership, and the trustee(s) in the case of a mutual fund established as a unit trust). A mutual fund of this type escapes regulation altogether and therefore is not required to be registered with CIMA.

Offering document

2.37 The Mutual Funds Law does not prescribe a format for the content of the offering document of a mutual fund, but it does require the offering document to describe the equity interests offered thereby in all material respects and to contain such other information as is necessary to enable a prospective investor in the mutual fund to make an informed decision as to whether or not to subscribe for or purchase such equity interests.

Investment restrictions

2.38 There are no statutory restrictions on the investment policies of mutual funds in the Cayman Islands. Restrictions can, of course, be laid down by the fund's offering document or its constitutional documents. These are often

2.38 Offshore Fund Domiciles – The Caribbean

dictated by listing rules requirements and are most prevalent in funds which have their equity securities listed on a recognised exchange.

Borrowing

2.39 There are no statutory restrictions on the power of mutual funds to borrow (whether in the form of traditional borrowing or stock lending transactions). The fund's offering document or its constitutional documents may (but need not) impose restrictions on leverage. Again, these are often dictated by listing rules requirements and are most prevalent in funds which have their equity securities listed on a recognised exchange.

Accounts

2.40 Mutual funds are required to prepare audited financial statements which must be reviewed and signed by an approved firm of auditors in the Cayman Islands (notwithstanding the fact that the audit is often conducted outside the Cayman Islands) and submitted to CIMA within six months following the end of the financial period to which the accounts relate.

Fund ownership

2.41 There are no legal restrictions on the percentage of equity interests in a mutual fund which may be held or subscribed for by any one person or related group of persons.

The regulatory process

2.42 Where a fund is a mutual fund (other than an exempted mutual fund with fewer than 16 investors[1]), it is required to submit to regulation by CIMA. The regulatory supervision by CIMA will depend upon the category of registration. As one would expect, regulatory supervision is greatest for a licensed mutual fund. Only licensed mutual funds require the approval of CIMA prior to commencing trading. Although they are subject to regulation by CIMA, administered mutual funds and mutual funds with fewer than 16 investors do not require CIMA's approval prior to commencing trading. Accordingly, the regulatory elements of the establishment of a hedge fund in the Cayman Islands should not, for the most part, extend the timeline for the fund's establishment.

[1] See para **2.36** above.

2.43 All regulated mutual funds are required to:

- submit to CIMA and keep current a copy of their most recent offering document;
- submit to CIMA audited annual accounts (filed electronically by the mutual fund's auditor together with a synopsis of key details relating to the mutual fund); and
- pay the prescribed annual fee (approximately US$4,300 for a feeder fund and approximately US$3,050 for a master fund).

2.44 Licensed mutual funds or administered mutual funds may only be administered by reputable persons with sufficient expertise. CIMA or the licensed mutual fund administrator will have to be satisfied that the business of the mutual fund and any offering which it makes is to be carried out in a proper way.

2.45 The Mutual Funds Law also contains enforcement provisions allowing CIMA to inspect books and records, call for accounting and take action to protect investors where appropriate. The penalties imposed by the Mutual Funds Law for breach of any statutory requirement are relatively stringent.

2.46 Pursuant to the Directors Registration and Licencing Law of the Cayman Islands, which came into force in 2014, directors of Cayman Islands companies that are registered with CIMA must themselves be directly registered with CIMA[1].

[1] For further details, see paras **8.89–8.90** in CHAPTER 8.

Investment managers and advisers

2.47 Any company, foreign company or partnership incorporated or registered in the Cayman Islands and carrying on securities investment business anywhere in the world, or any entity which has established a place of business in the Cayman Islands through which securities investment business is carried on will be subject to the Securities Investment Business Law of the Cayman Islands. Such persons are required to obtain a licence under the terms of that Law unless the conduct of the relevant services is in respect of persons who are (i) subject to regulation by a recognised overseas regulated authority, (ii) within the same group as the provider of the relevant services, and/or (iii) sophisticated or high net worth persons; in which case, the relevant entity is not required to obtain a full licence but instead can avail itself of an exemption from licensing upon the filing of an exemption certification form and payment of an annual fee. Cayman Islands investment managers and/or advisers are generally able to avail themselves of an exemption from licensing under the Securities Investment Business Law.

Anti-money laundering

2.48 Mutual fund business falls within the definition of 'relevant financial business' under the Cayman Islands' Proceeds of Crime Law[1]; as a result, mutual funds need to ensure compliance with the Anti-money Laundering Regulations of the Cayman Islands (the 'Regulations').

[1] Section 2 of the Proceeds of Crime Law.

2.49 Compliance with the Regulations is the ultimate responsibility of the mutual fund and its board of directors (or the general partner if the mutual fund is a partnership or the trustee if the mutual fund is a unit trust). This includes the need to have in place procedures for identifying and reporting suspicious activity and to identify an appropriate person to receive internal

2.49 Offshore Fund Domiciles – The Caribbean

suspicion reports (commonly called a Money Laundering Reporting Officer or 'MLRO').

2.50 CIMA recognises that a number of mutual funds have no permanent staff and so cannot have procedures in place to identify or report in the manner required by the Regulations. Accordingly, CIMA has issued guidance notes which provide that it is acceptable for such mutual funds to address compliance with the Regulations by identifying an MLRO for the mutual fund (being a board member or a suitable independent third party) or by delegating the functions of the MLRO to a regulated person in the Cayman Islands or in an approved jurisdiction (as set out in the Regulations). Where the issue and administration of subscriptions and redemptions is carried out by a person subject to the regulatory regime in the Cayman Islands or in an approved jurisdiction, compliance with such jurisdiction's requirements will be deemed sufficient by CIMA.

2.51 The mutual fund should keep records, such as appropriate board minutes, showing how it has complied with its obligations under the Regulations.

Taxation

2.52 There is no taxation in the Cayman Islands on the income or capital gains of individuals, companies, partnerships or trusts, including in relation to the payment of dividends or distributions to shareholders, limited partners or unitholders or capital gains on a redemption or sale of shares, limited partnership interests or units in a trust. Furthermore, a tax exemption undertaking can be applied for pursuant to which the Cayman Islands government guarantees that no such taxes will be imposed upon the entity in question for a specified period of time (30 years in the case of a company and up to 50 years in the case of a limited partnership and a unit trust).

2.53 There are no exchange controls in the Cayman Islands.

2.54 The Cayman Islands has signed two inter-governmental agreements to improve international tax compliance and the exchange of information – one with the US (the 'US IGA'), which gives effect to the automatic tax information exchange requirements of the US Foreign Account Tax Compliance Act ('FATCA'), and one with the UK with respect to the automatic exchange of tax information relating to UK tax resident persons and entities (the 'UK IGA'). The Cayman Islands is also one of multiple jurisdictions which have agreed to the automatic exchange of financial account information on the basis of the standard published by the Organisation for Economic Co-operation and Development (the Common Reporting Standard or 'CRS').

2.55 In order to give effect to its obligations under the US IGA, the UK IGA and the CRS, the Cayman Islands has adopted regulations (the 'AEOI Regulations'). Pursuant to the AEOI Regulations, the Cayman Islands Tax Information Authority (the 'Cayman TIA') has also published guidance notes on the application of the IGAs and the CRS. Reporting under the UK IGA was expected to be phased out in 2017 as the UK transitions to the CRS.

2.56 Under the AEOI Regulations, all Cayman Islands 'financial institutions' are classified as 'reporting financial institutions' ('Reporting FIs') unless a particular financial institution may rely on an exemption, in which case it will be classified as a 'non-reporting financial institution'. Most Cayman Islands funds will be classified as Reporting FIs. A Reporting FI is required to: (i) register with the US Internal Revenue Service (the 'IRS') to obtain a Global Intermediary Identification Number (under FATCA); (ii) register with and notify the Cayman TIA of its status as a Reporting FI; (iii) conduct due diligence on its investors to identify whether accounts are reportable under the AEOI Regulations; and (iv) report account information on reportable accounts to the Cayman TIA. The Cayman TIA will exchange the information reported to it with the IRS and other foreign fiscal authorities annually on an automatic basis.

B THE BRITISH VIRGIN ISLANDS

Marianne Rajic, Partner, Campbells

Introduction

2.57 The British Virgin Islands (the 'BVI') is a group of some 32 islands, 188 rocks and 20 cays situated 60 miles east of Puerto Rico and at the top of the Leeward Islands chain. It follows US Eastern Standard Time and is connected by frequent daily flights to San Juan in Puerto Rico with connecting international flights to the US, South America and Europe. Since 1959, the official currency of the BVI has been the US dollar.

2.58 As a British Overseas Territory, the BVI offers the security and stability traditionally associated with the British flag. The territory is responsible for its own internal self-government, whilst the UK remains responsible for the territory's external affairs, defence, internal security and the courts. However, the British Government has devolved responsibility to the BVI for developing and managing its financial services industry.

2.59 The BVI has an independent legal and judicial system based on English common law, with a right of final appeal to the Privy Council of the UK. The opening of a dedicated Commercial Division of the Eastern Caribbean Supreme Court on 4 May 2009 and the Commercial Court building on 30 October 2009 has brought a new and dynamic dimension to the specialist practice of cross-border litigation in the BVI. Since its inception, the Commercial Court has become renowned for facilitating the speedy and efficient resolution of commercial cases in the BVI in a manner that permits the Court and the BVI to maintain a competitive international profile and thereby provide support to the international business community.

2.60 The political and economic stability, well established international standing and respectability and the close relationship between the BVI government and the private sector, which ensures that policies and legislation meet the financial community's needs and interests, make the BVI one of the world's premier financial services centres.

2.61 BVI entities are extensively present in some of the most significant global transactions, such as the recent US$1.35 billion take-private acquisition of UTi Worldwide, the NASDAQ-listed logistics group, and many high value mergers, takeovers and acquisitions. BVI companies are listed on all of the world's ma-

2.61 Offshore Fund Domiciles – The Caribbean

jor stock exchanges with market capitalisations ranging from a few million to several billion US dollars. By way of example, Winsway Enterprises Holding Limited is a BVI company listed on the Hong Kong Stock Exchange and one of the leading suppliers of imported coking coal into mainland China, and Tianhe Chemicals Group Ltd, China's largest producer of lubricant oil and leading global producer of specialty chemicals and a BVI company, was recently listed on the Hong Kong Stock Exchange, raising US$654 million. Furthermore, the majority of Chinese companies incorporated outside of China and listed in Hong Kong (also known as red-chip stocks) have BVI holding companies.

The finance industry

2.62 The finance industry in the BVI developed rapidly following the introduction of the International Business Companies Act in 1986. Since 1986, some 900,000 international business companies ('IBCs') have been incorporated in the BVI, with 416,784 companies active on 31 December 2016. Since the introduction of the BVI Business Companies Act, 2004 (commonly known as the 'BC Act'), the BVI has benefited from having one of the most flexible and convenient company law statutes in the world.

2.63 The BC Act is based on English company law; however, whilst retaining established principles of English company law, the BC Act provides much greater flexibility than the UK's Companies Act 2006. The BC Act does not contain any maintenance of capital requirements. In addition, English common law restrictions on financial assistance are excluded by the BC Act. The BC Act enables BVI companies to enter into types of transaction which simply are not available to English companies, such as mergers/consolidations with a BVI or foreign company with either being the surviving company and continuations/migrations between the BVI and another jurisdiction. In financing transactions, banks are comfortable with BVI company structures, with the BC Act allowing for both BVI and foreign law governed security to be given by a BVI company over its assets or by its shareholders over their shares. Coupled with modern insolvency legislation (the Insolvency Act, 2003), the BVI possesses a modern legislative infrastructure for the finance industry.

2.64 The BVI's policies and legislation have been developed in close partnership with the private sector, ensuring that they continue to meet the needs of the financial community and maintain BVI's position in the global markets. Through this partnership, the BVI government has established sophisticated and efficient supervision and regulation which safeguards the integrity of the BVI and creates an operating environment that is highly attractive to private enterprise.

2.65 The BVI positioned itself as a funds formation jurisdiction in 1996 with the introduction of the Mutual Funds Act, and soon became a home jurisdiction for some of the world's largest investment funds, such as funds in the GAM family of funds. Now, the BVI is home to the second largest number of regulated investment funds globally, and is becoming increasingly popular as a jurisdiction for the establishment of start-up offshore investment funds, in addition to the traditional professional and private funds. Following the implementation of the Securities and Investment Business Act ('SIBA') and the

Mutual Funds Regulations in 2010, the BVI continues to offer an efficient framework for the establishment of professional and private funds to operate as stand-alone corporate or limited partnership vehicles, or as a part of a master-feeder structure. With the introduction of the Securities and Investment Business (Incubator and Approved Funds) Regulations, 2015 (the 'Incubator and Approved Funds Regulations') on 1 June 2015, the BVI expanded its offering with two new funds products, incubator funds and approved funds, to cater for start-up managers and those managing funds for small groups of closely-connected investors, such as family offices.

The funds regime and regulation

The Securities and Investment Business Act

2.66 SIBA defines a 'mutual fund' or a 'fund' as a company or any other body, a partnership or a unit trust which:

- collects and pools investor funds for the purpose of collective investment; and
- issues fund interests that entitle the holder to receive on demand or within a specified period after demand an amount computed by reference to the value of a proportionate interest in the whole or in a part of the net assets of the company or other body, partnership or unit trust, as the case may be.

2.67 'Fund interests' are defined as the rights or interests, however described, of the investors in a mutual fund with regard to the property of the fund, excluding debt.

2.68 The above definition means that closed-ended funds (ie those funds that do not permit investors to redeem their interest) are generally excluded from the scope of SIBA and are not regulated in the BVI.

2.69 Under SIBA, there are four categories of open-ended funds (also referred to as mutual funds under SIBA) that are required to be registered or recognised, namely:

- professional funds[1];
- private funds[2];
- public funds[3]; and
- recognised foreign funds[4].

[1] See paras 2.70–2.72 below.
[2] See paras 2.73–2.74 below.
[3] See para 2.75 below.
[4] See para 2.76 below.

PROFESSIONAL FUNDS

2.70 Only 'professional investors' can invest in a professional fund. The initial investment of each investor in a professional fund, other than an 'exempted investor', must be not less than US$100,000 or equivalent in other currency in order for that fund to qualify as a professional fund under BVI law.

2.71 *Offshore Fund Domiciles – The Caribbean*

2.71 A 'professional investor' is a person:

- whose ordinary business involves, whether for his account or the account of others, the acquisition or disposal of property of the same kind as the property, or a substantial part of the property, of the fund; or
- who has signed a declaration that he, whether individually or jointly with his spouse has a net worth in excess of US$1 million or its equivalent in any other currency and that he consents to being treated as a professional investor.

2.72 An 'exempted investor' is:

- the manager, administrator, promoter or underwriter of the fund; or
- any employee of the manager or promoter of the fund.

PRIVATE FUNDS

2.73 A private fund:

- offers and sells its shares or similar interests on a 'private basis'; or
- has constitutional documents which limit the number of investors to less than 50.

2.74 Whilst 'private basis' is not defined, SIBA provides that an invitation to subscribe for, or purchase, fund interests issued on a private basis includes an invitation which is made:

- to specified persons (however described) and is not calculated to result in fund interests becoming available to other persons or to a large number of persons; or
- by reason of a private or business connection between the person making the invitation and the investor.

PUBLIC FUNDS

2.75 A public fund is generally a fund that offers its shares to the public. There is no specified definition of the 'public' for these purposes; however, a public fund is generally regarded as a fund that is not otherwise a private fund or a professional fund.

RECOGNISED FOREIGN FUNDS

2.76 Recognised foreign funds are those funds which are marketed in the BVI and which have been recognised by the BVI Financial Services Commission.

The Incubator and Approved Funds Regulations

2.77 In addition to the four fund categories under SIBA, two new categories of funds, namely incubator and approved funds, were introduced by the Incubator and Approved Funds Regulations, which came into force on 1 June 2015.

INCUBATOR FUNDS

2.78 The incubator fund is aimed at start-up managers seeking a low-cost option to set up quickly and establish a track record, without having to comply with significant regulatory obligations.

2.79 Incubator funds are permitted to operate without appointing an administrator, custodian, investment manager or auditor but are restricted to sophisticated private investors and must operate within the following thresholds:

- a maximum of 20 investors;
- a minimum initial investment of US$20,000 per investor; and
- a maximum fund net asset value of US$20 million.

2.80 If an incubator fund exceeds the maximum number of investors or the maximum net asset value threshold over a period of two consecutive months, it is required to submit an application for conversion into a private, professional or approved fund.

2.81 Incubator funds are permitted to operate for up to two years (with the possibility of a one-year extension). After the end of the relevant term an incubator fund must either:

- apply to the BVI Financial Services Commission for recognition as a private or professional fund (which involves preparing an offering document and audited financial statements, as well as appointing an administrator, custodian, investment manager and auditor, unless certain exemptions are available); or
- apply to the BVI Financial Services Commission for approval as an approved fund.

2.82 If it is not viable for the fund to continue at the end of its term, the fund must commence the process of voluntary liquidation or amend its constitutional documents so as to cease to be a fund under SIBA.

APPROVED FUNDS

2.83 The approved fund is aimed at managers seeking to establish a low-cost, unsupervised fund for the longer term but on the basis of a more private investor offering. The approved fund is particularly suited to family offices.

2.84 Approved funds are entitled to operate without appointing a custodian or investment manager. An approved fund must appoint an administrator but is not required to appoint an auditor. There is no minimum investment requirement for investors and an approved fund is not subject to a limited period of operation. Approved funds are suitable for sophisticated private investors and are limited to:

- a maximum of 20 investors; and
- a maximum fund net asset value of US$100 million.

2.85 An approved fund may, at any time, voluntarily apply to the BVI Financial Services Commission for recognition as a private or professional

2.85 Offshore Fund Domiciles – The Caribbean

fund, and is required to convert into a private or professional fund if it exceeds one of the applicable thresholds over a period of two consecutive months.

Functionaries of SIBA registered or recognised funds

2.86 All BVI professional, private and public funds must at all times have the following fund functionaries:

- a fund manager;
- a fund administrator; and
- a custodian.

2.87 The custodian must be 'functionally independent' from the manager and administrator. Where the custodian role is performed either by the administrator or the manager, that functionary must have systems and controls that ensure that the persons fulfilling the custodial function are functionally independent from the persons fulfilling the fund management or fund administration functions.

2.88 The BVI Financial Services Commission may exempt a professional or private fund from the requirements to have a manager or a custodian, on a case-by-case basis.

Investment restrictions

2.89 There are no restrictions on the investment policies of mutual funds in the BVI other than those specifically contained in a fund's prospectus or its memorandum and articles of association, trust deed or memorandum and articles of partnership.

Borrowing

2.90 There are no legal restrictions on the power of mutual funds in the BVI to borrow other than those specifically contained in a fund's prospectus or its memorandum and articles of association, trust deed or memorandum and articles of partnership.

Offering documents and prospectus

2.91 Private and professional funds are required to file their offering documents with the BVI Financial Services Commission on application for recognition, and they must update their offering documents in the event of any material change to their terms and file the revised offering documents with the BVI Financial Services Commission within 14 days of such change taking effect. Documents which are filed with the BVI Financial Services Commission are not publicly available.

2.92 Prior to offering its shares or interests to the public, a registered public fund is required to register with the BVI Financial Services Commission a prospectus in writing which must comply with the terms of the Public Funds Code, and must be signed by or on behalf of the fund's board of directors in the case of a BVI company, or equivalent governing body in the case of other vehicles, who have approved its contents or authorised its registration.

2.93 SIBA requires that a public fund's prospectus must provide 'full and accurate disclosure of all such information as investors would reasonably require and expect to find for the purpose of making an informed investment decision'. A prospectus must also contain a summary statement of the statutory rights of investors as provided in SIBA.

2.94 Incubator and approved funds are required to provide a written description of their investment strategy and a document containing certain risk warnings to investors, but they are not required to have an offering document.

Accounts and audit

2.95 Registered public funds and recognised private and professional funds are required to appoint an auditor for the purposes of auditing their financial statements annually, although there is no requirement to have the audited financial statements signed off by a local (BVI based) auditor. A fund must provide a copy of its audited financial statements to the BVI Financial Services Commission within six months of its financial year end.

2.96 The requirement to appoint an auditor and submit annual accounts is subject to a case-by-case exemption from the BVI Financial Services Commission.

2.97 The annual financial statements must be prepared in compliance with any of the following:

(a)   International Financial Reporting Standards;
(b)   UK Generally Accepted Accounting Principles;
(c)   US Generally Accepted Accounting Principles;
(d)   Canadian Generally Accepted Accounting Principles; or
(e)   international recognised and generally accepted accounting standards equivalent to the standards in (a)–(d) above, as determined by the directors in the case of private and professional funds, or as may be approved by the BVI Financial Services Commission in case of a public fund.

2.98 All SIBA registered or recognised funds must also submit a mutual fund annual return ('MFAR') which contains information about the activities of the fund during the preceding year. The MFAR must be submitted on or before 30 June in respect of the calendar year immediately preceding the filing.

2.99 Incubator and approved funds are required to submit to the BVI Financial Services Commission:

- annual financial statements (unaudited); and
- semi-annual returns regarding their eligibility to remain an incubator or approved fund.

2.100 *Offshore Fund Domiciles – The Caribbean*

Statutory rights of investors

2.100 SIBA provides that if a public fund issues a prospectus that contains any misrepresentation relating to any of the disclosures required under SIBA, a person who purchased any fund interests on the basis of the prospectus is deemed to have relied upon the misrepresentation and will have a right of action:

- for the rescission of the purchase; or
- for damages, jointly and severally against the fund, and every director of the fund, or in the case of a unit trust, every member of the equivalent governing body who, while aware of the misrepresentation, or would have been aware of the misrepresentation had he made reasonable investigations consistent with his duties, authorised the signing of, or approved, the prospectus and consented to its issue.

2.101 There are no statutory protections for investors in recognised private and professional funds, or incubator and approved funds.

Fund ownership

2.102 There are no legal restrictions on the percentage of units in a mutual fund that may be held by one person or related group of persons.

The regulatory process

2.103 Public funds are subject to the supervision of the BVI Financial Services Commission and are required by the Public Funds Code and the Mutual Funds Regulations to submit to the BVI Financial Services certain information and documents. Information, material or documents submitted to or filed with the BVI Financial Services Commission are not publicly available.

2.104 All funds ordinarily prepare a detailed offering memorandum and subscription agreement which are filed with the BVI Financial Services Commission, together with the appropriate application form, fee and constitutional documents of the fund. The BVI Financial Services Commission reviews the documentation to ensure compliance with the legislation (essentially that it contains the required investment warning, disclosure as to the type of fund, and the availability of audited financial statements) and issues a certificate of recognition once it is satisfied that the fund meets the relevant criteria.

2.105 A private or professional fund must be 'recognised' by the BVI Financial Services Commission in order to carry on business or hold itself out as carrying on business as a mutual fund 'in or from within' the BVI. A professional fund can benefit from a fast track procedure whereby it may commence operation up to 21 days before it is recognised by the BVI Financial Services Commission. The recognition procedure itself has been designed to be quick and efficient.

2.106 A public fund must apply for and obtain registration with the BVI Financial Services Commission to carry on business or hold itself out as carrying on business as a mutual fund in or from within the BVI, and it must have its prospectus registered with the BVI Financial Services Commission. In most instances the registration process will be quick and straightforward.

2.107 SIBA also applies to funds that carry on business or hold themselves out as carrying on business as a mutual fund in or from within the BVI. The term 'in or from within the BVI' has been interpreted to include:
- a BVI constituted entity that carries on business in the BVI;
- a BVI constituted entity that carries on business elsewhere; and
- a foreign constituted entity that carries on business in the BVI (that is, it operates from a place of business in the BVI, or it solicits an individual within the BVI to subscribe for, or purchase, any of its fund interests).

2.108 A mutual fund incorporated, formed or organised outside the BVI is generally not regarded as soliciting an individual within the BVI in circumstances where the subscription or purchase is a result of an approach made by the individual to the fund without any solicitation being made by or on behalf of the fund.

Types of fund vehicle

2.109 Funds may be established in the BVI as corporate entities, unit trusts or limited partnerships.

2.110 By virtue of the greater flexibility provided by the corporate form for listing on stock exchanges and the wider acceptability of companies for marketing purposes, the majority of the mutual funds established in the BVI in recent years have been open-ended investment companies ('OEICs').

Corporate entities

2.111 BVI business companies incorporated under the BC Act (known as 'BCs') are very flexible vehicles with no minimum capital requirements, and they may acquire and hold their own shares as treasury stock subject to certain specified restrictions. BCs are able to offer redeemable shares which can be redeemed from any source provided the company satisfies a solvency test (which comprises both cash flow and balance sheets tests) immediately following the redemption in question. Whilst the directors of a BC need not be based or domiciled in the BVI, a BC must have a registered office and registered agent in the BVI.

Segregated portfolio companies

2.112 Under the BC Act, a company limited by shares may be incorporated or, if it has already been incorporated, registered by the registrar as a segregated portfolio company (an 'SPC'), provided that the BVI Financial Services Commission has given its written approval and the company:
- is, or on its incorporation will be, licensed as an insurer under the Insurance Act, 1994 (now the Insurance Act, 2008);
- is, or on its incorporation will be, recognised as a professional or private fund or registered as a public fund under SIBA; or
- is, or on its incorporation will be, of such class or description as may be prescribed by regulations made under section 159 of the BC Act.

2.113 At present, only licensed insurers and recognised or registered mutual funds can incorporate or register as an SPC under the BC Act.

2.114 An SPC is a single corporate legal entity that benefits from the statutory segregation of assets and liabilities between segregated portfolios established within the same company. SPCs can establish segregated portfolios to segregate the assets relating to classes of shares with different investment criteria, thereby protecting shareholders from cross liability arising from the adverse investment performance of other classes of shares. To achieve that segregation, the SPC must identify the relevant segregated portfolio(s) and make clear that business is being transacted in the name of, or by or for the account of, the particular named segregated portfolio(s). The capacity in which the SPC contracts and the name(s) of the relevant segregated portfolio(s) must be set out in writing in the relevant transaction documentation. Although each segregated portfolio must be separately identified it will not have separate legal personality from the company.

2.115 Creditors of an SPC have recourse to the assets of the segregated portfolio of that SPC in respect of which these creditors contracted with the SPC, and to any general assets of the company (being assets not comprised within any segregated portfolio) to the extent that the segregated portfolio assets attributable to such portfolio are insufficient. When dealing with an SPC a third party should clearly establish in respect of which segregated portfolio of the SPC it is contracting with the SPC (and therefore which of the relevant segregated assets it has recourse against).

Limited partnerships

2.116 Since 11 January 2018, limited partnerships are formed in the BVI under the Limited Partnership Act, 2017 (the 'Limited Partnership Act'). The main features of the Limited Partnership Act are as follows:

- the Limited Partnership Act codifies the law for limited partnerships into a single statute;
- the general partner can be a corporation and need not be registered or resident in the BVI;
- unless it elects to be registered without legal personality, a BVI limited partnership has legal personality but is not a body corporate;
- a limited partnership with legal personality has such specified legal personality rights as are set out in the Limited Partnership Act, including the right to institute legal proceedings in the name of the limited partnership; the right by an instrument in writing to create a charge over the assets of the partnership, which may be registered on the public register thus determining the statutory priority of enforcement; and the ability for a charge to be registered against the limited partnership and for such registration to provide priority under BVI law;
- a limited partnership is required to have a limited partnership agreement – upon formation, a model agreement is deemed to be adopted unless modified or excluded by the signed limited partnership agreement, allowing for a quick formation of limited partnerships;

- a general partner is required to act at all times in good faith and, subject to any contrary provision in the limited partnership agreement (most usual being formation of other limited partnership structures), in the interests of the limited partnership;
- a limited partner's liability is limited to the amount stated in the articles of limited partnership (also known as the limited partnership agreement) to be contributed by the limited partner;
- common law position on penalties, which may bring into question the enforceability of the forfeiture provisions in the event of default on a capital call, has been disapplied in the Limited Partnership Act, ensuring enforceability of any such forfeiture provisions;
- limited partnerships are given tax exempt status in the same way as BCs;
- there is no limit on the number of partners;
- limited partnerships are required to have a registered agent in the BVI; and
- limited partnerships can have a fixed term and bespoke dissolution events, with detailed provisions for the termination, deregistration and winding-up of a solvent limited partnership, as well as for the winding-up of an insolvent limited partnership – the Limited Partnership Act also allows the Registrar to strike off a limited partnership (for example, for non-payment of fees).

2.117 Limited partnerships formed under the old Partnership Act, 1996 continue to exist under the Partnership Act until they voluntarily reregister under the Limited Partnership Act. After a period of ten years, all limited partnerships remaining under the Partnership Act will be automatically reregistered under the Limited Partnership Act and will have two additional years to adopt a compliant limited partnership agreement.

2.118 The Limited Partnership Act provides that a limited partner is not liable for the debts and liabilities of a limited partnership beyond the amount of the limited partner's contribution or unpaid commitment to the limited partnership. A limited partner does not lose the benefit of limited liability by reason of the limited partnership not having a general partner. The Limited Partnership Act provides an extensive list of the safe harbour provisions for limited partners, drawing heavily on the provisions of Delaware and the Cayman Islands. Essentially, a limited partner loses its limited liability if it takes part in the management of the limited partnership to the same extent as the general partner and the person dealing with the limited partnership reasonably believed such limited partner to be the general partner based on its conduct.

2.119 Similarly to BCs, limited partnerships now have the ability to: continue to another jurisdiction, as well as for a foreign limited partnership to continue into the BVI; merge or consolidate with another limited partnership, including a foreign limited partnership where the foreign law permits mergers and consolidations of limited partnerships; redeem minority partnership interests (subject to the limited partnership agreement); and enter into a plan of arrangement or a scheme of arrangement. The limited partner also has the right to dissent on a merger, consolidation or mandatory redemption (subject to the limited partnership agreement).

2.120 *Offshore Fund Domiciles – The Caribbean*

Unit trusts

2.120 A unit trust which operates as a fund is a special kind of trust which in addition to being subject to the laws governing trusts is also subject to SIBA. A unit trust may be registered as one of the types of mutual fund under SIBA.

2.121 All assets of a unit trust are vested in a trustee under a trust deed or declaration of trust which divides the beneficial ownership into a number of units that are usually (but not necessarily) freely transferable and redeemable. The rights and obligations of the trustee and the unitholder, the terms of redemption and valuation rules are all set out in the trust deed.

2.122 A subscription agreement will contain the contractual provisions between the trustee and the unitholders. The contractual provisions governing the relationship between the trustee and other advisers to the trustee will be set out in agreements between the trustee and these advisers.

Managers, administrators, trustees and custodians

2.123 Individuals and entities wishing to carry on the business of management, custody or administration of mutual funds are required to apply for and obtain a licence under SIBA. It should be noted, however, that BVI funds need not engage local service providers other than an authorised representative and registered agent/registered office. SIBA does not apply to managers and administrators which are established under foreign law and whose operations are based entirely in a foreign jurisdiction, even though the manager or administrator may act for a BVI fund. The basic test for eligibility is that the service provider is a 'fit and proper' applicant.

2.124 The BVI Financial Services Commission generally will recognise and accept as fit and proper any functionary of a BVI fund that is established and located in a jurisdiction listed in the Schedule to the Securities and Investment Business (Recognised Jurisdictions) Notice, 2010 (the 'Notice').

2.125 Where a functionary of a fund is not established and located in a jurisdiction listed in the Notice, the BVI Financial Services Commission may recognise and accept that functionary if satisfied, upon application, that the functionary's jurisdiction of establishment and location has a system for the effective regulation of investment business, including funds.

Approved managers

2.126 The BVI approved manager regime was introduced by the Investment Business (Approved Managers) Regulations, 2012 (the 'Approved Managers Regulations'). The approved manager regime is aimed at non-institutional investment managers of BVI funds and provides an alternative streamlined regulatory framework for BVI investment managers currently required to be licensed under SIBA.

2.127 The ongoing obligations under the approved manager regime are less onerous than those under SIBA and the approval process streamlined. The BVI Financial Services Commission is able to raise objections to the application only during the seven-day period following the filing of the application, after which period the manager can commence business pending approval by the BVI Financial Services Commission.

2.128 To be eligible to be an approved investment manager under the approved manager regime, the applicant must be a BVI company or a BVI limited partnership and meet the BVI Financial Services Commission's 'fit and proper' test, and act as an investment manager or an investment adviser to a BVI private or professional fund under SIBA and certain foreign funds equivalent to BVI private or professional funds.

2.129 The approved investment manager is limited to having no more than US$400 million aggregate assets under management in respect of open-ended funds, and no more than US$1 billion aggregate capital commitments in the case of closed-ended funds. Where an investment manager manages an open-ended fund and a closed-ended fund, the aggregate assets under management in relation to the open-ended fund and the amount prescribed for the closed-ended fund must be segregated and treated separately.

Taxation

2.130 All dividends, interest, rents, royalties, compensations and other amounts paid by a fund established in the BVI to persons who are not resident in the BVI are exempt from the provisions of the BVI Income Tax Ordinance (Cap 206). Any capital gains realised with respect to any shares, debt obligations or other securities of a fund by persons who are not resident in the BVI are exempt from all forms of taxation in the BVI. No estate, inheritance, succession or gift tax, rate, duty, levy or other charge is payable by persons resident in the BVI with respect to any shares, debt obligation or other securities of the fund. All instruments relating to transfers of property to or by a fund, all instruments relating to transactions in respect of the shares, debt obligations or other securities of a fund, and all instruments relating to other transactions relating to the business of a fund are exempt from the payment of stamp duty in the BVI. There are currently no withholding taxes or exchange control regulations in the BVI.

The EU Savings Directive

2.131 Originally aimed at European Union ('EU') member states only, the EU Savings Directive[1] was extended to include their overseas territories, including the BVI and a number of non-EU countries (together, the 'applicable states').

[1] Council Directive 2003/48/EC of 3 June 2003.

2.132 The Directive came into effect on 1 July 2005 and applied to cross-border 'interest payments' made by a paying agent (such as a fund administrator) in an applicable state to a beneficial owner or residual entity resident for tax purposes in a different EU member state. The Directive has been largely superseded by the UK reporting regime similar to the US Foreign Account Tax Compliance Act ('FATCA') in relation to UK citizens ('UK FATCA', often referred to as 'UK CDOT') and the OECD's Standard for Automatic Exchange of Financial Information in Tax Matters (the Common

2.132 Offshore Fund Domiciles – The Caribbean

Reporting Standard or 'CRS'); as such, the Directive was repealed on 31 December 2016, and the reporting in respect thereof has been incorporated into UK FATCA and the CRS from that date.

FATCA and CRS

2.133 In order to facilitate reporting under and reduce the burden on BVI entities of compliance with FATCA, the BVI has signed a Model 1B intergovernmental agreement with the USA (the 'US IGA'). The US IGA allows a BVI entity that is a foreign financial institution ('FFI') for the purposes of FATCA to comply with the reporting obligations imposed by FATCA without having to enter into an agreement with the US Internal Revenue Service (the 'IRS'). Instead, a BVI FFI may report directly to the BVI International Tax Authority (the 'BVI Reporting Authority') and, provided it complies with the relevant procedures and reporting obligations, will be treated as a deemed compliant FFI that is not subject to automatic withholding on US source income and other US related payments.

2.134 Almost all BVI open-ended funds and private equity funds will be 'investment entities' and therefore qualify as FFIs under FATCA. The one exception is that funds where more than 50% of the gross revenues are from real estate (or other non-financial assets) will generally fall outside the definition of 'investment entity' (and therefore FFI) for the purposes of FATCA. There are some other limited exemptions available to open-ended funds and private equity funds, but these are expected to be of limited practical use for the vast majority of such funds.

2.135 BVI entities that act solely as the managers and advisers of BVI funds will typically not need to register and report as FFIs. Although BVI managers and advisers fall within the definition of 'investment entity' (and therefore FFI), the US IGA contains an exemption for a BVI FFI that qualifies as an investment entity solely because it (a) renders investment advice to, and acts on behalf of, or (b) manages portfolios for, and acts on behalf of, a customer for the purposes of investing, managing, or administering funds deposited in the name of the customer with a participating FFI. Accordingly, BVI managers and advisers will generally not be required to register with the IRS and report on their own account.

2.136 The US IGA requires the BVI Reporting Authority to provide information to the IRS by the end of nine months from the end of each calendar year. The annual reporting deadline for FATCA is 31 May in each year. The first reporting period covered by FATCA was 2015, with the reports in respect of that period being due for submission by 31 May 2016 on the BVI Financial Account Reporting System (the 'BVIFARS'). The deadline for enrolment on the BVIFARS was 30 April 2016.

2.137 The UK FATCA was implemented in the BVI by means of an intergovernmental agreement between the BVI and the UK (the 'UK IGA').

2.138 The UK IGA followed the US model very closely, although there were some important differences. In particular, it required BVI financial institutions to undertake due diligence to identify and then report on financial accounts of UK specified persons. As UK citizens are not subject to universal taxation, the definition of UK specified persons was not as extensive as under FATCA and generally included a UK resident and a UK incorporated entity. A non-UK entity which is controlled by UK specified persons is also subject to this reporting obligation. UK FATCA does not impose withholding on UK source income.

2.139 The UK IGA required BVI financial institutions to start carrying out due diligence on their accounts and identify specified persons, with the first reporting date being 31 May 2016. On the first reporting date, specified information on the accounts of specified persons and non-UK entities controlled by specified persons had to be reported to the BVI Reporting Authority.

2.140 The BVI implemented the CRS through the Mutual Legal Assistance (Tax Matters) Act, 2003. On 12 September 2016, the BVI Reporting Authority released guidance notes[1] on the CRS (the 'CRS Guidance Notes') and reiterated that the CRS notification to the BVI Reporting Authority was due by 30 April 2017 and that the CRS reporting to the BVI Reporting Authority was due by 31 May 2017. Reporting under the UK IGA has been phased out and replaced by reporting under CRS for 2018 and going forward.

[1] Available at www.bvi.gov.vg/aeoi-crs.

2.141 The CRS Guidance Notes provide for separate notification and reporting requirements. The notification of all existing BVI reporting financial institutions under the CRS was required to be completed by 30 April 2017. Each reporting financial institution need only enrol once by making a notification through the existing BVIFARS portal established for FATCA reporting regimes. Reporting financial institutions established from 2017 onwards will need to enrol by 30 April of the year which immediately follows their year of formation. Reporting must be made annually and must be undertaken through the BVIFARS portal. The first reporting period was in respect of the year to 31 December 2016, and the reporting deadline for that period was 31 May 2017. Subsequent reporting will be required by 31 May of each year in respect of the prior calendar year.

2.142 The BVI has identified as 'participating jurisdictions' all jurisdictions which have committed to commence exchanging information in 2017 or 2018, in order that reporting financial institutions do not need to change their due diligence procedures each time an automatic exchange agreement is entered into with participating jurisdictions.

2.143 'Reportable jurisdictions' are all jurisdictions with which an agreement is in place pursuant to which there is an obligation to provide the information specified in Section I of the CRS and which are identified in a published list. These comprise jurisdictions which have a competent authority agreement in place with the BVI and those jurisdictions that have completed the formalities required under the multilateral competent authority agreement. Such jurisdictions were required to complete all confidentiality and legal requirements as stipulated in the CRS for such arrangements.

2.144 There are a number of differences between FATCA and the CRS, some of the more notable being that unlike FATCA there is no sponsoring option available under the CRS, most of the exceptions available under FATCA do not exist under the CRS, the thresholds are applied differently for individual

2.144 Offshore Fund Domiciles – The Caribbean

and entity account holders, and there are certain changes to the method of reporting under the 'trustee-documented trust' option under the CRS.

2.145 No withholding tax will be imposed for non-compliant financial institutions under the CRS; however, the BVI implementing legislation imposes specific offences for BVI entities that fail to comply with the reporting obligations under the CRS.

The Alternative Investment Fund Managers Directive

2.146 The Alternative Investment Fund Managers Directive[1] ('AIFMD') was introduced to harmonise the regulation of alternative investment fund managers which manage and market alternative investment funds ('AIFs') in the EU. At present, non-EU fund managers and funds are required to comply with each EU country's national regime when they manage or market funds in that country, with non-EU fund managers largely precluded from marketing non-EU funds into the EU other than under the national private placement regimes ('NPPRs'). The extension of the AIFMD passport, which is currently only available to EU entities, would allow a BVI fund to be marketed in the EU and a BVI fund manager to market and manage funds in the EU, on a pan-EU basis, subject to compliance with the AIFMD regime.

[1] Directive 2011/61/EU of 8 June 2011.

2.147 The AIFMD definition of what constitutes an AIF is broader than current definition of funds under SIBA, and it includes closed-ended funds and all types of strategies, including private equity and property fund structures.

2.148 Prior to BVI funds being marketed in the EU, certain pre-conditions specified in AIFMD must be met. First, co-operation agreements must be in place between the regulators in the EU member states where the BVI fund is to be marketed and the BVI Financial Services Commission. The BVI Financial Services Commission has entered into a memorandum of understanding concerning consultation, co-operation and the exchange of information related to the supervision of AIF managers with most of the EU member states.

2.149 Second, neither the non-EU fund nor the non-EU manager can be established in a jurisdiction which the Financial Action Task Force ('FATF') has blacklisted. The BVI is not an FATF blacklisted jurisdiction, so this pre-condition has been satisfied in relation to BVI funds. In addition, whilst the BVI maintains its status as a 'tax-neutral' or 'tax-efficient' jurisdiction, in line with its commitment to the OECD principles of transparency and information exchange relating to tax matters, the BVI has signed Tax Information Sharing Agreements with 28 countries. Entering into a Tax Information Sharing Agreement with each EU jurisdiction in which the BVI fund is to be marketed under the passport will be a pre-condition to a BVI fund obtaining such a passport, and the continued negotiations with the remaining EU member states remains high on the BVI government's agenda.

2.150 On 19 July 2016, the European Securities and Markets Authority ('ESMA') published its latest advice to the European Parliament, the European Council and the European Commission on the application of the AIFMD passport regime to asset managers and investment funds domiciled in non-EU countries. On 29 September 2016, the BVI introduced the Securities and

Investment Business (AIFMD) Regulations, 2016 (the 'AIFMD Regulations'), which are not yet in force, to establish an 'opt in' regulatory regime to permit new or existing BVI open-ended and closed-ended funds and BVI fund managers to become approved as an 'EU Qualified BVI AIF' and 'EU Qualified BVI AIFM'.

2.151 The EU Qualified BVI AIF relates to both BVI domiciled open-ended and closed-ended funds which are either (a) managed by an EU based manager or (b) marketed to investors in EU jurisdictions in accordance with local law requirements. An EU Qualified BVI AIFM means a BVI entity or a foreign entity registered in the BVI whose regular business is managing one of more AIFs to which the AIFMD Regulations apply.

2.152 The AIFMD Regulations require EU Qualified BVI AIFMs to comply with obligations intended to reflect those applicable to EU managers authorised under AIFMD. The AIFMD Regulations also extend the enforcement powers of the BVI Financial Services Commission with respect to EU Qualified BVI AIFMs, to ensure that it is able to give full effect to its enforcement obligations under AIFMD in respect of EU Qualified BVI AIFMs, and to enhance compliance with information sharing obligations adopted by the BVI under the memoranda of understanding which the BVI Financial Services Commission has in place with various EU regulators.

2.153 Adopting an 'opt in' approach further demonstrates the BVI's commitment to implementing the best regulatory standards whilst always ensuring that the level of regulation is appropriate for the different types of users of its products. Non-EU managers and funds which do not intend to market in the EU will not be affected by the AIFMD Regulations. BVI managers that intend to continue to market BVI funds into the EU under the NPPRs need not opt in, whereas managers seeking to apply for an AIFMD passport will be able to opt in to AIFMD equivalent regulation.

2.154 Under the terms of AIFMD, ESMA is required to give an opinion to the European Commission as to whether non-EU countries would be able to take advantage of the AIFMD EU passport regime. The 'opt in' regime should ensure that the BVI is well positioned to receive a favourable recommendation from ESMA following its assessment on whether an AIFMD passport should be made available to BVI investment fund managers.

Anti-money laundering

2.155 Under the Anti-Money Laundering Regulations, 2008, as amended, and the Anti-Money Laundering and Terrorist Financing Code of Practice, 2008, as amended (together, the 'BVI AML laws'), all funds registered or recognised under SIBA are required to:

- appoint a Money Laundering Reporting Officer;
- implement and maintain certain anti-money laundering compliance procedures – primarily, the identification and verification of investors in the fund and related record-keeping, which in certain circumstances can be outsourced to the fund's administrator; and

2.155 Offshore Fund Domiciles – The Caribbean

- implement and maintain an independent compliance audit to ensure that the BVI fund is complying with its obligations under the BVI AML laws.

2.156 To ensure compliance with the BVI AML laws, and other generally accepted principles relating to anti-money laundering, the fund (usually through its administrator) will require verification of identity from any proposed investor. If a fund or the administrator (where the anti-money laundering compliance is outsourced by the fund) has a suspicion or belief that a payment to a fund (by way of investment, contribution or otherwise) is derived from or represents the proceeds of criminal conduct, that person is obliged to report such suspicion to the BVI Reporting Authority.

Chapter 3

OFFSHORE FUND DOMICILES – THE CHANNEL ISLANDS

A Jersey   3.1
B Guernsey   3.88

A JERSEY

Robert Milner, Partner, Carey Olsen

Introduction

3.1 Jersey is the largest of the Channel Islands, with a population of approximately 100,000. It is located about 14 miles from France and 85 miles from England. The Island enjoys first class air and sea links with the UK as well as some direct air links to major European cities. Jersey shares the same time zone as the UK.

3.2 In economic terms, Jersey is dominated by its finance industry, which employs over 13,000 people and contributes a significant portion of the Island's income. It is a mature industry, with a critical mass of expertise.

3.3 In recent years the finance industry has increasingly focused on the institutional market and sophisticated investors. The Island has repeatedly been endorsed by international bodies and has won numerous awards as an offshore and international financial centre.

3.4 The expertise that Jersey offers extends across all asset classes, with recent growth focused particularly on alternative asset classes and hedge funds, and Jersey is widely considered to be a key player in the world of domiciling, administering and managing hedge funds.

3.5 There has been a movement towards the relocation of hedge fund managers to Jersey in recent years. One potential structuring option is to incorporate the use of an independent management company (a 'ManCo') which will have significant substance for various regulatory purposes, including compliance with the OECD's Base Erosion and Profit Shifting ('BEPS') project. A ManCo can act as manager to virtually any fund established by a promoter and retain predefined levels of risk and/or portfolio management while delegating the remainder (where appropriate) to the promoter. A further option is to augment the substance of a new or existing offshore manager entity using resources supplied by an experienced fund administrator to effect a cost-efficient and practical alternative to establishing a full-presence office or branch in Jersey.

3.6 The use of a Jersey ManCo can provide fund managers and promoters with a degree of certainty regarding both market access and the ability to

3.6 *Offshore Fund Domiciles – The Channel Islands*

deploy capital that is difficult to replicate elsewhere. Jersey's ever-growing list of international tax agreements and endorsements by supranational agencies is evidence that this position can be maintained.

3.7 Following implementation of the Alternative Investment Fund Managers Directive[1] ('AIFMD') by EU member states, as a 'third country' non-EU jurisdiction, Jersey has ensured it can continue to offer fund managers a blend of stability and flexibility.

[1] Directive 2011/61/EU of 8 June 2011.

3.8 Jersey has a particular relationship with both the UK and the EU. It has been treated by the EU as a 'third country' for financial services purposes for many years and since the introduction of AIFMD has proven a popular location for managers and funds wishing to access EU/EEA markets using private placement routes. It has been assessed by the European Securities and Market Authority ('ESMA'), which has confirmed that no obstacles exist to the extension of the AIFMD passport (once available) to Jersey (and Guernsey).

3.9 Jersey's strategy in relation to AIFMD is to have the right frameworks in place to continue to provide fund establishment, management and administration services on a 'business as usual' basis. This has been achieved by placing an AIFMD 'overlay' on existing regulatory frameworks such that a Jersey fund need only comply with AIFMD to the extent that it is absolutely necessary.

A brief history

3.10 Jersey's position at the forefront of modern offshore centres is, in many ways, a natural result of its geographical situation and history. Jersey was, historically, part of the ancient duchy of Normandy that conquered England in 1066. When England lost mainland Normandy to the French king in 1204, the Channel Islands remained part of the English Crown. Through a series of Royal Charters, Jersey's liberties, immunities and privileges and relationship with the UK was formalised and the key principles have changed little since 1215: the Island is a dependency of the UK, yet is fully autonomous and makes its own laws through an elected chamber, the States of Jersey (the 'States') and has exclusive competence to collect taxes.

3.11 The States comprises the Bailiff (President), the Lieutenant-Governor, the Attorney General, the Solicitor General, the Dean of Jersey as well as 49 elected members (comprising eight Senators, the Connétables of the 12 Parishes of Jersey and 29 Deputies). The Council of Ministers forms the Executive branch of government and is drawn from the 49 elected members of the States. The Council of Ministers comprises a Chief Minister and ten departments, each headed by a minister supported by an assistant minister.

3.12 Jersey is neither a member nor an associate member of the EU and its relationship with the EU is governed by Protocol 3 of the EU Treaty of Accession of 1972. The effect of this is that Jersey falls within the common customs area and the common external tariff but is not required to comply with EU Directives and is free to maintain an independent fiscal policy.

Jersey's government closely monitors developments in the EU with a view to adhering to EU standards where possible.

3.13 A fund, whether established as a company, unit trust or limited partnership, is not generally subject to any local Jersey tax. In particular, there is no capital gains tax, capital transfer tax, wealth or inheritance tax payable in relation to the issue or realisation of investments in a Jersey investment fund (unless the fund invests in Jersey property or buildings). In addition, no corporation tax, profits tax or stamp duty is payable.

3.14 Jersey resident administrators and custodians are generally liable to Jersey income tax at the rate of 10%. However, Jersey-administered entities, such as general partners and managers that provide services to a fund, are taxed at 0%.

Jersey law

3.15 Jersey's close relationship with both England and France has influenced the development of Jersey law. Jersey's common law is based on Norman 'customary law' which, in large part, formed the basis of the modern French Civil Code. Whilst Jersey common law has evolved in line with international developments, and most modern laws and precedents will be familiar to English lawyers, lawyers in Jersey will always have regard to the customary law in relation to certain basic legal tenets. There are therefore various notable differences from English law. For example, there are certain technical differences in the law of contract, but outcomes and remedies are broadly in line with English principles.

3.16 Although Jersey's jurisprudence is rooted in Norman customary law, the legislation relating to the finance industry and investment structures such as companies, trusts and limited partnerships is substantively modelled and influenced by the judgements of other sophisticated jurisdictions. For example:

- The Companies (Jersey) Law 1991, as amended (the 'Companies Law'), is heavily drawn from the UK Companies Acts.
- The Trusts (Jersey) Law 1984, as amended, is based on trust law principles of England and other Commonwealth jurisdictions and provides flexibility and certainty in the establishment of unit trusts.
- Partnership law remains governed by the customary law, rather than by legislation. However, Jersey limited partnerships (which do not have a separate legal personality from their partners) are formed under the Limited Partnerships (Jersey) Law 1994, as amended (the 'LP Law'), which is similar to but frequently more flexible than limited partnership laws in other jurisdictions:
    - no Jersey general partner is required;
    - there is no upper limit on the number of limited partners nor any audit or annual return requirement;
    - confidentiality is assured; and
    - a limited partner may have greater involvement in management than is permitted in some other jurisdictions.

3.16 Offshore Fund Domiciles – The Channel Islands

Alternatively, partnerships may be established as separate limited partnerships (with separate legal personality) or incorporated limited partnerships (which are bodies corporate), which are particularly useful in management and carried interest structures.

3.17 Jersey has a mature legal system, which includes fully reported judgments, and a Court of Appeal manned by leading sitting and former UK judges. There is a final right of appeal to the UK Privy Council.

The finance industry in Jersey

3.18 For many years Jersey has collected a wide range of statistics in relation to its finance industry. The pattern has been one of steady, sustainable growth. Statistics are available from Jersey Finance Limited, with the latest figures[1] showing:

- bank deposits of £111.5 billion;
- net asset value of funds under administration increased by £14.1 billion to £237.3 billion during Q3 2016;
- 1,125 regulated funds with a total number of 1,863 separate investment pools and 120 active unregulated funds; and
- £19.7 billion total funds under management.

[1] Reflecting the position at the end of September 2016 (see www.jerseyfinance.je).

3.19 The States has an express policy of encouraging so-called 'high value/low footprint' businesses to move to Jersey, and over the past couple of years a number of hedge fund managers have relocated there, attracted by the high quality of life, first-class infrastructure and modest levels of personal taxation. The States has established a dedicated resource at its population office to provide a 'one stop shop' for businesses and principals wishing to relocate. In addition, there is a policy of allowing controlled population increase, and Jersey takes a proactive approach in encouraging ambitious and talented people to relocate, with a capacity for up to 500 new jobs to be created each year in high value businesses.

Hedge funds in Jersey and the new private funds regime

3.20 The Jersey Financial Services Commission (the 'JFSC') and industry bodies in Jersey have been co-operating to simplify the regulatory framework in Jersey, particularly for listed and sophisticated investor funds. Jersey regulatory classifications now provide a 'safe harbour' and three-day approval (or no approval) for the majority of non-retail funds:

- *Private funds* can benefit from a 'light touch' fast track regulatory process under the JFSC's new Jersey Private Fund Guide[1] and up to 50 offers may be made to investors who qualify as 'professional investors' and/or subscribe for interests with a value of at least £250,000. A ManCo may be established for this category of fund without the need for it to become regulated (save where the fund is an 'alternative investment fund' for the purposes of AIFMD).

- *Unregulated eligible investor funds* allow hedge funds to be established in Jersey without any Jersey service providers and without any regulatory approval under Jersey's funds legislation, thus providing fund promoters with unrivalled certainty, flexibility and speed when establishing new funds.
- *Regulated Jersey eligible investor funds ('JEIFs')* (aimed at sophisticated 'eligible investors', including those investing or committing a minimum of US$1 million or the foreign currency equivalent) benefit from a three-day 'fast track' approval process and a small number of structural requirements.
- *Expert funds* (aimed at 'expert investors', including those investing or committing a minimum of US$100,000 or the foreign currency equivalent) also benefit from a three-day 'fast track' approval process and a small number of structural requirements. This classification remains hugely successful.
- *Listed funds* are for closed-ended funds which are listed on recognised stock exchanges or markets and also benefit from a three-day 'fast track' approval process and a small number of structural requirements. They have no minimum investment requirement and no requirement for a custodian.

[1] Available at www.jerseyfsc.org/funds/policy-statements-guidance-notes.

3.21 Jersey also has an unregulated funds regime which is aimed specifically at hedge and alternative asset funds. Combined with Jersey's convenient time zone and strong international reputation, the unregulated funds regime has proved attractive to European fund managers and promoters and has been welcomed for providing a credible alternative to the Cayman Islands for new hedge funds. Additionally, since the introduction of AIFMD, JEIFs have proved popular as a regulated alternative to the unregulated eligible investor fund, and expert funds remain popular for hedge funds and similar structures.

Private funds

3.22 Prior to the publication of its Jersey Private Fund Guide, the JFSC had applied a similar proportionate and light-touch approach to very private structures (which permitted up to 15 offers to prospective investors) which resulted in a large number of those structures being established – they have been seen in particular as ideal for club investments, funds of one and co-investments. Now, the wider scope and the ability to make offers to up to 50 potential investors will allow many more funds to benefit from even more rapid 'fast track' (48-hour) authorisation by obtaining a simple consent under the Control of Borrowing (Jersey) Order 1958, as amended (the 'COBO'), and potentially reduce initial and ongoing costs. Jersey service providers such as general partners or managers set up specifically to service a particular private fund will not require regulation under the Financial Services (Jersey) Law 1998, as amended (the 'FSJL') (save in some circumstances where the AIFMD overlay applies).

3.23 Offshore Fund Domiciles – The Channel Islands

Unregulated funds

3.23 Unregulated eligible investor funds may be open-ended or closed-ended and are restricted to sophisticated investors (including those investing US$1 million). Unregulated funds can be established as companies (including incorporated cell and protected cell companies), unit trusts or limited partnerships. Key features of the regime include: no limit on the number of investors; no investment or borrowing restrictions; no audit requirement for limited partnerships or units trusts; and no need for Jersey service providers.

Regulated funds

3.24 The same structures (companies, limited partnerships and unit trusts) may be used for the regulated fund types listed above. The specific service provider and other requirements attaching to each regulated fund type may be found in the guidance notes published by the JFSC on its website[1].

[1] See www.jerseyfsc.org.

3.25 The JFSC adopts a balanced and pragmatic approach towards investor protection. It does not apply overly restrictive conditions to the authorisation of investment funds (especially hedge and other funds aimed at institutional, sophisticated or high net worth investors), whilst maintaining Jersey's international reputation as a well-regulated jurisdiction. The International Monetary Fund has stated that 'Jersey has a robust supervisory framework'.

3.26 The strength, speed and flexibility in Jersey's regulatory regime have been crucial to the strong growth in its funds industry, particularly in the alternative sector. Recent figures show that more than half of the assets of Jersey's funds industry are invested in the alternative market.

3.27 The JFSC has published a Code of Practice for Alternative Investment Funds and AIF Services Business (the 'AIF Code') which applies to Jersey-based alternative investment funds ('AIFs') and alternative investment fund managers ('AIFMs') to varying degrees[1].

[1] Available at https://www.jerseyfsc.org/the-commission/general-information/codes-of-practice.

3.28 Where a Jersey sub-threshold AIFM is appointed, a notification to the JFSC is needed and basic requirements regarding the monitoring of assets under management will apply. Where an AIFM opts to use the national private placement regimes of the EU/EEA states into which the AIF is marketed, additional requirements under the AIF Code will apply regarding matters such as transparency/disclosure and asset stripping. Finally, an AIFM may opt for full compliance with the AIF Code in preparation for seeking a marketing passport, in which case the more detailed operating conditions for AIFMs will also need to be complied with.

3.29 Private funds which qualify as AIFs will need to obtain an AIF certificate from the JFSC, while their AIFMs will need to obtain an AIF services business licence under the FSJL, to the extent that they are not already appropriately regulated. Public funds regulated under the CIF Law[1] and their AIFMs are exempt from these requirements.

[1] See para 3.57 below.

Regulation of the finance industry

3.30 As noted above, unregulated funds can be established in Jersey without any regulatory approval other than notifying the JFSC of their establishment. The consent of the JFSC will be required to establish a regulated fund (although the fund vehicle itself may be incorporated in advance of the application being made).

3.31 The authorisation and supervision of regulated investment funds in Jersey is performed by the JFSC as the principal regulatory authority in Jersey. In addition to regulation of the financial services sector under statute, the JFSC also exercises its regulatory function through the publication of guidelines and codes of practice for different industry sectors. These guidelines and codes of practice are promulgated after consultation with the relevant industry sector by way of the publication of various consultation papers.

3.32 To qualify as an expert fund, a listed fund or a JEIF, a fund will need to meet the criteria summarised below (or agree derogations from these criteria with the JFSC in advance of the fund's establishment).

3.33 For non-expert/listed/JEIF regulated public funds, the JFSC will have regard to the status and track record of the relevant parties in considering whether to grant consent to the establishment of the fund. Also, from a regulatory perspective, the minimum investment level will be important. In short, the higher the minimum investment level, the more flexible the JFSC will be as to the scheme proposed. A low minimum investment level will mean that the JFSC takes a more active role in considering the application.

Regulation of investment managers and service providers

3.34 In general:

- persons who perform defined functions for public funds in, or from within, Jersey must be authorised by the JFSC;
- persons who carry out investment business activities in, or from within, Jersey must obtain relevant licences, unless exempt;
- Jersey-based businesses holding investment business licences must comply with codes of practice;
- Jersey-based service providers which outsource activities should comply with the JFSC's outsourcing policy (as amended from time to time);
- all financial services and investment businesses are subject to Jersey's anti-money laundering legislation and 'know your customer' regulations; and
- Jersey hedge fund managers may also act for managed accounts which meet certain criteria without the need for further regulation, provided that the investment strategies of those accounts replicate (or comprise

material elements from) one or more hedge fund strategies currently employed by the manager in respect of its Jersey CIF(s) or unregulated fund(s).

3.35 An entity which provides services to funds (such as an administrator or investment manager) and is regulated in Jersey is not required to seek approval to act in relation to individual funds. Instead, its licence permits it to provide services to any fund, whether established in Jersey or overseas.

3.36 A custodian is not required for unregulated funds or for private or closed-ended schemes. There is no requirement for a Jersey hedge fund that qualifies as an expert fund or a JEIF to appoint a local custodian but, if open-ended, it should appoint a prime broker of international stature. There is no Jersey requirement for an AIF to appoint an AIF depositary but, if a decision is taken to appoint a local depositary for these purposes, that person will need to comply with the relevant provisions of the AIF Code.

3.37 The requirements for unregulated funds are set out below[1]. A regulated public Jersey scheme is required to have a manager or administrator incorporated and resident in Jersey. In the context of a limited partnership the management function is frequently discharged by the general partner. A closed-ended unit trust is only required to appoint a locally-based trustee.

[1] See para 3.47 below.

3.38 The JFSC has formalised its criteria for the investment manager/adviser of a Jersey expert fund, a Jersey listed fund and a JEIF[1].

[1] See para 3.67 et seq below.

3.39 For other public funds, the identity of the promoter and other entities involved in the scheme will be an important factor for the JFSC in deciding whether to grant the necessary regulatory approvals. The general policy of the JFSC is to further strengthen Jersey's reputation as a high quality and well-regulated centre for the establishment and administration of funds, whilst adopting a positive approach to new business opportunities.

Establishing a local investment manager

3.40 An increasing number of fund managers have relocated to or established a presence in Jersey and the tax and regulatory authorities in Jersey have been sympathetic to these new businesses. Jersey is now the sixth largest centre for hedge fund managers in the world.

3.41 Hedge fund promoters also often establish a 'special purpose' investment manager in Jersey to act for one or more funds, including to ensure that 'management and control' of the fund remains offshore. With the assistance of a recognised local administrator, this is generally a fast and straightforward process.

3.42 Broadly, where a financial services business is carried on in or from within Jersey, the provisions of the FSJL will apply. A person carries on a financial services business if, by way of business, that person carries on certain defined activities, including investment business and/or fund services business (each as described in the FSJL).

3.43 A person carries on fund services business if, by way of business, that person acts in one or more specified roles, including acting as the investment manager or investment adviser, in relation to a regulated or unregulated fund (which is not a recognised fund). An investment manager conducting fund services business in or from within Jersey will be required to register in accordance with the FSJL and act in accordance with the terms of its registration.

3.44 Investment management activities also fall within the definition of investment business for the purposes of the FSJL. There are a number of factors relevant to whether an investment business registration is required, including (i) the identity of the Jersey residents contacted and whether they are investors for the purpose of the FSJL and (ii) whether any exemptions are available, such as holding a registration to carry on fund services business (as described above).

3.45 To establish an investment management company in Jersey, an application would need to be made under the FSJL unless the activities of the investment manager were kept outside the scope of the FSJL regime or an exemption could be identified. Applications usually take between four to six weeks to be processed (unless the application is made in conjunction with a Jersey fund establishment and/or the investment manager is to be a managed entity, in which case the timeframe may be expedited) and a minimum of two local directors and a locally provided compliance function is required.

The new private funds regime

3.46 The key requirements under the JFSC's Jersey Private Fund Guide are that a private fund:

- can be established as a Jersey company (including a protected cell company (a 'PCC'), an incorporated cell company (an 'ICC') or any cell of any such company), limited partnership, limited liability partnership, separate limited partnership, incorporated limited partnership or unit trust;
- can also be established as virtually any non-Jersey structure so long as there is a relevant Jersey connection such that a COBO consent is required;
- may be established by obtaining a simple consent under the COBO under the JFSC's new fast track (48-hour) regime;
- is not specifically required to appoint any Jersey resident directors or Jersey resident general partner or trustee directors, as appropriate (although the JFSC would ordinarily expect a Jersey resident director to be appointed to the private fund's governing body);
- can be open-ended or closed-ended;
- is not required to appoint an auditor;

3.46 Offshore Fund Domiciles – The Channel Islands

- must appoint a Jersey regulated administrator (the 'designated service provider') to ensure that the necessary criteria and applicable anti-money laundering legislation are complied with and to carry out due diligence on the promoter;
- enables up to 50 offers to be made to investors who meet the below requirements;
- can only be marketed to specific categories of investors including those (i) who subscribe for interests with a value of at least £250,000 and/or (ii) who qualify as 'professional' (including whose ordinary business or professional activity includes acquiring or managing investments or who have at least US$1 million of investable assets); and
- must procure that investors receive and acknowledge a specified form of investment warning.

Establishing an unregulated fund – the 'notification only' requirement

3.47 An unregulated eligible investor fund:

- can be open-ended or closed-ended and may be sold to or held by an unlimited number of 'eligible investors' (see below);
- does not need to prepare audited accounts;
- may be listed, provided that the exchange permits transfer restrictions (to ensure that only eligible investors are allowed to invest in the fund); and
- must obtain a written acknowledgement from each investor confirming its acceptance of the risks involved in the fund (typically dealt with on the application form).

3.48 Clearly, the definition of an 'eligible investor' is crucial. This category comprises a person:

- who makes a minimum initial investment or commitment of US$1 million (or its foreign currency equivalent);
- whose ordinary business or professional activity includes dealing in, managing, underwriting or giving advice on investments (or an employee, director, consultant or shareholder of such a person);
- who is an individual with a net worth of over US$10 million or its foreign currency equivalent (calculated alone or jointly with his/her spouse and excluding his/her principal place of residence);
- which is a company, limited partnership, trust or other unincorporated association and which either (i) has a market value of US$10 million or equivalent (calculated either alone or together with its associates), or (ii) has only 'eligible investors' as members, partners or beneficiaries;
- which is, or acts for, a public sector body;
- which is the trustee of a trust which either (i) was established by an 'eligible investor', or (ii) is established for the benefit of one or more eligible investors; or
- which is, or is an associate of, a service provider to the fund (or an employee, director, consultant or shareholder of such a service provider or associate and who acquires the relevant investment by way of remuneration or reward).

3.49 The regime also expressly recognises that a discretionary investment manager may make investments on behalf of investors who do not qualify as 'eligible investors', provided that it is satisfied that the investment is suitable and the underlying investor is able to bear the economic consequences of the investment.

The fund vehicle

3.50 Once the fund vehicle is established in the usual way, no further regulatory approvals of any kind will be required if the fund meets the requirements for qualifying as an unregulated fund.

3.51 Unregulated funds can be established as a Jersey company, PCC or ICC, as a limited partnership with at least one general partner which is a Jersey company, or as a unit trust with at least one trustee or manager which is a Jersey company. PCCs and ICCs offer significant advantages and recent changes further increase their flexibility, whilst maintaining the 'bankruptcy remoteness' of each cell.

3.52 The usual application procedure for incorporating a company or registering a limited partnership will apply, each of which can often be completed on the same working day. Using a unit trust avoids even these requirements. Jersey public companies will be subject to an audit requirement under the Companies Law.

3.53 Unregulated funds must file a notice with the JFSC confirming that the relevant eligibility requirements are met.

3.54 An unregulated fund has no obligation to have any Jersey resident directors or any Jersey based administrator, custodian or other service providers.

Regulated investment funds

3.55 Jersey combines legislation and regulatory oversight meeting international standards with an approachable and flexible administration.

3.56 A key issue from a Jersey perspective is whether a regulated fund is to be classified as a collective investment fund or not. This depends, broadly, upon the number of people to whom it will be marketed. If the offer to subscribe to the fund is made to a restricted circle of fewer than 50 people, the fund will not be treated, for the purposes of Jersey law, as a collective investment fund. It is the number of people to whom the fund is marketed that is relevant for these purposes, rather than the number of people who actually invest in the fund.

3.57 Public funds are governed by the Collective Investment Funds (Jersey) Law 1988, as amended (the 'CIF Law'). Private funds are, broadly, those funds that are offered to a restricted circle of persons numbering 50 or less and whose units are not listed on a recognised stock exchange within one year of the initial offer. Private funds are regulated solely by the COBO which controls, among other things, the creation and issue of shares, securities, units in a unit trust scheme and limited partnership interests. These would include professional investor funds, single investor funds and venture capital funds.

3.58 *Offshore Fund Domiciles – The Channel Islands*

3.58 For regulated funds, the regulatory process depends largely upon the classification of the fund: recognised, unclassified (including expert, listed or JEIF) or private. At one extreme, there are recognised funds, very public funds which can be freely marketed in the UK and which are required to meet high standards prescribed in the Collective Investment Funds (Recognised Funds) (Rules) (Jersey) Order 2003 and other secondary legislation made under the CIF Law. At the other extreme are private funds[1].

[1] See para **3.46** above.

Unclassified funds

3.59 All regulated funds which are not recognised funds are termed 'unclassified funds' and accordingly this broad category includes the fast-tracked expert funds, listed funds and JEIFs, as well as retail products.

3.60 Expert funds, listed funds and JEIFs are established on certification by a licensed Jersey service provider (typically the fund's administrator) that the fund complies with the expert, listed or JEIF criteria (as appropriate). The JFSC generally processes the application within 72 hours of receipt. Any requests for clarification from the JFSC are usually raised and dealt with during that period. The JFSC does not typically review the draft fund documentation other than the final offer document. Any proposed departures from the expert fund, listed fund or JEIF requirements can be dealt with in advance of the 72-hour approval period by requesting the JFSC to grant relevant derogations. It is important to note that a fund will only need to satisfy the JFSC on those expert fund, listed fund or JEIF criteria that it fails to meet.

3.61 The expert fund, listed fund and JEIF process explained above seeks to allow the JFSC time to deal with derogations to the Jersey Expert Fund Guide, the Jersey Listed Fund Guide and the Jersey Eligible Investor Fund Guide (together, the 'Guides') on an expedited basis. Those unclassified funds that do not meet the terms of the Guides are subject to a more detailed application and review process by the JFSC, and the timescale for approval is generally four to six weeks.

3.62 A regulated fund can be established as a Jersey company, PCC, ICC, limited partnership or unit trust.

Expert funds

3.63 The expert fund regime enables funds aimed at expert investors[1] to be established quickly and cost effectively and to provide certainty for fund sponsors. In the first three years of the regime's operation over 300 expert funds were established in Jersey.

[1] Defined at **3.67** below.

3.64 The Jersey Expert Fund Guide is an extremely flexible regime which is able to accommodate funds of all types and has generally been the preferred route for establishing hedge funds in Jersey.

3.65 An expert fund may be open-ended or closed-ended. The 72-hour 'fast track' approval process is available to both open-ended and closed-ended funds and the structural requirements are the same for each, save that (subject to obtaining a derogation from the JFSC) an open-ended fund must appoint a Jersey custodian or trustee or, alternatively (in the case of hedge funds only), a prime broker that is part of a group with a minimum credit rating of A1/P1 or equivalent.

3.66 The key requirements of an expert fund are as follows:

- the investment manager/adviser and its principals should be approved by the relevant regulatory authority in an OECD state or a jurisdiction with which the JFSC has entered a memorandum of understanding or equivalent, be solvent, without disciplinary sanctions or convictions, be experienced in using similar investment strategies, have adequate span of control over the business, or otherwise be approved by the JFSC;
- the fund should have at least two directors resident in Jersey;
- the fund should have a Jersey resident administrator;
- all investors must sign a prescribed form of investment warning (usually contained in the fund's subscription documents); and
- the offer document must set out all material information in respect of the fund.

3.67 An expert fund investor must be one of the following:

- an investor making a minimum initial investment or commitment of US$100,000 (or its foreign currency equivalent);
- in the business of acquiring, underwriting, managing, holding or disposing of investments whether as principal or agent, or giving advice on investments;
- a person with a net worth (or joint net worth with that person's spouse) of more than US$1 million (or its foreign currency equivalent), excluding his/her principal residence;
- an entity with at least US$1 million (or its foreign currency equivalent) of assets available for investment, connected with the fund or a service provider of the fund (there is a flexible approach to carried interest arrangements); or
- a government, local authority, public authority, or supranational body in Jersey or elsewhere.

Listed funds

3.68 A 72-hour 'fast track' authorisation process is available for all funds qualifying as listed funds under the JFSC's Jersey Listed Fund Guide. The key requirements are that the fund is a closed-ended Jersey limited company, which has:

- at least two Jersey resident directors on its board;
- a majority of its board being independent of the investment manager;
- an administrator with a physical presence in Jersey;
- a listing on a recognised exchange (the list of recognised exchanges is numerous and global in scope, and includes all exchanges upon which listings are typically sought);

3.68 Offshore Fund Domiciles – The Channel Islands

- an investment manager able to demonstrate sufficient track record in the investment management industry; and
- an admission document containing all material information in relation to the fund and a prescribed form of investment warning.

3.69 The Jersey Listed Fund Guide does not place any restrictions on who can invest in the listed fund.

Jersey eligible investor funds

3.70 The JEIF regime is broadly similar to that governing expert funds and the key requirements set out above in relation to expert funds[1] apply equally to JEIFs. A lighter touch approach, however, is taken to the Jersey content requirements relating to the offering documents for JEIFs, given the nature of such funds' investors.

[1] See para 3.66 above.

3.71 Investors must qualify as 'eligible investors' in order to invest in a JEIF. There are eleven categories of eligible investor, including:

- those investing or committing a minimum of US$1 million or its foreign currency equivalent;
- those whose ordinary business or professional activity includes dealing in, managing, underwriting or giving advice on investments (or an employee, director, consultant or shareholder of such a person); and
- individuals who own assets which have a total market value of not less than US$10 million or its foreign currency equivalent.

Recognised funds

3.72 Recognised funds are not suitable for hedge funds or for other funds aimed at sophisticated investors. They are not frequently established in Jersey. Broadly speaking, recognised funds are prescriptive (investment powers and restrictions are set out in a prescriptive manner in the relevant legislation) and are designed so as to be able to be sold directly to retail investors in the UK.

Regulated funds – ongoing regulation and investment restrictions

3.73 No investment restrictions or gearing restrictions are placed on expert funds, listed funds or JEIFs.

3.74 An annual fee is payable by a regulated public fund, which varies according to the number of pools of assets in the fund, and the current annual fee for a private fund is £500.

3.75 Regulated funds are generally required to notify the JFSC of any failure to comply with the regulatory requirements pursuant to which they were approved (for example, any failure to comply with the requirements of the expert fund, listed fund or JEIF criteria).

Types of vehicle and relevant legislation

3.76 Funds in Jersey are typically established as companies (single class, multi-class, umbrella or protected cell or incorporated cell), limited partnerships or unit trusts. Hedge funds usually prefer a corporate structure (except where another vehicle is utilised to achieve tax transparency from the perspective of one or more 'onshore' jurisdictions). The legislation, regulation and policy governing this area are subject to constant review and are regularly updated to maintain Jersey's international reputation and competitive advantage.

3.77 Any Jersey fund, irrespective of its legal structure, may be open-ended or closed-ended. For Jersey regulatory purposes, a closed-ended fund is a fund which is not open for redemptions at the option of the holders of interests in that fund. The same regulatory categories apply to both open-ended and closed-ended funds and the regulatory treatment of each is therefore very similar, although it should be noted that a listed fund must be closed-ended.

Companies

3.78 In recent years the Companies Law has been modified to accommodate improvements for the funds industry, for example to permit the use of corporate directors and treasury shares, abolish financial assistance restrictions and further simplify the retention of capital requirements. These changes are of particular benefit to hedge funds which are structured as Jersey companies.

3.79 PCCs and ICCs are popular fund structures in Jersey. The PCC is a 'second generation' protected cell company that represents a significant advance from the PCC model used in other jurisdictions. For example, the segregated nature of the cellular structure is clearly provided for in statute and gives legal certainty. A PCC cell can also invest in another cell within the same PCC structure. The ICC was a true innovation, being very similar to and combining the flexibility of a PCC, whilst providing the secure ring fencing that can only be achieved through granting individual cells separate legal personality. PCCs and ICCs are particularly suited to umbrella structures, where a fund manager might seek to establish a number of funds, all using the same infrastructure but with different investment objectives, investor profiles or fee structures. Given their ring-fenced structure, PCCs and ICCs are particularly suitable as hedge fund vehicles.

Limited partnerships

3.80 Limited partnerships may be established under the LP Law. Limited partners enjoy limited liability in that their liability for the debts of the limited partnership cannot extend beyond their agreed capital contributions provided their activity does not amount to 'management' for the purposes of the LP Law. The LP Law provides a safe harbour for certain activities that would otherwise amount to 'management' and permits the limited partner a greater degree of involvement in the management of a limited partnership than some other jurisdictions.

3.81 Other advantages of a Jersey limited partnership include that there is no limit on the number of limited partners and that confidentiality is preserved, as the only document to be publicly filed is a short declaration of limited partnership that does not disclose the identity of the limited partners, the business of the limited partnership or the partnership contributions.

3.82 There are two additional forms of limited partnership under Jersey law, which may be used (for example) in management or carried interest structures: (i) the separate limited partnership (which, unlike a traditional limited partnership, has separate legal personality from that of its partners); and (ii) the incorporated limited partnership (which is a body corporate). Jersey has also enacted a limited liability partnerships law[1] with a view to enabling the use of Jersey limited liability structures by professional firms and other partnerships in which the partners take an active management role.

[1] Limited Liability Partnerships (Jersey) Law 1997.

Unit trusts

3.83 A unit trust is not a separate legal entity but a trust arrangement whereby the legal ownership of the scheme's assets is vested in a trustee who holds those assets on trust for the benefit of unitholders. A unit trust is constituted by an instrument of trust which is usually between a manager and a trustee in the case of an open-ended unit trust. The trust instrument governs the appointment and retirement of the trustee and manager, their respective duties, the distribution or accumulation of trust income, investment powers, dealing and valuation. The relevant trusts legislation in Jersey is the Trusts (Jersey) Law 1984.

The International Stock Exchange

3.84 Jersey shares the International Stock Exchange ('TISE') with Guernsey. An overview of TISE is provided in the Guernsey section of this chapter[1].

[1] See paras **3.146–3.148** below.

Taxation

3.85 Taxation is the responsibility of the Comptroller of Taxes under the Income Tax (Jersey) Law 1961, as amended. From a taxation perspective, the position in Jersey is very straightforward. A fund, whether established as a company, unit trust or limited partnership, will not be subject to any Jersey tax. There is no capital gains tax, capital transfer tax, wealth or inheritance tax payable in respect of the issue or realisation of investments in a Jersey investment fund (unless the fund invests in Jersey property or buildings). Nor is there any corporation tax, profits tax or stamp duty payable.

3.86 Jersey resident service administrators and custodians are generally liable to Jersey income tax at the rate of 10%. However, this does not apply to Jersey administered entities such as general partners and managers that provide services to a fund and which would be taxed at 0%.

3.87 The States of Jersey has been in discussions with (among others) the UK and the US with regard to the reporting of information and has recently signed inter-governmental agreements ('IGAs') with the UK and the US. In certain circumstances, information regarding investors' interests in funds may be provided by the Jersey Comptroller of Taxes in the future to the US, UK and other tax authorities in accordance with these IGAs and other international tax agreements that may apply to Jersey funds from time to time. Such future agreements would include the Common Reporting Standard, being the global standard for automatic exchange of financial account information released by the Organisation for Economic Co-operation and Development (the 'OECD') on 13 February 2014 and which may supersede some or all IGAs to which Jersey is a party.

B   GUERNSEY

Tom Carey, Partner, Carey Olsen

Introduction

3.88 The Island of Guernsey is the largest of the islands comprising the Bailiwick of Guernsey (the 'Bailiwick'), a group of islands located in the English Channel between England and France which form part of the Channel Islands. The Bailiwick has a resident population of approximately 65,000 and is around 35 minutes' flying time from London. The Bailiwick is a self-governing Crown Dependency, which means that it has strong constitutional links with England, but is not part of the UK (or the EU). Guernsey is in the same time zone as the UK.

3.89 Guernsey's governing body is known as the 'States of Deliberation' (the 'States'). The States comprises a Bailiff, HM Attorney General, HM Solicitor General and 40 peoples' deputies, including two representatives from the Island of Alderney (the second largest of the islands comprising the Bailiwick). Sark, with its own legislature, sends no representatives. The States is also the Executive, comprising a 'Senior Committee' (the Policy & Resources Committee) which has six subordinate 'Principal Committees' to which seven Authorities, Boards and Commissions answer.

3.90 Guernsey's relationship with the EU is governed by Protocol 3 of the EU Treaty of Accession of 1972. The effect of this is that the Bailiwick falls within the common customs area permitting freedom of travel, people and goods, but the Bailiwick is not bound by EU directives.

Guernsey law

3.91 Guernsey has governed its own taxation and fiscal policy and other domestic affairs through its own elected government and court system for more than 800 years. The unique constitutional position of Guernsey and each of the other Channel Islands has its origins in the integration of the Channel Islands into the Duchy of Normandy in France in the 10th and 11th centuries and the relationship between the Duchy of Normandy and England following the conquest of England in 1066 by William, Duke of Normandy. Whilst other

3.91 *Offshore Fund Domiciles – The Channel Islands*

French territories and provinces were eventually ceded to France, the Channel Islands remained possessions of the Crown of England. As a reward for their loyalty to the English Crown, the Islands were granted autonomy in relation to the management of their domestic affairs by Royal Charter and have governed themselves to this day.

3.92 Guernsey's close relationship with both England and France has influenced the development of Guernsey law. Guernsey's common law is based on Norman 'customary law' which, in large part, forms the basis of the modern French Civil Code. Whilst the common law has evolved in Guernsey in line with international developments, and most modern laws and precedents will be familiar to English lawyers, lawyers in Guernsey will always have regard to the customary law in relation to certain basic legal tenets. There are therefore various notable differences from English law, particularly in relation to land law and the laws of succession. However, the basic principles of Guernsey's contract law and laws relating to companies, trusts and partnerships will be familiar to international practitioners.

3.93 Legislation is made by the States, either in the form of Draft Orders in Council (which are ratified by England's Privy Council) or in the form of Ordinances (which do not require ratification by the English Crown).

3.94 The court structure in Guernsey is provided by the Royal Court of Guernsey. Rights of appeal are to a Court of Appeal which comprises senior English judges and, ultimately, to the Privy Council.

The finance industry in Guernsey

3.95 Guernsey's autonomy has enabled the creation of a regulatory and fiscal environment which is attractive to the finance industry. The finance industry became established in Guernsey approximately 50 years ago and encompasses banking, insurance, funds services and trust and company administration. In addition to favourable tax and regulatory regimes, Guernsey has a strong infrastructure with a motivated and well-qualified English-speaking workforce. Finance is the largest employer in the jurisdiction and produces 33% of Guernsey's gross domestic product.

3.96 In 1999, Guernsey won the backing of the International Financial Action Task Force for its impressive regulatory framework and in 2000 the Financial Stability Forum established by the G7 countries placed Guernsey in the Top Division of International Finance Centres, alongside countries such as Switzerland, Hong Kong and Singapore. In November 2003, the International Monetary Fund (the 'IMF') published a report commending Guernsey's standards of financial regulation, concluding that 'the jurisdiction has been assessed to have a high level of compliance with all of the standards against which it was assessed'. Guernsey was assessed by MONEYVAL in 2016 which found that it had the highest standard of any jurisdiction so far assessed: compliant or largely compliant with 48 out of 49 of the Financial Action Task Force (the 'FATF') recommendations on anti-money laundering and countering the financing of terrorism. MONEYVAL found that Guernsey has in place a range of measures to facilitate various forms of international co-operation and plays host to competent authorities and financial institutions that are highly efficient, knowledgeable and aware of their obligations.

3.97 Guernsey has a thriving funds industry: on 30 September 2017, 982 investment funds and 2,184 sub-funds with assets in excess of £269 billion were administered in Guernsey[1]. Of these, 141 (14%) were hedge funds or funds of hedge funds.

[1] Statistics are available from www.gfsc.gg.

3.98 The finance industry is overseen by an independent regulator, the Guernsey Financial Services Commission (the 'GFSC'). The GFSC was instrumental in establishing the Guernsey Training Agency in November 1996 and the Channel Islands Stock Exchange (now the International Stock Exchange[1]) in Guernsey in October 1998. In 2001, 'Guernsey Finance' (now operating under the brand name 'We Are Guernsey') was created as a joint initiative between the States of Guernsey and the finance sector to promote Guernsey as a finance centre.

[1] See paras **3.146–3.148** below.

Regulation of financial services

3.99 The GFSC is a body corporate established under the Financial Services Commission (Bailiwick of Guernsey) Law, 1987 to regulate the finance industry in Guernsey. The GFSC currently supervises and regulates over 2,800 licensees from within the banking, fiduciary, insurance and investment sectors in Guernsey. Currently, over 600 institutions are licensed to carry on investment business in Guernsey, comprising various fund management, administration and custody groups.

3.100 The financial services industry is governed by a range of statutes, the most significant of which is the Protection of Investors (Bailiwick of Guernsey) Law, 1987, as amended (the 'POI Law'), which establishes a regulatory framework for the licensing of service providers and authorisation of investment products and activities.

3.101 The GFSC has a wide remit to take such steps as it deems necessary for the development and effective supervision of the finance industry in Guernsey. It provides assistance to various governmental bodies on finance matters, as well as recommending schemes for the statutory regulation of finance (although it does not have the power to issue secondary legislation). As the Bailiwick's regulatory authority, the GFSC is also responsible for establishing anti-money laundering requirements, the prevention of financial fraud and liaising with other regulators and international bodies such as the IMF.

3.102 The GFSC's statutory functions include regulating, through four separate divisions, investment business, banking, insurance business and fiduciary business. Investment funds and their service providers which carry on controlled investment business[1] are regulated by the Investment Business Division of the GFSC. The POI Law requires the GFSC, in carrying out its functions, to have regard to the objectives of: protecting investors, the public and the reputation of the Bailiwick as a financial centre; ensuring that markets for

3.102 *Offshore Fund Domiciles – The Channel Islands*

controlled investments are fair, efficient and transparent; and reducing risks.

[1] 'Controlled investment business' occurs where 'restricted activities' are carried on in relation to 'controlled investments'. The definitions of controlled investments and restricted activities are set out in schedules to the POI Law.

Regulation of service providers

3.103 The POI Law specifies various activities which, when carried on in Guernsey in connection with a controlled investment, may only be carried on in accordance with the terms of a licence issued by the GFSC. Essentially, these activities encompass all forms of management administration, promotion or custody of securities or investment funds generally.

Regulation of investment funds

3.104 Investment funds established or administered in Guernsey are regulated by the GFSC under two regulatory regimes: 'authorised' or 'registered'. Broadly speaking, authorised funds are those which are *authorised by* the GFSC following a substantive review by the GFSC, whereas registered funds are those which are *registered with* the GFSC, with much of the scrutiny of the fund and the promoter (and the ongoing responsibility therefor) being conducted by the fund's administrator[1] (which must be a Guernsey entity licensed in Guernsey under the POI Law).

[1] This is described as the 'designated manager' in the POI Law and the 'designated manager' or 'designated administrator' in the various rules. For simplicity, the term 'administrator' is used here.

3.105 The POI Law enables the GFSC to create 'classes' of authorised and registered funds and rules which govern those classes. Classes may be exclusively open-ended or exclusively closed-ended, or either (depending upon the rules applicable to that class). An open-ended fund is broadly defined as an investment fund where investors have a right to redeem their investment from the investment fund[1]. In a closed-ended fund, investors have no right to redeem their investment during the fund's lifetime.

[1] Schedule 1, clause 1 of the POI Law. There is no prescribed period within which the redemption must occur or the moneys be paid.

3.106 The following table sets out the current classes of funds and the rules applicable to them (note that the POI Law is the governing legislation in all cases):

Type	Class	Rules	Open-ended/closed-ended
Registered	Registered collective investment scheme	The Registered Collective Investment Schemes Rules 2015 Prospectus Rules 2008	Both
Registered	Private investment fund	The Private Investment Fund Rules 2016	Both
Registered	Manager led product	Guidance note only	Both
Authorised	Class A	The Authorised Collective Investment Schemes (Class A) Rules 2008	Open
Authorised	Class B	The Authorised Collective Investment Schemes (Class B) Rules 2013	Open
Authorised	Class Q	The Collective Investment Schemes (Qualifying Professional Investor Funds) (Class Q) Rules 1998	Open
Authorised	Authorised closed-ended scheme	The Authorised Closed-Ended Investment Schemes Rules 2013	Closed

3.107 Typical forms of investment fund of any class established in Guernsey are limited liability companies, limited partnerships and unit trusts.

COMPANIES

3.108 Guernsey's companies law was completely revised by the enactment of the Companies (Guernsey) Law, 2008 (the 'Companies Law'), which came into force on 1 July 2008, to accommodate the requirements of the finance industry and a new electronic Companies Registry.

3.109 The Companies Law makes a range of corporate structures available in Guernsey. It also provides for a 'fast track' incorporation process, streamlined administration requirements and flexibility for capital structures, permitting the free increase, reduction and distribution of capital or income to investors without court or creditor intervention (provided the relevant company meets a standard 'solvency' test). This is of particular importance to any investment structures seeking to increase or return capital on a regular basis.

3.110 The range of corporate vehicles available in Guernsey includes single-class or multi-class limited liability companies, unlimited liability companies, companies limited by guarantee, hybrid companies (a combination of each type of company), protected cell companies and incorporated cell companies.

3.111 In 1997, Guernsey became the first jurisdiction in the world to introduce protected cell companies ('PCCs') as investment vehicles. With their ring-fenced structure and ease of administration, PCCs rapidly became popular as hedge fund vehicles (the concept has since been copied in many other jurisdictions). As at 30 September 2017, 94 PCCs were regulated as funds by the GFSC, representing 11% of all funds by number, and 41% of

3.111 *Offshore Fund Domiciles – The Channel Islands*

open-ended Guernsey domiciled funds by number[1].

[1] See www.gfsc.gg/industry-sectors/investment/statistics.

3.112 A PCC consists of a 'core' and separate and distinct 'cells'. The assets and liabilities of one cell are segregated and protected from those of the other cells under Guernsey law. Similarly, the assets and liabilities of the core are segregated and protected from those of the other cells. For investment funds, the attraction of a PCC is the avoidance of any cross-cell contagion if a cell within an 'umbrella' PCC fund becomes insolvent and the creditors attempt to enforce judgments against assets within other cells.

3.113 Guernsey added to the concept of PCCs by introducing incorporated cell companies ('ICCs'), which operate in a similar manner to PCCs but offer separate legal personality for each of the cells.

LIMITED PARTNERSHIPS

3.114 Limited partnerships may be established under the Limited Partnerships (Guernsey) Law, 1995 (the 'LP Law'). Limited partners enjoy limited liability: their liability for the debts of the limited partnership cannot extend beyond their agreed capital contributions provided their activity as limited partners does not amount to 'management' for the purposes of the LP Law. The LP Law provides a safe harbour for certain specified activities that would otherwise amount to 'management' and therefore permits limited partners a greater degree of involvement in the management of a limited partnership than some other jurisdictions, whilst maintaining their limited liability status.

3.115 Other advantages of a Guernsey limited partnership include no limit on the number of limited partners, the ability freely to transfer partnership interests and return capital contributions, as well as the preservation of investor confidentiality (as the only document to be filed publicly is a short declaration of limited partnership that does not disclose the identities of the limited partners or their contributions or commitments).

3.116 It is possible for limited partnerships in Guernsey to elect, at the time of formation, to have separate legal personality from the partners. If no election is made, the limited partnership will not have separate legal personality.

3.117 Guernsey limited partnerships are used extensively by the private equity industry and have also been used successfully for a number of innovative listed investment structures.

UNIT TRUSTS

3.118 Under Guernsey law, a unit trust is not a separate legal entity but is constituted by an agreement in writing, commonly known as a 'trust instrument', between a manager and a trustee. The concept of a trust is long recognised in Guernsey. Trusts are generally now governed by the provisions of the Trusts (Guernsey) Law, 2007.

3.119 The assets of a unit trust are held by its trustee on trust for the benefit of the beneficiaries (the unitholders (investors)) and are managed by the manager, which may appoint one or more investment managers or advisers to assist it.

3.120 Contracts in relation to the management and administration of the trust fund will be entered into by the manager, whereas the trustee will enter into contracts in relation to the assets themselves, such as bank deposits, borrowings and security agreements.

Investment fund regulatory approval process

3.121 As noted above, regulated funds are either *authorised by* (authorised funds) or *registered with* (registered funds) the GFSC. Accordingly, there are two distinct approval processes.

AUTHORISED FUNDS

3.122 Subject to the 'QIF' process outlined and defined below[1], the regulatory approval process for all classes of authorised funds in Guernsey by the GFSC is a three-stage process that can typically be completed in six to eight weeks.

[1] See paras 3.128–3.130 below.

3.123 The first stage is an application for approval in principle, setting out, amongst other things, details of the nature and purpose of the scheme, the names and addresses of the proposed administrator, manager and (if applicable) the trustee or custodian and the fees to be borne by the scheme.

3.124 If the promoter is new to Guernsey, there is a checklist[1] which must also be submitted. The new promoter will first have to satisfy the GFSC as to its fitness, propriety and track record in managing third party money before the GFSC will consider whether it is prepared in principle to approve the proposed fund. Normally, a demonstrable track record in the promotion and management of funds is required and the authorisation of intended promoters by regulatory authorities in other jurisdictions is not in itself generally sufficient. Newly established fund management groups may also be approved by the GFSC. The GFSC would take into account the track record of the individuals controlling and managing the operations of the promoter in determining whether the promoter is fit and proper and has the necessary track record.

[1] Promoters will normally approach the GFSC in advance of the fund application and should complete the New Promoter Checklist before doing so.

3.125 Once the GFSC has indicated that the promoter is acceptable and the fund is acceptable in principle, the GFSC will issue an 'outline authorisation', typically within 28 business days of receipt.

3.126 The second stage of the process involves filing a draft of the fund's prospectus or scheme particulars with the GFSC, together with a checklist of required disclosures. Once the GFSC is satisfied that the fund and the documentation comply with certain criteria (including an adequate spread of risk, comprehensive risk warnings, an appropriate investor profile, minimum subscription levels and full disclosure of all material facts), the GFSC will issue an 'interim authorisation', indicating that it will authorise the fund upon

3.126 *Offshore Fund Domiciles – The Channel Islands*

receipt of final certified documents. The GFSC aims to issue interim authorisations within ten business days of receipt.

3.127 The third stage involves filing dated, signed or certified copies of the final prospectus and all establishment documents (together with, in the case of Class B and Class Q schemes, a certificate from the manager of the scheme or an approved law firm, or a letter from the administrator, certifying the information in the relevant rules). The GFSC will then issue 'formal authorisation' by letter, typically within seven business days of receipt.

3.128 In addition to the three-stage authorisation regime referred to above, the GFSC offers 'fast track' authorisation for particular types of authorised funds known as qualifying investor funds ('QIFs'). All classes of authorised funds, with the exception of Class A Schemes (due to the retail nature of their investors), using any type of vehicle referred to above, can apply for fast track approval as a QIF.

3.129 QIFs are authorised investment funds whose investors are 'qualified investors', which are defined as 'professional investor', 'experienced investor' and/or a 'knowledgeable employee'[1].

[1] These definitions can be found in the GFSC's QIF Guidance Note (dated May 2007), in which the GFSC sets out the terms of regulation of QIFs.

3.130 The QIF regime guarantees that a QIF will be authorised by the GFSC on a fast track basis within a maximum of three business days from the date of application. It is a straightforward, single stage application and authorisation process that relies upon the proposed administrator in Guernsey (which must be a Guernsey entity licensed in Guernsey under the POI Law) taking responsibility[1] (as opposed to the GFSC) for assessing the suitability of the promoter (or investment manager) (new promoters are assessed on a similar basis to that set out above), ensuring that the fund will only be available to 'qualified investors', and verifying compliance with the applicable rules[2].

[1] The GFSC will require the administrator to carry out the same level of due diligence as the GFSC would carry out itself and provide appropriate warranties.
[2] QIFs are regulated in accordance with the GFSC's QIF Guidance Note (dated May 2007).

REGISTERED FUNDS

3.131 The regulatory approval process for all classes of registered funds is similar to that for QIFs in that an entity licensed under the POI Law, rather than the GFSC, takes responsibility for assessing the suitability of the promoter (or investment manager) and verifying compliance with the applicable rules.

Registered Collective Investment Scheme Rules

3.132 For funds seeking registration under the Registered Collective Investment Scheme Rules 2015, the GFSC must receive a copy of the application form, signed by the proposed administrator of the scheme, containing warranties given by the proposed administrator to the GFSC. The form must be accompanied by the final version of the prospectus (which must comply with the requirements of the Prospectus Rules 2008), together with the subscription/application form as well as the constitutional documents and all material agreements.

3.133 The GFSC aims to issue registration within three business days of receipt.

PRIVATE INVESTMENT FUNDS

3.134 In 2016, the GFSC introduced the Private Investment Fund Rules 2016 (the 'PIF Rules'), creating a new class of registered fund known as a 'private investment fund' (a 'PIF'). PIFs can be open-ended or closed-ended and must contain a maximum of 50 legal or natural persons (an agent acting on behalf of underlying investors will count as one person). A PIF can be marketed to an unlimited number of persons but only 30 additional investors can be added in any 12-month rolling period (excluding the first 12 months). The PIF Rules are predicated on the basis of a close relationship between the investors and the manager, which is required to confirm to the GFSC that the investors can bear potential losses from an investment in the PIF. For this reason, a PIF requires a separate manager and administrator (both POI licensed entities – the licence for the manager may be given as part of the PIF application). The PIF Rules dispense with any requirement for a prospectus, and do not require the manager to satisfy the capital adequacy rules or conduct of business rules.

3.135 For funds seeking registration under the PIF Rules, the GFSC must receive a copy of the application form, signed by both the administrator and the manager of the scheme, containing warranties given by both to the GFSC.

3.136 The GFSC aims to issue registration within one business day of receipt.

3.137 The introduction of the PIF provides Guernsey with a valuable and exciting new class of registered fund. A large number of funds established in Guernsey are essentially private and significant use of PIFs is expected in the future.

MANAGER LED PRODUCT

3.138 In 2016, Guernsey also introduced the manager led product ('MLP') regime. This was adopted in anticipation of the extension to Guernsey of the third country passport under the Alternative Investment Fund Managers Directive[1] ('AIFMD').

[1] Directive 2011/61/EU of 8 June 2011.

3.139 The regulatory focus of the MLP regime is on the investment manager (the 'AIFM') rather than the fund (ie the fund is *not* subject to additional regulatory requirements prescribed by GFSC rules as are the other classes of funds). This approach mimics the regulation adopted by member states.

3.140 The AIFM will be subject to the AIMFD Rules, 2013, which replicate the requirements of AIFMD. These Rules are designed to facilitate the use of the third country passport extension (which has not yet been extended to third country AIFMs, as discussed in more detail below[1]).

[1] See paras **3.144–3.145** below.

Hedge funds and funds of hedge funds in Guernsey

3.141 The GFSC adopts a pragmatic approach towards investor protection. It does not apply overly restrictive conditions to the regulation of investment funds, especially to those aimed at the institutional or high net worth investor market. This flexibility has helped the significant growth of the non-retail investment sector over the past 20 years or so since the first hedge fund was established in Guernsey. Nowadays, most funds formed in Guernsey tend to be for the institutional or high net worth individual[1] markets, with hedge funds, funds of hedge funds, private equity and property funds being especially popular.

[1] Although note that there is no definition of 'high net worth individual' under Guernsey law. Aside from Class Q schemes or QIFs, determination of investor base is by reference to the minimum amount to be invested. A person investing more than US$100,000 would be considered to be a high net worth individual.

3.142 Guernsey is particularly keen to attract high quality hedge fund business. In February 2004, the GFSC introduced a specific regulatory regime for hedge funds[1], setting out a more relaxed framework for the operation of hedge funds and including a number of waivers of various fund rules. Key changes are as follows:

- In relation to custody of investments (particularly for funds with an institutional and expert investor base), the GFSC is prepared to permit the fund's prime broker[2] to act as custodian, rather than a Guernsey domiciled and licensed entity, and will not require the prime broker to oversee the fund's manager.
- The GFSC is also prepared (again, for funds with an institutional and expert investor base) not to insist on complex segregation requirements for prime brokers holding fund assets.
- The GFSC is prepared to permit preliminary net asset value ('NAV') estimation processes in advance of final NAV determination[3] where the underlying assets do not easily permit frequent NAV determination.
- Where estimation is permitted, the GFSC will grant waivers of client money rules requiring segregation of subscription and redemption monies[4].

[1] See the GFSC's document, Hedge Funds: Flexible Approach to Authorisation Policy, published on 23 February 2004.
[2] Prime brokers will need to be located in a jurisdiction acceptable to the GFSC and have a substantial net worth.
[3] For example, to allow subscriptions and redemptions to be processed on estimated NAV, subject to adjustment on publication of final NAV.
[4] The Licensees (Conduct of Business Rules) 2016 define what constitutes client money and how client money accounts should be set up. The rules include record-keeping and reconciliation requirements.

3.143 Some of these waivers may also be available to hedge funds which are targeted at less sophisticated investors.

Guernsey and the Alternative Investment Fund Managers Directive

3.144 Guernsey is not a member of the EU and thus is a 'third country' for the purposes of AIFMD. Guernsey funds are eligible to be marketed in the EU through the national private placement regimes in accordance with Articles 36 and 42 of AIFMD. This has proved to be a highly effective means of access to EU markets (in particular, Guernsey enjoys easy access to the major UK investor market). Guernsey funds continue to be marketed in many EU countries, thereby avoiding the more onerous and costly AIFMD requirements.

3.145 Guernsey, Jersey and Switzerland were the first jurisdictions to be given an 'unqualified and positive assessment' for the purposes of the extension of the AIFMD passporting regime (which, subject to the satisfaction of certain conditions, would provide Guernsey managers and funds with full access to EU markets). It is currently unclear when the European Commission will extend the passport rights to third countries, although Guernsey is expected to be one of the first jurisdictions to be granted such rights.

The International Stock Exchange

3.146 The International Stock Exchange ('TISE') (previously known as the Channel Islands Securities Exchange ('CISE')) is a company limited by shares which was established in Guernsey in 2013 when it took over the business of the Channel Islands Stock Exchange. TISE is a shared exchange with Jersey and facilitates the listing and trading (via screen-based trading) of investment funds, debt instruments and shares in companies. More than 2,000 securities and over 400 open-ended and closed-ended funds appear on TISE's Official List, with a total market capitalisation of more than £300 billion. Admission to the Official List of TISE gives the advantage of greater transparency and may create a larger potential investor base (because some potential investors may be prohibited from investing in, or restricted in the amount they can invest in, unlisted vehicles). Listing also creates an additional source of oversight by TISE's market authority, which some investors may find comforting.

3.147 TISE is licensed to operate as an investment exchange under the POI Law and is regulated by the GFSC. In October 2003, TISE was approved as an affiliate member of the International Organisation of Securities Commissions. TISE was officially recognised by the Australian Stock Exchange in July 2000. In September 2002, TISE was recognised as a designated offshore securities market by the US Securities and Exchange Commission within the meaning of Rule 902(b) of Regulation S under the Securities Act of 1933. In December 2002, TISE was designated by the UK's Inland Revenue (now HM Revenue and Customs ('HMRC')) as a recognised stock exchange for the purposes of investment by Self-Invested Personal Pensions and Individual Savings Accounts. HMRC's recognition also means that products listed on TISE may be able to avail themselves of the Quoted Eurobond Exemption. In February 2004, the UK's (then) Financial Services Authority approved TISE as a recognised stock exchange within the meaning of the UK's Financial Services and Markets Act 2000. TISE is also an affiliate member of the World Federation of Exchanges.

3.148 Listing on TISE is straightforward, timely and cost effective. The listing process has two stages. The first stage is the submission of draft documentation and payment of an initial listing fee. These documents are reviewed by an analyst at TISE who provides a comments letter. The second stage is the submission of final documents, reflecting the written comments. Following approval and payment of the first annual listing fee, a listing letter is released and listing takes place.

Taxation

General

3.149 Taxation in Guernsey is the responsibility of the Director of Income Tax in Guernsey and the principal legislation is contained in the Income Tax (Guernsey) Law, 1975 as extensively amended. Guernsey does not levy any form of capital gains tax, inheritance tax or VAT.

3.150 No stamp or document duty is payable in respect of companies, unit trusts or limited partnerships.

Income tax

3.151 Unit trusts and companies authorised as investment funds may apply for exemption from income tax in Guernsey, subject to meeting certain criteria. The exemption has to be applied for annually and is subject to payment of a fee, which is currently fixed at £1,200. In the absence of such exemption, unit trusts and companies authorised as investment funds are subject to income tax at 0%.

3.152 A limited partnership is transparent for the purposes of Guernsey tax. There is no requirement for the partnership itself to make any returns or pay any fees to the Director of Income Tax and it is the responsibility of each partner to determine whether it has any liability in Guernsey to tax. A limited partner (whether an individual or a company) that is resident in Guernsey for Guernsey tax purposes is generally liable to tax on its share of the profits of a limited partnership whether those profits are generated in Guernsey or elsewhere. A limited partner that is an individual who is not solely or principally resident in Guernsey or a company which is not resident in Guernsey, is not liable to tax in Guernsey on any income derived from a limited partnership's international operations, defined as business operations conducted on behalf of a limited partnership with, and investments made on behalf of a limited partnership in, persons who are not resident in Guernsey for the purposes of the Income Tax (Guernsey) Law, 1975.

3.153 On 1 January 2008, in the light of competitive pressures following proposed reforms in the taxation regimes of competing financial services centres both onshore and offshore, the States of Guernsey introduced a package of measures proposing a broad direction as to future policy for a radical change in company taxation, including:

- the reduction in the general rate of income tax paid by Guernsey companies to 0% in respect of the tax year 2008 and subsequent years; and

- the imposition of a 10% and 20% rate of tax on companies receiving certain classes of income, including income from banking business and income arising in relation to certain utilities.

3.154 The current exemption regime, however, continues to be available for investment funds.

International tax initiatives

3.155 Guernsey has given its full support for the transparency principles central to the current G20[1], OECD and EU tax initiatives, and is working as part of the wider international community in the development and effective implementation of internationally agreed standards, including those set by the FATF and the OECD.

[1] The G20 (or G-20 or Group of Twenty) is an international forum for the governments and central bank governors from 20 major economies.

3.156 The co-operation with the EU began in 2003 when Guernsey voluntarily committed to the EU's Code of Conduct on Business Taxation.

3.157 In 2004, Guernsey also voluntarily entered into automatic information exchange and bilateral withholding arrangements with all member states under the EU Savings Directive[1] and has signed many tax information exchange agreements and double taxation agreements. Guernsey intends to complete negotiations and sign agreements with all G20, OECD and EU member states.

[1] Directive 2003/48/EC of 3 June 2003.

3.158 In May 2013, Guernsey committed to join the initiative of the G5 countries on establishing and piloting an international standard for the automatic exchange of information between tax authorities.

3.159 In December 2013, Guernsey entered into an inter-governmental agreement (an 'IGA') with the US in relation to the implementation of the US Foreign Account Tax Compliance Act ('FATCA'), which it implemented in June 2014. In October 2013, Guernsey also entered into an IGA with the UK in relation to the UK's own version of FATCA, which it also implemented in June 2014. However, the UK FATCA has now been superseded by the adoption by Guernsey (alongside numerous jurisdictions) of the much broader, global Common Reporting Standard (the 'CRS') on the automatic exchange of information.

3.160 Guernsey acceded to the OECD's Multilateral Convention on Mutual Administrative Assistance in Tax Matters in August 2014.

3.161 Guernsey joined in the joint statement on 19 March 2014 committing to the early adoption of the global CRS, with the first exchange of information in relation to new accounts and pre-existing individual high value accounts taking place by the end of September 2017.

3.162 On 29 October 2014, Guernsey was among over 50 jurisdictions to sign the OECD's Multilateral Competent Authority Agreement in Berlin as a

3.162 *Offshore Fund Domiciles – The Channel Islands*

further step towards implementation of the CRS. Guernsey, along with over 50 other jurisdictions, implemented the CRS into its domestic legislation with effect from 1 January 2016.

3.163 Following the repeal of the EU Savings Directive by the Council of the EU on 10 November 2015, in order to make way for the CRS, the existing arrangements between Guernsey and EU member states under the Directive will be suspended.

3.164 Guernsey sent letters to all member states within one week of the repeal of the Directive to confirm the suspension of the bilateral EU Savings Directive arrangements and to give the required notice of their termination, and to confirm the move to automatic exchange of information under the CRS from 1 January 2016 (with the first exchange by September 2017, except in the case of Austria which will be one year later).

3.165 Guernsey has established a dialogue with the European Parliament on tax issues. The Chief Minister of Guernsey met with the Chair of the European Parliament's Special Committee on Tax Rulings ('TAXE 1') in May 2015 and provided written submissions to the Committee. In March 2016, officials from Guernsey gave evidence at a hearing of the second Special Committee ('TAXE 2').

3.166 In 2016, in connection with the OECD's base erosion and profit shifting project ('BEPS'), Guernsey accepted the OECD's invitation to become a BEPS Associate and member of the newly established OECD BEPS Inclusive Framework. As a BEPS Associate, Guernsey is able to contribute to the overall development of the BEPS programme through policy dialogue and the exchange of information.

3.167 Guernsey is committed to adopting the BEPS minimum standards and has implemented country-by-country reporting in respect of accounting periods which began on or after 1 January 2016. Guernsey signed the OECD's Multilateral Instrument in June 2017 in order to implement tax treaty-related measures to combat BEPS.

Chapter 4

ONSHORE FUND DOMICILES

A	Hong Kong	4.1
B	Ireland	4.88
C	Luxembourg	4.201
D	Malta	4.324
E	Singapore	4.438
F	Switzerland	4.484

A   HONG KONG

Rolfe Hayden, Partner, Simmons & Simmons and Gaven Cheong, Partner, Simmons & Simmons

Introduction

4.1 Although the territory constituting Hong Kong reverted to the People's Republic of China (hereafter, China) in 1997, Hong Kong is an administratively autonomous region and has continued to maintain a common law legal system, based in the main on English law. Similarly, the regulators in Hong Kong, while operating increasingly closely with their counterparts on mainland China, are statutory bodies with their own Hong Kong-specific rules and requirements. The Securities and Futures Commission (the 'SFC') is the main regulator of investment funds and fund managers in Hong Kong and the primary legislation is the Securities and Futures Ordinance (Cap 571) (the 'SFO').

4.2 The hedge fund industry in Hong Kong has experienced tremendous and continued growth in the past decade. According to the SFC's latest report on hedge fund activities released in March 2015[1], the number of hedge funds managed by SFC-licensed hedge fund managers in Hong Kong increased from 676 in 2012 to 778 as of 30 September 2014.

[1] Report of the Survey on Hedge Fund Activities of SFC-licensed Managers/Advisers (March 2015) – see http://www.sfc.hk/web/EN/files/IS/publications/HF%20Survey%20Report%20EC%202015.pdf.

4.3 The diagram below, taken from the SFC's report, illustrates the upward trend of the volume of total hedge fund assets under management ('AUM') in Hong Kong, which expanded from US$87.1 billion in 2012 to US$120.9 billion as of 30 September 2014, representing an increase of 38.8%. It was also reported that the surveyed hedge fund managers invested mainly in the Asia Pacific region and that, as of 30 September 2014, 92% of investors in hedge funds were from outside of Hong Kong, consisting mostly of funds of hedge funds, insurance companies and other institutional investors.

4.3 Onshore Fund Domiciles

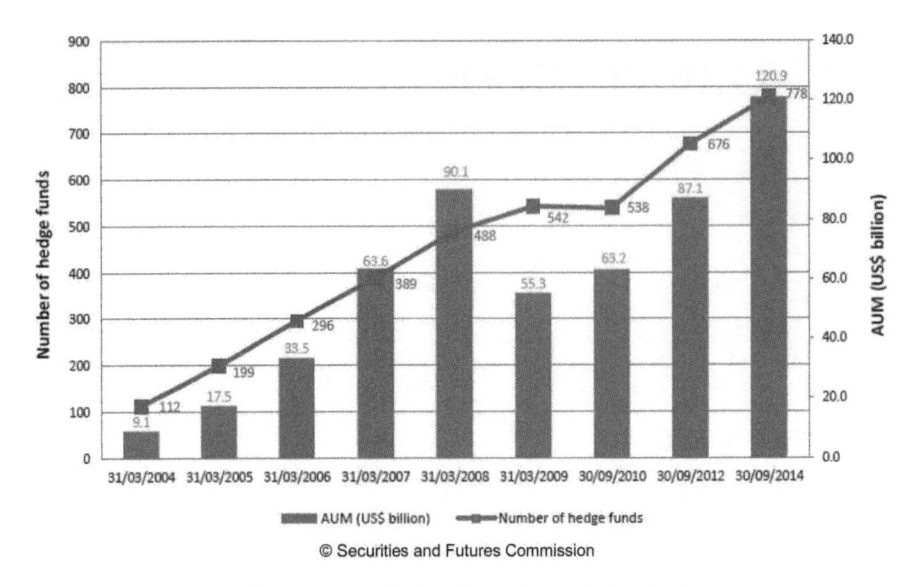

Analysis on total AUM and number of hedge funds
(Source: Securities and Futures Commission, Hong Kong, March 2015)

Typical fund structures

4.4 A vast majority of hedge funds managed in Hong Kong are established offshore in the Cayman Islands primarily for tax reasons. Generally, under the Inland Revenue Ordinance (Cap 112) (the 'IRO'), profits tax is payable by any person or entity that (i) carries on a trade or business in Hong Kong and (ii) earns profits which arise in or derive from Hong Kong, subject to specific exemptions available respectively to funds authorised by the SFC under the SFO (ie those which can be offered to the public) and non-Hong Kong resident funds in respect of certain specified transactions. Consequently, private (non-retail) funds which are managed in Hong Kong are usually established outside Hong Kong so as to take advantage of the profits tax exemption for offshore funds contained in the IRO.

4.5 Offshore hedge funds managed from Hong Kong commonly use mutual fund companies (including segregated portfolio companies), limited partnerships and unit trusts established in the Cayman Islands as the investment vehicle, and are typically organised into a combination of, or a variation on, the following structures:

- stand-alone funds[1];
- master-feeder funds[2]; and
- umbrella funds[3].

[1] See paras **4.6–4.9** below.
[2] See paras **4.10–4.13** below.
[3] See paras **4.14–4.16** below.

Stand-alone funds

4.6 The following diagram illustrates a typical stand-alone fund structure:

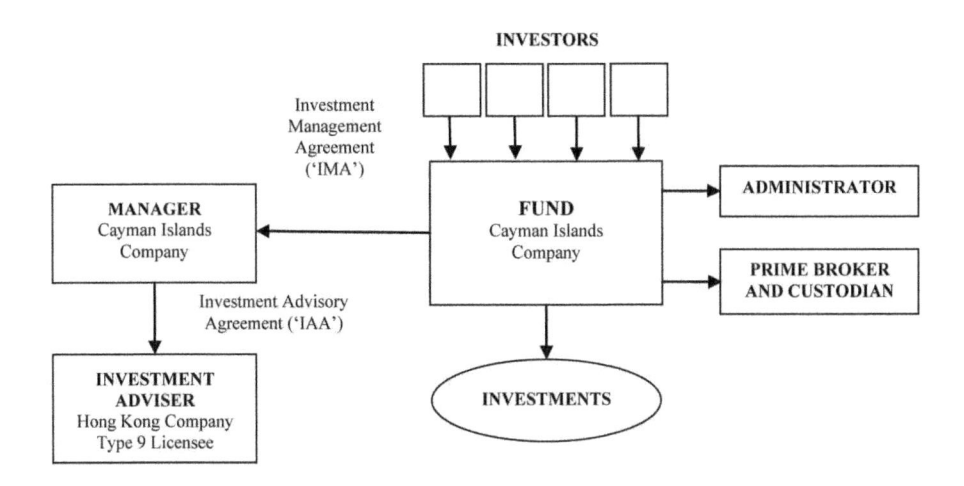

```
                              INVESTORS
                           ┌──┬──┬──┬──┐
                           │  │  │  │  │
         Investment        └┬─┴┬─┴┬─┴┬─┘
         Management         ▼  ▼  ▼  ▼
         Agreement
         ('IMA')                              ADMINISTRATOR
   ┌──────────────┐      ┌──────────────┐  ──►
   │   MANAGER    │ ◄────│    FUND      │
   │ Cayman Islands│     │ Cayman Islands│
   │   Company    │      │   Company    │     PRIME BROKER
   └──────┬───────┘      └──────┬───────┘  ──► AND CUSTODIAN
          │ Investment Advisory │
          │ Agreement ('IAA')   │
          ▼                     ▼
   ┌──────────────┐         INVESTMENTS
   │  INVESTMENT  │
   │   ADVISER    │
   │Hong Kong Company│
   │Type 9 Licensee │
   └──────────────┘
```

4.7 A stand-alone structure comprises a single vehicle with a single investment strategy. This type of fund most commonly uses an open-ended, limited liability company established in the Cayman Islands as its main vehicle.

4.8 Offshore fund structures often use a two-tiered management structure as set out in the diagram above. The management function of the board of directors of the fund company is delegated to a separate manager (often established as a Cayman Islands exempt limited liability company). From the manager, there is further delegation of investment and advisory functions down to an investment adviser, which would be a domestic entity (usually a Hong Kong private company incorporated with limited liability). The investment adviser employs the majority of the investment team, and is usually licensed to carry out 'regulated activities' in Hong Kong[1]. In terms of the economics of the fund, management and performance fees are paid to the manager. From this, a portion is allocated to the investment adviser (as an advisory fee) on a basis that equitably reflects the allocation of the fund's investment resources and the services provided by the respective entities.

[1] See paras 4.27–4.65 below.

4.9 There are three main drivers behind this management structure:

- *Taxation*: This structure is intended to achieve tax efficiency in relation to the economics of the fund structure; namely, the fund should not be liable to Hong Kong tax and, where it can be justified, the fees retained by the manager may not be taxed in Hong Kong.
- *Litigation risk management*: Removal of the management fee and performance fee from the fund vehicle into a distinct and separate entity (the investment manager) helps 'ring-fence' those amounts from trading/investment risks generated by the fund.

4.9 *Onshore Fund Domiciles*

- *Regulation*: The investment team is 'housed' at the investment adviser level, which is also the entity that is regulated by the SFC. This satisfies the requirements of the regulator and also provides reassurance to investors that there is regulatory oversight of the fund's activities.

Master-feeder funds

4.10 The following diagram illustrates a typical master-feeder fund structure:

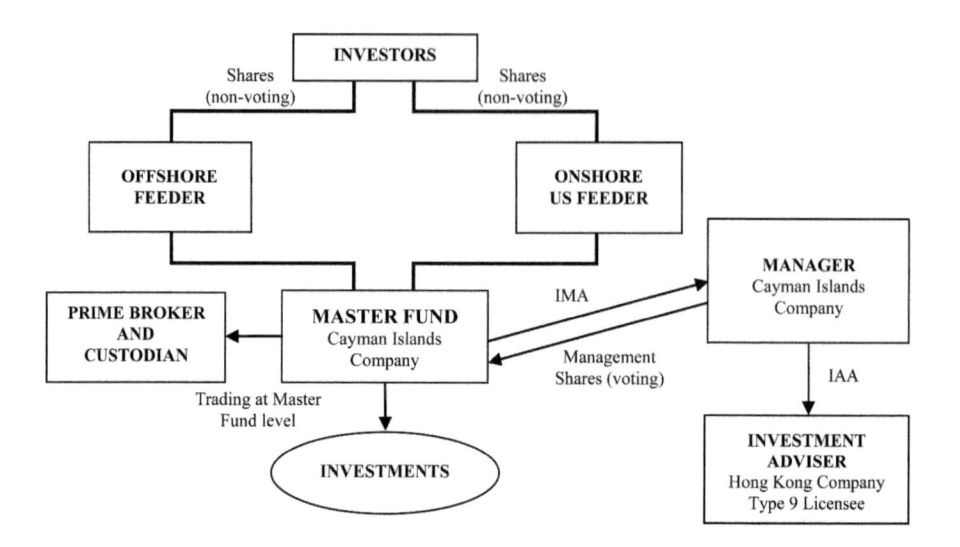

4.11 A master-feeder structure is one in which the assets from multiple funds (the 'feeder funds') catering for different investor groups are invested into a separate, central vehicle (the 'master fund'). Investors invest and pay management and performance fees at the feeder fund level, while trading and investment occurs at the master fund level. This is the preferred structure for most large scale institutional launches in Hong Kong. Often funds that are initially open only to non-US taxable investors are being launched in Hong Kong. These funds are structured as 'single-legged' master-feeder funds, that is, with only the offshore feeder and the master fund.

4.12 The onshore US feeder may be structured as a Cayman Islands open-ended investment company, limited partnership, or a Delaware limited partnership or limited liability company ('LLC'). In the past three to four years, however, the open-ended investment company (which then makes a 'check-the-box election' to be treated as a partnership for US tax purposes) has been the more popular choice for funds launched in Hong Kong. The main reason for this is the reduced time and cost involved in establishing the fund – documentation for the offshore fund can be more easily replicated for the onshore fund (with changes needed only for US tax, the Employee Retirement Income Security Act of 1974[1] ('ERISA') and securities law disclosure).

---

[1] Discussed in CHAPTER 11 – see paras **11.113–11.123**.

4.13 The principal benefits of a master-feeder structure are as follows:

- It allows the fund to comply with and benefit from the regulatory environment applicable to different target investors in the fund. In particular, it allows US taxable investors to invest in an offshore hedge fund in a tax efficient manner that does not compromise the tax position of other non-US or US tax-exempt investors.
- There is flexibility at the investor level since multiple feeder funds may be introduced to invest into a master fund, each of which may be tailored in accordance with different operating currencies, fees, subscription terms, liquidity and investment strategies.
- There is also flexibility at the investment level since different segregated pools may be created below the master fund (each structured as, for example, a wholly-owned subsidiary of the master fund) which may be used to trade different strategies, house its own pool of assets, and ensure there is segregation of liabilities.
- The pooling of assets means that the fund can benefit from greater economies of scale in relation to day-to-day management and administration of the fund and its portfolios, and therefore lower operational and transactional costs. Further reduction in costs is made possible by the use of a single investment vehicle which, for instance, eliminates the need to enter into duplicated agreements with counterparties. The increase in the critical mass of funds under management also allows the manager to more easily obtain and maintain credit lines and enhance the fund's ability to meet asset size-based investment qualifying tests.
- Segregation of US investors (sometimes regarded as more litigious) is preferred by non-US investors, as it lowers litigation risk that may involve non-US investors and also provides an additional layer of protection for the fund's assets (all of which are housed at the master fund level).

Umbrella funds

4.14 The following diagram illustrates a typical umbrella fund structure:

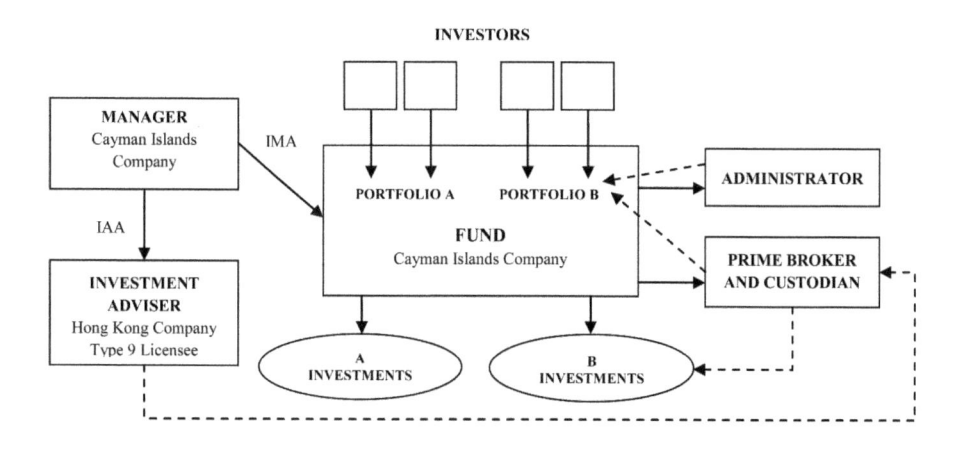

4.15 Onshore Fund Domiciles

4.15 An umbrella structure is a generic term for any overarching investment vehicle with sub-funds beneath it. Each sub-fund can have its own manager, pursue its own investment strategy and have its own pool of assets. Importantly, liabilities generated from the trading activities of each sub-fund are intended to be 'ring-fenced' to the assets only of that sub-fund.

4.16 A Cayman Islands segregated portfolio company ('SPC') is a popular choice for investment managers in Hong Kong looking to establish an umbrella structure. The ability to create multiple segregated portfolio sub-funds without needing to incorporate a new company every time is viewed as a distinct advantage in terms of time and costs. Cross-contamination of liabilities between different segregated portfolios is, of course, still an issue. For this reason, larger institutional hedge fund offerings tend to retain the 'master-feeder' structures, while the SPC structure is often seen for smaller, private long-only funds. It is possible to combine SPC structures with master-feeder structures – for example, each segregated sub-fund can be a feeder fund into a separate master fund.

Proposal for a Hong Kong open-ended fund company

4.17 Where investment funds are domiciled in Hong Kong, they are most usually established as unit trusts (because the capital maintenance rules and the restrictions on reduction of, and distributions out of, share capital under Hong Kong company law make it impractical to operate a Hong Kong company as an open-ended fund). In order to attract more funds to domicile in Hong Kong, on 15 January 2016, the Financial Services and the Treasury Bureau of Hong Kong (the 'FSTB') issued its consultation conclusions on the proposed regulatory framework for open-ended fund companies ('OFCs') as an additional form of investment fund vehicle to be established under the SFO[1]. On 10 June 2016, the Securities and Futures (Amendment) Ordinance 2016 (the '2016 Amendment Ordinance') was gazetted to introduce a new Part IVA into the SFO to provide the basic legal framework for the OFC regime in Hong Kong.

[1] Open-ended Fund Companies: Consultation Conclusions (January 2016) – see http://www.fstb.gov.hk/fsb/ppr/consult/doc/ofc_conclu_e.pdf.

4.18 To further provide for the regulatory landscape of the OFC regime, the SFC issued a consultation paper on 28 June 2017[1] to invite comments from the public regarding its proposals for the Securities and Futures (Open-ended Fund Companies) Rules (the 'OFC Rules') and the Code on Open-ended Fund Companies (the 'OFC Code'), which set out detailed legal and regulatory requirements for the new OFC vehicles based on the 2016 consultation conclusions. It is envisioned that the new OFC regime will be implemented in 2018 after the OFC Rules and the OFC Code become effective.

[1] Consultation Paper on the Securities and Futures (Open-ended Fund Companies) Rules and Code on Open-ended Fund Companies (June 2017) – see https://www.sfc.hk/edistribution Web/gateway/EN/consultation/doc?refNo=17CP5.

4.19 The OFC Rules are subsidiary legislation which will be made under the SFO. The proposed OFC Rules set out more detailed statutory requirements concerning: (i) company formation and maintenance; (ii) the key operators of the OFC (ie the directors, investment manager and custodian); (iii) the functions of the Hong Kong Companies Registry (the 'Companies Registry'); (iv) the segregated liability feature for umbrella and sub-funds structures and cross-investments of sub-funds of OFCs; (v) disqualification of directors; (vi) arrangements and compromises; (vii) winding-up; and (viii) offences. It is worthy to note that, with a view to ensuring that OFCs will only be operated as investment funds, the draft OFC Rules propose that any transaction entered into by an OFC which falls outside its operation as a collective investment scheme will be invalid.

4.20 The OFC Code will be issued by the SFC pursuant to its power to issue codes and guidelines under the SFO, and compliance with the OFC Code is expected to be a registration condition for the OFC. The proposed OFC Code is divided into two main sections. The first section sets out general principles as well as certain key structural and ongoing requirements applicable to all OFCs, including seven fundamental general principles which all OFCs and their key operators are expected to comply with. The second section sets out restrictions and requirements applicable only to private OFCs with respect to their investment scope, fund operations and disclosure. For example, the proposed OFC Code stipulates that at least 90% of the gross asset value of a private OFC must consist of (i) those asset types the management of which would constitute a Type 9 regulated activity, and/or (ii) cash, bank deposits, certificates of deposit, foreign currencies and foreign exchange contracts.

4.21 Under new Part IVA of the SFO, introduced by the 2016 Amendment Ordinance, an OFC will have a variable share capital and therefore the flexibility to meet shareholder redemption requests and to make distributions out of its share capital, subject only to solvency and disclosure requirements. New Part IVA also provides for a 'protected cell' regime, such that an OFC, like a Cayman Islands SPC, can be established as an umbrella fund with multiple sub-funds whose assets and liabilities are ring-fenced on a sub-fund by sub-fund basis.

4.22 An OFC will be established and incorporated under the SFO by obtaining a registration from the SFC and a certificate of incorporation from the Companies Registry. This is done via a one-stop process whereby the SFC will notify the Companies Registry of registration of the OFC, and the SFC's registration will take effect upon the issuance of a certificate of incorporation by the Companies Registry. The SFC is empowered to register an OFC and may impose any registration condition that it considers appropriate. The SFC may also refuse to register a proposed OFC and to cancel the registration of an OFC. In considering such registration, cancellation and/or imposition of conditions, the SFC will have regard to, amongst other things, compliance with the SFO, the OFC Rules, and relevant codes and guidelines issued by the SFC.

4.23 While private OFCs will not have to be licensed or authorised under the SFO, the SFC will exercise its supervisory function in relation to all OFCs through: (i) the SFC-licensed fund managers which will have to ensure compliance with the SFC's proposed OFC Code (in addition to compliance by the managers with the SFC's Code of Conduct for Persons Licensed or Registered with the Securities and Futures Commission and the Fund Manager Code of Conduct[1]); and (ii) their custodians, which will also have to

4.23 Onshore Fund Domiciles

comply with the proposed OFC Code. The SFC is also empowered under provisions introduced by the 2016 Amendment Ordinance to apply to Hong Kong courts to seek the appointment and removal of key operators of the OFC.

[1] See further paras 4.72–4.87 below.

4.24 The perceived advantages of an OFC are that, unlike a trust, it will have separate legal personality and its own board of directors, and hence will not require a trustee. This should lead to greater cost savings. As a company, an OFC may also be more marketable and easier to understand than unit trusts, which may not be common in jurisdictions throughout Asia. Additionally, the OFC may provide an attractive vehicle for the purpose of seeking mutual recognition in China under the proposed mutual fund recognition regime between Hong Kong and China. As an OFC would be clearly domiciled in Hong Kong, establishing tax residency in Hong Kong so as to take advantage of double tax agreements, including with China, may also be easier.

4.25 The Inland Revenue (Amendment) (No 4) Ordinance 2017 published by the Inland Revenue Department supplementing the OFC regime would appear to enhance Hong Kong's competitiveness in respect of the domiciliation of privately offered funds, as it extends the profits tax exemption in Hong Kong to private OFCs with their central management and control exercised in Hong Kong. Certain anti-tax avoidance measures are put in place, including the conditions that the OFC has to be non-closely held and that transactions must be carried through or arranged by an intermediary carrying a Type 9 licence.

4.26 Given possible cost advantages of OFCs over unit trusts, OFCs may become popular vehicles for both SFC-authorised, as well as certain non-authorised private funds. However, the role of the SFC and the limited permitted investments as well as regulation may make OFCs an unlikely choice for hedge funds.

Licensing

Regulated activities

4.27 Under the SFO, it is a criminal offence for any person to carry on a business in Hong Kong or hold himself out as carrying on a business in certain regulated activities, unless that person is licensed by or registered with the SFC. Financial institutions such as banks are primarily supervised by the Hong Kong Monetary Authority and will need to be registered with the SFC as 'registered institutions' if they also engage in securities or futures related activities. All other persons carrying on regulated activities should be licensed by the SFC as 'licensed corporations' or, in the case of individuals, be accredited to a licensed corporation to engage in the activity as 'licensed representatives'.

4.28 There are presently ten regulated activities set out in Schedule 5 of the SFO:

- Type 1 (dealing in securities);
- Type 2 (dealing in futures contracts);

Hong Kong 4.30

- Type 3 (leveraged foreign exchange trading);
- Type 4 (advising on securities);
- Type 5 (advising on futures contracts);
- Type 6 (advising on corporate finance);
- Type 7 (providing automated trading services);
- Type 8 (securities margin financing);
- Type 9 (asset management); and
- Type 10 (providing credit rating services).

4.29 For a hedge fund manager in Hong Kong, the three most relevant regulated activities are the following:

- *Type 1 (dealing in securities)*: This covers buying and selling of securities or inducing another party to enter into an agreement with a view to the buying or selling of securities. In this regard, the term 'securities' is defined in the widest possible sense under the SFO and includes, among other things and subject to exceptions, shares, stocks, bonds, debentures, interests in any collective investment scheme and interests 'commonly known as securities'.
- *Type 9 (asset management)*: This includes real estate investment scheme management or securities or futures contract management which, importantly, includes providing a service of managing a portfolio of securities for another person.
- *Type 4 (advising on securities)*: This covers giving advice or issuing analyses or reports on whether, which, the time at which, or the terms or conditions on which securities should be acquired or disposed of.

4.30 The definition of each of these regulated activities includes various, but limited, carve-outs. For example:

- A person licensed for Type 1 regulated activity does not need to be licensed for Type 9 regulated activity if he provides asset management service wholly incidental to the carrying on of Type 1 regulated activity; similarly, a Type 9 licensee does not need to be licensed for Type 1 regulated activity if he performs Type 1 regulated activity solely for the purpose of carrying on asset management activity. Accordingly, a Type 9 manager can place trades for a fund it manages and market a fund it manages without a Type 1 licence.
- A person does not need to be licensed for Type 1 regulated activity if he is acting as principal and dealing only with certain types of professional investors (for example, where the directors of a fund are marketing the fund).
- A Hong Kong based company does not need to be licensed for Type 9 or Type 4 regulated activity if it is providing such service solely to any of its wholly owned subsidiaries, 100% holding company, or other wholly owned subsidiaries of that parent company; however, the SFC considers, inter alia, that the exemption from a Type 9 licence can only be used if no third party funds are under management. Accordingly, if the Hong Kong company is an investment manager or sub-investment manager of a fund, this would not work.
- A person does not need to be licensed for Type 4 regulated activity if he is licensed for Type 1 regulated activity and is performing Type 4 regulated activity wholly incidentally to dealing in securities, or if he is

4.30 Onshore Fund Domiciles

licensed for Type 9 regulated activity and is providing advice to a fund for which he is managing the portfolio of securities solely for the purpose of providing the asset management service.

4.31 For these reasons all hedge fund managers managing funds in Hong Kong must hold a Type 9 licence and will usually not require a Type 1 licence. Whether or not a Type 4 licence is needed will depend on the nature of the hedge fund manager's activities in Hong Kong.

New OTC derivatives licensing regime

4.32 On 26 March 2014, the Legislative Council enacted the Securities and Futures (Amendment) Ordinance 2014 (the '2014 Amendment Ordinance'), which amends the SFO and provides a regulatory framework for the over-the-counter ('OTC') derivatives market in Hong Kong.

4.33 The 2014 Amendment Ordinance introduces two new regulated activities:

- Type 11 (dealing or advising in OTC derivative products); and
- Type 12 (providing clearing agency services for OTC derivative products).

4.34 It also expands two existing regulated activities:

- Type 9 (asset management) – to cover management of a portfolio of OTC derivative products; and
- Type 7 (providing automated trading services) – to cover the provision of automated trading services for OTC derivative products.

4.35 These provisions have not, to date, come into effect.

4.36 For fund managers in Hong Kong, the new Type 11 and expanded Type 9 regulated activities will be the most relevant. In particular, managers that intend to either deal or advise in relation to OTC derivatives and managers/funds that enter into an OTC derivatives transaction *other* than as a 'price taker' (ie primarily for the purpose of hedging) will have to obtain a Type 11 licence.

4.37 Managers that have, as part of the portfolio that they are managing, any OTC derivative, even purely as part of the fund's hedging strategy, will need to apply for an expanded Type 9 licence. In respect of both Type 9 and Type 11 regulated activities, there is a two-year Hong Kong experience (in relation to OTC derivatives) requirement.

Key licensing requirements

4.38 If none of the exemptions or carve-outs applies, a fund manager must apply to be licensed for the regulated activities which it engages in, and in doing so must satisfy the following criteria.

INCORPORATION

4.39 The fund manager seeking to be licensed must be either a Hong Kong incorporated company or a non-Hong Kong company registered with the Companies Registry under Part 16 of the Companies Ordinance (Cap 622). Sole proprietorship or partnership is not an acceptable form of business structure for licensing purposes. LLCs and LLPs which have legal and corporate personality may be licensed once registered under Part 16.

COMPETENCE

4.40 The fund manager must satisfy the SFC that it has a proper business structure, good internal control systems and qualified personnel status to ensure proper management of risks that it will encounter in carrying on its proposed business as detailed in its business plan. A business plan together with client documentation and a compliance manual must be submitted as part of the licence application.

FITNESS AND PROPERNESS

4.41 The SFC is obliged to refuse to grant a licence if the fund manager fails to satisfy the SFC that the fund manager itself, its substantial shareholders and officers, as well as any other person who is or is to be employed by or associated with the fund manager, are 'fit and proper' for the purpose of the regulated activity.

4.42 In determining whether a person is fit and proper, the SFC will take into account the following factors, in addition to any other matters that the SFC may consider relevant:

- financial status or insolvency;
- educational or other qualifications or experience having regard to the nature of the functions to be performed;
- ability to carry on the regulated activity concerned competently, honestly and fairly; and
- reputation, character, reliability and financial integrity.

RESPONSIBLE OFFICERS

4.43 Every fund manager must have at least two licensed representatives who are additionally approved by the SFC as responsible officers ('Responsible Officers') of the manager to supervise the conduct of each of the regulated activities it carries on. Applications for approval of the proposed Responsible Officers must be lodged with the SFC at the same time as the licence application.

4.44 For each regulated activity, at least one of the Responsible Officers must be an executive director which, in the licensing context, means a director of the licensed corporation who actively participates in, or is responsible for directly supervising, the business of a regulated activity for which the corporation is licensed. All of the fund manager's executive directors who are individuals must in any event seek the SFC's approval as Responsible Officers of the fund

4.45 Onshore Fund Domiciles

manager in relation to all the regulated activities it is licensed to carry on. Provided that there is no conflict of interest, a Responsible Officer may supervise more than one regulated activity.

4.45 The SFO further requires that, for each regulated activity, at least one of the Responsible Officers must be available at all times to supervise the business. This has been interpreted by the SFC as requiring at least one of the Responsible Officers to be based in Hong Kong, and at least one of them must be immediately contactable at all times by the SFC and by the fund manager's staff that are working from its Hong Kong office.

4.46 In order to qualify as a Responsible Officer, an individual must fulfil four competence requirements:

- management experience[1];
- industry experience[2];
- academic/industry qualification[3]; and
- regulatory knowledge[4].

[1] See para **4.47** below.
[2] See paras **4.48–4.49** below.
[3] See paras **4.50–4.53** below.
[4] See paras **4.54–4.57** below.

4.47 Management experience: The individual must have a minimum of two years' proven management skills and experience.

4.48 Industry experience: The individual must possess three years of relevant industry experience over the six years immediately prior to the date of application. Experience acquired by an individual from a broad range of activities and investment strategies, including asset management, proprietary trading, research, private equity, special situations, as well as experience in dealing with other alternative investments, will be considered as industry experience directly relevant to hedge fund management.

4.49 Where the individual has only acquired experience indirectly relevant to hedge fund management business (eg in sales, marketing or risk management of hedge funds), the SFC may exercise its discretion to accept him as a Responsible Officer but impose a licensing condition under which the individual must, when actively participating in or directly supervising the business for which the firm is licensed, do so under the advice of another Responsible Officer who possesses the required direct hedge fund management experience.

4.50 Academic/industry qualification: The individual must have obtained one of the recognised industry qualifications relevant to the regulated activities to be performed. For example, for Type 9 regulated activity, these are: (i) Papers 1 and 3 of the Hong Kong Securities Institute ('HKSI') Diploma Programme Examination ('DPE'); or (ii) Papers 7 and 12 of the HKSI Licensing Examination for Securities and Futures Intermediaries ('LE').

4.51 However, this requirement can alternatively be met by the following:

- a degree in accounting, business administration, economics, finance or law, or other degree but with passes in at least two courses in the aforesaid disciplines;

- internationally recognised professional qualifications in law, accounting or finance, such as Chartered Financial Analyst, Certified International Investment Analyst and Certified Financial Planner;
- passes in English or Chinese, and mathematics in the Hong Kong Certificate of Education Examination or equivalent high school public examinations and university entry examinations, plus an additional two years of relevant industry experience, which will be assessed by reference to any recognised industry qualifications, the role and functions to be performed and any experience that is closely related to such functions; or
- an additional five years of relevant industry experience (ie eight years in total).

4.52 Full and conditional exemptions from the academic/industry qualification requirement can be granted by the SFC. A full exemption is possible for individuals who are currently, or within the past three years have been, licensed representatives and would like to apply for: (i) a different type of regulated activity licence with the same competence requirements and in the same role; or (ii) a transfer of accreditation to another licensed corporation for the same regulated activities and in the same role.

4.53 An individual may be granted conditional exemption in exceptional circumstances if he is a current licensee with five years of related experience over the past eight years and is now applying to carry on a regulated activity with different competence requirements but in the same role. Where the exemption is granted, the SFC may impose restrictions on the scope of activities that may be undertaken, and the individual is required to complete an additional five hours of continuous professional training in industry/product knowledge in respect of the new regulated activity.

4.54 Regulatory knowledge: The individual must have passed one of the recognised local regulatory framework papers. For example, for a Type 9 licence, these are: (i) HKSI DPE Paper 2; (ii) Paper 1 of the HKSI Financial Market Principal Programme Examination; or (iii) HKSI LE Papers 1 and 6 (although Paper 1 is not required for an existing licensed representative applying to be a Responsible Officer). The SFC may grant an individual a six-month grace period in which to pass the relevant regulatory examinations; failure to obtain a pass within six months of obtaining approval may render the approval invalid unless a further extension of time is granted by the SFC in exceptional circumstances.

4.55 A full exemption from the regulatory knowledge examination requirement may be granted if the individual: (i) has been licensed with the SFC within the past three years for a regulated activity with the same competence requirements and in the same role as previously licensed; or (ii) has been actively involved in regulatory or compliance work in Hong Kong in the relevant industry for not less than three years over the past six years.

4.56 A conditional exemption from the regulatory knowledge examination requirement may be granted on such conditions as the SFC may consider necessary to impose, such as restricting the individual's activities within the same group of related companies or to non-retail clients, if the individual can demonstrate all of the following:

- *Substantial related experience:* The individual has proven substantial related experience, meaning he has at least: (i) eight years of related experience in recognised markets (eg in Hong Kong, the UK, the US or Japan); or (ii) six years of related experience with at least two years being licensed or acting as an executive officer or relevant individual of a registered institution (ie a bank) in Hong Kong, and in either case some part of the experience was gained in the past three years.
- *Restricted scope of permitted activities*: Either that the licensed corporation will only be carrying on a limited scope of business activities, or that the individual is only involved in a limited scope of activities for the licensed corporation (eg persons providing technical advice to clients on the structuring of corporate finance deals) or only assuming a very senior management level role (eg a Regional Head of Research coming to Hong Kong occasionally and accompanied by other local licensed staff in client meetings).
- *Regulatory support from other personnel*: There is designated by name to the SFC at least one approved Responsible Officer at the licensed corporation who is licensed for the relevant regulated activity and will be directly reporting to or otherwise responsible for advising the individual as well as supervising the daily operations of the regulated activity.
- *Internal control systems*: The licensed corporation has in place an appropriate risk and regulatory compliance infrastructure, including a comprehensive risk management system, internal audit, compliance staff and procedures.
- *Continuous professional training*: The individual has completed an extra five hours of continuous professional training within the six months preceding the application, or the licensed corporation undertakes to the SFC that the individual will complete the extra training hours within 12 months after the approval is granted.

4.57 A conditional exemption may also be granted to:

- an existing Responsible Officer applying to be approved for a regulated activity with different competence requirements where the individual: (i) has five years of related experience over the past eight years; and (ii) has completed or undertakes to complete an additional five extra hours of continuous professional training in regulatory knowledge in the relevant regulated activity; in such case, the SFC may impose restrictions on the scope of activities to be undertaken by that individual; or
- a licensed representative applying to be a Responsible Officer of the same regulated activity where the individual: (i) possesses at least three more years of relevant industry experience in addition to the other competence requirements set out above; and (ii) undertakes to complete an additional five extra hours of continuous professional training in regulatory knowledge in the relevant regulated activity.

TRANSFER OF ACCREDITATION

4.58 A fund manager may have, as its proposed Responsible Officer, a person who currently holds a licence to carry out the relevant regulated activity for another licensed corporation and who still works at that other licensed corporation while the new application is vetted. The SFC treats such an application in confidence. In such case, the individual should apply for a transfer of accreditation and pay the required application fee of HK$2,950 (for approval as a Responsible Officer) plus HK$200 (for transfer of accreditation) per regulated activity. The time limit for transfer of accreditation applications is 180 days after ceasing to act for a current principal.

MANAGER-IN-CHARGE REGIME

4.59 A 'manager-in-charge' (an 'MIC') is an individual appointed by the licensed corporation to be principally responsible, either alone or with others, for managing the relevant core function(s) of the licensed corporation. A licensed corporation is required to nominate an MIC for each of the following core functions:

- *Overall management oversight*: A function responsible for directing and overseeing the effective management of the overall operations of the licensed corporation on a day-to-day basis. This individual must also be a Responsible Officer.
- *Key business line*: A function responsible for directing and overseeing a line of business which comprises one or more types of regulated activities. This individual must also be a Responsible Officer.
- *Operational control and review*: A function responsible for: (i) establishing and maintaining adequate and effective systems of controls over the licensed corporation's operations; and (ii) reviewing the adherence to, and the adequacy and effectiveness of, the licensed corporation's internal control systems.
- *Risk management*: A function responsible for the identification, assessment, monitoring and reporting of risks arising from the licensed corporation's operations.
- *Finance and accounting*: A function responsible for ensuring the timely and accurate financial reporting and analyses of the operational results and financial positions of the licensed corporation.
- *Information technology*: A function responsible for the design, development, operation and maintenance of the computer systems of the licensed corporation.
- *Compliance*: A function responsible for: (i) setting the policies and procedures for adherence to legal and regulatory requirements in the jurisdiction(s) where the licensed corporation operates; (ii) monitoring the licensed corporation's compliance with the established policies and procedures; and (iii) reporting on compliance matters to senior management and the board of directors of the licensed corporation.
- *Anti-money laundering and counter-terrorist financing*: A function responsible for establishing and maintaining internal control procedures to safeguard the licensed corporation against involvement in money laundering activities or terrorist financing.

4.60 An individual may be an MIC for more than one core function. The purpose of the MIC regime is to have clearly identified individuals who can be held accountable for regulatory lapses in their area of responsibility.

4.61 *Onshore Fund Domiciles*

FINANCIAL RESOURCES

4.61 A licensed corporation must maintain at all times financial resources of no less than the specified levels of minimum paid-up share capital and liquid capital. The levels depend on the regulated activity for which the licensed corporation is licensed and are set out in the Securities and Futures (Financial Resources) Rules (Cap 571N) made under the SFO.

4.62 Generally, a fund manager seeking to be licensed for Type 1 (dealing in securities) regulated activity will be required to have a paid-up share capital of at least HK$5 million and a liquid capital of at least HK$3 million. The minimum paid-up share capital requirement will not apply to an applicant seeking to be licensed for Type 4 (advising on securities) or Type 9 (asset management) regulated activity if it is subject to the condition that it shall not hold client assets, but it must still maintain a liquid capital of at least HK$100,000. A licensed fund manager must notify the SFC within one business day when it becomes aware that its liquid capital has fallen below 120% of its required liquid capital.

Application forms

4.63 In general, three main applications need to be submitted: one for the licensed corporation, one for each individual seeking to be licensed as a licensed representative, and one for each individual seeking approval as a Responsible Officer. Application forms can be downloaded from the SFC's website[1].

[1] See http://www.sfc.hk.

Application processing time

4.64 For applications lodged by a new fund manager to become a licensed corporation, the SFC's estimated processing time is approximately 15 weeks once the relevant papers have been received in good order. However, this period refers only to the time taken by the SFC to process the application on its part; it does not include the time lapse between the issue of the SFC's requisitions and the applicant's responses. In addition, the SFC may reject an application and request additional information and clarifications. Accordingly, assuming there will be no significant issues, a more realistic time estimate would be 20 weeks from acceptance by the SFC of the application, although in some cases applications can be processed in less time.

4.65 Fund managers typically find that it will take up to four weeks to complete the application forms and provide the necessary information to lodge an application with the SFC. It would therefore be prudent to assume that the process from start to finish may take approximately 24 weeks. Variables which affect timing include: (i) Responsible Officers who are not eligible due to, for example, lack of obvious relevant industry experience; (ii) response time of overseas regulators; (iii) complex holding structures; and (iv) any record of regulatory breaches by group companies or proposed Responsible Officers. In addition, applications relating to certain regulated activities, such as Type 1 (dealing in securities), are subject to greater scrutiny by the SFC than for other regulated activities, such as Type 4 (advising on securities).

Ongoing obligations for licensed fund managers

Remaining fit and proper

4.66 Having successfully become licensed for the relevant regulated activities and therefore a licensed corporation, the fund manager and the licensed representatives accredited to it must remain fit and proper at all times. In particular, they must comply with all applicable provisions of the SFO and its subsidiary legislation, as well as the codes and guidelines issued by the SFC. Failure to comply with the applicable codes may be taken into account in considering whether the fund manager or the relevant representative is fit and proper to remain licensed.

Submission of audited accounts etc and annual fee

4.67 As a licensed corporation, the fund manager is also required to submit to the SFC the following documents and fees on a periodic basis:

Document	Time limit	Comment
Audited accounts	Within four months after the end of each financial year	Audited accounts and other required documents, made up to the date of cessation, should be submitted not later than four months after the date on which the corporation ceases to carry on all of the regulated activities for which it is licensed
Financial resources return	Within three weeks after the end of each month, except for corporations which are licensed for only Type 4, Type 5, Type 6, Type 9 and/or Type 10 regulated activities and are subject to the condition that they shall not hold client assets, in which case, within three weeks after the end of June and December each year	N/A
Business and risk management questionnaire	Within four months after the end of each financial year	N/A
Annual return	Within one month after each anniversary date of the licence	Failure to submit on time could result in suspension and revocation of the licence
Payment of annual fee	Within one month after each anniversary date of the licence	Monthly surcharges apply to outstanding amounts. Failure to pay on time could also result in suspension and revocation of the licence

4.68 Onshore Fund Domiciles

Notification of certain events and changes

4.68 All licensed corporations and licensed representatives are required to notify the SFC of certain events and changes within the specified time limit. Some of the more common changes and events that require notification are set out in the table below:

Types of change/events	Time limit on notification
Cessation of business	At least seven business days in advance for intended cessation of business
Ceasing to act as a licensed representative	Within seven business days
Ceasing to act as a Responsible Officer	Within seven business days
Change in name	Within seven business days
Change in business address	At least seven business days in advance for intended change in business address
Change in director or his particulars	Within seven business days
Change in complaints officer or his particulars	Within seven business days
Change in share capital or shareholding structure	Within seven business days
Change in contact information	Within seven business days
Change in bank accounts	Within seven business days
Change in associated entity or its particulars	Within seven business days
Change in auditor's name	Within seven business days
Giving notice of a motion to remove or change an auditor to be moved in general meeting, or cessation of an auditor before expiration of its term of office	Within one business day
Change in executive officer or his particulars	Within seven business days

4.69 In addition, licensed corporations and licensed representatives are required to seek prior approval of the SFC if they intend to make certain changes. Some of the more common changes that require such approval include:

- addition of regulated activity;
- reduction of regulated activity;
- modification or waiver of licensing or registration condition;
- change of financial year end;
- adoption of a period exceeding 12 months as financial year;
- extension of deadline for submission of audited accounts;
- new premises to be used for keeping records or documents;
- any person becoming a substantial shareholder of a licensed corporation;
- transfer or addition of accreditation; and
- any licensed representative becoming a Responsible Officer.

Continuous professional training

4.70 Fund managers, as licensed corporations, are held primarily responsible for designing and implementing continuous professional training ('CPT') programmes that are best suited to the training needs of the licensed representatives they engage. Such programmes should be able to enhance the individuals' industry knowledge, skills and professionalism. Sufficient records on the CPT programmes and activities undertaken by the individuals should be kept for a minimum of three years and be made available for inspection upon request by the SFC.

4.71 Licensed representatives are generally required to complete five CPT hours per calendar year for each regulated activity which they may carry out. They should also retain their own CPT compliance records for a minimum of three years.

Forthcoming regulatory change

Fund Manager Code of Conduct

4.72 Since 2003 with the introduction of the single licence under the SFO, there have been few direct changes to the oversight and supervision of fund managers in Hong Kong, in particular those whose focus is on the non-retail market, ie whose funds were sold to or invested by professional investors or offered on a non-retail basis (eg hedge funds). Indeed, there was a degree of satisfaction in Hong Kong that in the aftermath of 2008, Hong Kong's regime received no significant revision. This contrasted well with Singapore's overhaul of its 'exempt fund manager' regime and the new licensing regime under 'Dodd-Frank'[1] in the US as well as the Alternative Investment Fund Managers Directive[2] ('AIFMD') in the EU.

[1] Dodd-Frank Wall Street Reform and Consumer Protection Act of 2010.
[2] Directive 2011/61/EU of 8 June 2011.

4.73 Once a fund manager is licensed in Hong Kong under the SFO, it is subject to various SFC guidelines and circulars, compliance with which goes to the fund manager's fitness and properness. However, the key rules governing a fund manager's conduct are set out in the Fund Manager Code of Conduct (the 'FMCC'). The FMCC, like the Code of Conduct for Persons Licensed or Registered with the Securities and Futures Commission (the 'Code of Conduct'), is regulation not statute and to date has confined itself to the fund manager's obligations to clients and general guidance as to the SFC's expectations with regard to a fund manager licensed and operating in Hong Kong. Product specific requirements for retail funds are set out in the SFC's Code on Unit Trusts and Mutual Funds[1]. There are presently no structural or prescribed disclosure requirements on offshore funds arising from the fact that the fund manager is licensed under the SFO. In addition, unlike AIFMD in the EU and the registration regime in Singapore, Hong Kong has no filing, notification or registration requirements to offer interests in an offshore fund on a non-public basis[2].

[1] See http://www.sfc.hk/web/EN/rules-and-standards/codes-and-guidelines/codes for each of the Codes.

4.73 *Onshore Fund Domiciles*

[2] As mentioned in CHAPTER 13 – see para **13.182**.

4.74 The SFC has proposed (effective 17 November 2018) significant revisions to the FMCC, which herald material change to the existing regime. These will significantly affect fund managers, in particular fund managers of private funds. The driving force behind the changes to the FMCC – which will affect all Type 9 (asset management) licensed fund managers in Hong Kong – is not Hong Kong specific needs or identified risks. Rather it is the perceived need for Hong Kong to comply with broader international initiatives such as those of the International Organisation of Securities Commissions (the 'IOSCO'). The FMCC revisions relate specifically to: (i) securities lending and repurchase agreements ('repos'); (ii) custody; (iii) liquidity risk management; and (iv) disclosure of leverage. In addition, the scope of the FMCC is to be widened to apply to discretionary accounts.

4.75 A key aspect of the impending changes is that fund managers will have explicit responsibility under the FMCC for the funds they manage. In effect the new FMCC will stipulate minimum requirements for offshore and onshore private funds where the fund manager has (in the SFC's view) responsibility for the overall operation of the relevant fund. This will affect hedge funds managed and operated from Hong Kong.

Responsibility for funds

4.76 The FMCC has always governed Type 9 (asset management) licensed fund managers in respect of their management of funds. Paragraph 1.4 of the Code of Conduct, by contrast, presently states that to the extent a licensed person is managing a fund, the FMCC, not the Code, applies to that activity. The new FMCC will now make it clear that the Code applies as well as the FMCC and in the event of uncertainty the higher requirement will be applicable.

4.77 The present drafting in the FMCC is not concise and simply refers to 'client', where appropriate. The revised FMCC clarifies that the fund is a fund manager's client, not the fund investors – although in places the fund manager will have duties to fund investors under the new FMCC.

4.78 However, the revisions to the FMCC will broaden its scope so that it imposes duties on Hong Kong fund managers for funds where they have responsibility for the overall operation. The SFC considers this to be in line with relevant IOSCO principles. Certain duties will therefore be attached to the fund manager where it has, in substance, responsibility for the fund's operation, notwithstanding that legally the fund manager may not have formal responsibility. Whilst this is in effect the approach long adopted by the SFC with regard to managers of SFC-authorised funds, this is a departure for private funds which historically have had no such oversight. Regardless of, say, a corporate fund's board of directors, trustee or other legal structure, the revised FMCC provides that the fund manager will in effect be responsible for setting liquidity management policy and the selection of the custodian of any fund it operates. Similarly, for example, the new FMCC will require a fund manager to ensure fair treatment of fund investors when managing conflicts of interest despite fund investors not being the fund manager's client. A fund manager's decision to terminate a fund will be required to take into account the best interests of investors in the fund. The fund manager must also provide fund investors with information about itself. However, under the new FMCC the SFC has revised its previous suggestion that where a fund manager's and/or its affiliates' appointed representatives constitute a majority of the board of a fund, the fund would be controlled by the fund manager for this purpose.

4.79 Where a fund manager is appointed as a sub-investment manager, by contrast, the client of the fund manager would be the delegating primary manager. In that case, these additional requirements will not generally be imposed.

4.80 Specifically with regard to private funds (being funds, open-ended or closed-ended, which are not authorised by the SFC pursuant to the SFO), the SFC acknowledged that its 'proposed enhancements' may be perceived as more relevant to fund level regulation (and therefore not be subject to SFC regulation at all), but noted that IOSCO and other international regulations applicable to funds do not distinguish in their application as between private and public funds. The SFC emphasises that the FMCC changes are intended to be more principles-based, and proposes to issue FAQs from time to time to illustrate when it considers fund managers to be 'responsible for the overall operation of a fund'.

Securities lending and repos

4.81 The new FMCC will, in all material respects, adopt certain recommendations of the Financial Stability Board (the 'FSB') to address what the FSB refers to as shadow banking risks in respect of securities lending and repos transactions by funds. As stated in the new FMCC[1], the requirements are applicable to fund managers that engage in this activity for funds that they manage. Where a fund manager is involved in agreeing a securities lending mandate or in lending activities for a fund, the fund manager is considered to be engaging in such transactions and must comply with the requirements. It is important to note that the following provisions are not limited to fund managers in respect of funds for which the fund managers are responsible for the overall operation.

- *Collateral valuation and management policy*: Fund managers will be required to put such a policy in place to include certain minimum valuation and margin requirements. The key focus of the new requirements is to govern how fund managers manage collateral received.
- *Eligible collateral and haircut policy*: Fund managers will be required to also adopt a policy regarding the types of acceptable collateral and the methodology used to calculate 'haircuts' with due consideration to the specific nature of the fund it manages. The SFC will issue FAQs on the standards it will expect for designing the methodologies in this regard. From the SFC's perspective FAQs are a useful way of promulgating rules without requiring any public consultation process. It is hoped that the FAQs will not be as prescriptive as those for SFC-authorised funds.

4.81 Onshore Fund Domiciles

- *Reinvestment of cash collateral*: Fund managers will be required to also have in place a cash collateral reinvestment policy to ensure sufficient liquidity with transparent pricing and low risk to meet potential recalls. In addition, the SFC restates that for SFC-authorised funds, non-cash collateral should not generally be re-hypothecated.
- *Reporting to fund investors*: With regard to each of the foregoing, the fund manager must ensure that a summary of those policies are disclosed to fund investors of those funds for which it has responsibility for the overall operation at least annually and upon request. The SFC has clarified that such a summary need not be in the private placement memoranda of the fund. Where a third party agent conducts securities lending and repo activities on behalf of a fund, the SFC expects a fund manager to obtain access to such information (via a fund's board or a unit trust's trustee by agreement). The SFC appears to expect all fund documentation to be revisited for such contractual permissions as may be necessary to be given.

[1] See the introductory paragraph of the 'Securities Lending' section of the new FMCC, available at http://www.sfc.hk/web/EN/rules-and-standards/codes-and-guidelines/codes.

Custody

4.82 Regardless of the legal structure of the relevant fund, the SFC will expressly require that in cases where a fund manager is responsible for the operation of a fund, it must select and arrange for the appointment of a functionally independent custodian. Regardless of necessity, a private fund managed from Hong Kong must appoint a custodian unless the fund or fund manager adopts a 'self-custody' arrangement. In a self-custody arrangement (the meaning of which remains unclear), the SFC will require the fund manager to have policies and internal controls to ensure that the persons managing custody are functionally independent from those managing the fund investments. Although the requirement for an independent custodian or trustee to perform safe-keeping of fund assets is already applied to retail funds in Hong Kong, such functional independence is a new requirement for private funds which may prove difficult in practice and expensive for many smaller private equity funds in Hong Kong. However, the SFC makes clear that a custodian can be within the same group as the fund manager yet also be functionally independent.

4.83 The FMCC will be amended to explicitly require a fund manager to exercise due skill, care and diligence in the selection and ongoing monitoring of the relevant fund's custodian. The fund manager will also have to ensure a formal written custody agreement (which as regards unit trusts is the trust deed) is entered into and ensure its contents are sufficient. This new FMCC duty, despite industry protests, cuts across the usual responsibilities of directors and trustees in most fund structures.

4.84 The SFC will also require that fund managers ensure proper disclosure of custody arrangements and material risks associated with those (including any changes) to fund investors.

Liquidity risk

4.85 The new FMCC will impose certain liquidity related requirements to fund managers of private funds. The key proposals are as follows:

- *Liquidity management policy*: All fund managers will be required to maintain such policies and monitor the liquidity risk of the relevant fund or funds with reference to its obligations and redemption policy (if any). Regardless of whether or not a fund is closed-ended or open-ended, the new FMCC will require a fund manager in Hong Kong to have a compliant policy regarding liquidity.
- *Stress testing*: This will be required to be undertaken by the fund manager to assess and monitor liquidity risk. Although the extent and frequency of such testing may vary depending on the nature of the relevant fund, the new FMCC requires that such testing will be ongoing. The SFC says that, in adopting a proportionate approach, the extent and frequency of the testing may vary, depending on the nature and liquidity profile of each fund.
- *Tools*: Where fund documentation provides 'tools', such as redemption deferral or suspension, to assist with liquidity management, the new FMCC imposes on the fund manager a positive duty to consider the appropriateness of using such tools at all times.
- *Side letters*: In a footnote, the revised FMCC states that where side letters have been entered into, a fund manager should disclose this fact and the material terms in relation to redemption in the side letters to all potential and existing fund investors.

Leverage

4.86 In line with greater scrutiny of the use of leverage in the US and in the EU under AIFMD, the SFC says that when a fund manager is responsible for the operation of a fund, the fund manager should disclose the expected maximum level of leverage it may employ for the relevant fund to the fund's investors. Disclosure must be fair and not materially misleading. At this stage, the SFC acknowledges that there is no general consensus on how leverage is calculated. Accordingly, the SFC is not proposing to prescribe any method although it expects the basis of calculation to be disclosed and to take into account synthetic leverage from the use of derivatives. However, the SFC says it will keep this issue under review and it is possible that FAQs will be issued in future.

Other changes

4.87 In addition to the key changes outlined above, the SFC is also proposing other updates to the FMCC which are intended to codify what it expects already and to clarify the drafting. These include the following:

4.87 *Onshore Fund Domiciles*

- *Fund valuation*: The SFC proposes to require independent valuation of a fund's portfolio, separate from a fund's investment function. Valuation methodologies must be consistently applied to the valuation of similar types of fund assets. 'Independence' for this purpose does not mean that a third party value need be outside a fund manager's group.
- *Auditors*: Where a fund manager is responsible for the overall operation of a fund, it must ensure the appointment of an independent auditor (even if this is not required by the fund's jurisdiction of domicile).
- *Side pockets*: The new FMCC requires that a fund manager responsible for the overall operation of a fund discloses to fund investors the structure and operation of side pockets (including fees) before side pockets are created. In addition to generic disclosure, say in a private placement memorandum, additional notifications are required to fund investors when illiquid assets are side pocketed.
- *Reporting to the SFC*: A more express requirement is included in the new FMCC under which all fund managers must provide appropriate information to the SFC on an ongoing basis upon request, for example with regard to leverage or securities lending and repo or OTC transactions on behalf of funds. Fund managers, the new FMCC states, must respond promptly and in an open and co-operative manner. Any mistake in data provided must also be notified to the SFC promptly. All information provided by a fund manager (and on its behalf) to the SFC must in all material respects be 'complete and not misleading'.
- *House accounts*: The SFC will not include this requirement in the new FMCC but states that 'institutional professional investors' (as defined in the Code of Conduct) may request a different allocation priority than taking priority over house orders with regard to partially filled orders.

B   IRELAND

Iain Ferguson, Partner, Investment Management Group, McCann FitzGerald

Introduction

4.88 Ireland is an EU member state and is part of the Eurozone. Funds established in Ireland as undertakings for collective investment in transferable securities ('UCITS') or alternative investment funds ('AIFs') benefit from an EU-wide passporting regime.

4.89 Ireland has an excellent reputation as a location for robust and efficient regulation which facilitates market and product developments whilst protecting the interests of investors. Both the Central Bank of Ireland (the 'Central Bank') and the Irish Stock Exchange have a proven track record in adapting and developing their regulation to keep pace with industry developments. The Central Bank authorised the first AIFM in Europe, following Ireland's early implementation of the Alternative Investment Fund Managers Directive[1] ('AIFMD').

[1]   Directive 2011/61/EU of 8 June 2011.

4.90 Ireland is an internationally recognised, open and tax efficient jurisdiction with a 12.5% corporate tax rate and tax exempt status for funds and investors. It has one of the most developed and favourable tax treaty networks in the world, including double taxation treaties with 72 countries. In 2017, Ireland was one of only three jurisdictions awarded the highest international rating on tax transparency from the Organisation for Economic Co-operation and Development (the 'OECD').

The investment funds industry

4.91 Since its establishment in the late 1980s, Ireland's international financial services sector has grown spectacularly, attracting significant levels of foreign investment. Overall, the funds industry has in excess of €4.1 trillion assets under administration with €2 trillion of this amount in Irish domiciled funds. 18 of the top 20 global asset managers have Irish domiciled funds. According to recent figures released by the Irish Funds Industry Association ('Irish Funds')[1], the local industry body, there are over 887 fund promoters represented in the Irish funds industry and over 14,000 professionals are employed exclusively in the servicing of investment funds, offering deep expertise in services including fund administration, transfer agency, custody, legal, tax and audit services, stock exchange listing, compliance and consultancy services.

[1] Why Ireland: Excellence, Innovation, Reach (March 2017) – see https://files.irishfunds.ie/1489525513-IF_WhyIreland_Brochure_euro_03-2017.pdf.

4.92 Ireland is one of the leading regulated domiciles for internationally distributed investment funds. Irish funds are sold in over 70 countries across Europe, the Americas, Asia and the Pacific, the Middle East and Africa. Ireland is Europe's top hedge fund domicile and is the largest hedge fund administration centre in the world, servicing over 40% of global hedge fund assets. It is also a centre of excellence for UCITS and the fastest growing major domicile for UCITS in the world. Ireland is the leading European jurisdiction for both exchange-traded funds and money market funds.

Regulatory framework for investment funds

4.93 In Ireland, a collective investment scheme is usually established as either a UCITS or an AIF, each of which has its origins in EU legislation. Both UCITS and AIFs are regulated by the Central Bank, which is the regulatory authority responsible for the authorisation and supervision of all collective investment schemes established in Ireland.

4.94 Regulated funds and fund service providers must also comply with the Central Bank's fitness and probity requirements for persons performing certain functions within those entities.

Undertakings for collective investment in transferable securities

4.95 UCITS are open-ended investment funds that have the sole object of collective investment in transferable securities or in other liquid financial assets. A UCITS can invest in a diverse range of investments, including

4.95 *Onshore Fund Domiciles*

transferable securities, units in collective investment schemes, approved money market instruments, derivatives and forward transactions and deposits.

4.96 Once a UCITS is authorised in a European Economic Area ('EEA') member state, such as Ireland, it can be freely marketed on a retail basis throughout the EEA (subject to a simple registration process) without needing to comply with local securities laws in each member state. UCITS can also be sold globally (particularly throughout Asia) and can be restricted to institutional investors if the promoter wishes. The marketing passport is one of the key advantages of UCITS.

4.97 A UCITS must operate on the principle of risk-spreading and is subject to investment and borrowing restrictions as well as requirements regarding dealing frequency. These include the following:

- *Investment restrictions*: Amongst other things, a UCITS may invest no more than 10% of its net assets in unlisted transferable securities and money market instruments. A UCITS is also prohibited from investing more than a certain percentage of its assets in various securities issued by certain issuers, collective investment schemes and deposits with a particular credit institution. The risk exposure of a UCITS to a counterparty to an over-the-counter ('OTC') derivative may not exceed 5% of its net assets (which can be raised to 10% in certain circumstances).
- *Borrowing restrictions*: In general, a UCITS may not borrow money, grant loans or act as a guarantor for third parties. However, a UCITS may borrow up to 10% of its net asset value on a temporary basis, for example, to fund redemption requests.
- *Dealing frequency*: A UCITS must be open for redemption at least twice a month, at regular intervals.

4.98 At EU level, UCITS are regulated by the UCITS Directive[1], as well as by a number of delegated and implementing regulations and directives which set out the relevant requirements in more detail. The European Securities and Markets Authority ('ESMA') and its predecessor, the Committee of European Securities Regulators ('CESR') have also issued further guidance about UCITS.

[1] Directive 2009/65/EC of 13 July 2009, as most recently amended by Directive 2014/91/EU of 23 July 2014.

4.99 The UCITS Directive was transposed into Irish law by the European Communities (Undertakings for Collective Investment in Transferable Securities) Regulations 2011, as amended[1] (the 'UCITS Regulations').

[1] SI 2011/352.

4.100 UCITS, UCITS management companies and UCITS depositaries are also subject to the Central Bank (Supervision and Enforcement) Act 2013 (Section 48(1)) (Undertakings for Collective Investment in Transferable Securities) Regulations 2015[1], as amended (the 'Central Bank UCITS Regulations'). In addition to setting out the requirements for the authorisation of investment funds, the Central Bank UCITS Regulations cover issues such as the content of prospectuses and disclosure requirements, the administrative activities which must be carried out in Ireland, the duties of fund administrators and depositaries and the continuing reporting obligations of authorised funds.

[1] SI 2015/420.

4.101 The Central Bank has also published guidance on a number of topics to assist users of the UCITS Regulations, as well as UCITS Q&As which set out answers to queries which are likely to arise in relation to UCITS. In general, Ireland's domestic law on UCITS reflects the corresponding EU legislation, without any significant additional national requirements or 'gold-plating'.

4.102 UCITS benefit from an EEA-wide 'passport', which means that once a UCITS is authorised in an EEA member state (comprising 28 EU member states together with Iceland, Liechtenstein and Norway), it can be marketed in any other EEA member state without the need for any additional authorisation, subject to a notification procedure.

4.103 It is also straightforward to register a UCITS for public distribution in other non-EU jurisdictions. Irish funds are registered for sale in, for example, Switzerland, Singapore, Hong Kong, Macau, Taiwan, Chile, Peru, South Africa and Bahrain.

Alternative investment fund

4.104 An AIF can be established in Ireland as either a qualifying investor alternative investment fund ('QIAIF') or a retail investor alternative investment fund ('RIAIF'), depending on whether the relevant AIF is targeted at retail or institutional investors. Whilst both types of AIFs have a wider choice of eligible assets and are subject to fewer investment restrictions than a UCITS, the requirements applicable to RIAIFs are more restrictive than those applicable to QIAIFs.

RIAIFs

4.105 A RIAIF is an AIF which is authorised by the Central Bank and which may be marketed to retail investors. A RIAIF has no regulatory minimum subscription. The Central Bank has set out, in its AIF Rulebook, general investment and borrowing restrictions which are applicable to RIAIFs.

4.106 Under Central Bank rules, a RIAIF may only have a fully authorised AIFM. Consequently, non-EU managers which do not have a fully authorised EU-based AIFM and sub-threshold AIFMs cannot manage a RIAIF.

QIAIFs

4.107 At the name suggests, a QIAIF is a regulated AIF which is targeted at sophisticated and institutional investors. The minimum subscription must be at least €100,000 or its equivalent in another currency.

4.108 The QIAIF has a number of advantages over other fund structures, not least the fact that it is able to take advantage of a 24-hour 'fast track' approval

4.108 *Onshore Fund Domiciles*

process with the Central Bank. It is also able to take advantage of an EU-wide marketing passport if it is managed by an EU-based AIFM. Other advantages include the fact that a QIAIF:

- is not subject to Central Bank investment restrictions or to any borrowing or leverage limits;
- is not subject to risk diversification requirements, save that, in the case of investment companies, a QIAIF must observe the general principle of risk spreading (an 'Irish Collective Asset-management Vehicle' or 'ICAV'[1] is not subject to this requirement); and
- is subject to a favourable tax regime which ensures that Irish QIAIFs are not subject to Irish tax on their income or gains or dividends paid to non-Irish investors.

[1] See paras **4.121–4.125** below.

4.109 Once authorised, a QIAIF could seek to:

- carry on short selling without restriction;
- enter into borrowing arrangements without restriction;
- enter into derivative contracts (including the buying and selling of futures and options), repurchase, reverse repurchase and stock-lending arrangements in order to pursue hedge fund strategies.

4.110 A QIAIF can also be established for the purpose of engaging in loan origination, and a loan originating QIAIF is able to invest in a broad range of fixed income and credit securities as part of its overall investment strategy as well as the activities of direct lensing and acquiring loans on the secondary market. Ireland was one of the first member states to introduce a bespoke framework for loan originating investment funds.

4.111 As mentioned, once authorised, an Irish QIAIF which is managed by an EU-based AIFM can avail itself of an EU-wide marketing passport and can be distributed to professional investors across the EU. As the RIAIF is a retail fund product, it cannot avail itself of the automatic right to market throughout the EU under the AIFMD market passport as this is only available for professional investors. Access to individual markets may, however, be granted on a case-by-case basis.

4.112 At EU level, both these types of AIF are indirectly regulated by AIFMD, which provides a harmonised regulatory framework across the EU for AIFMs operating in the EU. Key issues covered in AIFMD include authorisation, capital requirements, conduct of business standards, remuneration, the valuation of assets, delegation, depositaries, transparency, and marketing.

4.113 The European Commission has set out the AIFMD requirements in more detail by way of delegated and implementing acts. In addition, ESMA has issued guidance and Q&As providing further information on what is required in order to comply with AIFMD.

4.114 AIFMD was implemented into Irish law by the European Union (Alternative Investment Fund Managers) Regulations 2013[1] (the 'AIFM Regulations'). The Central Bank has also published an AIF Rulebook which contains its requirements applicable to RIAIFs, QIAIFs, fund administrators,

AIFMs and AIF depositaries.

[1] SI 2013/257.

4.115 In addition, the Central Bank has published guidance on a number of topics to assist users of the AIF Rulebook, as well as AIFMD Q&As which set out the answers to queries which are likely to arise in relation to the implementation of AIFMD. As is the case with UCITS, in general, Ireland's domestic law on AIFMs reflects that applicable at EU level without any significant gold-plating.

Fitness and probity

4.116 Persons performing certain prescribed controlled functions or pre-approval controlled functions for a regulated fund or a fund service provider must comply with the Central Bank's fitness and probity requirements, which focus on competence, capability, honesty, integrity and financial prudence.

4.117 These requirements are set out in the Central Bank Reform Act (Sections 20 and 22) Regulations 2011[1] (as amended) and in the Central Bank's Fitness and Probity Standards[2].

[1] SI 2011/437.
[2] See https://www.centralbank.ie/regulation/how-we-regulate/authorisation/fitness-probity.

Corporate Governance Code

4.118 The Irish Funds' Corporate Governance Code applies to Irish regulated funds and their managers. It aims to provide a framework for the organisation and operation of investment funds to ensure that funds operate efficiently and in the interests of shareholders. The Irish Funds has also published a corporate governance code for fund service providers[1].

[1] See https://www.irishfunds.ie/regulatory-technical/corporate-governance for the Codes.

Investment fund vehicles

4.119 The recently established Irish Collective Asset-management Vehicle ('ICAV') has become the vehicle of choice for funds established in Ireland. Other types of fund vehicles are the investment company, the unit trust, the common contractual fund and the investment limited partnership.

4.120 Various factors affect the choice of fund vehicle, including potential distribution channels and the location and preferences of prospective investors.

The Irish Collective Asset-management Vehicle

4.121 One of the primary advantages of the ICAV is that it has its own legislative regime. Consequently, unlike the traditional investment company, the ICAV is not subject to those aspects of company law which are irrelevant to, or inappropriate for, a collective investment scheme (thereby helping to

4.121 Onshore Fund Domiciles

reduce administrative burden and costs). Nor is it subject to the risk-spreading and diversification requirements which are currently applicable to investment companies.

4.122 In addition, an ICAV is entitled to elect (ie 'check the box') to be treated as a flow-through entity or partnership for US tax purposes.

4.123 An ICAV is a suitable fund vehicle for both UCITS and AIFs and can be used for self-managed or externally managed, open-ended or closed-ended collective investment schemes. An existing Irish investment company or certain foreign corporate funds can convert/redomicile to an ICAV by way of continuation. This means that the ICAV retains its corporate identity and the track record and performance data following conversion.

4.124 Establishing an ICAV involves a two-step process. The ICAV must first be registered with the Central Bank and then authorised either as a UCITS pursuant to the UCITS Regulations or as an AIF pursuant to the AIFMD Regulations. ICAVs are supervised by the Central Bank.

4.125 The introduction of ICAVs highlights the Irish government's commitment to the Irish funds industry and enhances Ireland's attractiveness as a leading global domicile for collective investment schemes.

Investment company

4.126 Until recently, the investment company was the most common vehicle used by funds established in Ireland. An investment company is incorporated under Irish law and is managed and controlled by its board of directors. Whilst the board of directors of an Irish investment company will usually have a minimum of three directors, under Central Bank rules it must have a minimum of two directors, each of whom is Irish resident. Although the board of directors may delegate certain duties to third parties (such as investment management duties to an investment manager, and administration functions to an administrator), the board of directors remains responsible for ensuring that the company is managed in its shareholders' best interests.

4.127 A UCITS is established under the UCITS Regulations and is generally subject to company law requirements save where specifically disapplied or varied by the UCITS Regulations. The UCITS Regulations introduced the concept of a variable capital company into Irish company law and allowed the creation of open-ended investment companies for the first time (since all UCITS must be open-ended).

4.128 A UCITS investment company will typically be incorporated with two types of shares: subscriber shares of €1 each (which are generally subscribed for by the promoter of the fund) and participating shares. These participating shares have no par value. The actual value of the paid-up share capital reflects the net asset value of the company.

4.129 If self-managed, the minimum capital requirement under the UCITS Regulations is €300,000 (or its foreign currency equivalent). If a management company is established to manage a UCITS, certain minimum capitalisation rules will apply to that management company rather than to the investment company, and the normal general company law rules will apply to the capitalisation of the investment company.

4.130 An AIF investment company is established under Part 24 of the Companies Act 2014 (previously Part XIII of the Companies Act 1990) and the AIF Rulebook. The provisions of the 2014 Act generally apply to Part 24 investment companies, save where specifically disapplied or varied.

4.131 An AIF investment company will typically be incorporated with two types of shares: subscriber shares and participating shares. The minimum issued share capital of an AIF investment company is two shares of €1 each.

4.132 An internally managed AIF must meet a minimum capital requirement of €300,000. If an AIFM is established to manage the AIF, certain minimum capitalisation requirements will apply to that AIFM.

4.133 Like an ICAV, establishing an investment company is a two-step process. However, the initial incorporation is completed with the Companies Registration Office ('CRO') by filing standardised forms together with a constitution. The second stage involves completing the Central Bank authorisation process described at paras **4.143–4.149** below.

Unit trust

4.134 A unit trust is a common form of fund vehicle used in Ireland and can be established as a UCITS or an AIF. Whilst this vehicle is often used by fund managers which are marketing a fund to Irish, UK, US or Japanese investors, it is not typically used by investment managers that wish to market their funds to continental European investors, which have traditionally preferred a corporate structure (many civil law jurisdictions do not recognise trusts).

4.135 A unit trust is constituted by a trust deed made between the trustee and the manager. The trust deed will set out the constitution of the unit trust and the rights of the unitholders in the unit trust. Although the assets of a unit trust are held by the trustee on trust for the unitholders in that unit trust, the beneficial ownership remains at all times with the unitholders. The trust comes into effect upon the signing of the trust deed, which typically occurs at the same time as completion of the Central Bank authorisation process described at paras **4.143–4.149** below.

Common contractual fund

4.136 The common contractual fund ('CCF') is available in Ireland for both a UCITS and an AIF. A CCF is a collective investment undertaking which is an unincorporated body established by a management company. The participants, by contractual arrangement, participate and share in the property of the collective investment undertaking as co-owners.

4.137 The CCF essentially provides a framework whereby investors may pool their resources to enable them to be commonly managed for investment purposes provided certain investor criteria are met. Importantly, the CCF is treated as being transparent for Irish tax purposes provided that all of its investors are institutional investors.

4.138 *Onshore Fund Domiciles*

4.138 The CCF tends to be popular with pension funds, given the efficiencies involved in pooling pension fund investments whilst preserving any tax advantage enjoyed by the relevant pension funds. Other institutional investors have, however, started to use the CCF.

4.139 The CCF comes into effect upon the signing of the deed of constitution, which typically occurs at the same time as completion of the Central Bank authorisation process described at paras **4.143–4.149** below.

Investment limited partnership

4.140 The investment limited partnership ('ILP') was introduced in 1994 and is available only for AIFs. The ILP is recognised under the laws of a number of jurisdictions, including the US, as tax transparent.

4.141 An ILP is governed by a limited partnership agreement. One general partner, which must be Irish resident, is appointed and this entity has responsibility for running and managing the fund. Investors become limited partners in the ILP. A limited partner is not liable for the debts or obligations of an ILP beyond the amount of capital contributed, except where that limited partner takes part in the management of the partnership.

4.142 The ILP comes into effect upon the signing of the limited partnership agreement, which typically occurs at the same time as completion of the Central Bank authorisation process described below.

Investment fund authorisation

4.143 Every investment fund, UCITS management company and AIFM established in Ireland is authorised by the Central Bank in accordance with the requirements set out in the Central Bank's UCITS Regulations or AIF Rulebook, as appropriate.

4.144 For investment funds other than QIAIFs, an initial submission of an application is made to the Central Bank with documentation in as final form as is possible. The fund's legal advisers will prepare, in consultation with the investment manager and other relevant parties, the following documentation in connection with any such application:

- the Central Bank application form;
- the prospectus or offering memorandum;
- the constitutional or governing documents of the relevant vehicle; and
- UCITS management agreement or AIFM agreement, investment management agreement, investment advisory agreement and distribution agreement or paying agency agreement.

4.145 The fund's legal advisers will negotiate the depositary agreement and administration agreement with the relevant service providers and will submit the negotiated drafts to the Central Bank as part of the application process. A review and comment process between the Central Bank, the legal advisers and fund promoters then follows with the aim of settling all documentation and dealing with any queries to the satisfaction of the Central Bank before the formal authorisation is provided.

4.146 Only the Central Bank application form, draft prospectus and depositary agreement are reviewed by the Central Bank. For all other documents, the Central Bank requires the fund's legal advisers to certify compliance with the relevant regulations and the documents are filed with the Central Bank immediately prior to authorisation of the fund.

4.147 QIAIFs are subject to a self-certification approval process. Provided the Central Bank receives a complete application for the authorisation of a QIAIF before 3pm on a particular day, a letter of authorisation for that QIAIF can be issued on the following business day.

4.148 The availability of the fast track authorisation process is dependent on the Central Bank having approved in advance the QIAIF's investment manager, depositary, administrator and all of its directors. Furthermore, any policy issues relating to the QIAIF must be cleared in advance with the Central Bank.

4.149 The fund or management company, as appropriate, is required to certify that all of the fund documentation complies, in all material respects, with the AIF Rulebook. In addition, the depositary of the QIAIF must provide a similar confirmation in relation to the depositary agreement (or trust deed or deed of constitution in the case of a QIAIF established as a unit trust or CCF).

Fund management companies

4.150 Ireland is a leading location for fund management companies ('FMCs'), particularly AIFMs and UCITS management companies which are appointed to manage Irish domiciled investment funds, which are drawn by the numerous advantages Ireland has to offer as a domicile for cross-border management companies.

4.151 A UCITS or an AIF which is established as an ICAV or an investment company does not require a management company and can either be managed directly by its board of directors or appoint an external manager. Where a UCITS or an AIF is managed by its board of directors, it is referred to as an internally managed or self-managed fund. By contrast, a unit trust and a CCF must always have a management company and an ILP must always have at least one general partner.

4.152 A UCITS management company is responsible for collective portfolio management, which in the context of the UCITS regime includes investment management, administration and marketing. However, it is possible for a UCITS management company to delegate some or all of these functions provided it does not become a 'letter box entity'.

4.153 An AIFM must, at a minimum, be responsible for the investment management function, which includes portfolio management and risk management with respect to the AIFs which it manages. An AIFM may also be authorised to provide administration and marketing services in respect of the AIFs which it manages. Similar to the UCITS regime, an AIFM may delegate part of the investment management function provided it does not fall foul of the 'letter box' test set out in article 82(d) of the Level 2 AIFM Regulations.

4.154 An Irish UCITS management company or an AIFM may delegate the day-to-day portfolio management function to an investment manager located

4.154 Onshore Fund Domiciles

outside Ireland (either within or outside the EU) provided that the relevant investment manager is subject to a comparable level of prudential supervision as that which would exist under the Markets in Financial Instruments Directive[1] ('MiFID') regime. Provided the UCITS management company or AIFM does not become a 'letter box entity' as a result of this delegation, the Irish FMC model permits day-to-day investment decisions to be taken outside Ireland, while at the same time, enabling the funds themselves (whether UCITS or AIFs) to be passported for sale throughout the EEA pursuant to the UCITS and AIFMD regimes, as the case may be.

[1] Directive 2014/65/EC of 15 May 2014 (OJ L 173, 12.6.2014, p 349).

4.155 Both the UCITS management company and AIFM regimes permit those entities to apply to be licensed to undertake certain additional MiFID-type services such as individual portfolio management, investment advice, and the receipt and transmission of orders.

4.156 Irish authorised UCITS management companies and AIFMs are entitled to manage funds in other EU member states on a passporting basis, subject to notification requirements. The Central Bank also permits a non-EU AIFM to manage Irish authorised QIAIFs and to market both EU and non-EU AIFs to professional investors in Ireland.

4.157 A single management company may be authorised to manage both UCITS and AIFs (known as a 'Super ManCo'). Establishing a 'Super ManCo' makes it possible to obtain access to the passporting regimes for UCITS and AIFs without the need to establish two separately regulated and capitalised entities. As the Central Bank has recently streamlined the authorisation, on-going supervision, managerial functions and governance of AIFMs and UCITS management companies, establishing an Irish Super ManCo is now an attractive option. The Central Bank has published on its website information on its authorisation requirements for FMCs. Although a UCITS ManCo can also be authorised as an AIFM (and vice versa), the Central Bank will treat them as two separate authorisations.

4.158 Establishing an Irish FMC for externally managed investment funds involves the following.

Establishing a corporate entity

4.159 An FMC must be incorporated as an Irish private company limited by shares. There are two types of private limited company, namely a designated activity company (a 'DAC') and a private company limited by shares (an 'LTD'). The establishment of a DAC or an LTD takes approximately two weeks, which may run concurrently with the Central Bank's authorisation process for an FMC.

The preliminary meeting

4.160 Prior to submitting an application form to the Central Bank, an applicant must first organise a preliminary meeting to familiarise the Central

Bank with the applicant's background and business credentials and to enable the Central Bank to identify at an early stage any potential issues with the proposed business.

Individual questionnaires

4.161 Each person performing controlled functions or pre-approval controlled functions must comply with the Central Bank's fitness and probity requirements as previously described.

4.162 The Central Bank must give its prior approval before an individual can be appointed to a pre-approval controlled function. The individual must complete an online individual questionnaire which is endorsed by the applicant and then submitted electronically to the Central Bank for assessment.

Application form and supporting documentation

4.163 An applicant may apply for authorisation as an FMC by submitting a completed application form, signed by two directors of the applicant, together with relevant supporting documentation. In the application form, the applicant must provide the following information:

- *Legal structure and ownership*: This includes information about the identities of all direct or indirect shareholders or members of the applicant which hold 10% or more of the shares in the applicant.
- *Proposed activities*: The applicant must identify the collective portfolio management services that it intends to provide. It must also provide specified information regarding its financial and business projections.
- *Capital, financial and business information*: The applicant must explain how it would meet the minimum capital requirements. An FMC must have initial capital of at least €125,000 plus 0.02% of the value of the portfolios of the funds that it manages in excess of €250 million, with a maximum total requirement not exceeding €10 million. Additional considerations in relation to capital requirements are necessary where the FMC will also carry out individual portfolio management functions.
- *Organisational structure*: The applicant must provide details of its organisational structure including its staffing arrangements. Whilst an FMC must have adequate levels of staff and expertise to carry out its proposed activities, it is not required to have a specific number of staff. The applicant must confirm that it has submitted individual questionnaires in respect of directors and persons proposing to carry out pre-approval controlled functions.

4.164 The application form must be accompanied by the following supporting documentation:

- a detailed business plan/programme of activity which complies with the Central Bank's recently finalised guidelines for FMCs[1];

4.164 Onshore Fund Domiciles

- details of minimum capital, financial projections and detailed assumptions on which projections are based, including a confirmation from the board in respect of capital, a bank statement evidencing compliance with the minimum capital requirements and accounts;
- all information regarding ownership structure;
- information regarding remuneration policies and practices;
- information about the funds that the applicant intends to manage;
- ancillary documents such as a statement of responsibility for the management functions and authorised signatory list; and
- organisational charts.

[1] Fund Management Companies: Guidance (December 2016) – see https://www.centralbank.ie/regulation/industry-market-sectors/funds/ucits/guidance/fund-management-companies.

Key requirements for FMCs

4.165 Key requirements for FMCs are as follows:

- An FMC must have at least two directors. The Central Bank treats a high level of directorships combined with high aggregate levels of annual professional commitments as a supervisory risk indicator. The risk indicator is currently set at having more than 20 directorships and an aggregate professional time commitment in excess of 2,000 hours.
- An FMC must appoint a designated person for each of six designated managerial functions, namely: regulatory compliance, fund risk management, operational risk management, investment management, capital and finance management and distribution. Individual directors may be designated persons.
- One of an FMC's independent directors should undertake an 'organisational effectiveness' role, the purpose of which is to ensure that the FMC continues to be organised and resourced in an appropriate manner, on an on-going basis.
- An FMC must have at least two Irish resident directors and at least half of its directors must be EEA resident. In addition, half of an FMC's managerial functions must be performed by at least two designated persons who are resident in the EEA. Where an FMC is viewed by the Central Bank as being 'medium risk' from a supervisory perspective, it must have either three Irish resident directors or, alternatively, at least two Irish resident directors and one designated person who is resident in Ireland.
- An FMC board may delegate certain tasks which form part of its management functions to a third party, provided it does not delegate to such an extent that it becomes a 'letter box entity'. An FMC board retains ultimate responsibility for any tasks which it delegates. In addition, an FMC board must take all major strategic and operational decisions affecting the FMC and any investment funds which it manages.

Investment fund service providers

4.166 Alongside the AIFM or UCITS management company (in the majority of instances), the principal service providers to an investment fund in Ireland are the investment manager, the administrator, the depositary and, for hedge funds, the prime broker. Whilst an investment manager and prime broker may be located outside Ireland (typically in either the UK or the US), the administrator and depositary must be located in Ireland.

4.167 An investment fund will need to ensure that agreements with its key service providers contain certain provisions stipulated by the Central Bank.

Investment manager

4.168 The function of the investment manager is to take the day-to-day discretionary investment decisions in relation to the fund. EEA-based investment management companies that meet certain requirements (such as under MiFID) are not subject to an approval process. The Central Bank will, however, require confirmation from the home state regulator of such a management company that it has the appropriate regulatory status. For non-EEA investment managers, the Central Bank will normally apply a review and approval process. The main criteria relates to the level of regulation and supervision to which that investment manager is subject in its home jurisdiction. The Central Bank will not approve any investment manager located in a jurisdiction which the Central Bank considers does not provide an equivalent level of authorisation and on-going supervision. Once an investment manager has been approved by the Central Bank, it does not need to undergo the approval process again each time it is appointed as the investment manager to an additional fund.

4.169 Whereas an investment manager (or a sub-investment manager) which retains the discretionary investment management function need to be approved by the Central Bank, an investment adviser with no discretion does not require approval from the Central Bank.

Administrator

4.170 The administrator of an Irish authorised fund must be incorporated in Ireland. The administration of collective investment schemes (whether Irish or non-Irish) is a regulated activity under the Investment Intermediaries Act 1995 (as amended) and any firm carrying out such activities in Ireland must be authorised by the Central Bank under that Act.

4.171 Irish authorised funds typically outsource administrative activities to a third party fund administrator (unless undertaken by the fund's AIFM or UCITS management company). Those outsourced activities generally include:

- the calculation of net asset value and dealing price, including pricing of the underlying securities;
- the maintenance and updating of accounting records;
- the preparation of annual and semi-annual financial statements;
- the reconciliation of investment and cash positions with custody records;

4.171 *Onshore Fund Domiciles*

- the maintenance and servicing of investor registers; and
- correspondence with investors, including the storage and issue of subscription and redemption documents.

4.172 Frequently, a separate division of the fund administrator (often referred to as 'transfer agency' or 'shareholder services') deals with the issue and redemption of shares or units and investor queries, although these can also be outsourced to a separate company.

4.173 In relation to Irish based fund administrators, the Central Bank imposes requirements on the outsourcing of administrative activities which are intended to promote greater consistency of approach and certainty in relation to the Central Bank's principles on outsourcing.

Depositary

4.174 An AIFM or UCITS management company must appoint a single depositary, in respect of each AIF or UCITS which it manages.

4.175 The AIFMD Regulations and the UCITS Regulations impose a number of obligations on a depositary, including monitoring cash flow, safekeeping of assets and detailed oversight, verification and monitoring obligations.

4.176 A depositary is subject to a strict liability standard in respect of the loss of a financial instrument held in custody, subject to certain limited exceptions. Additionally, the depositary is liable to the AIF or the UCITS and its investors for all losses suffered by them as a result of the depositary's negligent or intentional failure properly to fulfil its obligations under the Irish AIFM Regulations and UCITS Regulations respectively.

4.177 A depositary is also subject to stringent rules regarding delegation and must comply with specified, minimum ongoing monitoring requirements in relation to its delegates (including, in the case of AIFs, prime brokers).

Taxation of investment funds

4.178 All Irish investment funds authorised by the Central Bank which are available to the public are exempt from Irish tax on their income and gains irrespective of where their investors are resident. No Irish stamp, capital or other duties apply on the issue, transfer or redemption of share or units in a fund.

4.179 An exit tax regime applies to funds set up as an ICAV, investment company, unit trust or ILP. Under this regime, no withholding tax applies on payments to non-Irish resident investors and certain Irish resident investors once certain declarations have been put in place or the fund has received approval in respect of 'equivalent measures'.

4.180 Funds which are established as a CCF are treated as transparent for Irish tax purposes and as such the income and gains of a CCF are treated as if they directly accrue to the investors from the underlying assets of that CCF. No withholding tax applies on any payments made by a CCF. There is no Irish tax on income or gains for investors that are not within the scope of Irish tax. It should, however, be noted that individuals are not permitted to invest in CCFs.

4.181 Certain services supplied to a fund are VAT-exempt activities. The principal exemptions relate to discretionary investment management services, administration services (including corporate administration) and marketing services. Custodial services are also generally exempt from VAT. Other services provided to a fund may create a VAT liability. VAT recovery is, however, available to the extent that the fund has either non-EU assets or non-EU investors.

4.182 Ireland has an extensive network of double taxation agreements. Access by a fund to these treaties can, however, be restricted because of the tax exempt nature of Irish funds. Treaty benefits have been obtained from a number of Ireland's treaty partners, and each jurisdiction should be reviewed on a case-by-case basis to determine whether double taxation agreement access is possible.

4.183 It is important to ensure that an Irish authorised fund is resident in Ireland for the purposes of Irish taxation. A fund established as an ICAV or investment company will be regarded as tax resident in Ireland if its central management and control is exercised in Ireland. An Irish unit trust is generally regarded as tax resident in Ireland on the basis that the trustee is resident in Ireland. An Irish ILP is treated in Ireland, as well as in many other jurisdictions, as being tax transparent, in which case it is the residence of the individual limited partners which will be relevant in determining tax status. An Irish CCF is tax transparent and, therefore, does not have a 'residence' for the purposes of Irish tax.

The Irish Stock Exchange

4.184 The main reason for obtaining a stock exchange listing for an Irish fund is to facilitate the marketing of its shares or units to specific categories of investors. Institutional investors, in particular, are often restricted or prohibited from investing in unlisted securities or in securities which are not listed on a recognised or regulated stock exchange. For other categories of investors, a listing on a recognised stock exchange will often mean that the shares or units qualify as an eligible security under their internal investment parameters (such as permitted only to purchase listed securities).

4.185 Since 1989, the Irish Stock Exchange (the 'Exchange') has maintained a successful track record in the listing of investment funds. The Exchange is a recognised EU stock exchange and has been recognised by the regulatory authorities in all of the main jurisdictions, including the US and Japan.

4.186 The Exchange has a detailed set of rules which govern the listing of investment funds. These rules vary to some extent depending on the fund's domicile. The Exchange has developed listing rules that provide a streamlined approach for the listing of investment funds that are authorised by the Central Bank.

4.187 In general, an open-ended fund that is authorised in Ireland by the Central Bank and prepares combined listing particulars within the initial prospectus of that fund will be deemed to have complied with all of the Exchange's listing requirements. In the case of a closed-ended fund, certain additional requirements may apply by virtue of the application of the

4.187 *Onshore Fund Domiciles*

Prospectus Directive[1].

[1] Directive 2003/71/EC of 4 November 2003 (OJ L 345, 31.12.2003, p 64).

4.188 Before a fund can be listed on the Exchange, it must appoint an approved 'listing sponsor' which is registered at the Exchange. The listing sponsor is responsible for ensuring the fund's suitability for listing prior to submission of an application, for submission of the listing application and for dealing with the Exchange on all matters in relation to the application. In the case of an Irish domiciled fund, an application for listing will usually run in parallel with the Central Bank authorisation process.

Investment managers located in Ireland

4.189 Ireland is home to a significant number of investment firms which are authorised under the regulatory framework set out in MiFID. There are a number of advantages to being authorised in Ireland as a MiFID firm, including:

- the ability to passport throughout the EEA, either on a branch or a cross-border services basis;
- a favourable tax regime, due to a combination of a 12.5% corporate tax rate and an extensive and comprehensive network of double taxation agreements; and
- access to a sophisticated financial services industry with a deep pool of staff, managers, professional advisers, regulators and service providers comprising both native English speakers and a sizeable international population (roughly 17%).

Regulatory framework

4.190 MiFID firms are regulated under the European Union (Markets in Financial Instruments) Regulations 2017[1] (the 'MiFID Regulations'), which transpose MiFID into Irish law, and the Markets in Financial Instruments Regulation[2] ('MiFIR').

[1] SI 375/2017.
[2] Regulation (EU) No 600/2014 of 15 May 2014 (OJ L 173, 12.6.2014, p 84).

Passporting and third country firms

4.191 One of the main advantages of the MiFID legislation is that it enables an investment firm to carry on business covered by its authorisation throughout the EU without seeking further authorisation in another member state.

Safe harbour and third country firms

4.192 In certain instances, an investment firm authorised in a third country (a 'third country firm') will be able to offer investment services in Ireland without authorisation on a 'safe harbour' basis. Specifically, a third country firm can offer MiFID investment services to per se professional clients and eligible counterparties without authorisation once it satisfies certain requirements, namely:

- the third country firm's head or registered office must be in a non-EEA member state and it must not have a branch in Ireland;
- the third country firm must be subject to authorisation and supervision in the third country in which it is established, and the relevant competent authority must pay due regard to any recommendations of the Financial Action Task Force (the 'FATF') in the context of anti-money laundering and countering the financing of terrorism; and
- co-operation arrangements must be in place between the Central Bank and the competent authorities of the third country that include provisions regulating the exchange of information for the purpose of preserving the integrity of the market and protecting investors.

4.193 MiFIR also provides an EU-wide right for a third country firm to provide investment services or perform investment activities to professional clients and eligible counterparties without establishing a branch once it is registered in the register of third country firms kept by ESMA. In order to be included on the register, a firm must meet a number of requirements. In particular, the European Commission must have adopted an equivalence decision in relation to the legal and supervisory arrangements in place in the third country.

4.194 Third country firms will be able to continue to provide services and activities in Ireland under the MiFID Regulations until three years after the adoption of such an equivalence decision.

4.195 Third country firms must establish a branch in Ireland and obtain prior authorisation from the Central Bank if they intend to offer investment services to a retail or opted-up professional client, unless the relevant investment service is being offered at the client's exclusive initiative.

The MiFID authorisation process

4.196 An entity that wishes to become authorised as a MiFID firm must submit an application for authorisation to the Central Bank. Prior to seeking authorisation, an entity should submit to the Central Bank a Key Facts Document. It should also arrange a preliminary meeting with the Central Bank, at which the Central Bank will outline the authorisation process and indicate whether there are any significant issues that might negatively affect its determination of the application.

4.197 Once it receives a complete application, the Central Bank will issue comments to the applicant firm within 40 working days, and the applicant will be expected to respond to those comments within 20 working days. The Central Bank will issue a second round of comments to the applicant firm within 20 working days of receipt by the Central Bank of the first round of responses, and the applicant has ten working days to respond to those comments. The Central Bank will reach a decision on authorisation within six months of receipt of a complete application. The Central Bank has published guidance on completing an application for authorisation under MiFID, which

4.197 *Onshore Fund Domiciles*

is available on its website[1].

[1] Guidance Note for Authorisation as an Investment Firm under MiFID (2017) – see https://www.centralbank.ie/regulation/industry-market-sectors/investment-firms/mifid-firms/authorisation-process.

Key considerations

4.198 An entity that wishes to obtain a MiFID authorisation under Irish law must fulfil a number of requirements. For existing groups with substantial operations outside Ireland, an important requirement will be the Central Bank's emphasis on ensuring that the applicant's 'heart and mind' will be located in Ireland. This essentially means that the Central Bank will need to be satisfied that the applicant will be properly run in Ireland and that the Central Bank will be able to supervise it effectively. Among other things, the Central Bank will expect the following presence in Ireland:

- a senior management team with strength and depth overseen and directed by a strong board of directors; and
- organisation structure and reporting lines which ensure there is appropriate separation and oversight of all activities.

4.199 There is no requirement for any specific individual to be resident in Ireland. However, ideally, the personnel who are to fulfil the applicant's core functions should perform such functions out of Ireland.

4.200 An Irish authorised branch may outsource/delegate some of its activities to entities in other jurisdictions, subject to compliance with the MiFID Regulations. However, the investment firm will need to be able to satisfy the Central Bank that there are objective reasons for the outsourcing arrangements and that they do not lead to the creation of letter box entities or allow the circumvention of the MiFID framework and the responsibilities of the investment firms.

C   LUXEMBOURG

Dr Marcel Bartnik, Counsel, DLA Piper, Luxembourg

Introduction

Europe's number one fund jurisdiction

4.201 As far as investment funds are concerned, Luxembourg's position is a rather unusual one. Whilst geographically speaking it is rather small with just 2,600 square kilometres and around 560,000 inhabitants, the Grand Duchy is by a substantial margin Europe's largest fund domicile, second only to the US.

4.202 This leading position is a consequence of Luxembourg's focus on the development of its financial sector since the 1980s. It is helped by its location in the centre of Western Europe, national legislation that is innovative and quick to react to new developments, and the presence of a substantial number of international banks (around 140) and other service providers to the financial sector (currently well over 300[1]) in Luxembourg. In addition, important institutions of the EU such as the European Court of Justice and the

European Investment Bank are established in the city of Luxembourg.

[1] As at 31 December 2017 (source: CSSF – see http://www.cssf.lu).

4.203 The concentration of such an extraordinary business community of the financial sector is the logical consequence of the rapid growth of Luxembourg's investment fund industry. Since 1983, when the first comprehensive investment fund legislation was introduced in Luxembourg[1], the number of investment funds, known as undertakings for collective investment ('UCIs'), has grown substantially with currently over 4,000 UCIs and €4,160 billion of assets under management[2]. Even these impressive numbers are not the full picture – due in particular to the implementation of the AIFMD rules, there is an increasing number of unregulated investment funds for which no reliable statistical data exists. The fact, however, that Luxembourg currently ranks fourth (behind Germany, France and the Netherlands) in terms of countries of domiciliation of alternative investment funds ('AIFs'), with around €656 billion of net assets[3], is an indication of the attractiveness of Luxembourg to this sector.

[1] See para **4.208** below.
[2] As at 31 December 2017 (source: CSSF); the RAIFs or unregulated fund structures are not counted in these figures.
[3] EFAMA quarterly statistical report for Q3/2017 – see http://www.efama.org.

4.204 The sponsors of Luxembourg investment funds are based in a wide range of countries. In terms of net assets, the US ranks first with a market share of 20.5%, followed by the UK (17.6%), Germany (14.6%) and Switzerland (13.6%)[1]. They use Luxembourg as a hub for distribution of their products within the EU. Indeed, in 2015 alone, the Luxembourg regulator received 3,477 notifications about the cross-border distribution of UCITS, and 1,758 notifications about the cross-border distribution of AIFs[2]. It is expected that these numbers will increase further in the coming years.

[1] As at 31 December 2017 (source: CSSF).
[2] CSSF Annual Report for 2015.

4.205 Luxembourg's hedge fund and fund of hedge funds sector has also seen remarkable growth in recent years. Between 2011 and 2015, Luxembourg's worldwide market share of hedge funds increased from 6% to 15.6%. This market is currently dominated by the Cayman Islands (26.7%) and the State of Delaware, USA (21.1%). Nevertheless, about half of all hedge funds which are based in Europe are domiciled in Luxembourg, and it is clear that there is a growing trend to move from offshore jurisdictions such as the Cayman Islands or the British Virgin Islands which have steadily declining market shares to onshore jurisdictions, with Luxembourg being the top choice.

Definition of hedge funds in Luxembourg

4.206 As indicated in CHAPTER 1, the term 'hedge fund' is an expression that is used in a variety of different contexts. Generally, it is considered that the term initially referred to the hedging of an open position against a particular risk. At the time, hedge funds exclusively operated on a market neutral basis using the strategy of buying securities assumed to be undervalued (long

4.206 Onshore Fund Domiciles

positions) and, at the same time, selling short securities assumed to be overvalued (short positions), thus resulting in the long position being hedged by the short position. The aim was for the hedge fund portfolio to be neutral to market movements and to be exposed only to the unsystemic risk inherent to the securities bought and sold short. Since then, numerous hedge fund investment strategies have been developed and the original hedging concept represents a relatively small element of today's hedge fund strategies: long-short equity, fixed income arbitrage, convertible bond arbitrage, absolute value strategies, to name but a few.

4.207 No definition of the term 'hedge fund' can be found in any Luxembourg law or regulation, and although the industry itself is very much aware of their existence and distinctive features, the Luxembourg legislator has so far abstained from providing a specific guidance in relation thereto.

The origin of Luxembourg's fund legislation

4.208 Luxembourg did not have a specific law on investment funds until 1983[1], when it introduced a comprehensive legislation – the Law of 25 August 1983 on undertakings for collective investment (the '1983 Law'). The 1983 Law was the first law on investment funds and provided for a great variety of permitted investment policies. It also introduced the 'investment company with variable capital'[2] as a specific type of company, which proved to be of particular interest for investors from Belgium and France to whom the use of an investment fund in corporate form presented fiscal advantages.

[1] A very brief Grand-Ducal Degree was issued in 1972 which severely lacked a detailed framework.
[2] *Société d'investissement à capital variable* or 'SICAV' – see paras **4.242–4.254** below.

4.209 The next important stimulus to the Luxembourg fund industry was the UCITS Directive of 20 December 1985[1] ('Directive 85/611'). Luxembourg was the first member state of the EU to transpose the Directive by its Law of 30 March 1988 on undertakings for collective investment (the '1988 Law').

[1] Council Directive 85/611/EEC of 20 December 1985.

4.210 The purpose of the 1988 Law was not limited to transposing, in its Part I, Directive 85/611 into Luxembourg law. Part II of the 1988 Law set out provisions for the establishment of retail UCIs, the object of which was the investment in assets other than transferable securities (such as real estate UCIs), or UCIs intending to pursue an investment strategy more flexible than permitted for UCITS, which at that time did not permit an extensive use of derivatives. It was under Part II of the 1988 Law that the first hedge funds were established. Due in particular to an intense use of derivative instruments and employing substantial leverage, their investment strategies did not fit into the much more conservative and restrictive UCITS rules. As a consequence, however, they could not avail themselves of the marketing passport reserved to UCITS, and therefore their distribution outside Luxembourg was difficult, or limited to private placement.

4.211 In order to provide at least some rules for this type of funds, the Luxembourg regulator subsequently issued IML[1] Circular 91/75, dated

21 January 1991 ('Circular 91/75'). That circular set out conditions for the establishment of UCIs using so-called alternative investment strategies, such as managed futures, use of leverage or carrying out short sales of securities, as well as funds of hedge funds. Since Circular 91/75 did not provide for a lot of details regarding UCIs adopting alternative investment strategies and only reflects the administrative policy of the regulator (ie without the binding force of a law or a regulation), the CSSF had been able to adopt a flexible approach in approving hedge funds and funds of hedge funds, and to permit investment and management techniques (such as securities lending) even though these were not explicitly envisaged in Circular 91/75.

[1] The Institut Monétaire Luxembourgeois (the 'IML') was the predecessor of the Commission de Surveillance du Secteur Financier (the 'CSSF'), the current financial regulator in Luxembourg.

4.212 The 1988 Law, which dealt exclusively with funds intended to be marketed to retail investors, was complemented shortly afterwards by the Law of 19 July 1991 on UCIs the units of which were not intended to be placed with the public and which were reserved for one or more institutional investors (the '1991 Law'). Under the 1991 Law it was also possible to establish hedge funds that were exclusively aimed at institutional investors, a category that also nowadays is one of the pillars of the demand for AIFs in general.

4.213 The revision of the UCITS regime through Directive 2001/107/EC[1] (the 'Management Directive') and Directive 2001/108/EC[2] (the 'Product Directive') (together known as 'UCITS III') resulted in the replacement of the 1988 Law by a new law dated 20 December 2002 relating to UCIs (the '2002 Law'), which entered into force on 1 January 2003. On 13 February 2007, the 2002 Law replaced the 1988 Law entirely[3]. As with the 1988 Law, the transposition of UCITS III into Luxembourg law was effected mainly by Part I of the 2002 Law, while Part II continued to deal with retail funds outside of the UCITS regime and was largely left untouched.

[1] Directive 2001/107/EC of 21 January 2002.
[2] Directive 2001/108/EC of 21 January 2002.
[3] The transitional period allowed UCITS to benefit from certain grandfathering clauses in the Product Directive.

4.214 One notable effect on hedge funds was, however, that UCITS III for the first time permitted UCITS to be exclusively invested in financial derivative instruments, thus enabling UCITS funds at least partially to use investment strategies that had been until then the exclusive domain of hedge funds. This laid the foundation for convergence between traditional hedge funds and UCITS, resulting in fund sponsors devising sophisticated strategies similar to those of traditional hedge funds, but still within the UCITS regime.

Current fund regulation in Luxembourg

The 2010 Law: UCITS

4.215 The next two main revisions of the legislative framework for funds in Luxembourg resulted from the amendment of the UCITS rules. As a first step, the transposition of Directive 2009/65/EC[1] ('UCITS IV') saw the replacement of the 2002 Law by the Law of 17 December 2010 (the '2010 Law'). In 2016,

4.215 *Onshore Fund Domiciles*

the 2010 Law was further revised by virtue of the transposition of Directive 2014/91/EU ('UCITS V')[2]. These two Directives did not change the structure of the original 2002 Law fundamentally, as the 2010 Law continues to be divided into a Part I which concerns UCITS and a Part II which concerns retail UCIs that do not comply with the UCITS regime. The effect of such changes for hedge funds was, however, rather limited, as the relevant UCITS Directives dealt with topics such as the management company passport or depositary rules that only tangentially concern hedge funds.

[1] Directive 2009/65/EC of 13 July 2009.
[2] Directive 2014/91/EU of 23 July 2014. The transposition was made by way of the Law dated 10 May 2016, published in the official Luxembourg gazette, *Mémorial A* No 88 of 12 May 2016.

4.216 In addition to these more fundamental revisions of the UCITS regime, Commission Directive 2007/16/EC[1] (referred to as the 'Eligible Assets Directive' or 'EAD') clarified certain definitions in the UCITS Directive concerning eligible assets for investment by UCITS and was transposed into Luxembourg law through a Grand-Ducal Regulation dated 8 February 2008[2]. It is complemented by CSSF Circular 08/339 (as amended by CSSF Circular 08/380) which reproduces the guidelines issued by the Committee of European Securities Regulators[3] and clarifies the interpretation of the EAD. This reflects an acknowledgement of the aforementioned convergence between hedge funds and UCITS: among other issues, these guidelines permit a UCITS to invest in financial derivative instruments that use hedge fund indices as underlying instruments, or into structured products such as certificates. Furthermore, the administrative practice of the CSSF had already previously admitted certain strategies such as the '130/30 approach'[4] to be employed by a UCITS, thus allowing for a flexibility which prior to such time was exclusive to hedge funds established under Part II of the 2002 and 2010 Laws.

[1] Commission Directive 2007/16/EC of 19 March 2007.
[2] Published in the official Luxembourg gazette, *Mémorial A* No 19 of 19 February 2008.
[3] The 'CESR', which has since been replaced by the European Securities and Markets Authority ('ESMA').
[4] This refers to limiting the exposure of a UCITS to 100% of its net assets by compensating a 130% long strategy with a 30% short strategy within the same market segment.

The 2010 Law: Part II funds

4.217 Currently, UCIs which are subject to Part II of the 2010 Law fall into three categories:

- venture capital funds, the principal object of which is investment in unlisted companies;
- real estate funds; and
- alternative investment funds.

4.218 The particular provisions applicable to the first two of those categories of funds are set out in Chapter I of Circular 91/75. In practical terms, the first category is of little interest today as more suitable vehicles for private equity and venture capital funds have been introduced. In terms of the third category, on 5 December 2002 the CSSF issued Circular 02/80 concerning the rules applicable to Luxembourg UCIs which adopt alternative investment strategies

('Circular 02/80'). That circular largely supplements the existing regime for funds which fall into its scope and clarifies the regulatory framework applicable to these UCIs. It is under this regime that – until 2007 – almost all Luxembourg hedge funds were established and Circular 02/80 provided for a sharp increase in the number of hedge funds created under Part II of the 2002 and 2010 Laws, as well as the 1991 Law. In total, there are currently 323 Part II funds established in Luxembourg, with assets under management of around €154 billion[1].

[1] As at 31 December 2017 (source: CSSF). This number is, however, steadily declining, from over 500 vehicles at the end of 2013.

The SICAR – a dedicated product for private equity

4.219 The first main piece of legislation based (at the time) on the 2002 Law which was aimed at a very specific class of assets was the Law of 15 June 2004 on investment companies in risk capital[1] (the 'SICAR Law'). The SICAR Law also introduced the concept of 'well-informed investors', which are the only eligible investors in a SICAR, and set out the principle that a SICAR has to exclusively invest in assets that can be considered as risk capital. It provided for a lighter regulatory regime than the 2002 or 1991 Laws and did not require the SICAR to diversify its investments.

[1] *Société d'investissement en capital à risque*, known as 'SICAR'.

4.220 CSSF Circular 06/241 later defined the notion of risk capital in further detail, setting out that investments need to exhibit an increased level of risk (beyond a mere market risk) and contribute to a development of the target companies of a SICAR's portfolio. With currently 286 SICARs investing approximately €46 billion of net assets[1], it should today be considered as a niche product[2].

[1] As at 31 December 2017 (source: CSSF).
[2] As a vehicle dedicated to private equity and venture capital investments, the SICAR does not have any bearing on hedge funds and shall therefore be excluded from further examination in the present chapter.

Specialised investment funds: the SIF Law

4.221 For alternative asset classes including hedge funds, the replacement of the 1991 Law by the Law of 13 February 2007 on specialised investment funds (the 'SIF Law') was of much greater effect. UCIs established under the 1991 Law were automatically converted into specialised investment funds ('SIFs') when the 1991 Law was repealed. The SIF Law introduced a much more flexible regime by, in particular, broadening the scope of eligible investors and lightening the degree of supervision[1]. Perhaps even more importantly, the flexibility as regards investment restrictions was increased: whereas under Circular 02/80 a substantial number of very detailed investment restrictions are imposed on hedge funds, the SIF Law does not contain any specific investment restrictions other than the overarching principle of risk diversification. As a result, the SIF Law has been widely accepted by market participants and over 1,570 SIFs have been created, managing over €472

4.221 Onshore Fund Domiciles

billion of assets[2]. Due to its greater flexibility as compared to Part II of the 2010 Law, it is safe to say that hedge funds which are not publicly distributed to retail investors have for the most part been established under the SIF Law.

[1] Initially, it was possible to establish a SIF without any prior approval from the CSSF; however, this possibility was removed by a revision of the SIF Law in 2012.
[2] As at 31 December 2017 (source: CSSF).

Transposition of AIFMD: the 2013 Law

4.222 The Alternative Investment Fund Managers Directive[1] ('AIFMD') introduced a paradigm change in the investment funds industry in Luxembourg. For the first time, it was not the investment fund itself that was the target of regulation, but rather its manager. For Luxembourg, the transposition into national law by way of a law dated 12 July 2013 (the '2013 Law') involved a substantial overhaul of its product related legislation such as the SIF Law, the SICAR Law and Part II of the 2010 Law. The 2013 Law itself is a faithful transposition of AIFMD and does not introduce any additional regulatory burden. It is complemented on a Luxembourg level by additional guidance through the CSSF's FAQs[2]. By the end of 2017, there were more than 220 fully authorised AIFMs in Luxembourg[3], as well as more than 600 registered sub-threshold AIFMs, which attests to the successful implementation of this regime in Luxembourg.

[1] Directive 2011/61/EU of 8 June 2011.
[2] See http://www.cssf.lu/surveillance/vgi/gfia-aifm/questionsreponses.
[3] As at 31 December 2017 (source: CSSF).

Reserved alternative investment funds: the RAIF Law

4.223 As a result of the regulation of the managers of AIFs, Luxembourg found itself with a double layer of regulatory supervision. One for the AIFs themselves (Part II funds, SIFs and SICARs), and another one for their managers to the extent these were established in Luxembourg. This had a negative impact on the time to market for AIFs and led to a further innovation of the Luxembourg legislator. The reserved alternative investment fund[1] ('RAIF') was introduced by way of a law dated 23 July 2016 (the 'RAIF Law'). The RAIF Law basically replicates the SIF and SICAR regimes[2] but without the need to be approved or supervised by the CSSF. As a counterpart, any RAIF has to be managed by a fully licensed AIFM. It has seen a marked success in the Luxembourg fund landscape, and already more than 300 RAIFs are currently established and registered as such in Luxembourg[3].

[1] *Fond d'investissement alternatif réservé.*
[2] As the possibility to set up a RAIF with SICAR characteristics is of no relevance to hedge funds, this additional variant will not be explored further. Any reference to the RAIF should be read as a reference to a RAIF with SIF features.
[3] As at February 2018 (source: Luxembourg register of commerce and companies – see https://www.rcsl.lu).

Summary of options

4.224 The current legislation in Luxembourg permits the establishment of: (i) UCITS using certain strategies of hedge funds under Part I of the 2010 Law; (ii) retail hedge funds subject to Part II of the 2010 Law and Circular 02/80; and (iii) hedge funds aimed at well-informed investors pursuant to the SIF Law as well as the RAIF Law.

Distinction between FCP and SICAV structures

4.225 Any Luxembourg investment fund established pursuant to the 2010 Law, the SIF Law or the RAIF Law can choose between two different structures: either a corporate vehicle (the investment company with variable capital or SICAV[1]) or a contractual arrangement that is called a *fonds commun de placement* or 'FCP'[2].

[1] *Société d'investissement à capital variable.*
[2] There is also a third category, the investment company with fixed capital (*société d'investissement à capital fixe* or 'SICAF'), which is of no practical importance, however, and will therefore not be explored in further detail in the present chapter.

Fonds commun de placement

LEGAL CONCEPT

4.226 An FCP is a contractual arrangement without legal personality which can be compared to the *Sondervermögen* in Germany. Investors subscribe for units of the relevant fund, which entitles them to a proportional share of its net assets without however granting them the power to intervene in the management of the FCP itself. The FCP is established by contractual arrangement and is not a trust under Luxembourg law.

4.227 The FCP is defined by the 2010 Law[1], the SIF Law[2] and the RAIF Law[3] as 'an undivided collection of assets made up and managed according to the principle of risk-spreading on behalf of joint owners who are liable only up to the amount contributed by them and whose rights are represented by units . . . '. Although the concept of the FCP may be compared to the concept of 'indivision' under the Luxembourg Civil Code (ie the legal situation where several persons hold a right in common in respect of an asset or a collection of assets) and the civil law concept of 'co-ownership', the FCP is actually governed by sui generis provisions which differ from both of these traditional legal concepts. First, the assets of an FCP are not static but vary over time, being managed on an ongoing basis. Second, the management of its assets is entrusted by law to a management company. Third, its assets are segregated from the assets of its unitholders.

[1] Article 5 of the 2010 Law.
[2] Article 4 of the SIF Law.
[3] Article 6 of the RAIF Law.

4.228 *Onshore Fund Domiciles*

Role of the management company

4.228 Due to the absence of legal personality, the FCP cannot itself enter into agreements or any obligations and its unitholders are not vested with the power to manage and administer the FCP. Such power is reserved to a corporate entity called a 'management company' that can be in Luxembourg or in another member state of the EU. This management company decides on the investment policies and strategies of the FCP and generally manages it on behalf of its unitholders.

4.229 Management companies established in Luxembourg that manage FCPs which are subject to Part I of the 2010 Law (that is, UCITS) are necessarily governed by the provisions of Chapter 15 of the 2010 Law[1], whereas FCPs subject to Part II of the 2010 Law, the SIF Law or the RAIF Law may be administered by management companies that comply with the provisions of either Chapter 15 or Chapter 16 of the 2010 Law[2].

[1] In the case of a foreign management company, it must have an equivalent licence in its home jurisdiction.
[2] The conditions to be complied with are set out in articles 101 to 124 of the 2010 Law for management companies subject to Chapter 15, and in articles 125-1 to 126-1 of the 2010 Law for management companies subject to Chapter 16. The main difference between the two regimes is that management companies subject to Chapter 15 need to comply with so-called 'substance requirements', ie certain technical and human infrastructure which needs to be present, such as two conducting persons supervising the management company. As a consequence, the approval procedure with the CSSF for a management company subject to Chapter 15 of the 2010 Law is much more in-depth and therefore time consuming than for management companies subject to Chapter 16 of the 2010 Law.

4.230 For those FCPs which qualify as AIFs (this is necessarily the case for Part II FCPs as well as RAIFs), the management company itself needs to be licensed as an AIFM[1], or it needs to appoint an entity that holds such a licence. As a matter of course, management companies can delegate part or all of their duties to third parties, such as the administration, portfolio management or risk management. However, in that case, a number of rules set out in the 2010 Law[2] and the 2013 Law[3] need to be complied with, such as a notification to the CSSF or appropriate disclosure to investors.

[1] Management companies subject to Chapter 15 of the 2010 Law may also acquire an AIFM licence (see article 101-1 of the 2010 Law). These are sometimes referred to as 'Super ManCos'.
[2] Article 110 of the 2010 Law, concerning management companies subject to Chapter 15 of the 2010 Law.
[3] Article 18 of the 2013 Law, if the management company also has an AIFM licence.

4.231 As a general rule, Luxembourg management companies may be incorporated in the form of a public limited company (*société anonyme*), a limited liability company (*société à responsabilité limitée*), a co-operative company (*société coopérative*) or a partnership limited by shares (*société en commandite par actions*). In practice, most management companies are established in the form of public limited companies. A management company may manage one or several FCPs, irrespective of the law to which the relevant FCPs are subject.

4.232 As the FCP has no legal personality, the management company is vested with the power to represent the FCP's investors vis-à-vis third parties, to enter into agreements on behalf of the FCP and to sue in court on behalf of the FCP.

Luxembourg 4.237

The management company acts in such instances in its own name but on behalf of the FCP. Furthermore, the management company exercises all rights attached to the assets which constitute the portfolio of the relevant FCP[1].

[1] Article 14(3) of the 2010 Law and article 13 of the SIF Law.

Rules of operation

4.233 An FCP is established and operates on the basis of two contractual arrangements. Its so-called management regulations which govern its functioning and are referred to as the 'constitutive document' of the FCP, and the subscription agreement under which the unitholders subscribe for units of the FCP.

4.234 The management company draws up and executes the management regulations, and they are in practice typically countersigned by the FCP's depositary bank[1]. The unitholders are not a party to the management regulations and are deemed to accept them by acquiring units in the FCP[2]. The unitholders do not have the power to amend the management regulations and any amendment thereof is effected at the initiative of the management company.

[1] From a strictly legal perspective, execution by the depositary bank is not required. In practice, however, the vast majority of management regulations are also executed by the depositary bank.
[2] Article 13(1) of the 2010 Law, article 12(1) of the SIF Law and article 13(1) of the RAIF Law. It could also be argued that the unitholders accept such provisions by virtue of the provisions of the subscription agreement which typically incorporates the management regulations by reference.

4.235 The management regulations deal with any substantial aspect of the operation of the FCP and contain a certain number of minimum provisions set out in the 2010 Law, the SIF Law and the RAIF Law[1]. These include its investment policy, the fees to be paid by the FCP, the identity of the main service providers and the procedure for the issue (and redemption, if the relevant FCP is open-ended) of its units.

[1] See article 13(2) for UCIs subject to Part I of the 2010 Law, article 13(2)(a)–(i) for UCIs subject to Part II of the 2010 Law, article 12 of the SIF Law and article 13(2) of the RAIF Law.

4.236 Subsequent to their execution, the management regulations are deposited with the Luxembourg register of commerce and companies[1] and a notice of such deposit is published in the official Luxembourg gazette, the *Mémorial*[2]. In addition, every FCP has to be registered with the RCS and provide such information as its name and date of establishment or the name and registered office of its management company[3].

[1] *Registre de Commerce et des Sociétés* or 'RCS'.
[2] Article 13(1) of the 2010 Law, article 12 of the SIF Law and article 13(1) of the RAIF Law.
[3] Law dated 27 May 2016 on the publication of legal notices in Luxembourg; see also Circular RCSL 16/01.

4.237 The RAIF Law provides for an additional obligation in view of the absence of any review by a supervisory authority. The establishment of a RAIF-FCP needs to be documented by a notarial deed[1], obliging the relevant

115

notary to verify a number of key elements.

[1] Article 34(1) of the RAIF Law.

INVESTORS' RIGHTS

4.238 As the management company draws its powers directly from the relevant law, it cannot be considered as an agent of the unitholders of the relevant FCP. Therefore, the management company is, in principle, under no obligation to comply with any instructions received from the unitholders, but has complete freedom regarding the management of the FCP (subject to compliance with the management regulations and the prospectus or offering document). As a consequence, investors of an FCP usually do not have any voting rights and an FCP can therefore be protected from hostile takeovers. This is the main advantage of that legal form when compared to an investment fund in corporate form.

4.239 However, if investor participation is considered to be important (for example, for marketing purposes or due to the specifics of the relevant fund's investor base), voting rights may be granted in respect of certain matters, such as in the case of amendments to the management regulations or the extension of the term of the FCP. Moreover, committees in which investors are represented may be established. Such committees, however, are not corporate bodies and may not substitute themselves for the management company. Indeed, the management company remains the ultimate decision-making body regarding the management of an FCP and unitholders do not have the right either to terminate the FCP[1] or to remove the management company[2]. This is of particular relevance to any decision relating to portfolio management in the case of FCPs that are AIFs, as such decisions must be taken by the relevant AIFM and any such committee can only have an advisory role.

[1] Article 11(1) of the 2010 Law (applicable through article 90 also for UCIs subject to Part II of the 2010 Law), article 10 of the SIF Law and article 12 of the RAIF Law.
[2] The management regulations may entitle unitholders to remove the management company. However, in such case, the FCP may only continue to exist if a new management company is appointed at the same time (and previously approved by the CSSF in the case of Part II FCPs and SIFs).

4.240 Similarly to the shareholders of a public limited company, the liability of the unitholders of an FCP is limited to the amount contributed by them. The creditors of the FCP do not have any right of recourse against the unitholders of the FCP. The FCP is not liable for the debts of the unitholders or those of the management company, only for the liabilities and charges that can be imposed on it in accordance with the provisions of the management regulations.

4.241 As the FCP is not a legal entity, it is in most jurisdictions considered as being transparent for tax purposes. In such case, the income of the FCP is attributed to its investors in proportion to their respective interests in the FCP, and an investor in a jurisdiction which has a double tax treaty with Luxembourg may be able to take advantage of treaty benefits, for example by offsetting its tax liability in its own jurisdiction against the withholding taxes incurred by the FCP in jurisdictions in which the FCP has made investments.

Société d'investissement à capital variable

LEGAL CONCEPT

4.242 As an alternative to establishing an FCP, UCIs subject to the 2010 Law, the SIF Law and the RAIF Law can adopt a corporate form. Such investment companies – except for the special limited partnership – have a legal personality separate from that of their investors.

4.243 As a consequence: (i) such company has its own assets, which may not be co-mingled with the assets of investors; (ii) the investors do not have any obligations as between themselves, but only vis-à-vis the company; (iii) the company has the power to bind itself by contractual agreement; (iv) the company acts through representatives which are corporate bodies; and (v) the company has a name, a registered office and a nationality[1]. In most cases, such investment companies adopt the form of an investment company with variable capital (a 'SICAV'), even though it is also possible to establish an investment company with fixed capital (a 'SICAF').

[1] It should be noted in this context that the Luxembourg legislator has provided for these characteristics also for the special limited partnership, even in the absence of legal personality.

AVAILABLE CORPORATE TYPES

4.244 SICAVs subject to the 2010 Law may only be established as a public limited company (*société anonyme* or 'SA')[1], whereas SICAVs subject to the SIF Law ('SICAV-SIFs') and the RAIF Law ('SICAV-RAIFs') may adopt a number of different corporate forms:

- public limited company (*société anonyme* or 'SA');
- partnership limited by shares (*société en commandite par actions* or 'SCA');
- limited liability company (*société à responsabilité limitée* or 'SARL');
- common limited partnership (*société en commandite simple* or 'SCS');
- special limited partnership (*société en commandite spéciale* or 'SCSp'); and
- co-operative in the form of a public limited company[2].

[1] Article 25 of the 2010 Law; SICAFs could also adopt different corporate forms such as the SCA.
[2] Article 25 of the SIF Law and article 23 of the RAIF Law.

4.245 The SA and the SARL have in common that the liability of their shareholders or partners is limited to their capital contribution. The three types of partnerships, on the other hand, have two categories of shareholders (or partners): one or more shareholders that are jointly and severally liable without limitation (general partners) and other shareholders whose liability is limited to their capital contribution (limited partners). In practice however, in order to limit their liability, the general partners are often established in the form of a SARL, owned and managed by the sponsor or manager of the partnership.

4.246 There are a number of differences between the different forms of investment funds in corporate form. Whilst the SA and the SCA may have an

4.246 Onshore Fund Domiciles

unlimited number of shareholders, the SARL may only have a maximum of 100 shareholders[1], and the transfer of shares to a new partner is subject to the approval of a general meeting that decides with a majority of shareholders which hold at least half of its shares[2]. Although the SARL has the advantage of slightly lighter administrative obligations[3], most SICAVs are established in the form of an SA or as a partnership.

[1] Article 710-4 of the 1915 Law.
[2] Article 710-12(1) of the 1915 Law; in principle, the quorum is set at 75% of the shares, but can be reduced to 50% of the shares by the articles of association of the relevant company.
[3] For example, no annual general meeting is necessary if the number of partners does not exceed 25; the minimum capital for incorporation is €12,000, whereas for an SA it is €30,000.

4.247 As far as the SA and the SCA are concerned, the rules governing both are for the most part identical. The major difference relates to the specifics of the partnership structure of the SCA. In light of its unlimited liability, the general partner is typically granted a veto right for any decision taken by the partners, thus allowing it to control and veto if desired any decision taken by the limited partners. This mechanism achieves a similar result that also is a key characteristic of an FCP, that is, the ability to prevent a hostile takeover through the control of its managing entity. Whereas for an FCP a regulated management company is required, a simple (and unregulated) general partner is sufficient in the case of an SCA.

4.248 The above considerations apply equally to the two other types of partnerships (SCS and SCSp). They are, however, generally considered to be tax transparent, unlike the SCA, which is one reason determining the choice between these structures. Between the SCS and the SCSp, the main difference is that the SCS has a separate legal personality. Therefore, the SCSp is closest to the traditional English limited partnership. In practical terms this makes little difference, however, as the Luxembourg legislator has inserted provisions regarding the SCSp which allow it to function as if it had a separate legal personality, such as concerning the registration of ownership of assets (which can be made in the name of the partnership and not its partners)[1].

[1] See Article 320-1 et seq of the 1915 Law.

VARIABLE CAPITAL

4.249 The defining feature (and advantage) of a SICAV is its variable share capital, which will always be equal to the net assets of the SICAV, as opposed to a traditional corporate entity such as an SA whose capital is set out in its constitutive documents, which therefore would need to be amended each time a new shareholder is admitted or an existing investor leaves.

4.250 For a SICAV, the share capital is always equal to its net asset value which is calculated by its central administration agent, and therefore automatically fluctuates on each valuation day[1] to reflect the subscription and redemption of shares, as well as the value of the underlying investments of the SICAV. As a consequence, no amendment to the SICAV's articles of incorporation are necessary during its lifetime in order to reflect the amount of its share capital. Also, there are no limits as to the part of the SICAV's capital that can be distributed to its shareholders (eg concerning its income or profit), except for the rule that its capital must not fall below the minimum capital requirement of €1.25 million[2].

[1] The frequency of the net asset value calculation depends mainly on the asset class and the regulatory regime. Whereas with liquid securities, a daily valuation is common (and in the case of UCITS, a frequency of twice a month is obligatory), there can be as few as one net asset value calculation each year for private equity and real estate structures.
[2] Articles 27 and 31 of the 2010 Law, articles 27 and 31 of the SIF Law and articles 25 and 29 of the RAIF Law.

MANAGEMENT

4.251 Unless more specific rules are set out in the 2010 Law, the SIF Law or the RAIF Law, the provisions of the Luxembourg Law of 10 August 1915 on commercial companies (the '1915 Law') apply to any SICAV. One consequence is that at the time of their incorporation, SICAVs must adhere to the provisions of the 1915 Law as to the minimum capital required for each legal form[1]. However, pursuant to the 2010 Law, the SIF Law and the RAIF Law, the subscribed share capital[2] of a SICAV may not be less than €1.25 million[3].

[1] See footnote 3 to para **4.246** above; the minimum capital for an SCA is also €30,000.
[2] For a SICAV working with a commitments and drawdowns mechanism, at the latest once all drawdowns have been made, the reference in the relevant law should be read as a reference to such drawn-down capital, and not only to the subscribed (committed) capital.
[3] The same rule also applies to FCPs; such subscribed capital must be reached within six months (for SICAVs and FCPs subject to the 2010 Law) or 12 months (for SIFs and RAIFs). It should be noted that in the case of SIFs and RAIFs whose structure reflects commitments and capital calls, it is sufficient that the relevant amount is committed to the relevant fund.

4.252 In accordance with the 1915 Law, SICAVs established in the form of an SA are typically managed by a board of directors which comprises at least three members[1]. The three partnership structures are typically managed by a general partner, although the 1915 Law also allows the SCS and the SCSp the flexibility to entrust the management function to a third party manager. The SARL may be managed by a single manager or by a board of managers.

[1] It is also possible to use a two-tier structure for the management of an SA, that is, to divide its management between a management board and a supervisory board (similar to the concept of a German *Aktiengesellschaft*). However, in practice such possibility is extremely rare as it mainly increases the operational complexity.

4.253 For the SA, SCA and the SARL important decisions concerning the company, such as amendments to its articles of incorporation, have to be made at a general meeting of shareholders. At least one such general meeting must be held in each year, during which the reports of the board of directors and auditors are reviewed, the annual accounts are approved and the directors and auditors are discharged (or dismissed, as the case may be). In practice, the shareholders of a SICAV do not use their voting rights very often. It should not, however, be assumed that a general meeting of shareholders will never exercise an influence over the management of the SICAV or its investment policy. This is particularly true for the SA which can at any time remove its board of directors.

4.254 Onshore Fund Domiciles

4.254 The SCS and SCSp are more flexible in terms of corporate governance, and the 1915 Law has made it clear that their limited partnership agreements can freely determine such mechanisms. However, limited partners are not permitted to be involved in the management of the partnership vis-à-vis third parties.

Umbrella funds with multiple compartments

4.255 The 2010 Law, as well as the SIF Law and the RAIF Law, permit the creation of umbrella funds[1]. These are funds formed as FCPs or SICAVs with several sub-funds within a single legal entity, where each sub-fund corresponds to a distinct portfolio of assets and liabilities of such UCI. The umbrella structure allows for a single UCI to have a number of sub-funds, each of which may have a different investment policy, a different base currency and different types of investors. Each investor determines the sub-fund of the UCI in which it wishes to subscribe for units or shares and, by such subscription, participates in the gains or losses which the relevant sub-fund realises. Due to its practical advantages, an umbrella structure is frequently chosen for Luxembourg investment funds. 64% of all Luxembourg investment funds are established as an umbrella, and there are currently almost 13,300 compartments in total that have been established[2].

[1] Cf article 181 of the 2010 Law, article 71 of the SIF Law and article 49 of the RAIF Law.
[2] As at February 2018 (source: CSSF); this figure does not include RAIFs as these are not subject to the supervision of the CSSF and therefore no reliable statistical data exists for them.

4.256 An umbrella fund as a whole constitutes a single legal entity. This implies that an umbrella fund can only be governed by one specific set of rules. It is not possible, for example, to establish an umbrella fund where one sub-fund is subject to the provisions of Part I of the 2010 Law while other sub-funds are subject to the provisions of Part II of the 2010 Law or to the SIF Law.

4.257 The different sub-funds of an umbrella UCI do not have a separate legal personality and, as a consequence, cannot enter into any agreements themselves. It is therefore the umbrella UCI (or its management company in the case of an FCP, or the general partner in the case of a partnership) that acts in respect of the sub-fund(s) and concludes any agreements on behalf of the relevant sub-fund(s).

4.258 In accordance with the provisions of the 2010 Law, the SIF Law and the RAIF Law, umbrella funds may be established if the constitutional documents expressly provide for such possibility and the specific investment policy of each sub-fund is described in the prospectus or offering document of the umbrella fund. Each sub-fund is only responsible for its own debts, engagements and other obligations, unless its constitutional documents provide otherwise. As a result of such ring-fencing, under Luxembourg law, the creditors of a sub-fund only have recourse against the assets of a specific sub-fund and do not have recourse to the assets of other sub-funds of the same umbrella fund. Each sub-fund of an umbrella fund is therefore protected under Luxembourg law against the insolvency of other sub-funds of the same structure.

4.259 An additional advantage of an umbrella structure lies in the fact that only a single depositary and central administration agent is required, and only a single audit is carried out for the umbrella fund encompassing all sub-funds. Although this also provides less of a choice for fund sponsors, it simplifies the operational process and will typically result in lower fees for these service providers, due to economies of scale.

4.260 Furthermore, once the umbrella fund with its documentation and service providers has been approved by the CSSF, the establishment of any additional sub-fund can usually be done in a more timely fashion than establishing a completely new UCI. Only the additional provisions relating to such new sub-fund will have to be approved by the CSSF and no recourse to a notary for its establishment will be necessary.

4.261 To a more limited extent this advantage also applies to RAIFs which do not need to be approved by the CSSF, as even for these funds the existing organisational structure and contractual relationship with their service providers remains identical, thus accelerating considerably the time to market for additional sub-funds that are added to an existing RAIF umbrella.

4.262 Within an umbrella fund, investors may be granted the right to convert their shares or units in one sub-fund into shares or units in another sub-fund of that umbrella fund. In general, conversion from one sub-fund to another sub-fund within the same umbrella fund does not give rise to the payment of commissions (except if there is a difference in the level of sales commissions charged in relation to the relevant sub-funds).

Service providers required for investment funds

Management companies

4.263 As described above[1], any FCP requires a Luxembourg management company to act for it. This is not necessarily true for SICAVs as they (or their general partner in partnerships) have a legal personality of their own. However, in the case of UCITS the appointment of a management company is standard market practice, as otherwise the SICAV itself would need to comply with all applicable substance requirements[2]. Although these so-called 'self-managed' SICAVs exist, it is a model that is in the process of being abandoned. On the one hand, it is more efficient and less costly to use a third party management company to provide the relevant substance, and on the other hand, some countries such as Switzerland have difficulties accepting self-managed SICAVs due to pretended lack of substance, which causes difficulty for their distribution.

[1] See para **4.228** above.
[2] See article 17 of the 2010 Law.

4.264 SICAVs that are not subject to the UCITS regime and its substance requirements do not usually appoint a management company, except as a service provider for specific tasks such as portfolio management, risk management or to act as their central administration agent.

4.265 Onshore Fund Domiciles

Alternative investment fund managers

4.265 Funds that are subject to Part II of the 2010 Law, as well as RAIFs, are per se alternative investment funds within the meaning of the 2013 Law and therefore have to appoint a fully licensed AIFM[1]. This can be an entity located in Luxembourg or elsewhere in the EU, and through the passport of such AIFM the relevant fund can be publicly marketed within the EU. It is also possible to appoint AIFMs established outside the EU and to delegate the portfolio and risk management to such an entity. However, as the passport for third countries has not yet been implemented under AIFMD, the distribution and marketing of such fund would mostly be limited to private placement.

[1] Article 88-1 of the 2010 Law and article 4(1) of the RAIF Law. Exceptions to this principle only apply in very limited circumstances in relation to RAIFs.

4.266 SIFs may, under certain circumstances, such as where they fall under one of the exemptions of the 2013 Law, not be considered as AIFs and therefore would not need to appoint a fully licensed AIFM[1]. They could either perform the portfolio and risk management functions themselves or appoint an entity that is a registered AIFM to fulfil those functions. In the case of partnerships, the general partner often assumes those functions.

[1] See article 2bis of the SIF Law. If a SIF falls within the scope of the 2013 Law, Part II of the SIF Law applies.

4.267 Among its, currently, more than 220 AIFMs, Luxembourg offers a wide choice for fund sponsors. Many of these are specialised in certain asset classes, and whilst in the majority of cases portfolio management is delegated to an entity outside Luxembourg, there are more and more AIFMs located in Luxembourg that also offer these services.

Depositary

4.268 As a general rule, all Luxembourg investment funds must appoint a depositary[1], which must either be a bank established as a Luxembourg corporation or a Luxembourg branch of a foreign bank. In the case of closed-ended funds that invest in assets that are typically not taken 'into custody' (such as private equity or real estate funds), such role can also be assumed by a depositary which is subject to a lighter supervisory regime[2].

[1] Articles 17, 33, 90 and 95 of the 2010 Law, articles 16 and 33 of the SIF Law and article 5 of the RAIF Law.
[2] See Article 26-1 of the Law of 5 April 1993 on the financial sector (the '1993 Law').

4.269 The depositary is entrusted with the custody of the assets of the fund. Since the transposition of AIFMD as well as UCITS V, the term 'custody' is defined in great detail. It means an obligation of safekeeping in respect of transferable securities, a duty of record-keeping and ownership verification for other assets, and a monitoring obligation concerning cash and other liquid assets. These rules, set out in the 2010 Law[1] and the 2013 Law[2], as well as the Commission Delegated Regulation (EU) 2016/438 of 17 December 2015, are supplemented for UCITS by CSSF Circular 16/644. For SIFs that are not AIFs, a lighter regime under the SIF Law applies[3]. The applicable depositary regime for Part II funds has recently been clarified: only Part II funds distributed to retail investors in Luxembourg are subject to a depositary regime similar to the UCITS depositary regime, whereas all other Part II funds fall under the AIFM depositary regime[4].

[1] Article 18 et seq and article 34 et seq of the 2010 Law.
[2] Article 19 of the 2013 Law.
[3] Article 16 et seq and article 34 et seq of the SIF Law.
[4] See draft bill of law no 7024, which was expected to enter into force between March and May 2018.

4.270 Until recently, hedge funds frequently used a prime broker that often held the majority, if not all, of their assets. Since the transposition of UCITS V and AIFMD into Luxembourg law[1], the depositary remains, in principle, responsible for the restitution of the relevant fund's assets. Such duty of restitution is independent of a delegation of the safekeeping functions to another bank[2] and therefore a liability unrelated to any breach of contract of the depositary itself. Therefore, the delegation itself needs to comply with a number of requirements[3].

[1] See also Article 91 of Commission Delegated Regulation (EU) No 231/2013 of 19 December 2012 for reporting obligations for prime brokers.
[2] Articles 19(1) and 35(1) of the 2010 Law and article 19(12) of the 2013 Law.
[3] Articles 18bis and 34bis of the 2010 Law and article 19(11) of the 2013 Law.

4.271 As a consequence of these additional rules and the obligation resulting therefrom to appoint the prime broker as a sub-depositary, as well as the ultimate liability of the Luxembourg depositary for the restitution of the relevant fund's assets, the preliminary due diligence to be made in relation to the prime broker and the operational procedures which are put in place between depositaries and prime brokers have become substantially more complex. Therefore, depositaries can usually only deal with a limited number of prime brokers, and the sponsor of a hedge fund that intends to employ a specific prime broker should verify whether the relevant depositary is able to establish such a relationship without undue difficulty.

Central administration

4.272 Certain administrative tasks (sometimes referred to as 'central administration tasks') need to be carried out in relation to each Luxembourg investment fund. These include the following:

- keeping the fund's accounts;
- keeping the share register of the fund;
- effecting the issue and redemption of shares or units;
- drafting and updating the prospectus and financial reports;
- sending notices and reports to investors; and
- calculation of the net asset value.

4.273 Typically, the relevant fund or its management company delegate these tasks to an appropriate service provider. This would, in principle, need to be a Luxembourg service provider, and Luxembourg has a considerable network of these service providers. Where a Luxembourg UCITS is managed by a

4.273 Onshore Fund Domiciles

foreign management company, these services could also be provided by a foreign service provider. In the case of AIFs such as a SIF or a RAIF, these services could be provided by the relevant AIFM[1].

[1] See Annex I of the 2013 Law.

4.274 The provision of the above central administration tasks in Luxembourg does not preclude the use of a computing network based outside Luxembourg for technical support, nor does it prevent a fund from employing distributors, nominees and other intermediaries for placement activities and for the redemption of shares and units.

Auditor

4.275 Every UCI (including RAIFs) as well as any Luxembourg management company and AIFM must appoint an independent Luxembourg auditor to review its annual accounts. Since 2009, auditors have been subject to the provisions of a specific law[1] and are registered on an official list which is maintained by the CSSF.

[1] The Law of 18 December 2009 on the Audit Profession, replaced by the Law of 23 July 2016 on the Audit Profession.

4.276 Where UCIs which are subject to the supervision of the CSSF, the auditor has additional tasks such as the establishment of a so-called long form report (for UCITS and Part II funds)[1], transmitting information to the CSSF and performing specific audit tasks when requested to do so by the CSSF[2].

[1] See CSSF Circular 02/81.
[2] See Article 154(3) of the 2010 Law and article 55(3) of the SIF Law.

Hedge funds for retail investors

UCITS with hedge fund strategies: Newcits

4.277 Whilst the use of derivative instruments has been possible for UCITS since the transposition of UCITS III into Luxembourg law, and therefore UCITS were already able to use hedge fund related strategies (such as long-short equity, global macro and convertible arbitrage), the major inflow into this sector started in the aftermath of the financial crisis and the Madoff scandal in the US. The appetite of managers and investors of hedge funds established in offshore jurisdictions such as the Cayman Islands diminished, the liquidity and the pan-European marketing passport available under the UCITS regime became more attractive. As a consequence, in the last two years the total assets under management of alternative UCITS (the term 'Newcits' is also sometimes used) has increased from approximately €260 billion to €469 billion[1].

[1] As at 31 January 2018 (source: LuxHedge – see http://www.luxhedge.com).

4.278 Although this is still only a small portion of the entire UCITS market, it can be expected that the alternative UCITS market will grow further over the coming years[1]. As the fixed income markets (in which a large portion of UCITS invest) do not continue to perform well, investors and fund sponsors are looking for alternative ways to generate returns.

[1] Deutsche Bank Global Prime Finance, 2016 Alternative UCITS Survey, October 2016.

4.279 The stricter regulation of UCITS – which can appeal to investors due to a higher level of investor protection and liquidity – also imposes limits on alternative UCITS which traditional hedge funds do not have to deal with. For instance, physical short sales are prohibited for UCITS[1], the global exposure relating to derivative instruments is limited to the total net asset value[2] and borrowing is not allowed[3]. In addition, a high level of diversification is required. The exposure to a single underlying asset for derivatives is limited to between 5% and 10%[4]. However, due to the clarifications provided in Commission Directive 2007/16/EC that was transposed into Luxembourg law through a Grand-Ducal Regulation dated 8 February 2008[5], a significant number of strategies can nevertheless be implemented through synthetic shorting and the use of over-the-counter ('OTC') derivatives or structured products. Also, the growing market for alternative UCITS opens up the possibility of establishing fund of hedge funds products in Luxembourg.

[1] Article 52 of the 2010 Law.
[2] Article 42(3) of the 2010 Law.
[3] Article 50 of the 2010 Law.
[4] Article 43(1) of the 2010 Law.
[5] Published in the official Luxembourg gazette, *Mémorial A* No 19 of 19 February 2008.

4.280 Luxembourg, in its role as the major domicile for UCITS in the EU by a fairly large margin, is ideally suited to offer hedge fund sponsors an environment where it is straightforward to establish alternative UCITS. In particular, a substantial number of service providers such as management companies and central administration agents exist in Luxembourg which are specialised in providing services for UCITS that wish to pursue alternative strategies, not least in terms of distribution within and outside the EU.

UCIs pursuant to Part II of the 2010 Law

4.281 Whilst the permitted investment policies and investment restrictions for UCITS established under the UCITS Directive are set out in detail under Part I of the 2010 Law[1], Part II of the 2010 Law does not restrict the types of investment strategies that can be used by such UCIs or impose diversification requirements on such UCIs. Indeed, the 2010 Law only obliges UCIs to follow the principle of risk diversification[2]. Therefore, the applicable rules have been set out for the most part in Circular 02/80. As a consequence of the absence of risk diversification requirements set out by law, the CSSF may approve provisions that are more flexible than those set out in the circular, subject to being provided with a reasonable justification for doing so. Following below is an overview of a number of issues set out in Circular 02/80 that are of particular importance to hedge funds.

[1] Article 41 et seq of the 2010 Law.
[2] Articles 89(1) and 93 of the 2010 Law.

4.282 *Onshore Fund Domiciles*

RISK DIVERSIFICATION

4.282 Pursuant to Circular 02/80, hedge funds subject to Part II of the 2010 Law may not invest more than 20% of their assets in securities issued by the same issuer. Furthermore, those hedge fund may not, in principle, (i) acquire more than 10% of the securities of the same kind issued by the same issuer, and (ii) invest more than 10% of their assets in transferable securities which are not admitted or dealt in on a regulated market. Such rules are not applicable to funds that exclusively invest in other UCIs, for which separate rules exist[1].

[1] See para 4.287 below.

SHORT SALES

4.283 Unlike UCITS, UCIs established under Part II of the 2010 Law may perform physical short sales. Circular 02/80 sets out conditions for risk diversification regarding short sales and imposes liquidity requirements where a fund holds short positions. For example, a UCI may hold short positions in transferable securities which are not quoted and not dealt on a regulated market, but only if such securities are highly liquid and do not represent more than 10% of the assets of the UCI. Other liquidity provisions include a requirement that a UCI may not take a short position in transferable securities where that position represents more than 10% of the securities of the same type issued by the same issuer. Short positions in transferable securities of the same issuer are also prohibited if the aggregate amount of the initial sales price of the relevant position represents more than 10% of the assets of the fund or the commitment in relation to that short position exceeds 5% of the fund's assets.

BORROWING

4.284 Circular 02/80 permits hedge funds and funds of hedge funds which are subject to Part II of the 2010 Law to borrow permanently for investment purposes. Leveraging in this context is, in principle, limited to 200% of the net assets of the relevant UCI. However, UCIs pursuing a strategy which entails a high degree of correlation between long positions and short positions are authorised to borrow up to 400% of their net assets.

DERIVATIVE FINANCIAL INSTRUMENTS

4.285 Under Circular 02/80, the use of both derivative financial instruments dealt in on an organised market and OTC instruments is permitted, provided that the OTC instruments are entered into with first class professionals which specialise in these types of transactions. The derivative financial instruments used may include options, forward contracts in financial instruments and options on such contracts, as well as swap contracts by private agreement on any type of financial instruments.

4.286 The use of such instruments requires a disclosure of the maximum leverage and of the risks resulting from such use in the prospectus of the relevant fund. The UCIs furthermore have to comply with, among others[1], the following diversification rules in relation to derivative instruments:

- margin deposits may not exceed 50% of the assets of the UCI;
- the UCI may not borrow to finance margin deposits;
- the UCI may not hold an open position in any single contract for which the required margin represents 5% or more of its assets; and
- the UCI may not hold an open position in derivative financial instruments relating to a single commodity or a single category of financial futures for which the required margin represents 20% or more of its assets.

[1] For an exhaustive list, see Chapter E1 of Circular 02/80.

Investment in other UCIs (funds of hedge funds)

4.287 UCIs which are subject to the provisions of Circular 02/80 are permitted to invest in securities issued by other open-ended UCIs[1]. In principle, investment in securities issued by the same UCI is limited to not more than 20% of the fund's net assets. However, where an umbrella fund is the investment target, each sub-fund of such umbrella structure is treated as a distinct UCI, provided that the segregation of the commitments of the different sub-funds towards third parties is ensured. Furthermore, it is also permissible to hold more than 50% of the units of a target UCI on the condition that, if the target UCI is an umbrella fund, the investment in the target UCI represents less than 50% of the net assets of the fund making the investment.

[1] Closed-ended UCIs are considered to be transferable securities, so that in this respect the rules set out at para **4.282** above apply.

Fund vehicles for sophisticated investors

Definition of the term 'well-informed investor'

4.288 Unlike UCITS and UCIs subject to Part II of the 2010 Law which can be marketed to any investor, including retail investors, the SIF and the RAIF are only available to so-called 'well-informed investors'[1]. Under both of these laws, that term includes three categories: institutional investors, professional investors and other (individual) investors.

[1] Article 2 of the SIF Law and article 2 of the RAIF Law.

4.289 Whilst the notion of a 'professional investor' is defined under MiFID[1], no definition of the term of 'institutional investor' is provided in any Luxembourg law. It was first used in the 1991 Law, and further details as to its meaning can be found in the parliamentary documents of that period[2]. That term includes professionals of the financial sector[3] (such as investment firms), insurance companies, pension funds, large financial corporations, social security institutions and local authorities investing their own funds. Where a discretionary management mandate exists, financial institutions investing their clients' monies can also qualify as institutional investors. Furthermore, any investment fund is per se considered to be an institutional investor.

[1] See article 1(5) of the 1993 Law, together with its Annex III.
[2] Parliamentary document No 3467, comments on the articles (3).

4.289 *Onshore Fund Domiciles*

[3] This is a translation of the French term *professionnel du secteur financier* which defines the entities such as banks and other service providers pursuant to the 1993 Law and supervised by the CSSF.

4.290 The third category of well-informed investors is individual investors who must comply with two conditions. First, the relevant person needs to confirm in writing that he adheres to the status of well-informed investor[1]. Second, he needs to either invest a minimum of €125,000 in the relevant fund or provide a certificate from a bank or investment firm that confirms his experience and knowledge. In practice, the second alternative is rarely used, as the relevant issuer is liable for its assessment.

[1] Such confirmation is typically given in the relevant subscription documentation.

4.291 The above conditions do not apply to persons involved in the management of the relevant SIF or RAIF. It is assumed that its directors, managers and staff have the relevant expertise and experience to assess an investment in such vehicle. They can therefore become investors in the relevant SIF or RAIF.

4.292 It should be mentioned in this context that the marketing passport granted to the AIFM that manages the relevant RAIF or SIF only extends to distribution to professional investors within the EU[1]. As a consequence, a distribution of shares to private individuals outside Luxembourg would need to be carried out in accordance with the relevant jurisdiction and may be prohibited or limited to private placement.

[1] For AIFMs in Luxembourg, see article 29 of the 2013 Law.

Specialised investment funds

4.293 Out of all the Luxembourg investment vehicles, the SIF represents the most flexible option for fund sponsors that do not seek (public) distribution to retail investors and seek a product that is regulated by the CSSF. Since the transposition of AIFMD into Luxembourg law, the SIF Law is divided in two parts: the first part deals with general provisions that apply to all SIFs, and the second part deals with the specific requirements for SIFs that are AIFs and therefore need to appoint an AIFM.

4.294 SIFs which do not qualify as AIFs must still comply with a number of rules in relation to the persons which have the responsibility for portfolio management. These persons require prior CSSF approval and need to be of sufficiently good repute as well as have the necessary experience[1]. So far as the delegation of portfolio management is concerned, the relevant delegate must, in principle, be a regulated entity, although it is possible to appoint individual persons or an entity without any licence in this respect[2]. The CSSF is, however, reluctant to approve individuals to have responsibility for portfolio management and has a clear preference for delegation to a regulated corporate entity.

[1] Article 42(4) of the SIF Law.
[2] Article 42b(b) of the SIF Law. Article 42b(c) also provides for the possibility to appoint an unregulated manager.

4.295 In any event, appropriate risk management procedures and conflict of interest policies need to be in place[1].

[1] Article 42a of the SIF Law.

RISK DIVERSIFICATION

4.296 As with UCIs which are subject to Part II of the 2010 Law, the SIF Law only imposes a requirement to follow the principle of risk diversification[1]. The CSSF has, however, given further guidance in CSSF Circular 07/309 ('Circular 07/309'), which is substantially more flexible than Circular 02/80 or the UCITS provisions. It sets out the main principle that a SIF may not invest more than 30% of its assets or of its commitments in securities of the same kind issued by the same issuer. As a consequence, it would be sufficient to invest in securities of four different issuers in order to comply with such rule.

[1] Articles 4 and 25 of the SIF Law. This principle applies for each sub-fund separately.

SHORT SALES

4.297 In terms of short sales, the only restriction imposed by Circular 07/309 is that uncovered sales may not, in principle, cause a SIF to hold an uncovered position in securities of the same kind issued by the same issuer which represent more than 30% of its assets.

BORROWING

4.298 Neither Circular 07/309 nor the SIF Law provides for any precise limit on the use of borrowing. In practice, the CSSF authorises borrowings without further justification within the same limits as under Circular 02/80. However, in view of the fact that SIFs are aimed at well-informed investors, the CSSF may approve borrowings in excess of such limits on a case-by-case basis and with appropriate justification.

DERIVATIVE FINANCIAL INSTRUMENTS

4.299 Under Circular 07/309, when using financial derivative instruments, a SIF must ensure a risk diversification comparable to the requirements for direct investments into securities, by means of an appropriate diversification of the underlying assets. This means that no more than 30% of the relevant SIF's assets (or its commitments) may be invested in a single financial derivative instrument. In the case of an OTC transaction, the relevant counterparty risk to which the SIF is exposed must be limited according to the quality and the qualification of the counterparty. In this respect, the CSSF generally assumes that the counterparty risk should not exceed 30% of the relevant SIF's assets. More flexibility may, however, be granted on a case-by-case basis.

INVESTMENT IN OTHER UCIS (FUNDS OF HEDGE FUNDS)

4.300 The limit of 20% set out under Circular 02/80 is raised to 30% under Circular 07/309 for UCIs which invest in other UCIs. Furthermore, a SIF may

4.300 Onshore Fund Domiciles

invest more than 30% of its assets in the same fund, provided that that fund itself is subject to risk diversification requirements at least comparable to those applicable to SIFs.

4.301 That means it is also possible to establish master-feeder structures whereby a SIF invests substantially all of its assets in a single fund. However, it should be kept in mind that where the SIF qualifies as an AIF, its AIFM can only use the EU marketing passport in relation to that SIF under the condition that the master fund is also an AIF established in the EU[1].

[1] Article 29(1) of the 2013 Law.

Reserved alternative investment funds

4.302 As the RAIF Law is to a large extent based on the SIF Law, it similarly imposes the general obligation that each RAIF must adhere to the principle of risk diversification[1]. However, due to the absence of any direct supervision by the CSSF, there are currently no specific guidelines as to how RAIFs may comply with the principle of risk diversification. There is a tendency to use Circular 07/309 as an indication in this respect, even if it cannot be considered as binding and different rules could be put in place for a given RAIF.

[1] Article 1(1)(b) of the RAIF Law.

4.303 Even though RAIFs do not need to be authorised by the CSSF, they nevertheless have to prepare an offering document and an annual report, as a SIF does[1]. The contents of both the offering document and the annual report need to take into account the requirements of the 2013 Law in this respect[2].

[1] Article 38(1) of the RAIF Law.
[2] Articles 38(4) and 41 of the RAIF Law and articles 20 and 21 of the 2013 Law.

4.304 In this context it should also be mentioned that it is possible to convert an existing SIF into a RAIF, or vice versa. Similarly, it is also possible to convert an unregulated special limited partnership into a RAIF.

Unregulated special limited partnership qualifying as an AIF

4.305 As a consequence of the transposition of AIFMD into Luxembourg law, vehicles that are not subject to any specific investment fund related legislation can qualify as an AIF[1]. Prior to the enactment of the RAIF Law, this possibility was used in particular in order to provide a quicker time to market for such AIFs and to avoid any delays caused by an approval procedure with the CSSF. As ordinary commercial companies cannot benefit from a favourable tax treatment under Luxembourg law that is available under Luxembourg investment fund laws, the most popular vehicle was typically the special limited partnership[2]. Due to its lack of legal personality and partnership attributes, it was generally accepted as being tax transparent. In addition, its flexibility and closeness to the limited partnership legislation available in many common law jurisdictions was attractive. It is also frequently used for AIFs which, due to one of the sub-threshold exemptions, do not need to appoint a fully licensed AIFM but can function as an internally managed AIFM that is only subject to a registration requirement with the CSSF[3]. It should be mentioned, however, that since a recent reform of the 1915 Law, the common limited partnership (*société en commandite simple*)[4] offers many of the same advantages and is therefore frequently used for the same purpose, the main difference being that it has a legal personality (as opposed to the absence thereof for the special limited partnership)[5].

[1] See article 1(39) of the 2013 Law for the definition of an AIF.
[2] Article 320-1 et seq of the 1915 Law.
[3] Article 3(2) of the 2013 Law.
[4] See article 310-1 et seq of the 1915 Law.
[5] See article 100-2 of the 1915 Law.

4.306 There are also some disadvantages of using such a structure instead of a dedicated investment fund vehicle. First, an unregulated special limited partnership cannot be established in the form of an umbrella fund with several compartments. Second, a RAIF or a SIF can be established using other corporate forms than the special limited partnership due to the applicable tax exemption. However, in particular since the enactment of the RAIF Law, there is an alternative to an unregulated special limited partnership that combines the advantages of a quick time to market with a wide range of structuring possibilities as well as a tax exemption, subject to the need to appoint a fully licensed AIFM.

Process for establishing an investment fund in Luxembourg

4.307 A distinction needs to be made in particular between investment funds that require prior CSSF approval (such as the UCIs subject to the 2010 Law and SIFs) and those that can be established without the intervention of the regulator (such as RAIFs and unregulated partnership structures).

Regulated investment funds: prior CSSF approval

UCIs subject to the 2010 Law

4.308 All UCIs that are subject to the 2010 Law must, in order to carry out their activities, be previously authorised by the CSSF[1]. In order to receive such approval, a written application based on several standard forms[2] must be filed with the CSSF. The main documents which need to be submitted to the CSSF are as follows:

- drafts of the constitutional documents (that is, management regulations for an FCP or articles of incorporation for a SICAV) and the prospectus[3];
- documentation in relation to the directors of the fund (in the case of a SICAV);
- draft agreements to be entered into between the fund and its service providers (such as depositary, central administration agent, investment manager and distributor); and
- description of the risk management process (for UCIs subject to Part I

4.308 *Onshore Fund Domiciles*

of the 2010 Law).

[1] Article 129(1) of the 2010 Law.
[2] All such forms can be found online at http://www.cssf.lu/surveillance/vgi/opcvm/formulaires.
[3] For UCITS subject to Part I of the 2010 Law, a draft of the Key Investor Information Document must also be submitted.

4.309 These documents can be submitted in French, English or German. The CSSF reviews the documents and provides comments or questions in relation to them. Once any requested documentation has been provided and the CSSF is satisfied with the answers to its questions, the CSSF will provide written approval of the relevant fund. The approval is finally put into effect by registering the relevant fund on the official list of Luxembourg funds[1], which is published in the official gazette and is available to the public.

[1] Article 130 of the 2010 Law. The list can also be consulted on the CSSF's website – see http://www.cssf.lu.

4.310 The marketing of units or shares in such UCIs can be carried out from the day of such registration. However, in practice, the CSSF issues a verbal approval some time prior to the registration of the UCI on the official list. At that time, the relevant fund can be established and marketed, as the inscription on the official list has a retrospective effect to the time of verbal approval. As a consequence, as soon as such verbal approval is received, the fund can be incorporated (in the case of a SICAV) or established by the management company by issuing the management regulations (in the case of an FCP). At such time, the relevant agreements with the service providers also need to be executed.

SPECIALISED INVESTMENT FUNDS

4.311 For some time after the SIF Law was first enacted, it was possible to establish a SIF without requiring prior approval from the CSSF, which could be sought afterwards. However, this flexibility was removed through a revision of the SIF Law in 2012 and since then all SIFs have to request prior approval of the CSSF.

4.312 As a consequence, the process for establishing a SIF is similar to that for establishing the investment funds subject to the 2010 Law, including the documentation that has to be filed with the CSSF for approval. The additional requirements of AIFMD also need to be taken into account.

Reserved alternative investment funds

4.313 As the RAIF is not subject to the supervision of the CSSF, no approval process is necessary. However, it should be kept in mind that due to the requirement to appoint a fully licensed AIFM, the regulator of such AIFM is in charge of verifying the compliance of the AIFs managed by that AIFM with the AIFMD provisions as transposed in the relevant jurisdiction. As a consequence, the relevant AIFM will, in its own interest, conduct a thorough review of the documentation of the RAIF and verify its compliance with the provisions of the 2013 Law.

4.314 Consequently, the time required to establish a RAIF depends on a number of variables: (i) whether the service providers (depositary, central administration, AIFM and auditor) have been identified and are ready and willing to work together from an operational perspective; (ii) the complexity of the proposed RAIF, which will influence how much time is needed for the drafting of the documentation; (iii) the time required for the review of this documentation by the AIFM; and (iv) the familiarity of the fund sponsor with the Luxembourg regulatory and corporate rules.

4.315 The final steps in terms for incorporating a RAIF are similar to those for other investment vehicles: in the case of a RAIF in the form of a SICAV, the founding shareholder(s) subscribes for the minimum capital and incorporates the company; the presence of a notary is required for certain corporate forms pursuant to the provisions of the 1915 Law (SA, SCA, SARL), while for RAIFs that can be established under private seal (SCS, SCSp), the notary has to make a record of their constitution within five days[1]. For a RAIF in the form of an FCP, the mere execution of the management regulations is sufficient, although that again has to be evidenced by way of a notarial deed. Following this, the service provider agreements need to be executed, and any RAIF has to be registered with the Luxembourg commercial register within ten days of its establishment.

[1] Article 34(1) of the RAIF Law which provides that the constitution of any RAIF has to be recorded by a notary. The aim of the legislator was clearly to involve a notary even where this was not required by other corporate rules. As a consequence, it is obvious that in relation to companies where the 1915 Law already requires their establishment through notarial deed (eg SA or SARL), such recording of the constitution is made by way of the notarial deed of its constitution and there is no additional deed required. The diverging view of the Luxembourg Chamber of Notaries in this respect (Circular 17/2016 dated 2 August 2016), claiming that two separate notarial deeds were required even in this case, has no foundation in law, its objective or the intention of the legislator.

Special limited partnerships

4.316 Pursuant to the 1915 Law, a special limited partnership can be established under private seal and does not require the participation of a notary. The mere act of signing the relevant limited partnership agreement between a general partner[1] and at least one limited partner is therefore sufficient for the establishment of a special limited partnership. Unlike other corporate forms, there are also no minimum capital requirements which need to be complied with.

[1] It should be noted, however, that due to the fact that the general partner is typically established in the form of a SARL, it would need to be incorporated (with a notary) before the partnership could be established.

Taxation

Taxation of Luxembourg investment funds

4.317 UCIs subject to the 2010 Law and to the SIF Law, as well as RAIFs, benefit from a general exemption from tax under Luxembourg law so that only

4.317 Onshore Fund Domiciles

a limited taxation regime applies. Indeed, all of these vehicles are only subject to an annual subscription tax (*taxe d'abonnement*) calculated on the basis of the relevant fund's net assets[1].

[1] Article 173 of the 2010 Law, article 66 of the SIF Law and article 45 of the RAIF Law.

4.318 The rate of the subscription tax is 0.05% per annum for UCIs subject to the 2010 Law and 0.01% per annum for SIFs and RAIFs with the features of a SIF. For UCITS and UCIs subject to Part II of the 2010 Law, the securities of which are marketed exclusively to institutional investors, the rate is reduced to 0.01% per annum.

4.319 In addition, in the following cases the relevant funds may be entirely exempt from the subscription tax:

- in relation to assets held which have already been subject to the subscription tax (due to an investment into other Luxembourg UCIs);
- UCIs that are money market funds; and
- UCIs the securities of which are reserved for issue to occupational retirement institutions and similar vehicles.

4.320 As regards unregulated fund structures such as a Luxembourg partnership (SCS or SCSp), these can generally be structured in a tax neutral fashion for Luxembourg tax purposes (due to their tax transparency).

Taxation of investors

4.321 Foreign investors having no taxable presence in Luxembourg are generally not subject to taxation in Luxembourg.

4.322 Investors, whether foreign or Luxembourg residents, which invest in FCPs or SICAVs (such as investment funds subject to the 2010 Law, SIFs or RAIFs) are not subject to withholding taxes in Luxembourg on distributions made by those FCPs or SICAVs.

4.323 Investors, whether foreign or Luxembourg residents, which invest in an unregulated fund in the form of a Luxembourg partnership (SCS or SCSp) are not subject to withholding taxes in Luxembourg on distributions made by such partnership.

D   MALTA

David Borg-Carbott, Senior Associate, GANADO Advocates, Malta

Introduction

4.324 The Republic of Malta is the smallest member state of the EU and one of the smallest sovereign states in the world. Malta joined the EU as a full member state in 2004 and adopted the euro as its national currency in 2008. Situated in the Mediterranean Sea approximately 50 miles south of Sicily (Italy) and 207 miles north of North Africa, Malta shares the same time zone as Berlin, Paris and Rome (CET, one hour ahead of GMT).

4.325 Due in no small part to its history as a British colony (1800–1964), most Maltese are native English speakers (typically bilingual together with the Maltese language or trilingual with Italian or French as a third language). English is both the business language as well as one of the two official languages, with all laws published in both English and Maltese.

4.326 Malta comprises an archipelago of three inhabited islands with a land mass of 122 square miles and a population of approximately 400,000. Malta is one of the most densely populated countries in the world and yet arguably one of the best places to work and live[1]. Blessed with the Mediterranean climate and lifestyle, deep natural harbours and idyllic beaches, a rich cultural heritage and, according to the United Nations' World Risk Report[2], the second safest country in the world, it is no wonder that Malta's economy was historically focused on maritime trade, tourism and as a prime retirement destination.

[1] Best climate on earth (tied first) and third best quality of life in the world (after US and New Zealand), both by International Living Magazine (2011). See further https://internationalliving.com/countries/malta.
[2] See http://www.WorldRiskReport.org.

4.327 In the past 25 or so years, Malta has successfully developed a well-diversified service economy with relatively new knowledge-based sectors such as information and communications technology, financial services, electronics manufacturing and pharmaceuticals, which have increasingly become mainstays of the economy. As one of the most resilient Euro-zone economies during the 2008/09 financial crisis, Malta's economy continues to buck the trend within the Euro-zone and remains one of the fastest-growing economies in Europe[1].

[1] IMF Country Report No 18/19 on Malta (January 2018) – see http://www.imf.org/en/Countries/MLT.

4.328 Reflecting its diverse history, Malta's legal system is a hybrid system with common law elements such as its company, banking, maritime, tax, trust and administrative laws, which are based on English law, superimposed over a codified civil law system owing its origins to Napoleonic laws. As an EU member state with one of the quickest rates of transposition of EU law into Maltese law, Maltese law also incorporates all EU legislation which is in force.

The finance industry

4.329 Malta was a late-bloomer, in that its foray into becoming a financial centre began in about 1989 with the adoption of a suite of, then in vogue, offshore-focused legislation and the establishment of the Malta International Business Authority. The experiment proved to be a disappointment and just four years later, perhaps with premonition, Malta reversed course. In 1994, Malta overhauled its financial services legislation, replacing the offshore-focused legislation with a suite of firmly onshore legislation reflecting equivalent legislation in force in other EU countries (notably that in the UK) and the establishment of a single regulator for financial services, now called the Malta Financial Services Authority (the 'MFSA'). Although the new suite of legis-

4.329 Onshore Fund Domiciles

lation already largely mirrored EU financial services laws at the time, it took EU membership in 2004 to truly catalyse Malta's aspirations to establish a modern financial services centre.

4.330 Spurred on by access to the EU common market, legal and regulatory innovation, a robust regulatory environment, competitive costs and an efficient but rigorous authorisation process, Malta's financial services offering has steadily grown in size, diversity and stature. Malta in early 2017 was home to, amongst others, 69 banks and other financial institutions, over 146 investment services licence holders, the majority of which are fund management companies, 27 fund administrators, 61 insurance companies, including captive (re)insurers and protected cell companies, 11 insurance managers, and 48 pension schemes and funds. Similarly, from just 48 locally based collective investment schemes ('CIS') (including sub-funds) in 2003, approximately 1,300 CIS (including sub-funds) have been licensed in Malta since then. The Maltese financial services sector is supported by over 10,000 skilled professionals and employees renowned for their skills, hardworking attitude and multilingual abilities.

4.331 Despite its slow start, Malta has blossomed into a reputable fund domicile and is widely considered as a competitive alternative to other EU fund domiciles. Indeed, since 2013 Malta has increasingly featured at the top of ranking tables in influential hedge fund publications as the most favoured EU fund domicile, particularly for fund management companies and start-up funds. Although Malta's competitive offering has broad appeal, fund managers and start-up funds particularly appreciate Malta's reasonable establishment and ongoing costs, accessible and well regarded regulator, skilful and multilingual workforce, first class infrastructure, as well as, for expatriates who choose to relocate to Malta, its climate and lifestyle.

The regulatory regime for funds

4.332 The Maltese regulatory regime for CIS was introduced on 13 September 1994 with the adoption of the Investment Services Act (Cap 370, Laws of Malta) (the 'IS Act') which introduced the concept of 'collective investment scheme' into Maltese law as well as a licensing requirement for CIS and their service providers. The IS Act has, over the years, been significantly revised and supplemented including in order to transpose relevant EU legislation such as the UCITS Directive[1], the Alternative Investment Fund Managers Directive[2] ('AIFMD') and the Markets in Financial Instruments Directive (recast)[3] ('MiFID'). The IS Act remains, however, the cornerstone of fund regulation in Malta.

[1] Directive 2009/65/EC of 13 July 2009, as amended by Directive 2014/91/EU of 23 July 2014.
[2] Directive 2011/61/EU of 8 June 2011.
[3] Directive 2014/65/EU of 15 May 2014.

4.333 Under the IS Act[1] it is an offence for a CIS to:

- issue or create any units or carry on any activity in or from Malta (wherever it may be based), or

- be formed in accordance with or exist under the laws of Malta (even if exclusively issuing or creating units or carrying on activities outside Malta),

without a valid CIS licence issued by the MFSA.

[1] Article 4 of the IS Act.

What is a collective investment scheme?

4.334 The IS Act defines[1] a CIS as:

'*any scheme or arrangement* which has *as its object* or as one of its objects the *collective investment of capital* acquired by means of *an offer of units* for subscription, sale or exchange *and which* has the following characteristics:
(a) the scheme or arrangement operates according to the principle of risk spreading; and either:
(b) the contributions of the participants and the profits or income out of which payments are to be made to them are pooled; or
(c) at the request of the holders, units are or are to be repurchased or redeemed out of the assets of the scheme or arrangement, continuously or in blocks at short intervals; or
(d) units are, or have been, or will be issued continuously or in blocks at short intervals . . . '

[1] Article 2 of the IS Act (emphasis added).

4.335 The definition is purposely broad and covers both open-ended and closed-ended funds, retail and non-retail funds as well as funds where the contributions of investors are not pooled. The definition of a CIS under the IS Act also covers alternative investment funds ('AIFs') as defined under AIFMD[1], undertakings for collective investment in transferable securities ('UCITS') defined under the UCITS Directive[2], as well as, since pooling is an optional element, funds that fall outside either category.

[1] Article 4(1)(a) of AIFMD defines an AIF as:

'collective investment undertakings, including investment compartments thereof, which: (i) raise capital from a number of investors, with a view to investing it in accordance with a defined investment policy for the benefit of those investors; and (ii) do not require authorisation under the UCITS Directive.'

[2] Article 1(2) of the UCITS Directive defines a UCITS as:

'an undertaking: (a) with the sole object of collective investment in transferable securities or in other liquid financial assets . . . of capital raised from the public and which operate on the principle of risk-spreading; and (b) with units which are, at the request of holders, repurchased or redeemed, directly or indirectly, out of those undertakings' assets.'

4.336 The definition of a CIS mandates risk spreading. Certain categories of CIS for non-retail investors are, however, exempt from that requirement (being AIFs marketed to professional investors and professional investor funds targeting qualifying or extraordinary investors)[1].

[1] Regulation 6(1) of the Investment Services Act (Exemption) Regulations (SL 370.02, Laws of Malta) (the 'Exemption Regulations'). See para **4.370** et seq below for details about such non-retail funds.

4.337 Onshore Fund Domiciles

4.337 By means of regulations issued under the IS Act, a number of schemes or arrangements which otherwise could satisfy the definition of a CIS are either expressly exempt from the licensing requirement (such as commercial joint ventures, employee share ownership schemes or family office vehicles)[1], subject to a less onerous recognition or notification regime (such as private collective investment schemes restricted to a small number of close friends or relatives of the promoters[2] or notified alternative investment funds[3]), or deemed not to amount to a CIS altogether (such as securitisation vehicles)[4].

[1] Regulation 5(1) of the Exemption Regulations. These exemptions are not automatically operative and require a determination in writing by the MFSA that the exemption applies (regulation 5(2)).
[2] Regulation 2 of the Investment Services Act (Recognition of Private Collective Investment Schemes) Regulations (SL 370.06, Laws of Malta).
[3] Regulation 5(1)(d) of the Exemption Regulations with reference to the Investment Services Act (List of Notified AIFs) Regulations (SL 370.34, Laws of Malta).
[4] Article 6 of the Securitisation Act (Cap 484, Laws of Malta).

4.338 Equally, (i) UCITS that have exercised their marketing right under the UCITS Directive, (ii) EU AIFs managed by an EU alternative investment fund manager ('AIFM') that has exercised its marketing right under AIFMD, or (iii) AIFs whose AIFM has completed the appropriate registration for private placement in Malta, are exempt from the licensing requirement.

4.339 CHAPTER 13 includes a detailed overview of the process for marketing interests in non-Maltese funds in Malta, whether under the marketing passport or by way of private placement[1].

[1] See paras **13.246–13.291** in CHAPTER 13.

Types of fund vehicle

4.340 Since the definition of a CIS under the IS Act is neutral as regards a fund's legal form[1], promoters are granted significant latitude under Maltese law as to the appropriate legal form for a fund, which will typically depend on the desired tax treatment, investor expectations or other relevant factors. Malta accordingly permits funds to be established as companies, limited partnerships, unit trusts, foundations or mere contractual arrangements.

[1] Through the use of the generic expression 'scheme or arrangement'.

Companies

4.341 CIS in Malta are usually established as companies under the Companies Act (Cap 386, Laws of Malta) (the 'Companies Act'). Adopting a corporate form means that the CIS is a separate legal entity managed by its board of directors (typically composed of three or more directors) and can enter into contracts in its own name. A CIS established as a company may either appoint an external fund manager or be self-managed.

4.342 Under the Companies Act, a promoter may establish a CIS as an investment company with fixed share capital ('INVCO') or an investment company with variable share capital (*société d'investissement à capital vari-*

able or 'SICAV'). In addition, the Companies Act requires the promoter to select whether the CIS should be registered as a public liability company or a private limited liability company[1]. That choice would typically be driven by, among other things, whether the limit of 50 shareholders and the limitations on the transferability and listing of securities issued by private limited liability companies are acceptable[2].

[1] An INVCO can only be established as a public limited company (article 194(6) of the Companies Act).
[2] A private limited liability company must have restrictions on transfers of its shares (article 209(1)(a) of the Companies Act) (ie they cannot be freely transferable) and its securities cannot be admitted to listing or trading (article 209(2)(c)).

4.343 The INVCO is a legal vehicle primarily designed for closed-ended fund structures. The INVCO benefits from one main exemption from the typical strictures of public companies (unlike the SICAV, an INVCO must always be a public limited company) in that it is able, provided certain conditions are satisfied, to distribute profits from certain typically undistributable reserves. Perhaps understandably, this structure has fallen into disuse in favour of the far more established and flexible SICAV which can, in addition to open-ended structures, also adequately serve as a closed-ended vehicle.

4.344 The SICAV is, by a large margin, Malta's most popular legal form for funds. SICAVs are exempt from the strictures of private and public companies that are inappropriate for funds and accordingly may, among other things, issue and redeem shares continually according to investor demand, issue fractional or discounted shares, and distribute by way of dividend amounts in excess of the profits and capital which are typically available for distribution by ordinary companies.

4.345 Malta has long catered for segregated cell structures (and recently incorporated cell structures) including in areas as diverse as charitable organisations, insurance and securitisation. The SICAV was, however, the first Maltese vehicle to offer these features and is the structure that offers the most flexibility. A SICAV may be established as a multi-class SICAV (that is, a fund with multiple unsegregated classes) or a multi-fund SICAV (that is, an umbrella fund with multiple sub-funds which may or may not have legal segregation between sub-funds). Subject to regulatory constraints, a sub-fund of a multi-fund SICAV may cross-invest into another sub-fund of that SICAV.

4.346 Although benefiting from robust and detailed provisions about the legal segregation of sub-funds, sub-funds within a multi-fund SICAV do not have a separate legal personality from the SICAV of which they form part. Promoters, particularly platform operators, wishing to establish an umbrella fund with the highest level of segregation may opt for an incorporated cell company whereby the main company is a multi-fund SICAV which can either create sub-funds (without separate legal personality) or create incorporated cells each of which is a multi-class SICAV company in its own right. A relatively recent innovation in this area is the recognised incorporated cell company which is an ordinary private or public company whose activity is restricted to providing administrative services to its incorporated cells and which can create incorporated cells each of which may be a multi-class or a multi-fund SICAV company.

4.347 Onshore Fund Domiciles

4.347 In addition to the incorporation of new companies under Maltese law, the IS Act and the Companies Act permit the migration or redomiciliation of funds in the form of a body corporate into and out of Malta[1].

[1] Article 31 of the IS Act and the Continuation of Companies Regulations (SL 386.05, Laws of Malta).

Limited partnerships

4.348 A limited partnership, or *partnership en commandite*, can have its capital divided into interests or shares and be licensed as a CIS under the IS Act. Limited partnerships which are established as funds will have objects limited to the collective investment of funds in securities and other property, with the partners benefiting from the proceeds of the management of those funds. Limited partnerships expressly set up as and licensed as a CIS are regulated by the Tenth Schedule to the Companies Act.

4.349 A limited partnership may be formed by two or more partners, with at least one general partner and one limited partner, as is typical in common law jurisdictions. Unlike conventional common law limited partnerships, however, a Maltese law limited partnership has a separate legal personality distinct from that of its partners and, accordingly, can transact business and own assets in its own name.

4.350 Any person (including a limited liability company) can be a partner (general or limited) in a limited partnership, regardless of where it is resident. The limited partnership itself, however, must have a registered office in Malta.

4.351 A general partner of a Maltese limited partnership is jointly and severally liable (with any other general partners of that limited partnership) for all debts of that limited partnership without limitation[1]. The liability of the general partners is, however, subordinate to that of the limited partnership itself, so that the assets of the limited partnership must be exhausted before any action can be taken against a general partner[2]. Limited partners are not liable for any debts of the limited partnership beyond the amount so contributed or agreed to be contributed and not yet paid[3].

[1] Paragraph 5(1)(a) of the Tenth Schedule to the Companies Act.
[2] Paragraph 5(1)(a) of the Tenth Schedule to the Companies Act.
[3] Paragraph 5(1)(b) of the Tenth Schedule to the Companies Act.

4.352 Like the SICAV, a limited partnership may be established as a multi-class limited partnership (that is, a fund with multiple unsegregated classes) or a multi-fund limited partnership (that is, an umbrella fund with multiple sub-funds with a choice as to whether or not to have legal segregation between the sub-funds).

Unit trusts

4.353 A CIS may be constituted as a trust, and the Trusts and Trustees Act (Cap 331, Laws of Malta) (the 'Trusts Act') and the IS Act contain provisions which permit a unit trust arrangement to operate much the same way as a SICAV.

4.354 Maltese trust law, notably the Trusts Act, is based on English common law principles and it also has contract-like flexibility which is expressly provided for at law[1]. As is typical with ordinary Maltese trusts, a CIS which is structured as a unit trust will not have legal personality separate from that of its trustee; however, the assets of the trust will constitute a separate, distinct estate to that of the trustee.

[1] Unit trusts along with other 'commercial transactions' (which includes CIS) are exempt from many of the formal requirements under the Trusts Act, instead leaving this up to the trust deed (article 6(6) of the Trusts Act).

4.355 A unit trust is constituted by an instrument of trust usually between the investment manager and the trustee. The trust instrument will govern matters such as the appointment and retirement of the investment manager and the trustee (the two main functionaries), their respective powers and duties as well as how the trust will operate.

4.356 Both foreign trusts and foreign trustees are recognised in Malta, but trustees carrying on business in Malta would need to be approved by the MFSA.

Foundations

4.357 It is possible for a CIS to take the form of a foundation, which is an organisation that comprises a 'universality of things' constituted by a founder for (i) the fulfilment of a specified purpose or (ii) the benefit of a named person or class of persons, and whose assets are administered by a designated person.

4.358 Foundations can be used to further any legitimate business or activity; however, unlike trusts, foundations are granted legal personality by statute. Typically, a foundation would have a finite existence, but when used for collective investment purposes there is no limit on its life.

Contractual funds

4.359 A CIS can be established by a 'deed of constitution' – a contract – between an investment manager and a custodian[1]. Contractual funds will not have legal personality, can be open-ended or closed-ended, and the interests in the fund can be divided into units, title to which will be evidenced by certificates or contract notes issued jointly by the investment manager and the custodian.

[1] The Investment Services Act (Contractual Funds) Regulations (SL 370.16, Laws of Malta).

4.360 A contractual fund can be a single fund or an umbrella fund, with separate strategies or different investors housed across sub-funds, as is the case for SICAVs.

Types of authorisation for funds

4.361 From a regulatory standpoint, CIS in Malta can be categorised into two main types: (a) UCITS authorised under the UCITS Directive, and (b) AIFs as

4.361 Onshore Fund Domiciles

defined under AIFMD. In addition, as noted above, since the definition of a CIS under Maltese law is broader than those two types, there is a third category of non-EU harmonised CIS that can be established in Malta.

4.362 Malta presently offers fund promoters a plethora of regulatory regimes under which to authorise and operate their investment vehicles, each with their own benefits and features.

The MFSA is in the process of finalising a fund regime consolidation exercise[1], so the main features of the current regime and the proposed regime are described below.

[1] MFSA's 'Circular to the Financial Services Industry on the Consolidation of the Maltese Fund Frameworks' dated 26 May 2016.

Retail investors (UCITS, retail non-UCITS and retail AIFs)

4.363 A CIS which is available for distribution to retail clients (as defined under MiFID)[1] ('retail investors') may be authorised as (a) a UCITS, (b) a retail non-UCITS, or (c) a retail AIF, each of which has its own dedicated MFSA Rulebook. Each fund may be externally managed or, if additional requirements are complied with, self-managed.

[1] A retail client is defined in Article 4(11) of MiFID as a client who does not qualify as a professional client.

UCITS

4.364 Malta has recently seen a resurgence of UCITS being established, and the number of UCITS authorised in Malta has almost doubled since 2010. This is primarily as a result of promoters and fund managers actively seeking out jurisdictions within the EU, such as Malta, which offer lower establishment and operating costs for what is essentially a harmonised fund product.

4.365 Although not historically associated with hedge funds, UCITS have over the past 14 years[1] successfully been used to replicate hedge fund strategies. With the advent of AIFMD, the entry into force of 'MiFID II' in 2018[2] as well as the UCITS VI consultation[3], the use of UCITS to replicate hedge fund strategies is likely be curtailed over the medium term.

[1] Since the entry into force of UCITS III (Directives 2001/107/EC and 2001/108/EC of 21 January 2002) in 2004.
[2] MiFID, as recast with effect from 3 January 2018, introduces a distinction between ordinary and structured UCITS making the latter harder to distribute to retail investors.
[3] European Commission Consultation, dated 26 July 2012, on UCITS product rules, liquidity management, depositary, money market funds, and long-term investments.

Retail non-UCITS

4.366 As a non-harmonised retail fund-type, the retail non-UCITS has increasingly fallen into disuse in Malta with promoters instead opting for the more established and easier to distribute UCITS. Additionally, following the transposition of AIFMD into Maltese law, a retail non-UCITS qualifies as an AIF and accordingly the AIFM will, if within AIFMD's scope, need to comply with the Directive without the benefit of a passport to market to the retail investors which this type of fund was originally designed for. As part of the MFSA's fund regime consolidation exercise, with effect from 3 June 2016, the MFSA no longer accepts new applications for retail non-UCITS, so this regime will gradually be phased out.

4.367 Retail non-UCITS are subject to a number of UCITS-like investment restrictions, including limits on eligible assets, diversification requirements and counterparty exposure limits, as well as local restrictions such as a prohibition on sub-funds of umbrella funds cross-investing into another sub-fund of that same umbrella fund. Retail non-UCITS are, in certain respects, subject to more onerous investment restrictions than UCITS, such as outright prohibitions on the use of financial derivatives for investment purposes and leverage. Unlike UCITS, a retail non-UCITS could, however, be established as a closed-ended CIS.

Retail AIFs

4.368 As part of Malta's transposition of AIFMD, the MFSA created a new type of fund for EU AIFMs, the aptly named 'alternative investment fund' (an 'AI fund')[1]. In recognition of the flexibility afforded by Article 43 of AIFMD for EU member states to permit the marketing of AIFs to retail investors, the AI fund may also be authorised as a 'retail AIF'.

[1] See further paras 4.377–4.382 below.

4.369 Retail AIFs are subject to similar investment restrictions to retail non-UCITS and can be established as closed-ended CIS. A retail AIF may only be managed by a Maltese or EU authorised AIFM and will be subject to a number of licensing conditions designed to reflect the AIFM's duties under AIFMD.

Professional investors and high net worth individuals (PIFs and AI funds)

4.370 A CIS which is available for distribution to professional clients (as defined under MiFID) ('professional investors') may be authorised as (a) a professional investor fund ('PIF') or (b) an AI fund, each of which has its own dedicated MFSA Rulebook. Each of these funds may be externally managed or self-managed. Additionally, EU AIFMs have a third option, the notified alternative investment fund ('NAIF'), which is an AIF under AIFMD that is not authorised by the MFSA but whose existence must merely be notified to MFSA.

Professional investor funds

4.371 Malta's flagship non-retail fund regime, the PIF, was retained largely unaltered following the implementation of AIFMD. A PIF may be structured as an AIF or otherwise as an open-ended or closed-ended CIS, may have a single or multiple custodians (or none at all, with prime brokers carrying out safekeeping), may appoint service providers based outside Malta (ideally based

4.371 Onshore Fund Domiciles

in a recognised jurisdiction[1]), does not require local directors, may pursue any investment strategy, and is subject to little or no investment restrictions. PIFs are also subject to a 'fast track' processing commitment by the MFSA[2].

[1] If service providers are based in recognised jurisdictions, the PIF is eligible for the MFSA's 'fast track' process. A recognised jurisdiction under MFSA rules is any EU jurisdiction or a jurisdiction with whose competent authority the MFSA has a relevant multilateral or bilateral memorandum of understanding ('MoU') in place. The current list of MoUs can be found on the MFSA's website – see http://www.mfsa.com.mt.

[2] Provided the PIF is externally managed and all service providers are based and regulated in recognised jurisdictions, the MFSA is committed to reviewing the application form and supporting documents and providing its comments to the applicant within (a) seven business days from receipt of an application for a PIF targeting experienced or qualifying investors, or (b) three business days from receipt of an application for a PIF targeting extraordinary investors.

4.372 The rules applicable to a PIF will depend on two main factors: (a) the location and type of AIFM which that PIF appoints, and (b) the type of investors which it is authorised to target.

4.373 Location and type of AIFM: A PIF may appoint as its external fund manager: (a) a full-scope EU AIFM[1], (b) a de minimis AIFM (that is, an AIFM which falls below the thresholds for assets under management which are set out in Article 3(2) of AIFMD[2] (the 'AUM thresholds')), or (c) a non-EU AIFM. Additionally, a PIF may be a self-managed PIF provided that it expects to remain below the AUM thresholds[3]. Where a PIF appoints a full-scope EU AIFM and qualifies as an AIF, the AIFM will need to ensure in accordance with AIFMD, among other things, that the PIF appoints a single custodian which is established in Malta or which is a credit institution established in another EU member state[4], that the offering documentation contains appropriate disclosures, and that it or an external valuer retains responsibility for the valuation of the AIF's assets. In all other cases, the PIF (and the AIFM) only needs to comply with the MFSA's PIF Rulebook. The position for full-scope non-EU AIFMs may be subject to change once AIFMD's third country regime comes into effect.

[1] As part of the MFSA's fund regime consolidation exercise, PIFs will be limited to de minimis and non-EU AIFMs in order clearly to differentiate between EU AIFs managed by full EU AIFMs in accordance with AIFMD and other funds.

[2] These are (a) €100 million, or (b) €500 million if unleveraged and investors have no redemption rights exercisable during a period of five years from the date of initial investment in the fund.

[3] If a self-managed PIF is expected to exceed these thresholds it will need to restructure and probably apply for authorisation as an AI fund or appoint an external AIFM.

[4] Malta's implementation of AIFMD included a derogation under Article 61(5) (also known as the 'Malta clause') which permitted a Maltese AIF to appoint a credit institution established in another EU member state as its single depositary until 22 July 2017. This derogation was not extended beyond 22 July 2017.

4.374 Type of investors targeted: PIFs fall into different categories depending on the type of investors targeted, ranging from quasi-retail to ultra-high net worth or institutional investors, which will, in turn, dictate the level of minimum investment required, the applicable investment restrictions and various other requirements. There are essentially three investor categories:

- *Experienced investors*: A PIF targeting experienced investors[1] (an 'ExpIF') is subject to the lowest minimum investment requirement (€10,000 or its equivalent in any other currency) and is subject to the most onerous requirements including detailed investment restrictions and limits (over and above those which are self-imposed). Among other things, an ExpIF:
    - may not borrow or employ leverage for investment purposes in excess of 100% of its net asset value ('NAV');
    - must comply with the principle of risk spreading as well as adhere to the diversification requirements in the MFSA PIF Rulebook (such as restrictions on exposure to any one counterparty, credit institution or issuer, as well as a minimum number of funds in which an ExpIF which is a fund of funds must invest);
    - may not, where the ExpIF is established as an umbrella fund, cross-invest into another sub-fund of that same umbrella fund (similar to the retail categories above); and
    - must appoint a single custodian with both a safekeeping and a monitoring and oversight role.

  As part of the MFSA's fund regime consolidation exercise, this category is being phased out and, with effect from 3 June 2016, the MFSA will not accept new applications for ExpIFs.

- *Qualifying investors*: A PIF targeting qualifying investors[2] (a 'QIF') is subject to a medium minimum investment requirement (€100,000[3] or its equivalent in any other currency) and is generally[4] not subject to any investment restrictions (other than those which are self-imposed). In addition, a QIF:
    - is not required to comply with the principle of risk spreading;
    - can, if the QIF is established as an umbrella fund with segregated sub-funds, cross-invest into another sub-fund of that same umbrella fund up to a limit of 50% of NAV in any one other sub-fund (can invest up to 100% of NAV in the aggregate); and
    - can have multiple custodians or none at all if the MFSA is satisfied that there are alternative safekeeping arrangements (such as through the use of prime brokers) – there is no requirement for the custodians or prime brokers to carry out a monitoring and oversight role[5].

  The QIF is proposed to be retained following the MFSA's fund regime consolidation exercise.

- *Extraordinary investors*: A PIF targeting extraordinary investors[6] (an 'ExtraIF') is subject to the highest minimum investment requirement (€750,000 or its equivalent in any other currency) but is subject to the lowest level of supervision, including no investment restrictions (other than those which are self-imposed). An ExtraIF has the same features as a QIF (as outlined above) and in addition:
    - does not need a formal offering document and can issue a brief marketing document; and
    - need simply notify the MFSA of changes to the offering document or marketing document as well as to service providers (such as custodian(s), manager, administrator or advisers) rather than seeking the MFSA's prior approval.

4.374 *Onshore Fund Domiciles*

As part of the MFSA's fund regime consolidation exercise, this category is also being phased out and, with effect from 3 June 2016, new applications for ExtraIFs are no longer accepted by the MFSA.

[1] The MFSA's PIF Rulebook defines an 'experienced investor' as 'a person having the expertise, experience and knowledge to be in a position to make his own investment decisions and understand the risks involved'. An investor in such a PIF must state the basis on which he satisfies this definition, either by confirming relevant work experience, reasonable experience of investing in the type of assets invested in by that PIF, particular volumes and frequencies of investments, or by providing any other appropriate justification. A person qualifying as a 'professional client' under MiFID automatically qualifies as an experienced investor.

[2] The MFSA's PIF Rulebook defines a 'qualifying investor' as a person who meets one or more of the following criteria:
- a body corporate which has (or which is part of a group which has) net assets in excess of €750,000 (or its equivalent in any other currency);
- an unincorporated body of persons or association, a trust or an individual (alone or together with his/her spouse) which has net assets in excess of that amount;
- an individual, or in the case of a body corporate, the majority of its board of directors or general partner (as applicable), who has reasonable experience in the acquisition and/or disposal of funds of a similar nature or risk profile or property of the same kind as the property, or a substantial part of the property, to which the PIF in question relates;
- a senior employee or director of service providers to the PIF;
- a relation or close friend of the promoters limited to a total of ten persons per PIF;
- an entity with (or which is part of a group with) €3.75 million (or equivalent) or more under discretionary management, investing on its own account;
- an investor which qualifies as a QIF or an ExtraIF; or
- a special purpose vehicle ('SPV') wholly owned by persons or entities satisfying any of the other criteria listed above.

The MFSA's fund regime consolidation exercise will, once complete, replace the definition of qualifying investor such that it covers any one of:
- a body corporate which has net assets in excess of €750,000 or which is part of a group which has net assets in excess of €750,000 or, in each case, the equivalent in any other currency;
- an unincorporated body of persons or association which has net assets in excess of €750,000 or the equivalent in any other currency;
- a trust where the net value of the trust's assets is in excess of €750,000 or the equivalent in any other currency;
- an individual whose net worth or joint net worth with that of the person's spouse exceeds €750,000 or the equivalent in any other currency; or
- a senior employee or director of a service provider to the PIF.

[3] QIFs established before 3 June 2016 may retain the previously applicable minimum investment of €75,000 or equivalent.

[4] The sole investment restriction imposed on QIFs is in relation to the use of leverage (a limit of 50% of NAV) where the QIF invests in real estate.

[5] Naturally, if the QIF is managed by an EU AIFM, the AIFM would need to ensure that these are implemented in order to comply with its obligations under AIFMD.

[6] The MFSA's PIF Rulebook defines an 'extraordinary investor' as a person who meets one or more of the following criteria:
- a body corporate which has (or which is part of a group which has) net assets in excess of €7.5 million or equivalent in any other currency;
- an unincorporated body of persons or association, a trust or an individual (alone or together with his/her spouse) which has net assets in excess of that amount;
- a senior employee or director of service providers to the PIF;
- an investor which qualifies as an ExtraIF; or
- an SPV wholly owned by persons or entities satisfying any of the other criteria listed above.

4.375 Of the three categories, the QIF is by far the most popular since promoters find that it strikes a good balance between the type of investor that may be targeted and the minimum investment level, on the one hand, and regulatory requirements on the other. Indeed, the MFSA's fund regime consolidation exercise means that, with effect from 3 June 2016, the QIF is the only available option for applicants, thereby gradually phasing out the ExpIF and the ExtraIF.

4.376 All PIFs need to appoint an AIFM (unless they are self-managed), a compliance officer, a money laundering reporting officer and a statutory auditor. Where the PIF does not appoint an administrator the AIFM would be required to assume that role. PIFs set up in corporate form are expected to have at least three directors one of whom should be independent. There are no residency requirements for directors of a PIF (unless that PIF is self-managed); however, if all directors and service providers are resident outside Malta, that PIF will need to appoint a local representative to act as a point of liaison with the MFSA.

ALTERNATIVE INVESTMENT FUNDS

4.377 As noted above[1], as part of Malta's transposition of AIFMD, the 'alternative investment fund' ('AI fund') was added as a new type of fund alongside the PIF. The AI fund is designed for full-scope EU AIFMs seeking a regulated type of fund as well as for self-managed AIFs that exceed the AUM thresholds[2].

[1] See para **4.368** above.
[2] See footnote 2 to para **4.373** above.

4.378 In order to support full-scope EU AIFMs in ensuring that the AIFs which they manage satisfy and continue to satisfy the requirements under AIFMD, the licensing conditions for AI funds mirror the requirements which apply to EU AIFMs in relation to the AIFs that they manage. Accordingly, an AI fund must appoint a single full-scope EU AIFM (or be self-managed), appoint a single custodian satisfying the requirements of Article 21 of AIFMD, ensure that its offering documents include the disclosures required under Article 23 of AIFMD, and ensure that the AIFM or a duly appointed external valuer is responsible for the valuation of the assets of the AI fund.

4.379 With the exception of the retail AIF described above[1], all AI funds may be marketed to (under AIFMD), and accept subscriptions from, professional investors. An AI fund which is available to professional investors is not subject to any minimum investment requirements or investment restrictions. Since the definition of professional investor reflects that under MiFID, subscriptions (even if based on reverse solicitation) from non-'per se' professional investors such as ultra-high net worth individuals, local authorities or medium-sized companies cannot be accepted unless such investors elect, and are eligible, to be treated as elective professional investors.

[1] See para **4.369** above.

4.380 Similarly to a PIF, an AI fund may, by imposing a minimum investment amount and certain investment restrictions (where applicable), opt to be authorised as an AI fund available to a slightly broader category of investors[1]:

4.380 Onshore Fund Domiciles

- *Experienced investors*: An AI fund which is available to experienced investors is subject to the same minimum investment requirement (€10,000 or its equivalent in any other currency) and investment restrictions, including leverage restrictions, as an ExpIF[2] (this category is being phased out with no new applications accepted since 3 June 2016).
- *Qualifying investors*: An AI fund which is available to qualifying investors is subject to the same minimum investment requirement (€100,000 or its equivalent in any other currency) as a QIF[3]. An AI fund targeting qualifying investors is not subject to any investment restrictions other than in relation to real estate.
- *Extraordinary investors*: An AI fund which is available to extraordinary investors is subject to the same minimum investment requirement (€750,000 or its equivalent in any other currency) as an ExtraIF[4]. Unlike the ExtraIF, an AI fund which is available to extraordinary investors does not benefit from additional derogations from the MFSA's AIF Rulebook beyond the lack of investment restrictions (this category is being phased out with no new applications accepted since 3 June 2016).

[1] An AI fund opting to be available to investors other than 'professional investors' should ensure that it either complies with the Investment Services Act (Prospectus of Collective Investment Schemes) Regulations (SL 370.04, Laws of Malta) or is suitably exempt. These rules, which partially implement the Prospectus Directive (Directive 2003/71/EC of 4 November 2003) and are normally of relevance to retail funds, apply where a CIS, other than a PIF, makes an offer of its securities to the public.
[2] See para **4.374** above.
[3] See para **4.374** above. AI funds available to qualifying investors and established before 3 June 2016 may retain the previously applicable minimum investment of €75,000 or equivalent.
[4] See para **4.374** above.

4.381 Besides the already effective increase in the minimum investment for AI funds available to qualifying investors (€100,000 instead of €75,000 or equivalent), the MFSA's fund regime consolidation exercise will, once complete, replace the definition of a qualifying investor (with the new definition included in footnote 2 to para **4.374** above).

4.382 Again similarly to a PIF, an AI fund must appoint, besides a single AIFM and custodian, a compliance officer, a money laundering reporting officer and a statutory auditor. An AI fund which is established in corporate form is expected to have at least three directors, one of whom should be independent. There are also no residency requirements for the directors of an AI fund (unless that AI fund is self-managed).

NOTIFIED ALTERNATIVE INVESTMENT FUNDS

4.383 A relatively recent introduction, the NAIF offers full-scope EU AIFMs a fund vehicle that qualifies as an AIF under AIFMD and can be launched within ten working days from notification to the MFSA. Unlike the AI fund described above, the NAIF is restricted to particular structures and strategies and is not authorised by the MFSA but notified by the AIFM to the MFSA. A NAIF is not regulated by the MFSA and, instead, the AIFM of that NAIF assumes responsibility for complying with the MFSA's requirements.

4.384 A NAIF must be managed by a full-scope EU AIFM authorised and regulated under AIFMD which must hold all of the voting rights in the NAIF. Thus, non-EU AIFMs may not establish NAIFs, at least until third country passport rights are granted under AIFMD. The NAIF regime may not be availed of by AIFs which (a) are self-managed, (b) are loan funds and are authorised to invest through loans[1], or (c) invest in non-financial assets (other than private equity funds or funds which invest in immovable property, infrastructure or certain non-financial assets determined by the MFSA to be permissible[2]).

[1] See para **4.386** below.
[2] To date, these are vintage cars, works of art, precious metals and antiques.

4.385 A NAIF may be made available to professional investors or qualifying investors[1] subject to a minimum investment of €100,000 or its equivalent in any other currency.

[1] See footnote 2 to para **4.374** above.

FUNDS WITH SPECIFIC INVESTMENT STRATEGIES

4.386 Whilst the regimes which govern PIFs, AI funds and NAIFs have historically been investment strategy neutral, the MFSA has recently issued dedicated rulebooks or supplementary licence conditions for funds pursuing particular strategies. To date, the MFSA has issued additional guidance[1] on PIFs or AI funds seeking to be authorised as (a) money market funds, (b) short-term money market funds, (c) lending funds (loan origination or loan acquisition), and (d) PIFs (and in future AI funds or NAIFs) which invest in virtual currencies, each with specific investment restrictions, diversification and eligibility criteria.

[1] Available on the MFSA website – see https://www.mfsa.com.mt.

4.387 PIFs, AI funds or NAIFs may be used to structure particular EU AIFs such as the EU venture capital fund or the EU social entrepreneurship fund.

Private collective investment schemes

4.388 As mentioned above[1], the IS Act contemplates the 'recognition' (a type of authorisation) of private collective investment schemes, which are a particular investment vehicle restricted to not more than 15 individuals who must all be close friends or relatives of the promoters. Since this type of fund is limited in scope and is not generally treated as a CIS, including for tax purposes (it is not authorised but recognised by the MFSA), this vehicle is rarely used.

[1] See para **4.337** above.

4.389 *Onshore Fund Domiciles*

The regulatory process

4.389 The MFSA describes its approval process for a CIS as being divided into three phases:

- the preparatory phase[1];
- the pre-licensing phase[2]; and
- the post-licensing phase[3].

[1] See paras **4.390–4.393** below.
[2] See paras **4.394–4.395** below.
[3] See paras **4.396–4.398** below.

Preparatory phase

4.390 The preparatory phase covers the submission in draft to the MFSA of application documentation, offering documents and other supporting documents in respect of the relevant CIS. Since the MFSA's approval process focuses on the governance (board composition and competence) of the CIS and the reputation of its core service providers (the manager, the administrator and the custodian(s)), the MFSA does not impose a sponsor requirement on any type of fund nor does it have capital or other eligibility requirements for fund promoters. The MFSA will, where a particular person retains the majority of voting rights or control of the CIS (such as through management shares), assess whether that person (together with the directors and service providers) is a 'fit and proper' person as part of the application process. This assessment is normally done on the basis of a personal questionnaire completed and submitted by the relevant person.

4.391 The MFSA typically recommends organising a preliminary meeting with promoters prior to submission of the application, though this is becoming less common except for novel products or where the promoters are unknown to the MFSA or wish to discuss certain issues with the MFSA in advance.

4.392 Upon submission of the draft application, the MFSA will proceed to review that application as well as the offering documentation and carry out its 'fit and proper' assessment on directors, controllers and service providers. The MFSA's review of the offering documentation is normally limited to ensuring that it includes all relevant risk and other disclosures and otherwise complies with the applicable legislation and rules. It is quite usual for the MFSA to revert with comments or requests for clarification.

4.393 Subject to 'fast track' commitments for PIFs, the duration of the preliminary phase will depend on the completeness and quality of the application, the complexity or novelty of the structure and whether or not all service providers are known to the MFSA. In the ordinary course of events, this phase will generally take one to three months from the initial submission of an application to the MFSA. The MFSA is usually amenable to working within timeframes pre-agreed with the promoters.

Pre-licensing phase

4.394 Once the MFSA has completed its 'fit and proper' assessments, obtained satisfactory replies to its comments and queries (if any) and is generally satisfied with the proposed CIS, its service providers and its draft offering documentation, the MFSA will send its 'in principle' approval. This approval is in the form of a letter noting that the MFSA is minded to authorise the CIS and will state the pre-licensing conditions, which will include matters such as finalisation of the draft documents submitted as well as (if applicable) incorporation of the CIS and signature of the relevant service agreements. The 'in principle' approval will typically also include post-licensing and pre-commencement of business conditions as well as, if the CIS is self-managed, post-licensing and post-commencement of business conditions.

4.395 Once the pre-licensing conditions are satisfied, the MFSA will issue its authorisation and stamp the cover page of the offering documentation to indicate its approval.

Post-licensing phase

4.396 Following the issue of its licence and before commencing business, the CIS would typically address its post-licensing and pre-commencement of business requirements (which would normally be administrative in nature). If the CIS is self-managed it may also be subject to post-licensing and post-commencement of business conditions which would have dates by which these requirements would need to be satisfied.

4.397 On an ongoing basis, once licensed, a CIS is required to adhere to the standard licensing conditions set out in the applicable MFSA Rulebook, which include items requiring either prior notification to and/or consent of the MFSA, reporting requirements, conduct of business obligations and similar obligations.

4.398 Solely in relation to NAIFs, the application process is replaced by a notification process under which the AIFM submits a notification pack to the MFSA. The notification pack would include the final offering documents approved by the governing body of the NAIF[1]. Provided that the notification pack is complete and in compliance with the MFSA's requirements, the MFSA must include the NAIF on the official list of NAIFs within ten working days from notification.

[1] The notification must be made within 30 calendar days from the date of adoption by the NAIF's governing body of the relevant offering documents.

Service providers and corporate governance

Fund managers/AIFMs

4.399 A CIS under Maltese law may be externally managed or, if it adopts a corporate structure, may be authorised as a self-managed CIS.

4.400 If the fund manager or AIFM is established in Malta it will need to hold a Category 2 licence issued under the IS Act, the requirements for which depend on whether the fund manager will qualify as a UCITS management company (that is, a fund manager that can manage UCITS), a de minimis AIFM (that is, an AIFM whose AIF assets under management are below the

4.400 Onshore Fund Domiciles

AUM thresholds), or a full scope AIFM (that is, an AIFM whose AIF assets under management exceed the AUM thresholds and accordingly is subject to AIFMD).

4.401 If the fund manager or AIFM is established in another EU member state and qualifies as a UCITS management company or a full scope AIFM (relevant to UCITS, AI funds or NAIFs in particular), it will first need to exercise its management passport under the relevant EU Directive.

4.402 If, on the other hand, the fund manager or AIFM is established outside the EU or qualifies as a de minimis AIFM (mainly relevant to retail non-UCITS and PIFs), provided that the MFSA is generally satisfied that the fund manager is adequately regulated in its country of residence and is of sufficient standing and repute, that fund manager is exempt from authorisation by the MFSA. This assessment would be carried out as part of the application for authorisation of the CIS.

4.403 If the CIS is to be established as a self-managed CIS, it would generally be required to have at least one locally resident director, establish an investment committee composed of no fewer than three persons with verifiable competence in portfolio management and, for AI funds, NAIFs and UCITS, have hierarchically segregated risk and valuation functions. A self-managed CIS may, subject to the rules applying to particular types of funds, delegate portfolio management or risk management to third parties acceptable to the MFSA.

Investment advisers

4.404 Similar considerations as those above for AIFMs apply to investment advisers appointed by the CIS. If the investment adviser is established outside Malta, provided that the MFSA is generally satisfied that it is adequately regulated in its country of residence and is of sufficient standing and repute, the investment adviser is exempt from authorisation by the MFSA. Again, this assessment would be carried out as part of the application for authorisation of the CIS.

Administrators

4.405 A CIS (or its AIFM on its behalf) may (a) appoint an external fund administrator to provide fund administration services such as the calculation of its NAV, fund accounting or transfer agency, (b) appoint the AIFM or the fund manager to provide those services, or (c) if self-managed, provide those services internally.

4.406 If the person (be it the external administrator, the AIFM or fund manager, or the self-managed CIS itself) is established in Malta, it will need to hold a 'recognition certificate' issued by the MFSA.

4.407 Although most major administrators have set up operations in Malta, Maltese CIS of any type are, unlike in many other jurisdictions, not required to appoint a Maltese administrator. Provided that the MFSA is generally satisfied that the administrator is adequately regulated in its country of residence and is of sufficient standing and repute, an administrator established outside Malta is exempt from authorisation by the MFSA. This assessment would, as for non-EU AIFMs, be carried out as part of the application for authorisation of the CIS.

Trustees and custodians of CIS

4.408 With the exception of UCITS (which must have a depositary in Malta) and retail non-UCITS, AI funds or NAIFs (which must have a depositary which is either resident in Malta or is a credit institution established in another EU member state[1]), Maltese CIS (essentially, ExpIFs, QIFs or ExtraIFs) are not required to appoint a Maltese custodian and can appoint a custodian established outside Malta.

[1] As noted in footnote 4 to para **4.373** above, this is a transitional derogation under Article 61(5) of AIFMD which remained in force until 22 July 2017.

4.409 If the custodian is established in Malta it must hold a Category 4a licence issued under the IS Act. Broadly, only credit institutions, certain investment services firms with not less than €730,000 in own funds, or branches or subsidiaries of such entities are eligible to apply for a Category 4a licence. Alternatively, if the CIS has no redemption rights during a period of five years from the date of initial investment in the fund and generally invests in assets that do not need to be held in custody under AIFMD, it can appoint a custodian in possession of a Category 4b licence (known as 'depositary lite'). The eligibility criteria for a Category 4b licence are wider and include, in addition to investment services firms, any fund administrator which has own funds of not less than €125,000.

4.410 A custodian for a PIF which is established outside Malta is exempt from authorisation by the MFSA provided that the MFSA is generally satisfied that the custodian is adequately regulated in its country of residence and is of sufficient standing and repute. This assessment would be carried out as part of the application for authorisation of the PIF.

4.411 Maltese custodians are permitted to (and most do) delegate safekeeping to a global custodian (and its sub-custody network) or to one or more sub-custodians.

Prime brokers

4.412 Maltese CIS may appoint local or foreign prime brokers. Where, as is permitted for QIFs, the prime broker also has a safekeeping role, the MFSA would need to be satisfied that the prime broker is adequately regulated in its country of residence and is of sufficient standing and repute.

Corporate governance

4.413 The MFSA has published a corporate governance manual[1] for directors of collective investment schemes (established as investment companies) which, to the extent proportionate or applicable, directors of Maltese CIS are

4.413 Onshore Fund Domiciles

expected to abide by.

[1] Available on the MFSA website – see https://www.mfsa.com.mt.

Marketing

4.414 The ability to market units or shares in Maltese CIS outside Malta depends on a number of factors, including the type of fund, the type and place of establishment of the AIFM, whether the countries targeted are in or outside the EU, and the type(s) of investors targeted. In addition, the local distribution rules in the target country are also relevant.

4.415 CIS which are authorised as UCITS benefit from an EU passport which enables them to be sold in all EU countries following a notification to that effect to the MFSA. Maltese UCITS have also been successfully registered for sale in non-EU countries (such as South Africa) though this is subject to local approvals.

4.416 AIFMD introduced a passport for EU AIFMs managing EU AIFs such as PIFs, AI funds (including self-managed AI funds) and NAIFs to market units or shares in those AIFs to investors that qualify as professional clients under MiFID. Similar to the process for UCITS, the process to be followed involves a notification to the 'home' regulator of the EU AIFM which is then transmitted to the 'host' EU regulator.

4.417 Marketing to other types of investors (such as retail investors) or marketing by AIFMs that do not have a passport under AIFMD (such as de minimis AIFMs or non-EU AIFMs) will require compliance with the local distribution or private placement rules (if any) in the relevant country or countries targeted.

4.418 An overview of the considerations when marketing units or shares in a CIS in Malta is provided in CHAPTER 13 – see paras **13.246–13.291**.

Malta Stock Exchange listing

4.419 An increasing number of local and foreign CIS are seeking either a primary or secondary listing on the Malta Stock Exchange (the 'MSE') in order to facilitate subscriptions by a broader range of investors. The MSE is Malta's primary stock exchange and central securities depositary and forms part of the Clearstream settlement network.

4.420 The MFSA as listing authority under the Financial Markets Act (Cap 345, Laws of Malta) has issued a dedicated chapter of the listing rules for CIS seeking to list on the MSE. A CIS seeking a listing will need to appoint a listing sponsor which will, with support from the CIS's legal advisers, prepare the CIS for admission to listing. In order to be admissible for listing on the MSE, a CIS (a) must ensure that its units are freely transferable, (b) must publish a prospectus or other offering document containing the disclosures required by the listing rules, (c) must have at least one independent director, (d) cannot have corporate directors (unless the corporate director is the AIFM), and (e) must adopt rules governing dealings by directors of the CIS in its units.

4.421 In order to facilitate and expedite listings by new applicants, so long as the MFSA is advised of a CIS's intention to be admitted to listing at application stage, the MFSA will review the application for admissibility to listing concurrently with the application for authorisation of the CIS and will issue a single approval.

Anti-money laundering

4.422 As a full EU member state, Maltese law incorporates the requirements of the Fourth Anti-Money Laundering Directive[1] on measures for the prevention of money laundering and countering the financing of terrorism ('AML/CFT').

[1] Directive (EU) 2015/849 of 20 May 2015.

4.423 Maltese CIS, whether externally managed or self-managed, are required to appoint a money laundering reporting officer ('MLRO') who must be resident in Malta and of sufficient seniority and command within the CIS (typically a Malta resident director). In terms of guidance issued by Malta's competent authority for AML/CFT, the Financial Intelligence Analysis Unit, a Maltese CIS may alternatively enter into a contractual arrangement with its administrator (whether or not established in Malta) under which the MLRO duties of the CIS are to be carried out by the MLRO of the administrator.

Taxation

Maltese CIS

4.424 Maltese CIS are classified under Maltese tax legislation as either 'prescribed' or 'non-prescribed' funds. In general, a prescribed fund is defined as a CIS (or a sub-fund if the CIS is divided into sub-funds), formed in accordance with the laws of Malta, which has declared to the Commissioner of Inland Revenue in Malta that the value of its assets situated in Malta amounts to at least 85% of the value of its total assets. Maltese CIS which do not have such an exposure to Maltese assets and made a declaration to that effect are classified as non-prescribed funds.

4.425 Broadly, a non-prescribed fund is exempt from Maltese income tax on any income and capital gains other than income derived from immovable property situated in Malta. The latter income would be subject to a 35% tax or a final withholding tax of 8% or 10% on income derived from the transfer of immovable property situated in Malta.

4.426 A prescribed fund is also exempt from tax in Malta except for certain types of investment income which are subject to a withholding tax of 10% or 15%. Furthermore, similar to a non-prescribed fund, any income derived from immovable property is subject to tax at 35% or subject to a final withholding tax of 8% or 10% on income derived from the transfer of immovable property situated in Malta. Maltese feeder funds into Maltese master funds would be classified as prescribed funds; however, any income derived from another

4.426 Onshore Fund Domiciles

Maltese CIS (whether by way of dividend or as capital gains derived on the disposal of shares) is exempt from income tax in Malta.

4.427 Fund administration, fund management and fund custody services are generally exempt activities for the purposes of Maltese VAT. To the extent that a Maltese CIS incurs VAT on services it receives, that Maltese CIS would generally not be able to recover that VAT since the services of a CIS are considered to be exempt without credit.

4.428 Capital gains derived from the disposal of units in or dividends received from a Maltese non-prescribed fund by investors who are not resident in Malta are generally not subject to tax in Malta. Malta resident investors deriving dividends and capital gains from a non-prescribed Maltese CIS are generally subject to a 15% withholding tax on gains from the disposal of units in a non-prescribed CIS. Any dividends derived from a non-prescribed CIS by a Maltese resident investor are subject to a withholding tax of 15%.

4.429 Capital gains derived from the disposal of shares or units in a prescribed fund that are listed on a recognised exchange are exempt from any tax in Malta irrespective of whether or not the investor is resident in Malta.

4.430 Redemptions of shares or units in a Maltese CIS and transfers of such shares or units to third parties are exempt from duty on documents and transfers in Malta, provided that that CIS is in possession of a valid stamp duty exemption.

4.431 Malta has an extensive network of double taxation treaties which may, depending on the type of CIS and the provisions of the particular treaty, be available to the CIS.

4.432 As a full EU member state, Malta has implemented Council Directive 2014/107/EU of 9 December 2014 (which amended the Directive on Administrative Co-operation[1]) and the Common Reporting Standard. As regards the US Foreign Account Tax Compliance Act ('FATCA'), Malta has entered into a Model 1A inter-governmental agreement with the US Internal Revenue Service so that a Maltese CIS must report to the Maltese tax authorities.

[1] Council Directive 2011/16/EU of 15 February 2011.

Non-Maltese CIS (Maltese investors)

4.433 Profits distributed by a non-Maltese CIS and capital gains arising on the disposal (redemption or transfer) of units or shares in a non-Maltese CIS are generally subject to tax if paid to an investor who is resident and domiciled in Malta. Profits distributed by a non-Maltese CIS to an investor who is resident but not domiciled in Malta are taxable in Malta if such profits are received by the investor in Malta.

4.434 If the payment is made through the services of an authorised financial intermediary[1], the Maltese resident investor will, unless he has previously made an election not to deduct such tax, be subject to a 15% withholding tax. If the payment is not made through a local paying agent or if the withholding tax is otherwise not deducted, the Maltese resident investor will be obliged to declare the income or gains in his personal income tax return and will be subject to tax at the investor's ordinary progressive income tax rate (up to a maximum of 35%).

[1] Under the Collective Investment Schemes (Investment Income) Regulations (SL 123.51, Laws of Malta) an authorised financial intermediary (paying agent) is a person resident in Malta who holds an investment services licence issued under the IS Act and has been registered by the Malta Commissioner of Inland Revenue for such purpose. Only Category 2 or Category 3 IS Act licence holders are eligible to be registered as a local paying agent.

4.435 Switches within sub-funds of the same non-Maltese CIS are not deemed to give rise to a gain or loss to a Maltese resident investor (subject to the satisfaction of certain conditions). Instead, upon final disposal of the new units or shares in the non-Maltese CIS, capital gains may be calculated by deducting the cost of acquisition of the initial units or shares from the proceeds arising upon disposal of the new units or shares.

4.436 Issues or redemption of units or shares in non-Maltese CIS to/from Malta resident investors generally do not attract stamp duty in Malta unless the non-Maltese CIS holds, directly or indirectly, immovable property situated in Malta.

Service providers

4.437 Maltese fund managers, administrators, custodians and other Maltese companies (other than CIS) are subject to a flat tax rate of 35% on taxable profits. However, shareholders of Maltese companies may be entitled to claim a tax refund of part of the tax suffered by the Maltese company once it distributes the taxable profits to its shareholders.

E SINGAPORE

Danny Tan, Partner, Allen & Gledhill LLP

Introduction

4.438 Singapore is a cosmopolitan city-state that sits in the middle of the South-East Asia region. Home to about five million people from ethnic Chinese, Malay, Indian and Eurasian origins as well as a large expatriate community, Singapore stands out as a multiracial and multicultural city in the region. Singapore is very easily accessible. Being a busy air hub and voted the world's best airport since 2013[1], Changi Airport serves many international airlines daily and is very well connected to other cities around the world.

[1] Skytrax, World Airport Awards (2017) – see http://www.worldairportawards.com/Awards/worlds_best_airport.html.

4.439 Known in the early days as a trading port called Temasek ('Sea Town'), thereafter Singapura ('Lion City'), modern Singapore was founded by Sir Stamford Raffles in 1819 and became part of the British Straits Settlement. It declared independence from the UK in 1963 to be part of Malaysia and then separated from Malaysia in 1965.

4.440 Forced to fend for itself, the tiny island with no natural resources focused on its strengths to develop and grow. Leveraging on its geographically

4.440 Onshore Fund Domiciles

strategic location, the Port of Singapore Authority, Changi Airport and Singapore Airlines grew into the world class brands they are known as today. With its political stability, British heritage, favourable time zone and a diverse and hardworking immigrant population, the banking and finance industry also grew quickly, placing Singapore firmly on the global financial services map.

4.441 Today, Singapore has a highly developed market economy and one of the highest GDP per capita in the world. It has a sterling reputation as an investor and business friendly jurisdiction and has been consistently ranked as one of the world's easiest places in which to do business[1], among the world's most competitive economies[2] and globalised countries[3], and cited as having the best business environment worldwide[4]. It also has a growing reputation as Asia's premier wealth management hub, offering investors a plethora of regional investment opportunities.

[1] World Bank, Doing Business 2018 (31 October 2017) – see http://www.doingbusiness.org/~/media/WBG/DoingBusiness/Documents/Annual-Reports/English/DB2018-Full-Report.pdf.
[2] World Economic Forum, Global Competitiveness Report 2016–2017 – see https://www.weforum.org/reports/the-global-competitiveness-report-2016-2017-1.
[3] ETH Zürich, KOF Index of Globalization – see http://globalization.kof.ethz.ch.
[4] Economist Intelligence Unit, Country Forecasts Report (17 April 2017) – see http://country.eiu.com/article.aspx?articleid=505360834&Country=Singapore&topic=Business&subtopic=Business+environment&subsubtopic=Rankings+overview.

Singapore law

4.442 Given its colonial history, Singapore's legal system has its roots in English law and practice. Singapore inherited the English common law traditions, especially in contract, tort and restitution, and thus the stability, certainty and acceptance that such law enjoys among other nations.

4.443 Whilst Singapore courts still refer to case law emerging from England, Singapore law has evolved its own distinctive jurisprudence, as it continues to absorb and modify the common law as well as best practices from other mature legal systems. Developments in Singapore law reflect an acute awareness of the need to recognise and accommodate current international business and commercial practices.

4.444 Singapore has a comprehensive judicial system. The State Courts and the Family Justice Courts form the first tier in the judicial hierarchy to administer justice amongst the people. The former comprises the District Courts, Magistrates' Courts, Coroner's Court, Small Claims Tribunals and the State Courts Centre for Dispute Resolution, whilst the latter comprises the Family Division of the High Court, the Family Courts and the Youth Courts. The second tier is the Supreme Court, which comprises the High Court and the Court of Appeal, the latter being the highest court in the land. The Chief Justice, Judges of Appeal, Judges and Judicial Commissioners are appointed by the President on the advice of the Prime Minister.

4.445 The legal system in Singapore has received numerous international accolades for its efficiency and integrity[1]. As a consequence, Singapore is now widely recognised as a leading legal hub in Asia. Moreover, the Singapore authorities have taken various initiatives over the years to further develop Singapore as the region's legal hub, most notably with the establishment of the

Singapore International Arbitration Centre (the 'SIAC') and through the use of international treaties which make arbitral awards rendered in Singapore potentially enforceable in more than 140 foreign jurisdictions[2].

[1] For example, the World Justice Project, WJP Rule of Law Index 2017 (2017) – see http://worldjusticeproject.org/rule-of-law-index.
[2] For example, the 1958 New York Convention on the Recognition and Enforcement of Foreign Arbitral Awards.

4.446 Singapore is also widely recognised as a leading arbitration hub. Apart from being one of the most popular seats of arbitration in the world, Singapore has also been recognised as the most improved seat over the past five years[1]. The SIAC too is a popular choice as an arbitral institution[2]. In 2017, the International Chamber of Commerce announced that it will set up a case management office in Singapore, and plans to establish its first office in Asia, in Singapore, were also released by the Permanent Court of Arbitration to cater to the growing demand in the region for arbitration as an alternative means of dispute resolution[3].

[1] White and Case, 2015 International Arbitration Survey: Improvements and Innovations in International Arbitration (London, 2015).
[2] White and Case, 2015 International Arbitration Survey: Improvements and Innovations in International Arbitration (London, 2015).
[3] Singapore Ministry of Law, Permanent Court of Arbitration to set up office in Singapore (25 July 2017) – see https://www.mlaw.gov.sg/content/minlaw/en/news/press-releases/permanent-court-of-arbitration-to-set-up-office-in-singapore-.html.

4.447 In addition, in light of increasing cross-border transactions and disputes, the Ministry of Law (the 'Ministry') established the Singapore International Commercial Court (the 'SICC') in 2015 as an international forum for court-based commercial dispute resolution, which has cemented Singapore's position as a leading forum for legal services and international commercial dispute resolution. The SICC is a division of the Singapore High Court and is staffed by a panel of experienced judges comprising specialist commercial judges drawn from the ranks of the existing Justices of the Supreme Court of Singapore, as well as international judges from both civil law and common law jurisdictions. To ensure the enforceability of SICC judgments internationally, Singapore has been a party to the Hague Convention on Choice of Courts Agreements since 1 October 2016.

4.448 Further, following the recommendations of a Working Group on International Commercial Mediation established by the Ministry, the Singapore International Mediation Institute ('SIMI') and the Singapore International Mediation Centre ('SIMC') were launched in 2014[1]. SIMI serves as a professional body to set standards and provide accreditation for mediators, whilst SIMC serves as an international mediation service provider offering a quality panel of international mediators and experts, and together they represent part of a concerted effort by the Ministry to build a credible offering of an entire suite of dispute resolution services in Singapore.

[1] See http://simc.com.sg/mediation-goes-global-in-singapore.

4.449 Onshore Fund Domiciles

The finance industry in Singapore

4.449 Singapore is a highly regarded financial centre and ranks as a leading financial centre in the world[1]. The city skyline is defined by towering skyscrapers which house international and domestic financial institutions. Banking and finance has been the powerhouse behind Singapore's economic success for decades. In more recent years, with growth and development in Asia, Singapore has risen as a global centre for fund management and wealth management.

[1] Long Finance, The Global Financial Centres Index 22 (London, September 2017).

4.450 Based on the annual survey conducted by the Monetary Authority of Singapore (the 'MAS'), at the end of 2016[1], total assets managed by Singapore-based asset managers stood at a new high of S$2.744 trillion, a 7% increase over the S$2.566 trillion at the end of 2015. This represents a five-year compound annual growth rate of 15% per annum in assets under management ('AUM'), underscoring the resilience and dynamism of the fund management industry in Singapore, against the backdrop of an uncertain global economic environment. In particular, overall hedge fund AUM grew by 16% to reach S$138 billion at the end of 2016.

[1] Monetary Authority of Singapore, 2016 Singapore Asset Management Survey (Singapore, 2017).

4.451 Like many things in Singapore, this growth did not result by chance. This is due, in no small part, to the meticulous planning by the Singapore authorities over the years to cultivate a conducive legal, regulatory and tax environment tailored to meet the needs of the fund management industry so that Singapore may become an attractive jurisdiction for fund managers, including hedge fund managers, to establish their operations and domicile their funds.

Hedge funds in Singapore

4.452 There is no statutory or judicial definition of a hedge fund under Singapore law. However, a hedge fund would normally be a collective investment scheme (a 'CIS') as defined under the Securities and Futures Act, Chapter 289 of Singapore (the 'SFA').

4.453 The Code on Collective Investment Schemes (the 'CIS Code') issued by the MAS (which sets out certain guidelines pertaining to the retail marketing of CIS in Singapore) provides that there are different characteristics and investment strategies that define hedge funds. Specifically, the CIS Code states that, in general, a hedge fund refers to a scheme which aims to achieve a high return through the use of advanced investment strategies.

4.454 In considering whether a fund falls within the MAS guidelines for hedge funds, the CIS Code provides that the MAS would look at, among other aspects, the use of advanced investment strategies which may involve financial instruments which are not liquid, financial derivatives, the concentration of investments, the use of leverage or short selling, and the use of alternative asset classes. In this regard, it would appear that the MAS has full discretion in deciding whether a CIS is a hedge fund for the purposes of the CIS Code.

Regulation of investment managers

4.455 Hedge fund management is regulated under the general fund management regulatory regime in Singapore. Fund management is one of the 'regulated activities'[1] under the SFA. 'Fund management' is defined under the SFA as undertaking on behalf of a customer (whether under discretionary authority granted by the customer or otherwise) the management of a portfolio of securities or futures contracts, or foreign exchange trading or leveraged foreign exchange trading, for the purpose of managing the customer's funds. It does not include real estate investment trust management.

[1] The other 'regulated activities' under the SFA are: dealing in securities; trading in futures contracts; leveraged foreign exchange trading; advising on corporate finance; real estate investment trust management; securities financing; providing credit rating services; and providing custodial services for securities.

4.456 A corporation which carries on a business of fund management in Singapore is prima facie required to hold a capital markets services licence (a 'CMS licence') for fund management under the SFA (and its staff who conduct the regulated activities must be individually notified as representatives under the Representative Notification Framework), unless one of the licensing exemptions under the SFA can be invoked.

4.457 On 7 August 2012, the MAS introduced an enhanced regulatory regime for fund management companies ('FMCs') in Singapore. Under this regime, FMCs operating in Singapore will be regulated under one of three categories:

- *Registered FMC*: An FMC whose AUM is below S$250 million, and which serves not more than 30 'qualified investors', of which not more than 15 are funds.
- *Licensed accredited/institutional investor FMC* ('A/I LFMC'): A licensed FMC which serves an unrestricted number of 'qualified investors' only. An FMC whose AUM is less than S$250 million may also apply for a CMS licence under this category, provided that it meets all the admission criteria.
- *Licensed retail FMC* ('retail LFMC'): A licensed FMC which serves all types of investors, including retail (ie non-accredited and non-institutional) investors, for example licensed FMCs which manage retail unit trust funds and collective investment schemes.

Establishing a local investment manager

4.458 Under the enhanced fund management regulatory regime, FMCs seeking to be licensed or registered in Singapore need to meet the enhanced business conduct and capital requirements which are set out below in brief:

- *Singapore incorporated*: An FMC should be a Singapore incorporated company with a permanent physical office in Singapore.

4.458 Onshore Fund Domiciles

- *Base capital*: An FMC must at all times meet the base capital thresholds which range from S$250,000 to S$1 million depending on the type of fund management activity that is carried out.
- *Risk-based capital*: A licensed FMC (ie A/I LFMCs and retail LFMCs – collectively, 'LFMCs') is required to meet the requisite risk-based capital requirements at all times and ensure that its financial resources are at least 120% of its operational risk requirement.
- *Competency requirements*: An FMC should ensure that its staff who conduct fund management or other regulated activities which are integral to fund management have the relevant experience and meet the relevant entry and examination requirements (if applicable). An FMC should also satisfy the MAS that its shareholders, directors, representatives and employees, as well as the FMC itself, are 'fit and proper'.
- *Compliance arrangements*: An FMC needs to have in place compliance arrangements that are commensurate with the nature, scale and complexity of its business.
- *Risk management framework*: An FMC has to put in place a risk management framework which identifies, addresses and monitors the risks associated with assets under its management. The risk management function should be segregated from and independent of the portfolio management function.
- *Internal audit*: The business activities of an FMC must be subject to adequate internal audit. The internal audit may be conducted by the internal audit function or outsourced.
- *Independent annual audits*: An FMC is required to meet annual audit requirements.
- *Professional indemnity insurance*: The MAS may impose a licence condition requiring a retail LFMC to obtain professional indemnity insurance that meets specified minimum requirements.
- *Letter of responsibility*: Where appropriate, the MAS may require an LFMC to obtain a letter of responsibility from its parent company.

4.459 FMCs are further required to comply with the following on an on-going basis:

- *Independent custody*: An FMC must ensure that the assets it manages are subject to independent custody. Independent custodians include prime brokers, depositories and banks that are regulated in their respective jurisdictions.
- *Independent valuation*: An FMC must ensure that the assets it manages are subject to independent valuation and customer reporting.
- *Mitigating conflicts of interest*: An FMC has to mitigate any actual or potential conflict of interest that may arise from the management of assets and, where appropriate, disclose such conflict to the customer.
- *Disclosure*: An FMC should ensure that there is adequate disclosure to its customers in respect of each fund or account that it manages. Information that should be disclosed includes, inter alia, the investment policy and strategy and the risks associated with the strategy.
- *AML/CFT requirements*: An FMC must comply with the requirements on anti-money laundering and countering the financing of terrorism requirements.

- *Reporting of misconduct*: All LFMCs are required to comply with the misconduct reporting requirements.
- *Use of service providers*: Prior to entering into arrangements with service providers (such as a compliance service provider or a fund administrator), an FMC should take into account the MAS requirements on outsourcing.
- *Approvals, notifications and periodic returns*: An FMC must comply with its obligations to notify MAS of, or to seek MAS approval for, as the case may be, relevant transactions and changes in particulars, and to submit periodic regulatory returns in relation to its fund management activities.

Establishing a fund

4.460 Singapore has seen increasing interest from fund managers looking to domicile their funds in Singapore. Some funds seek to take advantage of the extensive network of double taxation treaties that Singapore has entered into when making investments. For others, there appears to be a preference for funds to be domiciled in reputable jurisdictions such as Singapore as opposed to traditional offshore 'tax havens'.

4.461 Funds established in Singapore typically take the form of limited liability companies, limited partnerships and unit trusts.

4.462 Singapore-managed hedge funds have typically been domiciled offshore. These funds will typically delegate their management to a Singapore-based fund manager or appoint a Singapore-based investment adviser/sub-manager if the fund manager is based outside Singapore. Hedge funds established in Singapore have typically been structured as unit trusts.

4.463 However, this is likely to change soon. The Singapore authorities have been studying the benefits of an open-ended investment corporation and have embarked on a public consultation to solicit feedback on the new corporate structure, the Singapore variable capital company ('S-VACC')[1]. Key features of the S-VACC that have been proposed include providing for the creation of sub-funds with segregated assets and liabilities, allowing for the redemption of shares and the payment of dividends out of capital, and eliminating the need for the register of shareholders to be made available to the public. In addition, proposals for an inward re-domiciliation regime which will allow foreign structures that are equivalent to the S-VACC to re-domicile as an S-VACC in Singapore are also being considered. If introduced, the S-VACC could be a very attractive option for hedge funds that wish to domicile in Singapore and would further enhance the attractiveness of Singapore as a fund management centre.

---

[1] Monetary Authority of Singapore, Keynote address by Mr Lawrence Wong, Minister for National Development and Second Minister for Finance, at the Investment Management Association of Singapore's 20th Anniversary Conference, 23 March 2017 – see http://www.mas.gov.sg/News-and-Publications/Speeches-and-Monetary-Policy-Statements/Speeches.aspx.

4.464 *Onshore Fund Domiciles*

Types of vehicles and relevant legislation

Companies

4.464 The incorporation and management of companies in Singapore is governed by the Companies Act, Chapter 50 of Singapore (the 'Companies Act') and regulated by the Accounting and Corporate Regulatory Authority ('ACRA').

4.465 Companies limited by shares can be public or private, with the key difference being that a public company can have more than 50 shareholders and is subject to greater regulation than a private company.

4.466 Every company incorporated in Singapore must have at least one director who is ordinarily resident in Singapore[1] and at least one company secretary whose principal or only place of residence is Singapore[2]. In addition, companies must have a registered office from the date of incorporation and appoint an auditor within three months of this date[3]. Subject to certain exceptions, a company's accounts must be audited once a year.

[1] Section 145(1) of the Companies Act.
[2] Section 171(1) of the Companies Act.
[3] Section 205(1) of the Companies Act.

4.467 In Singapore, the incorporation of companies is effected online via BizFile, an electronic filing and information retrieval system maintained by ACRA. Incorporation can be done within the day, where the proposed company name has been reserved, and provided that all the incorporation documents are in order.

4.468 An advantage of a company is that it has a separate legal personality, and therefore may hold property in its own name. Members of a limited company further enjoy limited liability and would not be held personally liable for the debts and liabilities of the company. The disadvantages of a company would be that there is a higher level of statutory regulation than for some other vehicles, the dissolution of a company is complex and time-consuming, and a company must also meet the requirements for corporate transparency such as disclosure of shareholders and filing of accounts with ACRA.

Limited partnerships

4.469 The limited partnership is a well-established fund vehicle in many jurisdictions.

4.470 With the rise in popularity of Singapore as a fund domicile, in 2009 the Singapore authorities enacted the Limited Partnerships Act, Chapter 163B of Singapore, which introduced the Singapore limited partnership. Rather than reinvent the vehicle, the draftsman based that legislation on limited partnership legislation in England, Jersey and the US State of Delaware, which ensured that the Singapore limited partnership is able to capitalise on the familiarity of the worldwide investor community with such vehicles.

4.471 A Singapore limited partnership must consist of at least one limited partner and one general partner. Limited partners and general partners may be individuals or corporations. A general partner is liable for all of the debts and obligations of the limited partnership incurred while it is a general partner in the limited partnership. A limited partner, on the other hand, will not be liable for the debts and obligations of the limited partnership beyond the amount of its agreed contribution, subject to certain exceptions. In particular, to enjoy limited liability, limited partners must not take part in the management of a limited partnership. Limited partners do not have the power to bind a limited partnership.

4.472 Singapore limited partnerships are regulated by ACRA and the registration of a limited partnership may be made via BizFile. Every registration of a limited partnership will be valid for such period as the registrar may specify. The registration is valid for one year from the date of registration. The registration must be renewed annually on or before the expiry date.

4.473 The Singapore limited partnership provides an attractive framework for a fund structure. It is tax transparent, provides limited liability for investors, and provides for relative ease of cash repatriation even in the absence of profits. Annual audits of the accounts of the limited partnership are not required. One disadvantage of a limited partnership is that it does not have separate legal personality. In addition, unlike companies, it is not currently possible to list interests of a limited partnership.

Unit trusts

4.474 A unit trust is a trust arrangement whereby the legal ownership of the scheme's assets is vested in a trustee which holds those assets on trust for the benefit of unitholders. A unit trust is constituted by an instrument of trust which is usually made between a manager and a trustee. The trust instrument typically governs the appointment and retirement of the trustee and the manager, their respective duties, the distribution or accumulation of trust income, investment powers, dealings in units and valuation. The applicable legislation with regard to trusts in Singapore is the Trustees Act, Chapter 337 of Singapore (the 'Trustees Act').

4.475 The primary obligation of the trustee of a unit trust which is established under Singapore law is to manage the assets of the fund. It is not mandatory for a private unit trust established in Singapore to be managed by an investment manager although that is not common for private funds. Under the Trustees Act, a private unit trust can be established in Singapore without a manager and with the trustee of such trust carrying out its duties and functions as set out under the Trustees Act, including that of investment management.

4.476 A unit trust structure is largely contractual and as such is fairly flexible. Like a limited partnership, it is tax transparent, and can provide limited liability for investors as well as relative ease of cash repatriation even in the absence of profits. One disadvantage of a unit trust is that it does not have separate legal personality. The requirement to have a trustee may add costs to the structure and it may also not be as familiar to investors in certain jurisdictions.

4.477 *Onshore Fund Domiciles*

Taxation

4.477 Singapore is regarded as having one of the most attractive tax regimes in the world for funds and fund managers. Singapore's comprehensive tax treaty network, coupled with a relatively low corporate tax rate of 17%, has drawn many multinational corporations, including fund management companies and fund companies, to establish and build a presence on the island. Additionally, in recent years the Singapore authorities have introduced a wide range of tax concessions and incentives to promote Singapore as a centre for financial services activities, and in particular the fund management industry.

Tax treaties

4.478 As of February 2018, Singapore has approximately 84 comprehensive avoidance of double taxation agreements (agreements that generally cover all types of income), eight limited treaties (agreements that generally cover only income from shipping or air transport), and three treaties that are signed but not ratified (either comprehensive agreements or limited treaties that are not ratified and therefore do not have the force of law)[1]. Singapore has also entered into an exchange of information agreement with Bermuda.

[1] A list of tax treaties can be accessed on the Inland Revenue Authority of Singapore's website – see https://www.iras.gov.sg/irashome/Quick-Links/International-Tax.

4.479 Avoidance of double taxation agreements between Singapore and other countries not only serve to prevent double taxation of income, they also clarify the taxing rights between Singapore and its treaty partner on different types of income arising from cross-border economic activities between the two countries. The agreements also provide for the reduction or exemption of tax on certain types of income.

Taxation of funds and fund managers

4.480 A taxable presence could be created by a person in Singapore which manages a fund, regardless of whether the fund is based in Singapore or offshore. Generally, all income and gains of the fund which are attributable to the activities of a fund manager in Singapore may be taxable in Singapore, regardless of whether the fund is established in Singapore or elsewhere. However, Singapore's taxation framework does provide certain 'safe harbours' for such funds.

4.481 The main tax incentive schemes relevant to the fund management industry are as follows:

- *Qualifying fund scheme for offshore funds*: This scheme is applicable to non-resident or offshore companies and trusts pursuant to section 13CA of the Income Tax Act, Chapter 134 of Singapore (the 'Income Tax Act').
- *Resident fund scheme*: This scheme is applicable to Singapore-resident companies which are incorporated in Singapore pursuant to section 13R of the Income Tax Act.

- *Enhanced tier fund scheme*: This scheme is applicable to onshore or offshore companies, limited partnerships and trusts (other than certain trusts, such as approved pension or approved provident funds, Central Provident Fund unit trusts, designated unit trusts and real estate investment trusts) pursuant to section 13X of the Income Tax Act.

4.482 The scope of tax exemptions under each of the tax incentive schemes above is the same, that is 'specified income' from 'designated investments' of such funds under each of such schemes would be exempt from tax in Singapore, subject to the conditions of each respective scheme being met. It should also be noted that all the above tax exemptions require that the relevant funds be managed by a fund manager in Singapore (which is licensed or exempt from licensing by the MAS). In particular, the enhanced tier fund scheme affords considerable flexibility in that it imposes no restrictions on the residency status of the fund vehicles or that of the funds' investors, and applies equally to limited partnerships. There is, however, a S$50 million minimum fund size requirement, and the fund will need to incur at least S$200,000 in local business spending in each basis period relating to any year of assessment.

4.483 The Financial Sector Incentive Fund Management award is also available to fund managers. Under this award, concessionary rates of tax of 10% are available to fund managers on income derived from providing fund management or investment advisory services to a fund which qualifies under the three tax incentive schemes mentioned above, subject to certain conditions being met. Only fund managers with AUM of at least S$250 million are eligible for this award.

F SWITZERLAND

Olivier Stahler, Partner, Lenz & Staehelin and Charlotte Gilliéron, Associate, Lenz & Staehelin

The finance industry

4.484 Due to its long tradition of providing banking services, Switzerland is one of the world's leaders in the asset management industry. Switzerland is an important market for the distribution of interests in Swiss and non-Swiss funds. Further, Swiss investment fund managers manage a significant portion of European undertakings for collective investment in transferable securities ('UCITS') and alternative investment funds ('AIFs').

4.485 At the end of December 2016, Swiss investors had invested CHF 911.7 billion in Swiss and non-Swiss funds. At the end of 2016, 8,952 Swiss and non-Swiss funds were registered for distribution in Switzerland. Of these, 1,551 were funds established under Swiss law and 7,401 were funds established under foreign law[1]. These statistics do not take into account non-Swiss hedge funds, which in practice cannot be registered for distribution in Switzerland to 'non-qualified investors'[2].

---

[1] Swiss Funds & Asset Management Association's review of 2016 and outlook (SFAMA media release 02/2017) – see https://www.sfama.ch/en/media/media-releases.
[2] See paras 13.375–13.379 in CHAPTER 13 for the definition of 'non-qualified investors'.

4.486 Onshore Fund Domiciles

4.486 Switzerland is not a jurisdiction in which hedge funds are established. Rather, it is a jurisdiction in which fund related services are provided, such as marketing and distribution activities and investment management activities. The majority of the hedge funds which are managed by Swiss investment managers are established abroad in traditional offshore jurisdictions such as the Cayman Islands.

4.487 Since the entry into force of the Swiss Federal Act of 23 June 2006 on Collective Investment Schemes (the 'CISA') on 1 October 2007, the Swiss regime which governs investment funds aims at offering a more flexible legal framework for hedge funds in Switzerland. The CISA introduced new legal forms for funds, some of which may be suitable for hedge funds. That being said, the relevant legal and regulatory framework still imposes relatively strict investment restrictions (such as on the scope of permitted investments and leverage). In this context, Switzerland is disadvantaged compared to the traditional jurisdictions for the establishment of hedge funds.

Regulation of investment funds

4.488 Swiss hedge funds are governed by the CISA and its implementing ordinances, the Swiss Federal Ordinance of 22 November 2006 on Collective Investment Schemes (the 'CISO') and the Ordinance of the Swiss Financial Market Supervisory Authority ('FINMA') of 27 August 2014 on Collective Investment Schemes (the 'CISO-FINMA'). The CISA and the CISO have been subject to an important revision. The revised CISA and CISO entered into force on 1 March 2013 and mainly affected the distribution, safekeeping and administration of Swiss funds. The Swiss fund regulations do not contain a legal definition of hedge funds.

Types of fund vehicle

4.489 The CISA provides for four types of Swiss funds, which could in theory be suitable for alternative investments, namely:

- contractual funds[1];
- investment company with variable capital[2];
- limited partnership for collective investments[3]; and
- investment company with fixed capital[4].

[1] See paras **4.490–4.492** below.
[2] See paras **4.493–4.497** below.
[3] See paras **4.498–4.501** below.
[4] See paras **4.502–4.505** below.

Contractual funds

4.490 Contractual funds are the most commonly used vehicles in the Swiss investment management industry. A Swiss contractual fund is an open-ended fund. It is a contractual pool of assets the purpose of which is common investment. It does not have the legal capacity to act and is represented by a Swiss fund management company according to article 28 et seq of the CISA.

4.491 A fund management company must be established as a stock corporation which is incorporated and managed in Switzerland[1]. The fund management company's primary purpose is the management of contractual funds[2]. The fund management company must be authorised by FINMA[3] prior to carrying out its activities. The fund management company holds the contractual fund's assets on a fiduciary basis on behalf of the contractual fund's investors. The custody of the contractual fund's assets lies with a custodian bank. The Swiss custodian must be a Swiss bank pursuant to the Swiss Federal Act of 8 November 1934 on Banks and Savings Banks. In particular, the Swiss custodian is in charge of the safekeeping of the contractual fund's assets and exercises certain supervisory duties in relation to the contractual fund.

[1] Article 28 para 1 of the CISA.
[2] Article 29 para 1 of the CISA.
[3] Article 13 para 2(a) of the CISA.

4.492 The fund management company, the Swiss custodian and each investor are bound by a fund contract which sets out the rights and obligations of all parties[1]. The fund contract is the document which governs the contractual fund[2] and, as such, must be approved by FINMA[3].

[1] Article 26 para 2 of the CISA.
[2] Article 8 para 3 of the CISA.
[3] Article 15 para 1(a) of the CISA.

Investment company with variable capital

4.493 The investment company with variable capital ('SICAV') is an open-ended company with variable share capital[1]. It is subject to the supervision of FINMA. The most significant structural difference between a SICAV and a typical Swiss stock corporation is that a SICAV may issue shares to so-called investing shareholders in a straightforward fashion whilst a more burdensome procedure is necessary to increase and decrease the share capital of a typical Swiss stock corporation. The second major difference between a SICAV and a Swiss stock corporation is that a SICAV's sole corporate purpose is collectively to manage its own assets[2].

[1] Article 36 para 1(a) of the CISA.
[2] Article 36 para 1(d) of the CISA.

4.494 A SICAV may be either 'self-managed' or 'non-self-managed'. In the case of a self-managed SICAV, the administration of the SICAV lies with the general management; in the case of a non-self-managed SICAV, the administration of the SICAV is delegated to a fund management company[1]. The concept of administration does not include 'investment management' of the SICAV. The management of the SICAV's assets may therefore be delegated to an investment manager, provided that the relevant investment manager is licensed by FINMA[2].

[1] Article 51 paras 2 and 5 of the CISA.
[2] Article 13 para 2(f) of the CISA.

4.495 Onshore Fund Domiciles

4.495 A key feature of the Swiss SICAV is that it must provide for a special category of shares, namely sponsor's shares. The sponsor's shares form a separate sub-fund of the SICAV, which must be separate from any sub-fund in which the investors invest. As a rule, both types of shares, ie sponsor's shares and investor's shares, have the same rights and obligations. That being said, there are some exceptions to the principle of equal treatment among the shareholders of a SICAV. In particular, the holders of sponsor's shares have the exclusive right to decide upon the dissolution of the SICAV, to close a sub-fund of the SICAV or to request FINMA to liquidate the SICAV.

4.496 The board of directors of the SICAV must appoint a Swiss custodian. The tasks of the Swiss custodian of a SICAV are the same as for the Swiss custodian of a contractual fund.

4.497 The fund regulations of the SICAV consist of the SICAVs articles of association and investment regulations[1], each of which is subject to the approval of FINMA[2].

[1] Article 8 para 3 of the CISA.
[2] Article 15 para 1(b) of the CISA.

Limited partnership for collective investments

4.498 The Swiss limited partnership for collective investments ('SCPC') has been designed to mirror the legal form of certain offshore limited partnership vehicles. An SCPC may invest in alternative investments[1]. Prior to carrying out its activities, an SCPC must be authorised by FINMA[2]. The partnership agreement[3] which governs an SCPC is subject to the approval of FINMA[4].

[1] Article 103 para 2 of the CISA; article 121 para 1(b) of the CISO.
[2] Article 13 para 2(c) of the CISA.
[3] Article 9 para 3 of the CISA.
[4] Article 15 para 1(c) of the CISA.

4.499 SCPCs comprise one or more general partners (each, a 'general partner') and several limited partners (each, a 'limited partner'). The limited partners must be qualified investors as defined in the CISA[1].

[1] See paras **13.375–13.379** in CHAPTER 13 for the definition of 'qualified investors'.

4.500 The management of an SCPC lies with the general partner to the exclusion of the limited partners. The general partner can delegate the management of the SCPC to qualified third parties (such as an authorised fund management company)[1].

[1] Article 102 para 1(i) of the CISA.

4.501 The SCPC is a closed-ended collective investment scheme. The limited partners are in principle not entitled to request the SCPC to redeem their interests in the SCPC. The SCPC partnership agreement may however deviate from this prohibition[1].

[1] Article 102 para 1(f) of the CISA.

Investment company with fixed capital

4.502 The SICAF is defined as a closed-ended corporation (i) whose corporate purpose is limited to the management of its own assets, (ii) in which 'non-qualified investors'[1] may invest, and (iii) which is not listed on a Swiss stock exchange[2]. With the exception of certain rules provided in the CISA and the CISO, SICAFs are mainly governed by the relevant provisions of the Swiss Code of Obligations of 30 March 1911 (the 'Swiss Code of Obligations') which applies to Swiss corporations. If the shares are listed on a stock exchange or if the SICAF is exclusively reserved to qualified investors and its shares are registered shares, the SICAF falls outside the scope of the CISA. It would appear that all Swiss SICAFs have so far relied on this regulatory exemption. In this context, there is currently no Swiss SICAF which is regulated by FINMA.

[1] See paras **13.375–13.379** in Chapter 13 for the definition of 'non-qualified investors'.
[2] Article 110 of the CISA.

4.503 The SICAF is more suitable than the SCPC for pursuing long-term investment strategies. The main difference between a SICAF and an SCPC lies in the absence of a requirement for the investors in the SICAF to be qualified investors within the meaning of the CISA[1].

[1] See paras **13.375–13.379** in Chapter 13 for the definition of 'qualified investors'.

4.504 The fund regulations of the SICAF consist of the SICAF's articles of association and investment regulations[1], each of which is subject to the approval of FINMA[2].

[1] Article 9 para 4 of the CISA.
[2] Article 15 para 1(d) of the CISA.

4.505 As a corporation, SICAF is managed by a board of directors which may delegate investment decisions as well as any other tasks, provided that this is in the best interest of the SICAF[1]. SICAFs may only manage their own assets[2].

[1] Article 122 para 2 of the CISO.
[2] Article 122 para 1 of the CISO.

Investment restrictions

4.506 The CISA, the CISO and the CISO-FINMA contain numerous investment restrictions. The scope of those restrictions differs depending on (i) the structure of the funds (namely, contractual fund, SICAV, SCPC or SICAF) and (ii) the investment strategy of the relevant Swiss fund (for example, whether the relevant Swiss fund is a securities fund, a real estate fund, a so-called traditional investments fund or an alternative investment fund ('AIF')). For instance, AIFs are entitled to borrow up to 50% of their net assets[1]. They may pledge or transfer as collateral up to 100% of their assets and may commit to an overall exposure of up to 600% of their net assets[2].

[1] Article 100 para 2(a) of the CISO.
[2] Article 100 para 2(b) and (c) of the CISO.

4.507 *Onshore Fund Domiciles*

Regulation of investment managers

4.507 As mentioned above, Switzerland is not a jurisdiction in which hedge funds are established. References to 'Swiss hedge funds' should therefore be understood as references to non-Swiss hedge funds which are managed by Swiss-based investment managers.

4.508 Before the revision of the CISA, which came into force on 1 March 2013, only investment managers of Swiss funds had to be licensed by FINMA. Under certain conditions (for example, if foreign law required a regulated status for the investment manager), the Swiss investment managers of non-Swiss funds could apply for authorisation from FINMA. This voluntary submission to FINMA supervision aimed at allowing Swiss investment managers to fulfil the requirements of the Undertakings for Collective Investment in Transferable Securities Directive[1] (the 'UCITS Directive'), and thereby to provide investment management services to UCITS. The investment managers of foreign non-UCITS, whose investment management did not require prudential supervision, could in principle not obtain authorisation as investment managers from FINMA.

[1] Directive 2009/65/EC of 13 July 2009.

4.509 Since the entry into force of the revised CISA on 1 March 2013, Swiss investment managers of both Swiss and non-Swiss funds must now be authorised by FINMA.

The de minimis exemptions

4.510 The CISA provides for certain de minimis exemptions. By virtue of these exemptions, investment managers of both Swiss and non-Swiss funds whose investors are qualified investors as defined in the CISA[1] are not regulated if one or more of the following conditions is met:

- the assets under management, including those resulting from the use of leverage, do not exceed CHF 100 million;
- the assets under management do not exceed CHF 500 million, and the funds are unleveraged and closed-ended for a five-year period from the date of the initial investment; or
- the investors are exclusively group companies.

[1] See paras 13.375–13.379 in Chapter 13 for the definition of 'qualified investors'.

Investment manager licence

4.511 The conditions for authorisation as an investment manager are inspired by the conditions for authorisation as a bank or securities dealer in Switzerland.

4.512 Pursuant to the CISA and the CISO, FINMA will grant a licence to a Swiss investment manager if the following conditions (see paras 4.513–4.536 below) are met:

SHAREHOLDERS

4.513 Holders of qualified shareholding interests (ie persons which hold 10% or more of the equity) must have a good reputation and must not exercise their influence to the detriment of cautious and sound management[1].

[1] Article 14 para 1(b) of the CISA; article 11 of the CISO.

GOVERNANCE STRUCTURE

4.514 The governance structure of an investment manager must comprise the following:

- *A management board*: The management board of the investment manager determines the strategy of the investment manager and acts as senior management of the investment manager. The management board must have practical experience of the asset classes of the funds which the investment manager manages, risk management and compliance in order to exercise its supervisory function appropriately.

  The management board must comprise at least three members. Based on the principle of checks and balances, FINMA requires that a majority of the members of the management board do not carry out operational tasks on behalf of the investment manager and that at least one third of the members of the management board are independent, in particular from the majority shareholders.

  The members of the management board must have a good reputation and offer all the guarantees of proper management[1].

- *An executive committee*: The principal task of the executive committee is to deal with the day-to-day business of the investment manager in accordance with the instructions of the management board in relation to strategy and risks.

  The executive committee must consist of at least two members who must have their place of residence in a location that enables them to exercise the effective management of the business[2].

  Like the members of the management board, the members of the executive committee must have a good reputation and offer all the guarantees of proper management. They must also have appropriate professional qualifications and experience in the relevant fields, ie portfolio management, compliance and risk management[3].

[1] Article 14 para 1(a) of the CISA, article 10 of the CISO.
[2] Article 12 para 1 of the CISO.
[3] Article 14 para 1(a) of the CISA, article 10 of the CISO.

AUDIT FIRM

4.515 The investment manager must appoint an external audit firm to carry out the audit of its annual accounts and its regulatory audit. The annual accounts audit and the regulatory audit must be carried out each year. An investment manager is not required to appoint the same firm to carry out the

4.515 Onshore Fund Domiciles

annual accounts audit and the regulatory audit, although in practice it typically does so. Only firms which are approved by the Federal Audit Oversight Authority with a specific authorisation may be appointed for this purpose[1].

[1] Article 126 para 1(e) of the CISA.

4.516 An audit firm must be appointed to issue the report which accompanies the application for authorisation. The task of the auditor is to conduct an audit during the authorisation procedure and to submit a report to FINMA indicating whether the applicant is able to fulfil all the authorisation conditions.

4.517 For the purpose of ensuring the independence of the authorisation auditor, it does not have the right to carry out the audit of the annual accounts or the regulatory audit of an investment manager in relation to which it submitted a report to FINMA for three years following the granting of the licence for that investment manager.

Legal form of the company

4.518 The investment manager must be a legal entity which is established under Swiss law or a Swiss branch of an entity which is established under foreign law. Swiss investment managers may choose one of the legal forms provided for by Swiss corporate law[1]. In practice, Swiss corporations limited by shares are the most frequently used legal form for investment managers.

[1] Article 18 para 1 of the CISA.

Corporate governance

4.519 The corporate governance of the investment manager must guarantee the fulfilment of its legal obligations[1]. The corporate governance must be appropriate and adequate, particularly in the fields of risk management, internal control system and compliance.

[1] Article 14 para 1(c) of the CISA.

4.520 There must be a clear division of expertise and responsibilities from an operational perspective and some key functions must be separated. The control functions must be separated from the operational functions (such as investment management) and the front office functions must be separated from those of the back office.

4.521 As regards delegation, only the activities for which the investment manager is able to establish an adequate control system may be outsourced.

Risk management, internal control system and compliance

4.522 The investment manager must ensure appropriate and adequate risk management as well as an internal control system and a compliance system which covers all of its activities. The specific organisation must be adapted to the type, scope and complexity of the operations and to the risks involved[1].

[1] Article 14 para 1ter of the CISA, article 12a of the CISO.

4.523 The investment manager will separate the risk management, the internal control system and the compliance functions from the operational functions of the investment manager, specifically those connected to portfolio management activities.

4.524 The risk management function must be organised in such a way that it can detect, assess and monitor sufficiently the main risks[1].

[1] Article 12a para 2 of the CISO.

4.525 The purpose of the internal control system is to monitor the investment manager's most important activities. This involves all the processes, methods and actions of the management board and of the executive committee of the investment manager that ensure the proper conduct of the operational activities of the investment manager.

4.526 The compliance function is responsible for checking compliance with the regulations applicable to the investment manager as well as the internal policies of the investment manager.

INTERNAL REGULATIONS

4.527 The investment manager must put in place internal regulations to ensure compliance with the obligations provided for in the Swiss fund regulations[1].

[1] Article 14 para 1(c) of the CISA.

4.528 The organisational regulations must describe the organisation of the investment manager[1]. They must reflect the actual structures and competencies within the investment manager and must define precisely the scope and geographical radius of the activities of the investment manager, unless this information is already included in the articles of incorporation or the partnership agreement of the investment manager[2]. The regulations must also state the essential tasks which the investment manager has delegated to third parties[3]. The organisational regulations of an investment manager are subject to the approval of FINMA.

[1] Article 12 para 3 of the CISO.
[2] Article 24 para 1 of the CISO.
[3] Article 66 of the CISO-FINMA.

4.529 An investment policy must describe the investment strategy and the investment process of the investment manager. A risk management and risk control policy will lay down appropriate principles for the management and control of risks as well as the organisation of the management and control of risks[1]. Other internal directives may be required depending on the activities of the investment manager (eg a distribution directive). Unlike the organisational regulations, internal directives are reviewed by FINMA during the authorisa-

4.529 Onshore Fund Domiciles

tion procedure but are not approved by FINMA.

[1] Article 68 para 4 of the CISO-FINMA.

Anti-money laundering

4.530 Investment managers fall within the scope of the Swiss Anti-Money Laundering Act of 10 October 1997 (the 'AMLA') and are therefore subject to FINMA supervision where they distribute funds and/or conduct other business activities which are subject to the AMLA, such as individual asset management activities[1].

[1] Article 2 paras 2(b^{bis}) and 3 of the AMLA.

Rules of conduct

4.531 Investment managers are required to comply with the rules of conduct set out in article 20 et seq of the CISA and article 31 et seq of the CISO, in particular with regard to the obligations of loyalty, diligence and information.

4.532 These obligations are embodied in the code of conduct issued by the Swiss Funds & Asset Management Association (the 'SFAMA') on 7 October 2014[1] (the 'SFAMA Code of Conduct'). FINMA has recognised the SFAMA Code of Conduct as a minimum standard. All investment managers must therefore comply with that code.

[1] Available at http://www.sfama.ch/en/self-regulation-model-documents/codes-of-conduct.

4.533 Where an investment manager engages in activities which are subject to other rules of conduct, such as fund distribution activities or individual asset management activities, the investment manager must also comply with the relevant rules of conduct. When distributing funds, an investment manager is therefore required to comply with the SFAMA directive for the distribution of collective investment schemes. If the investment manager manages the assets of individual clients, it must also observe the rules of conduct issued by a self-regulatory organisation recognised by FINMA.

4.534 The audit firm appointed by the investment manager is responsible for checking that the investment manager has complied with the relevant rules of conduct.

Financial guarantees

4.535 The investment manager must have sufficient financial resources which are mainly intended to ensure the survival of the company during periods of low profitability and to cover possible legal actions.

4.536 The investment manager must have a minimum share capital of CHF 200,000 (CHF 500,000 under certain specific circumstances), fully paid up in cash. Further, the investment manager must hold shareholders' equity equal to 0.02% of the portion of its total assets under management which exceeds CHF 250 million but always at least one quarter of the fixed costs of the investment manager during the last financial year. The maximum amount of shareholders' equity required is CHF 20 million. The investment manager must also either hold additional shareholders' equity amounting to 0.01% of its total assets under management, or take out professional civil liability insurance[1].

[1] Article 14 para 1(d) of the CISA, articles 19 and 21 of the CISO.

Swiss branches of foreign investment managers

4.537 As mentioned above, the CISA permits a foreign investment manager to operate in Switzerland through a branch in relation to the investment management of both Swiss and non-Swiss funds. A Swiss branch of a foreign investment manager must obtain an authorisation from FINMA. It must comply with (i) the general conditions of article 14 of the CISO, as described above, and (ii) all three of the special conditions set out in article 18 para 1(c) of the CISA, as follows (see paras **4.538–4.544** below).

APPROPRIATE SUPERVISION

4.538 The investment manager must be subject to adequate supervision, including in respect of its Swiss branch, by its home regulator.

4.539 The text submitted by the Swiss government to the Swiss Parliament referred to 'equivalent regulations'. The Swiss Parliament decided to replace the reference to 'equivalent regulations' with the requirement for 'appropriate supervision'. This less stringent requirement was adopted to ensure that each application for authorisation does not give rise to a mere comparison of the legislation to which the foreign investment manager and its Swiss branch are subject.

ADEQUATE CORPORATE GOVERNANCE AND SUFFICIENT FINANCIAL RESOURCES

4.540 The investment manager must have adequate corporate governance, sufficient financial resources and competent staff to operate a branch in Switzerland.

4.541 The Swiss branch of the foreign investment manager must have an internal regulation which defines exactly its scope of activities and its organisation[1]. Further, FINMA may require that the Swiss branch of a foreign investment manager has sufficient local financial resources if the protection of investors so requires[2].

[1] Article 29b para 2(f) of the CISO.
[2] Article 29b para 4 of the CISO.

CO-OPERATION BETWEEN FINMA AND THE INVESTMENT MANAGER'S HOME REGULATOR

4.542 FINMA and the foreign investment manager's home regulator must have entered into a co-operation agreement.

4.543 Onshore Fund Domiciles

4.543 Article 29b para 2(c) of the CISO provides that the foreign regulator must not have any objection to the opening of a branch in Switzerland. FINMA requires the submission of a document issued by the investment manager's home supervisory authority which confirms that it has no objection to the foreign investment manager opening a branch in Switzerland.

4.544 The competent foreign regulator must undertake immediately to inform FINMA of any event that is likely seriously to endanger the interests of investors, their assets or the funds managed by the foreign investment manager[1].

[1] Article 29b para 2(d) of the CISO.

4.545 FINMA granted licences to foreign investment managers to open Swiss branches during the last quarter of 2015.

Forthcoming amendments to the legal and regulatory framework

4.546 The regulatory framework applicable to the Swiss investment funds industry will be amended by the enactment of the Swiss Federal Act on Financial Institutions (the 'FAFI') together with the Swiss Federal Financial Services Act (the 'FFSA').

4.547 The FAFI and the FFSA are a response by the Swiss government to the 2009 global financial crisis in general and, furthermore, to international developments in financial regulation. The FAFI and the FFSA are also a response to the so-called 'third country provisions' of the Markets in Financial Instruments Directive[1] ('MiFID'), as amended, and the Regulation on Markets in Financial Instruments[2] ('MiFIR').

[1] Directive 2014/65/EU of 15 May 2014.
[2] Regulation (EU) No 600/2014 of 15 May 2014.

4.548 The objective of the FAFI and the FFSA is to provide for a new legal framework which governs the supervision of all Swiss financial institutions, with the exception of banks and insurance companies which will remain regulated by specific legislation, and the provision of financial services.

4.549 The likely impact of the FAFI and of the FFSA on the Swiss investment funds industry is as follows:

- the CISA will be product-related legislation, that is it will only govern funds;
- investment managers (as well as fund management companies), which are currently supervised under the CISA, will be subject to supervision under the FAFI; and
- investment managers will be subject to the rules of conduct set out in the FFSA, such as obligations of loyalty, diligence and information.

4.550 Major changes for the Swiss investment funds industry are not anticipated since, unlike various other financial products and services, investment funds products and services are already regulated to a large extent.

4.551 The FAFI together with the FFSA were submitted by the Swiss government to the Swiss Parliament on 4 November 2015, after a consultation process in 2015 which had led to many substantial amendments to the initial drafts. The Council of States was the first chamber of the Swiss Parliament to debate those draft Acts on 14 December 2016. As a result of the debates in the Council of States, a number of amendments were made to the draft Acts.

4.552 The FFSA and the FAFI were submitted for debate in the second chamber of the Swiss Parliament, the National Council, on 13 September 2017. Following those debates, there were some differences between the versions of the two chambers. In this context, the Commission on Financial Affairs of the Council of States (the 'Commission') undertook the review and elimination of the remaining differences between the versions of the two chambers. On 24 January 2018, the Commission issued a press release in which it explained that it had finalised its deliberations. The draft Acts will thus be discussed during the Council of States' 2018 spring session, with any remaining differences being dealt with in the 2018 summer session.

4.553 Upon the agreement of the Council of States and the National Council on all provisions of the FAFI and the FFSA, the new legislation will be final. This will allow the Swiss Federal Financial Department to proceed with the formal consultation process on the implementing ordinances to the FAFI and the FFSA, which will specify many key provisions of the new legislation.

4.554 The earliest likely date on which the FAFI and the FFSA will come into force is currently 1 January 2020. Most of the detailed transitional deadlines to implement the new rules, which are key for the Swiss investment funds industry, will be defined in the implementing ordinances.

Taxation

Taxation of the fund

4.555 Under Swiss tax legislation, Swiss funds are not subject to Swiss corporate income tax. They are regarded as transparent vehicles for Swiss tax purposes (unless they directly hold real estate). This holds true for Swiss contractual funds, SICAVs and SCPCs. SICAFs are, however, treated as corporate vehicles which are subject to Swiss corporate income tax.

4.556 The main Swiss tax connected to Swiss funds is the Swiss withholding tax which is payable on distributions by Swiss funds of ordinary income. Ordinary income realised by Swiss funds is indeed subject to a Swiss withholding tax levied at the rate of 35% irrespective of whether that income is effectively distributed or reinvested. Such withholding tax is not, however, payable on capital gains realised by a Swiss fund.

4.557 Swiss legislation also contains a mechanism which allows non-Swiss residents to benefit from an exemption from Swiss withholding tax if more than 80% of the assets held by the fund are of a foreign source (the 'affidavit procedure').

4.558 Foreign investors which invest in Swiss funds that do not benefit from the affidavit procedure may obtain, upon request to the Swiss Federal Tax

4.558 *Onshore Fund Domiciles*

Administration, a partial or total relief from Swiss withholding tax under the double tax treaty (if any) between Switzerland and their country of residence.

Taxation of the investors

4.559 The tax treatment of Swiss resident investors in Swiss or foreign funds may be summarised as follows:

- Swiss corporate investors as well as individual professional investors are subject to Swiss ordinary income tax on any income or gain derived from the investment in the Swiss or foreign fund.
- Swiss private investors (that is, individual investors who hold the investment as part of their private assets) are subject to Swiss income tax on their share of the ordinary income derived by the fund. They are, however, exempt from any Swiss tax on capital gains derived by the fund as well as from any Swiss tax on capital gains realised upon disposal or redemption of interests in the fund.

Taxation of Swiss investment managers

4.560 The Swiss tax treatment of Swiss resident investment managers may be summarised as follows:

- Investment management fees (or investment advisory fees) represent taxable income subject to tax at the ordinary rate. This holds true irrespective of whether those fees are received by a Swiss company or a Swiss individual. The main aim is therefore to determine the share of the fees that should be allocated to Switzerland versus other jurisdictions (which involves transfer pricing analysis).
- On a case-by-case basis, careful structuring, notably of the performance fee or of the carried interest, may generate a more attractive result. Similarly, the personal investment that is typically required by investment managers may continue to qualify as a private investment (notwithstanding the connection with the fund). This allows the investment manager's team to realise tax exempt capital gains as a private investor.

Chapter 5

ESTABLISHMENT OPTIONS – LEGAL FORM

Dale Gabbert, Partner, Simmons & Simmons and Andrew Wylie, Partner and Head of Investment Funds, DLA Piper

A	Introduction	5.1
B	Companies	5.2
C	Partnerships	5.15
D	Unit trusts	5.25
E	Master-feeder structure	5.31

A INTRODUCTION

5.1 This chapter considers the forms of business organisation that can be used for a hedge fund. There is no particular magic to this – in theory the choice of vehicle is limited only by the forms of legal entity available and the appetite of investors for a particular structure. However, in practice the predominant choice is that of a company, followed by limited partnerships, which are frequently used together in a 'master-feeder' structure[1]. Less common vehicles include unit trusts, which this chapter also considers.

[1] Described in paras **5.31–5.37** below.

B COMPANIES

5.2 The diagram below illustrates the structure of a simple hedge fund which is established as an offshore company:

5.2 Establishment Options – Legal Form

CONTROL – COMPANY STRUCTURE

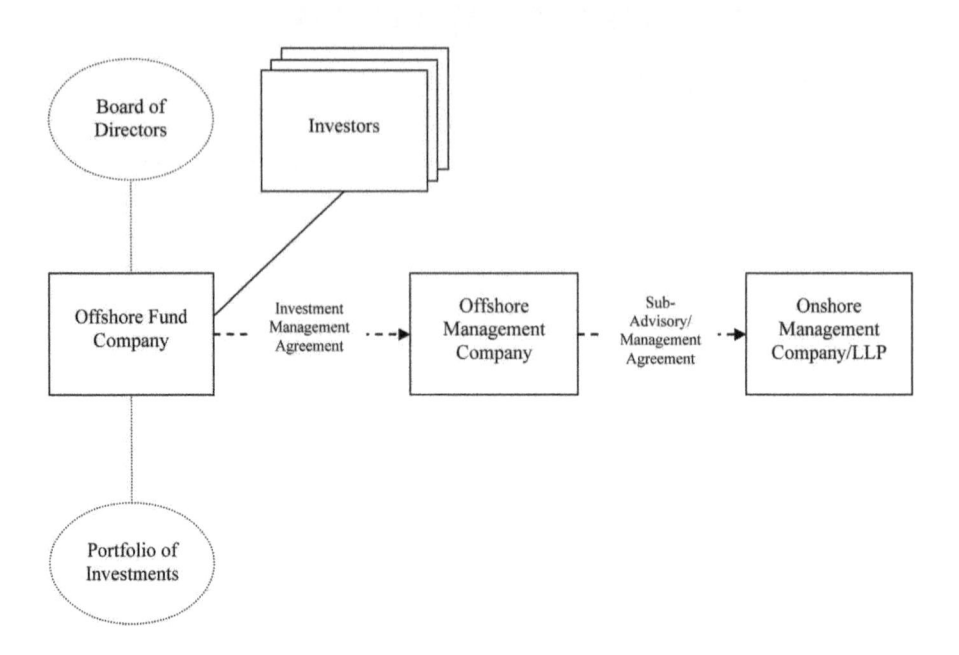

[Diagram: Board of Directors and Investors connect to Offshore Fund Company, which links via Investment Management Agreement to Offshore Management Company, then via Sub-Advisory/Management Agreement to Onshore Management Company/LLP. Offshore Fund Company also connects to Portfolio of Investments.]

5.3 The company is by far the most common and well understood form of business organisation in the world. This is a result of its ubiquity in the modern world and its apparent simplicity. Companies have legal personality separate from that of their shareholders, which means that they can enter into contracts, hold property, sue and be sued in their own name and enjoy broadly the same capacity as a natural person. The primary benefit of such separate legal personality for a company is that the liability of its shareholders will, in the ordinary course of business, be limited to the amount which they have paid up, or agreed to pay up, in respect of their shares.

5.4 A key feature of companies is that they are generally treated as 'tax opaque'. That means that they are subject to tax in their own right. Where they are incorporated in onshore jurisdictions, charges to tax are likely to arise at two levels, upon the company itself in respect of its income and profits (entity level taxation) and upon the shareholder in respect of dividend income which it receives from the company and capital gains which it realises on the disposal of its shares in the company. Where the company is incorporated in an offshore jurisdiction, no corporation tax will be payable, so that double taxation is avoided. However, many offshore jurisdictions have legislation which punitively taxes offshore investment companies. This is because such offshore companies have in the past sometimes been used as vehicles for tax avoidance, including schemes which attempted to take advantage of differential taxation rates for income and capital gains. In the UK, the offshore funds rules punitively tax investors in offshore funds unless they distribute the vast majority of their income. Similarly, the US has anti-avoidance legislation which targets offshore investment companies.

5.5 Of course, most companies are closed-ended, which means that they issue shares that are not capable of being redeemed, save pursuant to schemes of arrangement whereby they are cancelled or taken into 'treasury stock' (that is, acquired by the company itself). Hedge funds are typically open-ended, that is, they allow investors to redeem their shares in order to realise their investment. Accordingly, the typical closed-ended company structure would be an inefficient method of structuring a hedge fund because in order to generate liquidity for investors one would have to return cash by way of dividends (which would be subject to legal constraints, such as having sufficient distributable profits) or by cumbersome reorganisations (which typically require court and creditor consent).

5.6 Fortunately, a large number of jurisdictions allow the creation of companies with a variable share capital (or no share capital) and permit those companies to issue redeemable shares. This allows the use of companies, with their advantages of simplicity, limited liability, familiarity and predictability, to be used as fund vehicles. Offshore jurisdictions such as the Cayman Islands, the British Virgin Islands, Guernsey and Jersey all have forms of company with redeemable shares.

5.7 One issue to consider when structuring hedge funds as companies is whether the shares will have voting rights. Deciding whether to give investors a vote in the absence of a requirement to do so is usually fairly easy from a manager perspective – investors are simply not given a vote. Giving investors a vote would allow them to remove the board of directors of the hedge fund and change its constitution, which may embody key fund characteristics such as liquidity rights. This is something that fund promoters are typically keen to avoid. Accordingly, most hedge funds issue non-voting redeemable shares to investors that carry the exclusive right to participate in the profits and income of the fund. Any company must issue some shares which have voting rights, and hedge funds typically issue voting shares to the promoter of the hedge fund or to one of its affiliates. Typically, those voting shares carry no rights to participate in the profits or income of the fund, other than a return of any amount paid up on those shares on the liquidation of the fund. This allows the fund promoter (typically the manager of the fund or a member of its group) to control the fund both by means of its shareholding, which allows it to amend the constitution of the fund (including the rights attaching to shares), and the right to appoint and remove the board of directors of the hedge fund. This level of control and convenience is unsurprisingly popular with fund promoters and accordingly most hedge funds established as companies follow this dual share structure. From an investor perspective this presents certain corporate governance issues, which are discussed in CHAPTER **16**.

5.8 Another factor in deciding whether to give shares voting rights is whether and on which stock exchange the shares will be listed. Some listing regimes will require that the shares to be listed have voting rights. However, a number of jurisdictions permit the listing of shares which do not have voting rights. A listing of shares need not be an admission to trading, and may simply be an admission to listing. Such listings of convenience do not provide investor liquidity but do serve a number of other purposes. First, a number of investors will not or cannot invest in unlisted securities, or may have a limited allocation to unlisted securities all of which may, in practice, be applied to direct or indirect private equity investments. Listing allows such investors to acquire (or

5.8 Establishment Options – Legal Form

acquire to a greater extent) shares in listed hedge funds. Second, investors derive a certain level of comfort from the fact that shares are listed. It is an additional layer of regulation in the broader sense. In order to list its shares, the fund will need to comply with the relevant stock exchange's rules on admission to listing. Where the listing occurs after the shares have been issued this will typically include an auditor's report. Lawyers and a listing agent will have to be engaged to ensure that the company meets the requirements of the relevant listing rules, and appropriate listing particulars will have to be produced. These all provide additional comfort from an investor perspective. Once admitted to listing there will also be ongoing obligations under the relevant listing rules which will provide some comfort on issues such as changes in investment policy, disclosure and the equal treatment of shareholders.

5.9 Where investors hold non-voting shares, their rights are extremely limited. However, most jurisdictions do not allow a variation of class rights without a vote of the shareholders which hold the shares of that class. Class rights are rights that attach to a particular class of shares. In most jurisdictions class rights can only be varied by a favourable vote of the relevant portion of the shareholders which hold the shares of the relevant class. This is often offered by fund promoters as justification (or mitigation) for the failure to give participating shares voting rights. In practice, however, it is often difficult to establish that a particular entitlement is one that attaches to a given class, rather than applying to shareholders generally. This is particularly the case where more than one class of participating shares is in issue. For example, one might assume that rights of redemption are class rights, but are they? If the redemption provisions are drafted so as to apply to all classes of participating shares, it is hard to see how they are capable of being characterised as a 'class right' unless one concludes that each class has an identical, and yet distinct, class right, which is clearly a difficult analysis. Second, a number of the issues one would want comfort on as an investor are not 'rights' but liabilities or impositions. For example, should the amount of fees paid by a class of shares properly be characterised as a 'right' of that class? One could treat it as a right to pay fees which do not exceed the relevant amount, but again that is arguably simply an attempt to create a class right out of what is essentially a class burden.

5.10 Allied to the notion of redeemable shares is the absence of a requirement for significant capital. Whilst the promoter or the manager of a hedge fund may be required to maintain a minimum amount of capital for regulatory reasons, funds which are established with participating redeemable shares will typically have no or very limited capital maintenance obligations. This is not troublesome where the participating shares have the right to participate in capital, profits and income and where the third party creditors such as the manager, the prime broker and the administrator are aware of the fund's capital structure.

5.11 In the absence of investor voting rights, annual general meetings have less relevance since the only persons that are entitled to vote (unless there is a proposal to vary class rights attaching to non-voting participating shares) are the holders of the founder shares. Accordingly, any statutory requirement to hold an annual general meeting can normally be satisfied by the use of a representative or proxy.

5.12 So, in the absence of a voting right, what comfort do investors have? It is often asserted by fund counsel that there is a duty to treat all shareholders equally. This is almost universally not the case for companies that are established in common law jurisdictions which are based on English common law. There is no such duty under English law.

5.13 In practice there are very limited remedies which are available to individual shareholders, typically only where they can fall within limited minority protection doctrines which are enshrined in common law or specific statutory remedies under the laws of the jurisdiction in which the fund is incorporated. However, the real source of comfort is the ability to redeem their shares. Where liquidity is limited or the rights of redemption are subject to long notice periods, it is possible for funds to introduce adverse changes before investors have the opportunity to redeem their shares. However, this is not good practice and fund counsel will normally advise that any material amendments that may be considered materially detrimental to shareholders should only be introduced after affected shareholders have been given notice and the opportunity to redeem their shares. The articles of association of most hedge funds will contain the power to waive notice periods and/or create additional dealing days, thereby giving the flexibility to introduce changes quickly whilst allowing investors to redeem their shares before those changes take effect.

5.14 The absence of shareholder rights and corporate governance has been one reason for the prevalence of side letters between hedge funds and their investors[1]. Side letters clearly do not provide for equal treatment of all shareholders.

[1] Discussed in CHAPTER 16 – see paras **16.34–16.41**.

C PARTNERSHIPS

5.15 The diagram below illustrates the structure of a simple hedge fund which is established as an offshore limited partnership:

5.15 Establishment Options – Legal Form

CONTROL – PARTNERSHIP STRUCTURE

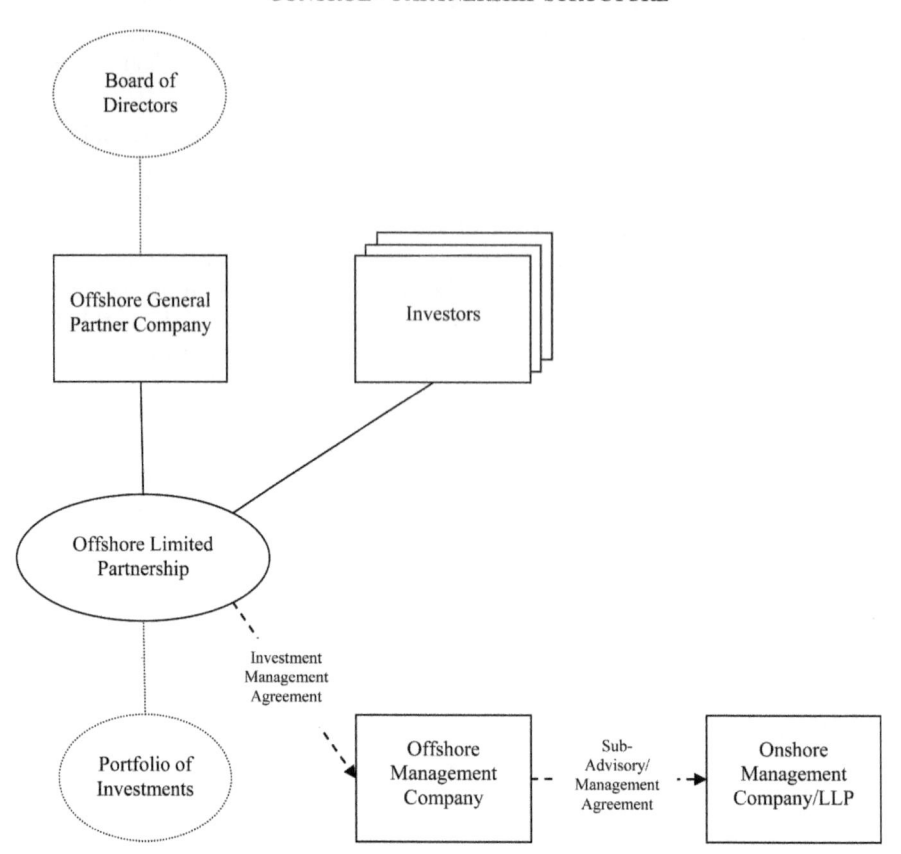

[Diagram: Board of Directors connects to Offshore General Partner Company, which connects to Offshore Limited Partnership. Investors also connect to Offshore Limited Partnership. Offshore Limited Partnership connects to Portfolio of Investments, and via Investment Management Agreement to Offshore Management Company, which links via Sub-Advisory/Management Agreement to Onshore Management Company/LLP.]

5.16 Partnerships are an ancient form of business organisation and preceded the establishment of the company in English law. Partnerships in England and overseas now typically have one or more governing statutes. In the UK these are the Partnership Act 1890 (the '1890 Act') and the Limited Partnerships Act 1907 (the '1907 Act'). A body of common law is also germane to partnership law under the laws of most common law jurisdictions.

5.17 Unlike companies, partnerships are not normally incorporated. They can be created by conduct as well as, more usually, in writing by entering into a partnership agreement. It is important to bear in mind that the partnership was never developed by the common law as an investment vehicle. It was intended to be a useful form of general business organisation. Many of the relevant legal cases therefore concern small businesses. It is doubtful that Parliament, when it enacted the 1907 Act, ever imagined the scale or extent of the use of English limited partnerships as investment vehicles.

5.18 Funds which are established as partnerships are invariably established as limited partnerships, under the relevant limited partnership legislation. It is important to establish whether the limited partnership created under these laws is a different type of entity to a general partnership or whether it is the same type of entity but with an additional 'cloak' of limited liability conferred by the relevant statute. If the latter (which is more common), the limited partnership will typically be subject to the law applicable to general partnerships, save to the extent this is excluded by the limited partnership statute itself. This is the case for English limited partnerships, and section 7 of the 1907 Act expressly states that the general law relating to partnerships is preserved to the extent not inconsistent with the 1907 Act or the 1890 Act. This has considerable significance since the law which relates to partnerships is arguably more arcane and consequently less predictable than that which relates to companies. This is a reflection both of the common law origin of partnerships and the fact that the greater popularity of companies as forms of business organisation has meant that more disputes concerning companies have been judicially considered and hence there are more judicial decisions about company law than partnership law.

5.19 Limited partnerships will be established with one or more limited partners and one or more general partners. The general partner will have unlimited liability for the debts and obligations of the limited partnership. The liability of a limited partner will be limited to the amount which it has agreed to commit to the limited partnership. Some jurisdictions, such as England, allow partnerships to combine capital and debt, so that limited partners' subscription amounts can comprise partly loan and partly capital. In most jurisdictions the entire commitment of a limited partner will be capital.

5.20 If capital is returned to a limited partner prior to the termination of the limited partnership, that limited partner may be liable to return it to satisfy the claims of creditors. It may also be necessary for a limited partnership to register the identity and capital contributions of its limited partners. This is so that any person that deals with the limited partnership may ascertain how much capital is available to meet the claims of creditors. Where confidentiality is required and the names of limited partners are available publicly, it may be necessary to invest through a nominee. Of course, the nominee must be an entity whose ownership information is not available to the public. Depending on the jurisdiction, default in registration may prejudice the limited liability of the limited partners. Maintenance of the register in accordance with the law will be the duty of the general partner and, if it fails to do so, the limited partners may enforce their obligation to do so under the relevant limited partnership agreement. In practice, however, it is unlikely that they will become aware of any such default in registration unless they are unusually vigilant. This is a disadvantage of the limited partnership regime.

5.21 One key advantage of limited partnerships as fund structures is that they are generally treated as transparent for tax purposes under the laws of most jurisdictions. This means that no tax is levied on the limited partnership itself and that limited partners have a proportionate share of the partnership assets. Whilst the first factor is of no relevance where the limited partnership is established in an offshore jurisdiction, the latter factor will be relevant to investors which are subject to tax. This is not always a blessing, however, because where disposals are made of partnership assets or new investors are admitted, the partners will be treated as having made a disposal equivalent to their share of the assets disposed of or the amount by which their partnership share has been diluted by the newly admitted investors. Where this is not desirable, investors may elect to participate indirectly in the limited partner-

5.21 *Establishment Options – Legal Form*

ship through a corporate 'feeder fund'[1].

[1] Described in paras 5.31–5.37 below.

5.22 Partnerships have several distinctive features. Partners owe fiduciary duties to each other, whereas shareholders in a company do not owe fiduciary duties to each other.

5.23 The general partner of a limited partnership owes fiduciary duties to the limited partners in that limited partnership and the overriding duty is to act in good faith. Most of the fiduciary duties may be regarded as a subset of this overriding duty. Specific examples of fiduciary duties are the duty not to take a secret profit and not to compete with the business of the partnership. It is unclear to what extent, if any, these fiduciary duties can be excluded, but many limited partnership agreements attempt to do so. Usually this is done by using the slightly cryptic phrase, 'to the maximum extent permitted by law, partners' fiduciary duties to one another shall be excluded'. Not all funds established as limited partnerships take this approach however. Certainly, it is difficult to conclude that one could exclude fiduciary duties entirely under English law.

5.24 Another difference between limited partnerships and companies is that limited partnerships in many jurisdictions do not have legal personality separate from that of their partners. This can lead to difficulties in practice. Jurisdictions which do not consider partnerships to have a separate legal personality include England and Wales and the Cayman Islands. Those that do give limited partnerships a separate legal personality include Scotland and many states in the US, including the state of Delaware and the state of New York. This leads to a number of practical consequences, including the fact that a limited partnership which does not have legal personality may not be able to hold property in its own name and it may not be attractive for that limited partnership to become a partner in another limited partnership.

D   UNIT TRUSTS

5.25 The diagram below illustrates the structure of a simple hedge fund which is structured as an offshore unit trust:

CONTROL – UNIT TRUST STRUCTURE

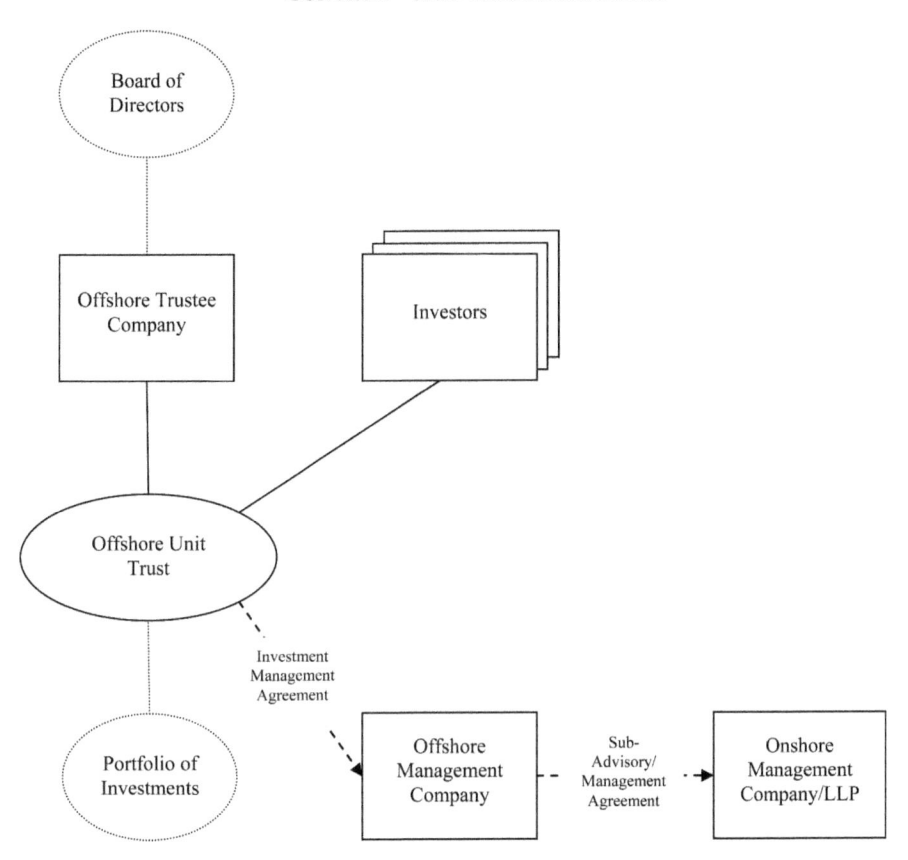

```
         Board of
         Directors
            |
            |
   ┌────────────────┐         ┌──────────┐
   │ Offshore Trustee│         │ Investors│
   │    Company     │         └──────────┘
   └────────────────┘              │
            │                      │
            │                      │
      ┌───────────┐                │
      │Offshore Unit│───────────────┘
      │    Trust   │
      └───────────┘
            │    ╲
            │     ╲ Investment
            │      Management
            │      Agreement
            │        ╲
   ┌──────────┐   ┌───────────┐  Sub-      ┌───────────┐
   │Portfolio │   │ Offshore  │─Advisory/──│ Onshore   │
   │   of     │   │Management │─Management─│Management │
   │Investments│  │ Company   │  Agreement │Company/LLP│
   └──────────┘   └───────────┘            └───────────┘
```

5.26 Unit trusts are much less frequently used as hedge fund vehicles than companies or partnerships. Unit trusts are, as the name suggests, trusts where the beneficiaries receive units that give the unitholders the right to share in the trust property, as participating shares or limited partnership interests do in funds which are established as companies or limited partnerships respectively. Like limited partnerships, unit trusts are often tax advantaged.

5.27 The first and most obvious point is that a unit trust must have a trustee. This will usually be an independent professional trustee. A trustee owes fiduciary duties to the beneficiaries of the trust of which it is a trustee. For this reason, it is unwise to appoint an entity which is in the same group as the manager of a unit trust as the trustee of that unit trust. Investors will typically require a robust third party trustee, not a newly incorporated company established by the promoter of the unit trust. The rights of unitholders will be contained in the trust deed which governs the unit trust. The trust deed must be comprehensive as it is more difficult to amend a trust deed than the memorandum and articles of a company where the promoter holds the founder shares. Amendments of any substance will typically require unitholder consent and, even if this is not a strict legal requirement, the trustee of the unit

5.27 Establishment Options – Legal Form

trust may require that such consent is obtained before making material amendments to the trust deed. Unit trusts are therefore usually less flexible as a fund vehicle than companies. They are also less flexible than limited partnerships in practical terms because the trustee is frequently entirely independent of the manager's group, whereas the general partner of a fund which is established as a limited partnership is usually under common control with the manager of the limited partnership.

5.28 It would be a mistake, however, to analyse unit trusts purely in the context of a trustee/beneficiary relationship. As Sin observes in *The Legal Nature of the Unit Trust*[1]:

> 'The unit trust is somewhat of a hybrid with characteristics of both the trust and the contract. This is because the management function is carried out by a third party manager, not the trustee itself. The manager is usually a party to the trust deed which forms the contract pursuant to which the settlor appoints the manager to manage the assets of the trust.'

[1] Sin, K F, *The Legal Nature of the Unit Trust* (1997) Oxford University Press.

5.29 Unit trusts also differ from private trusts in the scope of the rights which are given to unitholders. In a unit trust deed there will typically be provisions for unitholder voting and meetings in a similar way to funds which are established as companies.

5.30 One of the barriers to the greater use of the unit trust as a vehicle for hedge funds is uncertainty as to the degree to which it is possible to characterise the manager as a fiduciary. In both the company form and the partnership form, the manager will not normally owe fiduciary duties to any person and it will simply enter into a contractual relationship with the relevant fund. Of course, the directors of a fund which is established as a company owe fiduciary duties to the members of that company, as does the general partner of a limited partnership to the limited partners of that limited partnership, but the manager of either entity will not generally owe fiduciary duties to the person which appointed it to act as the manager. In the case of a unit trust, the analysis is more complicated because not only does the manager supplant the activities of a fiduciary (the trustee) it also does so by reason of its adherence to the trust instrument itself. This goes further than, and can be distinguished from, the situation where the general partner of a limited partnership appoints a manager by means of a contract. Whilst the manager of a unit trust does not have legal title to the trust assets, if the trust deed effectively substitutes the manager for all other purposes, it is certainly arguable that the degree of control the manager has over the trust property should cause it to be treated as owing fiduciary duties to the unitholders.

E   MASTER-FEEDER STRUCTURE

5.31 The diagram below illustrates the structure of a fund which is established as a master-feeder fund:

Master-feeder structure 5.33

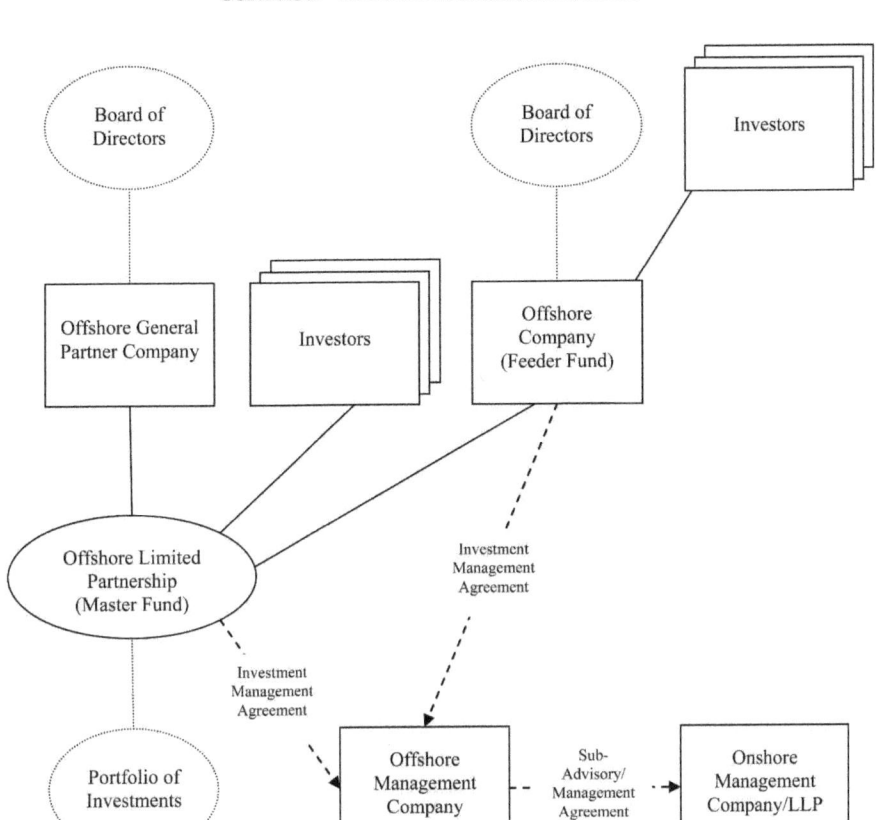

CONTROL – MASTER-FEEDER STRUCTURE

[Diagram: Board of Directors connects to Offshore General Partner Company, which connects to Offshore Limited Partnership (Master Fund). Investors connect to Offshore Limited Partnership. Board of Directors connects to Offshore Company (Feeder Fund), which has Investors and connects to Offshore Limited Partnership (Master Fund). Offshore Limited Partnership connects to Portfolio of Investments (Investment Management Agreement) and to Offshore Management Company (Investment Management Agreement). Offshore Company (Feeder Fund) has Investment Management Agreement with Offshore Management Company. Offshore Management Company has Sub-Advisory/Management Agreement with Onshore Management Company/LLP.]

5.32 The master-feeder structure combines the corporate and partnership forms to create a dual-tiered structure which offers different tax treatments to investors by combining a tax opaque vehicle (a company) with a tax transparent one (a limited partnership). The company invests as a limited partner in (or 'feeds into') the limited partnership and the limited partnership holds the portfolio (and hence is referred to as the 'master fund'). This is why the structure is known as a 'master-feeder' structure. Investors that wish to invest in a tax transparent vehicle will invest directly into the limited partnership or through a limited partnership which is a feeder fund into the underlying limited partnership. Investors that do not wish to invest in a tax transparent vehicle will invest in the company which in turn invests in the limited partnership.

5.33 The classic master-feeder structure would typically have all of the assets of the corporate feeder fund invested in the master fund. No additional fees should be levied at the level of the feeder fund other than those which relate to its own costs of establishment and operation. In practice, many service providers provide a single fee proposal for servicing a master-feeder fund rather than charging the feeder fund and master fund separately.

5.34 Establishment Options – Legal Form

5.34 The analysis of the rights of a shareholder in a feeder fund is, however, more complex because that shareholder is removed from the underlying assets of the hedge fund by two vehicles rather than one (because that shareholder has to exercise its rights as an investor in the feeder fund which in turn has to exercise its rights as an investor in the master fund). This can lead to problems of effective enforcement – instead of being able to exercise its rights directly an investor needs to procure that the feeder fund enforces its rights as a limited partner in the master fund. The board of directors of a feeder fund typically comprises directors selected by the promoter and the promoter holds the voting shares in the feeder fund. The promoter can therefore effectively determine whether or not the feeder fund enforces its rights as a limited partner in the master fund. In ordinary circumstances this is not a concern, but in troubled circumstances the promoter may not wish to enforce these rights against the master fund.

5.35 It should be noted that where all of the assets of a feeder fund are invested in limited partnership interests of the master fund, there is strictly no need to have an investment management agreement in place for the feeder fund since technically there is no investment discretion to exercise (assuming the timing of investments and redemptions of interests in the feeder fund are not discretionary and are simply mechanical, based on subscription and redemption requests at the feeder fund level). Typically, however, there will be an investment management agreement in place for administrative and regulatory convenience.

5.36 A related point for fund promoters is that they should not have identical boards of directors of the feeder fund company and the general partner of the master fund limited partnership because their interests may conflict in the event that the master fund faces difficulties. In those circumstances the directors may not be able to resolve the conflict between their interests and duties as directors of the feeder fund and as directors of the general partner of the master fund.

5.37 Notwithstanding these issues, the simplicity and flexibility of this structure has made it extremely popular for hedge funds, particularly because most service providers are able to accommodate this dual-tiered structure without a significant effect on the overall cost.

Chapter 6

SERVICE PROVIDERS – MAKING IT HAPPEN

Dale Gabbert, Partner, Simmons & Simmons and Andrew Wylie, Partner and Head of Investment Funds, DLA Piper

A	Introduction	6.1
B	Directors of the fund	6.5
C	The investment manager	6.11
D	The administrator	6.22
E	The prime broker	6.44
F	Other service providers	6.62

A INTRODUCTION

6.1 Hedge funds are legal constructs. The hedge fund itself has no employees or officers other than a few directors. Therefore everything a hedge fund does is done by someone else. They are heavily reliant both in their day-to-day existence and for their long-term success on the quality of the service providers which support them and without whom they would not be able to function properly. In a very real sense, the service providers make the fund happen.

6.2 It should therefore come as no surprise that the manner in which hedge funds are structured has fundamental importance for the relationships which it has with various third parties. In order to maintain the favourable taxation and regulatory treatment of the hedge fund, to facilitate its smooth establishment and operation, and to maximise returns, the hedge fund will be required to appoint a number of specialist service providers.

6.3 This chapter explains the role played by each of the key service providers, how they make the fund happen and the terms on which they are generally appointed. The key service providers to a hedge fund are:

- the investment manager[1];
- the administrator[2]; and
- the prime broker[3].

[1] See paras **6.11–6.21** below.
[2] See paras **6.22–6.43** below.
[3] See paras **6.44–6.61** below.

6.4 The diagram below illustrates the relationships between each of the key service providers. There are, however, other service providers, including auditors, accountants and legal advisers, whose importance should not be overlooked.

6.4 Service Providers – Making it Happen

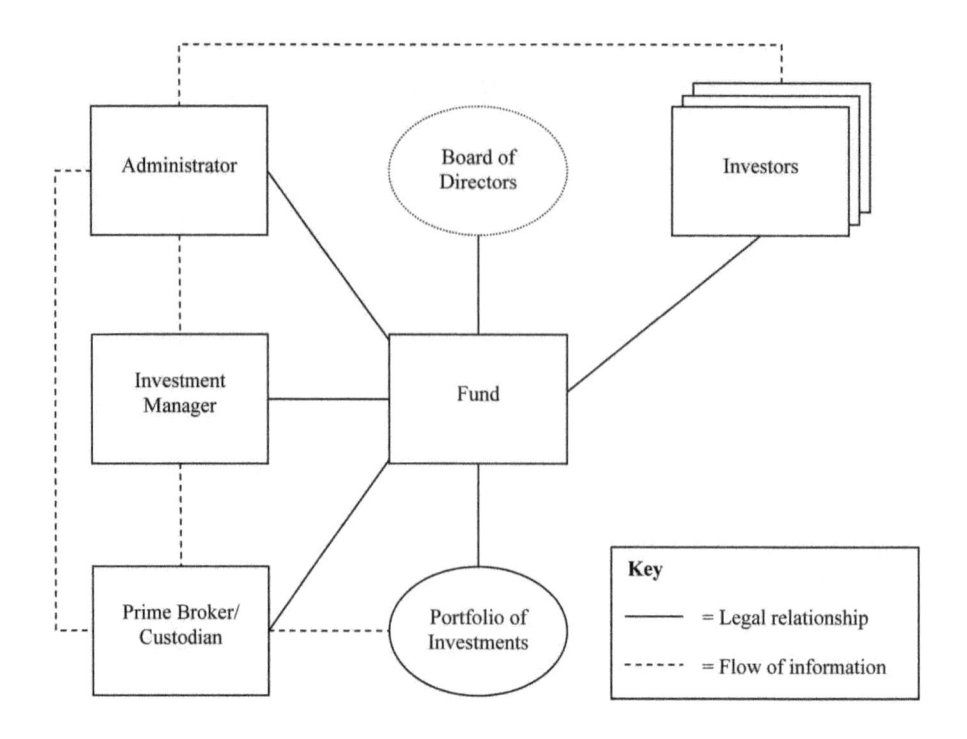

[Diagram: Fund structure showing relationships between Administrator, Board of Directors, Investors, Investment Manager, Fund, Prime Broker/Custodian, and Portfolio of Investments. Key: solid line = Legal relationship; dashed line = Flow of information]

B   DIRECTORS OF THE FUND

6.5 Whilst a hedge fund delegates management of that hedge fund to its investment manager and delegates its day-to-day operation to its administrator, it should be remembered that the fund (or the general partner of a hedge fund which is structured as a limited partnership) has a board of directors which remains responsible for the appointment and supervision of the service providers which the fund has appointed and for providing general oversight of the activities of the hedge fund in accordance with principles of good corporate governance. Directors are typically the only personnel which a fund directly employs.

6.6 Accordingly, whilst it is true that the day-to-day role of the board of directors of a hedge fund (or the general partner in the case of a hedge fund which is structured as a limited partnership) is minimal, it is not an insignificant function. The directors can terminate the appointment of all the service providers to the hedge fund, including the investment manager. Whilst this might seem radical given that the investment manager typically establishes the fund, it is simply a function of the way funds are structured, splitting the vehicle holding the assets (the fund) from the staff managing the fund (the principals and employees of the investment manager).

6.7 The role of a director of a hedge fund is not pedestrian. The directors are responsible for the appointment, monitoring and, if necessary, the termination of the appointment of service providers to the hedge fund, resolving conflicts of interest that arise between service providers and the fund, maintaining the offshore tax status of the fund, and dealing with investor complaints and pending or threatened litigation.

6.8 The composition of the board of directors of a hedge fund should therefore be considered carefully. This should take into account:

- relevant tax considerations, including critically demonstrating offshore management and control[1];
- the need to have directors available to take decisions and execute documents, potentially on short notice if required;
- the need to demonstrate a suitable level of independence, competence and oversight both from an investor and a regulatory perspective; and
- the ability to have a board of directors that can consider the merits of appointing and supervising the performance of all of the service providers to that hedge fund (by having a sufficient number and diversity of directors so that there will be at least one director who is independent of the relevant service provider and therefore able to take a decision without being in a position of conflict of interest).

[1] Discussed in CHAPTER 14 – see paras 14.24–14.58.

6.9 It is fair to say that there is a divergence of practice about the composition of the boards of directors of hedge funds. Hedge funds which are sponsored by US investment managers frequently have fewer independent directors and may comprise entirely principals of the onshore investment manager. Hedge funds which are sponsored by UK investment managers tend to have a majority of directors who are independent of the manager because of UK sensitivities in relation to central management and control. The board of directors of a hedge fund which is managed by a UK investment manager will typically have at least two offshore directors who will frequently be current or former employees of local service providers (typically an administrator, an accountant or a law firm) and possibly one representative of the investment manager. It is important from an investor perspective that the board of directors of a hedge fund comprises experienced directors who take their responsibilities seriously.

6.10 Obviously, directors who are principals or employees of a service provider will have to excuse themselves from any discussion about the performance of the service provider with which they are connected. For that reason it is unwise for all of the directors of a hedge fund to be connected to a single business. Another point that is often overlooked is that in the case of a master-feeder structure[1], because the feeder fund is an investor in the master fund, if the same individuals are directors of the feeder fund and the master fund they will have an irreconcilable conflict of interest if a dispute arises between the feeder fund and the master fund. Therefore it is advisable to have some divergence of personnel on each board. Nevertheless, many investment managers do not want to incur additional expense in relation to a risk which they view as theoretical.

[1] Discussed in CHAPTER 5 – see paras 5.31–5.37.

6.11 *Service Providers – Making it Happen*

C   THE INVESTMENT MANAGER

6.11 Whilst the investment manager of a hedge fund often holds the voting shares in that hedge fund and has the power to appoint its board of directors, it is nonetheless a service provider to the fund. The investment manager should be engaged on arm's length terms in accordance with the terms of an investment management agreement (an 'IMA'). The IMA is one of the core contractual agreements of a hedge fund and sets out the duties of the investment manager, the fees it is entitled to receive, the parameters within which it may exercise its discretionary investment powers, and its obligations in respect of other service providers to that hedge fund.

6.12 If the investment manager is a regulated entity, the rules of the relevant regulator will also require the IMA to contain mandatory terms or disclosures concerning matters such as the management of conflicts of interest, 'soft dollar' commissions, the extent of the obligation of the investment manager to provide 'best execution', reporting to the hedge fund and its complaints procedure. The IMA will often deal with issues such as the investment objective, investment policy and investment restrictions of the hedge fund by cross-referring to the offering document of the fund (and will usually contain a provision requiring the investment manager always to have regard to the fund's offering memorandum in the fulfilment of its duties).

6.13 Hedge funds will often have an offshore investment manager which delegates substantially all of its rights and obligations to an onshore investment manager. The offshore investment manager is typically established in the same jurisdiction as the hedge fund itself and will generally have few directors, officers and employees. By contrast, the onshore investment manager will be the entity with premises and staff and will be subject to regulatory supervision and capital adequacy requirements. Offshore investment managers can serve a number of purposes in the structure, including the ability to pay fees or rebates to third parties which are resident offshore without first bringing the payments onshore, and enabling a tax-efficient disposal of interests in the investment manager where its principals are tax resident in a more favourable jurisdiction than the jurisdiction in which the investment manager is resident.

Discretionary management

6.14 A hedge fund almost always appoints its investment manager to manage its portfolio on a fully discretionary basis. This has certain regulatory implications, which together with other regulatory aspects of the role of the investment manager are explored in more detail in CHAPTER 9 and CHAPTER 11.

6.15 Notwithstanding the term 'discretionary', the degree to which the investment manager of a hedge fund may deal with the assets of that hedge fund will be limited by reference to the investment policy and the mandate of the investment manager, which are usually set out as a schedule to the IMA (or incorporated in the IMA by reference to the hedge fund's offering documents). In addition, the investment manager will be required to act in the best interests of the hedge fund and in accordance with applicable legal and regulatory requirements (including the rules of any stock exchange on which the shares in the hedge fund are listed).

6.16 Other than being required to comply with the investment policy and restrictions described above, the consequence of discretionary management is that the entire responsibility for managing the hedge fund's portfolio lies with the investment manager. The activities for which the investment manager is responsible include buying and selling securities, employing various hedging techniques, analysing the returns of the fund, formulating and reviewing strategies, complying with regulatory requirements, exercising any voting rights it may hold in the hedge fund's underlying investments, investing uninvested cash on a short-term basis, and keeping proper books and records. The prime broker will be authorised to act on the proper instructions of the investment manager.

Additional duties

6.17 In addition to the discretionary management of the hedge fund's portfolio, the duties of the investment manager will be set out in the IMA and are likely to include observing and complying with legal and regulatory requirements, reporting any issues to the board of directors of the hedge fund, conducting research and engaging in risk assessments. The investment manager may also be appointed to market interests in the hedge fund to prospective investors, particularly where it is an onshore authorised entity.

Fees

6.18 The investment manager receives two fees from the fund in connection with the performance of its duties: the management fee and the performance fee.

6.19 The management fee is intended to cover the costs and expenses which the investment manager incurs in providing its services to the hedge fund and is typically equal to between 1% and 2% per annum of the hedge fund's assets from time to time (before payment of the performance fee). This is calculated by the administrator and is paid either monthly or quarterly in advance or in arrears.

6.20 The performance fee is intended to incentivise the investment manager to make profits and is calculated by reference to the positive returns generated by the fund. A typical performance fee is equal to 20% of the appreciation in the fund's net asset value above a high-water mark (which is generally equal to the greater of the initial issue price of the shares of the fund and the prior highest net asset value at which a performance fee was last paid). The performance fee is also calculated by the administrator and is payable on an annual basis (the period by reference to which it is calculated is often referred to as a 'calculation period'). Where the fund is established in a corporate form and the hedge fund issues additional shares in the fund during a calculation period, it will be necessary to have some form of 'equalisation' procedure to ensure performance fees are borne equitably between investors. The fees paid to the investment manager are dealt with in more detail in CHAPTER 15.

6.21 Service Providers – Making it Happen

Appointing agents

6.21 The IMA will usually permit the investment manager of a hedge fund to delegate certain of its duties to other persons. As has already been alluded to, it is not uncommon for the investment manager of a hedge fund to appoint an investment adviser for legal or regulatory reasons, although in such circumstances the investment manager should remain liable for the performance by the investment adviser of the delegated duties because there is no contract between the hedge fund and the investment adviser (and therefore no right of action for damages for breach of contract).

D THE ADMINISTRATOR

6.22 The role of the administrator of a hedge fund encompasses almost every aspect of the operation of that hedge fund. It is generally the first point of contact for investors and will be required to deal with all of the other service providers to that hedge fund. The administrator is therefore a crucial part of a hedge fund's day-to-day operational infrastructure.

6.23 Fund administration has grown to become a global business, with the larger organisations operating in a number of onshore and offshore jurisdictions and generating significant revenues. At the opposite end of the spectrum are smaller operations which focus on a single jurisdiction. The choice of administrator will depend on a number of factors, including legal requirements, experience, resources, track record and, inevitably, price. It is obviously critical that the administrator's systems are compatible with those of the fund's prime broker(s) and this should be confirmed at an early stage. Different jurisdictions have different views as to whether a hedge fund must have a local administrator. The law of the Cayman Islands does not require hedge funds which are established in the Cayman Islands to appoint a local administrator (and such hedge funds which have UK investment managers frequently appoint administrators located in Ireland) although both Jersey and Guernsey do require a local entity to act as the administrator.

6.24 The administrator plays a key role prior to the establishment of a hedge fund and accordingly should be selected and appointed as soon as possible. This is even more important in the Channel Islands where the newly established 'registered fund' regimes allow for the fast track approval of a hedge fund where the administrator gives certain warranties to the local regulator. Whilst this has enabled a very fast establishment time it has transferred much of the regulatory burden to the administrator. Inevitably, this means that the administrator will need to be involved from a very early stage so that it can commence its diligence on the investment manager and the sponsor as soon as possible.

6.25 From a practical perspective, administrators are likely to have been engaged by a number of funds and can offer a useful perspective prior to the establishment of a hedge fund in terms of structure, taxation, local legal issues and bank account arrangements. Their experience is also valuable when incorporating the necessary local anti-money laundering requirements into the subscription agreement to be completed by any prospective investors in a hedge fund.

Pre-establishment activities

6.26 The role of the administrator prior to the establishment of a hedge fund varies depending on the jurisdiction in which the hedge fund is established. In the Cayman Islands it will be required to submit a letter to the Cayman Islands Monetary Authority stating that it consents to act as the administrator of the hedge fund, whereas in the Channel Islands it will be required to engage in a more detailed dialogue with the local regulator, the precise content of which will vary depending on the type of fund authorisation that is being sought.

6.27 The second significant involvement of the administrator prior to the establishment of a hedge fund will be the negotiation and finalisation of its administration agreement. This agreement sets out the key duties of the hedge fund and the administrator, the circumstances under which the appointment of the administrator may be terminated and its remuneration (which is typically a percentage of the fund's net asset value, possibly with additional fixed fees for certain corporate and investor relations functions).

6.28 The board of directors of a hedge fund usually contains at least one director who is independent of the investment manager and sponsor and it is common for the administrator to provide this individual. This individual is often a director of many hedge funds and is able to offer a useful perspective.

Accepting investors

6.29 The responsibility for processing the subscription agreements submitted by potential investors lies with the administrator. In addition to the various practical matters that this entails, the administrator (usually in conjunction with the fund's legal counsel) will consider the representations made by each potential investor to determine whether it is suitable for admission as an investor in the hedge fund. This will involve an analysis of tax and regulatory issues, which are dealt with by the use of a detailed subscription form which seeks to elicit the required representations and information. The administrator needs to ensure this is correctly completed and retain records of the information obtained about the investors in the hedge fund so that appropriate checks can be made.

6.30 The hedge fund is not able to admit investors until the relevant anti-money laundering requirements of each relevant jurisdiction have been complied with. The administrator is responsible for collating the relevant documentation and liaising with prospective investors in respect of any additional requirements. Investors should always be encouraged to deal with these issues as soon as possible.

6.31 Once the administrator is satisfied that all anti-money laundering requirements have been fulfilled, subscription monies (less any amounts required to satisfy the liabilities of the fund) will be released to the prime broker to enable the investment manager to commence trading. The hedge fund will also issue shares to subscribing investors, usually in book entry form (meaning that no share certificates are issued so that the title to those shares is evidenced by an entry in the fund's register of shareholders which the administrator maintains).

6.32 *Service Providers – Making it Happen*

Post-establishment

6.32 After the establishment of the fund and the acceptance of subscription monies from the initial investors, the administrator plays a key role in the operation of the fund. As well as dealing with any additional subscriptions on subsequent dealing days, and handling redemption and exchange requests from current investors, the key duties of the administrator are as follows.

Calculating net asset value and performance fees

6.33 Perhaps the most important aspect of the administrator's role is the calculation of the fund's net asset value and the performance fee payable to the investment manager. The administrator is usually required to calculate the net asset value on the subscription days and redemption days of the fund, since this will determine the price by reference to which subscription and redemption requests will be processed. The days on which valuations are required to be finalised are often referred to as 'valuation days' and may occur as often as monthly. In order to calculate the net asset value of a hedge fund, the administrator will rely upon the investment manager to provide it with all relevant information about the portfolio, and the administration agreement usually contains an express agreement by the investment manager to provide that information in a timely manner in advance of each valuation day. The investment manager will also require the co-operation of other third party service providers (such as the prime broker and the fund's accountants) to assist it in this role (and often the investment manager will be required to agree to procure their co-operation).

6.34 The ability to determine accurately the price of the securities of a hedge fund should always be a key factor when selecting an administrator, as the use of incorrect pricing is likely to have adverse legal and regulatory implications for the hedge fund. The valuation of listed equity securities is generally not problematic because their prices are readily available. An administrator may be required to rely on the executing broker or its counterparty in the case of unquoted stock. However, thinly traded securities (such as distressed debt) or complex securities (such as rights under non-exchange traded derivative contracts) may require assistance from the investment manager in order to determine their value. Since the valuation of the assets of the fund has a direct bearing on the fees payable to the investment manager, a detailed disclosure of the valuation policy of the fund must be made in its offering materials. This is one of the key potential areas where conflicts of interest may arise and it is always preferable for the administrator to value the fund's assets based on independent information.

6.35 Once the administrator has calculated the gross value of the fund's assets and its costs and expenses, it can calculate the net asset value of the fund. It will then be allocated between the various classes of interest according to their rights to share in those assets. Where there is a master-feeder structure in place, the feeder fund's net asset value will be the value of its interest in the master fund less any expenses borne by the feeder fund itself plus any assets that the feeder fund has in addition to its interest in the master fund, such as cash awaiting investment (if any).

6.36 The net asset value will then be used to calculate both the management fee (because it is expressed as a percentage of the net assets of the hedge fund) and the amount of any performance fee payable to the investment manager. This can be a time consuming and complicated process, particularly where interests in the hedge fund are issued or redeemed during the performance fee calculation period, requiring the application of a procedure called 'equalisation' to ensure that fees are fairly borne between investors (and, in the case of redemptions, that the investment manager receives a performance fee in respect of the shares which are to be redeemed). Further complications also arise where the investment manager is able to defer some of its fees and obtain a notional return on the deferred amount (a common practice amongst US hedge fund managers). The calculation of the performance fee is discussed in more detail in CHAPTER 15. It is, of course, crucial that the mechanism for the valuation of the hedge fund, its interests and the calculation of the management and performance fee is clearly explained in the administration agreement (whether directly or by reference to the description in the fund's offering memorandum).

Reporting

6.37 The administrator will also be responsible for producing the hedge fund's financial statements (which are usually produced on an annual and semi-annual basis), liaising with the hedge fund's auditors in connection with their production and sending these statements to the fund's investors. Where the hedge fund also produces monthly fact sheet summaries (and other ad hoc reporting requested by certain investors, for example, reporting of any fee rebates paid to them), the administrator will also co-ordinate their production and circulation.

Monitoring and settling trades

6.38 The portfolio of the hedge fund will frequently change and the administrator will be required to monitor and record this. This is another area in which active co-operation by the administrator with the investment manager and the prime broker is required.

6.39 All investments which a hedge fund makes should reflect its investment policy and current asset allocations (both of which will be set out in its offering documents). The administrator may monitor the fund's compliance with the investment policy as set out in the offering documents (although it will not wish to be responsible for any non-compliance). Performance of this monitoring function by another person, such as the investment manager, may give rise to a conflict of interest.

6.40 From the perspective of the fund, assets are acquired or disposed of when the investment manager executes a trade on behalf of the fund in the market. However, the trade is not actually completed until the prime broker effects it through the relevant clearing system. The administrator will ensure that the prime broker is reflecting the same trades and holding the same positions as the administrator records in the books and records of the hedge fund. Unmatched or unsettled transactions can result in the cancellation of a trade and have

6.40 *Service Providers – Making it Happen*

implications for the calculation of net asset value. More seriously, they may result in pricing errors that require reporting to the relevant regulatory authority.

6.41 In order for the administrator to be able to fulfil this (and other) function, it relies on the prompt flow of accurate and high quality information from the prime broker. For this reason it is common for the administration agreement to exclude liability on the part of the administrator for any loss which the fund suffers as a result of a delay in the flow of information, or the receipt of inaccurate information, from the prime broker. As previously mentioned, the compatibility of the computer systems of the administrator and the prime broker is crucial in this respect.

Registered office and company secretarial functions

6.42 The law of any jurisdiction in which a hedge fund is established will always require that hedge fund to have a registered office in that jurisdiction, and will often require corporate and regulatory filings to be made within prescribed timescales, notifications to investors to be made, and the minute book and register of members to be kept up to date. Either the administrator or a local company secretary may perform this role. Where a separate service provider performs this role, the administrator will be required to liaise with that entity to ensure that the books and records of the hedge fund are accurate and up to date.

Other duties

6.43 The administrator is also often responsible for performing a number of other functions, including monitoring the expenses which the hedge fund incurs, issuing instructions to the fund's bankers to settle any liabilities (including to other service providers) and co-ordinating stock exchange listings and adhering to the requirements of the relevant exchange (where relevant).

E   THE PRIME BROKER

6.44 Prime brokerage is a well-established global business which is dominated by global investment banks, and when an investment manager wishes to appoint a prime broker, it will rarely be able to negotiate provisions that are significantly different from the standard terms and conditions of the relevant prime broker. This is essentially an issue of bargaining power as although in theory many funds could operate without a prime broker, in practice most funds will not be able to maximise returns (or indeed implement their strategies) without appointing a prime broker which has access to a wide pool of investment opportunities.

6.45 The traditional role of the prime broker in clearing and settling trades and providing custody services has widened over the last few decades to include the provision of leverage and securities lending facilities. Whilst hedge funds are able to obtain these services from separate service providers, the ability of prime brokers to provide them all on an integrated basis on a single platform is a significant benefit. Nevertheless, some funds may engage separate execution brokers, particularly where trade commissions can be reduced by doing so.

6.46 Prime brokers are required to be regulated by the Financial Conduct Authority in the UK and the Securities and Exchange Commission in the US.

6.47 The role of the prime broker in relation to a hedge fund also gives a considerable regulatory benefit and comfort to investors. Prime brokers are invariably very large banks and are therefore highly regulated, with sophisticated systems and controls. The presence of the prime broker in the structure alleviates a number of concerns arising from the offshore nature of hedge funds and the fact that hedge funds, particularly start-ups, are frequently lightly staffed at the level of the investment manager.

6.48 The prime broker in a very real sense has an overview of and controls the hedge fund's assets on a day-to-day basis. The prime broker can close the fund down irrespective of the wishes of the investment manager if it considers that the fund is entering insolvency and it is strongly incentivised to do so because of its combined roles as lender, service provider, broker and counterparty to the hedge fund. This is one reason why hedge funds normally do not become insolvent and are simply wound up.

6.49 From a regulator's perspective the prime broker is a source of information and oversight that lends considerable comfort because of its resources, the fact that it is normally established in an onshore jurisdiction and therefore subject to the regulator's jurisdiction, and because of its economic incentive to ensure the fund is successful. This, combined with the fact that the investment manager (or in the case of an onshore-offshore management structure, the sub-investment manager or investment adviser) is also normally located onshore, makes the hedge fund industry significantly more regulated than is commonly perceived. However, prime brokers can also fail, as happened with Bear Stearns in 2008, which had to be rescued by a takeover by JP Morgan Chase. One alleged cause of its collapse was the withdrawal by prime brokerage clients of their assets.

Choice of prime broker

6.50 The choice of prime broker will depend on a number of factors, although it would be rare for a fund to engage a prime broker that is not well-established on a global scale. The level of trade commissions, credit rating and reputation are all relevant considerations. Since the financial crisis, it has become increasingly common for a hedge fund to appoint more than one prime broker, particularly in the case of multi-strategy hedge funds.

6.51 Once the fund has been established, the prime broker will open the prime brokerage and custodial accounts. It will receive the monies subscribed by investors and will await trading instructions from the investment manager.

Clearing trades

6.52 When a hedge fund enters into a trade, the investment manager will inform the executing broker that the prime broker will act as clearing agent.

6.52 *Service Providers – Making it Happen*

The investment manager and the executing broker will then report the trade details to the prime broker, which will verify that those instructions match each other. If so, the trade will be confirmed and the relevant securities will be transferred to the fund's brokerage account with the prime broker. If the trade does not match, the prime broker will seek to resolve it. In settling a trade, the prime broker will deliver funds to pay for acquisitions of securities and receive funds as a result of disposals.

6.53 Reporting and confirming trades is one of the key interactions between the investment manager, the administrator and the prime broker in relation to a hedge fund. The prime broker is required to identify any discrepancies between the trade envisaged by the investment manager and the executing broker. The sector has increasingly relied on technology in order to fulfil this role.

6.54 Whether the prime broker is acting as principal or as agent on behalf of the hedge fund will depend on the type of transaction involved, although generally the prime broker acts as agent in the settlement process.

Custody

6.55 A key role of the prime broker is to hold the assets of the fund on a global basis, which may or may not be in a segregated account. The manner in which assets will be held should be considered in advance as the relevant client money protection rules may not always apply. The prime broker will also have security over the assets that it holds as collateral against any cash and securities which the prime broker has lent to the hedge fund, which may be taken in the form of fixed or floating charges. In granting custody over the assets of the fund, the extent to which the prime broker is able to pledge those assets should be carefully considered and a maximum percentage should be specified in the prime brokerage agreement with the prime broker. For both of these reasons, the fund will need to be comfortable with the prime broker's financial security and credit rating.

Securities lending

6.56 The success of a hedge fund that engages in short selling strategies is highly dependent on the ability of the prime broker to provide securities lending services. This is the most significant factor for the success of such strategies.

6.57 The prime broker's securities lending desk will identify the stock that the fund wishes to 'short' (generally from another investor although it may be sourced from another broker) and will arrange for the relevant stock to be delivered in order to settle the trade. The prime broker will provide security to the lender of the securities and is required to maintain a collateral balance to ensure that any calls can be met.

Leverage

6.58 A fundamental service which a prime broker provides is to make leverage available to the hedge fund. Leverage can be provided in the form of margin financing (that is, where the fund borrows a portion of the value of the security that it wishes to acquire from the prime broker) or through the use of derivatives.

6.59 The amount of leverage that a prime broker is willing to provide for a particular asset is expressed as a 'haircut' of the value of the asset for which it is intended to be used, which is usually a percentage discount to its value. The fund will be required to provide the discounted amount from its own assets in order to acquire the relevant asset. The prime broker will calculate the fund's overall margin on a daily basis and if that exceeds the overall leverage limit of the hedge fund the prime broker may make a 'margin call' which requires the fund to take immediate remedial action. Since the margin calculations are made on a daily basis, the prime broker may refuse to settle trades where it considers that the fund will not be able to satisfy any connected margin call and will be able to take remedial action by unwinding some or all of the fund's positions.

Reporting

6.60 A prime broker will produce various reports, including daily transaction reports, cash balance reports and margin reports. The investment manager uses these reports to manage the fund's portfolio and to compile the reports which it in turn provides to investors.

Fees

6.61 Prime brokers are not remunerated on a whole services basis but instead receive income from a number of sources, including the spreads that they receive on financing and lending, trading commissions and settlement fees. These fees are generally charged as a percentage of the value of the assets provided and/or transactions effected.

F OTHER SERVICE PROVIDERS

6.62 This chapter has examined the roles played by the key service providers who 'make the fund happen' and work closely together to ensure that the hedge fund operates smoothly and successfully. In addition to those described above, the fund may also engage:

- placing agents/distributors to seek out prospective investors;
- listing sponsors (if any of the interests in the fund are to be listed on a stock exchange);
- auditors; and
- lawyers (often in a number of relevant jurisdictions).

Chapter 7

THE PRIME BROKER

Allan Yip, Partner, Simmons & Simmons

A	Introduction	7.1
B	What is a prime broker?	7.3
C	Custody services	7.11
D	Clearing and settlement	7.15
E	Financing	7.17
F	Ancillary and 'value add' services	7.20
G	Other roles	7.23
H	Key documentation	7.27

A   INTRODUCTION

7.1 If the investment manager is the metaphorical brain of a hedge fund, performing the 'front office' functions such as making trading decisions, the prime broker could perhaps be best categorised as the hands, carrying out the 'middle office' and 'back office' functions such as ensuring that such trades are accurately captured and settled.

7.2 However, this would be a gross over-simplification of the role performed by the prime broker. Alongside the investment manager and the administrator, the prime broker is one of the three key pillars on which a hedge fund relies for its day-to-day existence. This chapter explores the relationship between a prime broker and a hedge fund.

B   WHAT IS A PRIME BROKER?

7.3 In the UK, the Financial Conduct Authority (the 'FCA') provides two separate regulatory definitions of a prime broker. The most recent definition was introduced by the FCA in its Investment Funds Sourcebook ('FUND') as a direct result of the Alternative Investment Fund Managers Directive[1] ('AIFMD'). This definition[2] tracks the one set out in AIFMD:

> 'a credit institution, regulated investment firm or another entity subject to prudential regulation and ongoing supervision, offering services to professional clients primarily to finance or execute transactions in financial instruments as counterparty and which may also provide other services, such as clearing and settlement of trades, custodial services, stock lending, customised technology and operational support facilities.'

[1]   Directive 2011/61/EU of 8 June 2011.
[2]   See 'prime brokerage firm' in the Glossary to the FCA Handbook.

7.4 The FUND definition of the role of a prime broker is, unfortunately, so broad in its drafting that it could arguably include entities that are clearly not

7.4 The Prime Broker

prime brokers within its scope. For example, with its reference to 'primarily to . . . execute transactions in financial instruments as counterparty', it potentially captures simple trading counterparties (such as executing brokers or derivatives counterparties).

7.5 Therefore, whilst a hedge fund will clearly be obliged to use such definition in connection with its consideration of AIFMD, for the purposes of this chapter, it can be put to one side as an unhelpful and unclear regulatory definition.

7.6 Somewhat closer to the mark is the earlier definition published by the FCA in connection with its enhancement of its Client Assets Sourcebook ('CASS') to cater for prime brokerage arrangements, after the collapse of Lehman Brothers. In this context, a prime broker is defined[1] as an authorised firm that provides:

> 'a package of services provided under a prime brokerage agreement which gives a prime brokerage firm a right to use safe custody assets for its own account and which comprises each of the following:
> (a) custody or arranging safeguarding and administration of assets;
> (b) clearing services; and
> (c) financing, the provision of which includes one or more of the following:
> (i) capital introduction;
> (ii) margin financing;
> (iii) stock lending;
> (iv) stock borrowing;
> (v) entering into repurchase or reverse repurchase transactions,
> and which, in addition, may comprise consolidated reporting and other operational support.'

[1] See 'prime brokerage firm' and 'prime brokerage services' in the Glossary to the FCA Handbook.

7.7 The CASS definition of a prime broker still contains deficiencies. For instance, from the wording in the opening paragraph, it appears to require a prime broker to have a right of re-use, suggesting that if a prime broker were to agree to forego such right, but whilst still providing all the other prime brokerage services, it would no longer be a prime broker. In addition, the apparent reference to 'capital introduction' as a form of financing is odd, to say the least.

7.8 However, the CASS definition does capture the essence of the role of the prime broker in describing it as the provider of a 'package of services'. It is this notion of a provision of a service that forms the backbone of the relationship between a hedge fund and its prime broker, driving the commercial considerations such as where any credit or market risk should lie and legal considerations such as the direction of indemnity and limitation of liability provisions.

7.9 Although there are some providers of prime brokerage who operate on a smaller, local scale, the major players tend to be global investment banks. As such, they will tend to be highly regulated entities, with sophisticated systems and controls, and they were placed under even more regulatory scrutiny following the near-collapse of Bear Stearns and the collapse of Lehman Brothers in 2008, who were two of the largest global prime brokers at the time.

7.10 Whilst different prime brokerages will provide differing packages of service, they will each at least provide the core services of:

- custody of securities and cash[1];
- clearing and settlement[2]; and
- financing[3].

[1] See paras **7.11–7.14** below.
[2] See paras **7.15–7.16** below.
[3] See paras **7.17–7.19** below.

C CUSTODY SERVICES

7.11 The most basic role played by a prime broker is that of a custodian. A prime broker will hold securities and cash belonging to the hedge fund and will provide administration services in relation to securities, such as collecting dividends and other income and processing corporate actions.

7.12 One of the key issues in respect of the custody service is the treatment of securities and cash held in custody following the insolvency of the prime broker. This will depend primarily on the jurisdiction in which the prime broker is established, as that is most likely to be the jurisdiction whose insolvency laws will govern.

7.13 In the UK, the treatment of a hedge fund's assets will differ depending on whether those assets are securities or cash. In the case of securities, as long as they are still held in custody (as opposed to being 're-used' or 'rehypothecated'[1]), such securities should be held segregated away from the prime broker's own assets and therefore be held outside the prime broker's insolvent estate. However, in relation to cash, unless a hedge fund has requested client money protection under the FCA's client money rules[2], the hedge fund will be an unsecured and general creditor in respect of such cash and will therefore be fully exposed to the credit risk of the prime broker.

[1] See para **7.29** below.
[2] See Chapter 7 of the Client Assets Sourcebook in the FCA Handbook.

7.14 In the same way as a traditional custodian does, a prime broker will usually employ sub-custodians in certain markets where they do not have a custody presence themselves. The use of sub-custodians can introduce additional risk to treatment of securities described above, as in certain jurisdictions the prime broker may hold a hedge fund's securities with a sub-custodian on a commingled basis with the prime broker's own securities.

D CLEARING AND SETTLEMENT

7.15 When a hedge fund enters into a trade, it is the prime broker that will take steps to ensure that the trade settles in accordance with its agreed terms. This will involve communicating with the hedge fund's executing broker to match the relevant trade details, resolve any discrepancies and ultimately to ensure that the trade settles by transferring or receiving from or into the hedge fund's prime brokerage account the relevant amount of securities or cash.

7.16 *The Prime Broker*

7.16 The clearing and settlement service provided by a prime broker is critical to the well-running of the hedge fund. The key issues in relation to this part of the prime broker service tend to be of an operational nature. There is heavy reliance on technology and systems, and the best prime brokers will distinguish themselves by being able to provide a strong clearing and settlement service.

E   FINANCING

7.17 The prime broker will also typically provide financing to a hedge fund, which permits that hedge fund to employ leverage in executing its trading strategy. This can take the form of a cash loan to the hedge fund, but can also be in the form of securities lending.

7.18 As holding cash in its prime brokerage account is generally not the optimal allocation of assets, a cash loan extended by a prime broker to a hedge fund will generally not take the form of cash being credited to the cash account. Instead, it would usually take the form of a hedge fund purchasing securities from an executing broker and the prime broker using its own cash to settle that purchase transaction on behalf of the hedge fund. Upon settlement, the securities would be credited to the hedge fund's securities account with the prime broker and a cash amount representing the amount loaned to the hedge fund would be debited to the hedge fund's cash account with the prime broker.

7.19 A hedge fund which employs shorting strategies will need a prime broker with a strong securities lending service. Shorting involves a hedge fund entering into a sale transaction in respect of securities that it does not currently own. Therefore, it is important to the hedge fund to know that its prime broker will be able to source the relevant securities and to settle the sale transaction using those 'lent' securities.

F   ANCILLARY AND 'VALUE ADD' SERVICES

7.20 In addition to the above core services, a prime broker will often provide ancillary and other additional 'value add' services to support the establishment and ongoing running of a hedge fund.

7.21 The key ancillary service is probably that of reporting. In the UK, the FCA's CASS rules[1] now require a prime broker to make available daily reports to its clients on a close-of-business-day basis. These daily reports are required to set out the key information about the portfolio, including the total value of securities held in custody and any client money, the value of any cash or securities loans, the value of securities rehypothecated by the prime broker, and the value of all claims and obligations between the hedge fund and the prime broker. In summary, the daily report must provide a hedge fund with all the detail in respect of its exposure to the prime broker.

[1] See CASS 9.2.

7.22 The 'value add' services usually include capital introduction, pursuant to which a prime broker might organise events and provide introductions of a hedge fund to potential investors, and consultancy services, pursuant to which a prime broker would provide assistance to start-up hedge funds in respect of recommendations of service providers, provision of office space and IT support. In respect of capital introduction, the key concern is to ensure that the prime broker does not stray into the realm of marketing the fund, and the prime broker will usually have strict guidelines and policies to ensure that it does not fall foul of this.

G　OTHER ROLES

7.23 As well as providing the prime brokerage services described above, a prime broker will often have additional contractual relationships with the hedge fund. These could include acting as an OTC derivatives counterparty pursuant to an ISDA Master Agreement, a futures executing and clearing broker, an FX prime broker, a repo counterparty or an OTC derivatives clearing broker.

7.24 Despite the fact that the contractual relationship is between the hedge fund and the same legal entity, it is important to remember that each of these relationships is distinct from the prime brokerage relationship that a hedge fund has with that entity. In some cases, it will be analogous to a prime brokerage relationship in that there is a service provider and a service consumer. However, in other cases the relationship will be one of counterparty to counterparty, and this shift in roles is important in considering the balance of commercial, credit and legal risks to be assumed by each party. In addition, each distinct contractual relationship is likely to involve additional documentation, which brings with it its own risks and issues for a hedge fund.

7.25 A prime broker may seek to connect some of the credit, legal and documentation issues by offering a 'cross-product margining' structure. Through such a structure, the prime broker would assess the credit exposure to a hedge fund across all the distinct contractual relationships and calculate a single margin/collateral amount rather than separate margin amounts for each relationship. This can be beneficial to the hedge fund in that the single margin amount is likely to be lower than the aggregate of the separate margin amounts that would otherwise be required, and it can also ease the operational burden of having to post separate margin amounts.

7.26 From a legal and documentation perspective, a cross-product margining structure is usually achieved by entering into a separate agreement (called a 'master netting agreement' or similar), pursuant to which an event which gives rise to a termination right in respect of one contractual relationship would also give rise to a termination right in respect of all other contractual relationships and amounts owing between the parties under one contractual relationship would be netting against amounts owing under each other contractual relationships.

H　KEY DOCUMENTATION

7.27 There is no industry-standard agreement governing prime brokerage. A prime broker will invariably have its own version which is traditionally designed to protect it against the default of the hedge fund, rather than protecting the hedge fund against the default of the prime broker. As many

7.27 The Prime Broker

hedge funds which appointed Lehman Brothers as their prime broker discovered in 2008, this arrangement can leave hedge funds exposed upon a prime broker insolvency.

7.28 One of the key central issues is the level of protection provided by segregation of assets and the speed with which assets can be returned to the hedge fund following a prime broker insolvency. The treatment of assets held in custody following a prime broker insolvency has already been discussed above. In relation to the issue of the timely return of assets, the use by prime brokers of group entities as sub-custodians and the grant of liens in favour of those affiliate sub-custodians can hinder the retrieval of assets in an insolvency scenario. In addition, the traditional existence of a broad security interest in favour not only of the prime broker but also the prime broker's affiliates can also cause shortfall and delay in the return of assets to a hedge fund.

7.29 Another key issue is the common market practice of 'rehypothecation' – that is, the right of the prime broker to 're-use' a hedge fund's securities for its own purposes. Under English law, when its securities are rehypothecated, a hedge fund will lose title to those securities and instead be left with a contractual right to redelivery of those securities. Upon the insolvency of the prime broker, that contractual right represents only a general and unsecured claim against the prime broker's insolvent estate, as contrasted against the treatment of segregated securities which are held outside the prime broker's insolvent estate.

7.30 Importantly, under English law (unlike in the US) there is no regulatory limit on the amount of a hedge fund's securities that can be rehypothecated by the prime broker. The well-advised hedge fund will therefore seek to impose a contractual limit in its prime brokerage agreement. The traditional way in which this is achieved in prime brokerage agreements governed by English law is by applying the agreed percentage against the value of any indebtedness of the hedge fund to the prime broker.

7.31 In the UK, there are prime brokerage rules which involve, as discussed at the beginning of this chapter, not only the FCA formally introducing a regulatory definition of prime brokerage services for the first time, but also the enshrinement of formal daily reporting by prime brokers to their clients and the obligation to disclose certain risks associated to a prime brokerage relationship.

7.32 The relationship between a prime broker and a hedge fund has indisputably changed in the post-Lehman world. Whilst the role of the prime broker has remained largely the same, it can no longer be assumed automatically that the prime broker will always be the safer credit risk.

7.33 Arguably, even the term 'prime broker' is a slight misnomer in today's market. 'Prime' suggests first in importance, a single broker that provides services to the hedge fund that no other broker can. So perhaps the most apparent way in which the relationship change is demonstrated lies in the fact that most hedge funds will usually appoint at least two (but often as many as three or four) prime brokers, each of whom will vie for the lion's share of the hedge fund's business and assets.

Chapter 8

DIRECTORS' DUTIES

Dale Gabbert, Partner, Simmons & Simmons and Catherine O'Connell, Associate, Simmons & Simmons

A	Introduction	8.1
B	UK common law principles	8.5
C	The Cayman Islands	8.53

A INTRODUCTION

8.1 When considering directors' duties in connection with hedge funds, they must be considered in context. Unlike most commercial companies, market practice for hedge funds is for boards to delegate day-to-day management authority. Hedge funds generally delegate all their duties to service providers, including the investment manager, administrator, and depositary/custodian. Hedge funds commonly have no executive directors or staff and are, to some extent, a legal construct.

8.2 Hedge funds are typically established in offshore jurisdictions to minimise tax at the fund level. The duties that apply to the directors of the fund will be determined by the law of the place of incorporation of the fund (or, if the fund is a partnership, the place of incorporation of its general partner). In order to establish the nature and scope of directors' duties, it will therefore be necessary to look at the statute law and common law of the relevant jurisdiction. Some jurisdictions codify directors' duties in their company law statutes. The UK underwent such a process of codification in the Companies Act 2006 ('CA 2006').

8.3 CA 2006 enshrines in statute certain common law and equitable duties owed by directors of UK companies. In particular, it sets out the statement of directors' general duties[1]. The purpose of codification was to provide greater clarity regarding what is required of directors and to make the law in this area more accessible to directors and others, in addition to making developments in the law on directors' duties more predictable. The statutory statement of directors' general duties does not cover all duties owed by a director to a company; many are imposed elsewhere in legislation or remain uncodified (such as the duty not to defraud the company).

[1] See CA 2006, ss 170–177.

8.4 By contrast, there is no statutory codification of directors' duties under Cayman Islands law; duties of directors are founded in common law, which is derived from the principles of English common law (before the enactment of CA 2006). As such, this chapter addresses those common law rules and principles upon which directors' statutory duties now codified in CA 2006 are based. These principles will continue to be highly persuasive in common law

8.4 *Directors' Duties*

jurisdictions, like the Cayman Islands, that follow English law but have not codified directors' duties into their own statute law (or have done so but retain elements of the common law, such as the British Virgin Islands). This chapter does not intend to address all duties owed by a director to a company generally; rather, it intends to address those most relevant to directors of hedge funds.

B UK COMMON LAW PRINCIPLES

To whom are directors' duties owed?

8.5 As a fundamental principle of common law, company directors owe duties to the company of which they are a director and do not, by virtue of the legal relationship between the directors and the company, owe fiduciary duties to the company's shareholders or creditors (although shareholders may be able to bring derivative actions[1] in certain limited circumstances). Therefore, it is only the company that will be able to enforce the duties owed to it by its directors. The general duties, arising by virtue of the relationship between the company and the directors, are owed in all circumstances and owed by each director individually.

[1] See paras 8.50–8.52 below.

8.6 It is worth noting that under the pre-CA 2006 regime, in certain circumstances directors owed duties to persons other than the company, notably:

- The interests of employees insofar as it is in the best interests of the company.
- The interests of the company's creditors, as laid down by certain provisions of the Insolvency Act 1986 ('IA 1986').
  It was held in *Lonrho Ltd v Shell Petroleum Co Ltd*[1] that the interests of the company are 'not exclusively those of the shareholders but may include those of its creditors'. Reinforced by IA 1986, directors are obligated to take every step they would be expected to take to minimise any loss to creditors from the moment it becomes apparent that the company cannot avoid insolvent liquidation.
- The interests of other stakeholders.
  Obligations exist in various pieces of legislation to ensure companies pay due regard to the interests of various parties impacted by the company's operations.

[1] [1980] 1 WLR 627, 124 Sol Jo 412, HL.

8.7 This chapter focuses on the general duties owed by directors to a company under the previous common law regime in the UK.

Insolvency

8.8 The obligations on directors are particularly pertinent where the company is in a precarious financial situation. Once a company is insolvent, or the directors are aware that there is no reasonable prospect that the company will avoid going into liquidation, directors' duties are owed to creditors and directors are obligated to prioritise such interests over those of the shareholders, as creditors have a prior claim on the assets of the company.

Delegation

8.9 Directors are permitted to delegate their powers; however, their duties to the company remain intact and, as such, they will continue to be responsible for the exercise of such powers.

The general duties

8.10 It has long been established in common law that a director owes three types of general direct duty to the company:

- duty to act within powers[1];
- duty of care[2] – this concerns the degree of care, diligence and skill exercised in discharging one's duties so as not to be considered negligent in carrying out such duties; and
- fiduciary duties[3] imposed upon directors in connection with the management of the company.

[1] See paras **8.12–8.13** below.
[2] See paras **8.14–8.24** below.
[3] See paras **8.25–8.47** below.

8.11 Further, common law prohibits the personal interests of directors from conflicting with those of the company and does not allow directors to derive any personal profit from their position beyond that paid by the company in recognition of their role as director.

Duty to act within powers

8.12 A board of directors must ensure that it acts within the powers conferred on it in the memorandum and articles of association ('articles') of the company. A board is not permitted to act beyond the capacity of the company laid down in its constitutional documents, unless expressly approved by the shareholders (either in advance of the particular action or subsequently ratified at a general meeting of the company).

8.13 Where directors' actions go beyond the powers conferred upon them, the transaction may be voidable or the directors authorising the transaction may be in breach of their duties and may be personally liable for any loss to the company or any third party.

Duty of care

8.14 The duty of care principle requires directors to act with a certain standard of care, diligence and skill in discharging their duties. The test is principally subjective, in that it requires a director to exercise his duties with

8.14 Directors' Duties

a degree of care and skill that may reasonably be expected of a director in his position; however, this will be considered in conjunction with the actual knowledge, skill and experience of the particular director in question.

8.15 The leading authority on the nature and extent of this duty is *Re City Equitable Fire Insurance Company Ltd*[1], in which the following three basic principles were established by the Court of Appeal:

- directors need only display the skills they can reasonably be expected to possess; they cannot be expected to exercise a level of skill they do not have;
- directors are not required to devote their continuous attention to the affairs of the company; and
- in the absence of suspicious circumstances, directors are entitled to rely on the expertise and experience of co-directors and officers of the company in the performance of duties that they are entitled to delegate.

[1] [1925] Ch 407, [1924] All ER Rep 485, CA.

Degree of skill

8.16 Directors are therefore not required to possess any particular skills; rather, they are expected to diligently apply any skills that they do possess. As such, the test is a subjective one, assessing the way in which a director carries out any skills he actually has. It follows that honest incompetence is a ground for exoneration under common law, on the grounds that a director can do no better.

8.17 Subsequent developments in the law following *City Equitable* have added an objective element to the test, extending the duties owed by directors and the manner in which they must be carried out. Under IA 1986, where a company is insolvent, in order to avoid personal liability for wrongful trading, directors must display both the general knowledge, skill and experience that may reasonably be expected of a person carrying out the director's specific duties *and* the general knowledge, skill and experience that the director has, if higher than the objective minimum standard. It is now considered that this test has been generally applied by the courts in respect of directors' duties, whether or not the relevant company is insolvent.

8.18 The existence of a service contract stipulating tasks in respect of a director's particular skills, knowledge and experience will imply an objective level of skill. For example, in *Bairstow v Queens Moat Houses plc*[1], the High Court held that the level of competence expected of an executive director is commensurate with his responsibilities, noting the substantial remuneration which he would be paid.

[1] [2000] 1 BCLC 549, [1999] All ER (D) 1378, QBD.

8.19 It is also important to note that the basic standard is flexible, ie what can reasonably be expected of a director of a multinational, listed company may differ to that of a small, private company. The director of a hedge fund might therefore be expected to have a reasonable degree of financial sophistication.

UK common law principles **8.24**

ATTENTION TO THE BUSINESS

8.20 The extent to which a director is required to devote his personal attention to the affairs of the company will largely depend on the size and nature of the company's business. In order to determine the appropriate level of attention that is required, it will be necessary to consider the particular business. Note that a service contract would ordinarily require a director to devote his full attention to the company. In *City Equitable* it was held that[1]:

> 'In one company, for instance, matters may normally be attended to by the manager or other members of the staff that in another company are attended to by the directors themselves. The larger the business carried on by the company the more numerous, and the more important, the matters that must of necessity be left to the managers, the accountants and the rest of the staff.'

[1] *Re City Equitable Fire Insurance Company Ltd* [1925] Ch 407, p 426, CA.

8.21 In a hedge fund, where it is common practice for directors to delegate the primary investment management and administrative functions to third parties, it will be more appropriate for directors to assume a supervisory role; however, appropriate oversight and scrutiny will still be required in order for directors to discharge their duties sufficiently.

RELIANCE ON OTHERS

8.22 Directors are entitled, in the absence of grounds for suspicion, to rely on co-directors and officers of the company in the performance of duties which may be properly delegated. It follows that powers may legitimately be delegated to properly constituted committees of the board. As such, one director's breach of duty does not necessarily render another director liable where it would be considered reasonable to place one's trust in the delegate: '[a director] is, in the absence of grounds for suspicion, justified in trusting that official to perform such duties honestly'[1].

[1] *Re City Equitable Fire Insurance Company Ltd* [1925] Ch 407, p 408, CA.

8.23 Indeed, depending on the size of the business, a degree of delegation may be essential to the company's operating efficiently. However, as has been noted[1], a director's overall responsibility may not be delegated. Accordingly, whilst certain tasks may be outsourced, a director is still required to oversee their performance. Further, directors will be expected to scrutinise any delegated tasks and use their own independent judgement; ignorance is no defence and directors may be held liable where they ought to have been aware, even if they weren't.

[1] See para **8.9** above.

8.24 In particular, it should be remembered that directors will not be able to absolve themselves of responsibility where a company goes into liquidation by claiming that they took no part in the management of the company. A director will be expected to take a diligent interest in the affairs of the company and the information available to him in supervising the activities of another.

8.25 Directors' Duties

Fiduciary duties

8.25 It is important to distinguish between 'fiduciary' duties and 'non-fiduciary' duties because they are fundamentally different and, as such, the consequences of breach will be different. As explained by Millett LJ in the Court of Appeal in *Bristol and West Building Society v Mothew (t/a Stapley & Co)*[1]:

> 'A fiduciary is someone who has undertaken to act for or on behalf of another in a particular matter in circumstances which give rise to a relationship of trust and confidence. The distinguishing obligation of a fiduciary is the obligation of loyalty. The principal is entitled to the single-minded loyalty of his fiduciary. This core liability has several facets. A fiduciary must act in good faith; he must not make a profit out of his trust; he must not place himself in a position where his duty and his interest may conflict; he may not act for his own benefit or the benefit of a third person without the informed consent of his principal.'

[1] [1998] Ch 1, [1996] 4 All ER 698 at 712, CA Civ.

8.26 Directors must therefore act in a faithful or trustful manner towards or on behalf of the company, exercise the powers conferred on them and fulfil their duties of office honestly.

DUTY TO ACT IN GOOD FAITH IN THE INTERESTS OF THE COMPANY

8.27 In the Court of Appeal in *Re Smith and Fawcett Ltd*, Lord Greene MR iterated that directors must act 'bone fide in what they consider – not what a court may consider – to be in the interests of the company, and not for any collateral purpose'[1]. The duty to act bona fide in the best interests of the company is a subjective duty; crucially, this duty is concerned with what the particular director believes to be in the best interests of the company. It requires directors to act in good faith free from any personal motive when making decisions in respect of the company. As such, directors should not use their powers for the benefit of third parties or themselves.

[1] [1942] Ch 304, [1942] 1 All ER 542 at 543, CA.

8.28 In carrying out their duty to act bona fide in the best interests of the company, directors may be faced with a number of difficulties. Most notably, perhaps, in circumstances such as the insolvency or pending insolvency of a company, directors may be subject to conflicting demands. Fundamental to understanding this duty is an appreciation that, in acting bona fide for the company, the interests of the company will not necessarily be identical to the interests of the collective shareholders, for example by virtue of the duties owed by a company to its creditors not to dissipate its assets, or a company's duty to have regards to the interests of its employees in general.

8.29 The courts will interfere only if no reasonable director would have concluded that a particular transaction was in the best interests of the company. As such, it is possible to be in breach of this duty without any conscious dishonesty on the part of the director. However, the courts are generally reluctant to intervene, recognising that what is in the best interests of a company is often a matter of subjective opinion. Further, the test is what the *director* believes to be in the best interests of the company, rather than what the *court* believes. The courts will therefore only intervene where the breach of good faith is demonstrable, for example where directors have refused to take into account matters which should have been properly considered.

8.30 Directors would not normally be subject to claims of breach of duty where they have acted honestly with a genuine belief that their actions were in the best interests of the company. It may be possible for shareholders to ratify an act that is in breach of this duty. Further, a court may excuse a director in breach of the bona fide rule where he acted honestly and reasonably and the court considers that he ought fairly to be excused. However, where his actions were not in the best interests of the company, a director will be in breach of the bona fide duty despite having acted honestly.

Duty to act for proper purpose

8.31 A company's memorandum and articles, relevant shareholders' resolutions and board minutes will determine the specific powers conferred on directors, and the manner and context in which they can be exercised. Such powers must be used for the proper purpose intended; acting honestly in the best interests of the company alone will not prevent a director from being in breach of this duty if a transaction is based on an improper use of the director's powers.

8.32 In *Hogg v Cramphorn Ltd*[1], directors considered it to be in the best interests of the company to issue shares with special voting rights for the benefit of the company's employees in order to block a takeover bid. Whilst it was held by the High Court that the directors had acted in good faith, they were in breach of their duty to the company by making improper use of their powers to issue shares. In a fund context, this may be relevant where incoming investors wish changes to be made to the fund's memorandum and articles that benefit one group of shareholders over another, or give undue power to one interest grouping, without a corresponding benefit to the fund.

[1] [1967] Ch 254, [1966] 3 All ER 420, Ch D.

8.33 In certain circumstances an improper use of powers may be ratified by the members in a general meeting. However, shareholders are not permitted to ratify a breach of this duty where the company is insolvent.

Duty not to make secret profits

8.34 As a fiduciary, a director is prohibited from profiting personally from any opportunities arising as a result of his position as a director, even if he is acting honestly and in the interests of the company. If a director makes a personal profit in such circumstances without it being disclosed to the company (and authorised by the shareholders), he is under a duty to account for such profit and it must be repaid to the company.

8.35 This principle has been interpreted to include profits arising from seizing a business opportunity. In *Regal (Hastings) Ltd v Gulliver*[1], the House of Lords found that the company (under the control of a new board) was entitled

8.35 *Directors' Duties*

to personal profit made by the former directors, because the opportunity to make such profit arose only as a result of knowledge they had gained as directors. Despite the fact that the profit would not have accrued to the company, the directors were liable to account for such profit to the company, given that the opportunity to make the profit arose as a result of their directorship.

[1] [1967] 2 AC 134, [1942] 1 All ER 378, HL.

8.36 A director will be in breach of this duty even if he has acted in good faith or the action in question benefited the company as well as the director. Whether or not the director's profit was at the company's expense will not be relevant. Provided that the actions of the director led to him receiving a profit, which was not disclosed to and permitted by the company, and which came about in the course of the director's management of the company (or by virtue of his opportunities or knowledge as a director), the director will be under a duty to account for such profit to the company. Furthermore, this duty continues even after a director leaves a company; resigning before taking his profit will not absolve a director of the duty to account for personal profit made in the applicable circumstances.

8.37 In order for a director to benefit from situations in which he could use his particular knowledge for personal gain, a director must disclose the profit and the circumstances of the opportunity, and ensure that the retention of that profit is approved by the company (and recorded in the minutes of a general meeting).

8.38 Shareholders can often ratify directors' actions in these circumstances and thereby allow them to retain any profit. Whilst it is not a defence that a director acted honestly and in good faith, this will certainly be relevant in whether a company decides to ratify the actions of the director. Where profit has been obtained dishonestly or by way of misapplication of the company's assets, ratification by the shareholders will not be possible.

8.39 In a hedge fund context, this is likely to be relevant where directors are appointed by service providers (such as the investment manager or administrator) or have outside interests (or investments) that overlap with the fund's investment objective, strategy or investments. In such cases, care must be taken to ensure that these interests are fully disclosed. Where directors are the personnel of a regulated entity, such as the investment manager, they are often subject to a compliance regime that supplements and assists with this disclosure obligation.

Duty to avoid conflicts of interest

8.40 Directors must ensure that their personal interests do not conflict with their duty to the company. Where there is a potential conflict of interest, the interests of the company must always override the personal interests of the director. Further, unless permitted in the company's articles or approved by the shareholders, a director must account to the company for any benefit accrued through a transaction in which he has an interest. A director will be liable to account for the benefit of any such transaction even where he was unaware of the decision in question.

8.41 A conflict of interest will arise where a director exploits the assets or opportunities of the company for his own benefit. In particular, a conflict of interest may arise in respect of information gained through the company and used for the director's own benefit, even where the company does not use the information on its own account. Further, a conflict of interest may arise where a company enters into a transaction with another company in which the director has an interest. Under the pre-CA 2006 common law regime, the test was objective: a conflict could arise where 'the reasonable man looking at the relevant facts and circumstances of the particular case would think that there was a real sensible possibility of conflict'[1].

[1] *Boardman v Phipps* [1967] 2 AC 46, [1966] 3 All ER 721 at 756, HL.

8.42 It is a well-established practice that disclosure of any interest by a director will serve to validate the proposed transaction. Usually, provisions in the company's articles will render such contracts enforceable where the director in question has fully disclosed his interest to the board in advance (ideally the full board). The duty to avoid conflicts of interest may even be circumvented to permit a person to be a director of competing companies. Courts have held that this may be permitted where approval of the directors of both companies has been obtained. However, in such circumstances, a director must ensure the treatment of one company does not become preferential to that of the other[1]. Standard form articles for hedge funds typically have broad powers with regard to conflicts, but whilst these may prevent a director from acting outside the scope of his powers, they generally won't cure a conflict of interest in the absence of full disclosure and consent of the non-conflicted members of the board or the shareholders.

[1] *Scottish Co-operative Wholesale Society Ltd v Meyer* [1959] AC 324, [1958] 3 All ER 66, HL.

8.43 In a hedge fund context, a director may have a conflict of interest because of his activities as a member of other hedge fund boards, or where he is a functionary of the investment manager or another service provider. The proper course of action for a director is to disclose these conflicts and to excuse himself from any board decision on a topic in connection with which he has a conflicting interest (eg discussion of how to remunerate a service provider of which he is an executive or whether or not to terminate the service provider's contract). Another issue that can arise in a fund context is where a director is on the board of more than one entity in a fund structure, for example the board of the master fund and the feeder fund that participates in the master fund. This situation should generally be avoided because if the interests of the two entities conflict (eg the feeder fund's rights are not being respected or it needs to enforce them), the director may have an irreconcilable conflict of duty. In this case the only solution is to step down. In addition, there may be issues around the use of information gained in one capacity (eg as a director of the master fund) in another capacity (eg as a director of the feeder fund). Often these nuances only become apparent once a serious problem occurs. As a general rule, simplicity is preferable; where a fund structure has multiple entities, it is inadvisable to serve on the board of more than one entity in the same fund structure.

8.44 Where a contract is voidable by virtue of a director's conflict of interest, this can be ratified by the company's shareholders in certain circumstances.

Duty to declare an interest

8.45 Directors are required to disclose all interests to the board. It is common for a company's articles to permit conflicting interests where a director has disclosed the relevant interest to the company in advance, and they will usually specify that the relevant director may not vote in any proceedings relating to the contract.

8.46 Any interests a director may have ideally should be disclosed at the first board meeting at which the particular transaction is discussed. As noted above, any profit made as a result of a transaction in which a director has an interest may be due to the company, and any such contract or transaction may subsequently be voided by the company where the director has failed to disclose his interest and receive the appropriate authority to retain such profit. Directors are still bound by this duty even where an interest arises after a particular transaction has been completed; where this occurs, directors should declare such interest at the following board meeting. A company may authorise a particular transaction in advance or ratify it at a later date.

Fettering of discretion

8.47 Directors must take care when they agree to fetter the exercise of their future discretion. In *Fulham Football Club Ltd v Cabra Estates Plc*[1], the Court of Appeal considered whether directors could be released from an undertaking given in relation to future support of a planning application, on the basis that it was an unlawful restraint of their fiduciary duty to act bona fide in the best interests of the company. The Court of Appeal, citing with approval a decision of the Australian High Court in *Thorby v Goldberg*[2], rejected the illegality argument and held that, as the arrangements had conferred substantial benefits upon the company, it could not be said that the directors improperly fettered the future exercise of their discretion. The thrust of the decision in this case is that directors may enter into contractual arrangements that fetter the future exercise of their discretion provided that they bona fide believe at the time they enter into the contract that it is in the best interests of the company. That may seem a straightforward proposition, but the inverse of this is that if there is no tangible benefit to the contract that creates the fetter, it may be harder as a practical matter to establish the required bona fide belief. The greater the future fettering and the more removed it is from the achievement of a specific contractual purpose, the more difficult it will be to credibly establish the necessary belief. In a fund context, this is most likely to arise in relation to the issue of side letters[3] which restrict or direct the exercise of certain powers or require the consent of a third party (typically the investor). Care must be taken when granting such rights that the directors consider and record the reasons why they believe the overall arrangements are in the best interests of the fund.

[1] [1994] 1 BCLC 363, [1993] 1 PLR 29, CA Civ.
[2] (1964) 112 CLR 597, Aus HC.
[3] See paras **16.34–16.41** in Chapter 16.

Consequences of breach of duty

8.48 Where a director has breached one of his duties owed to the company, a number of potential actions are available to the company:

- injunctive relief to prevent the director from breaching or continuing to breach his duty;
- ratification of the action by the company; although, certain actions are not capable of ratification;
- rescission of a contract entered into improperly; however, if a third party has entered into a contract in good faith, the company would be unlikely to succeed in a claim for rescission;
- restitution for loss of company property; again, a company will need to be mindful of third parties who have acted in good faith;
- where secret profits have been made in breach of a director's duty, recovery of those profits by the company;
- seeking damages against the director, to indemnify the company for any loss suffered as a result of the breach;
- suing the director for negligent performance; and/or
- the director's dismissal, because the director's breach of duty is considered to be a breach of the terms of his service contract.

8.49 It is important to note that these are actions available to the company in respect of a director in circumstances where one of the director's general duties has been breached. Additionally, there are a number of statutory provisions which impose criminal liability, the breach of which could lead to criminal prosecution.

Derivative actions

8.50 In addition to the above actions which may be brought on behalf of the company, in certain limited circumstances individual shareholders may choose to bring a derivative action on behalf of the company.

8.51 Ultimately, a director's duties are owed to the company as a whole, and the prima facie principle, as laid down in *Foss v Harbottle*[1], is that a duty owed to the company may only be enforced by the company, rather than individual shareholders. Subject to certain exceptions, shareholders are generally bound under English law by the principle of majority rule. As such, if a breach of duty were capable of being ratified by the shareholders of a company, this may often be achieved by a bare majority. Consequently, shareholders will usually be unable to challenge actions approved by the majority; this is particularly so, given that the courts are generally reluctant to intervene in the internal management of a company.

[1] 2 Hare 461, 67 ER 189, VC Ct.

8.52 In order to allow some recourse of action for minority shareholders, there are limited circumstances in which an individual shareholder may bring an action in name of the company; however, the principle laid down in *Foss v Harbottle* creates a difficult hurdle for an individual investor to surpass in order to sue directors personally.

8.53 *Directors' Duties*

C THE CAYMAN ISLANDS

8.53 The principles of English common law (upon which directors' duties in the Cayman Islands are largely based) have been substantively confirmed by the courts of the Cayman Islands, most notably in the case of *Weavering Macro Fixed Income Fund Ltd (in liquidation) v Stefan Peterson and Hans Ekstrom*[1], as discussed below[2].

[1] CICA 10 of 2011 (unreported, 12 February 2015); [2011] 2 CILR 203, CIGC.
[2] See paras **8.68–8.87** below.

8.54 As is the case under English common law, the role of directors in the context of hedge funds must be considered in light of the fact that, unlike other companies, most management and administrative functions will be delegated to third parties. Integral to the law on directors' duties therefore is the fact that directors may delegate any and all of their duties to other directors, committees, officers, service providers etc, provided such power to delegate is provided for in the articles of the company. However, a fundamental caveat to this is that delegation will not relieve directors of their duties entirely; the ultimate responsibility for exercising supervision of any delegates will still be borne by the directors in question. The precise extent to which a director will be required to exercise supervision and control over a delegate in order to fulfil his duties will depend on the particular circumstances.

8.55 Under Cayman Islands law, directors' duties are categorised into (i) fiduciary duties[1] and (ii) duty of care, diligence and skill[2].

[1] See paras **8.59–8.63** below.
[2] See para **8.58** below.

To whom are the duties owed?

8.56 Directors owe their duties to the company (which equates to the interests of the shareholders, as the individuals with the principal economic interest in the company and how it is managed). However, directors' duties to the company cannot be divided into individual obligations owed to separate shareholders. Directors owe their duties to the company as a whole and, as such, the shareholders as a collective body. As under English common law, shareholders are usually entitled to ratify decisions of the board that would otherwise constitute a breach of duty, in the absence of fraud. Further, a director's duties are owed to the particular company of which he is a director; a director is not entitled to consider the interests of another company within the same group, for example.

Insolvency/doubtful solvency

8.57 As is the case with an English company, where a Cayman Islands company becomes insolvent or its solvency is reasonably considered to be doubtful, the question of to whom the directors' duties are owed shifts away from the company and towards the company's creditors. Upon insolvency or doubtful solvency, the general body of creditors have the principal economic interest in the company. Directors must not prefer the interests of one creditor or group of creditors over the general body of creditors in the absence of a legitimate commercial reason.

What are the duties?

Duty of care, diligence and skill

8.58 This principle requires directors to act with care, diligence and skill in discharging their duties. The test is principally subjective in that it requires a director to exercise his duties with a degree of care and skill that may reasonably be expected of a director in his position. However, the courts will also have regard to the actual knowledge, skill and experience of the particular director in question. As such, the precise requirements of this duty will be established on a case-by-case basis. It is worth noting that a benchmark in determining whether or not a director has complied with the duty of care, diligence and skill is whether the director is considered to be an executive or a non-executive director. As a general guide, whilst executive directors are expected to take a more active role in the management of a company, a non-executive director's role may be more focused on ensuring effective supervision of the executive management of a company.

Fiduciary duties

8.59 Directors' fiduciary duties are composed of the following four elements, discussed below:

- 'bona fides' principle;
- 'proper purpose' principle;
- unfettered discretion;
- avoidance of conflicts of duty and interest.

BONA FIDES PRINCIPLE

8.60 The bona fides principle requires directors to act in good faith in what they consider to be the best interests of the company. This principle focuses on what the particular director believes to be in the best interests of the company and is therefore a subjective test. As such, if a decision of a director were to be challenged, the courts would not look at the merits of the particular decision. To demonstrate subsequently that a particular decision caused loss to the company will not necessarily equate to a breach of a director's duty, provided that the director believed in good faith at the time in question, on the basis of the information available to him at that time, that the decision was in the best interests of the company. The courts will generally only interfere where it is determined that no reasonable person could have concluded that a particular course of action was in the best interests of the company.

8.61 *Directors' Duties*

PROPER PURPOSE PRINCIPLE

8.61 The proper purpose principle requires that powers vested in directors are exercised for the purpose for which they were conferred and that actions are not taken for a collateral purpose. For example, if directors waived a redemption fee for a particular investor, at the request of the investment manager, as a means to entice that investor to invest in another fund managed by the investment manager, this would be acting with a collateral purpose without benefit to the company. As such, the directors could be said to have breached their duties to the company.

UNFETTERED DISCRETION

8.62 Directors must not improperly fetter the exercise of their future discretion, for example by contractually binding themselves to vote in a particular manner at future board meetings. By doing so, directors may subsequently be in a position where to vote in such a way would no longer be in the best interests of the company, but to do otherwise would be in breach of their contractual obligation.

AVOIDANCE OF CONFLICTS OF DUTY AND INTEREST

8.63 Directors are required to avoid situations in which there is a conflict between their duty to the company and any personal interest that may exist. The basic presumption is that directors should not participate in decisions in which such conflicts arise. However, it is common for this requirement to be addressed in the company's articles, rendering it possible for directors still to contract with the company whilst having a personal interest in transactions, provided such interest has been disclosed to the board. This may be particularly pertinent where directors are shareholders in the relevant company or are owners of a service provider, such as the investment manager.

Consequences of breach of duties

8.64 Where a director has breached his duties to the company, he may be personally liable to pay damages to the company. This may take the form of damages for the loss suffered by the company or for any improper profit made by the director. Furthermore, a company may be able to pursue an injunction to prevent a director from breaching (or continuing to breach) a duty owed to the company. Where applicable, a company may also be entitled to seek restoration of company property improperly in the hands of a director.

8.65 As is the case under English common law, because directors' duties are owed to the company, enforcement lies in the hands of the company. The limited exceptions in which a shareholder can bring a derivative action also apply in the case of a Cayman Islands company; however, as with English companies, the principle in *Foss v Harbottle*[1] presents a difficult hurdle for individual shareholders who might want the ability to sue a director personally. This would require the director to have committed an illegal act or perpetrated fraud on the minority shareholders. In most circumstances there will be no direct cause of action available to individual shareholders against directors.

[1] See para 8.51 above.

8.66 Where a company is insolvent or in liquidation, it will be up to the liquidator to bring any action against the directors for breach of duty. There may also be certain other criminal offences, particularly in the case of insolvency, which can result in directors facing criminal prosecution.

8.67 As a matter of general practice, there is usually a provision in the articles of a Cayman hedge fund that directors will be entitled to indemnification and exculpation. Depending on how these provisions are drafted, a director may not be liable for loss caused to a company as a result of his breach of duty.

The Weavering case

8.68 In *Weavering*[1], the Grand Court of the Cayman Islands (the 'Grand Court'), in finding two directors of an investment fund liable in damages for the fund's losses by virtue of their breaches of duty, examined duties of fund directors more generally and provided important commentary on the type of practices and procedures which should be in place in order for such duties to be effectively discharged.

[1] *Weavering Macro Fixed Income Fund Ltd (in liquidation) v Stefan Peterson and Hans Ekstrom* CICA 10 of 2011 (unreported, 12 February 2015); [2011] 2 CILR 203, CIGC.

8.69 The Grand Court found that the directors were guilty of wilful neglect or default and that their conduct fell well below that required of them. In reaching this conclusion, the Grand Court confirmed that whilst a fund may outsource much of its day-to-day management functions, directors must take an active role in supervising the business and must exercise independent judgement when making decisions and executing documents provided by any such service providers.

Background to the case

8.70 The proceedings concerned Weavering Macro Fixed Income Fund Limited ('Weavering Ltd'), which collapsed in 2009. Despite consistently reporting steady returns, the Weavering Ltd fund had in fact for many years been making huge losses on its trading activities, and had been engaging in fictitious trades (namely, interest rate swaps) marked at inflated prices with a related party, Weavering Capital Fund. Weavering Capital Fund was controlled by one of the directors of Weavering Ltd. The directors claimed that they were not aware that the counterparty had been Weavering Capital Fund, believing that the trades had been with international financial institutions.

8.71 Weavering Ltd had been structured conventionally; that is to say, the investment management and trading had been delegated to a third party investment manager and various accounting responsibilities to a third party administrator. However, the sole directors of Weavering Ltd were the brother and father of the principal of the investment manager. The proceedings were

8.71 Directors' Duties

brought by the liquidators of Weavering Ltd, who sought damages from the two directors, Mr Peterson and Mr Ekstrom, for breach of duty, including breach of fiduciary duty. The principal allegation was that the directors had wilfully breached their duty to exercise reasonable skill and care in their lack of supervision of the performance of Weavering Ltd's service providers. The argument was that had the directors carried out their supervisory role to the requisite standard of skill and care, they would have discovered that the counterparty to the interest rate swaps was a related entity and that redemption payments were being made on the basis of grossly inflated net asset values.

8.72 The constitutional documents of Weavering Ltd provided an indemnity for the directors, common to many Cayman Islands investment funds, exculpating the directors by providing that there could be no cause of action against them, except for losses arising from the directors' own wilful neglect or default.

Grand Court decision

8.73 The Grand Court accepted the central allegation of the liquidators and held that the directors had wilfully breached their duty to exercise reasonable skill and care[1]. Jones J acknowledged that, as is common with funds structured in this way, the directors' supervisory duties were 'high level'; however, he found that the directors had wholly and wilfully failed to perform even that high level role. It was held that as a result of the directors' wilful neglect, Weavering Ltd had suffered losses of at least US$111 million (the difference between what was actually paid out by Weavering Ltd and what would have been paid out on the basis of accurate net asset value figures). As such, Jones J awarded damages in that amount against the directors.

[1] [2011] 2 CILR 203, CIGC.

8.74 In considering the facts of the case, Jones J's obiter comments provided helpful, practical guidance as to how independent non-executive directors of Cayman Islands funds should approach a number of their various functions, in order to meet the skill, care and diligence threshold required of them. Jones J split the case into three key periods of a fund's life cycle: (i) launch of the fund; (ii) life cycle of fund; and (iii) where the fund gets into distress. He explained what he considered to be the appropriate actions required from a board in respect of each stage.

8.75 Jones J held that the board had so significantly failed in respect of its duties that intentional default had to be construed. In order to rely on the indemnity contained in Weavering Ltd's articles, Jones J explained that the directors had only needed to perform their 'incompetent best'; however, he inferred from the countless failures to act that there was wilful breach. That decision was overturned on appeal[1], but the judgment of Jones J at first instance remains a helpful overview of the duties of fund directors under Cayman Islands law.

[1] See paras 8.85–8.87 below.

Practical guidance for independent non-executive fund directors

Launch

8.76 Directors need to be involved and engaged with the launch of the fund. They have a duty to understand the structure of the fund and ensure that both the structure and the terms on which the fund is engaging with service providers are in line with industry standards. Moreover, they should have a clear understanding of the roles and responsibilities being delegated, so as to enable their effective supervision, ensuring all parties appreciate their respective roles. Whilst Jones J did not specify the exact level of detail required, he commented that a mechanical review of service agreements with the various third parties would be inadequate to meet the relevant threshold. Further, he stated that directors should be actively involved in the selection and appointment of the fund's auditors and the contractual terms on which they enter into a relationship.

8.77 Directors should also be actively engaged with verification of the fund's offering documents; one's duties will not be sufficiently discharged simply by appointing reputable third parties to prepare the offering memoranda. Directors should ensure that the fund's offering documents properly describe the fund's strategy and the roles and responsibilities of the fund's various service providers.

8.78 Jones J found in *Weavering* that the directors had had no involvement at all, citing the fact that the launch board minutes of Weavering Ltd specified a different prime broker, administrator and auditor to those actually retained. He held it was clear that the directors had not engaged in any stage of the launch process in order to gain an understanding of the fund's structure, business or terms, and in particular it's trading counterparties. Jones J used the opportunity to reiterate that whilst there is nothing improper with directors delegating certain functions to service providers, if they fail to delegate a particular task, it will continue to be the directors' sole responsibility.

During the ordinary course of business

8.79 During the lifecycle of a fund, once a director has delegated a particular task, he will still retain supervisory responsibilities. Jones J compared the role to one of 'high level supervision', rather than a 'mindless automaton'. Board meetings should be convened to provide the directors with an opportunity substantively to discuss matters, rather than simply 'rubber stamp' matters raised by the investment manager. Further, board minutes should be prepared contemporaneously and should be scrutinised to ensure they are an accurate reflection of what was discussed and agreed. Where appropriate, directors should request reports from the fund's investment manager, auditor and administrator. Directors should fully engage with the documents sent to them, ensuring they have a comprehensive understanding of those documents and asking questions where necessary. Directors should review the fund's monthly or quarterly management accounts to ensure they are fully aware of the fund's financial/net asset value position.

8.80 *Directors' Duties*

8.80 In the case of *Weavering*, the directors signed board documents within minutes of them being received, including minutes of board meetings that never happened.

DISTRESS MODE

8.81 When a fund enters a crisis management stage, how a director discharges his duties will change (although the underlying law does not). During this stage of a fund's life cycle, a director's duty to be engaged with the affairs of the fund is enhanced and would include, for example, ascertaining the fund's solvency and financial forecast, ensuring the fund's service providers are complying with their heightened duties that exist during such time, together with considering the interests of creditors in addition to the best interests of the fund. Directors should frequently hold meetings during such time to remain informed of the financial status of the fund and make appropriate decisions.

GENERAL GUIDANCE

8.82 There is an expectation that independent directors will be proactive, rather than simply reactive to the issues brought to their attention by the fund's service providers. Jones J made clear that directors are not entitled to absolve themselves completely of responsibility upon delegation, or to assume that service providers have performed all of their respective obligations without the need for any supervision.

8.83 In addition, Jones J considered that the court was entitled to have regard to the amount of fees paid to directors, inferring that the more substantial the fee, the more onerous the responsibilities that may be expected. He did note however that a director may not absolve himself of responsibility entirely by virtue of receiving no fee at all.

8.84 What should always be borne in mind when considering this guidance is that what will be expected of one independent non-executive director may vary to what is reasonably expected of another. What is required of a director in order to discharge his duties in a particular situation will need to be considered on a case-by-case basis. As such, Jones J's obiter statements should be approached as guidance rather than an exhaustive and definitive list of actions to be taken in order to satisfy a director's duties.

Court of Appeal decision

8.85 The Cayman Islands Court of Appeal agreed with Jones J that the directors had failed to perform their supervisory roles to the requisite standard in respect of their delegation to the fund's service providers[1]. However, the Court of Appeal held that the evidence available to the Grand Court was not sufficiently demonstrative to enable Jones J to find that the directors had *wilfully* breached their duties. The Court of Appeal confirmed that the correct test for wilful neglect or default was the English authority laid down in *City Equitable*[2], that negligence is wilful if a person either: (i) knows he is committing and intends to commit a breach of duty; or (ii) is recklessly careless in that he does not care whether or not his act or omission is a breach of duty.

The Court of Appeal found that the Grand Court had erred in its finding that the directors fell within the first limb of this test, finding that Jones J did not have the evidence to determine the directors' state of mind necessary for a finding of wilful default. Both directors had in fact given evidence that they honestly believed they were complying with their duties and, crucially, it was never put to them during cross-examination that they knowingly and intentionally breached their duties. Further, Jones J did not provide any justification for disbelieving them. As such, the Court of Appeal was bound to find the directors merely negligent, in the absence of evidential support that the directors knew they were being negligent. Consequently, the directors were entitled to rely on the indemnification and exculpation provisions in Weavering Ltd's articles.

[1] CICA 10 of 2011 (unreported, 12 February 2015).
[2] See para 8.15 above.

8.86 The Court of Appeal also considered whether the second limb of wilful neglect or default applied under the circumstances and found that in order to establish recklessness (and thereby satisfy the second limb), it was necessary to establish that a director appreciated that his conduct might be a breach of duty and continued with such conduct despite this awareness. As with the Court's finding in respect of the first limb, ie the directors' evidence as to their honest belief, and the lack of evidence to the contrary, the second limb was also not established.

8.87 Crucially, the Court of Appeal's decision was solely due to the evidence available to the Court in respect of supporting a finding that the directors knew that what they were doing was in breach of their duties. With regards to the legal principles governing directors' duties and wilful neglect or default, Jones J's obiter guidance remains valid as the Court of Appeal did not disagree with it. Indeed, the Statement of Guidance for Regulated Mutual Funds, issued by the Cayman Islands Monetary Authority ('CIMA') on 13 January 2014[1], codified a number of the principles reflected in Jones J's guidance. Whilst the Statement of Guidance has no regulatory effect, nor any penalties for non-compliance, it will serve to inform the regulator and the courts as to whether a director has discharged his duties.

[1] Available at https://www.cima.ky/investment-funds-regulatory-measures.

Documentation

8.88 As a matter of good corporate governance, decisions of the board should be properly documented by way of appropriate board minutes and resolutions. If directors' decisions are subsequently challenged, board minutes may play an important evidentiary role in demonstrating that a director has complied with his duties. The level of detail required to meet the appropriate standard will vary depending on the circumstances; as a general rule, the more significant the meeting and the decisions taken, the more detail should be included in the corresponding minutes.

8.89 *Directors' Duties*

Directors' registration and licensing regime

8.89 The Directors Registration and Licensing Law, 2014 came into force in the Cayman Islands on 14 June 2014 and introduced a new registration and licensing regime for directors of 'covered entities', defined as companies regulated as mutual funds under the Mutual Funds Law and management companies registered as excluded persons under the Securities Investment Business Law. Under the regime, every director of a covered entity must either be registered or licensed as a 'professional director'. Whether a director is required to be registered or licensed will depend on the number of covered entities of which he is a director. Directors of up to 19 covered entities must be registered; directors of 20 or more covered entities must be licensed as professional directors.

8.90 Once registered or licensed with CIMA, there are ongoing obligations to notify CIMA of all changes to information within 21 days of such change, together with an annual fee. The register is not public; rather, it is for CIMA's internal purposes and co-operation with other regulators. Directors should be aware that there may be material penalties for breach of the regime, including fines and imprisonment. Furthermore, these are personal obligations on the directors themselves, not the fund. However, in practice, CIMA will usually enforce any action through the fund, for example by refusing to register a fund with an unregistered and/or unlicensed director on its board.

Chapter 9

REGULATORY OVERVIEW – THE UNITED KINGDOM

Andrew Wylie, Partner and Head of Investment Funds, DLA Piper and Tony Katz, Partner and Head of Financial Services Regulation, DLA Piper

A	Introduction	9.1
B	Regulated activities	9.3
C	Promotion of hedge funds	9.30
D	Market abuse	9.56

A INTRODUCTION

9.1 Hedge funds are usually established in an offshore jurisdiction. However, onshore regulatory regimes remain relevant to various activities relating to hedge funds.

9.2 This chapter considers the types of regulated activity that might be undertaken in the UK by the manager of a hedge fund, restrictions on the promotion of interests in hedge funds, and the relevance of the UK market abuse regime to the activities of hedge funds. The Markets in Financial Instruments Directives fall outside the scope of this chapter save insofar as they relate to market abuse.

B REGULATED ACTIVITIES

9.3 Under the Financial Services and Markets Act 2000 ('FSMA 2000'), it is a criminal offence for any person to carry on, or purport to carry on, a regulated activity in the UK unless that person is authorised by the Financial Conduct Authority (the 'FCA') or is an exempt person (the 'general prohibition'[1]). A person who contravenes the general prohibition is liable, in the case of summary conviction, to up to six months' imprisonment or a fine, and in the case of conviction on indictment, to up to two years' imprisonment or a fine. It is a defence in proceedings for such an offence for the accused to show that he took all reasonable precautions and exercised all due diligence to avoid committing the offence. An agreement made by a person in the course of carrying on a regulated activity (other than that of accepting deposits) in contravention of the general prohibition is unenforceable against the other party to that agreement. That other party is entitled to recover any money or other property which that party paid or transferred under that agreement, and compensation for any loss which that party sustained as a result of having parted with that money or other property.

[1] FSMA 2000, s 19.

9.4 Regulatory Overview – The United Kingdom

9.4 An activity is a regulated activity for the purposes of FSMA 2000 if it is an activity which is specified as such in the Financial Services and Markets Act 2000 (Regulated Activities) Order 2001[1], as amended (the 'Regulated Activities Order'), is carried on by way of business and relates to an investment which is specified in that Order. Part II of the Regulated Activities Order lists specified activities and specific exclusions applicable to those particular activities[2]. It also lists exclusions which apply to several specified kinds of activity[3]. Part III of the Regulated Activities Order sets out a list of specified investments[4]. Carrying on a specified activity in relation to a specified investment without the benefit of an exclusion amounts to carrying out a regulated activity.

[1] SI 2001/544.
[2] See SI 2001/544, arts 4–64.
[3] See SI 2001/544, arts 65–72I.
[4] See SI 2001/544, arts 73–89.

Specified investments

9.5 Part III of the Regulated Activities Order prescribes a wide range of specified investments ranging from ordinary shares to complex derivative instruments:

- Article 76 of the Order covers shares and stock in the share capital of any body corporate, whether incorporated or not, or any unincorporated body corporate constituted under the law of a country outside the UK.
- Articles 77 and 78 of the Order deal with two broad categories of debt instruments. The first covers a wide range of instruments including loan stock, debentures, bonds and any other instrument creating or acknowledging indebtedness. The second covers instruments acknowledging or creating indebtedness issued by or on behalf of the UK government, the government of any country outside the UK, a local authority in the UK or elsewhere, and certain international organisations.
- Article 81 of the Order relates to units in a collective investment scheme within the meaning of FSMA 2000, s 235.
- Articles 83, 84 and 85 of the Order encompass options, futures and contracts for difference respectively.

Specified activities

Dealing in investments as principal or agent

9.6 Article 14 of the Regulated Activities Order provides that buying, selling, subscribing for or underwriting securities and certain other investments as principal is a specified activity for the purposes of the Order.

9.7 The issue by a company of its own shares or share warrants and the issue by any person of its own debentures or debenture warrants is expressly excluded from article 14 of the Regulated Activities Order (by virtue of article 18 of the Order). Any transaction into which a person enters as principal with another person is excluded from article 14 if that other person is also acting as principal and they are members of the same group or they are, or propose to become, participators in a joint enterprise and the transaction is entered into for the purposes of or in connection with that enterprise (by virtue of article 69 of the Regulated Activities Order).

9.8 Article 21 of the Regulated Activities Order provides that buying, selling, subscribing for or underwriting securities and certain other investments as agent is a specified activity for the purposes of the Order. A person which is not an authorised person is regarded as not carrying on such an activity by entering into a qualifying transaction as agent for another person with or through an authorised person (by virtue of article 22 of the Regulated Activities Order).

Arranging deals in investments

9.9 Article 25 of the Regulated Activities Order provides that making arrangements for another person (whether as principal or agent) to buy, sell, subscribe for or underwrite a particular investment which is a security, a contractually-based investment or a specified investment is a specified activity. Making arrangements with a view to a person which participates in the arrangements buying, selling, subscribing for or underwriting shares is also a specified activity.

9.10 Arrangements which do not or would not bring about the transaction to which those arrangements relate will be ignored for these purposes (by virtue of article 26 of the Regulated Activities Order). It is, of course, likely that any person which seeks to raise funds for a hedge fund, such as its investment manager or a placing agent, would be regarded as arranging deals in investments under the Regulated Activities Order.

Managing investments

9.11 Article 37 of the Regulated Activities Order provides that managing qualifying investments belonging to another person, in circumstances involving the exercise of discretion, is a specified activity for the purposes of the Order. That article does not therefore apply to non-discretionary management arrangements. The investment manager of a hedge fund would almost invariably be regarded as carrying on discretionary investment management.

Safeguarding and administering investments

9.12 Article 40 of the Regulated Activities Order provides that the activity consisting of both the safeguarding of assets belonging to another and the administration of those assets is a specified activity for the purposes of the Order where those assets include qualifying investments.

Investment advice

9.13 Article 53 of the Regulated Activities Order provides that advising a person is a specified activity for the purposes of the Order if that advice (a) is given to that person in its capacity as an investor or potential investor, or as

9.13 Regulatory Overview – The United Kingdom

agent for an investor or a potential investor, and (b) relates to the merits (whether as principal or agent) of buying, selling, subscribing for, exchanging, redeeming, holding, underwriting or exercising any right conferred by any qualifying investment.

9.14 It is likely that the investment manager of a hedge fund would provide advice to the board of directors of that hedge fund from time to time, in addition to managing the assets of that hedge fund. It is also possible that a sub-adviser to the investment manager of a hedge fund would simply provide advice (and no other services) to that investment manager.

Certain activities in relation to UCITS

9.15 Article 51ZA of the Regulated Activities Order provides that managing an undertaking for collective investments in transferable securities ('UCITS'), which involves carrying on collective portfolio management of that UCITS, is a specified activity for the purposes of the Order.

9.16 Article 51ZB of the Regulated Activities Order provides that acting as the trustee of an authorised unit trust scheme, or the depositary of an open-ended investment company (an 'OEIC') or authorised contractual scheme, where that scheme or company is a UCITS, is a specified activity for the purposes of the Order.

Certain activities in relation to AIFs

9.17 Article 51ZC of the Regulated Activities Order provides that managing an alternative investment fund (an 'AIF'), which involves performing at least risk management or portfolio management for the AIF, is a specified activity for the purposes of the Order. A person will not be regarded as managing an AIF if that person performs functions for that AIF which another person has delegated to it, provided that other person is not an alternative investment fund manager (an 'AIFM') which has delegated those functions to the extent that it is a 'letter box entity'. On that basis, the sub-investment manager of a hedge fund will often not be regarded as managing that hedge fund for the purposes of the Regulated Activities Order.

9.18 Article 51ZD of the Regulated Activities Order provides that acting as:

(a) the depositary of an AIF which is managed by a full scope UK AIFM or a UK AIF which is managed by an EEA AIFM, or
(b) the trustee of an authorised unit trust scheme which is an AIF that does not fall within (a), or
(c) the depositary of an OEIC or authorised contractual scheme which is an AIF that does not fall within (a),

is a specified activity for the purposes of the Order.

Establishing a collective investment scheme

9.19 Article 51ZE of the Regulated Activities Order provides that establishing, operating or winding up a collective investment scheme (a 'CIS') is a specified activity for the purposes of the Order. A hedge fund which is structured as an OEIC or a limited partnership will almost invariably be a CIS for UK regulatory purposes.

Exclusions

9.20 A significant number of exclusions apply to activities which would otherwise be treated as specified activities for the purposes of the Regulated Activities Order, two of which are considered below.

Activities in connection with the sale of a body corporate

9.21 Article 69 of the Regulated Activities Order excludes from the scope of the Order various dealing, arranging and advisory activities in connection with a transaction to acquire or dispose of shares in a body corporate other than an OEIC, or for the purposes of such an acquisition or disposal, which broadly relates to 50% or more of the voting shares in that body corporate.

Overseas persons

9.22 Article 72 of the Regulated Activities Order provides an important exclusion for 'overseas persons', under certain circumstances, from the regulated activities of dealing in investments as principal, dealing in investments as agent, arranging deals in investments, advising on investments and agreeing to carry on any of those activities. An 'overseas person' for these purposes is a person which carries on certain specified activities but does not carry on any such activities, or offer to do so, from a permanent place of business which it maintains in the UK.

9.23 By way of example, an overseas person will be treated as not carrying on the regulated activity of giving advice as a result of a 'legitimate approach'. For these purposes, a legitimate approach means (a) an approach made to the overseas person which it has not solicited in any way, or which it solicited in a way which does not contravene the UK financial promotion regime, or (b) an approach made by or on behalf of the overseas person in a way which does not contravene that regime.

9.24 It should be noted, however, that the FCA is reluctant to accept that in practice customers contact firms on an unsolicited basis (rather than the firm contacting its customers) with any frequency. Accordingly, it will usually be safer for a firm to rely on the second of these tests.

Obtaining authorisation from the FCA

9.25 Persons which propose to provide services to hedge funds that would amount to carrying on one or more regulated activities in the UK, in circumstances where no exemption would be available, will need to apply for authorisation from the FCA to become an authorised person. This is known as a 'Part IV permission'. When applying for a Part IV permission, the applicant needs to obtain permission for each of the regulated activities that it wishes to

9.25 Regulatory Overview – The United Kingdom

carry on (and an authorised firm may apply to the FCA following its authorisation to vary its existing permissions). For example, the manager of a hedge fund might apply for permission to deal in investments as agent, arrange deals, manage investments, provide investment advice and act as an AIFM.

9.26 To obtain authorisation, the applicant must satisfy the 'threshold conditions' in relation to all of the activities for which it is applying for permission from the FCA. The threshold conditions are set out in FSMA 2000, Sch 6 and include conditions relating to the applicant's legal status, the location of its offices, effective supervision, adequacy of resources, the suitability of the applicant and its business model. Additionally, the FCA will make an assessment as to whether the persons who control the applicant are fit and proper.

9.27 Once submitted, the FCA will allocate a case officer who will make an initial determination as to whether an application is routine or non-routine. An application will be treated as non-routine if it is particularly complex or unusual or if there is any question about the fitness or propriety of any of the persons who control the applicant. Where the FCA considers an application to be non-routine, it will scrutinise that application. The relevant case officer at the FCA may ask for further information or clarification from the applicant about its application.

9.28 Firms typically wish to avoid incurring unnecessary expenditure prior to becoming an authorised person – for example, a firm may not wish to inject the relevant regulatory capital or put professional indemnity insurance in place until it is clear that the FCA will grant it authorisation. Each of these can usually be accommodated by judicious timing.

9.29 If an application for authorisation is successful, the FCA will write to the applicant confirming its authorisation and enclosing the 'Scope of Permission Notice' setting out when the permission starts, which regulated activities the firm has permission to carry on and any limitations the FCA wishes to impose. If an application is not successful, there is a procedure for the firm to challenge the FCA's decision.

C   PROMOTION OF HEDGE FUNDS

The financial promotion restriction

9.30 Section 21 of FSMA 2000 provides that a person must not, in the course of business, communicate an invitation or inducement to engage in investment activity (such as buying shares in a company or interests in a limited partnership) (known as the 'financial promotion restriction').

9.31 The financial promotion restriction does not apply to communications made by authorised persons, or by any person where the content of the communication has been approved by an authorised person (in respect of communications which are eligible for approval by an authorised person). The financial promotion restriction will only apply to a communication which originates outside the UK if that communication is capable of having an effect in the UK.

9.32 A person who contravenes the financial promotion restriction is guilty of an offence and is liable, in the case of summary conviction, to up to six months' imprisonment or a fine, and in the case of conviction on indictment, to up to two years' imprisonment or a fine. It is a defence in proceedings for such an offence for the accused to show that he took all reasonable precautions and exercised all due diligence to avoid committing the offence. If a person enters as a customer into an agreement in consequence of a communication which breaches the financial promotion restriction, that agreement is unenforceable against that person. That person is entitled to recover any money or other property which he paid or transferred under that agreement, and compensation for any loss which he sustained as a result of having parted with that money or other property. A court may, however, allow any such agreement to be enforced, or money or property paid or transferred under any such agreement to be retained, if that court is satisfied that it is just and equitable in the circumstances.

9.33 Any document promoting investment into a hedge fund, or any oral communication of the same nature, will be a financial promotion. The words 'invitation or inducement' are given a very broad meaning and, in practice, documents relating to hedge funds would be scrutinised closely if it were claimed that they did not amount to an invitation or inducement. For example, even statements about the successful establishment of a particular hedge fund might be seen as an invitation or inducement to further investors, or in relation to the services of the investment manager of that hedge fund.

9.34 HM Treasury and the FCA are both permitted to specify circumstances in which the financial promotion restriction does not apply, and have done so in the Financial Services and Markets Act 2000 (Financial Promotion) Order 2005[1], as amended (the 'Financial Promotion Order').

[1] SI 2005/1529.

The promotion of collective investment schemes

9.35 Section 238 of FSMA 2000 provides that an authorised person must not communicate an invitation or inducement to participate in a CIS other than an authorised unit trust scheme, an authorised contractual scheme, an authorised OEIC or a recognised scheme (collectively known as 'regulated CIS'), or a CIS which falls within the Financial Services and Markets Act 2000 (Promotion of Collective Investment Schemes) (Exemptions Order) 2001[1], as amended (the 'CIS Exemptions Order'). This restriction is known as the 'scheme promotion restriction' and will only apply to a communication which originates outside the UK if that communication is capable of having an effect in the UK.

[1] SI 2001/1060.

9.36 An authorised person that wishes to promote units in a regulated CIS to the general public in the UK is not subject to the scheme promotion restriction. However, a unit in a CIS is a 'controlled investment' for the purpose of the financial promotion restriction, so an authorised person must comply with the financial promotion rules in Chapter 4 of the Conduct of Business Sourcebook[1] in the FCA Handbook unless that authorised person is able to take advantage of any of the exemptions in the CIS Exemptions Order.

[1] See www.handbook.fca.org.uk/handbook/COBS.

9.37 Furthermore, an authorised person may not approve, for the purposes of FSMA 2000, s 21, the content of a communication relating to any CIS, including a hedge fund, if it would be prohibited by the scheme promotion restriction from effecting that communication itself (by virtue of the application of FSMA 2000, s 240).

The CIS Exemptions Order

9.38 The CIS Exemptions Order and Chapter 4 of the Conduct of Business Sourcebook in the FCA Handbook set out circumstances in which authorised persons may communicate financial promotions about interests in any hedge fund which is an unauthorised OEIC, an unauthorised unit trust or a limited partnership. A person may rely on more than one exclusion in respect of the same communication. The principal exclusions are as follows.

Investment professionals

9.39 The scheme promotion restriction does not apply to any communication which is made only to recipients whom the person making the communication believes on reasonable grounds to be investment professionals, or may reasonably be regarded as directed only at such persons[1]. For these purposes, 'investment professionals' include authorised persons, certain exempt persons, any other person whose ordinary business activities involve it in participating in unregulated schemes for business purposes, and a government, local authority or international organisation.

[1] SI 2001/1060, art 14.

9.40 The relevant communication must be accompanied by appropriate wording, and there must be proper systems and procedures in place to prevent recipients other than investment professionals from acquiring units in the scheme to which the communication relates.

One-off non-real time communications and solicited real time communications

9.41 The financial promotion restriction does not apply to a one-off communication that is either a non-real time communication (eg in writing) or a solicited real time communication (eg an oral promotion)[1]. This exemption is most commonly used for non-real time communications.

[1] SI 2001/1060, art 15.

9.42 If both of the conditions set out below are met in relation to a relevant communication, it will be regarded as a one-off communication. Nevertheless, a relevant communication may still be regarded as a one-off communication even if neither of these conditions is met. The conditions are as follows:

- the communication must be made to one recipient or a group of recipients in the expectation that they would engage in any investment activity jointly (eg a group of investors into a hedge fund); and
- the communication must not be part of an organised marketing campaign.

Existing participants in an unregulated CIS

9.43 The scheme promotion restriction does not apply to any communication by the operator of a hedge fund (which will usually be its investment manager) which is a non-real time communication or a solicited real time communication to persons whom the operator believes on reasonable grounds to be persons who are entitled to interests in that hedge fund[1].

[1] SI 2001/1060, art 18.

Group companies

9.44 The scheme promotion restriction does not apply to any communication made by one body corporate in a group to another body corporate in the same group[1].

[1] SI 2001/1060, art 19.

Certified high net worth individuals

9.45 The scheme promotion restriction does not apply to any communication which is a non-real time communication or a solicited real time communication made to an individual whom the person making the communication believes on reasonable grounds to be a certified high net worth individual[1]. The communication must relate to an unregulated scheme which invests wholly or predominantly in the shares or debentures of one or more unlisted companies. An unlisted company for these purposes and for purposes of the CIS Exemptions Order generally is a body corporate the shares in which are not listed or quoted on an investment exchange whether in the UK or elsewhere. This exemption will therefore not be available to the promoters of hedge funds which invest in assets other than the shares or debentures of unlisted companies.

[1] SI 2001/1060, art 21.

9.46 A certified high net worth individual means an individual who has signed, within the period of 12 months ending on the day on which the communication is made, a statement in the form prescribed in Part I of the Schedule to the CIS Exemptions Order which states that during the financial year immediately preceding the statement, the individual had an annual income of £100,000 or more and net assets to the value of £250,000 or more (ignoring his primary residence and certain other assets). The relevant communication must also contain appropriate regulatory language and warnings.

High net worth companies, unincorporated associations, etc

9.47 The scheme promotion restriction does not apply to any communication which is made only to recipients whom the person making the communication believes on reasonable grounds to be the following persons, or which may reasonably be regarded as directed only at such persons[1]:

(a) any body corporate which has, or which is a member of the same group as an undertaking which has, a called-up share capital or net assets of not less than £5 million (or £500,000 if the body corporate has more than 20 members or is a subsidiary undertaking of an undertaking which has more than 20 members;
(b) any unincorporated association or partnership which has net assets of not less than £5 million;
(c) the trustee of a high value trust (being a trust whose gross asset value is £10 million or more); and
(d) any director, officer or employee of any person within (a)–(c) above, acting in that capacity.

[1] SI 2001/1060, art 22.

9.48 The relevant communication must be accompanied by appropriate wording, and proper systems and procedures must be in place to prevent recipients other than such persons from acquiring units in the scheme to which the communication relates.

Sophisticated investors

9.49 The scheme promotion restriction does not apply to any communication which is made to a certified sophisticated investor[1]. A 'certified sophisticated investor' means a person who has a current certificate in writing signed by an authorised person to the effect that he is sufficiently knowledgeable to understand the risks associated with participating in unregulated schemes and who has signed a statement which contains the relevant language contained in the CIS Exemptions Order. A certificate will be current if it is signed and dated not more than three years before the date on which the communication is made. In practice, many authorised persons are reluctant to sign such certificates in light of the potential liability.

[1] SI 2001/1060, art 23.

9.50 The relevant communication must not be made by the operator of the unregulated scheme to which that communication relates. In the case of a hedge fund, it is likely that its operator for these purposes would be its investment manager. The relevant communication must also contain appropriate regulatory language and warnings.

Self-certified sophisticated investors

9.51 The scheme promotion restriction does not apply to any communication which is made to an individual whom the person making the communication believes on reasonable grounds to be a self-certified sophisticated investor[1].

Promotion of hedge funds **9.54**

The communication must relate to an unregulated scheme which invests wholly or predominantly in the shares or debentures of one or more unlisted companies. This exemption will therefore not be available to the promoters of hedge funds which invest in assets other than the shares or debentures of unlisted companies. The relevant communication must contain appropriate regulatory language and warnings.

[1] SI 2001/1060, art 23A.

9.52 A 'self-certified sophisticated investor' means an individual who has signed, within the period of 12 months ending on the day on which the communication is made, a statement in the form prescribed in Part II of the Schedule to the CIS Exemptions Order and which includes confirmation that at least one of the following applies to the relevant individual:

- he is a member of a network or syndicate of business angels and has been so for at least the last six months prior to the date of that statement;
- he has made more than one investment in an unlisted company in the two years prior to the date of that statement;
- he is working, or has worked in the two years prior to the date of that statement, in a professional capacity in the private equity sector, or in the provision of finance for small and medium enterprises; and
- he is currently, or has been in the two years prior to the date of that statement, a director of a company with an annual turnover of at least £1 million.

The Financial Promotion Order

9.53 The Financial Promotion Order provides that the financial promotion restriction will not apply in certain circumstances to the promotion by any person which is not an authorised person, in the course of business, of any investment which does not amount to a CIS to certain persons which fall within the Financial Promotion Order. Most hedge funds are open-ended companies which are established outside the UK and are almost invariably CIS for UK regulatory purposes. The Financial Promotion Order is therefore likely to be relevant to the promotion by a person which is not an authorised person of interests in most hedge funds in the UK.

9.54 A person may rely on more than one exclusion in respect of the same communication. The categories of person which are excluded from the application of the financial promotion restriction under the Financial Promotion Order are largely the same as the categories of person which are excluded from the application of the scheme promotion restriction under the CIS Exemptions Order. These include investment professionals, high net worth companies, unincorporated associations etc and sophisticated investors. Whilst both the Financial Promotion Order and the CIS Exemptions Order contain exclusions for certified high net worth individuals and self-certified sophisticated investors, those exclusions in the former statutory instrument are broader than in the latter (and are not simply restricted to shares in unlisted companies).

9.55 Regulatory Overview – The United Kingdom

Overseas marketing restrictions

9.55 Almost all jurisdictions, whether sophisticated or unsophisticated, impose legal restrictions on marketing interests in hedge funds, and other investments, in or from their respective jurisdictions. Examples would include Australia, Canada, the EU, each member state of the EU, Japan, New Zealand, Switzerland, Russia and the US. A breach of the relevant securities laws may give rise to criminal liability and penalties and may render any relevant agreement unenforceable.

D MARKET ABUSE

9.56 The market abuse regime was introduced in the UK by FSMA 2000 on 1 December 2001. Changes to the regime were made in order to implement the Market Abuse Directive[1] ('EU MAD'), which came into force on 1 July 2005. EU MAD was repealed by the Market Abuse Regulation[2] ('EU MAR'), which came into effect on 3 July 2016. EU MAR strengthened the previous UK market abuse regime by extending its scope to new platforms, including multilateral trading facilities ('MTFs'), organised trading facilities ('OTFs') and new behaviours. By virtue of being a Regulation, EU MAR has direct effect in the UK and changes have been made to the UK's domestic regime (including the repeal of FSMA 2000, ss 118–122 and changes to the FCA Handbook[3]) to ensure that UK national law complies with EU MAR[4].

[1] Directive 2003/6/EC of 28 January 2013.
[2] Regulation (EU) No 596/2014 of 16 April 2014.
[3] See paras **9.60–9.61** below.
[4] See the Financial Services and Markets Act 2000 (Market Abuse) Regulations 2016 (SI 2016/680).

9.57 EU MAR is made under the 'Lamfalussy process' for financial services legislation in the EU[1] which comprises three levels, each of which focuses on a specific stage of implementation of legislation:

- Level 1: EU MAR;
- Level 2: Implementing measures: European Securities and Markets Authority ('ESMA') technical standards and Commission Delegated Acts; and
- Level 3: ESMA Guidelines and ESMA Q&As.

[1] See para 4.3 of the FCA's guide to the EU and its legislative processes – www.fca.org.uk/publication/archive/european-union-legislative-process.pdf.

9.58 Further, the market abuse regime supplements the criminal regime for market abuse which is set out in Part V of the Criminal Justice Act 1993 ('CJA 1993') and Part 7 of the Financial Services Act 2012 ('FSA 2012'). The existence of both civil and criminal regimes means that a number of regulations need to be considered and that the FCA has a choice as to whether to pursue a criminal prosecution and/or take civil action in respect of the same behaviour.

9.59 Under EU MAD, the market abuse regime was set out in the Disclosure and Transparency Rules (the 'DTR'), the Model Code and the Code of

Market Conduct (the 'CoMC') in the FCA Handbook. However, the introduction of EU MAR necessitated major changes to these provisions. Given that EU MAR has direct effect in UK law, the FCA's approach was not to 'copy out' EU MAR into the FCA Handbook but rather to include 'signposts' to the relevant provisions of EU MAR. The FCA's amendment process also involved aligning the pre-existing UK criminal regime with EU MAR.

9.60 Following a detailed consultation process with firms, the FCA made the following changes to the DTR, the Model Code and the CoMC respectively:

- The DTR were repealed and replaced with signposts to the relevant provisions in EU MAR. Under the previous regime, the DTR set out the rules for issuers on the disclosure and control of inside information and transactions by persons discharging managerial responsibilities and their connected persons. These rules are now set out in EU MAR itself, but where possible, helpful elements of the DTR have been retained in the FCA Handbook as 'Disclosure Guidance'.
- The Model Code was found to be partially incompatible with EU MAR and was revoked. The Model Code formed part of the Listing Rules and imposed restrictions on dealing in the securities of a listed company. The FCA has stated that it proposes to replace the Model Code with guidance for firms to use when developing their processes to allow persons discharging managerial responsibilities to apply for clearance to deal. ICSA: The Governance Institute has since published a 'specimen' share dealing policy (broadly, an industry-led equivalent of the Model Code) which has been widely adopted in the market[1].
- The CoMC was repealed and recast as guidance. Under EU MAD, the FCA was required to issue a code with provisions that provided guidance to those determining whether or not behaviour would amount to market abuse. The requirement for such a code was repealed by EU MAR; however, the FCA chose to keep the CoMC, albeit recast as guidance and generally referred to as 'MAR 1'.

[1] See www.icsa.org.uk/knowledge/resources/mar-dealing-code.

9.61 A number of other provisions were included in different sections of the FCA Handbook, namely:

- SYSC 18, which requires firms to have whistleblowing arrangements in place for reporting infringements;
- COBS 12.4, which sets out the FCA's specific requirements about the production and dissemination of investment recommendations; and
- SUP 15.10, which sets out the notification requirements for reporting suspicious transactions.

9.62 It is worth noting that the FCA's Principles for Businesses ('PRIN'), Statements of Principle and Code of Practice for Approved Persons ('APER') and Code of Conduct ('COCON') are also relevant and applicable to EU MAR.

9.63 The following sections highlight the principal market abuse offences, and in particular those provisions in EU MAR which are most relevant to the hedge fund industry.

9.64 *Regulatory Overview – The United Kingdom*

Disciplinary powers of the FCA

9.64 In brief, where a person's behaviour amounts to market abuse, the FCA may:

- impose an unlimited civil fine;
- make a public statement that that person has engaged in market abuse;
- apply to the court for an injunction to restrain threatened or continued market abuse, an injunction requiring a person to take steps to remedy market abuse, or a freezing order;
- apply to the court for a restitution order; or
- require the payment of compensation to victims.

9.65 The imposition of penalties for market abuse transactions does not make the transaction void or unenforceable in itself[1].

[1] See FSMA 2000, s 131.

9.66 In the case of authorised firms or approved persons, market abuse could lead to the loss of a Part IV permission for an authorised person or approved person status for an individual.

9.67 Section 401 of FSMA 2000 empowers the FCA to prosecute criminal offences under FSA 2012, Pt 7 and CJA 1993, Pt V in England and Wales. For insider dealing and market manipulation, potential criminal sanctions include custodial sentences of up to seven years and unlimited fines.

Market abuse (civil regime)

Scope

9.68 EU MAR applies to:

(a) financial instruments admitted to trading on a regulated market or for which a request for admission to trading on a regulated market has been made;
(b) financial instruments traded on an MTF, admitted to trading on an MTF, or for which a request for admission to trading on a MTF has been made;
(c) financial instruments traded on an OTF; and
(d) financial instruments to which paragraphs (a), (b) or (c) do not apply, the price or value of which depends on or has an effect on the price or value of a financial instrument referred to in those paragraphs, including credit default swaps and contracts for difference[1].

[1] Article 2(1) of EU MAR.

9.69 The market manipulation prohibition under EU MAR also applies to:

- spot commodity contracts, which are not wholesale energy products, where the transaction, order or behaviour has or is likely or intended to have an effect on the price of a financial instrument within the scope of Article 2(1) of EU MAR;

- types of financial instrument, including derivative contracts or derivative instruments for the transfer of credit risk, where the transaction, order, bid or behaviour has or is likely to have an effect on the price or value of a spot commodity contract where the price or value depends on the price or value of those financial instruments; and
- behaviour in relation to benchmarks[1].

[1] Article 2(2) of EU MAR.

9.70 EU MAR is further expressed to apply to any transaction, order or behaviour concerning any financial instrument referred to in Article 2(1) and (2) of EU MAR irrespective of whether or not that transaction, order or behaviour takes place on a trading venue[1].

[1] Article 2(3) of EU MAR.

9.71 The delay to the implementation of the recast Markets in Financial Instruments Directive[1] ('MiFID') and the Markets in Financial Instruments Regulation[2] ('MiFIR') (collectively, 'MiFID II') has affected the application of EU MAR. As drafted, EU MAR was intended to sit alongside MiFID II to enhance investor protection, maximise market transparency and reduce market abuse. However, the 18-month period between the implementation of EU MAR and MiFID II respectively in UK law gave rise to a transitional phase during which EU MAR referred to definitions and concepts in MiFID II prior to MiFID II having come into force. Throughout that period, Article 39(4) of EU MAR clarified that all references to MiFID II in EU MAR were to be read as references to MiFID I[3], and all provisions of EU MAR which referred to concepts introduced by MiFID II would not apply until MiFID II came into force. Accordingly, those provisions in EU MAR which refer to OTFs, SME growth markets, emission allowances or related auctioned products came into force on 3 January 2018, ie the date on which MiFID II was implemented into UK law.

[1] Directive 2014/65/EU of 15 May 2014.
[2] Regulation (EU) No 600/2014 of 15 May 2014.
[3] Directive 2004/39/EC of 21 April 2004.

9.72 The extended scope is one of the key components of EU MAR. It revises the market abuse regime to reflect the changed nature of financial markets, which operate on different trading platforms and use different technologies from those which were prevalent when EU MAD came into force. However, for issuers of financial instruments which are traded on formerly unregulated exchanges (ie AIM companies), EU MAR creates a raft of new and onerous obligations.

9.73 Most notably, EU MAR contains an extra-territorial dimension to its scope. As an EU Regulation, EU MAR naturally applies to financial instruments which are traded in the EU, but it does not specify any geographical limit in terms of where the conduct in relation to that financial instrument takes place. As a result, a party with no connection to the EU could now be subject to EU MAR[1].

[1] Article 2(4) of EU MAR.

9.74 *Regulatory Overview – The United Kingdom*

Inside information

9.74 Certain of the market abuse provisions in EU MAR refer to the definition of 'inside information' which is broadly unchanged from the definition under EU MAD. However, EU MAR extends that definition to inside information about spot commodity contracts, and also introduces a new definition of inside information for emission allowances and auction products based on emission allowances.

9.75 'Inside information'[1] comprises the following types of information:

- Information of a precise nature, which has not been made public, relating, directly or indirectly, to one or more issuers or to one or more financial instruments, and which, if it were made public, would be likely to have a significant effect on the prices of those financial instruments or on the price of related derivative financial instruments. Article 7(4) of EU MAR clarifies that when determining whether information is inside information, a 'significant effect on the price' in relation to financial instruments, derivative financial instruments, related spot commodity contracts or auctioned products based on emission allowances means information which a reasonable investor would be likely to use as part of the basis of its investment decision[2].

- In relation to commodity derivatives, information of a precise nature, which has not been made public, relating, directly or indirectly, to one or more such derivatives or relating directly to the related spot commodity contract, and which, if it were made public, would be likely to have a significant effect on the prices of such derivatives or related spot commodity contracts. The information must be of a type that is reasonably expected, or required, to be disclosed on the relevant commodity derivatives markets or spot markets in accordance with legal or regulatory provisions at EU or national level, market rules, contract, practice or custom[3].

- In relation to emission allowances or auctioned products based on emission allowances, information of a precise nature, which has not been made public, relating, directly or indirectly, to one or more such instruments, and which, if it were made public, would be likely to have a significant effect on the prices of such instruments or on the prices of related derivative financial instruments.

- For persons charged with the execution of orders concerning financial instruments, information conveyed by a client and relating to the client's pending orders in financial instruments, which is of a precise nature, relating, directly or indirectly, to one or more issuers or to one or more financial instruments, and which, if it were made public, would be likely to have a significant effect on the prices of those financial instruments, the price of related spot commodity contracts, or the price of related derivative financial instruments.

[1] Article 7(1) of EU MAR.
[2] Article 7(4) of EU MAR.
[3] See also ESMA's Guidelines on MAR – information relating to commodity derivatives markets or related spot markets for the purpose of the definition of inside information on commodity derivatives (ESMA/2016/1412, 30 September 2016).

9.76 Information is deemed to be 'precise' if it indicates a set of circumstances which exists or which may reasonably be expected to come into existence, or an event which has occurred or which may reasonably be expected to occur, where it is specific enough to enable a conclusion to be drawn as to the possible effect of that set of circumstances or event on the prices of the financial instruments or the related derivative financial instrument, the related spot commodity contracts, or the auctioned products based on the emission allowances. In the case of a protracted process that is intended to bring about, or that results in, particular circumstances or a particular event, those future circumstances or that future event, and also the intermediate steps of that process which are connected with bringing about or resulting in those future circumstances or that future event, may be deemed to be precise information[1].

[1] Article 7(2) of EU MAR.

Prohibition of insider dealing (Article 14 of EU MAR)

9.77 Article 14 of EU MAR prohibits a person from:

- engaging or attempting to engage in insider dealing; or
- recommending that another person engage in insider dealing or inducing another person to engage in insider dealing.

9.78 Insider dealing arises where a person possesses inside information and uses that information by acquiring or disposing of, for his own account or for the account of a third party, directly or indirectly, financial instruments to which that information relates. EU MAR clarifies that the use of inside information by cancelling or amending an order concerning a financial instrument to which the information relates, where the order was placed before the person concerned possessed the inside information, is also insider dealing[1].

[1] Articles 8, 9 and 14 of EU MAR.

9.79 The recitals to EU MAR contain further helpful clarification about activities which amount to insider dealing:

- There is a rebuttable presumption that a person in possession of inside information who carries out transactions connected with that information is deemed to have used that information[1].
- Orders placed before a person possesses inside information should not be deemed to be insider dealing. However, where a person comes into possession of inside information there is a rebuttable presumption that any change relating to that information to orders placed before possession of that information (including the cancellation or amendment of an order, or an attempt to cancel or amend an order) constitutes insider dealing[2].
- The use or attempted use of inside information to trade on one's own account or on the account of a third party is clearly prohibited. Information regarding a market participant's own plans and strategies for trading should not be considered to be inside information, although information regarding a third party's plans and strategies for trading

may amount to inside information[3].

[1] Recital 24 to EU MAR.
[2] Recital 25 to EU MAR.
[3] Recital 54 to EU MAR.

9.80 MAR 1.3 in the FCA Handbook also provides more detailed guidance for market makers, brokers and about takeover and merger activity.

9.81 The substance of the offence of insider dealing is almost entirely the same under EU MAR as it was previously under EU MAD. It is therefore likely that firms will need to make no more than minimal changes to their policies and procedures regarding the cancellation and amendment of orders to ensure compliance with EU MAR.

Unlawful disclosure of inside information (Article 14 of EU MAR)

9.82 Article 14 of EU MAR prohibits a person from unlawfully disclosing inside information. Unlawful disclosure of inside information arises where a person possesses inside information and discloses that information to another person, except where the disclosure is made in the normal exercise of an employment, a profession or duties[1].

[1] Articles 10 and 14 of EU MAR.

9.83 The disclosure of recommendations or inducements will also amount to unlawful disclosure of inside information where the person who discloses that recommendation or inducement knows or ought to know that it was based on inside information[1].

[1] Article 10 of EU MAR.

9.84 The offence of unlawful disclosure of inside information is essentially unchanged under EU MAR.

9.85 MAR 1.4 in the FCA Handbook sets out various descriptions of behaviours that indicate the lawfulness of a disclosure, including:

- whether the disclosure is permitted by the rules of a trading venue, a prescribed auction platform, the FCA or the Takeover Code; or
- whether the disclosure is accompanied by the imposition of confidentiality requirements upon the person to whom the disclosure is made, and whether the disclosure is reasonable in the circumstances.

Legitimate behaviour (Article 9 of EU MAR)

9.86 In order to avoid inadvertently prohibiting forms of financial activity which are legitimate, namely where such activity does not in effect constitute market abuse, EU MAR recognises certain legitimate behaviour for the purposes of Article 8 (insider dealing) and Article 14 (prohibition of insider dealing and unlawful disclosure of inside information) of EU MAR.

9.87 Article 9(1) of EU MAR states that it will not be deemed from the mere fact that a legal person is, or has been, in possession of inside information that

that person has used that information and has thus engaged in insider dealing on the basis of an acquisition or disposal where that legal person:

- has established, implemented and maintained adequate and effective internal arrangements and procedures that effectively ensure that neither the natural person who made the decision on the legal person's behalf to acquire or dispose of financial instruments to which the information relates, nor another natural person who may have had an influence on that decision, was in possession of the inside information; and
- has not encouraged, made a recommendation to, induced or otherwise influenced the natural person who, on behalf of the legal person, acquired or disposed of financial instruments to which the information relates.

9.88 Article 9(2) of EU MAR further recognises the role of market makers, when acting in the legitimate capacity of providing market liquidity, stating that it will not be deemed from the mere fact that a person is in possession of inside information that that person has used that information and has thus engaged in insider dealing on the basis of an acquisition or disposal where that person:

- for the financial instrument to which that information relates, is a market maker or a person authorised to act as a counterparty, and the acquisition or disposal of financial instruments to which that information relates is made legitimately in the normal course of the exercise of its function as a market maker or as a counterparty for that financial instrument; or
- is authorised to execute orders on behalf of third parties, and the acquisition or disposal of financial instruments to which the order relates is made to carry out such an order legitimately in the normal course of the exercise of that person's employment, profession or duties.

9.89 Article 9(3) of EU MAR states that it will not be deemed from the mere fact that a person is in possession of inside information that that person has used that information and has thus engaged in insider dealing on the basis of an acquisition or disposal where that person conducts a transaction to acquire or dispose of financial instruments and that transaction is carried out in the discharge of an obligation that has become due in good faith and not to circumvent the prohibition against insider dealing, and:

- that obligation results from an order placed or an agreement concluded before the person concerned possessed inside information; or
- that transaction is carried out to satisfy a legal or regulatory obligation that arose before the person concerned possessed inside information.

9.90 Under Article 9(4) of EU MAR, it will not be deemed from the mere fact that a person is in possession of inside information that that person has used that information and has thus engaged in insider dealing where such person has obtained that inside information in the conduct of a public takeover or merger with a company and uses that inside information solely for the purpose of proceeding with that merger or public takeover, provided that at the point of approval of the merger or acceptance of the offer by the shareholders of that company, any inside information has been made public or has otherwise

9.90 Regulatory Overview – The United Kingdom

ceased to constitute inside information. Article 9(4) was expressed to not apply to stake-building (being an acquisition of securities in a company which does not trigger a legal or regulatory obligation to make an announcement of a takeover bid in relation to that company).

9.91 In addition, under Article 9(5) of EU MAR, the mere fact that a person uses its own knowledge that it has decided to acquire or dispose of financial instruments in the acquisition or disposal of those financial instruments will not of itself constitute use of inside information.

9.92 Notwithstanding the above, Article 9(6) of EU MAR states that an infringement of the prohibition of insider dealing set out in Article 14 of EU MAR may still be deemed to have occurred if the competent authority (being the FCA for the UK) establishes that there was an illegitimate reason for the orders to trade, transactions or behaviours concerned.

Market soundings (Article 11 of EU MAR)

9.93 One of the safe harbours contained in EU MAR relates to 'market soundings'. Market soundings are interactions between a seller of financial instruments or a third party on its behalf and one or more potential investors, prior to the announcement of a transaction, in order to gauge the interest of potential investors in a possible transaction and the conditions relating to such transaction such as its pricing, size and structuring[1].

[1] Article 11 of EU MAR; Commission Delegated Regulation (EU) 2016/960 of 17 May 2016, Commission Implementing Regulation (EU) 2016/959 of 17 May 2016.

9.94 Conducting market soundings may require disclosure of inside information which could conflict with the prohibition on the unlawful disclosure of inside information. The EU MAR regime seeks to regulate the way in which market soundings are conducted, regardless as to whether or not inside information is transmitted in the course of such soundings.

9.95 EU MAR provides that where a market sounding involves the disclosure of inside information, the disclosing party (a 'Disclosing Party') will be considered to be acting within the normal course of the person's employment, profession or duties where, at the time of making that disclosure, the Disclosing Party informs and receives the consent of the person to whom the disclosure is made that: (i) it may be given inside information; (ii) it will be restricted from trading or acting on that information; (iii) reasonable steps must be taken to protect the ongoing confidentiality of the information; and (iv) it must inform that Disclosing Party of the identity of all persons to whom the information is disclosed in the course of developing a response to the market sounding.

9.96 A recipient of market soundings is also subject to certain requirements under EU MAR and under the ESMA guidelines for market soundings[1]. Under EU MAR, any such recipient is required to conduct its own assessment as to whether it is in possession of inside information as a result of the market sounding. In conducting such assessment, any such recipient should consider other related information which it might possess in addition to the information received from the Disclosing Party.

[1] Guidelines on the Market Abuse Regulation – market soundings and delay of disclosure of inside information (ESMA/2016/1130, 13 July 2016).

9.97 The ESMA guidelines further require any such recipient to establish, implement and maintain internal procedures to control the flow of information within that recipient's business which are appropriate and proportionate to the scale, size and nature of any such recipient's business activity. In addition, the ESMA guidelines provide that all of the personnel of any such recipient which are entrusted with receiving and processing the information received in the course of the market sounding are properly trained with respect to the relevant internal procedures and the prohibitions arising from possessing inside information. Any such recipient is expected to designate a specific person or a contact point to receive market soundings, and to make that information available to any Disclosing Party.

9.98 EU MAR imposes record-keeping requirements with which any Disclosing Party and any such recipient of a market sounding must comply.

Market manipulation (Article 15 of EU MAR)

9.99 Article 15 of EU MAR prohibits a person from engaging or attempting to engage in market manipulation.

9.100 'Market manipulation'[1] includes:

- behaviour which gives, or is likely to give, false or misleading signals as to the supply of, demand for, or price of a financial instrument, or which secures, or is likely to secure, the price of a financial instrument at an abnormal or artificial level;
- behaviour which employs a fictitious device or any other form of deception or contrivance;
- disseminating information which gives, or is likely to give, false or misleading signals as to the supply of, demand for, or price of a financial instrument, or which secures, or is likely to secure, the price of a financial instrument at an abnormal or artificial level, including the dissemination of rumours, where the person who made the dissemination knew, or ought to have known, that the information was false or misleading; and
- behaviour which manipulates the calculation of a benchmark.

[1] Article 12 of EU MAR; Commission Delegated Regulation (EU) 2016/522 of 17 December 2015.

9.101 There is no requirement that a person needs to be an 'insider' (as is the case for insider dealing) in order to commit the offence of market manipulation.

9.102 Article 12(2) of EU MAR sets out a non-exhaustive list of behaviour that will be considered to amount to market manipulation:

9.102 Regulatory Overview – The United Kingdom

- the conduct by a person (or persons acting in collaboration) to secure a dominant position over the supply of or demand for a financial instrument which has, or is likely to have, the effect of fixing, directly or indirectly, purchase or sale prices, or creates, or is likely to create, other unfair trading conditions;
- the buying or selling of financial instruments at the opening or closing of the market, which has or is likely to have the effect of misleading investors acting on the basis of the prices displayed, including the opening or closing prices;
- the placing of orders to a trading venue (including any cancellation or modification thereof) by any available means of trading, including by electronic means such as algorithmic trading or high-frequency trading strategies, which has one of the effects of disrupting the regular trading function of the trading venue, making it more difficult for other persons to identify genuine orders on the trading venue, or creating, or being likely to create, a false or misleading signal about the supply of, demand for, or price of a financial instrument; or
- taking advantage of occasional or regular access to the media by voicing an opinion about a financial instrument (or indirectly about its issue) while having previously taken positions on that financial instrument and profiting subsequently from the effect of that opinion on the price of that instrument without having simultaneously disclosed that conflict of interest to the public in a proper and effective way.

9.103 The market manipulation offence was a key component of EU MAD, and remains so in EU MAR. It has been widened in scope expressly to prohibit attempted market manipulation as a separate offence. Manipulation of benchmarks also falls within scope, although this has been a criminal offence in the UK since the implementation of FSA 2012, Pt 7. As previously noted[1], the mention of algorithmic trading strategies reflects EU MAR's intention to take account of market trends and technologies. There are multiple factors set out in MAR 1 of the FCA Handbook which may be taken into account when considering whether or not behaviour could be regarded as market manipulation. These are all fairly self-explanatory: the FCA will consider the fact that the person has an illegitimate or actuating reason for committing a transaction, that the person's behaviour is intended to secure an abnormal or artificial price level or that the behaviour was intended to create an 'abusive squeeze' as likely indicators of an intention to manipulate the market[2].

[1] See para **9.72** above.
[2] See MAR 1.6 of the FCA Handbook.

Insider lists (Article 18 of EU MAR)

9.104 EU MAR places an obligation on issuers (or any person acting on their behalf or on their account), emission allowances market participants and parties involved in relevant auctions to maintain a list of all persons working for them that have access to inside information.

9.105 Insider lists must include prescribed content and be drawn up in accordance with a mandatory template in electronic format[1].

[1] Commission Implementing Regulation (EU) 2016/347 of 10 March 2016.

9.106 Any firm which is subject to Article 18 of EU MAR must promptly revise the insider list which it maintains whenever a person is added or removed as a person who has access to inside information, together with the date and time when that change occurred. Copies of each version of the list must be retained for five years. Firms will be required to send their insider lists to the FCA on request[1].

[1] Article 18 of EU MAR.

9.107 Although the principle of the insider list is not new, EU MAR is substantially more prescriptive in this respect than EU MAD, so firms should revisit their existing procedures to ensure compliance with EU MAR.

9.108 Under EU MAR there is a prescribed electronic format for insider lists which requires more information than previously. The new list must be kept up to date electronically. Listed companies must take reasonable steps to ensure insiders acknowledge in writing that they are aware of the obligations and the sanctions to which they are subject.

Investment recommendations (Article 20 of EU MAR)

9.109 EU MAR requires a person who produces or provides investment recommendations to ensure that the information is objectively presented and to disclose any conflicts of interest concerning the financial instruments to which that information relates[1]. Public institutions which disseminate statistics or forecasts that are liable to have a significant effect on financial markets must take care to disseminate them in an objective and transparent way[2].

[1] Article 20(1) of EU MAR; Commission Delegated Regulation (EU) 2016/958 of 9 March 2016.
[2] Article 20(2) of EU MAR.

9.110 EU MAR extends the scope of what constitutes an investment recommendation and the category of persons who may be regarded as having made an investment recommendation for the purposes of EU MAR. The definition now encompasses any information recommending or suggesting an investment strategy, either explicitly or implicitly, concerning one or several financial instruments or their issuers, including any opinion as to the present or future value or price of such instruments, intended for distribution channels or for the public[1]. This information may be produced by an independent analyst, an investment firm, a credit institution, any other person whose main business is to produce investment recommendations, and any other person who directly proposes a particular investment decision in respect of a financial instrument. This is a significant broadening of the previous definition under EU MAD to include anyone who produces or provides an investment recommendation, not just individuals who produce or provide recommendations in the course of their day-to-day business[2].

[1] Article 1(35) of EU MAR.

9.110 *Regulatory Overview – The United Kingdom*

[2] Article 1(34) of EU MAR.

9.111 Article 20(3) of EU MAR granted ESMA the power to produce and issue regulatory technical standards (the 'RTS') on the precise intricacies of investment recommendations[1]. The RTS specify how recommendations must be presented, identified and disseminated and what they must contain. They also contain guidelines on how conflicts of interest must be disclosed and other obligations with which individuals who produce investment recommendations must comply.

[1] Commission Delegated Regulation (EU) 2016/958 of 9 March 2016.

9.112 The amount of detail in EU MAR and the RTS means that much of the FCA's pre-existing guidance on the production and dissemination of investment recommendations in COBS 12.4 in the FCA Handbook is redundant and has been revoked. The remaining provisions are limited to a confirmation that graphs may be used as part of a 'fair presentation' of a recommendation and that persons who make investment recommendations may choose to disclose interests or conflicts of interest even where they have not crossed a threshold which requires disclosure of that information.

Whistleblowing (Article 32 of EU MAR)

9.113 EU MAR places requirements on regulators and firms to be able to receive whistleblowing notifications about suspected market abuse[1]. This is an extension of the market abuse regime under EU MAD. These whistleblowing mechanisms must include specific procedures governing the receipt of reports of breaches and their review. EU MAR provides protection for both the whistleblower and any person who is accused of market abuse by virtue of that whistleblowing. It requires that regulators and firms take steps to protect personal data, ensure confidentiality and prevent retaliation, discrimination or other unfair treatment.

[1] Article 32 of EU MAR; Commission Implementing Directive (EU) 2015/2392 of 17 December 2015.

9.114 Notably, EU MAR allows (but does not require) member states to provide financial incentives to whistleblowers who provide new information that leads to action against an infringer[1]. This is similar to the approach which exists under the equivalent US legislation. To date, however, neither the UK nor any other member state has chosen to adopt the relevant provisions of EU MAR.

[1] Article 32(4) of EU MAR.

9.115 The UK already had its own whistleblowing regime in place prior to the implementation of EU MAR, so these provisions should have limited effect for regulated firms which already comply with that existing UK regime. SYSC 18 in the FCA Handbook provides helpful guidance as to what an appropriate whistleblowing procedure may involve, although, in general, firms have discretion as to exactly how they implement their own whistleblowing mechanisms.

Market abuse (criminal regime)

Criminal insider dealing (Part V of CJA 1993)

9.116 As stated above, insider dealing is also a criminal offence. CJA 1993 makes it a criminal offence for an individual who has information as an insider to disclose that information or to deal or encourage another person to deal in securities whose price would be likely to be significantly affected if that information were to be made public.

9.117 In broad terms, CJA 1993 makes it a criminal offence, with a maximum penalty of seven years' imprisonment and an unlimited fine, for an individual who has non-public information to deal in price-affected securities (including derivatives relating to them) on a regulated market, or involving a professional intermediary, or by acting himself as a professional intermediary. Securities are 'price-affected' if the inside information, if made public, would be likely to have a significant effect on the price of the relevant securities.

Criminal market manipulation (Part 7 of FSA 2012)

9.118 Part 7 of FSA 2012 sets out three separate criminal offences for making false or misleading statements, creating false or misleading impressions, and making false or misleading statements or creating a false or misleading impression in relation to specified benchmarks.

9.119 The criminal offence under FSA 2012, s 89 applies to a person who:

- makes a statement that he knows is false or misleading in a material respect;
- makes a statement that is false or misleading in a material respect, being reckless as to whether it is; or
- dishonestly conceals any material facts, whether in connection with a statement made by that person or otherwise.

9.120 A person commits an offence under FSA 2012, 89 if he makes the statement or conceals the facts with the intention of inducing, or is reckless as to whether making the statement or concealing the facts may induce, another person (whether or not the person to whom the statement is made or from whom the facts are concealed):

- to enter or offer to enter into, or refrain from entering or offering to enter into, a relevant agreement; or
- to exercise, or refrain from exercising, any rights conferred by a relevant investment[1].

[1] See FSMA 2000, Sch 1, Pt 2, which sets out the investments which are specified for the purposes of FSA 2012, s 93(5).

9.121 A relevant agreement is an agreement the entering into or performance of which by either party constitutes an activity of a kind specified in an order made by HM Treasury which relates to a relevant investment. Under article 2 of the Financial Services Act 2012 (Misleading Statements and Impressions) Order 2013[1], the kinds of activity specified for those purposes include the following:

9.121 *Regulatory Overview – The United Kingdom*

- a controlled activity[2];
- sending dematerialised instructions;
- establishing a CIS;
- establishing a pension scheme; and
- managing the underwriting capacity of a Lloyd's syndicate.

[1] SI 2013/637.
[2] See FSMA 2000, Sch 1, Pt 2.

9.122 Under FSA 2012, s 90, an offence is committed by a person who does any act or engages in any course of conduct which creates a false or misleading impression as to the market in, or the price or value of, any relevant investment if the person intends to create the impression, and:

- the person intends, by creating the impression, to induce another person to acquire, dispose of, subscribe for or underwrite investments or to refrain from doing so, or to exercise or refrain from exercising any rights conferred by investments; and/or
- the person knows that the impression is false or misleading or reckless as to whether it is, and the person intends, by creating the impression, to make a gain for himself or another person, cause loss to another person, expose another person to the risk of loss, or is aware that creating the impression is likely to produce any of those results.

9.123 Under FSA 2012, s 91, an offence would be committed by a person ('A') who makes a false or misleading statement to another person ('B') if:

- A makes the statement in the course of arrangements for the setting of a relevant benchmark (such as LIBOR);
- A intends that the statement should be used by B for the purpose of setting a relevant benchmark; and
- A knows that the statement is false or misleading or is reckless as to whether it is.

9.124 It is also an offence for a person to do any act or engage in any course of conduct which creates a false or misleading impression as to the price or value of any investment, or as to the interest rate appropriate to any transaction, if:

- the person intends to create that impression;
- the impression may affect the setting of a relevant benchmark;
- the person knows that the impression is false or misleading or is reckless as to whether it is; and
- the person knows that the impression may affect the setting of a relevant benchmark.

'Principles'

9.125 A breach of the market abuse regime will also constitute a breach of the fifth of the FCA's Principles for Businesses, though the reverse may not be true, due to the fact the Principle is wider than the legislation. Consequently, for authorised firms, the FCA can take action for the breach of a Principle. This is particularly important when considering market abuse due to the fact that a

Principle ought to apply to innovative conduct which the FCA may view as questionable or objectionable, whereas the legislation, which is narrower, may not.

9.126 Under EU MAD, proceedings in respect of a breach of an FCA Principle for an authorised firm, or a Principle for an approved person, were more frequent than proceedings for alleged market abuse. Principles allow the regulator to enforce standards of behaviour where the nature of an objectionable activity does not fit with the statutory definitions of the market abuse regime; additionally, Principles can be applied to conduct that is outside the territorial scope of a particular rule.

The FCA's Principles for Businesses

9.127 The FCA often seeks to address market-related misconduct by the enforcement of duties under its Principles for Businesses ('PRIN'). The market abuse regime and the Principles exist side by side.

9.128 Of most importance is Principle 5, which states: 'A firm must observe proper standards of market conduct.'

9.129 Principle 2[1] and Principle 3[2] have historically been used by the FCA in respect of market conduct matters that did not amount to market abuse, most famously in relation to Citigroup and its 'Dr Evil' trades[3] on the European government bond markets.

[1] Principle 2 states: 'A firm must conduct its business with due skill, care and diligence.'
[2] Principle 3 states: 'A firm must take reasonable care to organise and control its affairs responsibly and effectively, with adequate risk management systems.'
[3] See FSA Final Notice to Citigroup Global Markets Limited, 28 June 2005.

The FCA's Statements of Principles and Code of Practice for Approved Persons

9.130 The FCA's Statement of Principles and Code of Practice for Approved Persons ('APER') have commonly been cited by the FCA where an approved person's behaviour is brought into question:

- Statement of Principle 2 states: 'An approved person must act with due skill, care and diligence in carrying out his accountable functions.'
- Statement of Principle 3 states: 'An approved person must observe proper standards of market conduct in carrying out his accountable functions.'

The FCA's Senior Managers Code of Conduct

9.131 The FCA has separate conduct rules for individuals within the scope of the Senior Managers and Certification Regime in its Senior Managers Code of Conduct ('COCON')[1]:

- Rule 2 states: 'You must act with due skill, care and diligence.'
- Rule 5 states: 'You must observe proper standards of market conduct.'

[1] See COCON 2.1 Individual conduct rules.

9.132 Persons who are designated as senior managers under the Senior Managers and Certification Regime in COCON must comply with additional specific rules[1].

[1] See COCON 2.2 Senior manager conduct rules.

9.133 In particular, Senior Manager Conduct Rule 2 states: 'You must take reasonable steps to ensure that the business of the firm for which you are responsible complies with relevant requirements and standards of the regulatory system.'

Case law

David Einhorn and Greenlight Capital, Inc

9.134 The case involving David Einhorn and Greenlight Capital, Inc[1] examined insider dealing in contravention of FSMA 2000, s 118(2).

[1] See FSA press release FSA/PN/005/2012, 25 January 2012.

9.135 Mr Einhorn, the sole owner, sole portfolio manager and President of US hedge fund Greenlight Capital, Inc ('Greenlight'), sold 11,656,000 shares in Punch Taverns Plc ('Punch') between 9 and 12 June 2009 ahead of Punch's announcement of a new issue of equity. This allowed Greenlight to avoid a loss of approximately £5.8 million. Mr Einhorn had specifically asked not to be 'wall-crossed' in relation to Punch and so participated in a phone call on 9 June 2009 with Punch's broker that was expressly set up on a 'non-wall crossed' basis. However, during the call Mr Einhorn was provided with confidential information that Punch was at an advanced stage of the process towards the issue of a significant amount of new equity, probably within a timescale of around a week. It was alleged that Mr Einhorn had therefore been 'wall-crossed', had become an 'insider' and was not permitted to trade in Punch once he had received the information.

9.136 Mr Einhorn and Greenlight were fined £3,638,000 and £3,650,795 respectively for market abuse.

MARKET ABUSE BY MR EINHORN

9.137 The former Financial Services Authority (the 'FSA') decided that Mr Einhorn engaged in market abuse within the meaning of FSMA 2000, s 118. Mr Einhorn's behaviour amounted to market abuse by reference to the five required elements under section 118(2) in that:

- Mr Einhorn's behaviour occurred in relation to shares in Punch, which are qualifying investments;
- Mr Einhorn was an insider;
- Mr Einhorn dealt in shares in Punch;
- Mr Einhorn had inside information; and
- Mr Einhorn dealt on the basis of that inside information.

9.138 Mr Einhorn was an insider because he had inside information as a result of having access to information by virtue of his employment at Greenlight and his duties as the President and portfolio manager of Greenlight.

9.139 Mr Einhorn dealt in the investment by directing traders to sell Greenlight's shares in Punch.

9.140 The information received by Mr Einhorn from Punch's broker was inside information for the following reasons:

- The information referred to Punch and shares in Punch.
- The information was precise because:
  - it indicated an event (the issue of new shares) that may reasonably have been expected to occur – it was not necessary for Mr Einhorn to be told that the issue would definitely proceed; and
  - it was specific enough to enable a conclusion to be drawn as to the possible effect of the share issue on the price of shares in Punch – Mr Einhorn received information about the size and purpose of the issue which was sufficient to allow him to conclude that the issue would cause the price of the relevant share to fall.
- The information was not generally available. Whilst there was some speculation in the market that Punch would have to raise capital, public statements by Punch indicated that it was pursuing a different strategy than that of raising additional capital. The timing, size and shareholder support for the issue was not available to the public.
- The information was likely to have a significant effect on the price of shares in Punch.

9.141 The fact that the Punch call was expressly set up on a 'non-wall crossed' basis did not prevent the information disclosed from being inside information. The FSA found that Mr Einhorn should have been aware of the risk of receiving inside information, should not have assumed that no inside information had been disclosed during the call, and should have made his own thorough and independent assessment of whether the matters discussed on the call constituted inside information.

9.142 Mr Einhorn dealt on the basis of the inside information. It is sufficient that a decision to deal is materially influenced by the inside information.

Ian Charles Hannam

9.143 The case of *Ian Charles Hannam v The Financial Conduct Authority*[1] examined unlawful disclosure of inside information in contravention of FSMA 2000, s 118(3).

[1] [2014] UKUT 0233 (TCC), [2014] All ER (D) 219 (May).

9.144 The FSA fined Mr Hannam £450,000 for market abuse arising out of unlawful disclosures made by Mr Hannam.

9.145 Mr Hannam, who was JP Morgan's Global Co-Head of UK Capital Markets at the time, made unlawful disclosures on two occasions. In an email to a potential investor on 9 September 2008, Mr Hannam disclosed that JP Morgan was engaged in discussions with a potential acquirer of Heritage Oil

9.145 *Regulatory Overview – The United Kingdom*

Plc ('Heritage') and that the CEO of Heritage, on advice from Mr Hannam, had decided to participate in those discussions. On 8 October 2008, Mr Hannam further disclosed to the investor that Heritage had made an oil discovery which was 'looking good'. It would have been easily deducible from publicly available information that this related to Heritage's Warthog-1 well in Uganda. These disclosures were made at a time when Mr Hannam knew that the recipient might recommend that the organisation he represented should enter into a corporate transaction with Heritage, whereby the organisation would purchase a stake in Heritage.

MARKET ABUSE BY MR HANNAM

9.146 The FSA decided that Mr Hannam had engaged in market abuse within the meaning of FSMA 2000, s 118. Mr Hannam's behaviour amounted to market abuse by reference to the three required elements under section 118(3) in that:

- Mr Hannam was an insider;
- Mr Hannam disclosed inside information to another person; and
- the disclosures were made other than in the proper course of the exercise of Mr Hannam's employment, profession or duties.

9.147 Mr Hannam was an insider because he had inside information as a result of having access to information by virtue of his employment at JP Morgan and his duties as Heritage's adviser.

9.148 The information disclosed by Mr Hannam on 9 September 2008 and 8 October 2008 was inside information for the following reasons:

- The information referred to Heritage and shares in Heritage.
- The information was precise because:
  - it indicated that Heritage's corporate advisers, JP Morgan, were engaged in ongoing discussions with a potential acquirer and that the CEO of Heritage decided to participate in those discussions; it also indicated that Heritage found oil in one of its wells and from publicly available information it was clear that the information related to Heritage's Warthog-1 well in Uganda; and
  - it was specific enough to enable a conclusion to be drawn as to the possible effect of the share issue on the price of shares in Heritage; from these disclosures, it was clear that Heritage's share price was likely to rise.
- The information was not generally available. There is no evidence that this information was generally available prior to the announcements by Heritage on 18 September 2008 and 21 October 2008.
- The information was likely to have a significant effect on the price of shares in Heritage. It was noted by the FSA that, in reality, the share price of Heritage rose from 204p to 240p after the announcement by Heritage about the existence of third party discussions on 18 September 2008.

9.149 The FSA concluded that Mr Hannam's disclosures were not made in the proper course of the exercise of his employment, profession or duties. Although Mr Hannam had implicit authority to make disclosures of the information contained in both emails, he did not consider whether he was disclosing inside information or whether it was necessary to disclose the information in order properly to discharge his responsibilities to Heritage. Mr Hannam's disclosures were not reasonable nor in fulfilment of a legal obligation.

9.150 Notably, it was not part of the case brought by the FSA that Mr Hannam deliberately set out to commit market abuse or that he lacked honesty or integrity. Furthermore, the FSA acknowledged that the inside information was not used by the investor to deal, so the information arguably remained confidential.

Upper Tribunal decision

9.151 Mr Hannam referred the decision of the FSA to the Upper Tribunal (Tax and Chancery Chamber) on 26 March 2012. On 27 May 2014, the Upper Tribunal affirmed the FSA's decision and held that Mr Hannam's disclosures on 9 September 2008 and 8 October 2008 amounted to behaviour which fell within FSMA 2000, s 118(3). The Upper Tribunal clarified that the appropriate standard to apply in a market abuse case is the civil standard of proof on the balance of probabilities.

Chapter 10

THE ALTERNATIVE INVESTMENT FUND MANAGERS DIRECTIVE

Dale Gabbert, Partner, Simmons & Simmons and Matthew Jones, Senior PSL, Simmons & Simmons

A	Introduction	10.1
B	Where to find AIFMD measures	10.4
C	What is an AIF?	10.13
D	What is an AIFM?	10.33
E	Exemptions	10.47
F	Authorisation or registration of the AIFM	10.58
G	Organisational issues	10.66
H	Managing an AIF	10.105
I	Marketing under AIFMD	10.118
J	Transparency	10.161
K	Service providers	10.194
L	Conclusion and next steps	10.263

A INTRODUCTION

10.1 22 July 2014 saw perhaps the most fundamental regulatory change to the UK (and European) hedge fund industry since its inception with the implementation in the UK of the Alternative Investment Fund Managers Directive[1] ('AIFMD').

[1] Directive 2011/61/EU of 8 June 2011. Since AIFMD is a Directive, the 28 member states of the EU (the 'member states') were required to transpose its provisions into their national laws by 22 July 2013, with the possibility of allowing a further one-year transitional period to 22 July 2014. In addition, Norway, Iceland and Liechtenstein, as members of the European Economic Area ('EEA'), are obliged, under the terms of the EEA Agreement, to implement AIFMD in their own jurisdictions.

10.2 AIFMD is a major element in the EU's work to reform the European financial sector generally in light of the financial crisis of the late 2000s. Its objective is to introduce a common regulatory regime for unregulated funds in the EU (ie for any fund that is not a UCITS fund[1]) with a view to (i) providing greater investor protection and (ii) enabling European regulators (referred to under AIFMD as 'national competent authorities') to obtain increased information in relation to funds being managed in, or marketed into, the EU so that they can better monitor systemic risk.

[1] That is, a fund which is required to be authorised under the Undertakings for Collective Investment in Transferable Securities Directive (2009/65/EC) (the 'UCITS Directive').

10.3 As such, AIFMD has significant implications not only for hedge fund managers based within the EU but also for those outside, not least those who

10.3 *The Alternative Investment Fund Managers Directive*

wish to market an alternative investment fund (an 'AIF'), such as a Cayman hedge fund, to professional investors within the EU.

B WHERE TO FIND AIFMD MEASURES

10.4 The provisions which make up the new regime imposed under AIFMD are to be found in a series of different documents, which have varying degrees of legal and/or regulatory authority.

European Union measures

10.5 The primary text is the Directive itself (the 'Level 1 text'), which was published in the Official Journal of the EU (the 'OJ') on 1 July 2011 and which sets out a framework for the new European regime.

10.6 The European Commission (the 'Commission') has used the powers delegated to it by the Council of the EU (the 'Council') and the European Parliament to adopt a number of Level 2 measures:

- a Delegated Regulation[1], dated 19 December 2012 and published in the OJ on 22 March 2013, which provides further detail around a number of key measures within the Level 1 text (for example, the calculation of leverage) (the 'Delegated Regulation');
- a further Delegated Regulation[2], dated 17 December 2013 and published in the OJ on 24 June 2014, which establishes the criteria by which an AIF is determined to be open-ended or closed-ended; and
- two Implementing Regulations[3], dated 15 May 2013 and published in the OJ the following day, which, respectively, set out procedures to be followed:
  - where a manager of an AIF (an 'AIFM') chooses to opt in to the provisions of AIFMD; and
  - to determine which should be the member state of reference for a non-EU AIFM.

As Regulations, these are directly applicable in all member states without the need for implementation.

[1] Commission Delegated Regulation (EU) No 231/2013 of 19 December 2012.
[2] Commission Delegated Regulation (EU) No 694/2014 of 17 December 2013.
[3] Commission Implementing Regulation (EU) No 447/2013 and Commission Implementing Regulation (EU) No 448/2013, each of 15 May 2013.

10.7 In addition, the European Securities and Markets Authority ('ESMA') was mandated to develop a series of guidelines, dealing with:

- sound remuneration policies under AIFMD (the 'Remuneration Guidelines')[1];
- key concepts of AIFMD (the 'Key Concepts Guidelines')[2]; and
- reporting obligations under Article 3(3)(d) and Article 24(1), (2) and (4) of AIFMD (the 'Reporting Guidelines')[3].

[1] See https://www.esma.europa.eu/sites/default/files/library/2015/11/2013-232_aifmd_guidelines_on_remuneration_-_en.pdf.
[2] See https://www.esma.europa.eu/sites/default/files/library/2015/11/2013-611_guidelines_on_key_concepts_of_the_aifmd_-_en.pdf.

[3] See https://www.esma.europa.eu/sites/default/files/library/2015/11/2014-869.pdf.

10.8 ESMA's guidelines are not binding on AIFMs per se, but the national competent authorities of the member states are obliged to implement them in their national rules (or explain to ESMA why they decide not to).

10.9 In addition, both the Commission and ESMA have published Q&As dealing with AIFMD[1]. Again, these are not technically binding but they do offer insights into the Commission's and ESMA's interpretation of issues arising from the Directive.

[1] See https://ec.europa.eu/info/sites/info/files/aifmd-commission-questions-answers_en.pdf and https://www.esma.europa.eu/sites/default/files/library/esma34-32-352_qa_aifmd.pdf.

10.10 Finally, looking ahead to the UK's forthcoming withdrawal from the EU ('Brexit'), on 31 May 2017, ESMA published a non-legally binding Opinion[1] on principles for supervisory convergence, intended to ensure that the national competent authorities of the remaining 27 member states take a consistent approach to the authorisation of UK entities which look to relocate into the EU post-Brexit. This was followed, on 13 July 2017, by three further sectoral Opinions (covering, respectively, investment management[2], investment firms[3] and secondary markets[4]).

[1] General principles to support supervisory convergence in the context of the United Kingdom withdrawing from the European Union (ESMA42-110-433).
[2] Opinion to support supervisory convergence in the area of investment management in the context of the United Kingdom withdrawing from the European Union (ESMA35-45-344).
[3] Opinion to support supervisory convergence in the area of investment firms in the context of the United Kingdom withdrawing from the European Union (ESMA35-43-762).
[4] Opinion to support supervisory convergence in the area of secondary markets in the context of the United Kingdom withdrawing from the European Union (ESMA70-154-270).

UK measures

10.11 As mentioned above, member states were required to transpose AIFMD into their national law. In the UK, this was achieved by a combination of:

- HM Treasury's Alternative Investment Fund Manager Regulations 2013 (as amended)[1] and Alternative Investment Fund Manager Order 2014 (as amended)[2] (together, the 'HMT Regulations'); and
- changes to the Financial Conduct Authority's ('FCA') Handbook of Rules and Guidance, in particular the Investment Funds Sourcebook[3] ('FUND') and Perimeter Guidance Manual[4] ('PERG').

[1] SI 2013/1773, as amended by SI 2013/1797.
[2] SI 2014/1292, as amended by SI 2014/1313.
[3] See http://fshandbook.info/FS/html/FCA/FUND.
[4] See http://fshandbook.info/FS/html/FCA/PERG.

10.12 The FCA's website also contains a useful section devoted to AIFMD, to which reference can be made[1].

[1] See https://www.fca.org.uk/firms/aifmd.

10.13 *The Alternative Investment Fund Managers Directive*

C WHAT IS AN AIF?

Definition of an AIF

10.13 By definition, in order to be an AIFM an entity must be managing an AIF. So the first question must be, 'what is an AIF?'

10.14 Under Article 4(1)(a) of AIFMD, an AIF is defined as being a collective investment undertaking (including investment compartments) which is not a UCITS fund and which:

- raises capital,
- from a number of investors,
- with a view to investing it in accordance with a defined investment policy for the benefit of those investors.

10.15 The Commission noted in its Q&As[1]:

> 'The definition of an AIF has been intentionally drafted broadly by the legislators in order to capture the variety of fund structures in all member states (hence the broad formulation "collective investment undertakings"). The intention behind such wording was to include investment funds in one of the two categories: AIFs or UCITS and to avoid any gaps.'

[1] See the third answer on page 1 – https://ec.europa.eu/info/sites/info/files/aifmd-commission-questions-answers_en.pdf.

10.16 ESMA's Key Concepts Guidelines (which are very largely mirrored in the FCA's PERG) provide further clarification on each of the key elements listed above. ESMA makes clear, however, that its Guidelines remain secondary to the Level 1 text – if the concepts set out above are present, based on the application of the Level 1 text alone, an undertaking should still be considered an AIF even if it shows none of the characteristics described in the Guidelines.

10.17 Each of the concepts is considered in turn below.

Collective investment undertaking

10.18 ESMA's Key Concepts Guidelines state that if all the following characteristics are shown, the entity should be considered to be a collective investment undertaking (a 'CIU'):

- no 'general commercial or industrial purpose';
- the pooling together of capital from investors with the aim of generating a pooled return for those investors (irrespective of whether different returns to different investors are generated); and
- the investors, as a collective group, have no day-to-day discretion or control – if one or more (though not all) the investors are granted day-to-day control, this is not indicative that the undertaking is not a CIU.

Investment compartments of an undertaking

10.19 If an investment compartment of an undertaking shows all the elements of a CIU set out in Article 4(1)(a) (ie it is itself a CIU; it raises capital from a number of investors etc), this should be enough to determine that the undertaking as a whole is an AIF.

Raising capital

10.20 Where the CIU (or someone on its behalf, such as the AIFM) takes direct or indirect steps 'to procure the transfer or commitment of capital by one or more investors to the undertaking for the purpose of investing it in accordance with a defined investment policy'[1], this commercial activity should amount to 'raising capital'.

[1] ESMA's Key Concepts Guidelines, Section VII Guidelines on 'raising capital', para 13.

10.21 It is immaterial whether the activity takes place only once, more than once or on an on-going basis.

Number of investors

10.22 Under ESMA's Key Concepts Guidelines, the principal element to be taken into consideration is whether or not there is a restriction whereby the undertaking may only raise capital from a single investor.

10.23 If there is no such restriction (whether in national law, in the rules or instruments of incorporation of the fund or in some other legally binding provision), the undertaking should be regarded as one which raises capital 'from a number of investors' even if, in fact, it has only one investor.

10.24 If such a restriction does exist, the undertaking will still be regarded as raising capital 'from a number of investors' if the sole investor:

- invests capital which it has raised from more than one person, with a view to investing it for their benefit; and
- consists of an arrangement or structure which in total has more than one investor – examples include:
  - a master-feeder structure where a single feeder fund invests in a master undertaking;
  - where a fund of funds is the sole investor in an underlying fund; or
  - where a nominee is acting as agent for more than one investor.

Defined investment policy

10.25 ESMA's Key Concepts Guidelines consider an undertaking as having a 'defined investment policy' where it has a policy as to how pooled capital is to be managed in order to generate a pooled return for the investors.

10.26 The Guidelines set out a number of factors, which would (either singly or cumulatively) tend to indicate the existence of such a policy. These include where the investment policy:

10.26 *The Alternative Investment Fund Managers Directive*

- is set out in a document which becomes part of or is referenced in the rules or instruments of incorporation of the undertaking;
- specifies investment guidelines, including any or all of the following:
  - to invest in certain categories of assets, or conform to restrictions on asset allocation;
  - to pursue certain strategies;
  - to invest in particular geographical regions;
  - to conform to restrictions on leverage, minimum holding periods or other restrictions designed to provide risk diversification.

10.27 The definition of an AIF above will therefore capture the following:

- most hedge funds/funds of hedge funds;
- private equity funds;
- listed closed-ended funds;
- real estate funds;
- infrastructure funds;
- commodity funds;
- long only funds which are not UCITS funds;
- other non-UCITS retail funds;
- feeder funds and master funds in a master-feeder structure.

What isn't an AIF?

10.28 As well as those which do not meet all of the criteria above, a number of entities are specifically excluded from the scope of AIFMD through exemptions in the Level 1 text. These include:

- holding companies;
- national central banks;
- employee participation schemes or employee savings schemes; and
- securitisation special purpose entities.

10.29 In addition, recitals 7 and 8 of the Level 1 text state that AIFMD does not apply to:

- family office vehicles; and
- insurance contracts.

Joint ventures

10.30 The position in respect of joint ventures, however, is slightly more complex. Although recital 8 of the Level 1 text states that the Directive 'should not apply to' such vehicles, the Commission's view[1] is that the recital cannot alter or amend the list of exemptions given in the core Level 1 text.

[1] See the second answer on page 19 – https://ec.europa.eu/info/sites/info/files/aifmd-commission-questions-answers_en.pdf.

10.31 A joint venture, in the Commission's opinion, can be excluded from being an AIF only if it falls under the exemptions listed in Article 2(3) or if its specific structure means that any of the defining criteria of an AIF examined above are not met.

10.32 The FCA, however, has taken a slightly more robust view. When considering[1] whether a joint venture would be caught by the definition of an AIF, the FCA believes that it would 'not normally' be. Although the analysis must be fact-based in each instance, the FCA feels that a joint venture is generally likely to fail the 'AIF test' on two counts, namely that (i) capital must be invested on behalf of investors, rather than the parties investing the capital for themselves, and (ii) a joint venture may well not be raising external capital.

[1] See PERG 16.2, Questions 2.46 to 2.49 – http://fshandbook.info/FS/html/FCA/PERG/16/2.

D WHAT IS AN AIFM?

Definition of an AIFM

10.33 Having determined whether or not a structure is an AIF, the next issue to consider is who, or what, is its AIFM. AIFMD defines an AIFM as a legal person 'whose regular business is managing one or more AIFs'. AIFMD also provides, at Article 6(1), that no AIFM may manage an AIF unless it is authorised in accordance with the Directive[1].

[1] At present, authorisation as an AIFM under the Directive is only relevant for EU AIFMs since the provisions in Article 67 of the Level 1 text regarding authorisation of non-EU AIFMs are not yet in force.

10.34 In the UK, the FCA has made clear[1] that an entity which is not a legal person (for example, a limited partnership) may still carry on the regulated activity of 'managing an AIF', since this regulated activity does not equate precisely to acting as an AIFM. (In the case of an AIF in the form of a limited partnership, the FCA has also confirmed that the general partner may be appointed as the AIFM, although it will be an external AIFM for the purposes of the Directive. For the distinction between internally and externally managed AIFs, see para **10.43** below.)

[1] See PERG 16.3, Question 3.15 – http://fshandbook.info/FS/html/FCA/PERG/16/3.

10.35 Note that AIFMD applies not only to all AIFMs based in the EU but also to any non-EU AIFM which has a point of contact with investors in the EU, either because it manages an AIF which is established in the EU or because it markets an AIF (whether EU or non-EU) into a member state.

10.36 Further, Article 5(1) of the Level 1 text requires that each AIF managed within the scope of AIFMD must have only one AIFM. However, this provision will not apply to non-EU AIFMs in respect of non-EU AIFs while they continue to market into a member state under that country's national private placement regime, unless the jurisdiction in question has imposed additional requirements on non-EU AIFs above those imposed under the Directive. National private placement regimes may be withdrawn in the future, but this will not be required to happen under AIFMD in the immediate future[1].

[1] See further para **10.149** below.

10.37 *The Alternative Investment Fund Managers Directive*

What activities must an AIFM perform?

10.37 In order to be 'managing' an AIF, an AIFM must be performing either, or both, (i) risk management or (ii) portfolio management for the AIF. Although it is only necessary for one of these activities to be performed to render an entity an AIFM, the entity cannot be authorised as an AIFM to carry out only one of these activities without the other.

10.38 An AIFM may delegate one or other of these activities to an appropriate third party to perform but may not delegate both (or delegate to the extent that the AIFM becomes a 'letter box entity'[1]).

[1] See further paras **10.253–10.254** below.

10.39 In addition to risk management and portfolio management, AIFMD permits an AIFM to perform certain ancillary activities, as set out in Annex 1 of the Level 1 text. These include:

- administration:
  - legal and fund management accounting services;
  - valuation and pricing;
  - unit issues and redemptions;
  - record-keeping;
- marketing; and
- activities related to the AIF's assets.

10.40 However, the AIFM may only perform the ancillary services if it is also performing the risk management and/or portfolio management activity.

The UK regulated activity of 'managing an AIF'

10.41 In the UK regulatory regime, a new regulated activity, that of 'managing an AIF', was created in order to implement the requirements of AIFMD. This activity does not align precisely with that of being an AIFM, as pointed out above in the context of legal persons. To comply with the requirements of the Directive, a UK regulated firm will need permission from the FCA to perform both risk and portfolio management activities, even where it will only, in practice, be performing one.

10.42 The firm will not, though, be 'managing an AIF' if it performs only ancillary services. Nor will a delegate be considered to be 'managing an AIF' unless the AIFM has delegated to such an extent that it has become a letter box entity[1].

[1] See further paras **10.253–10.254** below.

Internal and external AIFMs

10.43 AIFs may be either externally managed or, where the legal form of the AIF permits this, internally managed:
- An external manager is a legal person appointed by or on behalf of the AIF and which is responsible for managing the AIF.

- The AIF will be internally managed, on the other hand, where its governing body chooses not to appoint an external AIFM but, instead, is responsible for the risk and/or portfolio management of the AIF itself.

10.44 An AIF may, however, only have one AIFM.

AIFMD and MiFID

10.45 An AIFM is subject to AIFMD, and not to the Markets in Financial Instruments Directive ('MiFID'), on the basis that it will be providing the function of collective portfolio management and not that of individual portfolio management. (Individual portfolio management is, however, included among the activities listed in Article 6(4) of the Level 1 text which member states may allow an AIFM to perform.)

10.46 However, where an AIFM has delegated part of its investment management functions to another entity, the latter will be providing the investment service of individual portfolio management and, if within the EU, will be subject to MiFID II[1] (the recast MiFID) and the Markets in Financial Instruments Regulation[2] ('MiFIR').

[1] Directive 2014/65/EU of 15 May 2014.
[2] Regulation (EU) No 600/2014 of 15 May 2014.

E   EXEMPTIONS

Threshold requirements

10.47 Article 3 of the Level 1 text specifies certain AIFMs to which AIFMD will not apply to its full extent.

10.48 AIFMs which manage AIFs whose only investors are the AIFM itself or its parent undertakings or subsidiaries (either of the AIFM or the parent undertaking) are out of scope of the Directive altogether, provided that none of the investors is itself an AIF.

10.49 The more significant exemption, however, applies to AIFMs which manage portfolios of AIFs whose total assets under management ('AUM') are below either:

- €500 million, where the AIFs are unleveraged and have no redemption rights exercisable for five years following the date of initial investment; or
- €100 million in all other cases.

10.50 Note that, in the latter case, the AUM includes assets acquired through the use of leverage. The Delegated Regulation gives further detail[1] as to the calculation of AUM for the purposes of determining whether or not the AIFM falls within the threshold. AIFMs are permitted to occasionally – and temporarily – exceed the threshold without automatically triggering the need to become authorised. Again, the Delegated Regulation sets out the relevant criteria[2] to be considered.

[1] Article 2 of the Delegated Regulation.

10.50 *The Alternative Investment Fund Managers Directive*

[2] Article 4 of the Delegated Regulation.

10.51 AIFMs falling into either of the above categories are required to register with, and must provide certain limited information to, their national competent authority. Other than that, sub-threshold AIFMs are not obliged to comply with AIFMD.

10.52 However, for such AIFMs, there will be a choice to be made. It is possible for the AIFM to opt in to the AIFMD regime. For each AIFM this will be a balance between, on the one hand, the perceived disadvantages (for example, the additional disclosure and reporting obligations which AIFMD imposes[1] and which will be potentially costly to comply with, especially for smaller managers) and, on the other hand, obtaining the benefit of rights granted under the Directive, such as the marketing passport[2], which is available only to authorised AIFMs.

[1] See further paras **10.161–10.193** below.
[2] See further paras **10.118–10.160** below.

Categorisation of AIFMs under the UK's regulatory regime

10.53 In the UK, in order to merge the requirements of AIFMD within the existing regulatory framework, the HMT Regulations create three types of UK AIFM.

10.54 A *full scope UK AIFM* is a UK AIFM that either does not fall under the threshold described above or which does but has elected to opt in.

10.55 *Small UK AIFMs* are those which fall under the threshold but have chosen to remain outside the scope of AIFMD. There are two types of small UK AIFMs, namely small registered UK AIFMs and small authorised UK AIFMs.

10.56 A *small registered UK AIFM* is defined in the HMT Regulations[1] as one which is, in broad terms, (a) the internal manager of a body corporate which is not a collective investment scheme, (b) the external AIFM of certain real estate funds which have an FCA-authorised operator, or (c) an external AIFM that has applied to be registered as a manager of an EU social entrepreneurship or venture capital fund.

[1] See SI 2013/1773, reg 10.

10.57 *Small authorised UK AIFMs* are those sub-threshold UK AIFMs which are not small registered UK AIFMs. Since these will still be conducting a regulated activity – ie managing an AIF – failure to be authorised by the FCA would be a breach of the general prohibition set out in section 19 of the Financial Services and Markets Act 2000 ('FSMA 2000').

F AUTHORISATION OR REGISTRATION OF THE AIFM

Requirement for an AIFM to be authorised under AIFMD

10.58 As mentioned above, an AIFM may not manage an AIF unless it is either authorised in accordance with the Directive or falls within one of the exemptions referred to above.

10.59 The Level 1 text requires the national competent authority of an AIFM's home member state (the AIFM's 'home regulator') to obtain certain specified information from the AIFM when it applies for authorisation. This includes:

- information on the persons effectively conducting the business of the AIFM;
- information on the identity of the AIFM's shareholders or members, whether direct or indirect, natural or legal persons, that have qualifying holdings and on the amounts of those holdings;
- a programme of activity setting out the organisational structure of the AIFM, including information on how the AIFM intends to comply with its obligations under the Directive including those relating to authorisation, operating conditions and transparency requirements;
- information on the AIFM's remuneration policies and practices; and
- information on arrangements made for the delegation and sub-delegation to third parties of certain functions.

10.60 An AIFM applying for authorisation must also provide its home regulator with details regarding the AIFs which it intends to manage, including information about:

- the investment strategies, including the types of underlying funds if the AIF is a fund of funds;
- the AIFM's policy as regards the use of leverage;
- the risk profiles and other characteristics of the AIFs it manages or intends to manage, including information about the member states or third countries in which such AIFs are established or are expected to be established;
- where the master AIF is established, if the AIF is a feeder AIF;
- the rules or instruments of incorporation of each AIF the AIFM intends to manage; and
- the arrangements made for the appointment of the depositary for each AIF the AIFM intends to manage.

Authorisation or registration with the FCA

10.61 In the UK, the FCA has specified that a UK AIFM's application for authorisation or, where applicable, for variation of an existing permission ('VoP') to manage an AIF should be made on the relevant form, set out on the UK AIFMs webpage of the FCA's website[1], depending on whether the AIFM is a full scope UK AIFM or a small authorised UK AIFM.

[1] See https://www.fca.org.uk/firms/aifmd/uk-aifm.

10.62 In each case, the AIFM must submit a completed VoP form and a schedule of AIFs. Full scope UK AIFMs (but not small authorised UK AIFMs) must also submit a disclosure checklist to confirm compliance with FUND 3.2.2 R.

10.63 Firms applying for a new authorisation (whether as a full scope or as a small authorised UK AIFM) must in addition submit a wholesale investment firm application.

10.64 Small registered UK AIFMs must complete an application for entry on the register (again, the form may be found on the FCA's website, as referred to above), along with a schedule of the AIFs which it intends to manage.

10.65 The FCA has three months in which to determine a complete application, though this may be extended to six months in certain circumstances.

G   ORGANISATIONAL ISSUES

10.66 AIFMD imposes a number of operational obligations on AIFMs, including in respect of:

- risk management[1];
- leverage[2]; and
- valuation[3].

[1] See paras **10.67–10.79** below.
[2] See paras **10.80–10.92** below.
[3] See paras **10.93–10.104** below.

Risk management

Functional and hierarchical separation of the risk management function

10.67 An AIFM must functionally and hierarchically separate its risk management function from its operating units, including its portfolio management function. The AIFM's home regulator must, however, apply the principle of proportionality when reviewing the AIFM's compliance with this requirement. Functional and hierarchical separation of the function will be considered achieved where:

- persons engaged in the performance of risk management are not supervised by those responsible for portfolio management;
- persons engaged in the performance of risk management are not engaged in activities within the operating units, including portfolio management;
- persons engaged in the performance of risk management are compensated in accordance with the achievement of the objectives linked to that function, not to portfolio management; and
- the remuneration of senior officers in the risk management function is directly overseen by the remuneration committee, where such a committee has been established.

10.68 The AIFM will also need to demonstrate that it has specific safeguards in place against conflicts of interest which allow for the independent performance of risk management activities and that the risk management process is consistently effective.

Implementation of 'risk management systems'

10.69 An AIFM is required to implement adequate risk management systems[1] to identify, measure, manage and monitor all risks relevant to each AIF's investment strategy and to which the AIF may be exposed. This must include:

- an appropriate documented due diligence process when investing;
- procedures to identify, measure, manage and monitor investment position risks; and
- a process to ensure an AIF's risk profile corresponds to its offering and constitutional documents.

[1] Risk management systems are described in Article 38 of the Delegated Regulation as comprising:

'relevant elements of the organisational structure of the AIFM, with a central role for a permanent risk management function, policies and procedures related to the management of risk relevant to each AIF's investment strategy, and arrangements, processes and techniques related to risk measurement and management by the AIFM in relation to each AIF it manages.'

10.70 Such risk management systems must be reviewed at least annually and on the occurrence of certain events and adapted as necessary.

Permanent risk management function

10.71 Under AIFMD, an AIFM must establish and maintain a permanent risk management function which implements effective risk management policies and procedures in order to identify, measure, manage and monitor, on an ongoing basis, all risks relevant to each AIF's investment strategy. Moreover, the AIFM should ensure that the risk profile of the AIF disclosed to investors is consistent with the risk limits set by the AIFM.

10.72 The AIFM should also monitor compliance with the risk limits it sets for each AIF and provide regular updates to the governing body of the AIFM regarding its compliance with those risk limits and their adequacy and effectiveness. Senior management of the AIFM should be provided with regular updates regarding the current level of risk incurred by each managed AIF and any actual or foreseeable breaches of any risk limits so as to ensure that prompt and appropriate action can be taken.

Policies and procedures

10.73 An AIFM is required to establish, implement and maintain an adequate and documented risk management policy which identifies all the relevant risks to which the AIFs it manages are or may be exposed.

Risk measurement and management

10.74 An AIFM is required to put in place such risk management arrangements, processes and techniques as are necessary to ensure that the risk

10.74 The Alternative Investment Fund Managers Directive

positions taken and their contribution to the overall risk profile are accurately measured on the basis of sound and reliable data. Periodic back-tests and stress tests should be performed, and procedures should be put in place to ensure that any breaches are remedied in a timely fashion.

Assessment, monitoring and review of risk management systems

10.75 Periodically (and at least once a year) an AIFM must assess, monitor and review the adequacy and effectiveness of the risk management policy and the arrangements, processes and techniques put in place.

10.76 This review should also consider:

- the degree of compliance with the policy;
- the adequacy and effectiveness of measures taken to address any deficiencies in the risk management processes;
- the performance of the risk management function generally; and
- the adequacy and effectiveness of the functional and hierarchical separation of risk management and portfolio management.

10.77 Where changes are required to the risk management policy an AIFM is required to notify the regulatory authority of its home member state.

Risk limits

10.78 An AIFM is required to establish and implement quantitative and/or qualitative risk limits for each AIF it manages. Where only qualitative limits are set, an AIFM must be able to justify this approach to its home regulator.

10.79 Risk limits should at least cover:

- market risks;
- credit risks;
- liquidity risks;
- counterparty risks; and
- operational risks.

Leverage

10.80 AIFMD makes the use of leverage[1] subject to several obligations.

[1] Article 4(1)(v) of AIFMD defines leverage as 'any method by which the AIFM increases the exposure of an AIF it manages whether through borrowing of cash or securities, or leverage embedded in derivatives positions or by any other means'.

Application for authorisation

10.81 As part of the application for authorisation, the AIFM is required to provide the national competent authority of its home member state with information about the AIFM's policy as regards the use of leverage.

Setting a maximum level of leverage

10.82 As part of its risk management function[1], the AIFM is required to set a maximum level of leverage which it may employ on behalf of each AIF it manages and with which it must comply at all times. The AIFM must also demonstrate to its home regulator that the limit which it has set is reasonable.

[1] See paras 10.67–10.79 above.

10.83 It should also be noted that an AIFM's home regulator is authorised under AIFMD to impose limits on the level of leverage that an AIFM is entitled to employ (or other restrictions on the management of the AIF which it manages) in order to limit the extent to which the use of leverage contributes to the build-up of systemic risk in the financial system or the risk of disorderly markets. Where this power is to be used, however, notification must first be given to ESMA, the European Systemic Risk Board and (where it concerns an EU AIF) the national competent authorities of the AIF.

Leverage – disclosure to investors

10.84 For each EU AIF it manages which employs leverage, and for each AIF (whether EU or non-EU) that it markets in the EU which employs leverage, the AIFM must disclose to investors prior to their investment in the AIF[1]:

- the types and sources of leverage permitted and the associated risks;
- any restrictions on the use of leverage and of any collateral and asset re-use arrangements; and
- the maximum level of leverage which the AIFM is entitled to employ on behalf of the AIF.

[1] Article 23(1)(a) of AIFMD.

10.85 The AIFM must also make disclosure to investors whenever there are any material changes to the circumstances in which the AIF may use leverage.

10.86 In addition, AIFMs (i) managing EU AIFs which employ leverage or (ii) marketing AIFs in the EU which employ leverage must regularly disclose to investors 'without undue delay' any changes to the maximum level of leverage which the AIFM may employ on the AIF's behalf and changes to the re-use of collateral or guarantee granted under the leveraging arrangement, along with the total amount of leverage employed by that AIF.

Leverage – disclosure to regulators

10.87 Where an AIFM manages an AIF employing leverage 'on a substantial basis', it must disclose to its home regulator:

- information about the overall level of leverage employed by each AIF it manages;
- a break down between leverage arising from borrowing of cash or securities and leverage embedded in financial derivatives; and
- the extent to which the AIF's assets have been re-used under leveraging arrangements.

10.88 *The Alternative Investment Fund Managers Directive*

10.88 The Delegated Regulation[1] specifies that leverage is employed 'on a substantial basis' for the purposes of AIFMD when the exposure of an AIF, calculated according to the commitment method, exceeds three times its net asset value.

[1] Article 111 of the Delegated Regulation.

10.89 The information disclosed must include:

- the identity of the five largest sources of borrowed cash or securities for each of the AIFs managed by the AIFM; and
- the amounts of leverage received from each of those sources for each of those AIFs.

Calculation of leverage

10.90 The AIFM must have appropriately documented procedures to calculate the exposures of each AIF under its management in accordance with both the methods set out in the Delegated Regulation, and this calculation must be applied consistently over time.

10.91 By Articles 6 to 11 of the Delegated Regulation, an AIFM is required to calculate the exposure of the AIFs it manages in accordance with both the gross method and the commitment method.

10.92 Article 6(2) of the Delegated Regulation required the Commission to review the calculation methods by 21 July 2015, in light of market conditions, in order to determine whether they are sufficient and appropriate for all types of AIFs or whether an additional or optional method for calculating leverage should be developed. To date, no changes to the methodology have been proposed.

Valuation

AIFM and performance of the valuation function

10.93 Article 19 of AIFMD imposes a number of new obligations upon hedge fund managers. Rather than being a responsibility of the fund (one which the board of the fund would typically have delegated to the investment manager before AIFMD), the valuation function is now the legal responsibility of the AIFM and must be performed with 'all due skill, care and diligence'.

10.94 The valuation function may be performed either by the AIFM itself or by an independent external valuer appointed by the AIFM by way of delegation. The AIFM's liability to the AIF and its investors will not be affected by the fact that the valuation function has been delegated to an external valuer.

10.95 In its Quarterly Consultation Paper No 8 (CP15/8)[1], the FCA set out guidance, in the form of Q&As, clarifying a number of issues around valuation, including what constitutes the valuation function itself. Although the consultation period closed in May 2015, the Q&As have not yet been incorporated within the FCA Handbook.

[1] See http://www.fca.org.uk/your-fca/documents/consultation-papers/cp15-08.

Requirement to determine valuation methodologies and policies and procedures

10.96 Although the Directive recognises that AIFMs employ different methodologies, systems and models for valuing assets, depending on the assets and markets in which they invest, it nevertheless requires an AIFM to determine and describe the valuation methodologies it uses, to ensure that written policies and procedures are established, maintained, implemented and reviewed so that a sound, transparent, comprehensive and appropriately documented valuation process is in place.

Valuation of assets and calculation and disclosure of net asset value

10.97 Under AIFMD[1], the AIFM is responsible for the proper valuation of the AIF's assets, the calculation of the net asset value and its disclosure to investors. It must also ensure that the procedures and methodology for calculating the net asset value per share are fully documented and that it subjects these procedures and methodologies (and their application) to regular verification by the AIFM.

[1] Article 19(10) of AIFMD.

10.98 The AIFM must ensure both that remedial procedures are in place should the net asset value be incorrectly calculated and that the number of shares or interests in issue is subject to regular verification, at least as often as the share or interest price is calculated.

Functional independence and staffing

10.99 Where the AIFM performs the valuation function itself, the valuation task must be functionally independent from the AIFM's portfolio management activity to ensure that conflicts of interest are mitigated.

External valuer

10.100 Where the AIFM appoints an external valuer, the latter must be subject to mandatory professional registration and must be able to provide sufficient professional guarantees to demonstrate its ability to perform the valuation function.

10.101 An external valuer cannot delegate the valuation function to a third party, while a depositary may only be appointed as external valuer if it has functionally and hierarchically separated the performance of its depositary functions from its tasks as external valuer.

10.102 Notwithstanding the above (and irrespective of any contractual arrangements which might provide otherwise), where an external valuer is

10.102 *The Alternative Investment Fund Managers Directive*

appointed, it will be liable to the AIFM for any losses suffered by the AIFM as a result of the external valuer's negligence or intentional failure to perform its tasks.

10.103 Note, however, that recital 80 of the Delegated Regulation provides that:

> '[a] third party that carries out the calculation of the net asset value for an AIF should not be considered an external valuer for the purposes of [the Directive], as long as it does not provide valuations for individual assets, including those requiring subjective judgment, but incorporates into the calculation process values which are obtained from the AIFM, pricing sources or an external valuer.'

Frequency of valuation

10.104 Valuation should be carried out at least once a year or on each subscription, redemption or cancellation of shares or interests. In the case of open-ended funds, valuation should be carried out at a frequency which is both appropriate to the assets held by the AIF and its issuance and redemption frequency. In the case of closed-ended funds, valuations should be carried out in case of an increase or decrease of the capital of the AIF.

H   MANAGING AN AIF

10.105 AIFMD sets out a number of requirements with which an AIFM managing an AIF must comply. The specific requirements vary depending on whether the AIFM or the AIF (or both) is established in the EU.

EU AIFM managing an EU AIF

10.106 An EU AIFM[1] may not manage an AIF unless the AIFM is authorised in accordance with AIFMD. An EU AIFM must apply for authorisation to the national competent authority of its home member state.

[1] Article 4(1)(l) of AIFMD defines 'EU AIFM' as 'an AIFM which has its registered office in a member state'.

10.107 Once authorised, an EU AIFM is permitted to manage an EU AIF established in another member state either directly or by establishing a branch, provided that the AIFM is authorised to manage that type of AIF.

10.108 Where it intends to manage an EU AIF in another member state for the first time, the EU AIFM must communicate to its home regulator:

- the member state in which it intends to manage the AIF directly or establish a branch; and
- a programme of operations stating, in particular, the services which it intends to perform and identifying the AIF it intends to manage.

10.109 Where a branch is to be established, the EU AIFM must also provide:

- the organisational structure of the branch;
- the address in the AIF's home member state from which documents may be obtained; and

- the names and contact details of the persons responsible for the management of the branch.

10.110 Following receipt of the complete documentation, the AIFM's home regulator has one month (or two months where a branch is to be established) in which to transmit the documentation on to the national competent authorities of the intended host member state(s), together with a statement to the effect that the AIFM concerned is authorised by it.

10.111 The AIFM's home regulator must also immediately notify the AIFM of the transmission of documentation. Once it has received this notification, the AIFM may start to provide its services in the host member state. The host member state of the AIFM must not impose any additional requirements on the AIFM in respect of the matters covered by AIFMD.

10.112 If any of the information provided to the home member state changes, the AIFM must give written notice of that change to its home regulator at least one month before implementing the planned changes (or immediately where the change was unplanned). Provided the changes do not affect the AIFM's compliance with AIFMD (either in its management of the AIF or otherwise), its home regulator must inform the national competent authorities of the host member state(s) of those changes without undue delay.

EU AIFM managing (but not marketing) a non-EU AIF

10.113 An EU AIFM may manage a non-EU AIF which is not marketed in the EU provided that the AIFM complies with all of the requirements of AIFMD other than the provisions in respect of depositaries (Article 21) and the annual report (Article 22).

10.114 There must also be co-operation arrangements in place between the AIFM's home state regulator and the supervisory authorities of the third (ie non-EU) country in which the AIF is established[1], ensuring sufficient information exchange to allow the AIFM's regulator to carry out its duties under the Directive. (See paras **10.128–10.148** below in respect of the rules applicable to an EU AIFM which manages a non-EU AIF and markets its shares or interests in the EU.)

[1] Note that the AIF need not necessarily be registered with, or supervised by, the third country supervisory authority.

Non-EU AIFM managing (but not marketing) an EU AIF

10.115 Prior to the introduction (if any) of a European passport regime[1], a non-EU AIFM which manages an EU AIF but does not market it in the EU is not subject to any requirements under AIFMD, including the requirement to be authorised. However, the laws of the jurisdiction in which the EU AIF is domiciled may impose specific requirements.

[1] See further paras **10.149–10.153** below.

10.116 In the event that a European passport is introduced in respect of its home jurisdiction, a non-EU AIFM managing an EU AIF will be required to obtain authorisation pursuant to the Directive whether or not it markets that EU AIF in the EU. This will involve the AIFM becoming authorised in a 'member state of reference' and having a 'legal representative' in that member state[1]. (See paras **10.149–10.160** below in respect of the rules applicable to a non-EU AIFM which manages an AIF and markets its shares or interests in the EU.)

[1] See further Article 37 of AIFMD and Commission Implementing Regulation EU (No) 448/2013 of 15 May 2013.

Non-EU AIFM managing (but not marketing) a non-EU AIF

10.117 Where a non-EU AIFM manages a non-EU AIF but does not market interests in that non-EU AIF in the EU, that non-EU AIFM is not subject to AIFMD (simply because there is no nexus with the EU).

I MARKETING UNDER AIFMD

General provisions

Definition of 'marketing'

10.118 Under AIFMD[1], the term 'marketing' has a specific meaning, namely:

> 'a direct or indirect offering or placement at the initiative of an AIFM or on behalf of an AIFM of units or shares of an AIF which it manages to or with investors domiciled or with a registered office in the EU.'

[1] Article 4(1)(x) of AIFMD.

10.119 In order to constitute 'marketing' for these purposes, the offering or placement of interests in an AIF must be carried out 'at the initiative' of the AIFM or on its behalf. Consequently, 'passive' or 'reverse enquiry/solicitation' type activity will not be caught within the definition and is therefore outside the scope of the Directive.

10.120 Although the substantive provisions of the Level 1 text are silent as to what is meant by 'passive marketing' in its various forms, the recitals make it clear that the Directive is not intended to affect the existing situation pre-AIFMD, whereby a professional investor established in the EU may invest in an AIF on its own initiative, irrespective of where the AIFM or the AIF is domiciled. However, the question of whether passive marketing is permitted in a particular member state will depend on that member state's national law.

10.121 In the UK, the relevant offering documents must be in essentially final form to constitute AIFMD marketing. In its PERG guidance[1], the FCA sets out that in its view (which, it notes, may not be shared by the national competent authorities of other member states) communications relating to draft offering will not fall within the meaning of an 'offer' or 'placement' for the purposes of AIFMD, as the AIFM cannot apply for permission to market the AIF at this point. Thus, a promotional presentation or a pathfinder version of the private

Marketing under AIFMD **10.126**

placement memorandum would not constitute an offer or placement, provided such documents cannot be used by a potential investor to make an investment in the AIF.

[1] See PERG 8.37.6G – https://www.handbook.fca.org.uk/handbook/PERG/8/37.html.

'To or with investors domiciled or with a registered office in the EU'

10.122 The concept of 'domicile' is potentially ambiguous. In certain member states, the term has connotations of 'residence' only, whereas in the UK it has a specific legal meaning which can be quite complex (and can occasionally lead to counter-intuitive results). In the UK context, it is thought (though the position is not certain) that the 'residence' interpretation is the one which the FCA would accept.

Investors – professional and retail

10.123 AIFMD relates primarily to the marketing of AIFs to 'professional investors'. For the purposes of AIFMD, investors are those within the meaning of Annex II of MiFID – that is, MiFID per se professional clients or investors that may, on request, be treated as professional clients[1].

[1] Note that, after 3 January 2018, the applicable definition of 'professional investor' is that in Annex II of MiFID II, the recast MiFID.

10.124 AIFs that are managed and marketed by the AIFM may only be marketed to professional investors, unless the member state in which the AIF is marketed allows the AIFM to market to retail investors in its territory pursuant to the derogation in Article 43 of AIFMD.

10.125 Marketing of AIFs (both EU and non-EU) to retail investors in the UK, for example, remains permissible following the implementation of AIFMD provided that:

- the AIF, where it is a UK AIFM, is registered with the FCA under either Article 31 or Article 36 of AIFMD;
- the additional disclosures required under COBS[1] 18.5 are made where the AIFM is an FCA-authorised AIFM;
- marketing is undertaken only to retail investors falling within the exemptions in COBS 4.12 (note that these exemptions were further restricted by legislative changes which came into force on 1 January 2014).

[1] The FCA's Conduct of Business Sourcebook – see http://fshandbook.info/FS/html/FCA/COBS.

10.126 Where marketing is to be undertaken by an FCA-regulated investment firm which is not an AIFM:

- where a condition must be met before an AIFM may market an AIF, the investment firm may not market that AIF unless that condition is met; and

10.126 *The Alternative Investment Fund Managers Directive*

- the UK's financial promotion regime will continue to apply, so marketing must fall within an exemption to FSMA 2000, s 238 (as amended), such as COBS 4.12 or the Financial Services and Markets Act 2000 (Promotion of Collective Investment Schemes) (Exemptions) Order 2001 (as amended)[1].

[1] SI 2001/1060.

10.127 Further, under the terms of the Prospectus Directive[1], shares in a listed company may currently be marketed generally throughout the EU to certain retail investors (ie investors which fall outside AIFMD's definition of 'professional investor'[2]). While there is no specific exemption for listed AIFs (such as UK investment trust companies), it is clear that member states may allow listed AIFs to be marketed to retail investors in their territory pursuant to the derogation in Article 43 of the Directive if, as is the case in the UK, they elect to do so.

[1] Directive 2003/71/EC of 4 November 2003.
[2] See para **10.123** above.

Marketing by EU AIFMs

Marketing an EU AIF

MARKETING IN THE EU AIFM'S HOME MEMBER STATE (ARTICLE 31 OF AIFMD)

10.128 An AIFM may market an EU AIF that it manages to professional investors in its home member state once it has provided its home regulator with certain specified documentation and information, including:

- a form of notification, including:
  - a programme of operations identifying the AIFs which the AIFM intends to market; and
  - information on where the AIFs are established;
- the AIF's rules or instruments of incorporation;
- identification of the AIF's depositary;
- a description of, or any information on, the AIF which is available to investors;
- information on where the master AIF is established, if the AIF is a feeder AIF; and
- where relevant, information on the arrangements established to prevent the AIF from being marketed to retail investors, including where the AIFM relies on activities of independent entities to provide investment services in respect of the AIF.

10.129 An AIFM may only market an EU AIF which is a feeder fund if the master AIF is also an EU AIF managed by an authorised EU AIFM.

10.130 Once it has received a complete notification, the AIFM's home regulator must inform the AIFM within 20 working days whether it may begin marketing the AIF(s) in question. Where the AIF is established in a different member state, the AIFM's home regulator must also inform the national competent authorities of that member state that the AIFM may start marketing shares in the AIF.

10.131 For a full scope UK AIFM seeking to market an EU AIF within the UK, a link to the relevant notification form can be found on the FCA's website[1].

[1] See https://www.fca.org.uk/firms/aifmd/notifications/forms.

MARKETING IN ANOTHER MEMBER STATE (ARTICLE 32 OF AIFMD)

10.132 An EU AIFM may market an EU AIF that it manages to professional investors in another member state (the 'host member state'). However, it must first obtain a European passport permitting it to do so by providing its home regulator with the same documentation and information as referred to in para 10.128 above, but including, in addition, an indication of the member state(s) in which it intends to market the AIF.

10.133 In the UK, the relevant notification form may be found on the FCA's website[1].

[1] See https://www.fca.org.uk/firms/aifmd/notifications/forms.

10.134 The EU AIFM's home regulator has 20 days in which to notify the national competent authorities in each of the other member states in which the AIFM wishes to market the EU AIF. The EU AIFM may commence marketing in those host member states as soon as it has been informed by its home regulator that such notification has been made.

10.135 As with the UCITS passport, the AIFM must, when exercising the marketing passport under the Directive, comply with the marketing rules of each of the other member states in which it markets an EU AIF and such marketing is subject to the supervision of the national competent authorities in those member states.

10.136 Where the EU AIF is a feeder AIF, the passport may only be obtained if the master AIF is also an EU AIF which is managed by an authorised EU AIFM.

10.137 For a full scope UK AIFM seeking to market an EU AIF into another member state, a link to the relevant notification form can be found on the FCA's website.

Marketing a non-EU AIF

MARKETING WITH A PASSPORT (ARTICLE 35 OF AIFMD)

10.138 Article 67 of AIFMD required ESMA, by 22 July 2015, to have issued an Opinion to the Commission, the Council and the European Parliament on, among other things, the functioning of the marketing of non-EU AIFs by EU AIFMs under national private placement regimes. ESMA was also mandated to advise the Commission on the possible application of the European passport to the marketing of non-EU AIFs by EU AIFMs.

10.139 In the event of ESMA's advice being positive, the Commission was then required[1], within three months, to adopt a delegated act to introduce a passport. Following adoption, the European Parliament and the Council would have three months (extendable to six months) in which to make objections to the Commission's proposal. To date, however, the provisions of Article 67 have not been complied with.

[1] Article 67(6) of AIFMD.

10.140 ESMA produced its initial Opinion[1] and Advice[2] on 30 July 2015, having completed its assessment of only six non-EU jurisdictions. Of these, ESMA concluded that only in respect of Jersey and Guernsey were there no obstacles to the extension of the passport (although positive advice in respect of Switzerland depended only on certain pending amendments to the Swiss Federal Act being enacted). ESMA noted, however, that the Commission, the Council and the European Parliament might wish to delay 'until ESMA has delivered positive advice on a sufficient (though unspecified) number of non-EU countries, before introducing the passport in order to avoid any adverse market impact that a decision to extend the passport to only a few non-EU countries might have'.

[1] See https://www.esma.europa.eu/sites/default/files/library/2015/11/2015-1235_opinion_to_ep-council-com_on_aifmd_passport_for_publication.pdf.
[2] See https://www.esma.europa.eu/sites/default/files/library/2015/11/2015-1236_advice_to_ep-council-com_on_aifmd_passport.pdf.

10.141 ESMA's further Advice[1] followed on July 2016 (revised on 12 September 2016) and covered an additional six jurisdictions beyond those in the initial Opinion. Of the 12 countries assessed, ESMA provided positive advice in respect of five (with Canada and Japan joining Jersey, Guernsey and Switzerland) and offered a qualified opinion on the others (the US, Bermuda, the Cayman Islands, Hong Kong, the Isle of Man, Australia and Singapore).

[1] See https://www.esma.europa.eu/sites/default/files/library/2016-1140_aifmd_passport.pdf.

10.142 The Commission has taken no further steps to adopt a delegated act under Article 67(6) of AIFMD and ESMA has given no indication of its further intentions in respect of this work.

10.143 In the event that the European passport is eventually made available, EU AIFMs marketing non-EU AIFs will be required to comply with all of the requirements of the Directive, as well as with three further conditions:

- Co-operation arrangements must be in place between the AIFM's home regulator and the supervisory authority of the third country where the non-EU AIF is established, ensuring sufficient information exchange to allow the AIFM's regulator to carry out its duties under the Directive.
- The third country where the non-EU AIF is established must not be listed as a Non-Cooperative Country and Territory by the Financial Action Task Force (the 'FATF').

- The third country where the non-EU AIF is established must have signed an agreement with (i) the AIFM's home member state and (ii) each other member state in which the AIF is intended to be marketed which complies with the standards set out in the OECD's Model Tax Convention on Income and Capital.

MARKETING PURSUANT TO NPPRS (ARTICLE 36 OF AIFMD)

10.144 EU AIFMs that do not wish to take advantage of the passport (when available) could continue to market non-EU AIFs under the national private placement regime ('NPPR') of the relevant host member state (where such a regime exists) until such date as NPPRs are abolished (foreseen as being at least three years after the delegated act required under Article 67(6) of AIFMD has entered into force) or until the NPPR in question ceases to be available in the jurisdiction in which the AIFM intends to market shares or interests of the non-EU AIF.

10.145 It should be noted that NPPRs are optional and are not harmonised. Some member states do not maintain such a regime and others have abolished regimes that were in operation prior to implementation of AIFMD.

10.146 Nevertheless, under Article 36 of AIFMD, member states may (but are not required to) allow an authorised EU AIFM to market non-EU AIFs that it manages (and also EU feeder AIFs that do not invest in a master AIF, which is also an EU AIF managed by an authorised EU AIFM) to professional investors in their territory, subject to the following conditions:

- The AIFM is required to comply with all of the requirements of the Directive except for the requirement to appoint a depositary under Article 21. The AIFM must, instead, ensure that one or more entities are appointed to carry out the duties referred to in Article 21(7) (cash monitoring), Article 21(8) (safe-keeping of assets) and Article 21(9) (certain oversight functions). This is referred to as the 'depositary lite' regime[1].
  The AIFM itself cannot perform the Article 21(7), Article 21(8) and Article 21(9) functions but must identify to its home regulator the entity or entities responsible for carrying out the three duties.
- Appropriate co-operation arrangements must be in place between the AIFM's home regulator and the supervisory authorities of the non-EU country where the non-EU AIF is established in order to ensure an efficient exchange of information that allows the AIFM's home regulator to carry out its duties in accordance with the Directive.
- The third country where the non-EU AIF is established must not be listed as a Non-Cooperative Country and Territory by the FATF.

[1] See further paras 10.233–10.244 below.

10.147 Member states are permitted to impose stricter rules on the AIFM in respect of the marketing of shares or interests in non-EU AIFs to investors in their territory. The UK has chosen not to impose any additional rules for the marketing of non-EU AIFs in the UK by EU AIFMs.

10.148 *The Alternative Investment Fund Managers Directive*

10.148 For a full scope UK AIFM wishing to market non-EU AIFs into another member state, a link to the relevant notification form may be found on the FCA's website[1].

[1] See https://www.fca.org.uk/firms/nppr.

Marketing by non-EU AIFMs

Marketing AIFs pursuant to NPPRs (Article 42 of AIFMD)

10.149 Until at least three years after the delegated act required under Article 67(6) of AIFMD[1] has entered into force, member states may (but are not required to) allow a non-EU AIFM to market an AIF (whether EU or non-EU) that it manages to professional investors in that member state under an NPPR. This is subject to certain conditions set out in Article 42 of the Directive, although member states can impose stricter marketing rules on a non-EU AIFM than are provided for under AIFMD.

[1] See paras **10.138–10.143** above.

10.150 Accordingly, whilst a non-EU AIFM which markets an AIF is not generally required to comply with AIFMD, it must nevertheless comply with:

- the transparency requirements of the Directive (in respect of each AIF so marketed), namely:
    - Article 22 – publication of an annual report[1];
    - Article 23 – disclosure to investors[2]; and
    - Article 24 – reporting to national competent authorities[3];
- where relevant, the AIFMD requirements applicable to AIFs which acquire control of non-listed companies and issuers[4], set out at Articles 26 to 30 of the Directive[5].

[1] See paras **10.161–10.167** below.
[2] See paras **10.168–10.176** below.
[3] See paras **10.177–10.193** below.
[4] Both terms, 'non-listed company' and 'issuers', are defined under Article 4 of AIFMD.
[5] Where any of the requirements under Articles 26 to 30 refer to 'competent authorities' or 'AIF investors', this means the national competent authorities and investors in the member state(s) in which the relevant AIF is marketed.

10.151 Furthermore, appropriate co-operation arrangements to enable the member state national competent authorities to carry out their duties under the Directive must be in place between:

- the national competent authorities of the member state(s) in which the AIF is marketed;
- the national competent authorities of the EU AIF (where relevant);
- the supervisory authorities of the third country where the non-EU AIF is established (where relevant); and
- the supervisory authorities of the third country where the non-EU AIFM is established.

10.152 In addition, the third country where the non-EU AIF or the non-EU AIFM is established must not be listed as a Non-Cooperative Country and Territory by the FATF.

10.153 For non-EU AIFMs seeking to market AIFs into the UK, a link to the relevant notification form can be found on the FCA's website[1].

[1] See https://www.fca.org.uk/firms/aifmd/notifications/forms.

Marketing AIFs pursuant to a passport (Articles 39 to 41 of AIFMD)

10.154 Article 67 of AIFMD required ESMA, by 22 July 2015, to have issued an Opinion to the Commission, the Council and the European Parliament on, among other things, the functioning of the marketing of AIFs (whether EU or non-EU) in the EU by non-EU AIFMs under NPPRs. ESMA was also mandated to advise the Commission on the possible application of the European passport to the marketing of AIFs in the EU by non-EU AIFMs.

10.155 In the event of ESMA's advice being positive, the Commission was then required[1], within three months, to adopt a delegated act to introduce a passport. Following adoption, the European Parliament and the Council would have three months (extendable to six months) in which to make objections to the Commission's proposal. To date, however, the provisions of Article 67 have not been complied with.

[1] Article 67(6) of AIFMD.

10.156 See paras **10.138–10.143** above for the current position in respect of the extension of the passport to non-EU AIFMs. (Note that if the passport is granted, a non-EU AIFM which manages an EU AIF will be obliged to obtain authorisation pursuant to the Directive whether or not it markets that EU AIF in the EU.)

10.157 The Directive sets out further conditions to which a non-EU AIFM marketing an EU AIF[1] or a non-EU AIF[2] would be subject (including the need for co-operation and tax agreements between the member state of reference and the country in which the AIF is established, and the requirement that the AIF's state of establishment is not a Non-Cooperative Country or Territory for FATF purposes as well as the relevant notification regime).

[1] See Article 39 of AIFMD.
[2] See Article 40 of AIFMD.

10.158 As and when the European passport becomes available to a non-EU AIFM, the AIFM will have a choice whether to (a) market under the passport, which would entail compliance with the full scope of the Directive's provisions, or (b) continue to use existing NPPRs, where these are available, complying only with the specified provisions of AIFMD which apply in the particular jurisdiction.

10.159 Three years after the introduction of a passport those NPPRs which remain in force may be terminated. At that point, the European passport regime would be the sole marketing regime applicable in all member states to the marketing by a non-EU AIFM of a non-EU AIF[1].

[1] Article 68 of AIFMD.

10.160 It should be noted, however, that member states are not required to maintain NPPRs for three years following the introduction of a passport – indeed, some member states have already determined to end their NPPRs early.

J TRANSPARENCY

Annual report (Article 22 of AIFMD)

10.161 AIFMD requires an AIFM to make available an annual report for each EU AIF it manages and for each AIF it markets in the EU in respect of each financial year. The AIFM must do this by no later than six months following the end of the financial year.

10.162 The annual report must be made available to investors on request and must also be made available to the AIFM's home regulator and, where applicable, the national competent authority of the AIF's home member state.

10.163 It should be noted that, under Article 24(3)(a) of AIFMD, as part of its reporting obligation an AIFM must make an annual report available 'on request' to its home regulator for each EU AIF it manages and for each AIF it markets in the EU.

Content requirements of the annual report

10.164 The information provided in the annual report must be materially relevant, reliable, comparable and clear. In addition, AIFMD and the Delegated Regulation together specify that the annual report must contain:

- a balance sheet or statement of assets and liabilities[1];
- an income and expenditure account for the financial year;
- a report on the activities of the financial year;
- any material changes in matters disclosed to investors during the financial year covered by the report[2];
- the total amount of remuneration for the financial year, split into fixed and variable remuneration, paid by the AIFM to its staff, and number of beneficiaries, and where relevant, carried interest paid by the AIF; and
- the aggregate amount of remuneration broken down by senior management and members of staff of the AIFM whose actions have a material impact on the risk profile of the AIFM[3].

[1] See further Articles 104 and 105 of the Delegated Regulation.
[2] For clarification as to the meaning of 'material changes', see Article 106 of the Delegated Regulation.
[3] See further Article 107 of the Delegated Regulation.

10.165 Accounting information given in the annual report must be prepared in accordance with the accounting standards of the AIF's home member state (or, where the AIF is non-EU, in accordance with the accounting standards of the AIF's domicile) and with the accounting rules laid down in the AIF's rules or instruments of incorporation. Although the information must be audited by an auditor established in the EU, member states may permit an AIFM which markets a non-EU AIF to have such accounting information audited according to international auditing standards in force in the domicile of the AIF.

10.166 Where an AIF is required to make public an annual financial report in accordance with the Transparency Directive[1], a derogation is allowed under AIFMD so that any additional information which AIFMD requires to be included in the annual report need only be provided to investors on request, either separately or as an additional part of such annual financial report. If provided as part of the annual financial report, the whole annual financial report must be made public no later than four months following the end of the relevant financial year.

[1] Directive 2004/109/EC of 15 December 2004.

Date of first annual report

10.167 The FCA has confirmed[1] that a full scope UK AIFM will be responsible for producing an AIFMD-compliant annual report and making it available to the FCA within six months (or four months, where the AIF is required to make public an annual financial report under the Transparency Directive) of the first financial year end of the AIF which follows the date on which the AIFM was authorised.

[1] See FUND 3.3.2R and 3.3.3R.

Disclosure to investors (Article 23 of AIFMD)

10.168 AIFMD requires an AIFM to ensure that certain specified information is made available to investors, in respect of:

- each EU AIF it manages; and
- each of the AIFs that it markets in the EU.

10.169 Different requirements apply in respect of (a) information which must be disclosed prior to the investor's investment in the AIF (along with any material changes to such information), and (b) information which must be disclosed on a periodic basis. Additionally, certain regular disclosures must be made by the AIFM where the AIF in question is employing leverage.

10.170 Information which AIFMD requires to be disclosed does not have to be provided in the AIF's prospectus or other offering document – it may be provided to investors separately, for example, by way of an AIFM disclosure statement or through newsletters.

10.171 *The Alternative Investment Fund Managers Directive*

Disclosure prior to investment

10.171 Article 23(1) of AIFMD sets out what information must be provided to an investor prior to investment in an AIF. This includes (but is not limited to) the following:

- a description of the investment strategy and objectives of the AIF;
- where any master fund or (where the AIF is a fund of funds) underlying funds are domiciled;
- the types of assets in which the AIF may invest;
- the techniques the AIF may employ and all associated risks;
- any applicable investment restrictions;
- the circumstances in which the AIF may use leverage, the types and sources of leverage permitted and the associated risks;
- any restrictions on the use of leverage and any collateral and asset re-use arrangements;
- the maximum level of leverage which the AIFM is entitled to employ on behalf of the AIF;
- the identity of the depositary and other service providers of the AIF, as well as a description of their duties and investors' rights;
- the identity of, and description of any material arrangements with, prime brokers and how conflicts of interest between the AIF and its prime brokers are managed;
- all fees, charges and expenses and the maximum amounts directly or indirectly borne by the investors;
- any preferential treatment, or the right to obtain such treatment given to an investor, and a description of the preferential treatment, the type of investor who obtains it and their legal or economic links with the AIFM or AIF – this would, for example, cover side letters entered into by the AIF;
- the latest annual report;
- where the depositary has sub-delegated custody arrangements to a prime broker and has transferred the liability for the loss of financial instruments held in custody to the prime broker;
- the latest net asset value of an AIF and also, where available, the historical performance of the AIF;
- a description of how the AIFM is complying with AIFMD's professional liability risks requirements (ie whether it is providing additional own funds or obtaining professional indemnity insurance).

Periodic disclosure requirements

10.172 The AIFM must also make certain periodic disclosures to investors in respect of:

- each EU AIF that it manages; and
- each AIF that it markets in the EU.

10.173 Such disclosures should cover:

- the percentage of the AIF's assets which are subject to special arrangements arising from their illiquid nature;

- any new arrangements for managing the liquidity of the AIF and the current risk profile of the AIF; and
- the risk management systems employed by the AIFM to manage those risks.

10.174 The Delegated Regulation requires such disclosures to be presented 'in a clear and understandable way'. Periodic disclosures must be made to investors, at a minimum, at the same time as the annual report is made available, or on a more frequent basis as required by the AIF's rules or instruments of incorporation.

Regular disclosures regarding use of leverage

10.175 In addition, where an AIFM is managing an EU AIF or marketing an AIF in the EU which, in either case, employs leverage, the AIFM must regularly disclose to investors (again, in a clear and understandable way):

- any changes to the maximum level of leverage which the AIFM may employ on the AIF's behalf;
- changes to the right of re-use of collateral or any guarantee granted under the leveraging arrangement; and
- the total amount of leverage employed by that AIF.

10.176 The information relating to the maximum level of leverage and the right of re-use or guarantee must be provided to investors 'without undue delay', and information about the total amount of leverage employed by the AIF must be provided to investors along with the periodic disclosures[1].

[1] See paras 10.172–10.174 above.

Reporting to regulators (Article 24 of AIFMD)

General reporting requirements

10.177 AIFMD requires an AIFM to make regular reports to its home regulator in respect of specified types of information. The Delegated Regulation and ESMA's Reporting Guidelines expand on these requirements.

10.178 The AIFM must, for example, report regularly to its home regulator on behalf of each AIF it manages as to:

- the principal markets and instruments in which it trades;
- information on the main markets of which it is a member or on which it actively trades; and
- the principal exposures and most important concentrations of each AIF.

10.179 For each of the EU AIFs it manages and for each of the AIFs it markets in the EU, the AIFM must also provide certain information ('Article 24(2) information') to its home regulator, including:

- the percentage of the AIF's assets which are subject to special arrangements arising from their illiquid nature;
- any new arrangements for managing the liquidity of the AIF;

10.179 *The Alternative Investment Fund Managers Directive*

- the current risk profile of the AIF and the risk management tools employed by the AIFM to manage market risk, liquidity risk, counterparty risk and other risks including operational risk;
- the main categories of assets in which the AIF is invested, and
- the results of the periodic stress tests which the AIFM is required to perform under the Directive.

ESMA's Opinion

10.180 Alongside its Reporting Guidelines, on 1 October 2013, ESMA published an Opinion[1], 'Collection of information for the effective monitoring of systemic risk under Article 24(5), first sub-paragraph, of the AIFMD' (the 'Opinion'). In it, ESMA sets out details of information which is not required to be reported under AIFMD but which ESMA considers it would be desirable for all EU national competent authorities to require AIFMs to report, in order better to monitor systemic risk in the EU's financial markets.

[1] See esma.europa.eu/system/files/2013-esma-1340_opinion_on_collection_of_information_under_aifmd_for_publication.pdf.

10.181 Among other matters raised in the Opinion, ESMA notes that the Article 24(2) information covers only (i) EU AIFs or (ii) AIFs which are marketed in the EU. AIFMs are not required under AIFMD to report Article 24(2) information for non-EU AIFs if these are not marketed in the EU.

10.182 To ensure a comprehensive set of information is collected, ESMA recommends that EU national competent authorities should require AIFMs that manage a non-EU master AIF which is not marketed in the EU to report Article 24(2) information in respect of that master fund where one of its feeder AIFs is either an EU AIF or is marketed in the EU. However, ESMA's view is that this information need not be provided if the non-EU master AIFs and the feeder AIFs do not have the same AIFM.

10.183 Although the Opinion is not legally binding, a number of EU national competent authorities (though not all) have elected to comply with ESMA's recommendation. In the UK, the FCA originally decided not to require non-EU AIFMs to report information to the FCA in respect of the non-EU master AIF if only the feeder is marketed in the UK. However, in January 2017, the FCA confirmed that it would extend its rules to require master fund level reporting, with such rule changes coming into force on 29 June 2017.

Additional information requests

10.184 An AIFM must also provide, when requested to do so by its home regulator, the annual report of each EU AIF it manages and of each AIF it markets in the EU, as well as a detailed list of all AIFs it manages as at the end of each quarter.

10.185 The AIFM's home regulator may request additional information, not provided for in the Directive or Delegated Regulation, in order to carry out effective monitoring of systemic risk in the markets.

10.186 ESMA also has the power to request that the national competent authorities in member states impose additional reporting requirements upon AIFMs, but it may do so only 'in exceptional circumstances and where required in order to ensure the stability and integrity of the financial system, or to promote long-term sustainable growth'[1].

[1] Article 24(5) of AIFMD.

Information on leverage

10.187 Additional reporting requirements are applicable where the AIFM manages an AIF which employs leverage 'on a substantial basis'. Article 111 of the Delegated Regulation specifies that leverage will be considered to be employed 'on a substantial basis' when the AIF's exposure as calculated according to the commitment method exceeds three times its net asset value.

10.188 Where this is the case, the AIFM must make available to its home regulator:

- information about the overall level of leverage employed by each AIF it manages;
- a breakdown between leverage arising from borrowing of cash or securities and leverage embedded in financial derivatives; and
- the extent to which the AIF's assets have been re-used under leveraging arrangements.

Reporting frequency and timeframes

10.189 The Delegated Regulation and ESMA's Reporting Guidelines provide templates and timeframes for delivery of the information to the home member state national competent authorities.

10.190 Frequency of reporting will depend on the size and type of AIF which the AIFM manages, as follows:

Frequency of reporting	When the reporting frequency applies	In respect of which AIFs
Quarterly	Where the AIFM manages portfolios of AIFs whose total AUM exceeds €1 billion	Each EU AIF which the AIFM manages and each AIF which it markets into the EU
Quarterly	Where the AIFM manages portfolios of AIFs whose total AUM exceeds the threshold in Article 3(2) of AIFMD (see para **10.49** above) but does not exceed €1 billion	Each AIF whose AUM exceeds €500 million
Half-yearly	Where the AIFM manages portfolios of AIFs whose total AUM exceeds the threshold in Article 3(2) of AIFMD (see para **10.49** above) but does not exceed €1 billion	Each EU AIF which the AIFM manages and each AIF which it markets into the EU

10.190 *The Alternative Investment Fund Managers Directive*

Frequency of reporting	When the reporting frequency applies	In respect of which AIFs
Annually	Where the AIFM manages an unleveraged AIF, which invests in non-listed companies and issuers in order to acquire control	Each such unleveraged AIF

10.191 The information must be delivered no later than one month after the end of the relevant period, though this period may be extended by 15 days where the AIF is a fund of funds. There is provision in the Delegated Regulation for member states to require all or part of the reported information to be provided on a more frequent basis.

10.192 As far as timing of the first report is concerned, the ESMA Reporting Guidelines state that an AIFM should start reporting to its regulator as from the first day of the following quarter after the AIFM 'has information to report' (ie from the date of its authorisation, registration or notification), until the end of the first reporting period. Reporting periods end on the last day of March, June, September and December.

10.193 By way of example, an AIFM subject to a half-yearly reporting obligation and which is authorised on (and therefore has 'information to report' from) 15 February 2020, would start to report as from 1 April 2020 (the first day of the full quarter following the end of March) to 30 June 2020 (the last day of the first half-year period). Its next report would cover the period 1 July to 31 December 2020.

K   SERVICE PROVIDERS

10.194 In addition to the obligations which it imposes upon AIFMs, AIFMD also sets out rules in relation to a number of the typical service providers of an AIF.

Depositaries (Article 21 of AIFMD)

10.195 Given that one of the key drivers which led to AIFMD was perceived weakness in investor protection exposed by the financial crisis in the late 2000s (not least the losses suffered by investors through the collapse and subsequent insolvency of Lehman Brothers), it is little surprise that much attention in the Level 1 text and Delegated Regulation is devoted to the issue of safe-keeping the assets of investors.

10.196 By Article 21, AIFMD introduces the requirement that an AIFM must ensure that, for each AIF it manages, a single depositary is appointed to fulfil certain functions. (A lighter touch regime, generally termed 'depositary lite', applies in respect of EU AIFMs which market non-EU AIFs into the EU[1].)

[1] See paras 10.233–10.244 below.

10.197 The provisions under Article 21 of the Level 1 text and the associated Articles of the Delegated Regulation together set out a framework as to:

- who can act as a depositary and where it should be located;
- what duties a depositary must perform;
- how a depositary must act (and when, and to whom, it may delegate its functions); and
- what liability a depositary must assume.

Who can act as a depositary and where should it be located?

10.198 The depositary of an EU AIF must generally be located in the AIF's home member state[1] and must be:

- an 'EU bank' (ie a credit institution which has its registered office in the EU);
- a regulated investment firm authorised to provide safe-keeping and administration services and whose own funds are not less than €730,000; or
- another entity, provided that it is subject to prudential regulation and ongoing supervision and falls within a category of institutions authorised to act as a UCITS depositary.

[1] For a transitional period, until 22 July 2017, member states were permitted to relax the requirement that an EU AIF's depositary must be located in the AIF's home member state, provided that the institution appointed as a depositary is an EU bank.

10.199 Where the main business of an AIF is private equity or real estate investment and the AIF satisfies certain conditions (ie there are no redemption rights exercisable for five years from the date of initial investment), the AIFM may appoint as a depositary persons who carry out depositary activities as part of their professional activities, for example law firms, notaries or other authorised investment firms.

10.200 A prime broker cannot act as depositary to an AIF for which it also acts as counterparty, unless it has functionally and hierarchically separated the performance of its depositary functions from its prime brokerage tasks and potential conflicts of interest are properly identified, managed, monitored or disclosed to the AIF's investors.

What duties must a depositary perform?

10.201 AIFMD establishes that, in complying with the single depositary requirement, the AIFM must ensure a single depositary is appointed to carry out the three principal functions of:

- monitoring cash flows[1];
- safe-keeping of assets[2]; and
- oversight[3].

[1] Article 21(7) of AIFMD. See paras **10.202–10.203** below.
[2] Article 21(8) of AIFMD. See paras **10.204–10.208** below.
[3] Article 21(9) of AIFMD. See paras **10.209–10.212** below.

Monitoring cash flows

10.202 The depositary must ensure that, among other matters, cash flows are properly monitored, investor payments are received and that cash is properly booked to the correct accounts.

10.203 The depositary must also ensure that all cash of the AIF is properly booked to accounts opened in the name of the 'relevant account holder' (ie the AIF, the AIFM acting on behalf of the AIF or the depositary itself when acting on behalf of the AIF) with an entity that is either an EU bank or a bank or similar authorised third country entity.

Safe-keeping of assets

10.204 In respect of the safe-keeping function, AIFMD distinguishes between financial instruments which can be held in custody, and those which cannot – the latter include instruments, such as derivatives, interests in partnerships and investments in privately held companies, which can only be directly registered in the name of the AIF with the issuer itself, the registrar or other agent.

10.205 Financial instruments which belong to an AIF but which are subject to collateral arrangements must be treated as custody assets as the AIF (or the AIFM on behalf of the AIF) remains the legal owner of the instrument until such time as the security interest is exercised or, where there is a right of re-use, where that right has been exercised.

10.206 Financial instruments subject to title transfer collateral arrangements where the legal ownership in the financial instrument has been transferred from the AIF (or AIFM acting on behalf of the AIF) to the collateral taker will not be custody assets. Equally, as they are no longer the assets of the AIF (or the AIFM acting on behalf of the AIF), they will not be considered non-custody assets.

10.207 In broad terms, the safe-keeping function requires custody assets to be registered in a segregated account in the books of the safe-keeping entity in the name of the AIF or the AIFM acting on behalf of the AIF, so that they can be clearly identified as belonging to the AIF in accordance with the applicable law at all times.

10.208 ESMA's Opinion[1], 'Asset segregation and application of depositary delegation rules to CSDs', dated 20 July 2017, provides recommendations to the Commission, the Council and the European Parliament for possible clarification of the legislative provisions under both AIFMD and the UCITS Directive relating to the asset segregation requirements and the application of depositary delegation rules to central securities depositaries ('CSDs'). This follows two public consultations in which ESMA proposed a number of options (all of which received significant criticism from respondents), in particular, in respect of the practical application of the required segregation at the level of a delegated third party.

---

[1] See https://www.esma.europa.eu/sites/default/files/library/esma34-45-277_opinion_34_on_asset_segregation_and_custody_services.pdf.

OVERSIGHT

10.209 The depositary must maintain oversight of various functions, including those of:

- subscriptions and redemptions;
- valuation of shares or interests;
- carrying out of the AIFM's instructions;
- timely settlement of transactions; and
- the AIF's income distribution.

10.210 Alongside the specified components of the oversight role, the depositary is also expected, at the time of its appointment, to (i) assess the risks associated with the nature, scale and complexity of the AIF's strategy and the AIFM's organisation, and (ii) establish oversight procedures which are appropriate to the AIF and AIFM.

10.211 These oversight procedures must be regularly updated. Although the Delegated Regulation does not specify what 'regularly' means in this context, it is probably fair to assume at least annual updates.

10.212 In performing its oversight duties, the depositary should:

- ensure that an appropriate verification and reconciliation procedure exists which is implemented and applied and frequently reviewed;
- perform ex-post controls and verification of processes and procedures that are under the responsibility of the AIFM, the AIF or an appointed third party; and
- establish a clear and comprehensive escalation procedure to deal with situations where potential irregularities are detected in the course of its oversight duties.

How must a depositary act?

10.213 A depositary must act honestly, fairly, professionally, independently and in the interests of the AIF and the investors of the AIF.

10.214 To avoid conflicts of interest between the depositary, the AIFM and/or the AIF and/or its investors:

- an AIFM may not act as depositary; and
- a counterparty prime broker to an AIF cannot act as depositary to that AIF unless it has functionally and hierarchically separated the performance of its depositary functions from its prime brokerage tasks and potential conflicts of interest are properly identified, managed, monitored or disclosed to the AIF's investors.

10.215 Nor may a depositary carry out activities that give rise to conflicts of interest unless it has functionally and hierarchically separated the performance of its depositary tasks from those other tasks which potentially might give rise to a conflict of interest, and properly identified, managed, monitored and disclosed these conflicts to the investors of the AIF.

10.216 *The Alternative Investment Fund Managers Directive*

Delegation of the depositary function

RESTRICTIONS ON DELEGATION

10.216 AIFMD imposes a general prohibition on delegating the functions of monitoring of cash flows and oversight to a third party.

10.217 While a depositary may delegate safe-keeping duties to a third party, in order to do so it must fulfil a number of criteria, including that:

- the tasks are not delegated with the intention of avoiding the requirements of the Directive;
- the depositary must be able to demonstrate that there is an 'objective reason' for the delegation;
- the depositary must have exercised, and must continue to exercise, all due skill, care and diligence in when selecting and appointing the third party; and
- the depositary must ensure that the third party meets a number of conditions at all times during the performance of the tasks delegated to it.

10.218 The Delegated Regulation sets out in further detail what is expected of a depositary when selecting and appointing a third party. Robust policies and processes will be needed to effect and monitor a delegation in compliance with the Directive.

10.219 A third party delegate may, in turn, sub-delegate safe-keeping functions, subject to the same requirements.

10.220 Provided that it satisfies the delegation criteria (including the requirements around management of conflicts of interest), there is no prohibition against a depositary appointing a prime broker as sub-custodian.

10.221 Where local law requires custody assets to be held in custody by a local, non-EU, entity, but no local entity satisfies the delegation criteria relating to prudential regulation and supervision, the depositary may delegate its functions to a 'non-compliant' local entity provided that delegation is only to the extent required by the law of that third country and remains in place only for as long as there are no local entities that satisfy the delegation requirements, subject to the following requirements:

- the investors of the relevant AIF must be duly informed prior to their investment; and
- the AIF, or the AIFM on behalf of the AIF, must instruct the depositary to delegate custody of such financial instruments to the local entity.

DELEGATION DISCLOSURE REQUIREMENTS

10.222 An AIFM must disclose to an AIF's investors details of any delegation of the safe-keeping function by the depositary, including details of the delegate and any conflicts of interest that may arise from such delegation. Additional disclosure requirements are imposed where the depositary makes any arrangements pursuant to which the depositary contractually discharges itself of liability in accordance with AIFMD. There is, however, no obligation to identify delegates of a sub-custodian (ie sub-sub-custodians).

10.223 Since the disclosure must be made to the investors, it is likely that a high level disclosure would be made in the prospectus or other offering document. However, the AIFM may well choose to produce a separate disclosure document in relation to each AIF that it manages in order to provide investors with all of the disclosures required under the Directive, including those relating to delegation by the depositary.

Depositary liability

General provisions

10.224 AIFMD provides that the depositary will be liable to the AIF or to the investors of the AIF for the loss of custody assets by the depositary or by a third party delegate.

10.225 The Directive further sets out that a depositary must return assets of an 'identical type' or 'corresponding amount' to the AIF (or AIFM acting on behalf of the AIF) without undue delay.

10.226 A loss will be deemed to have occurred if:

- a stated right of ownership of the AIF is demonstrated not to be valid because it has either ceased to exist or never existed;
- the AIF has been definitively deprived of its right of ownership over the financial instrument (unless the instrument is substituted by, or converted into, another financial instrument); or
- the AIF is definitively unable, directly or indirectly, to dispose of the financial instrument.

10.227 The liability is, to all intents, strict – the only circumstance in which a depositary will not be liable is where it can prove that the loss has arisen 'as a result of an external event beyond its reasonable control, the consequences of which would been unavoidable despite all reasonable efforts to the contrary'[1].

[1] Article 21(12) of AIFMD.

10.228 AIFMD also provides that the depositary will be liable to the AIF or to the investors of the AIF for all other losses suffered by them as a result of the depositary's negligent or intentional failure properly to fulfil its obligations pursuant to the Directive.

10.229 As a general rule, a depositary's liability for other losses will not be affected by any delegation (where permitted) as the Directive does not permit a depositary to contract out of its liability.

Discharge of liability to a third party

10.230 Where a depositary has delegated the custody of financial instruments held in custody ('custody assets') to a third party, the depositary can discharge itself of its liability in respect of the loss of the custody assets if it can prove that each of the following conditions are met:

- the delegation criteria set out in para **10.217** above are satisfied;
- there is a written contract between the depositary and the third party that:
    - explicitly transfers the liability of the depositary to that third party; and
    - makes it possible for (i) the AIF (or the AIFM on behalf of the AIF) to make a claim against the third party in respect of the loss of financial instruments, or (ii) the depositary to make such a claim on the AIF's behalf; and
- there is a separate contract between the depositary and the AIF (or the AIFM on behalf of the AIF) which expressly allows a discharge of the depositary's liability and establishes an 'objective reason' for such a discharge.

Contractual arrangements and depositaries

10.231 The Delegated Regulation contemplates that a depositary contract may be entered into by the depositary on the one hand and the AIF and/or the AIFM on the other hand. It is an open question as to whether an AIFM will typically become a party to the contract – it is likely that AIFMs will argue that they should not as the Directive does not require them to be a party.

10.232 Whilst the Directive clearly sets out a number of measures that an AIFM will need to fulfil in its dealings with a depositary (for example, in relation to access to information), it is likely to be the case that these measures can be addressed in the relevant fund administration and investment management agreements.

Depositary lite (Article 36 of AIFMD)

10.233 For an EU AIFM managing a non-EU AIF which is marketed in the EU, Article 36 of AIFMD imposes a more limited set of depositary requirements (generally termed 'depositary lite').

10.234 The AIFM is required to ensure that the primary depositary functions of cash monitoring, safe-keeping and oversight are carried out[1]. However, the other rules contained within Article 21 of AIFMD, such as those relating to independence, segregation and liability, are expressly disapplied.

[1] See paras 10.201–10.212 above.

10.235 Whilst the Directive imposes an obligation upon the AIFM to ensure that depositary lite providers are appointed, in practice it is likely that it will be the AIF (or the AIFM on its behalf) which will make the appointment.

Who can provide depositary lite services?

10.236 The Directive does not set out specific eligibility criteria as to what type of entity can provide depositary lite services other than to state that the AIFM may not perform these functions itself.

10.237 A key feature of the Directive that distinguishes the depositary lite regime from the single depositary regime pursuant to Article 21 is that the AIFM may appoint more than one entity to fulfil the different depositary lite functions.

10.238 Notwithstanding the absence of eligibility criteria, an element of regulatory oversight exists, as Article 36 of AIFMD sets out that an AIFM must provide its home regulator with the identity of the entity/entities providing the depositary lite functions.

Liability and ability to delegate

10.239 Whilst the Directive's provisions relating to delegation by, and liability of, the depositary[1] have caused significant concern within the industry, these do not apply to the depositary lite regime.

[1] See paras **10.216–10.230** above.

10.240 As such, a depositary lite provider will be able to delegate tasks it has agreed to perform under an AIF's services agreement to affiliates and third parties without being constrained by the Directive.

10.241 Equally, a depositary lite provider may limit its liability contractually without any constraints being imposed by the Directive and, as such, will be free to negotiate with the AIF as to the extent of its liability.

Conflicts of interest

10.242 It is clear that an entity which both acts as a fund administrator and carries out the general oversight function will be exposed to significant conflicts of interest: for example, in the context of overseeing the subscription and redemption process that it is administering, or in respect of the valuation process that it undertakes in relation to the assets of the AIF.

10.243 AIFMD does not prescribe how a depositary lite provider should manage its conflicts of interest; however, clearly, robust Chinese walls within a single entity in respect of the general oversight function are likely to be necessary in order to manage any conflicts that might arise.

10.244 Whilst the Directive does not mandate functional and hierarchical separation between an entity which is both acting as a fund administrator and performing depositary lite services for the same AIF, having a separate legal entity within a group performing, at the very least, the oversight duties required by the depositary lite regime may be the most appropriate way to manage these types of conflicts of interest.

Delegation (Article 20 of AIFMD)

Duty to notify regulator and comply with certain conditions

10.245 Any delegation by an AIFM of any of its functions must be notified to the AIFM's home regulator before the delegation arrangements become effective.

10.246 Any delegation must comply with certain conditions, including a requirement that the AIFM must be able to justify the delegation with objective reasons. These include[1]:

- optimising business functions and processes;
- cost saving;
- the delegate's expertise in administration or in specific markets or investments; and
- access of the delegate to global trading capabilities.

[1] Article 76 of the Delegated Regulation.

10.247 The delegation agreement must also contain certain specified provisions.

To whom can an AIFM delegate?

10.248 Where delegation is of portfolio or risk management, the third party to whom this function is delegated must itself be authorised or registered for the purpose of asset management and subject to supervision[1]. Where this condition cannot be satisfied, prior approval of the delegation must be obtained from the AIFM's home regulator.

[1] Article 20(1)(c) of AIFMD.

10.249 Delegation of portfolio or risk management without such prior approval may therefore only be made to:

- UCITS management companies;
- investment firms authorised under MiFID to perform portfolio management services;
- credit institutions authorised under the Capital Requirements Directive[1] and authorised under MiFID to perform portfolio management;
- external AIFMs authorised under AIFMD; or
- third country entities authorised or registered to perform asset management and supervised by a national competent authority in their home country.

[1] Directive 2013/36/EU of 26 June 2013.

Non-EU delegates

10.250 Where the delegate is domiciled outside the EU, AIFMD requires that a written arrangement must exist between the AIFM's home regulator and the supervisory authorities of the third country in which the delegate is domiciled. The agreement must allow the AIFM's home regulator to request information, access documents, carry out inspections and, in the event of a breach, obtain immediate information from the relevant third country supervisory authority and co-operate in enforcement.

10.251 Reference should also be made to ESMA's Opinion on supervisory convergence following Brexit[1] (at which point the UK will presumably become a non-EU jurisdiction) and its subsequent sectoral Opinion on investment management, in which ESMA sets out its views on, among other matters, the ability of a UK authorised firm to seek authorisation, post-Brexit, in an EU member state and delegate functions back to an operation which is within the UK. While many in industry regard ESMA's stance as being somewhat hard line, others will regard ESMA as drawing a line in the sand to avoid a regulatory 'race to the bottom' as remaining member states potentially lower their requirements in order to attract UK firms that wish to relocate from the UK, thereby threatening to harm investor protection and the orderly functioning and financial stability of Europe's markets.

[1] See para 10.10 above.

Effective supervision

10.252 The delegation must not prevent the effectiveness of supervision of the AIFM, or prevent the AIFM acting and the relevant AIF being managed in the best interests of the AIF investors. An AIFM seeking to delegate must be able to demonstrate that the delegate is qualified and capable and has been selected with due care. The AIFM should review the services provided by each delegate on an ongoing basis.

Letter box entity

10.253 An AIFM may not, however, delegate its functions in respect of an AIF to the extent that it becomes a 'letter box entity' and can no longer be considered to be the manager of that AIF.

10.254 Article 82 of the Delegated Regulation provides guidance as to when an AIFM will be deemed a letter box entity[1]. This will be the case if the AIFM:

- no longer retains the necessary expertise and resources to supervise the delegated tasks and manage the risks associated with the delegation;
- no longer has the power to take decisions in key areas which fall under the responsibility of senior management and implement the investment policy and strategy;
- loses its contractual rights to inquire, inspect, have access or to give instructions to its delegates; or
- delegates the performance of investment management functions to such an extent that exceeds by a substantial margin the investment management functions performed by the AIFM itself.

[1] Guidance on the FCA's interpretation of when an AIFM is, and when it is not, a letter box entity can be found at Q.3.13 in PERG 16.3.

Giving instructions and withdrawal of delegation

10.255 The AIFM must also be able to monitor the delegated activity, to give further instructions to a delegate at any time and to withdraw the delegation with immediate effect when this is in the interests of investors.

10.256 *The Alternative Investment Fund Managers Directive*

Sub-delegation

10.256 A delegate may sub-delegate any of the functions delegated to it provided that:

- the AIFM consents to the sub-delegation;
- the AIFM notifies the relevant authorities of the sub-delegation; and
- the sub-delegate satisfies the conditions of delegation applicable to the AIFM.

10.257 Note that delegation may not be conferred on the depositary or a delegate of the depositary or on any other entity whose interest may conflict with those of the AIFM or the AIF investors.

Remuneration and delegates

10.258 Where delegation to a third party is of portfolio or risk management, ESMA's Remuneration Guidelines state that the delegate should be subject to:

- regulatory requirements on remuneration which are equally effective as the guidelines applicable to AIFMs; or
- appropriate contractual arrangements to avoid circumvention of the remuneration rules.

Delegation and liability of the AIFM

10.259 An AIFM's liability towards the AIF and its investors is not affected by the fact that the AIFM has delegated functions to a third party, or by any further sub-delegation.

10.260 In the November 2016 update of its Q&As on the application of AIFMD[1], ESMA indicated that where a third party, rather than the AIFM itself, performed any of the functions set out in points 1 or 2 of Annex I of the Directive, the AIFM is not released from its responsibility to ensure compliance of the relevant function(s) with AIFMD. In ESMA's view, where the third party performs such a function, this should be considered as having been delegated by the AIFM to the third party, leaving the AIFM still responsible for ensuring compliance with the delegation requirements under Article 20 of AIFMD and the principle in Article 5(1) (ie the single AIFM appointed for an AIF is responsible for ensuring compliance with AIFMD).

[1] See para 10.9 above.

10.261 This reading, however, seems at odds with the Level 1 text, Annex I, point 2 of which refers to 'other functions that AIFMD *may* additionally perform in the course of the collective management of AIF' (emphasis added). By way of example, following the logic of the ESMA Q&As, the appointment by any AIF of an administrator, where the AIFM was an EU AIFM, would need to be restructured such that the administrator is appointed by the AIFM.

10.262 The discussion at ESMA which led to agreement of the revised Q&As has been described as 'heated' and the vote was split, significantly between the jurisdictions which are commonly regarded as being 'fund friendly' and the other member states. The Q&As themselves are not legally binding and it remains to be seen which of the member states will follow them.

L CONCLUSION AND NEXT STEPS

10.263 AIFMD was the product of lengthy gestation – the Commission's original proposal for a Directive was published in April 2009 while the negotiations between the European Parliament and the Council, which developed the proposal into the final agreed Level 1 text, were concluded in November 2010. The Directive was not published in the Official Journal until 1 July 2011, which in turn established its implementation date as 22 July 2013, with provision for member states to allow a further one-year transitional period.

10.264 From proposal to final implementation, therefore, was over five years. Even so, a number of aspects of the Directive and its interpretation remain unclear and/or incomplete.

10.265 While it is beyond doubt that the Directive has had a fundamental impact on the way in which AIFMs do business in the EU, it is still uncertain, as the new regime beds down, exactly what the consequences of these changes will be, not least (given that introducing many of the changes involves a cost to the AIFM) when it comes to what returns investors will receive.

10.266 The key legislation and guidance is, however, finally in place and the Directive is in force.

10.267 Article 69 of AIFMD required the Commission to have started a review on the application and scope of the Directive by 22 July 2017. Tender documents were invited[1] for conducting a backward-looking analysis as to the extent to which the objectives of AIFMD have been achieved. This analysis is expected to take one year, following which the Commission will presumably publish a formal report.

[1] See https://etendering.ted.europa.eu/cft/cft-display.html?cftId=2214.

10.268 It remains to be seen how (or, indeed, whether) the work by ESMA and the Commission on extending the passport regime to non-EU AIFMs and to non-EU AIFs being marketed by EU AIFMs will be pursued. Although the availability of the passport will not spell the immediate end of the NPPR route, it would represent an important step on the path to a single regulatory framework covering all AIFMs with a connection to EU investors. Nevertheless, NPPRs will be able to continue to exist for the time being at least (unless individual member states elect to switch them off beforehand) while limiting distribution activities to reverse enquiries will remain outside the scope of AIFMD marketing in any event.

10.269 In addition, the implications of the UK's decision to leave the EU, particularly in the asset management sector, are likely to be wide ranging for both the UK and the remaining member states. It remains to be seen what impact this will have on the Commission's view of how the alternative investment management regime in the EU should develop in the longer term.

Chapter 11

THE US DIMENSION

Patricia A Poglinco, Partner, Seward & Kissel LLP and Robert B Van Grover, Partner, Seward & Kissel LLP

A	Introduction	11.1
B	Securities (SEC) regulation	11.5
C	Commodities (CFTC) regulation	11.46
D	US marketing of hedge fund interests	11.92
E	Other US issues affecting hedge fund managers	11.113

A INTRODUCTION

11.1 There is no harmonised source of the US financial services laws regulating the activities of hedge funds and their managers. Rather, the US financial services laws have arisen over time from a mosaic of disparate federal and state legislation with a range of sometimes competing regulators. For hedge fund purposes, the most important of these laws are the various securities laws, including the Securities Act of 1933, as amended (the 'Securities Act'), the Securities Exchange Act of 1934, as amended (the 'Exchange Act'), the Investment Company Act of 1940, as amended (the '1940 Act') and the Investment Advisers Act of 1940, as amended (the 'Advisers Act'), which are administered by the Securities and Exchange Commission (the 'SEC'). Other important laws include the commodities laws (the Commodity Exchange Act of 1936, as amended (the 'CEA')), which are administered by the Commodity Futures Trading Commission (the 'CFTC'), and the Employee Retirement Income Security Act of 1974, as amended ('ERISA'), which is administered by the Department of Labor (the 'DOL').

11.2 In the US, the 'regulation' of hedge funds is primarily concerned with compliance with exemptions from regulations that would otherwise require registration as a retail fund or as a public offering of securities.

11.3 This chapter provides an overview of the US securities and commodities laws and regulations (and the exemptions and exceptions from them) potentially applicable to hedge funds and their managers, and of certain other US laws and issues commonly encountered by them.

11.4 The following table lists the principal US financial services statutes and laws referred to in this chapter and notes certain aspects of their potential relevance to hedge funds and hedge fund managers:

11.4 The US Dimension

US law	Regulator	Fund investments	Relevant activities
Securities Act of 1933	SEC	Any	Marketing/distribution
Securities Exchange Act of 1934	SEC	Any	Marketing/distribution
Investment Company Act of 1940	SEC	Securities	Marketing/distribution
Investment Advisers Act of 1940	SEC	Securities	Investment management
Commodity Exchange Act of 1936	CFTC	'Commodity' interests	Marketing/distribution and investment management
Employee Retirement Income Security Act of 1974	DOL	Any	Investment management
State 'blue sky' laws	US states	Any	Marketing/distribution

B   SECURITIES (SEC) REGULATION

11.5 The SEC administers four main US securities Acts which are potentially relevant to hedge funds and their managers:

- the Securities Act, which regulates public offers of 'securities'[1] generally (including interests in hedge funds) and the issuers of such securities;
- the Exchange Act, which establishes a regulatory regime for secondary market trading in 'securities' and brokers, dealers and exchanges trading securities;
- the 1940 Act, which regulates publicly offered collective investment vehicles investing in securities and provides exceptions for privately offered collective investment vehicles; and
- the Advisers Act, which regulates persons engaged in the business of providing investment advice (including discretionary management) about securities.

[1] The definition of 'securities' in the US securities laws is broad. For example, section 2(a)(1) of the Securities Act (15 United States Code ('USC') § 77b(a)(1)) defines 'security' to include the following:

'any note, stock, treasury stock, security future, security-based swap, bond, debenture, evidence of indebtedness, certificate of interest or participation in any profit-sharing agreement, collateral-trust certificate, preorganization certificate or subscription, transferable share, investment contract, voting-trust certificate, certificate of deposit for a security, fractional undivided interest in oil, gas, or other mineral rights, any put, call, straddle, option, or privilege on any security, certificate of deposit, or group or index of securities (including any interest therein or based on the value thereof), or any put, call, straddle, option, or privilege entered into on a national securities exchange relating to foreign currency, or, in general, any interest or instrument commonly known as a 'security', or any certificate of interest or participation in, temporary or interim certificate for, receipt for, guarantee of, or warrant or right to subscribe to or purchase, any of the foregoing.'

11.6 Of these, the 1940 Act and the Advisers Act, and the exceptions and exemptions from them, are perhaps the most important for hedge funds principally trading securities and the managers of such funds, and will be addressed in the sections immediately below. The Securities Act and the Exchange Act are relevant to hedge funds and their managers in marketing fund interests in the US or, in certain circumstances, to US persons abroad, regardless of whether the fund concerned trades principally securities or commodities, and will be addressed separately further below[1].

[1] See paras **11.92–11.112** below.

Fund regulation – exceptions from the 1940 Act

11.7 Section 7 of the 1940 Act makes it illegal for a US 'investment company' (or, if the investment company does not have a board, its depositor, trustee or underwriter) to offer, sell or redeem its own securities or to buy or sell securities for its own portfolio, unless that investment company is registered with the SEC under section 8 of the 1940 Act[1]. The 1940 Act's definition of 'investment company'[2] includes (in part):

> 'any issuer which:
> (A) is or holds itself out as being engaged primarily, or proposes to engage primarily, in the business of investing, reinvesting, or trading in securities; or
> . . .
> (C) is engaged or proposes to engage in the business of investing, reinvesting, owning, holding, or trading in securities, and owns or proposes to acquire investment securities having a value exceeding 40 per centum of the value of such issuer's total assets (exclusive of Government securities and cash items) on an unconsolidated basis.'

[1] 1940 Act § 7(a) and (b), 15 USC § 80a-7(a) and (b).
[2] 1940 Act § 3(a)(1), 15 USC § 80-3(a)(1).

11.8 Consequently, since a securities nexus is a requirement for regulation under the 1940 Act, the term 'investment company' does not cover operators of pure commodity pools, which are regulated by the CFTC.

11.9 In a 1983 no-action letter, the SEC staff set forth the 'primary business engagement' test for determining whether a commodity pool would be deemed an 'investment company' under the 1940 Act. In *Peavey*[1], the SEC staff took the position that a pool that would otherwise be deemed an 'investment company' under the 1940 Act will be excepted from the definition of 'investment company' if the pool is primarily engaged in investing in futures and options on futures. To make this determination, the staff considered, among other factors, the composition of the pool's assets, the sources of the pool's income and the pool's expected gains or losses from futures trading compared to other activities.

[1] *Peavey Commodity Futures Fund*, SEC Staff No-Action Letter (2 June 1983).

11.10 For further discussion on the regulation of commodity pools and their advisers, see paras **11.46–11.91** below.

11.11 The 1940 Act also makes it illegal for a non-US investment company and its depositor, trustees and underwriters to make any direct or indirect US public offering unless that investment company is registered with the SEC[1]. As a practical matter, however, the SEC will not allow non-US funds to register under the 1940 Act. Therefore, all non-US funds must rely on an exception

11.11 *The US Dimension*

from registration.

[1] 1940 Act § 7(d), 15 USC § 80a-7(d).

11.12 The 1940 Act contains various exceptions from the definition of 'investment company', two of which exempt certain 'private' investment companies and are regularly relied on by both US and non-US hedge funds to avoid the 1940 Act's registration requirements.

11.13 The *section 3(c)(1) exception* requires that:

- the fund must not make or propose to make a public offering of its securities in the US (essentially imposing the 'accredited investor' requirements under Regulation D[1]); and
- the outstanding securities of the fund must not be beneficially owned by more than 100 persons[2] – in counting US persons, the fund must 'look through' to the beneficial owners of any investing entity which owns 10% or more of the voting securities of the fund and which is itself a US registered investment company or an exempt private investment company (for example, a fund of funds).

[1] Discussed at para **11.94** below.
[2] For section 3(c)(1) counting purposes, non-US private funds need only count beneficial owners that are resident in the US. See *Touche, Remnant & Co*, SEC Staff No-Action Letter (27 July 1984). An investor's US residence is assessed at the time of investment, and the section 3(c)(1) exception is not affected by a non-US investor's subsequent relocation to the US. See *Investment Funds Institute of Canada*, SEC Staff No-Action Letter (4 March 1996). A US private fund relying on section 3(c)(1) is required to count all beneficial owners.

11.14 The *section 3(c)(7) exception* requires that:

- the fund must not make or propose to make a public offering of its securities in the US; and
- the beneficial owners of the fund[1] must be limited exclusively to persons who, at the time of their investment, are 'qualified purchasers' which include (i) natural persons who own at least US$5 million in 'investments'[2], which is limited to assets that are held for investment purposes only, (ii) certain family companies which own at least US$5 million in investments, (iii) other persons that, in the aggregate, own and invest on a discretionary basis at least US$25 million in investments, and (iv) trusts where each trustee and settlor is a qualified purchaser within (i), (ii) or (iii).

[1] For section 3(c)(7) purposes, only investors in a non-US fund that are 'US persons' (defined, in general, as that term is used in SEC Rule 902 of Regulation S under the Securities Act (17 Code of Federal Regulations ('CFR') § 230.902)) are required to be qualified purchasers. See *Goodwin, Proctor & Hoar LLP*, SEC Staff No-Action Letter (28 February 1997). All investors in a US private fund relying on section 3(c)(7) are required to be qualified purchasers.
[2] For purposes of defining 'qualified purchaser' under 3(c)(7), the definition of 'investments' includes (i) securities (except controlling interests) as discussed in footnote 1 in para **11.5** above and (ii) when held for investment purposes, real estate, commodity interests, physical commodities, financial contracts, unfunded capital commitments and cash or cash equivalents (1940 Act Rule 2a51-1, 17 CFR § 270.2a51-1).

11.15 There is a further exclusion available under both section 3(c)(1) (for the purposes of counting beneficial owners) and section 3(c)(7) (for the purposes of determining whether beneficial ownership is limited exclusively to qualified purchasers) for 'knowledgeable employees' of the fund or its investment manager and for companies owned exclusively by such knowledgeable employees[1]. The term 'knowledgeable employee' includes executive officers (ie the president, any vice president in charge of a principal business unit, division or function (such as sales, administration or finance), or any other person who performs similar policy-making functions), directors, trustees, general partners and advisory board members of the fund or its investment manager and certain other employees[2] whose regular duties for at least 12 months have included participation in investment activities[3].

[1] 1940 Act Rule 3c-5(b), 17 CFR § 270.3c-5(b).
[2] The SEC staff has indicated that a facts and circumstances approach should be used in determining whether an individual may qualify as a knowledgeable employee for the purposes of Rule 3c-5, and recommends that investment advisers both maintain a written record of those employees permitted to invest as knowledgeable employees and be able to explain the basis in the rule pursuant to which the employee qualifies as a knowledgeable employee. See Response of the Investment Adviser Regulation Office and Chief Counsel's Office, Division of Investment Management (6 February 2014).
[3] 1940 Act Rule 3c-5(a)(4), 17 CFR § 270.3c-5(a)(4).

11.16 No SEC filing is required for either the section 3(c)(1) exception or the section 3(c)(7) exception.

11.17 Because a hedge fund's acceptance of one or more non-qualified purchaser US investors permitted under the section 3(c)(1) exception will prevent the fund from relying on the section 3(c)(7) exception, a hedge fund will need to determine prior to offering its securities to US investors whether it will seek to rely on section 3(c)(1) or section 3(c)(7) and to build the relevant requirements into its offering documents.

11.18 Notwithstanding section 3(c)(7)'s qualified purchaser restriction, most hedge funds find this exception preferable because it (i) allows a greater number of US investors and (ii) does not have section 3(c)(1)'s look-through provisions. However, an entity formed for the purpose of making an investment in a 3(c)(7) fund must be owned exclusively by qualified purchasers.

Investment adviser regulation

11.19 Section 203(a) of the Advisers Act makes it illegal, subject to certain exemptions, for an investment adviser to 'make use of the mails or any means or instrumentality of interstate commerce'[1] unless registered with the SEC. The term 'investment adviser' is defined to include 'any person who, for compensation, engages in the business of advising others, either directly or through publications or writings, as to the value of securities or as to the advisability of investing in, purchasing, or selling securities . . . '[2].

[1] The reference to 'interstate commerce' derives from the Commerce Clause of the US Constitution: 'The Congress shall have power . . . To regulate commerce with foreign nations, and among the several states' (US Constitution, Article I, § 8, cl 3).
[2] Advisers Act § 202(a)(11), 15 USC § 80b-2(a)(11).

11.20 *The US Dimension*

11.20 'Advice' is the primary regulatory focus of the Advisers Act rather than the exercise of discretionary management authority over a portfolio used to implement that advice.

11.21 Whilst the Advisers Act registration requirement is subject to a wide range of exemptions, the passage of the Dodd-Frank Wall Street Reform and Consumer Protection Act (the 'Dodd-Frank Act') eliminated the so-called 'de minimis exemption', which had provided that no SEC registration was required for an investment adviser which: (1) had fewer than 15 clients in the preceding 12 months, (2) did not act as investment adviser to any SEC-registered investment company and (3) did not hold itself out to the general public as an investment adviser[1]. Notwithstanding the elimination of this exemption, there are several exemptions to registration available to private fund advisers. Registered advisers and exempt reporting advisers (as described below) are subject to routine SEC examinations.

[1] Advisers Act § 203(b)(3), 15 USC § 80b-3(b)(3).

Private fund adviser exemptions

11.22 In 2011, pursuant to the Dodd-Frank Act, the SEC established a set of exemptions from SEC registration known as the 'private fund adviser' exemptions:

- *US private fund advisers*: An adviser with its principal office and place of business in the US is exempt from SEC registration if the adviser: (i) acts solely as an investment adviser to one or more 'qualifying private funds'[1]; and (ii) manages private fund assets[2] of less than US$150 million. An adviser who advises managed accounts is precluded from relying on this exemption.
- *Non-US private fund advisers*: An adviser with its principal office and place of business outside the US is exempt from SEC registration if: (i) the adviser has no client that is a US person except for one or more qualifying private funds; and (ii) all assets managed by the adviser from a place of business in the US are solely attributable to private fund assets and are less than US$150 million.

[1] 'Qualifying private fund' means any private fund that is not registered under section 8 of the Investment Company Act and has not elected to be treated as a business development company under the Investment Company Act. 3(c)(1) and 3(c)(7) funds are qualifying private funds.
[2] 'Private fund assets' mean the investment adviser's assets under management attributable to qualifying private funds. In determining whether the relevant monetary thresholds discussed in this paragraph are met, advisers must calculate 'Regulatory AUM', in accordance with Item 5.F of Form ADV Part 1A. As a general matter, 'Regulatory AUM' is equal to gross assets under management.

Foreign private adviser exemption

11.23 A non-US private adviser, which is defined in section 202(a)(30) of the Advisers Act, is exempt from SEC registration if: (i) it has no place of business in the US; (ii) it has, in total, fewer than 15 clients in the US and investors in the US in private funds advised by it; (iii) it has less than US$25 million in

Securities (SEC) regulation 11.25

aggregate in assets under management[1] attributable to such clients and investors; and (iv) it does not hold itself out generally to the public in the US as an investment adviser.

[1] In determining whether the relevant monetary thresholds discussed in this paragraph are met, advisers must calculate 'Regulatory AUM'.

Venture capital fund adviser exemption

11.24 An adviser (US or non-US) is exempt from SEC registration if it advises solely one or more venture capital funds. A venture capital fund means a private fund that: (i) holds no more than 20% of the fund's capital commitments in non-qualifying investments[1] (other than short-term holdings); (ii) does not borrow or otherwise incur leverage (other than short-term borrowing); (iii) does not offer its investors redemption or other similar liquidity rights except in extraordinary circumstances; (iv) represents itself as pursuing a venture capital strategy to investors and prospective investors; and (v) is not registered under the 1940 Act and has not elected to be treated as a business development company[2].

[1] 'Qualifying investments' generally consist of any equity security issued by a 'qualifying portfolio company' that is directly acquired by a qualifying fund and certain equity securities exchanged directly for the directly acquired securities. A 'qualifying portfolio company' is defined as any company that: (i) at the time of investment, is not a reporting or foreign traded company and does not have a control relationship with a reporting or foreign traded company; (ii) does not incur leverage in connection with the investment by the private fund and distribute the proceeds of any such borrowing to the private fund in exchange for the private fund investment; and (iii) is not itself a private fund or pooled investment vehicle.

[2] The SEC adopted a 'grandfathering provision' in the definition of a venture capital fund for any private fund that: (i) represented to investors and potential investors at the time the fund offered its securities that it pursues a venture capital strategy; (ii) has sold securities to one or more third party investors prior to 31 December 2010; and (iii) has not sold any securities to, including accepting any additional capital commitments from, any person after 21 July 2011.

Reporting obligations of exempt reporting advisers

11.25 Advisers who are relying on the private fund adviser exemption or the venture capital fund adviser exemption (collectively, 'exempt reporting advisers') are required to complete the following parts of and file with the SEC Form ADV Part 1A (and the corresponding sections of Schedules A, B, C and D thereto):

- Item 1 – Identifying information.
- Item 2.B – Qualification as an exempt reporting adviser.
- Item 3 – Form of organisation.
- Item 6 – Other business activities.
- Item 7 – Financial industry affiliations and private fund reporting.
  An exempt reporting adviser must provide detailed information about each private fund that it advises, such as organisational, operational and investment characteristics (including gross asset value), non-identifying information about beneficial owners, the identity of the general partner and directors, and certain information about service providers.

11.25 *The US Dimension*

- Item 10 – Control persons.
- Item 11 – Disciplinary information.

11.26 An exempt reporting adviser is required to amend its reports on Form ADV at least annually, within 90 days of its fiscal year-end, and more frequently if required by the instructions to Form ADV. For example, an exempt reporting adviser is required promptly to update Item 1 (Identifying information), Item 3 (Form of organisation), and Item 11 (Disciplinary information) if any such item becomes inaccurate in any way, and promptly to update Item 10 (Control persons) if it becomes materially inaccurate.

11.27 An exempt reporting adviser is required to provide its clients with an annual privacy notice describing the adviser's policies regarding its disclosure of clients' non-public personal information[1]. The annual notice must be provided at least once in any period of 12 consecutive months. The privacy notice must disclose the types of information the adviser collects and shares with others and the procedures the adviser has implemented to safeguard that information. If an adviser discloses non-public personal information about its clients to third parties (other than to affiliates and certain service providers), the adviser must also provide an 'opt-out' notice, giving the client the opportunity to request that the adviser not disclose the information to such third parties.

[1] Exempt reporting advisers are also subject to other requirements, which include a rule which imposes limitations on an adviser and its covered persons who make impermissible political donations (the 'pay-to-play rules').

Becoming SEC registered as an investment adviser

11.28 Where no exemption is available, assets under management and the thresholds of an SEC registration have been met, the hedge fund manager will need to register with the SEC as an investment adviser. An investment adviser registers with the SEC by completing Parts 1A and 2A of Form ADV and filing them (and any subsequent amendments) with the SEC electronically via the internet using the Investment Adviser Registration Depository ('IARD') system which is managed by the Financial Industry Regulatory Authority, Inc ('FINRA')[1]. Further, a registered investment adviser must complete and deliver Parts 2A and 2B of Form ADV to its advisory clients.

[1] See para **11.124** below.

11.29 The information required in Part 1A of Form ADV, which the SEC uses to inform its registration determination and to manage its regulatory and examination programs, includes:

- information regarding the basic organisational, operational and investment characteristics of each private fund advised by the investment adviser, including the fund's gross asset value, information about its beneficial owners, required minimum investment amounts, and identification of certain of its service providers (such as the prime broker, custodian, administrator, auditor and marketer (if any));
- identification of the firm's control persons (this requirement includes both owners and officers of the firm) and advisory affiliates[1]; and

Securities (SEC) regulation **11.34**

- disclosure of any regulatory enforcement actions and certain other litigation involving the firm, its controllers or its advisory affiliates.

[1] A firm's advisory affiliates include: (i) all of the firm's officers, partners or directors; (ii) all persons directly or indirectly controlling or controlled by the firm; and (iii) all of the firm's current employees (other than employees performing only clerical, administrative, support or similar functions).

11.30 The information required in Part 2A of Form ADV (the 'Brochure') includes a description of the adviser's advisory business, how it is compensated, its methods of analysis, investment strategies, and the risk of loss associated with an investment. Further, the Brochure includes disclosure of certain disciplinary events which have occurred in the preceding ten years, the adviser's code of ethics, and the factors considered in selecting or recommending broker-dealers.

11.31 The information required in Part 2B of Form ADV (the 'Brochure Supplement') includes the educational background, business experience and disciplinary history of certain specific individuals who provide advisory services to the adviser's clients in addition to the other business activities and additional compensation of such individuals.

11.32 In addition to any interim required amendments, each registered investment adviser must update its Form ADV within 90 days of its fiscal year-end. Each registered investment adviser must also file all amendments to the Brochure through IARD. Annually, no later than 120 days after the end of its fiscal year, a registered investment adviser must deliver the Brochure (or provide a summary of material changes to the Brochure with an offer to provide the Brochure) to its advisory clients. Whilst the Brochure Supplement is not required to be filed electronically, a registered investment adviser must complete and deliver the Brochure Supplement to its advisory clients.

11.33 The initial registration and annual updating amendment fees for filing Part 1A of Form ADV vary by the amount of assets under management by the investment manager[1].

[1] See IARD firm system processing fees, available at http://www.iard.com/fee_schedule.asp.

11.34 The SEC has 45 days after receipt of Form ADV to declare the registration effective[1]. This may be delayed, however, if the SEC requires additional information to process the application for registration, or institutes an administrative proceeding to determine whether registration should be denied. An adviser can check the status of its registration through IARD, and the SEC will send the adviser an order declaring the registration effective once SEC registration has been granted.

[1] Under the Advisers Act, the SEC must within 45 days after filing of a registration application – or within such longer period as to which the applicant consents – either: (a) grant the application; or (b) institute proceedings to determine whether registration should be denied. See Advisers Act § 203(c)(2), 15 USC § 80b-3(c)(2).

11.35 The US Dimension

Ongoing compliance – non-US SEC-registered investment advisers

11.35 In a series of no-action letters[1], the SEC staff established the principle that, subject to certain conditions, a non-US SEC-registered investment adviser may structure its business so that it is only required to apply the substantive provisions of the Advisers Act with respect to its US clients, and need not apply these requirements to its non-US clients[2]. Since it was first introduced, the SEC staff has consistently reaffirmed this principle.

[1] A no-action letter is formal guidance given by the SEC staff to particular persons to the effect that the SEC staff will not recommend enforcement action against those persons on the facts and circumstances set out in the letter. The legal interpretive positions taken by the SEC staff in a no-action letter are technically only binding on the SEC staff in respect of potential enforcement action against the persons to which it is addressed. However, the SEC often publishes no-action letters, effectively making them public guidance. These published no-action letters are therefore widely relied on by other persons in interpreting the securities laws and the SEC rules.
[2] See, for example, *Uniao de Bancos de Brasileiros SA*, SEC Staff No-Action Letter (28 July 1992).

11.36 A non-US SEC-registered adviser will be subject to the Advisers Act's general anti-fraud provisions with respect to its non-US clients as set forth in section 206 of the Advisers Act. Accordingly, even in respect of its non-US clients, a non-US SEC-registered investment adviser is prohibited from making any misstatement or misleading omissions of material facts and other fraudulent acts and practices in connection with the conduct of an investment advisory business.

11.37 Each registered adviser is required to (i) appoint a chief compliance officer, (ii) implement compliance policies and procedures designed to prevent the violation of the Advisers Act by the adviser and its supervised persons, including addressing portfolio management processes, trading practices, proprietary and personal trading, disclosures to investors, safeguarding of client assets, creation and maintenance of records, valuation of securities, protection of client information and business continuity plans, and (iii) perform an annual review of its compliance policies and procedures. The annual review must assess the adequacy of the compliance policies and procedures and the effectiveness of their implementation. The SEC has indicated that, in conducting its annual review, a registered adviser should consider any compliance matters that arose during the previous year, any changes in the business activities of the adviser or its affiliates, and any changes in the Advisers Act or applicable regulations that may suggest a need to revise the adviser's policies and procedures. In determining the adequacy of an annual review, the SEC has indicated that it will consider a number of factors, including the person(s) conducting the review, the scope and duration of the review, and the adviser's findings and recommendations resulting from the review.

11.38 A registered adviser that has or is deemed to have custody of a private investment fund client's assets may satisfy its obligations under the custody rule by providing audited financial statements of the fund to investors in the private investment fund within 120 days (180 days for funds of funds) after the end of the pool's fiscal year. The financial statements must be prepared in accordance with US generally accepted accounting principles ('GAAP')[1] by an independent public accountant registered with, and subject to regular inspection by, the Public Company Accounting Oversight Board. A registered adviser that has or is deemed to have custody of client funds and securities must engage an independent public accountant to verify by actual examination (surprise exam) at least once each calendar year such client accounts; provided, however, that if such client accounts are private funds that provide investors with audited financial statements (in accordance with the discussion above), the adviser does not have to comply with the surprise exam requirement.

[1] With respect to non-US SEC-registered advisers, the financial statements can be prepared in accordance with International Accounting Standards, provided that the financial statements contain a footnote reconciling any material variations between the accounting standard used and GAAP.

11.39 A registered adviser with at least US$150 million in regulatory assets under management[1] which are attributable to private funds must periodically file Form PF with the SEC through FINRA's Private Fund Reporting Depository system. The level and frequency of an adviser's Form PF reporting obligations will vary depending on the amount and type of private fund regulatory assets managed by such adviser.

[1] Determined in accordance with Part 1A, Instruction 5b of Form ADV.

11.40 Certain investment advisers that are subject to SEC and CFTC jurisdiction (including certain registered investment advisers, as well as firms that are subject to CFTC regulation as commodity trading advisers ('CTAs'), or commodity pool operators ('CPOs'))[1] are required to develop and implement written identity theft programs pursuant to Regulation S-ID. The programs must be designed to detect identity theft 'red flags' and prevent and mitigate such identity theft in connection with the opening of a covered account or any existing covered account. Registered advisers are also required to provide clients with an annual privacy notice[2].

[1] Any registered adviser, CTA or CPO which meets the SEC or CFTC definition of 'financial institution' or 'creditor' must develop and implement a written identity theft prevention program with respect to any covered account.
[2] See para **11.27** above.

11.41 The SEC adopted Rule 206(4)-8 under the Advisers Act which applies to registered and unregistered advisers to 'pooled investment vehicles' (defined as funds relying on the section 3(c)(1) or section 3(c)(7) exception) and provides that:

> '[i]t shall constitute a fraudulent, deceptive, or manipulative act, practice, or course of business . . . for any investment adviser to a pooled investment vehicle to:
> (1) make any untrue statement of a material fact or to omit to state a material fact necessary to make the statements made, in the light of the circumstances under which they were made, not misleading, to any investor or prospective investor in the pooled investment vehicle; or
> (2) otherwise engage in any act, practice, or course of business that is fraudulent, deceptive, or manipulative with respect to any investor or prospective investor in the pooled investment vehicle.'[1]

[1] Advisers Act Rule 206(4)-8(a), 17 CFR § 275.206(4)-8(a).

11.42 Rule 206(4)-8 applies to a non-US SEC-registered hedge fund manager's conduct in respect of US investors in non-US pooled investment vehicles

11.42 *The US Dimension*

within the rule's scope[1].

[1] In the rule's adopting release, the SEC stated:
'A few commenters requested that we clarify how we intend to apply rule 206(4)-8 to offshore advisers' interaction with non-US investors. . . . Our adoption of this rule will not alter our jurisdictional authority.'
(SEC Release No IA-2628, 72 Fed Reg 44,756, 44,758 n 16 (9 August 2007))

Withdrawal from SEC registration

11.43 Whilst the SEC has the authority to revoke the registration of a registered investment adviser pursuant to section 203(f) of the Advisers Act, an SEC-registered investment adviser can also apply to withdraw from SEC registration by filing Form ADV-W electronically via the IARD system.

11.44 The withdrawal application is effective on receipt, but the adviser's registration will continue for 60 days after filing for the purpose of allowing the SEC to take certain enforcement action[1].

[1] See Advisers Act Rule 203-2(c), 17 CFR § 275.203-2(c):
'Each Form ADV-W filed under this section is effective upon acceptance by the IARD, provided however that your investment adviser registration will continue for a period of sixty days after acceptance solely for the purpose of commencing a proceeding under section 203(e) of the Advisers Act (15 USC § 80b-3(e)).'

11.45 Registered advisers are required to comply with the Advisers Act's record retention requirements after withdrawal, and Form ADV-W requires the withdrawing adviser to disclose whether the adviser (i) has ceased conducting advisory business, (ii) has custody of client assets, (iii) has received advisory fees for services not yet rendered, (iv) has borrowed money from clients that has not been repaid, (v) has assigned advisory contracts to another person, and (vi) has any unsatisfied judgments or liens against it. Further, Form ADV-W requires the withdrawing adviser to disclose its financial condition if, at the time the form is filed, the withdrawing adviser still (i) has custody of any client assets, (ii) owes money to any client for prepaid advisory fees or under a client loan, or (iii) has any unsatisfied judgments or liens. The withdrawing adviser is also required to list the name and address of the person having custody of the adviser's books and records.

C   COMMODITIES (CFTC) REGULATION

11.46 The managers, general partners, advisers and promoters of hedge funds that trade commodity interests are potentially subject to regulation under the CEA. As with the US securities laws, however, there is a wide range of exemptions and exclusions from the CEA available to most hedge fund operators and managers.

11.47 The CFTC administers the CEA, and as such is responsible for regulating the US markets in futures, options on futures, swaps[1] and other derivatives and certain participants in these markets, including the operators of and advisers to funds investing in such derivatives – referred to as 'commodity pools'[2].

[1] The term 'swap' is very broad and includes foreign currency options (unless traded on a national securities exchange); commodity options; non-deliverable forwards in foreign exchange; cross-currency swaps; forward rate agreements; contracts for differences; options to enter into swaps; forward swaps; interest rate and other monetary rate swaps; total return swaps on a broad-based security index or on two or more loans; credit default swaps on a group of obligations constituting a broad-based security index; swaps on futures (other than security futures); and certain other derivatives. The term 'swap' also includes foreign exchange swaps and foreign exchange forwards, but only with respect to trade-reporting requirements, anti-evasion authority and business conduct standards.
[2] A 'commodity pool' is defined as 'any investment trust, syndicate or similar form of enterprise operated for the purpose of trading commodity interests.

11.48 Given that the SEC also regulates trading in certain securities derivative products, there exists a division of derivatives jurisdiction between the CFTC and SEC. The Dodd-Frank Act divided regulatory authority over swap agreements between the CFTC and the SEC, so that the SEC has regulatory authority over 'security-based swaps', the SEC and the CFTC share authority over 'mixed swaps' (that is, security-based swaps that also have a commodity component), and the CFTC has regulatory authority over all other swaps[1].

[1] The division of regulatory oversight can vary among different types of swaps such that a swap under the CFTC's jurisdiction that has a material term based on a security is regulated by the CFTC and also subject to certain SEC rules, including with respect to anti-fraud.

11.49 The main focuses of CFTC regulation under the CEA are the derivatives exchanges, swap execution facilities and clearing houses operating in the US and the intermediaries providing derivatives trading and advisory services to others. The National Futures Association (the 'NFA') serves as the industry's self-regulatory organisation (referred to as a 'registered futures association' in the CEA), under the CFTC's supervision.

11.50 In contrast to the 1940 Act, the CEA does not directly regulate the commodity pools themselves, only the advisers to and operators of such pools[1]. Nor will commodity pools generally qualify as 'investment companies' under the 1940 Act, unless they invest a significant proportion of their assets in securities[2]. Commodity pools offered to the public in the US will, however, be required to register their units with the SEC as securities under the Securities Act.

[1] See para **11.8** above.
[2] A commodity pool will come within the 1940 Act definition of 'investment company' if it is or holds itself out as being 'engaged primarily . . . in the business of investing, reinvesting, or trading in securities' (1940 Act § 3(a)(1), 15 USC § 80a-3(a)(1)), or if it is 'engaged . . . in the business of investing, reinvesting, or trading in securities, and owns . . . securities having a value exceeding 40 per centum of the value of [its] total assets (exclusive of Government securities and cash items) on an unconsolidated basis' (1940 Act § 3(a)(3), 15 USC § 80a-3(a)(3)).

11.51 There are six main categories of derivatives intermediaries which require CFTC registration[1]:

11.51 The US Dimension

- *Futures Commission Merchants ('FCMs')*: FCMs solicit and accept orders for commodity futures and options contracts and also accept client money and assets and/or extend margin credit to secure these contracts. FCMs may be clearing or non-clearing commodity exchange members.
- *Introducing Brokers ('IBs')*: IBs solicit and accept orders for commodity futures and options contracts and introduce these orders to an FCM. They are not able to accept client money or assets or extend margin credit.
- *Commodity Trading Advisors ('CTAs')*: CTAs, for a fee or profit, advise others on investing in commodity interests. Their advice may be given directly to clients or indirectly through issuing reports or publications.
- *Commodity Pool Operators ('CPOs')*: CPOs operate commodity pools and/or solicit investment in commodity pools. One CPO registration will cover a potentially unlimited number of pools.
- *Swap Dealers ('SDs')*[2]: Any person who engages in swap dealing activities (which are different from hedging or proprietary trading activities) that are neither exempt nor under specified de minimis thresholds is required to register as an SD. SDs are subject to requirements concerning, among other things, margin, capital and business conduct.
- *Major Swap Participants ('MSPs')*[3]: A person who is not an SD, but who is deemed by the CFTC to be systemically important, will be required to register as an MSP. MSPs are subject to similar regulations as SDs.

[1] This is not an exhaustive list of registration categories. Other categories include Retail Foreign Exchange Dealer, Floor Broker and Floor Trader.
[2] Subject to certain exceptions, a person is an SD if it: (i) holds itself out as a dealer in swaps; (ii) makes a market in swaps; (iii) regularly enters into swaps with counterparties as an ordinary course of business for its own account; or (iv) engages in any activity causing it to be commonly known in the trade as a swap dealer or market maker in swaps.
[3] Subject to certain exceptions, a person is an MSP if such person is not an SD and: (i) maintains a substantial position in swaps for any of the major swap categories, excluding certain positions, including those held for hedging or mitigating commercial risk; (ii) has outstanding swaps that create substantial counterparty exposure that could have serious adverse effects on the financial stability of the US banking system or financial markets; or (iii) is a financial entity that (a) is highly leveraged relative to the amount of capital such entity holds and is not subject to capital requirements established by an appropriate federal banking agency, and (b) maintains a substantial position in outstanding swaps in any major swap category.

11.52 As with SEC registration, exemptions from CFTC registration are available.

The CPO registration requirement and exemptions

11.53 The CEA makes it illegal for a CPO to 'make use of the mails or any means or instrumentality of US interstate commerce in connection with his business' as a CPO, unless the CPO is registered with the CFTC[1].

[1] CEA § 4m(1), 7 USC § 6m(1).

11.54 The CEA defines the term 'commodity pool operator' to include both the operation of the fund itself and the marketing of interests in the fund:

> 'any person engaged in a business that is of the nature of an investment trust, syndicate, or similar form of enterprise, and who, in connection therewith, solicits, accepts, or receives from others, funds, securities, or property, either directly or through capital contributions, the sale of stock or other forms of securities, or otherwise, for the purpose of trading in any commodity for future delivery on or subject to the rules of any contract market or derivatives transaction execution facility, except that the term does not include such persons not within the intent of the definition of the term as the Commission may specify by rule, regulation, or order.'[1]

[1] CEA § 1a(11), 7 USC § 1a(11).

11.55 Accordingly, the operator of a hedge fund is subject to CFTC regulation if the fund transacts in swaps, futures contracts or options on futures contracts or commodities. The CPOs of the fund include its general partner if the fund is a limited partnership and, potentially, the investment manager. Unless the CPO is registered with the CFTC or exempt from registration, the CPO and its employees may not solicit investors for the fund.

11.56 The CFTC Rules contain various exemptions from registration as a CPO. Of particular significance is the 'limited trading' exemption contained in CFTC Rule 4.13(a)(3) which exempts CPOs to certain private investment companies and is regularly relied on by both US and non-US hedge fund managers to avoid the CEA's CPO registration requirements. This exemption requires the following:

- Interests in the pool for which a CPO is seeking to claim relief are exempt from registration under the Securities Act – such as under SEC Regulation D[1] – and such interests are offered and sold without marketing to the public in the US.
- The pool for which a CPO is seeking to claim relief meets one of the following tests with respect to its commodity interest positions (including positions in security futures products) at all times:
  - the aggregate initial margin, premiums, and required minimum security deposit (for retail forex transactions) required to establish such positions, determined at the time the most recent position was established, do not exceed 5% of the liquidation value of the pool's portfolio, after taking into account unrealised profits and unrealised losses on such positions; or
  - the aggregate net notional value of such positions, determined at the time of the most recent position was established, does not exceed 100% of the liquidation value of the pool's portfolio, after taking into account unrealised profits and unrealised losses on such positions.
- The CPO reasonably believes, at the time of investment, that each person that participates in the pool is:
  - an 'accredited investor' under Securities Act Rule 501[2] of Regulation D;
  - a 'knowledgeable employee' under Exchange Act Rule 3c-5[3];

11.56 The US Dimension

- a 'qualified eligible person' as defined in CFTC Rule 4.7(a)(2)(viii)(A)[4];
- a trust formed by an accredited investor for the benefit of a family member; or
- a person who could participate in a Rule 4.13(a)(4) pool[5].
- Participations in the pool for which a CPO is seeking to claim relief are not marketed as or in a vehicle for trading in the commodity futures or commodity options markets.

[1] See para **11.93** below.
[2] 17 CFR § 230.501.
[3] 17 CFR § 270.3c-5.
[4] 17 CFR § 4.7(a)(2)(viii)(A).
[5] Rule 4.13(a)(4), which the CFTC repealed in 2012, applied to private investment funds in which (i) each participant that is a natural person is a 'qualified purchaser' (generally, a person owning investments of not less than US$5 million), a knowledgeable employee (including principals of the manager) or a non-US person; and (ii) each participant that is a non-natural person is a 'qualified eligible person' (generally, owning a securities portfolio of at least US$2 million), an accredited investor (generally, having assets in excess of US$5 million) or a non-US person or entity.

11.57 Any manager that claims an exemption under Rule 4.13(a)(3) will be required to make an initial filing with the NFA and maintain books and records relating to its commodity trading. The manager will also be subject to any special calls that the CFTC may impose relating to eligibility for and compliance with the exemption. In addition, the CFTC imposes a requirement that each manager claiming an exemption under Rule 4.13(a)(3) must make an annual filing with the NFA affirming its eligibility to rely on the exemption. Failure to affirm an exemption under Rule 4.13(a)(3) will be deemed as a request to withdraw the exemption and therefore result in the automatic withdrawal of the exemption once the 60-day period following the calendar year-end has elapsed.

11.58 The CFTC provides multiple exemptions from CPO registration for non-US managers. A CPO located outside the US is exempt from registration if the pool is located outside the US, all investors are located outside the US and no solicitations are directed into the US, provided that all commodity interest transactions are executed bilaterally or made on or subject to the rules of any designated contract market or swap execution facility and submitted for clearing through a registered futures commission merchant[1]. A CPO to a non-US pool is also exempt from registration if commodity interest transactions are limited to foreign futures and foreign options, provided that not more than 10% of the participants in, and value of the assets of, the pool are held by or on behalf of US investors[2]. In addition, a non-US CPO is exempt from registration, regardless of the percentage of US investors in the commodity pools or accounts it advises, provided that: (i) all commodity interest transactions are limited to transactions in foreign futures or foreign options; (ii) all permissible commodity interest transactions are carried out through a CFTC-registered futures commission merchant or a foreign broker who has received an exemption pursuant to CFTC Rule 30.10; and (iii) the CPO files a Form 7-R with the NFA and designates an agent for service of process in the US[3].

[1] 17 CFR § 3.10(C)(3).
[2] 17 CFR § 30.4.

[3] 17 CFR § 30.5.

The CTA registration requirement and exemptions

11.59 The CEA makes it illegal for a CTA to 'make use of the mails or any means or instrumentality of US interstate commerce in connection with his business' as a CTA, unless the CTA is registered with the CFTC[1].

[1] CEA § 4m(1), 7 USC § 6m(1).

11.60 The CEA defines the term 'commodity trading advisor' to include both direct advice to clients and indirect advice through reports and other publications. Specifically, the CEA defines a CTA to include:

'any person who–
  (i) for compensation or profit, engages in the business of advising others, either directly or through publications, writings, or electronic media, as to the value of or the advisability of trading in–
      (I) any contract of sale of a commodity for future delivery made or to be made on or subject to the rules of a contract market or derivatives transaction execution facility;
      (II) any commodity option authorized under CEA section 4c; or
      (III) any leverage transaction authorized under CEA section 19; or
  (ii) for compensation or profit, and as part of a regular business, issues or promulgates analyses or reports concerning any of the activities referred to in clause (i).'[1]

[1] CEA § 1a(12)(A), 7 USC § 1a(12)(A).

11.61 Thus, a hedge fund's investment manager (and possibly the general partner of a fund that is a limited partnership if residual contractual responsibility for investment management is retained) is potentially required to register as a CTA, unless it qualifies for an exclusion or exemption.

11.62 However, the CEA and CFTC Rules contain various exceptions and exemptions from the definition of CTA and from the CTA registration requirement.

11.63 Of particular relevance to hedge fund managers, the CTA registration requirement is subject to a 15 client de minimis exemption. Specifically, section 4m(1) of the CEA provides:

'The provisions of this section shall not apply to any commodity trading advisor who, during the course of the preceding twelve months, has not furnished commodity trading advice to more than fifteen persons and who does not hold himself out generally to the public as a commodity trading advisor'.

11.64 The CFTC adopted Rule 4.14(a)(10) to clarify the scope of this de minimis exemption, in particular as regards the manner of counting clients[1]. Rule 4.14(a)(10) is regularly relied on by both US and non-US hedge fund advisers to avoid the CEA's CTA registration requirements.

[1] See CFTC final rule release, 68 Fed Reg 47,221, 47,226 (8 August 2003).

11.65 The Rule 4.14(a)(10) exemption applies to a CTA which:

11.65 The US Dimension

- during the course of the preceding 12 months has not furnished commodity trading advice to more than 15 persons; and
- does not hold itself out generally to the public as a commodity trading advisor.

11.66 The rule's methodology for counting clients allows the general partner of a limited partnership, or other person acting as a CTA to the limited partnership, to count the limited partnership as one person. In addition, the rule provides further relief for non-US CTAs by only requiring them to count their US resident clients[1]. Consequently, the CTA registration exemption permits unregistered, non-US CTAs, which do not otherwise hold themselves out as CTAs, to provide commodity trading advice to an unlimited number of non-US commodity pools and up to 15 US commodity pools. The rule also provides that a CTA's participation 'in a non-public offering of interests in a collective investment vehicle under the Securities Act' (for example, a private placement of hedge fund interests under Regulation D) does not amount to 'holding out' for these purposes[2]. Consistent with the de minimis exemption in CEA § 4m(1), no CFTC or NFA filing is required to put the Rule 4.14(a)(10) exemption into effect.

[1] CFTC Rule 4.14(a)(10)(ii)(C), 17 CFR § 4.14(a)(10)(ii)(C).
[2] CFTC Rule 4.14(a)(10)(iii), 17 CFR § 4.14(a)(10)(iii).

11.67 It should also be noted that there are other exemptions not discussed here that are available for CPOs and CTAs.

Becoming CFTC/NFA registered

11.68 Where the CPO and CTA registration exemptions are insufficient, a hedge fund manager will need to file an application for registration as a CPO and/or a CTA with the NFA. The application will be filed through the NFA's Online Registration System ('ORS').

11.69 Regardless of whether the firm is registering as a CPO or a CTA (or both), the initial application is the same and consists of the following items:

- Form 7-R (an online application form to register the firm);
- Form 8-R (an online application form to register each natural person who is a principal or an associated person (as described below) of the firm);
- proof of passage of a qualifying examination (or exemption therefrom) for each associated person of the firm[1];
- a fingerprint card for each natural person who is a principal or an associated person of the firm; and
- registration fees and annual NFA dues[2].

[1] Discussed more fully in paras **11.72–11.74** below.
[2] Each as updated from time to time at the following website: https://www.nfa.futures.org/nfa manual/NFAManual.aspx?RuleID=RULE%20203&Section=8.

11.70 Additionally, all registered CPOs engaged in swap transactions are required to have at least one principal that is also an approved swap associated person.

Principals

11.71 Generally, a 'principal' of a CPO or CTA would be: (i) in the case of a sole proprietorship, a sole proprietor; (ii) in the case of a partnership, a general partner; (iii) a director, president, chief executive officer, chief operating officer, chief financial officer or a person in charge of a business unit, division or function subject to regulation by the CFTC of a corporation, limited liability company or limited liability partnership; (iv) a manager, managing member or a member with management authority for a limited liability company or limited liability partnership; (v) a chief compliance officer; (vi) an individual who, directly or indirectly, through agreement or otherwise, owns or controls 10% or more of the outstanding shares of any class of the applicant or has the power to exercise a controlling influence over the activities of the applicant; or (v) an individual who has contributed 10% or more of the capital of the applicant unless such capital contribution consists of certain subordinated debt[1].

[1] The full list of who is considered a 'principal' is available at https://www.nfa.futures.org/nfa-registration/principal/index.html.

Associated persons

11.72 The term 'associated person' means an individual who solicits orders, customers, or customer funds on behalf of the CPO, commodity pool or CTA (or any person in the supervising 'chain-of-command' who supervises such persons)[1].

[1] The full list of who is considered an 'associated person' is available at https://www.nfa.futures.org/nfa-registration/ap/index.html.

11.73 Each CPO and CTA is required to have at least one person who is both a principal and an associated person.

11.74 Associated persons also must pass a National Commodity Futures Examination (or obtain an exemption therefrom)[1] and submit proof of passing that examination with their application for registration and attend mandatory ethics training. Principals are not required to take an exam or attend ethics training in their capacity as principals, but would be required to take an exam (unless the requirement is waived) if also acting in the capacity of an associated person.

[1] There are multiple exemptions from the exam requirement. One exemption provides that, at the discretion of the NFA, the test may be waived entirely in certain circumstances. In general, it may be waived for associated persons of CPOs that operate pools satisfying the following criteria: (i) the pool is subject to SEC regulation (this includes unregistered, privately offered pools); (ii) the pool engages principally in securities transactions; (iii) the pool commits only a small percentage of its assets as initial margin deposits and premiums for futures and options on futures; and (iv) the pool uses futures and options on futures only for hedging or risk management purposes. The full list of the NFA's proficiency requirements indicating the instances in which testing requirements may be waived is available at https://www.nfa.futures.org/nfa-registration/proficiency-requirements.html.

11.75 *The US Dimension*

Light disclosure regime for registered CPOs and CTAs – CFTC Rule 4.7

11.75 Most hedge fund managers registered as CPOs or CTAs with the CFTC take advantage of the exemptions in CFTC Rule 4.7 that allow them to comply with less burdensome disclosure, record-keeping and reporting requirements on the basis that investors in the commodity pool and the commodity trading clients are 'qualified eligible persons'[1].

[1] Generally, 'qualified eligible persons' include government or regulated entities or persons capitalised above a certain threshold (US$5 million in most cases), persons who satisfy a US$2 million 'portfolio requirement', non-US persons, 'qualified purchasers' as defined in section 2(51)(A) of the 1940 Act (15 USC § 80a-2(51)(A)), and certain insiders of the entity.

11.76 The Rule 4.7 exemption is claimed by electronic filing with the NFA. For a CPO exemption, a notice must be filed with respect to each pool that the CPO operates for which it is claiming the exemption. For a CTA exemption, the CTA must represent that it only provides commodity trading advice to qualified eligible persons.

11.77 Summarised below are the disclosure, reporting, record-keeping and ongoing compliance requirements to which CPOs and CTAs that claim the Rule 4.7 exemption are subject.

Disclosure requirements

11.78 Rule 4.7 exempts qualifying CPOs and CTAs from almost all disclosure requirements other than the requirement that a specified disclosure legend must be included by the CPO in any offering memorandum for a commodity pool and by the CTA in any brochure or disclosure statement provided to clients[1].

[1] Any offering materials are also subject to general anti-fraud requirements and may not be misleading, either through affirmative misstatements or material omissions.

Registered CPO reporting requirements

11.79 Registered CPOs are required to comply with the following reporting requirements[1].

[1] CTAs have their own reporting requirements, which are not discussed here.

QUARTERLY REPORTS

11.80 For each pool that it operates, a Rule 4.7 exempt CPO is required to prepare quarterly reports for distribution to participants in that pool. The reports must be prepared and distributed within 30 days after the end of each quarter. Each report must contain the fund's net asset value as of the end of the quarter, the change in net asset value from the end of the previous quarter, and the net asset value per outstanding equity unit at the end of the quarter.

11.81 The quarterly report must contain a signed affirmation that the information in the report is accurate and complete to the best of the knowledge and belief of the person making the affirmation.

Form CPO-PQR

11.82 A CPO is required to file electronically Form CPO-PQR. A CPO with aggregate gross assets under management equal to or exceeding US$1.5 billion must file this form within 60 days of the end of each calendar quarter. All other CPOs must file the form within 60 days of each quarter ending March, June and September and within 90 days of each calendar year-end. A CPO that is also filing Form PF generally does not need to file certain portions of Form CPO-PQR relating to funds that were reported on Form PF.

Annual reports

11.83 A CPO is also required to prepare annual reports with respect to each pool that it operates. The reports must be filed with the NFA and distributed to pool participants within 90 days of the end of the pool's fiscal year.

11.84 The annual report must: (i) contain a statement of financial condition as of the end of the fiscal year, a statement of income (loss) for the year and appropriate disclosure of any other material information; (ii) be prepared in accordance with US GAAP (or reconciled, in certain respects, to US GAAP[1]; and (iii) include a legend on the cover page disclosing that the CPO has filed a claim for exemption under Rule 4.7 for the fund. The annual report must also contain the signed affirmation as described in para **11.81** above. Finally, the annual report must either be certified by an independent public accountant[2] or contain a statement on the cover page of the report that a certified audit will be provided upon the request of a majority of the participants in the pool who are unaffiliated with the CPO.

[1] Financial statements are, pursuant to Rule 4.7(b)(2)(v), allowed under certain circumstances to be presented using an alternative accounting methodology, including International Financial Reporting Standards ('IFRS').
[2] In this context, the term 'certified' means audited and reported upon with an opinion expressed by an independent certified public accountant or independent licensed public accountant.

Annual questionnaire and review

11.85 A CPO is required to submit electronically to the NFA an annual questionnaire with basic information about the CPO and its related entities. Further, a CPO is required to conduct an annual review of its operations using the self-examination questionnaire prescribed by the NFA and available on the NFA's website. Following the review, the CPO is required to sign a written attestation (in a form prescribed by the NFA) representing that it has performed such review.

Record-keeping

11.86 Under the Rule 4.7 exemption, CPOs and CTAs are exempt from most record-keeping requirements. A CPO must maintain copies of all quarterly and annual reports and CPOs and CTAs must maintain all books and records prepared in connection with operating the fund or advisory activities (including any records regarding the qualifications of investors as qualified eligible

11.86 *The US Dimension*

persons, any promotional materials[1], and records substantiating performance information). Records must be kept for five years and must be readily available for at least the first two years.

Withdrawal from CFTC and NFA registration

11.87 A registered CPO or CTA can apply to withdraw from CFTC and NFA regulation by filing Form 7-W electronically with the NFA. The withdrawal will generally become effective 30 days after the NFA's receipt of the form (or earlier if the NFA determines)[1].

[1] See CFTC Rule 3.33(f), 17 CFR § 3.33(f), NFA Rule 601(c).

11.88 The NFA's checks on the withdrawal application will focus on making sure that the withdrawing firm has no regulatory obligations as a CTA and/or CPO outstanding, including that all of its required filings and reports are up to date and all fees have been paid. The NFA will co-ordinate with the CFTC on the withdrawal, and the CFTC's acceptance will be required before the withdrawal is approved. If, while the withdrawal application is pending, the NFA or CFTC receives information that causes either regulatory body to initiate an investigation against the firm, the withdrawal is unlikely to be approved until the matter is resolved.

11.89 The registration of the withdrawing firm's associated persons will automatically terminate upon the firm's withdrawal from registration as a CPO and/or CTA, unless that associated person is also registered with another NFA member[1].

[1] See NFA Rule 206(d), which provides:

'A person registered in accordance with paragraphs (a) or (b) of this Rule, Rule 207 or Rule 301(e) and whose registration has not been revoked, shall continue to be so registered until the . . . withdrawal of the registration of each of the registrant's sponsors . . . '

11.90 After withdrawal, the formerly registered CPO/CTA will be required to maintain its relevant books and records for a period of five years following the date of withdrawal, during which time the firm may be asked to produce such records to the CFTC[1].

[1] See CFTC Rule 1.31, 17 CFR § 1.31, and CFTC Rule 3.33(b)(3), 17 CFR § 3.33(b)(3).

11.91 The CFTC will continue to retain enforcement jurisdiction over the formerly registered CPO/CTA firm for any misconduct committed while registered[1]. Also, a customer of the former CPO/CTA will be able to bring a claim for damages against the firm under the CFTC's Reparations Program, if the claim involves business for which the firm was CFTC registered at the time of the alleged wrongdoing or at the time the complaint is filed. Such reparations claims are, however, subject to a two-year statute of limitations[2].

[1] CFTC Rule 3.33(h), 17 CFR § 3.33(h) ('Withdrawal from registration does not constitute a release from liability for any violation of the CEA . . . or of any rule, regulation or order thereunder.'). See also NFA Rule 601(e).
[2] See CEA § 14(a)(1), 7 USC § 18(a)(1).

D US MARKETING OF HEDGE FUND INTERESTS

Securities Act issues – SEC Regulation D

11.92 Under the Securities Act, any US offer to sell securities must either be registered with the SEC or qualify for an exemption.

11.93 One such exemption is the 'private offering exemption' in section 4(a)(2) of the Securities Act, which, by its terms, exempts 'transactions by an issuer not involving any public offering'. However, given the vagueness of this language, the statutory exemption was not often used, which prompted the SEC to adopt Regulation D, which permits private offerings provided that an issuer does not engage in general solicitation or advertising. In 2013, the SEC amended Rule 506 and added Rule 506(c), which permits an issuer to conduct a private placement of securities under Rule 506 while engaging in general solicitation or general advertising in offering and selling securities provided that: (i) the offering complies with the general requirements for a Regulation D private placement, which are set forth in Rules 501 and 502; (ii) all purchasers of the securities are accredited investors, as defined under the Securities Act; and (iii) the issuer takes reasonable steps to verify that such purchasers are accredited investors. The amendment to Rule 506 also includes a non-exclusive list of methods that issuers may use to satisfy the verification requirement for purchasers who are natural persons. Finally, the SEC also added an informational item to Form D for issuers to indicate when they are relying on Rule 506(c). Under Rule 506 of Regulation D an issuer may offer and sell to a potentially unlimited number of 'accredited investors' and up to 35 other sophisticated purchasers.

11.94 For these purpose, an 'accredited investor' includes the following:

- *Natural person investors:* Generally, to be considered an accredited investor, an individual must either (i) have an annual income of US$200,000 (or US$300,000 jointly with his/her spouse) in each of the previous two years and a reasonable expectation of reaching the same level of income in the current year, or (ii) have a net worth of at least US$1 million at the time of purchase, excluding the value of such individual's primary residence.
- *Regulated investors:* Banks, savings and loan associations, SEC-registered broker-dealers, insurance companies, investment companies registered with the SEC under the 1940 Act, business development companies and small business investment companies are considered accredited investors without regard to their level of income or assets owned.
- *Other non-natural person investors:* The following entities are generally considered accredited investors if they have at least US$5 million in total assets:
  - an employee benefit plan, within the meaning of ERISA, if a bank, insurance company, or registered investment adviser makes the investment decisions, or if the plan has total assets in excess of US$5 million;
  - a charitable organisation, corporation, or partnership;

11.94 *The US Dimension*

- any trust not formed for the specific purpose of acquiring the securities offered whose purchase is directed by a sophisticated person; and
- any other entity in which all of the equity owners are accredited investors.

11.95 Within 15 days after securities are first sold in reliance on the Regulation D exemption, the issuer must file Form D, which is a brief notice that includes the names and addresses of the issuer's executive officers, the size of the offering and the date of the first sale. However, the Form D filing is not a precondition to the effectiveness of the Regulation D exemption. Further, an annual amendment to a private fund's Form D filing must be made electronically with the SEC for each private fund that (i) relies upon Rule 506 under the Securities Act, as a 'safe harbor' under the Securities Act's section 4(a)(2) private offering exemption from securities registration, and (ii) makes a continuous offering. In addition to the annual amendment, updates to a filing may be required if there are certain changes to the information included in the filing, for example the name or address of the issuer or the persons receiving sales compensation. A fund's annual amendment is due on or before the anniversary of its initial SEC Form D filing, or if an amendment has been made to its initial filing, on or before the anniversary of the most recently filed amendment.

11.96 Pursuant to the 'bad actor' disqualification provisions of Rule 506(d) and Rule 504(b) of the Securities Act, an issuer may not rely on the Rule 506 or Rule 504 offering exemptions if the issuer or certain other persons involved with the offering (including both placement agents and any beneficial owner of 20% or more of the issuer's outstanding voting equity securities) has a disqualifying event, unless the disqualification is waived or otherwise remedied[1]. Events occurring prior to 23 September 2013 that would be disqualifying events if they had occurred after such date will not disqualify an issuer from relying on Rule 506, but must be disclosed in writing to offerees a reasonable time prior to sale. An issuer that is disqualified from relying on Rule 506 and Rule 504 may, under certain circumstances, privately offer securities, but will be required to rely on the 'private offering exemption' in section 4(a)(2) of the Securities Act[2]. Any issuer that made sales at a time when there were unknown disqualifying events may still rely on Rule 506 and Rule 504 for those prior sales, if the issuer can establish that it did not know and, in the exercise of reasonable care, could not have known that such disqualifying events existed[3].

[1] Issuers that are subject to disqualification may apply for a waiver, which may be granted upon a showing of good cause if the SEC determines that disqualification is not necessary, or in the case of a final order (as discussed below), based on a determination of the issuing authority that disqualification is not necessary. Circumstances that may be relevant to a waiver request may include, but are not limited to, a change of control, change of supervisory personnel, absence of notice and opportunity for hearing and relief from a permanent bar for a person who does not intend to apply to reassociate with a regulated entity.
[2] See para **11.93** above.
[3] To establish that it has exercised reasonable care, an issuer must make, in light of the circumstances, factual inquiry into whether any disqualifications exist. For issuers that engage in continuous, delayed or long-lived offerings, reasonable care includes updating the factual inquiry on a reasonable basis, which may include contractual covenants from those involved in the offering to provide bring-down of representations, questionnaires and certifications,

negative consent letters, periodic rechecking of public databases, and other steps, depending on the circumstances.

Exchange Act issues – US marketing by non-US managers

11.97 The SEC takes an expansive view of its jurisdiction over the offer of securities in the US or to US persons, including interests in hedge funds. As a general matter, where a person's business involves effecting securities transactions in the US, that person must register with the SEC as a broker or rely on an exemption from such registration. This remains the case even if the securities are offered on a private placement basis under Regulation D.

11.98 There are three exemptions on which non-US hedge funds and/or hedge fund managers commonly rely in respect of US private placement activity: the so-called 'issuer exemption' and Rules 3a4-1[1] and 15a-6[2] of the Exchange Act. However, these exemptions cover only a very limited range of activities.

[1] 17 CFR § 240.3a4-1.
[2] 17 CFR § 240.15a-6.

The issuer exemption

11.99 The 'issuer exemption' is not specified in statute or rule, but instead arises from the structure of the Exchange Act's broker registration requirements. In summary, the Exchange Act's general definition of 'broker' includes 'any person engaged in the business of effecting transactions in securities for the account of others'[1]. When an issuer sells or buys its own securities, it is not a broker required to be registered under section 15(a)(1) of the Exchange Act[2]. The exemption thus covers an issuer's sales and purchases of its own securities where the purpose of this activity is to raise money to use in its business and the activity does not amount to a separate business intended to make profits on the transactions themselves.

[1] Exchange Act § 3(a)(4), 15 USC § 78c(a)(4).
[2] 15 USC § 78o(a)(1).

LIMITATION ON THE ISSUER EXEMPTION – EMPLOYEES

11.100 However, the issuer exemption may not cover the employees of the issuer involved in marketing and/or distributing the issuer's securities. These employees may individually be considered to be engaging in the business of effecting transactions in securities – particularly if distribution forms a significant part of their activities or compensation – and therefore be required to register with the SEC as brokers.

Exchange Act Rule 3a4-1

11.101 The Rule 3a4-1 exemption, which is a non-exclusive 'safe harbor', applies to employees of the fund or the manager – that is, the 'associated person[s] of an issuer of securities'. Associated persons include any partner, officer, director or employee of (i) the issuer (for example, a hedge fund), (ii)

11.101 *The US Dimension*

a corporate general partner of a limited partnership that is the issuer, and (iii) a company or partnership that controls, is controlled by, or is under common control with the issuer. Indicia of such 'control' generally include overlapping directors and/or share ownership.

11.102 Rule 3a4-1 permits such persons to carry on a limited range of offering activities with respect to investment vehicles, but only where the associated person of the issuer:

- is not subject to any statutory disqualification;
- has not been associated with a broker or dealer in the preceding 12 months;
- is not compensated in connection with his participation in the offering by the payment of commissions or other remuneration based directly or indirectly on transactions in securities; and
- complies with any one of the following three sets of conditions:
  (i) the person restricts his participation to transactions involving, among other things, offers and sales of securities (a) to certain US-registered or licensed entities (for example, brokers, dealers, investment companies), banks, savings and loan associations and certain trust companies and trusts, or (b) that are exempt from registration under the Securities Act by certain sections of the Securities Act;
  (ii) the person 'primarily' performs, or is intended primarily to perform, substantial duties for or on behalf of the issuer otherwise than in connection with transactions in securities and such person was not a broker or dealer or associated person of a broker or dealer within the preceding 12 months and the person does not participate in selling an offering of securities for any issuer more than once every 12 months; or
  (iii) the person restricts his activities to (a) preparing written communication or delivering such communication through the mail or other means that do not involve oral solicitation, (b) responding to inquiries from potential purchasers in a communication initiated by the potential purchaser, but only where the content of such response is limited to information contained in the fund's offering documents, or (c) performing ministerial and clerical work in effecting any transaction.

11.103 In short, Rule 3a4-1 enables associated persons of issuers to conduct specific activities relating to limited offerings without having to register with the SEC as a broker.

11.104 Many non-US hedge fund managers rely on condition (ii) above, which applies to infrequent offering activity in respect of US persons either by directors of the fund itself or by portfolio managers of an investment manager that is under common control with the fund.

Foreign broker exemption – Exchange Act Rule 15a-6

11.105 The foreign broker exemption provides relief, subject to certain conditions, from US broker registration for non-US brokers engaged in the offer and sale of securities (including hedge fund interests) to US persons, where the offering activities of the non-US broker are, in effect, supervised by a US registered broker[1].

[1] See Exchange Act Rule 15a-6(a)(3), 17 CFR § 240.15a-6(a)(3).

11.106 To qualify for this exemption, the non-US broker must:

- make an offer only to SEC-registered investment companies, SEC-registered investment advisers with greater than US$100 million under management, banks, savings and loan associations, insurance companies, certain employee benefit plans, certain charities, and other US institutional investors with total assets in excess of US$100 million ('institutional investors');
- effect any resulting transactions through a SEC-registered broker-dealer; and
- provide the SEC (upon request) with information and documents relating to the transactions.

11.107 In addition, the personnel of the non-US broker must conduct all marketing activities from outside the US and may only visit US institutional investors within the US if:

- accompanied on these visits by an associated person of an SEC-registered broker-dealer that (i) has satisfied itself that the non-US person is not prohibited by regulatory disqualification or otherwise from marketing to the institutional investor and (ii) has accepted responsibility for the non-US person's communications with that institutional investor; and
- any securities transactions discussed during the visit by the non-US person are effected only through the SEC-registered broker-dealer.

11.108 In order for the transactions to be 'effected through' the SEC-registered broker-dealer, the role of the non-US broker and its staff should be limited to negotiating the terms of the transaction. In particular, the SEC-registered broker-dealer must: (i) book all transaction fees; (ii) issue all required confirmations and statements; (iii) extend or arrange for the extension of any credit to the institutional investor in connection with the transaction; and (iv) maintain the books and records required by the SEC in relation to the transaction.

11.109 The SEC-registered broker-dealer also must participate in all oral communications between the non-US broker and the institutional investor. An exception to this requirement covers only oral communication with SEC-registered investment advisers with at least US$100 million in assets under management or any other institutional investor with total assets in excess of US$100 million.

11.110 Finally, transactions that have not been solicited by the non-US broker are generally outside the scope of the SEC broker registration requirement[1], as are a non-US broker's solicited or unsolicited transactions with SEC-registered broker-dealers (whether acting as principal or as agent for others) and certain US banks[2].

[1] See Exchange Act Rule 15a-6(a)(1), 17 CFR § 240.15a-6(a)(1).

11.110 *The US Dimension*

[2] See Exchange Act Rule 15a-6(a)(4)(i), 17 CFR § 240.15a-6(a)(4)(i).

US state 'blue sky' issues

11.111 The US states are separate sovereigns under the US federal constitutional structure. The US Constitution expressly reserves certain matters to the states and others to the federal government. In some areas, the Constitution is unclear or silent, which can result in parallel or overlapping federal and state jurisdiction and sometimes federal 'pre-emption' of jurisdiction previously exercised by states. In the case of securities laws, federal jurisdiction is largely based on the Constitution's Commerce Clause[1], which provides for exclusive federal jurisdiction over interstate and foreign commerce. Some purely intrastate offers of securities are therefore theoretically outside the SEC's jurisdiction[2].

[1] See footnote 1 in para **11.19** above.
[2] See, for example, Securities Act § 3(a)(11), 15 USC § 77c(a)(11), exempting from the Act's coverage:

'[a]ny security which is a part of an issue offered and sold only to persons resident within a single state or territory, where the issuer of such security is a person resident and doing business within or, if a corporation, incorporated by and doing business within, such state or territory.'

11.112 Accordingly, whilst federal law pre-empts much of the securities law arena, parallel state regulation continues to exist in some areas. The state securities laws (called 'blue sky laws') include registration requirements for securities offerings within the state and private placement exemptions from those registration requirements. These private placement exemptions often mirror the Securities Act's private placement exemption in Regulation D. However, where an issuer, including a hedge fund, relies on the Regulation D private placement exemption, compliance with the state private placement requirements is generally limited to a notice filing and payment of fees (each of which is actively monitored by state securities agencies – thus requiring that issuers track US investors for state blue sky purposes)[1]. Moreover, many states have exemptions from their blue sky filing requirements where there are only a few investors in that state or where the investors are institutional investors.

[1] See Securities Act § 18(b)(4)(D), 15 USC § 77r(b)(4)(D).

E   OTHER US ISSUES AFFECTING HEDGE FUND MANAGERS

The Employee Retirement Income Security Act of 1974

11.113 ERISA[1] establishes a federal regulatory structure for US employee pension and benefit schemes (referred to as 'plans') established or operated by private-sector employers, 'employee organisations', such as trade unions, and regulates the activities of certain 'parties in interest' (such as service providers and fiduciaries) to those plans. Amongst other things, ERISA imposes special duties on, and prohibits certain transactions by, plan 'fiduciaries', which are defined to include persons who exercise any discretionary authority or control over the plan or its assets and persons providing investment advice to the plan for a fee or other compensation[2]. Whether a hedge fund manager will be considered a discretionary ERISA fiduciary to an ERISA plan investor depends on whether assets of the fund in which the plan invests are deemed to include 'plan assets' covered by ERISA[3]. ERISA also imposes certain reporting and disclosure obligations on hedge fund managers, some of which apply even if the hedge fund does not hold 'plan assets'.

[1] 29 USC § 1001, et seq.
[2] See ERISA § 3(21)(A), 29 USC § 1002(21)(A); 29 CFR § 2510.3-21(c).
[3] The DOL adopted a regulation effective on 9 June 2017 that deems sellers of securities, including interests in private investment funds, to be 'advice fiduciaries' under ERISA. This regulation effectively prohibits hedge fund offerings to ERISA plans with less than US$50 million in plan assets, participant directed ERISA plan accounts and individual retirement accounts unless the investment is made by or based on advice from a bank, insurance company, registered investment adviser or registered broker-dealer. The applicability date for the bulk of the class exemption associated with this regulation has been postponed to July 2019, while the DOL further studies the regulation and potentially poses changes thereto.

11.114 A DOL regulation[1], which has been modified in application by section 3(42) of ERISA[2], provides that a fund's assets will not be treated as plan assets if, immediately after the most recent acquisition, redemption or transfer of any equity interest in the fund, less than 25% of the total value of each class of equity interests in the fund is held by 'benefit plan investors'. The term benefit plan investor means:

- 'an employee benefit plan subject to Part 4' of Title I of ERISA, which includes (a) most US private sector pension plans established by an employer or trade union and (b) 'employee welfare benefit plans' established by a private sector employer or trade union to provide other benefits including medical benefits and benefits in the event of disability, death or unemployment[3];
- 'any plan to which section 4975 of the Internal Revenue Code of 1986 applies', which includes various types of US tax-advantaged individual and employer-sponsored plans – the section 4975 definition includes all employer sponsored plans subject to Part 4 of Title I of ERISA, as well as individual retirement accounts and annuities, medical and health savings accounts and educational savings accounts[4]; and
- 'any entity whose underlying assets include plan assets by reason of a plan's investment in such entity' – for example, a fund where 25% or more of a class of the equity interests is held by benefit plan investors, certain bank collective trusts and certain insurance company general and separate accounts.

[1] 29 CFR § 2510.3-101.
[2] 29 USC § 1002(42).
[3] ERISA § 3(1)(A), 29 USC § 1002(1)(A).
[4] See Internal Revenue Code § 4975(e)(1), 26 USC § 4975(e)(1).

11.115 Significantly, the following are excepted from the definition of employee benefit plan and therefore also from the definition of benefit plan investor:

- *non-US plans*, that is, those 'maintained outside of the United States primarily for the benefit of persons substantially all of whom are non-resident aliens'[1];

11.115 *The US Dimension*

- *governmental plans*, including those established for employees of the federal government, any US state, county or city government, any government agency and certain tax-exempt international organisations[2];
- *certain church plans*, including plans established and maintained by conventions and associations of churches[3].

[1] ERISA § 4(b)(4), 29 USC § 1003(b)(4).
[2] See ERISA § 4(b)(1), 29 USC § 1003(b)(1); ERISA § 3(32), 29 USC § 1002(32).
[3] See ERISA § 4(b)(2), 29 USC § 1003(b)(2); ERISA § 3(33), 29 USC § 1002(33). Note that a church plan is permitted to make an election to be subject to the provisions of Title I of ERISA, in which case it would be a benefit plan investor.

11.116 If a hedge fund becomes subject to ERISA, the manager becomes a fiduciary to each plan subject to ERISA or section 4975 of the Internal Revenue Code invested in the fund and must manage the fund in compliance with ERISA and/or section 4975 of the Internal Revenue Code. Many hedge funds will limit and monitor ownership by benefit plan investors in the fund to keep each class of the fund below the 25% threshold described above.

11.117 Where a hedge fund does hold ERISA plan assets, the hedge fund's manager will be subject to ERISA's fiduciary duty and prohibited transaction regimes, as well as certain reporting and disclosure requirements imposed on plan fiduciaries.

ERISA fiduciary duties

11.118 The fund manager will be subject to ERISA's standard of care, which requires, in part, that a plan fiduciary act for the exclusive purpose of providing benefits to participants and their beneficiaries and with the care, skill, prudence, and diligence under the circumstances then prevailing that a prudent man acting in a like capacity and familiar with such matters would use in the conduct of an enterprise of a like character and with like aims[1]. ERISA provides that an individual fiduciary (such as the individual that serves as the hedge fund manager's portfolio manager) has joint and several personal liability for breaches of the standard of care[2]. ERISA also prohibits provisions that would require a plan to indemnify a fiduciary for breaches of its duties under ERISA, though ERISA fiduciaries are permitted to purchase insurance for such breaches[3].

[1] See ERISA § 404(a), 29 USC § 1104(a).
[2] See ERISA § 409(a), 29 USC § 1109(a).
[3] See ERISA § 410, 29 USC § 1110.

ERISA prohibited transaction requirements

11.119 The hedge fund manager will also become subject to ERISA's prohibited transaction rules[1]. These rules prohibit the hedge fund manager itself from entering into certain transactions with an ERISA plan asset fund[2]. The manager would also be prohibited from causing the fund to enter into certain transactions between the fund and a 'party in interest' to any benefit plan investor in the fund[3]. A party in interest is defined very broadly to include 'a person providing services to such plan', other fiduciaries to the plan, the employer or trade union whose employees are covered by the plans and certain affiliates[4].

[1] ERISA § 406, 29 USC § 1106.
[2] ERISA § 406(b), 29 USC § 1106(b).
[3] ERISA § 406(b)(1), 29 USC § 1106(b)(1). Section 4975 of the Internal Revenue Code also imposes special excise taxes on a similar list of prohibited transactions between the ERISA plan and 'disqualified persons'; see Internal Revenue Code § 4975(c)(1), 26 USC § 4975(c)(1).
[4] ERISA § 3(14), 29 USC § 1002(14). Section 4975 of the Internal Revenue Code also includes these categories in its definition of 'disqualified person'; see Internal Revenue Code § 4975(e)(2), 26 USC § 4975(e)(2).

11.120 The prohibited transaction rules present a number of potential compliance problems for a hedge fund manager that is an ERISA fiduciary. A benefit plan investor that is a large pension fund can potentially have hundreds of service providers and, therefore, hundreds of parties in interest. Hedge fund manages acting as ERISA fiduciaries will typically assume that everyone that transacts with the plan asset fund is a party in interest to the fund's underlying plan investors. However, statutory and class exemptions to the prohibited transaction rules provided under ERISA and by the DOL make these compliance issues manageable. Two of the more common exemptions used by hedge fund managers are as follows:

- *The QPAM exemption:* A hedge fund manager will qualify as a 'qualified professional asset manager' (a 'QPAM') if it (i) is SEC registered, (ii) has shareholders' or partners' equity in excess of US$1 million, (iii) had client assets under management in excess of US$85 million on the last day of its most recent accounting year, and (iv) has acknowledged its fiduciary status in writing in a written management agreement with the plan[1].

  The QPAM exemption is not available (i) if the QPAM or an affiliate has been convicted of certain crimes within the past ten years, (ii) with respect to certain securities lending and mortgage-related transactions, (iii) for transactions with a fiduciary that has appointed the hedge fund manager as QPAM for a plan if that plan represents 10% or more of the fund, and (iv) for transactions with parties of interest of plan investors that represent 20% or more of the hedge fund manager's total client assets under management.

  The QPAM exemption permits arm-length transactions, but it does not provide relief for any self-dealing prohibitions.

- *The service provider exemption:* This exemption provides an exemption for transactions between an ERISA plan and its service providers (excluding those managing plan assets or giving investment advice to the plan) 'but only if in connection with such transaction the plan receives no less, nor pays no more, than adequate consideration'[2].
  For this purpose, 'adequate consideration' means:
    - for a security traded on an SEC-registered exchange, the price prevailing on that exchange;
    - for a security traded on any other generally recognised market, a price not less favourable than the offering price for the security as established by the current bid and asked prices quoted by persons

11.120 The US Dimension

independent of the issuer and of the party in interest, taking into account factors such as transaction size and marketability of the security; and
– for any other security, the fair market value of the asset as determined in good faith by a fiduciary or fiduciaries in accordance with DOL regulations[3].

The service provider exemption permits certain transactions between a plan and specific parties in interest (such as service providers) to that plan for adequate consideration, but it does not provide relief for any self-dealing prohibitions.

[1] DOL Prohibited Transaction Exemption (PTE) 84-14, as amended, 75 Fed Reg 38,837 (6 July 2010).
[2] ERISA § 408(b)(17)(A), 29 USC § 1108(b)(17)(A).
[3] ERISA § 408(b)(17)(B), 29 USC § 1108(b)(17)(B). The DOL has not yet issued any regulations in this regard.

ERISA reporting and disclosure

11.121 Regardless of whether a hedge fund is deemed to include 'plan assets', plan investors in a hedge fund must identify all of its service providers that received more than US$5,000 during the year. To comply with the plan's reporting obligation, the manager must disclose to the plan investor remuneration it received (indirectly through the plan's investment in the fund) during the previous fiscal year. This remuneration includes management fees, performance fees or allocations, soft dollars, and gifts or entertainment from fund service providers in excess of certain de minimis thresholds.

11.122 For a manager of a plan asset fund, disclosures regarding the manager's remuneration that is required by Form 5500, described above, as well as the operating expenses and other fees associated with an investment in the fund, should be made to each ERISA plan investor in advance of the plan's investment in the fund (or within 30 days of becoming a plan asset fund, if applicable). Whilst most of these required disclosures are typically already made in a standard fund prospectus, the DOL suggests that plan asset fund managers should provide a 'roadmap' document that directs plan investors to the required disclosures, and many hedge fund managers already provide such a 'roadmap'. In addition, more detailed information about fund holdings may need to be provided by plan asset hedge funds, and certain financial disclosures made to union plans may be available to members of the union plan.

Miscellaneous

11.123 In addition to the issues described above, a hedge fund manager of a plan asset fund should be aware of the following points:

- ERISA requires that plan fiduciaries be bonded against acts of dishonesty and fraud, provides for limitations in indemnification for breaches of an ERISA fiduciary's duties, and imposes certain requirements on the way in which insurance is purchased by an ERISA fiduciary.
- Cross trades are generally prohibited if one or both sides of the trade are plan assets.

Other US issues affecting hedge fund managers **11.127**

- Soft dollar arrangements should comply with the 'safe harbor' provided by section 28(e) of the Exchange Act.
- ERISA generally requires indicia of ownership of plan assets to be maintained within the US. Exceptions to the rule are available with respect to non-US securities, but these exceptions require specific agreements with the fund custodian if the hedge fund manager does not have a principal place of business in the US.
- Prime brokers, International Swap Dealers Association ('ISDA') counterparties and other fund counterparties will typically require representations regarding ERISA compliance in the relevant agreement between the parties.
- Certain issuers of structured debt or asset backed securities will restrict (or altogether prohibit) plan asset funds from acquiring the securities. Careful attention should be paid to the issuer's offering materials.

FINRA Rules 5130 and 5131 – new issues

11.124 The Financial Industry Regulatory Authority, Inc ('FINRA') was created in 2007 by the merger of the National Association of Securities Dealers, Inc ('NASD') with the regulatory and arbitration divisions of the New York Stock Exchange. Accordingly, FINRA succeeded the NASD as the principal self-regulatory organisation under the Exchange Act. Substantially all SEC-registered broker-dealers are members of FINRA.

11.125 FINRA Rule 5130 generally prohibits a FINRA member from selling a 'new issue' to any account in which a 'restricted person' has a beneficial interest. For this purpose, 'new issue' includes any US IPO and any non-US IPO in which a FINRA member is part of the underwriting syndicate. 'Restricted persons' are, generally, FINRA members and other broker-dealers, their affiliates, and persons having portfolio management responsibility for collective investment vehicles or financial or other institutions, as well as the immediate family members of all such persons.

11.126 Significantly, FINRA Rule 5130 is subject to a de minimis exemption which exempts sales to and purchases by an account if the beneficial interests of restricted persons do not exceed in the aggregate 10% of such account. Whilst restricted persons may receive some benefit from new issues, nearly all of the benefit (90% or greater) must flow to non-restricted persons.

11.127 FINRA Rule 5131 prohibits the allocation of new issues by a FINRA broker-dealer[1] to an account in which an executive officer or director of a public company[2] or a covered non-public company[3] (each, a 'company'), or a person materially supported[4] by such executive officer or director (collectively, a 'covered investor'), has a beneficial interest if:

- the company is currently an investment banking services client of such FINRA broker-dealer (a 'related broker') or the related broker has received compensation from the company for investment banking services in the past 12 months;

11.127 The US Dimension

- the person responsible for making the allocation decision knows or has reason to know that the related broker intends to provide, or expects to be retained by the company for, investment banking services within the next three months; or
- new issues are allocated on the express or implied condition that such executive officer or director, on behalf of the company, will retain the related broker for the performance of future investment banking services.

[1] Rule 5131(b) will not apply to allocations of securities that are directed in writing by the issuer, its affiliates, or selling shareholders, so long as the FINRA broker-dealer has no involvement or influence, directly or indirectly, in the allocation decisions of the issuer, its affiliates, or selling shareholders, with respect to such issuer-directed securities.

[2] Rule 5131(e)(1) defines a 'public company' as any company that is registered under section 12 of the Securities and Exchange Act of 1934 or files periodic reports pursuant to section 15(d) thereof.

[3] Rule 5131(e)(3) defines a 'covered non-public company' as any non-public company with: (i) an income of at least US$1 million in the last fiscal year or in two of the last three fiscal years and shareholders' equity of at least US$15 million; (ii) shareholders' equity of at least US$30 million and a two-year operating history; or (iii) total assets and total revenue of at least US$75 million in the latest fiscal year or in two of the last three fiscal years.

[4] Rule 5131(e)(6) defines 'material support' as directly or indirectly providing more than 25% of a person's income in the prior calendar year. Persons living in the same household are deemed to be providing each other with material support.

11.128 Significantly, FINRA Rule 5131 is subject to a de minimis exemption which exempts sales to and purchases by an account if the beneficial interests of covered investors do not exceed in the aggregate 25% of such account. Whilst restricted persons may receive some benefit from new issues, nearly all of the benefit (75% or greater) must flow to non-covered investors.

11.129 Where the rule applies, allocating brokers which are FINRA members must, before selling any new issue to an account, have obtained within 12 months prior to the sale a representation from the beneficial owners or their conduit (such as their investment adviser, broker-dealer or bank) that the account is eligible to purchase new issues under the rule. Thus, in order to invest in new issues, a hedge fund manager will often be required to represent that the account purchasing the IPO shares is either: (1)(a) not held by any restricted persons or (b) complies with the 10% de minimis exemption; or (2)(a) not held by any covered investors or (b) complies with the 25% de minimis exemption. In practice, this means that a hedge fund that intends to invest in new issues will need to track the extent of the beneficial interests in the fund held by FINRA restricted persons.

Chapter 12

UCITS

Matthew Jones, Senior PSL, Simmons & Simmons and Neil Simmonds, Partner, Simmons & Simmons

A	UCITS: The 'gold' standard	12.1
B	UCITS: A brief history	12.3
C	UCITS: Key characteristics, features and requirements	12.44
D	Summary of UCITS investment powers	12.51
E	Spreading risk and investment limits	12.59
F	Financial derivative instruments	12.70
G	Investment restrictions applicable to derivatives	12.82
H	Financial indices	12.120
I	Securities and instruments that embed derivatives	12.124
J	Investment management techniques	12.130
K	Borrowing and lending	12.136
L	Short selling	12.139
M	Fund liquidity	12.145
N	Future legislative changes	12.146

A UCITS: THE 'GOLD' STANDARD

12.1 The appetite for alternative UCITS has increased in recent years as they provide access to hedge fund strategies within a regulated, transparent and liquid format. It would appear that this trend is likely to continue as pension funds and other financial institutions (particularly those managing money on behalf of individuals) seek hedge fund-related returns within a structure which offers the highest level of investor protection and regulation.

12.2 Hedge fund managers have been taking advantage of the opportunities presented by UCITS since 2001 when the implementation of UCITS III significantly widened the range of financial instruments available for investment by UCITS vehicles. Since the financial crisis, the use of UCITS vehicles by managers in the alternatives sector has gathered real momentum as more investors have demanded onshore, transparent, regulated vehicles.

B UCITS: A BRIEF HISTORY

Background

12.3 'UCITS' (or 'undertakings for collective investments in transferable securities') is a type of collective investment scheme ('CIS') which can trace its origins back to Europe in the 1980s and the European Community's drive to develop a single market, introduce free movement of capital between member states and remove restrictions on trade.

12.4 UCITS

12.4 On 20 December 1985, Council Directive 85/611/EEC (the original 'UCITS Directive') was published with the aim of harmonising the sale and marketing of open-ended CIS to retail investors, since distribution, at the time, varied widely from one member state to another. This new directive set standards for investment managers and sought to create a single market in the sale of open-ended CIS within the European Community through 'passporting'.

12.5 The reality was somewhat different. Varying marketing rules in the individual member states created obstacles to marketing, and the limited range of investments permitted under the original UCITS Directive prevented UCITS from using the increasing range of investments that were being developed in the market. Moreover, the passporting procedure by which UCITS were registered in other member states, which was intended to operate as an automatic notification, became instead a time-consuming and costly registration hurdle in many member states.

UCITS II

12.6 From 1985, European officials were involved in discussions to amend the UCITS Directive and rectify the investment and cross-border marketing restrictions. This led to a draft directive being developed ('UCITS II'), which was subsequently abandoned as agreement on its content could not be reached by the European Council of Ministers.

UCITS III

12.7 By 1998, the European Commission published a new proposal, drafted in two parts, which was finally adopted in 2001 and culminated in the publishing of two separate directives, together known as 'UCITS III':

- Directive 2001/107/EC of 21 January 2002 (the 'Management Directive'); and
- Directive 2001/108/EC of 21 January 2002 (the 'Product Directive').

12.8 The Management Directive set out minimum standards which a UCITS management company should comply with in terms of capital and risk control, rules of conduct and conditions relating to resources.

12.9 The primary aim of the Product Directive was to expand the nature and scope of investments that a UCITS could invest in to include new instruments (money market instruments, collective investment schemes, bank deposits and, most significantly, financial derivative instruments). The Product Directive also eased investment restrictions for index tracker funds.

UCITS IV

12.10 Directive 2009/65/EC of 13 July 2009, the recast 'UCITS Directive' (known as 'UCITS IV'), was required to be implemented by member states on 1 July 2011. UCITS IV introduced a management passport allowing a UCITS to be managed by a manager regulated in a member state other than the

UCITS' home member state. UCITS IV also set out a regime for merging UCITS on both a domestic and cross-border basis. Master-feeder structures[1] were introduced, enabling one or more feeder funds to invest the cash received from its own investors in a master fund, and the simplified prospectus was replaced by a 'key investor information document' which is intended to provide investors with important information about a particular fund in a clear way. Finally, the notification procedure for the marketing of UCITS in member states was streamlined and simplified by providing for a regulator-to-regulator notification procedure, bringing the process in line with equivalent passport procedures under other European directives.

[1] See paras **12.49–12.50** below.

UCITS V

12.11 On 18 March 2016, a further revision, Directive 2014/91/EU of 23 July 2014 (known as 'UCITS V'), came into effect. UCITS V introduced a number of significant amendments to the recast UCITS Directive, principally in the areas of:

- remuneration[1];
- depositaries[2]; and
- administrative sanctions[3].

[1] See paras **12.12–12.32** below.
[2] See paras **12.33–12.42** below.
[3] See para **12.43** below.

Remuneration

12.12 UCITS V requires the management body of any UCITS established within the EU (ie its management company or the fund itself where it is 'self-managed') to establish and apply remuneration policies and practices which (i) are consistent with and promote sound risk management and (ii) do not encourage risk taking inconsistent with the risk profile or rules of the UCITS.

12.13 By design, the remuneration provisions in UCITS V are similar in many respects to those in the Alternative Investment Fund Managers Directive[1] ('AIFMD') and the Capital Requirements Directive[2] and Capital Requirements Regulation[3] (together, 'CRD') – although those for UCITS include considerably more detail regarding the identification of material risk takers, payments to third parties, the operation of proportionality and disclosure.

[1] Directive 2011/61/EU of 8 June 2011.
[2] Directive 2013/36/EU of 26 June 2013.
[3] Regulation (EU) No 575/2013 of 26 June 2013.

12.14 The structuring requirements for UCITS management companies include 'pay out process' rules which are similar to those for AIFMs. Following is a summary.

12.15 UCITS

Deferral

12.15 Deferral requirements have been aligned with AIFMD, ie payment of at least 40% of variable remuneration should be deferred for at least three years and vest no faster than on a pro-rata basis. Where variable remuneration is 'a particularly high amount', at least 60% must be deferred.

Payment in units of the UCITS or equivalent instruments

12.16 At least half the variable remuneration paid to members of staff who are material risk takers[1] must be paid in units of the UCITS that they manage (or equivalent ownership interests, or share-linked instruments or equivalent non-cash instruments), unless the management of UCITS accounts for less than half the total portfolio managed by the management company.

[1] See paras 12.20–12.21 below.

Performance assessment

12.17 Where remuneration is performance related, the assessment of performance must be set in a multi-year framework 'appropriate to the holding period recommended to the investors of the UCITS managed by the management company'.

Performance adjustment

12.18 Variable remuneration must be subject to potential forfeiture in certain circumstances including through malus and clawback.

Guaranteed variable remuneration

12.19 As is the case under both CRD and AIFMD, guaranteed variable remuneration should be exceptional, occurring only in the context of new hires and limited to the first year only.

Material risk takers

12.20 In line with AIFMD, material risk takers ('MRTs') are defined to cover categories of staff, including:

- senior management;
- risk takers;
- control functions; and
- any employee receiving total remuneration that falls within the remuneration bracket of senior management and risk takers whose professional activities have a material impact on the risk profiles of the management companies or the UCITS they manage.

12.21 In addition, MRTs should include:

- any employee and any other member of staff at fund or sub-fund level who are decision takers, fund managers and persons who take real investment decisions;
- persons who have the power to exercise influence on such employees or members of staff, including investment policy advisers and analysts, and senior management; and
- any employees receiving total remuneration that takes them into the same remuneration bracket as senior management and decision takers.

APPLICATION TO DELEGATES

12.22 The European Securities and Markets Authority's ('ESMA') guidelines on sound remuneration policies under the UCITS Directive[1] (the 'Remuneration Guidelines') require the UCITS management company to ensure that either:

- entities to which investment management activities have been delegated are subject to remuneration requirements 'equally as effective' as those in the Remuneration Guidelines; or
- appropriate contractual arrangements are put in place which cover any payments made to the delegate's 'identified staff' as compensation for the performance of investment management activities on the management company's behalf.

[1] ESMA/2016/575, 14 October 2016 – seehttps://www.esma.europa.eu/sites/default/files/library/2016-575_ucits_remuneration_guidelines.pdf.

REMUNERATION DISCLOSURE

12.23 A prospectus issued by a UCITS must include details of the up-to-date remuneration policy, including but not limited to a description of how remuneration and benefits are calculated and the identities of persons responsible for awarding the remuneration and benefits, including the composition of the remuneration committee (if it exists), or a link/reference to a website containing that information.

12.24 The firm's annual report must also contain details of the total amount of remuneration for the financial year, split into fixed and variable remuneration paid by the management company and by the investment company to its staff, and the number of beneficiaries, and where relevant, any amount paid directly by the UCITS itself, including any performance fee.

12.25 The key investor information document must also include a statement that the details of the up-to-date remuneration policy, including but not limited to a description of how remuneration and benefits are calculated and the identities of persons responsible for awarding the remuneration and benefits, including the composition of the remuneration committee (if it exists), are available by means of a website (including a link/reference to that website).

12.26 UCITS

REMUNERATION COMMITTEE

12.26 Like AIFMs, UCITS management companies which are significant in (a) size, (b) the amount of the assets under management of the UCITS they manage, (c) their internal organisation, and (d) the nature, scope and complexity of their activities, will be required to establish a remuneration committee ('RemCo').

12.27 The RemCo members must be members of the management body who do not perform executive functions.

12.28 Moreover, where national law provides for employee representation on the management board, the RemCo must include one or more employee representatives.

12.29 Finally, the RemCo's decisions must take into account 'the long-term interests of shareholders, investors and the public interest'. It is unclear exactly how the RemCo's members are to assess where the public interest lies and no clarification is expected from either ESMA or the European Commission.

APPLYING THE REMUNERATION RULES PROPORTIONATELY

12.30 UCITS V states that proportionality should apply 'provided that UCITS management companies apply all the principles governing remuneration policies'.

12.31 UCITS management companies must then comply with the remuneration principles 'in a way and to the extent that is appropriate to their size, internal organisation and the nature, scope and complexity of their activities'. In assessing what is proportionate, the management company's focus should be on a combination of all the stated criteria (size, internal organisation and the nature, scope and complexity of the activities) and, as this list is not deemed to be exhaustive, it should also consider any other relevant criteria.

12.32 The Remuneration Guidelines should also, to the extent possible, be aligned with those for managers regulated under AIFMD and with rules applicable to other firms in the financial services sector.

Depositaries

12.33 UCITS V aims to align the rules on depositaries for UCITS with those under AIFMD, for example by requiring that for each UCITS – as for each AIF – a single depositary must be appointed, with responsibility for oversight, monitoring and safekeeping functions. The appointment must be evidenced by a written contract.

12.34 In carrying out its functions, the depositary will have to act honestly, fairly, professionally, independently and solely in the interest of the investors in the UCITS.

Who can be a depositary?

12.35 Depositaries are restricted, under UCITS V, to specified entities, namely:

- national central banks;
- EU credit institutions under CRD; or
- other legal entities which are authorised in a member state to act as depositaries, provided that they are subject to capital requirements and own funds not less than those required under CRD – note that entities in this category must also meet a number of minimum prudential and organisational requirements.

12.36 UCITS V also prohibits re-use by the depositary of UCITS assets which are held in custody unless certain specified criteria are met.

Liability of the depositary

12.37 Under UCITS V, the depositary is, to all intents and purposes, strictly liable to the fund and to its unitholders for the loss of financial instruments by the depositary or by a third party to whom the depositary has delegated custody.

12.38 Liability can be neither excluded nor limited by agreement and may only be avoided where the depositary can prove 'that the loss has arisen as a result of an external event beyond its reasonable control, the consequences of which would have been unavoidable despite all reasonable efforts to the contrary'[1] – these provisions closely reflect the position in the equivalent sections of the Level 1 AIFMD text, although a key difference is that for a UCITS the depositary is not able to contractually discharge itself of liability (as it may under AIFMD).

[1] Article 24 of the UCITS Directive.

12.39 Under UCITS V, a depositary cannot delegate the oversight or monitoring functions to a third party but may delegate the custody function to an appropriate third party provided certain conditions are met.

12.40 It seems likely that a third party to which the depositary has delegated any function may, in turn, sub-delegate on the same conditions.

12.41 Where custody functions are delegated to a third party, the third party must take all necessary steps to ensure that, should it become insolvent, the UCITS assets which it holds are not available to the third party's creditors.

Reporting obligations of the depositary

12.42 Under UCITS V, the depositary is obliged to make available to its competent authority, on request, all information which the depositary has received while performing its duties which may be necessary for the competent authority to carry out its duties. Where the depositary has a different competent authority from that of the UCITS management company, the depositary's competent authority must share information with that of the management company without delay.

Administrative sanctions

12.43 UCITS V provides for a number of 'effective, proportionate and dissuasive' sanctions to be available which competent authorities can apply where the Directive's provisions have been breached, and includes provisions by which competent authorities are able (a) to publish sanctions in an anonymised form in a number of specified circumstances, (b) to take into account, where appropriate, measures taken after the breach by the person responsible in order to avoid a repetition of the breach, and (c) to take into account additional factors beyond those contained in UCITS V when determining the type and level of administrative sanctions.

C UCITS: KEY CHARACTERISTICS, FEATURES AND REQUIREMENTS

Principal requirements for all UCITS

12.44 Under the UCITS Directive[1], the key requirements of a UCITS are as follows:

- The sole object of the fund must be the collective investment in transferable securities or in other liquid financial assets (as set out in the Directive) of capital raised from the public.
- The fund must operate on the principle of risk-spreading.
- The shares/units must, at the request of holders, be repurchased or redeemed, directly or indirectly, out of the fund's assets (ie the UCITS must be open-ended).
- The fund must not undertake any activities unless and until it has been authorised by the competent authority of its home member state. Under the Directive, a competent authority has up to two months to decide on whether to grant the relevant authorisation or not.
- Investment can only be made in certain eligible assets within specific restrictions relating to the spread of investments, leverage and exposures.
- The assets of a UCITS must be entrusted to an independent trustee/custodian/depositary which holds them for the benefit of the UCITS/investors depending on the legal nature of the fund.

[1] Directive 2009/65/EC of 13 July 2009, as amended by Directive 2014/91/EU of 23 July 2014.

Structuring options for a UCITS

12.45 In practice, the structuring options available for a UCITS depends on the domestic laws of the member state selected for its establishment. However, in principle, the UCITS Directive provides for the following:

- A UCITS may be constituted in accordance with contract law (as common funds managed by management companies), trust law (as unit trusts), or statute (as investment companies).
- A UCITS established as an investment company may be self-managed (so, it is not required to appoint a separate management company).

- A UCITS may take the form of an umbrella structure with sub-funds, in which case each sub-fund is regarded as a UCITS.
- The shares of a UCITS may be listed on a stock exchange.
- It is possible to have a master UCITS with feeder funds (which must also be UCITS).

12.46 Once a fund is established as a UCITS it cannot be converted or transformed into a non-UCITS fund.

Marketing UCITS

12.47 The UCITS Directive sets out common rules which allow a UCITS authorised and supervised in one member state to market its units in any other member state following a simplified notification procedure. The following is a summary of the notification process:

- A UCITS seeking to market its units in another member state informs its home authority of its intention and sends them the notification documents (prospectus, constitutional documents, reports, key investor information document).
- The home authority checks the completeness of the file and, if complete, transmits it to the host authority within ten working days, together with an attestation confirming that the UCITS fulfils its obligations under the Directive.
- The competent authority of the host member state will not be entitled to review, challenge or discuss the merits of the UCITS authorisation granted in the home member state.
- The home authority informs the UCITS about the transmission date and the UCITS is able to start marketing its units in the host member state following the transmission date.
- The host authority checks ex post that marketing is conducted in accordance with national rules.

12.48 Under the Directive, it should take no more than ten business days to obtain access to the markets of the relevant member states following notification to the home state regulator.

Master-feeder structures

12.49 Under the UCITS Directive, one or more feeder funds are able to pool their assets in a single master fund provided all feeder funds and the master fund are authorised as UCITS. This allows UCITS to have increased economies of scale and lower operational costs and makes the framework more attractive for creating funds for institutional investors.

12.50 The master-feeder structure allows the feeder UCITS to invest 85% or more of the net asset value ('NAV') into a master UCITS. Up to 15% of the NAV can be invested in ancillary liquid assets and derivatives for hedging purposes. The feeder UCITS de facto delegates portfolio management to the master UCITS and must therefore monitor the master UCITS. The feeder and master UCITS may be in the same or in different member states and may or may not have depositaries in the same group (each UCITS still needs a local

12.50 *UCITS*

depositary) although, if different, the management companies, depositaries and auditors must enter into information sharing agreements. A master UCITS is not permitted to be a feeder fund and it is not permitted to invest in other feeder funds.

D   SUMMARY OF UCITS INVESTMENT POWERS

12.51 Under the original UCITS Directive, a UCITS could only invest in 'transferable securities' (bonds and equities), although a UCITS was able to employ 'techniques and instruments' relating to transferable securities for the purposes of 'efficient portfolio management'. Since 1985, the availability and market acceptance of these techniques and instruments has grown rapidly. Due to the limited scope of the original Directive, UCITS were not able to keep up with these developments and there was a strong demand to extend the scope of the Directive to enable UCITS to compete with other investment funds.

12.52 As part of UCITS III, the Product Directive expanded the range of available investments, allowing money market instruments, units in collective investment schemes and deposits to all be eligible investments for a UCITS. Significantly, UCITS III permitted UCITS to invest in derivatives for investment purposes as well as for 'efficient portfolio management' and/or 'hedging'.

12.53 Article 53a of the original UCITS Directive[1] conferred delegated powers to the European Commission to clarify definitions in the Directive in order to ensure its uniform application throughout the EU. In this context, the Commission decided to make use of its powers and, on 19 March 2007, issued Commission Directive 2007/16/EC (referred to as the Eligible Assets Directive or 'EAD'). The EAD clarifies the meaning and the scope of the definitions included in the UCITS Directive as regards transferable securities, money market instruments and other liquid financial assets as well as how these definitions apply to certain financial instruments.

[1] Article 111(a) of the recast UCITS Directive.

12.54 Since the introduction of UCITS III and the EAD, the Committee of European Securities Regulators ('CESR') and its successor, ESMA, have published a number of guidance documents and opinions relating to UCITS eligible assets and investment techniques. In addition, various Q&As have been published with a view to promoting common supervisory approaches and practices. While the Q&As are primarily aimed at member states to ensure that their actions converge along the same lines as those adopted by ESMA, they are also helpful for management companies and their advisers by providing a further level of technical detail and clarity on the requirements under UCITS.

Eligible assets overview

12.55 Article 1(2) of the UCITS Directive states that UCITS are undertakings 'with the sole object of collective investment in transferable securities or in other liquid financial assets . . . of capital raised from the public and which operate on the principle of risk-spreading'.

12.56 The eligible assets for a UCITS can be summarised as follows:

- Transferable securities (including shares, bonds, units in closed-ended funds, structured financial instruments and other negotiable securities) which are:
  - admitted to official listing on a stock exchange in an EU member state or non-EU member state; or
  - dealt in on a market which is regulated, operating regularly, recognised and open to the public; or
  - recently issued transferable securities which will be admitted to official listing on a stock exchange or other market (as described above) within a year.
- Money market instruments ('MMIs') which are:
  - admitted to official listing on a stock exchange in an EU member state or non-EU member state; or
  - dealt in on a market which is regulated, operating regularly, recognised and open to the public; or
  - instruments, other than those dealt in on a regulated market, provided that the issue or the issuer is itself regulated for the purpose of protecting investors and savings and provided that the MMIs are issued or guaranteed by certain bodies.
- Units of UCITS and units of (some) non-UCITS collective investment schemes.
- Deposits with credit institutions.
- Financial derivative instruments that meet certain criteria.
- Transferable securities and MMIs other than those referred to above (subject to a maximum aggregate limit of 10% of the UCITS' assets) – often referred to as the 'trash bucket'.

12.57 Generally a UCITS is only permitted to acquire movable and immovable property if this is essential for the direct pursuit of its business. A UCITS is not permitted to acquire precious metals or certificates representing precious metals.

12.58 Direct exposure to commodities is not permissible, although it is possible to achieve indirect exposure to ineligible assets (such as commodities) by way of:

- derivatives on acceptable indices; and
- structured financial products backed by or linked to such assets.

E   SPREADING RISK AND INVESTMENT LIMITS

12.59 Article 1(2) of the UCITS Directive states that UCITS are undertakings ' . . . which operate on the principle of risk-spreading'. The Directive sets out various limits that apply when a UCITS invests in specific eligible asset classes as described below.

Transferable securities and MMIs issued by same body

12.60 A UCITS may not invest any more than 5% of its assets in transferable securities or MMIs issued by the same body (the '5% Limit'). However, the 5% Limit can be raised to 10% provided that the total value of the transferable securities and the MMIs held by the UCITS in the relevant issuing bodies in

12.60 UCITS

each of which it invests more than 5% of its assets does not exceed 40% of the value of its assets (the '5/10/40 Rule'). GAPS and Covered Bonds[1] are not taken into account when applying the 5/10/40 Rule.

[1] See para 12.62 below.

12.61 The 5% Limit referred to above may be raised to 35% if the transferable securities or MMIs are issued or guaranteed by a member state, by its local authorities, by a third country or by a public international body to which one or more member states belong (generally referred to as 'Government and Public Securities' or 'GAPS'). A UCITS may invest up to 100% of its assets in GAPS of a single issuer provided it does not hold more than 30% in GAPS of a single issue and holds GAPS from at least six separate issues.

12.62 The 5% Limit may also be raised to a maximum of 25% where bonds are issued by a credit institution which has its registered office in a member state and is subject by law to special public supervision designed to protect bond-holders as set out in the UCITS Directive (generally referred to as 'Covered Bonds'). However, where a UCITS invests more than 5% of its assets in Covered Bonds issued by a single issuer, the total value of the Covered Bonds must not exceed 80% of the value of the assets of the UCITS.

12.63 The 5% Limit may be increased to either 20% or 35% to allow investment in shares or debt securities issued by the same body for certain tracker funds, ie where the investment policy of the UCITS is to replicate the composition of a certain stock or debt securities index. Certain conditions need to be satisfied for this to apply.

Deposits with the same body

12.64 A UCITS may not invest any more than 20% of its assets in deposits made with the same body.

Counterparty exposure on an OTC derivative

12.65 The risk exposure to a counterparty of a UCITS in an over-the-counter ('OTC') derivative transaction may not exceed 5% of its assets (10% for banks and other approved credit institutions).

Combining the limits

12.66 A UCITS is not able to combine any of the limits referred to above where this would lead to investment of more than 20% of its assets in a single body, in any combination of the following:

- transferable securities or MMIs issued by that body (excluding GAPS and Covered Bonds);
- deposits made with that body; or
- exposures arising from OTC derivative transactions undertaken with that body.

12.67 Save for those circumstances where a UCITS may invest up to 100% of its assets in GAPS issued by the same issuer (ie where it does not hold more than 30% of its assets in GAPS of a single issue and holds GAPS from at least six separate issues), none of the limits referred to above may be combined such that investments in transferable securities or MMIs issued by the same body (including GAPS and Covered Bonds) or in deposits or derivative instruments made by such body exceeds 35% of the assets of the UCITS.

12.68 For the purposes of applying each of the limits, the UCITS Directive provides that companies that are included in the same group for the purposes of consolidated accounts shall be regarded as a single body.

Investment in CIS

12.69 A UCITS is not permitted to invest in any CIS that is not a UCITS or other CIS referred to in Article 50(1)(e) of the UCITS Directive (a 'UCITS Equivalent'). A UCITS may not invest more than 20% of its assets in a single UCITS or UCITS Equivalent. It may also not invest more than 30% of its assets, in aggregate, in CIS which are not UCITS (ie UCITS Equivalents) although it may invest up to 100% of its assets in other UCITS.

F   FINANCIAL DERIVATIVE INSTRUMENTS

12.70 Hedge funds are often characterised by their extensive use of derivatives and derivative based techniques. UCITS may invest in derivatives subject to a variety of conditions relating to the nature of the exposures taken, the leverage generated through such positions, the process employed by the UCITS to manage the risks arising from derivatives investment as well as rules relating to OTC counterparty exposure and to the valuation of derivatives exposure.

Rules applicable to all derivatives

12.71 Article 50(1)(g) of the UCITS Directive states that UCITS may invest in derivatives, including equivalent cash-settled instruments (whether dealt in on a regulated market or OTC derivatives) provided that the underlying consists of:

- otherwise eligible assets (other than assets which could only comprise the 10% trash bucket), although this may include financial instruments 'having one or several characteristics' of such eligible assets;
- interest rates;
- foreign exchange rates or currencies; or
- financial indices[1].

[1] See paras 12.120–12.123 below.

Rules specifically applicable to OTC derivatives

12.72 In the case of OTC derivatives, the UCITS Directive states that in addition to the requirements outlined above, those types of derivatives must also comply with the following criteria:

12.72 *UCITS*

- the counterparties to OTC derivative transactions must be institutions subject to prudential supervision, and belonging to categories approved by the relevant UCITS' competent authority; and
- the OTC derivatives must (i) be subject to 'reliable and verifiable valuation' (see below) on a daily basis and (ii) be able to be sold, liquidated or closed by an offsetting transaction at any time at their 'fair value' (see below) at the UCITS' initiative.

12.73 According to Article 8(4) of the EAD, the reference to 'reliable and verifiable valuation' referred to above is understood as a reference to a valuation corresponding to the 'fair value', which does not rely only on market quotations by the counterparty and which fulfils the following criteria:

- the basis for the valuation is either a reliable up-to-date market value of the instrument or, if such a value is not available, a pricing model using an adequate recognised methodology;
- verification of the valuation is carried out by one of the following:
  - an appropriate third party which is independent from the counterparty of the OTC derivative, at an adequate frequency and in such a way that the UCITS is able to check it;
  - a unit within the UCITS which is independent from the department in charge of managing the assets and which is adequately equipped for such purpose.

12.74 The reference to 'fair value' is understood as a reference to the amount for which an asset could be exchanged, or a liability settled, between knowledgeable, willing parties in an arm's length transaction.

Credit derivatives

12.75 Credit derivatives are eligible assets if they comply with the specified criteria set out in Article 8(2) of the EAD, namely:

- they allow the transfer of credit risk of an asset (independently of other risks associated with that asset) that is an acceptable underlying for derivatives as referred to above;
- they comply with the criteria for OTC derivative instruments as set out above;
- the end of the transaction can only result in the delivery or transfer of assets (including cash) which are, themselves, eligible for the UCITS;
- the risk management policy for credit derivatives should meet the same criteria as for OTC derivatives[1] but should additionally take into account the risks of asymmetry of information, in particular with related parties.

[1] See Article 19(1)(g) of the original UCITS Directive and Article 8(3) and (4) of the EAD.

12.76 The EAD makes it clear that the risks of asymmetry of information between the issuers/banks and the UCITS must be taken into account here. These risks are particularly great for credit derivatives which are concluded with counterparties that might have access to non-public information on issuers referenced by credit derivatives.

Commodity derivatives

12.77 The EAD expressly excludes derivatives on commodities as an eligible asset for UCITS. However, see below in relation to derivatives on financial indices (which may include commodity indices).

Derivatives on financial indices

12.78 Derivatives on financial indices which meet the criteria for financial indices[1] are eligible investments. These may be derivatives on financial indices of eligible and ineligible assets (such as commodities). Derivatives on indices which are composed of eligible assets, but which do not meet the criteria for financial indices, are treated as derivatives on a combination of eligible assets and will be eligible for investment provided the spread rules in relation to those underlying assets are met. 'True' indices that comply with the criteria for financial indices do not have to be combined with other assets in the fund in accordance with the spread and issuer concentration rules.

[1] See para **12.120** below.

Diversification and total return swaps

12.79 In the context of setting out guidelines in relation to the levels of diversification required of a UCITS' investment portfolio, ESMA has specifically highlighted the use of total return swaps or other derivative instruments with similar characteristics. ESMA's guidelines on ETFs and other UCITS issues[1] (the 'ETF Guidelines') state that where a UCITS enters into a total return swap ('TRS') or invests in other financial derivative instruments ('FDI') with similar characteristics, the underlying exposures of the FDI should be taken into account in calculating the investment limits set out in Article 52 of the UCITS Directive.

[1] ESMA/2014/937EN, 1 August 2014 – see https://www.esma.europa.eu/document/guidelines-etfs-and-other-ucits-issues-0.

12.80 ESMA has previously highlighted particular concerns where a UCITS enters into swaps which are not passively managed by the counterparty and the contract includes some discretionary elements (for example, where the counterparty selects assets backing the swap from an eligible pool) or where the swap is managed completely within the discretion of the counterparty without a clear objective methodology.

12.81 To address such concerns, the ETF Guidelines provide that where a counterparty has discretion over the composition/management of the UCITS' investment portfolio or of the underlying of the FDI, the agreement between it and the UCITS should be considered as an investment management delegation arrangement. This would therefore need to comply with the UCITS requirements on delegation.

G INVESTMENT RESTRICTIONS APPLICABLE TO DERIVATIVES

Spread

12.82 The exposure to the underlying assets of a derivative must not exceed the investment restrictions for such underlying assets (although does not apply in relation to derivatives on financial indices and its underlying reference assets).

OTC counterparty risk exposure

12.83 A UCITS' maximum OTC derivative counterparty exposure (including collateral posted as margin) must not exceed 5% of the UCITS' assets (or 10% if the counterparty is a bank or other approved credit institution).

Issuer concentration

12.84 However, it should be noted that a UCITS cannot combine OTC derivative counterparty exposure to a single body (which will include collateral received) with:

- investments in transferable securities and/or MMIs issued by, and/or
- deposits made with,

the same single body where such combined investments are in excess of 20% of the value of the UCITS' assets.

12.85 Compliance with issuer concentration limits are required to be calculated on the basis of the underlying exposure created through the use of derivative instruments using the 'commitment' approach[1].

[1] See paras 12.104–12.109 below.

Netting

12.86 Article 43 of Commission Directive 2010/43/EU (published on 1 July 2010 as part of the Level 2 measures under UCITS IV) (the 'Commission Directive') provides that when calculating a UCITS' exposure to a counterparty, management companies must use the positive mark-to-market value of the OTC derivative contract with that counterparty. For these purposes the management company is able to net the derivative positions of a UCITS held with the same counterparty, provided it can legally enforce netting agreements with the counterparty on behalf of the UCITS. Netting is only permissible with respect to OTC derivatives with the same counterparty and not in relation to any other exposures the UCITS may have with that counterparty.

Collateral

12.87 A UCITS' exposure to a counterparty of an OTC derivative may be reduced through the receipt of collateral. Such collateral must be sufficiently liquid so that it can be sold quickly at a price that is close to its pre-sale valuation.

12.88 Collateral must be taken into account when calculating counterparty exposure risk when collateral is posted from a UCITS to an OTC counterparty. Collateral passed to a counterparty in this way may be taken into account on a net basis if there are legally enforceable netting arrangements between the UCITS and the counterparty.

12.89 On 28 July 2010, CESR published its guidelines on risk measurement and the calculation of global exposure and counterparty risk for UCITS[1] (the 'Risk Measurement Guidelines'). These Guidelines accompanied the Commission Directive. As regards collateral, the Risk Measurement Guidelines were modified further by the ETF Guidelines issued in December 2012 (and revised in August 2014). Taken together the two sets of Guidelines confirm that collateral may be used to reduce counterparty risk exposure provided it complies with the following criteria at all times:

- *Liquidity*: Any collateral received other than cash should be highly liquid and traded on a regulated market or multilateral trading facility with transparent pricing in order that it can be sold quickly at a price that is close to pre-sale valuation. Collateral received should also comply with the provisions of Article 56 of the UCITS Directive.
- *Valuation*: Collateral received should be valued on at least a daily basis and assets that exhibit high price volatility should not be accepted as collateral unless suitably conservative haircuts are in place.
- *Issuer credit quality*: Collateral received should be of high quality.
- *Correlation*: The collateral received by the UCITS should be issued by an entity that is independent from the counterparty and is expected not to display a high correlation with the performance of the counterparty.
- *Collateral diversification (asset concentration)*: Collateral should be sufficiently diversified in terms of country, markets and issuers. As regards issuer concentration, this requirement will be regarded as satisfied if the UCITS receives from a counterparty a basket of collateral with a maximum exposure to a given issuer of 20% of its net asset value. When UCITS are exposed to different counterparties, the different baskets of collateral should be aggregated to calculate the 20% limit of exposure to a single issuer.
- *Operational and legal risks*: Risks linked to the management of the collateral should be identified, managed and mitigated by the risk management process.
- *Title transfer*: Where there is title transfer, the collateral received should be held by the depositary of the UCITS. For other types of collateral arrangement, the collateral can be held by a third party custodian which is subject to prudential supervision and which is unrelated to the provider of the collateral.
- *Enforceability of collateral*: Collateral received should be capable of being fully enforced by the UCITS at any time without reference to or approval from the counterparty.
- *Non-cash collateral*: Such collateral cannot be sold, reinvested or pledged.
- *Cash collateral*: Such collateral can only be:

12.89 *UCITS*

- placed on deposit with entities prescribed under the UCITS Directive;
- invested in high-quality government bonds;
- used for the purpose of reverse repo transactions provided the transactions are with credit institutions subject to prudential supervision and the UCITS is able to recall at any time the full amount of cash on an accrued basis;
- invested in short-term money market funds.

[1] CESR/10-788, 28 July 2010 – see https://www.esma.europa.eu/sites/default/files/library/2015/11/10_788.pdf.

12.90 The ETF Guidelines state that re-invested cash collateral should be diversified in accordance with the diversification requirements applicable to non-cash collateral.

12.91 A UCITS receiving collateral for at least 30% of its assets should have an appropriate stress testing policy in place to ensure regular stress tests are carried out under normal and exceptional liquidity conditions to enable the UCITS to assess liquidity risk attached to the collateral.

12.92 A UCITS is required to have in place a haircut policy adapted for each class of assets received as collateral. This policy is required to take into account the characteristics of the assets such as the credit standing or the price volatility, as well as the outcome of the relevant stress tests. The policy is required to be documented and should justify each decision to apply a specific haircut, to a certain class of assets.

12.93 The Risk Management Guidelines state that a UCITS cannot invest cash collateral in financial instruments providing a yield greater than the generally accepted risk-free return. The Guidelines go on to explain that it is generally accepted that in practice, markets use the return of short-dated (generally three-month) high-quality government bonds.

12.94 Collateral in the form of cash deposits in a currency other than the currency exposure should be subject to adjustment for currency mismatch. For collateral presenting a risk of value fluctuation, prudent discount rates can be determined by simulating the valuations of both securities and collateral over multiple holding periods.

12.95 Following publication in May 2015 of ESMA's Opinion[1] on the impact of the European Market Infrastructure Regulation[2] on the UCITS Directive, ESMA's view is that UCITS should no longer distinguish between OTC financial derivative transactions and exchange traded derivatives; rather, the distinction should be between cleared and non-cleared financial derivative transactions (ie irrespective of whether exchange traded or OTC).

[1] 2015/ESMA/880, 22 May 2015 – see www.esma.europa.eu/sites/default/files/library/2015/11/2015-880_esma_opinion_on_impact_of_emir_on_ucits.pdf.
[2] Regulation (EU) No 648/2012 of 4 July 2012.

Global exposure

12.96 Article 51(3) of the UCITS Directive requires a UCITS to ensure that its global exposure relating to derivative instruments does not exceed the total net value of its portfolio.

12.97 Article 41 of the Commission Directive provides that the global exposure of a managed UCITS may be calculated as either of the following:

- the incremental exposure and leverage generated by the managed UCITS through the use of financial derivative instruments including embedded derivatives, which may not exceed the total of the UCITS' net asset value; or
- the market risk of the UCITS' portfolio.

12.98 Global exposure is required to be calculated on at least a daily basis.

12.99 The Commission Directive provides that member states may allow management companies to calculate global exposure by using the commitment approach[1], the value at risk approach[2] ('VaR') or other advanced risk methodologies as may be appropriate. For these purposes, 'VaR' is said to mean a measure of the expected loss at a given confidence level over a specific time period.

[1] See further paras **12.104–12.109** below.
[2] See further paras **12.110–12.112** below.

12.100 The method selected for calculating global exposure must be appropriate to the UCITS, taking into account its investment strategy and the types and complexity of the derivative instruments used. Also, the proportion of the UCITS' portfolio which comprises financial derivative instruments should be considered.

12.101 If, as part of its efficient portfolio management, a UCITS employs techniques and instruments such as repos or securities lending with a view to generating additional leverage or exposure to market risk, such transactions are required to be taken into account for the purposes of calculating global exposure.

12.102 The Risk Measurement Guidelines state that a UCITS must use an advanced risk methodology (supported by a stress testing program) such as the VaR approach to calculate global exposure where:

- it engages in complex investment strategies which represent more than a negligible part of the UCITS' policy;
- it has more than a negligible exposure to exotic derivatives; or
- the commitment approach does not adequately capture the market risk of the portfolio.

12.103 The Risk Management Guidelines also state that managers are expected to use a 'maximum loss' approach to assess whether a complex investment strategy or the use of exotic derivatives represents more than a negligible exposure. Further, the Guidelines identify specific strategies that may be pursued by UCITS where the commitment approach is not considered adequate – such as the following hedge fund-like strategies:

- option strategies (for example, delta-neutral or volatility strategies);

12.103 *UCITS*

- arbitrage strategies (arbitrage on the interest rate curve, convertible bond arbitrage, etc);
- complex long-short and/or market neutral strategies.

Calculating global exposure using the commitment approach

12.104 According to the Risk Measurement Guidelines, using the commitment approach means applying the commitment conversion methodology which is the market value of the equivalent position in the underlying asset. This may be replaced by the notional value or the price of the futures contract where this is more conservative.

12.105 The Risk Measurement Guidelines set out the technical details for calculating global exposure using the commitment approach in the context of a range of different derivative types. They prescribe the conversion methodologies for standard derivatives such as futures, plain vanilla options, swaps and forwards and also set out the conversion methodologies to be used for embedded derivatives and non-standard (exotic) derivatives such as variance swaps and volatility swaps.

12.106 When calculating global exposure using the commitment approach the Risk Measurement Guidelines allow netting and hedging arrangements to be taken into account. For these purposes 'netting arrangements' are defined as combinations of trades on financial derivative instruments and/or security positions which refer to the same underlying asset, irrespective – in the case of financial derivative instruments – of the contracts' due date, and where the trades on financial derivative instruments and/or security positions are concluded with the sole aim of eliminating the risks linked to positions taken through the other financial derivative instruments and/or security positions.

12.107 Hedging arrangements are defined as combinations of trades on derivative instruments and/or security positions which do not necessarily refer to the same underlying asset and where the trades on financial derivative instruments and/or security positions are concluded with the sole aim of offsetting risks linked to positions taken through the other financial derivative instruments and/or security positions.

12.108 The Risk Management Guidelines state that if the UCITS uses a conservative calculation rather than an exact calculation of the commitment for each financial derivative instrument, hedging and netting arrangements cannot be taken into account if it results in an underestimation of the global exposure.

12.109 The Commission Directive states that where the use of financial derivative instruments does not generate incremental exposure for the UCITS, the underlying exposure need not be included in the commitment calculation[1]. Further, temporary borrowing arrangements entered into on behalf of the UCITS need not be included in the global exposure calculation.

[1] Article 42(4) of the Commission Directive.

Calculation of global exposure using the VaR approach

12.110 The VaR approach is a measure of the maximum potential loss due to market risk rather than leverage. The VaR approach measures the maximum potential loss at a given confidence level (probability) over a specific time period under normal market conditions.

12.111 A UCITS using VaR is required to establish, implement and maintain a documented system of internal limits concerning the measures used to manage and control the relevant risks for each UCITS. The VaR limits should be set according to the defined risk profile of the UCITS. All efficient portfolio management exposures should also be included as part of the UCITS' calculations and limits.

12.112 For the purposes of calculating global exposure a UCITS can use the relative VaR approach or the absolute VaR approach. The UCITS is responsible for deciding which VaR approach is the most appropriate given the risk profile and investment strategy of the UCITS. The Risk Measurement Guidelines include technical details for calculating and applying both methodologies. They also indicate where one method may be more appropriate than the other.

Cover rules for derivatives transactions

12.113 A UCITS must, at any given time, be capable of meeting all its payment and delivery obligations incurred by transactions involving financial derivative instruments. Monitoring to ensure that financial derivative transactions are adequately covered is required to form part of the risk management process described in more detail below. The Risk Measurement Guidelines set out in detail the cover requirements and how these can be satisfied in certain scenarios.

Risk management policy and process

12.114 All UCITS, whether or not they use financial derivative instruments, are required to establish, implement and maintain an adequate and documented risk management policy[1] which identifies the risks the UCITS is or may become exposed to. The policy must include procedures to assess market, liquidity and counterparty risks as well as all other risks a particular UCITS may be exposed to, including operational risks[2].

[1] Article 40 of the Commission Directive.
[2] Article 38 of the Commission Directive.

12.115 Further, under the Commission Directive, UCITS management companies are required to adopt adequate and effective arrangements, processes and techniques in order to:

- measure and manage at any time the risks which the UCITS they manage are or might be exposed to;
- ensure compliance with limits concerning global exposure and counterparty risk.

12.116 For these purposes, the Commission Directive requires management companies to take the following actions for each UCITS managed by them:

- put in place such risk measurement arrangements, processes and techniques as are necessary to ensure that the risks of its positions and their contribution to the overall risk profile are accurately measured on the basis of sound and reliable data and that the risk measurement arrangements, processes and techniques are adequately documented;
- conduct, where appropriate, periodic back-tests in order to review the validity of risk measurement arrangements which include model-based forecasts and estimates;
- conduct, where appropriate, periodic stress tests and scenario analyses to address risks arising from potential changes in market conditions that might adversely impact the UCITS;
- establish, implement and maintain a documented system of internal limits concerning the measures used to manage and control the relevant risks for each UCITS;
- ensure that the current level of risk complies with the risk limit system;
- establish, implement and maintain adequate procedures that, in the event of actual or anticipated breaches to the risk limit system, result in timely remedial actions in the best interests of unitholders.

12.117 Under Article 40(3) and (4) of the Commission Directive there is also a requirement to use an appropriate liquidity risk management process which should be subject to stress testing.

12.118 Prior to UCITS IV, CESR published its guidelines 'Risk management principles for UCITS'[1]. These guidelines remain valid and should be followed by UCITS management companies to the extent they remain compatible with the latest iteration of the UCITS Directive, the Commission Directive and the Risk Measurement Guidelines.

[1] CESR/09-178, February 2009 – see https://www.esma.europa.eu/sites/default/files/library/2015/11/09_178.pdf.

Reporting

12.119 The Commission Directive sets out requirements for UCITS management companies to deliver reports to the competent authorities of their home member states. These reports must be submitted on at least an annual basis and must contain information which reflects a true and fair view of the types of derivative instruments used for each UCITS, the underlying risks, the quantitative limits and the methods which are chosen to estimate the risks associated with the derivative transactions.

H FINANCIAL INDICES

General requirements for financial indices

12.120 In general, in order for an index to qualify for use as the underlying for a derivative transaction it must:

- be sufficiently diversified;
- represent an adequate benchmark for the market to which it refers; and
- be published in an appropriate manner.

12.121 The EAD explains the meaning of each of these terms and requirements in some detail.

Further requirements for derivatives on hedge fund indices

12.122 The issue of whether or not hedge fund indices can be classified as financial indices for the purposes of investment by UCITS was considered by CESR and published in its Level 3 text, 'Guidelines concerning eligible assets for investment by UCITS – The classification of hedge fund indices as financial indices'[1] (the 'HFI Guidelines'), in July 2007. The HFI Guidelines are broadly supportive of the concept of hedge fund indices and provide additional criteria (beyond those for other financial indices) which an index must meet in order to be eligible as the underlying for derivatives. These are that:

- pre-determined rules and objective criteria are applied for selecting and rebalancing components of the index;
- no payment may be made by constituents of the index to the index provider for inclusion in the index;
- the methodology of the index allows no backfilling, ie retrospective amendment to valuations of the index or its constituents;
- in the case of an OTC derivative on a hedge fund index, the OTC derivative rules apply (ie daily valuation, exposure rules and close out);
- the appropriate due diligence should be carried out to ascertain the quality of the index (this should take into account at least the following factors: the comprehensiveness of the index methodology; the availability of information about the index; and matters relating to the treatment of index components).

[1] CESR/07-434, July 2007 – see https://www.esma.europa.eu/sites/default/files/library/2015/11/07_434.pdf.

12.123 Accordingly, it is possible to construct a UCITS' portfolio solely consisting of synthetic exposure to an index meeting these criteria. Equally, indices can be used as part of a strategy to provide diversified exposure to alternative asset classes using indices on real estate, private equity or commodities.

I SECURITIES AND INSTRUMENTS THAT EMBED DERIVATIVES

12.124 If a transferable security or MMI embeds a derivative, a 'look through' will apply and, consequently, the global exposure[1] and issuer concentration[2] rules will apply to the embedded derivative element of the relevant security or instrument.

[1] See paras **12.96–12.112** above.
[2] See paras **12.84–12.85** above.

12.125 UCITS

12.125 The EAD provides that a transferable security or MMI will be considered to embed a derivative where it contains a component which fulfils the following criteria:

- by virtue of that component, some or all of the cash flows that otherwise would be required by the transferable security or MMI which functions as host contract can be modified according to a specified interest rate, financial instrument price, FX rate, index of prices or rates, credit rating or credit index, or other variable, and therefore vary in a way similar to a stand-alone derivative;
- its economic characteristics and risks are not closely related to the economic characteristics and risks of the host contract; and
- it has a significant impact on the risk profile and pricing of the transferable security or MMI in question.

12.126 If a transferable security or MMI contains a component which is contractually transferable independently of the transferable security or the MMI, it will not be regarded as embedding a derivative. Such a component will be regarded as a separate financial instrument and treated as such to determine whether it was an eligible asset and met any applicable investment restrictions.

12.127 Collateralised debt obligations ('CDOs') or asset-backed securities using derivatives, with or without an active management, will generally not be considered as embedding a derivative unless:

- they are leveraged, ie the CDOs or asset-backed securities are not limited recourse vehicles and the investors' loss can be higher than their initial investment; or
- they are not sufficiently diversified.

12.128 In its guidelines concerning eligible assets for investment by UCITS[1] (the 'Eligible Assets Guidelines'), published in March 2007, CESR set out the following list of transferable securities and MMIs which could be assumed to embed a derivative:

- credit-linked notes;
- transferable securities or MMIs whose performance is linked to the performance of a bond index;
- transferable securities or MMIs whose performance is linked to the performance of a basket of shares, with or without active management;
- transferable securities or MMIs with a fully guaranteed nominal value whose performance is linked to the performance of a basket of shares, with or without active management;
- convertible bonds; and
- exchangeable bonds.

[1] CESR/07-044, March 2007 – see https://www.esma.europa.eu/sites/default/files/library/2015/11/07_044.pdf.

12.129 It is the responsibility of the UCITS to check that investment in hybrid instruments embedding derivatives complies with these requirements. The nature, frequency and scope of checks performed will depend on the characteristics of the embedded derivatives and on their impact on the UCITS, taking into account its stated investment objective and risk profile.

J INVESTMENT MANAGEMENT TECHNIQUES

Efficient portfolio management

12.130 A UCITS may use techniques and instruments relating to transferable securities and MMIs (including derivatives) for the purpose of efficient portfolio management, which is usually taken to include (but is not limited to) hedging transactions.

12.131 The UCITS Directive and CESR's Eligible Assets Guidelines stress that techniques and instruments used for the purposes of efficient portfolio management must not cause the UCITS to diverge from its stated investment objective or add substantial supplementary risks in comparison to the UCITS' risk policy.

12.132 Efficient portfolio management involves investment transactions which are:

- economically appropriate (ie realised cost effectively);
- entered into for one or more of the following:
  - reduction of risk;
  - reduction of cost; or
  - the generation of additional capital or income with an appropriate level of risk, bearing in mind the risk profile set out in the prospectus of the UCITS and the general provisions of the UCITS Directive; and
- adequately captured by the risk management policy of the UCITS.

12.133 The 'techniques and instruments' which may be used for efficient portfolio management must be used in a way that:

- ensures compliance with the requirements of the risk management policy; and
- is in line with detailed risk-spreading requirements set out in Article 52 of the UCITS Directive.

12.134 Under CESR's Eligible Assets Guidelines, collateral, repos, reverse repos and securities lending all qualify as techniques and instruments relating to transferable securities. If a UCITS were to use repos or securities lending to generate leverage, these operations would need to be taken into account when calculating the global exposure of the UCITS.

12.135 Derivatives used for the purposes of efficient portfolio management must comply with both the requirements for efficient portfolio management and the requirements for financial derivatives instruments[1], simultaneously.

[1] See para **12.70** above.

K BORROWING AND LENDING

12.136 A UCITS is allowed to borrow up to 10% of the value of its assets on a temporary basis.

12.137 A UCITS may also borrow by means of a 'back-to-back' loan. This is a loan whereby the UCITS acquires an amount in one currency whilst

12.137 *UCITS*

maintaining an amount in a different currency at least equal to the first amount on deposit with the lender.

12.138 A UCITS is not entitled to grant loans or act as guarantor on behalf of third parties although this does not prevent a UCITS from acquiring eligible assets which are not fully paid.

L   SHORT SELLING

12.139 Short selling is the practice of selling a security that one does not own, and which one therefore borrows, in the hope or expectation of the price of that security falling before the obligation to return the borrowed asset to the lender arises (or one elects to effect such redelivery) and buying it back at that cheaper price – thereby realising a profit as a consequence. It is a practice commonly used by hedge funds, particularly those adopting long-short equity or market neutral strategies with shorting activities being supported by extensive stock borrowing programmes. It is clear that as a matter of policy a UCITS will not be permitted to physically short a security.

12.140 It is, however, possible to effect a short position using a derivative transaction such as a CFD/swap (although not where the intention is to create the potential for an uncovered sale). In this case, cover (in the form of cash or other liquid assets) is required from elsewhere in the UCITS' portfolio in order that a synthetic short sale may be effected.

Shorting in the UCITS environment

12.141 In a hedge fund environment, the security being shorted will be the subject of a stock borrow and then sold in the market at the then market price (the 'sale price'). The investment manager then buys the stock (hopefully at the subsequently deflated 'bought price') and redelivers the stock to the lender, thereby closing the fund's short position and making a profit of the difference between the sale price and the bought price.

12.142 Although, as mentioned above, UCITS are prevented from short selling in a physical sense, it is possible for UCITS to sell short 'synthetically' by the use of derivatives such as cash settled contracts for differences ('CFDs') or options which, although having the same financial profile of an uncovered sale, are not prohibited by the UCITS Directive.

12.143 A UCITS wishing to enter into derivatives to implement a long-short strategy would, of course, need to comply with the requirements mentioned at paras **12.82–12.119** above – for example, those regarding counterparty exposure and risk management.

12.144 Assuming that it has complied with these requirements (and any other applicable local rules relating to the use of derivative instruments), a UCITS can use CFDs to create the synthetic short (using its physical long positions as 'cover') to replicate a long-short or 'absolute return' strategy.

M FUND LIQUIDITY

12.145 Traditionally, one of the obstacles standing in the way of hedge fund managers that are considering offering a UCITS fund is liquidity. Most hedge funds will deal monthly or even quarterly, but in order to comply with the liquidity rules imposed by the UCITS Directive, managers must ensure that their strategy is liquid enough to support redemptions on at least a twice monthly basis. Although sometimes regarded as daily dealing products, UCITS are not required to be daily dealing.

N FUTURE LEGISLATIVE CHANGES

UCITS VI

12.146 On 26 July 2012, the European Commission published a consultation paper seeking views on the UCITS regime and whether further changes are needed to address its concerns about certain aspects of it. A number of issues contained in the consultation paper have since been made the subject of separate EU legislative initiatives in their own right – for example, the European Long-term Investment Funds ('ELTIF') Regulation[1] and the Money Market Funds Regulation[2] – and there currently appears to be little appetite on the part of the EU legislators to commence a further wholesale amendment of the UCITS Directive in the immediate future.

[1] Regulation (EU) 2015/760 of 29 April 2015.
[2] Regulation (EU) 2017/1131 of 14 June 2017.

12.147 In November 2017, however, the European Commission indicated that, in parallel with its review of AIFMD, it would examine certain limited elements of the UCITS Directive, restricted to issues of a technical or administrative nature, such as reporting problems. It appears unlikely that such review will lead to any specific proposals for change until late 2018 or, perhaps, 2019.

Proposals on the cross-border distribution of funds

12.148 Separately, in March 2018, the European Commission adopted a proposal for a Directive and a Regulation to amend a number of legislative texts, including AIFMD and the UCITS Directive, to eliminate perceived barriers to the cross-border distribution of funds within the EU. This follows the Commission's public consultation[1], which ran from June to October 2016 and formed part of its plan to develop a deeper Capital Markets Union across the EU. Once the final text of the Directive has been agreed with the Council of the EU and the European Parliament, the Commission has proposed a two-year transposition period, making it unlikely that the final rules would be in place until Q3 2020 at the earliest.

[1] CMU Action on cross-border distribution of funds (UCITS, AIF, ELTIF, EuVECA and EuSEF) across the EU, 2 June 2016 – see http://ec.europa.eu/finance/consultations/2016/cross-borders-investment-funds/docs/consultation-document_en.pdf.

12.149 *UCITS*

The PRIIPs Regulation

12.149 On 29 December 2014, the EU Regulation on key information documents for packaged retail and insurance-based investment products[1] (the 'PRIIPs Regulation') formally entered into force, introducing a new mandatory pre-contractual disclosure key information document to replace the key investor information document currently required under the UCITS Directive.

[1] Regulation (EU) No 1286/2014 of 26 November 2014.

12.150 The PRIIPs Regulation was originally intended to become applicable from 31 December 2016 but, following agreement between the Council of the EU, the European Parliament and the Commission, its date of application was moved back to 1 January 2018, except for UCITS, which have until 1 January 2019 by which to comply.

Chapter 13

MARKETING – SELECTED JURISDICTIONS

A	Australia	13.1
B	China	13.26
C	France	13.84
D	Germany	13.114
E	Hong Kong	13.158
F	Italy	13.197
G	Malta	13.246
H	Netherlands	13.292
I	Singapore	13.325
J	Spain	13.347
K	Switzerland	13.367

A   AUSTRALIA

Martin Jamieson, Partner, DLA Piper, Australia

Legal and regulatory framework

13.1 Hedge funds are subject to the same rules as any other funds which are offered in Australia. The one exception to this is the additional disclosure and reporting obligations for hedge funds that are offered to retail clients in Australia.

13.2 Since February 2014, retail hedge funds have been subject to the specific mandatory additional disclosure and ongoing reporting obligations provided for by the Australian Securities and Investments Commission's Regulatory Guide 240: Hedge funds: improving disclosure[1] ('RG 240'). A retail fund must comply with these additional 'hedge fund' requirements where the fund is promoted as a hedge fund or where it exhibits two or more of the following characteristics:

- complexity of investment strategy or structure (determined by reference to multiple interposed entities);
- the use of leverage;
- the use of derivatives (other than for the dominant purpose of managing foreign exchange or interest rate risk, gaining economic exposure on a limited temporary basis or the use of exchange traded derivatives);
- the use of short selling; and
- charging a performance fee out of the fund's assets.

[1] Available on the ASIC website – see http://asic.gov.au/regulatory-resources/find-a-document/regulatory-guides.

373

13.3 Marketing – Selected Jurisdictions

13.3 The scope of the definition of a hedge fund in RG 240 means that a fund which might not expressly identify itself as a hedge fund may be required to comply with the disclosure requirements of RG 240. RG 240 does not, however, impose any investment constraints or any other operational constraints upon funds which are subject to RG 240; it merely requires those funds to disclose against benchmarks on valuation and periodic reporting and against nine disclosure principles.

Structure of Australian hedge funds

13.4 As already noted, Australian law does not prescribe specific rules for hedge funds other than the additional disclosure obligations provided for in RG 240 for hedge funds which are offered to retail clients. An Australian resident hedge fund is typically structured as a unit trust and would ordinarily fall within the definition of a 'managed investment scheme' under the Australian Corporations Act 2001 (Cth) (the 'Corporations Act').

13.5 Australian unit trusts are generally managed so they can be treated as a 'flow through' for Australian tax purposes, so that it is the investor and not the fund that is taxed on income and gains which arise to the fund. Investors are taxed on their share of the net income and capital gains earned by the fund.

13.6 A fund which is offered to 'retail clients' (as defined by the Corporations Act) must be registered with the Australian Securities and Investments Commission ('ASIC'), the principal Australian regulator of financial services entities.

13.7 The operator of a fund (whether a wholesale or retail fund) must usually hold an Australian financial services licence.

13.8 Australian funds, whether wholesale or retail, are not subject to investment constraints. Australia's regulatory regime instead focuses on the adequacy of disclosure made to investors in respect of a fund.

13.9 The Australian federal government announced in its 2016/17 budget the introduction of two new types of collective investment vehicles ('CIVs') as an alternative to the current Australian unit trust structure which is used by most Australian resident funds. The new vehicles will be a corporate CIV and a limited partnership CIV, along the lines of equivalent structures which are commonly utilised in foreign jurisdictions. The availability of these new CIVs is expected significantly to enhance the ability of Australian fund managers to offer Australian resident funds to international investors.

Marketing foreign hedge funds in Australia

Register of foreign funds

13.10 A foreign hedge fund would commonly be required to be registered in Australia and its offer documents would be subject to prescribed disclosure requirements if offered to retail clients in Australia. However, a foreign hedge fund which is offered solely to wholesale clients in Australia will commonly not be required to be registered in Australia or be subject to any prescription on disclosure documents.

13.11 An investor is deemed to be a 'wholesale client' for Australian law purposes where it has invested AU$500,000 or more in a particular fund. There are numerous other criteria for an investor to qualify as a wholesale client for Australian law purposes, including where an investor can produce a copy of a certificate given within the preceding two years by a qualified accountant that confirms that the investor has net assets of at least AU$2.5 million or has a gross income for each of the last two financial years of at least AU$250,000. Further, a person who has or controls gross assets of AU$10 million (including any assets held by an associate or under a trust which that person manages) is deemed to be a wholesale client no matter what the size of its investment.

Promoter of foreign hedge funds

13.12 The Corporations Act provides that a person which carries on a financial services business in Australia must either hold an Australian financial services licence (an 'AFSL') which permits it to provide the relevant financial services, or be able to take advantage of an appropriate exemption. As such, the promoter of a foreign hedge fund into Australia will need to obtain an AFSL, become appointed as an authorised representative of an AFSL or be able to take advantage of an appropriate exemption. This will need to be effected at or prior to the fund being marketed to investors in Australia, whether or not the fund is marketed physically in Australia (including if merely physically marketed in Australia on a classic 'fly-in, fly-out' basis) or by email or telephone from outside Australia to prospective investors in Australia.

13.13 Any person which markets or promotes a hedge fund within Australia would normally be considered to be carrying on a financial services business in Australia. This is because the marketing and promotion of a fund to prospective investors in Australia normally involves some degree of financial advice. A recommendation or a statement of opinion, or a report about either of those matters, constitutes 'financial product advice' if it is provided with the intention of influencing a person's decision in relation to the relevant financial product – even where the provider of the advice does not take into account any of the person's objectives, financial situation or needs. Any person which arranges for interests in a fund to be issued to investors would also be considered to be conducting a financial services business in Australia. This would include any marketing by email or telephone from a jurisdiction outside Australia which deliberately targets potential investors in Australia even though interests in the foreign hedge fund will be issued outside Australia.

13.14 The need for the promoter of a foreign hedge fund to hold an AFSL (or be authorised as a representative of an entity which holds an appropriate AFSL or be able to take advantage of an appropriate exemption from the need to hold an AFSL) applies to whoever is effecting the promotion of that fund in Australia. As such, it applies equally to any person which effects the promotion in Australia, whether a placement agent, the foreign hedge fund, the foreign manager of that hedge fund or anyone else.

13.15 It would commonly not be commercially viable or practicable for a foreign manager to obtain its own AFSL purely to facilitate the promotion of a foreign hedge fund in Australia. This is because in order to obtain an AFSL,

13.15 Marketing – Selected Jurisdictions

the licensee must (amongst other things) have employees (or a person engaged under contract) who have prior experience in being a responsible manager of a firm which has an AFSL (or who have significant prior experience in being a representative of a firm which holds an AFSL and the knowledge and skill of the obligations of an AFSL under Australian law). Responsible managers are the persons nominated to ASIC by an applicant for an AFSL who will be responsible for the significant day-to-day decisions about (in this instance) the promotion of the hedge fund in Australia.

13.16 An alternative to obtaining an AFSL would be for a promoter of the foreign hedge fund, and its relevant employees and other representatives, to become authorised by another firm which holds an AFSL to act on its behalf. This is facilitated by a firm which holds an AFSL appointing the promoter as its corporate authorised representative. However, this is not commonly done in respect of unaffiliated entities (unless the firm which holds the AFSL is also the placement agent and so will get a material marketing fee) as in appointing the authorised representative, the AFSL firm will take on all the liability for the activities of the authorised representative, which is an additional risk for which the AFSL firm would ordinarily seek to charge a material arm's length fee. Nonetheless, there are some non-placement agent providers (and some placement agent providers) which are potentially willing to provide this regulatory service for an arm's length fee and currently do so for foreign fund management groups in respect of their marketing activities in Australia.

13.17 ASIC does, however, provide that certain entities which are already regulated in other equivalently regulated foreign jurisdictions may be exempt from Australia's AFSL regime on the condition that they only provide services to wholesale clients as defined under the Corporations Act. ASIC has issued class order relief from the need to hold an AFSL for entities equivalently regulated in Germany, Hong Kong, Singapore, the UK and the US. While this class order relief is currently under review and operates under transitional arrangements, it is still able to be relied upon and applied for. It is expected that ASIC will merely refine the terms of the existing relief (rather than terminate it) as a result of the current review. Many foreign hedge fund managers rely on this class order relief to promote their foreign hedge funds to wholesale clients in Australia. Foreign hedge fund managers do have to apply to ASIC to rely on the class order relief. Pursuant to the terms of the relief, the foreign hedge fund manager can only conduct such marketing activities in Australia which it is permitted to conduct under the rules of its home jurisdiction, and must conduct such marketing in Australia in the same manner (so far as possible) as it would in its home jurisdiction.

13.18 There are a number of other very limited exemptions from the need to obtain an AFSL or to act under an authorisation from another entity holding an AFSL in order to promote a foreign fund in Australia to wholesale clients and these exemptions do not involve any application to ASIC. They include the following:

- Where the marketing to the Australian resident is conducted wholly outside Australia (which means that the Australian resident would have to receive the marketing material outside Australia). This must not involve any conduct which is intended, or would be likely, to induce people in Australia to acquire interests in a hedge fund.

- Where the marketing is done in Australia to a prospective client which itself holds an AFSL and is not acting as a trustee or on behalf of another person (given that Australian superannuation funds and Australian fund managers offer their products to their Australian clients via trusts, this limits the exemption to true proprietary investors which commonly do not have an AFSL as they do not generally need one under Australian law).
- Where the prospective Australian client makes enquiries of a foreign hedge fund without any prior solicitation by the foreign fund manager and it does not during this time actively solicit persons in Australia in respect of the relevant fund (other than in response to the enquiry initiated by the Australian client or the Australian client's agent).

Taxation

13.19 Previously, the offer of foreign funds to Australian investors was not generally regarded as tax effective for Australian investors because of the foreign investment fund ('FIF') rules. The FIF rules were very complex and imposed a requirement to attribute income to an Australian investor at the end of each financial year in respect of foreign investments (such as interests in foreign hedge funds) even though the foreign fund may not have made any distributions. This resulted in the Australian investor having to pay Australian income tax on the income attributed to it on an accruals basis in respect of its foreign investment at the end of each financial year. In 2010, the FIF rules were abolished.

13.20 The main consideration currently is whether a foreign fund is considered to be a controlled foreign company ('CFC'). A foreign fund which is structured as an Australian unit trust will generally not be a CFC. Only a foreign hedge fund which is structured as a company or a limited partnership will need to consider whether it is a CFC.

13.21 A foreign hedge fund will be a CFC for Australian tax purposes where any of the following are satisfied:

- five or fewer Australian entities together hold 50% or more of the interests in the foreign hedge fund;
- a single Australian entity holds 40% or more of the interests in that fund and is not controlled by another entity; or
- five or fewer Australian entities actually control that fund.

13.22 Where a foreign hedge fund is a CFC, the CFC rules provide for accruals taxation in respect of certain Australian resident investors. These CFC rules may impose tax on a yearly basis on the Australian investors which are attributable taxpayers in relation to that foreign fund in respect of realised gains of the underlying investment portfolio of that foreign fund even where these gains have not been distributed by the foreign hedge fund. Where a foreign hedge fund is a CFC, only an Australian resident investor which is an attributable taxpayer is subject to the CFC accruals taxation regime. An 'attributable taxpayer' is an Australian entity which holds an 'associate-inclusive control interest' of 10% or more in a CFC. 'Associate-inclusive

13.22 *Marketing – Selected Jurisdictions*

control interest' includes both direct and indirect control interests (ie voting rights, rights to dividend and rights to capital) in a CFC held by the Australian entity and its associates.

13.23 The CFC accruals taxation regime generally provides for a similar net tax treatment to that which would occur if an Australian resident investor were instead to invest in an Australian resident unit trust which directly holds the investment portfolio. Two of the exceptions to the general statement that the tax treatment of a CFC is comparable to the tax treatment of an Australian unit trust for an Australian resident are as follows:

- If the foreign hedge fund invests in Australian shares and derives Australian franking credits in respect of the dividends payable by an Australian company, the benefit of any such franking credits are generally lost to an Australian resident (resulting in higher net taxation in respect of the dividend income).
- Any capital gains derived from the disposal of shares held in the underlying investment portfolio where those shares had been held for more than 12 months will not be concessionally taxed in the hands of an Australian resident when derived from a foreign fund that is a CFC (whereas an Australian unit trust which qualifies as a 'managed investment trust' for Australian capital gains tax purposes and elected to be treated on capital account would obtain concessional tax treatment).

13.24 If a foreign hedge fund is not a CFC (or even if it is a CFC but the relevant Australian resident investor is not an 'attributable taxpayer'[1]), an Australian resident investor in that foreign hedge fund is not subject to any form of Australian accruals (ongoing) taxation (even where that foreign hedge fund does not physically distribute any income or capital gains on an ongoing basis).

[1] See para **13.22** above.

13.25 Accordingly, where a foreign hedge fund is not a CFC, an Australian resident investor may potentially be attracted to invest directly in that foreign hedge fund. This is because an Australian investor potentially receives the significant benefit of a deferral in paying tax until it ultimately disposes of its investment in that foreign hedge fund. This can be a significant advantage compared to investing in an Australian unit trust since Australian unit trusts distribute all the realised capital gains and income which they derive in a tax year each year and, as such, an Australian investor has to pay tax on such income as it arises. Whilst, however, an Australian resident investor in a foreign hedge fund which is not a CFC (or an Australian investor in a CFC which is not an 'attributable taxpayer') can obtain the significant benefit of deferral in taxation, any gain derived by virtue of the investor ultimately disposing of its interest in that fund normally would not be treated as a capital gain for Australian tax purposes and, as such, would not be concessionally taxed.

B CHINA

Melody Yang (Fan), Partner, Simmons & Simmons, Beijing

Background to hedge funds in China

13.26 Hedge funds are a fairly recent development in China. This is to be expected given that the stock market did not exist in the People's Republic of China until 1990. China's evolution from a planned economy to a market economy accelerated in the 1990s. This was accompanied by the promulgation of the Company Law in 1993 and the Securities Law in 1998. Although the first Securities Investment Fund Law (the '2003 SIF Law') was promulgated on 28 October 2003, it regulated only publicly offered securities investment funds, failing to address the regulation of privately offered funds investing in secondary markets, including hedge funds.

13.27 The market for privately offered funds has nevertheless continued to develop in China despite the absence of an overarching law regulating them. First, various financial institutions, including trust companies, securities companies, fund management companies and insurance companies, have been permitted to launch and operate various types of asset management products that invest in secondary markets, which are in fact different variations of 'privately offered funds'. They do so in accordance with specific, ad hoc regulations issued by the regulators who oversee these non-banking financial institutions. Second, a growing number of investment advisers who are not financial institutions under Chinese law have also launched privately offered funds investing in secondary markets. They have done so either through a cumbersome and costly contractual arrangement with trust companies and fund management companies, or simply by operating on their own in a legal grey area. Privately offered funds operated by these investment advisers through the channels of trust or fund management companies were known in China as 'sunshine privately offered funds' ('阳光私募').

13.28 With the development of China's asset management industry, the regulatory environment for privately offered funds has also developed rapidly in recent years. This encompasses changes in the regulation of such funds and the emergence of a self-regulatory organisation that regulates private fund businesses in China (such as hedge funds and private equity funds).

13.29 Under the supervision and authorisation of the China Securities Regulatory Commission (the 'CSRC'), the Asset Management Association of China ('AMAC') was established in 2012. AMAC is a self-regulatory industrial association but is empowered by China's State Council and the CSRC as the de facto private fund regulator. Therefore, from 2013, privately offered funds began to be regularised and they were redefined as 'private securities investment funds' in the CSRC's Interim Measures for the Supervision and Administration of Privately Offered Investment Funds[1].

---

[1] See further para **13.38** below.

13.30 There is no specific definition of 'hedge fund' under related Chinese laws and regulations. 'Private securities investment funds', discussed above, are generally considered to include hedge funds as they share certain common characteristics such as: being privately offered; requiring investors to have a

13.30 *Marketing – Selected Jurisdictions*

minimum net worth and/or level of financial sophistication; allowing flexibility in investment strategies; and being subject to limited regulatory supervision.

Supervising authorities

13.31 China's securities investment laws have evolved in the context of pre-existing agencies with their own regulatory scopes. China's regulation of the financial industry is divided into different authorities supervising different financial institutions and their financial products. In China, securities companies and fund management companies, and their financial products, are regulated by the CSRC. Commercial banks, trust companies and financial leasing companies, and their financial products, are regulated by the China Banking Regulatory Commission (the 'CBRC'). Insurance companies and their products are regulated by the China Insurance Regulatory Commission (the 'CIRC'). Thus, hedge fund-like products offered by different financial institutions may fall under the supervision of different regulators and may be subject to their respective regulations.

13.32 For example, the hedge fund-like products offered by trust companies are called 'collective investment trust schemes' and are regulated by the CBRC under the Measures for Administration of the Collective Investment Trust Schemes of Trust Companies, which took effect on 1 March 2007 and were amended on 4 February 2009. Similar products offered by securities companies are called 'collective asset management schemes' and are regulated by the CSRC under the Administrative Measures for the Client Asset Management Business of Securities Companies, which were first promulgated on 18 October 2012 and amended on 26 June 2013.

13.33 Since AMAC was established in 2012, most hedge fund-like products are required to be filed with AMAC and their manager must register with AMAC. The media has referred to this registration as 'licensing', but unlike licensing, it is not an authorisation in the strict sense.

13.34 AMAC is directly responsible for the registration and ongoing supervision of managers that manage private securities investment funds and the private funds themselves. To this end, AMAC has released a series of self-discipline rules (which in practice are strictly adhered to by market players) and established an online registration and filing system as a centralised information reporting and monitoring centre.

13.35 According to statistics published by AMAC[1], China's asset management business supervised by the CSRC and AMAC only (referring to asset management products launched by fund management companies and their subsidiaries, securities companies, futures companies and private fund management institutions) amounted to approximately RMB 53.6 trillion. The private fund industry showed an outstanding growth in 2017 with a total size exceeding RMB 11 trillion (with an annual growth of RMB 3.21 trillion). At the end of 2017, a total of 22,446 fund managers were registered with AMAC, together with 66,418 private fund products that have been filed accordingly.

[1] See AMAC's official website – http://www.amac.org.cn.

Regulatory framework

13.36 An amendment to the 2003 SIF Law took effect on 1 June 2013 (the '2013 SIF Law'), which was subsequently followed by a second revision on 24 April 2015 (the current '2015 SIF Law'). Notably, the 2013 SIF Law included privately offered funds within its scope for the first time and divided securities investment funds into publicly offered funds ('public funds') and non-publicly offered funds ('private funds'). In the chapter governing private funds, the 2013 SIF Law provides some general guidelines but lacks sufficient detail. Furthermore, initially, it was not entirely clear whether the provisions on private funds in the 2013 SIF Law were intended also to govern the similar privately offered funds previously regulated under the respective regulations promulgated by the financial regulators (ie the CBRC, CSRC and CIRC).

13.37 In order to address this uncertainty, in February 2013, the CSRC circulated for public comment a draft of the proposed Interim Measures for Private Securities Investment Funds (the 'IMPSIF'). In the draft notes to the IMPSIF, the CSRC clarified that, although the 2013 SIF Law was intended to govern all types of private funds, the various types of private fund managers that are financial institutions (ie trust companies, securities companies, fund management companies and insurance companies) would continue to be regulated by their respective supervising agencies in accordance with existing regulations, subject to necessary amendments to comply with the 2013 SIF Law. In contrast, the IMPSIF was intended only to regulate those investment advisers that are not financial institutions. However, the IMPSIF never entered into force.

13.38 Instead, the Interim Measures for the Supervision and Administration of Privately Offered Investment Funds[1] (the 'Interim Measures') were formally issued by the CSRC on 21 August 2014. The major difference between the IMPSIF and the Interim Measures is that the latter also include venture capital funds and private equity funds (which are all part of 'privately offered investment funds'). This is due to the fact that, in June 2013, the State Commission Office of Public Sectors Reform assigned the regulatory oversight of venture capital funds and private equity funds to the CSRC, resulting in a certain power struggle between the CSRC and other regulatory bodies.

[1] Decree No 105 of the China Securities Regulatory Commission (21 August 2014).

13.39 The Interim Measures set out detailed rules on the establishment, marketing and relevant filing procedures for private funds raised and operated by these non-financial institution fund managers.

13.40 The discussion below focuses on private funds regulated by the CSRC in accordance with the Interim Measures. The existing regulations, as amended to comply with the 2013 SIF Law, with respect to private funds operated by financial institutions are similar to the provisions of the Interim Measures.

Registration and filing

13.41 The registration and filing requirements are set forth in the Measures for the Registration of Private Investment Fund Managers and Filing of Private

13.41 *Marketing – Selected Jurisdictions*

Investment Funds (Trial Implementation), which were issued by AMAC on 17 January 2014 and came into effect on 7 February 2014 (the 'Registration and Filing Measures').

REGISTRATION REQUIREMENTS FOR PRIVATE FUND MANAGERS

13.42 Unlike managers of public funds, which are subject to authorisation by the CSRC, managers of private funds are only required to register with AMAC. Only AMAC-registered institutions can launch and operate private funds. Under AMAC's rules, in order to obtain (or maintain) the registration status, the fund managers need to satisfy the following requirements, among others:

- a certain number of the investment management team and risk/compliance management team must have passed the qualification exam (the first exam was held after the new regulations took effect on 23 April 2016; 11,272 people took the exam);
- they must have assets under management (no minimum amount stipulated);
- they must be supported by an official legal opinion issued by an external law firm on various aspects of the manager, including its corporate registration, team qualification, risk management policies and practice, type of trading, portfolio investment, etc.

13.43 In addition, pursuant to the Registration and Filing Measures, a private fund manager is required to report relevant information on itself, its employees and the funds under its management to AMAC on a regular or non-regular basis.

FILING REQUIREMENTS FOR PRIVATE FUNDS

13.44 Unlike public funds, which must be registered with the CSRC before offering, private funds are subject to a much more relaxed filing scheme. A private fund manager is only required to file the relevant information with AMAC after the fundraising is completed. The fund manager needs to submit a core details form to complete the filing of the fund, which requires factual information about the name, registered office, capitalisation, business structure, controllers, management and personnel, internal systems and controls, fund administration and custodian, etc.

13.45 A private fund is also subject to ongoing disclosure obligations.

Qualification of investors

13.46 According to the Interim Measures, a private fund may only raise funds from no more than 200 qualified investors. 'Qualified investors' are defined as those entities or individuals who can identify and bear the risks for investing in a private fund.

13.47 Generally speaking, private funds should only be promoted and marketed to a qualified investor. In addition to other 'softer' requirements, a qualified investor should meet the relevant assets threshold[1] (unless it qualifies for exemption), as follows:

- for entities, net assets of not less than RMB 10 million;
- for individuals, financial assets[2] of not less than RMB 3 million or average annual income of not less than RMB 500,000 in the previous three years.

[1] Article 12 of the Interim Measures.
[2] The term 'financial assets' includes, but is not limited to, bank deposits, stocks, bonds, fund shares, asset management plans, bank wealth management products, trust plans, insurance products, and futures equities.

13.48 The following entities are deemed as qualified investors even if they do not meet the assets threshold[1]:

- social security funds, corporate pension funds, charity funds and funds of similar nature;
- investment schemes that have been filed with AMAC;
- management teams and employees that have made investment into the private fund they are managing; and
- other investors that can be deemed to be qualified investors in accordance with the CSRC rules.

[1] Article 13 of the Interim Measures.

13.49 Each qualified investor is required to invest a minimum of RMB 1 million in a single private fund[1].

[1] Article 12 of the Interim Measures.

Marketing private funds in China

13.50 Public marketing activities for private funds are prohibited in China. According to the SIF Law, private funds may not be publicised or promoted to unspecific targets through public media such as newspapers, journals, radio or television stations or the Internet, or by such means as lectures, debriefing meetings or seminars[1].

[1] Article 91 of the 2015 SIF Law.

13.51 Private funds may be marketed by fund managers directly or through agency arrangements with other institutions. The fund managers and/or the distribution institutions of the fund are required to make sufficient disclosure to investors of the risks of investment and to sell products compatible with each investor's risk profile. Fund managers and distribution institutions must not promise investors that their investment is principal-protected or guaranteed with minimum returns[1].

[1] Articles 14 and 15 of the Interim Measures.

13.52 The fund offering/marketing process generally encompasses the following key steps:

13.52 Marketing – Selected Jurisdictions

- identifying the specific targets, having the potential investor sign an undertaking letter that it/he is a qualified investor ('特定对象确认');
- completing a suitability assessment by (i) circulating the form to collect the investor's details, (ii) asking the potential investor to fill out the risk assessment questionnaire, and (iii) issuing the confirmation letter to match the risk level of the investor and that of the fund or, when there is a risk mismatch, a warning letter ('投资者适当性匹配');
- circulating the PPM offering document to the potential investor ('推介');
- disclosing risks and having the potential investor sign the risk disclosure letter ('基金风险揭示');
- confirming that the potential investor is a qualified investor ('合格投资者确认');
- signing the fund contract ('签署基金合同');
- giving the potential investor a cooling-off period to rethink ('投资冷静期'); and
- confirming the investor's intention to effect the fund contract by holding a return interview ('回访确认').

13.53 Depending on the nature of the investors, ie whether they are professional qualified investors or ordinary qualified investors, some or all of the above procedures should apply.

LICENSING FOR MARKETING A PRIVATE FUND

13.54 An entity that undertakes promotion and marketing activities as an independent intermediary must already have obtained a fund marketing licence from the CSRC and registered with AMAC.

13.55 Self-promotion by a private fund manager is not subject to such licensing requirement.

13.56 The current licensing schemes were designed a few years ago and were intended for marketing mutual funds. Thus, such licences are held by the securities and mutual fund management companies. In other words, only certain securities and mutual fund management companies are qualified to promote and market private funds (that are not managed by them) until further rules are introduced.

RESTRICTIONS ON MARKETING ACTIVITIES

13.57 The promotion and marketing activities must not target any retail investors by means of public media, open lectures, social media and the like[1].

[1] Article 14 of the Interim Measures.

13.58 Any promised return in the offering materials is strictly prohibited (ie the materials must not give investors a no-principal-loss or minimum return guarantee)[1].

[1] Article 15 of the Interim Measures.

13.59 Any information published by the private fund managers to the non-specific public (such as the information on its website) is limited to the brand, development strategy, investment strategy, investment team, management team and other information that is made public by AMAC[1].

[1] Articles 23, 24 and 25 of AMAC's Administrative Measures on Fundraising Behaviours of Privately Offered Funds.

13.60 There should be no public disclosure of any information about the specific fund product[1]. Even for promotion and marketing to qualified investors, the rules on identifying and certifying a qualified investor and the risk disclosure requirements have been tightened up.

[1] Articles 23, 24 and 25 of AMAC's Administrative Measures on Fundraising Behaviours of Privately Offered Funds.

Liability for illegal marketing activities

13.61 A fund manager or distribution institution may be fined or barred from providing fund-related services, and its responsible personnel may be subject to warnings and fines, if: (i) it publicly offers a fund in violation of the 2015 SIF Law; (ii) it offers a private fund or transfers shares of such fund to any entity or individual other than a qualified investor; (iii) it uses the words 'fund' or 'fund management' or any similar name to engage in securities investment without registration with AMAC; or (iv) it fails to disclose risks to investors or misleads investors into purchasing any fund products incompatible with their risk profile[1].

[1] Articles 127, 133, 135 and 137 of the 2015 SIF Law.

The PFM WFOE regime

13.62 On 30 June 2016, AMAC issued an official notice confirming that foreign shareholding in a private fund manager ('PFM') (established in China) can be increased to 100% (including a hedge fund-type private fund)[1]. This was a breakthrough for all foreign asset managers that wished to launch and operate a hedge fund in China. It enables wholly foreign-owned enterprises ('WFOE') or joint ventures to register as private securities investment fund managers and provide investment management services to Chinese private funds (the 'PFM WFOE regime').

[1] AMAC's FAQs Regarding the Registration and Filing of Private Funds (No 10) (30 June 2016).

Characteristics of a foreign-invested PFM fund

13.63 Under the PFM WFOE regime, a foreign asset manager is allowed to establish a WFOE or a joint venture which serves as the private fund manager (a 'foreign-invested PFM'). The foreign-invested PFM then raises an open-ended fund targeted at qualified investors in China, ie a private securities investment fund defined under Chinese rules, structured as a contractual type

13.63 *Marketing – Selected Jurisdictions*

fund. The manager and the custodian are the de facto co-trustees of the private fund.

13.64 A private securities investment fund can invest in securities issued in China, including stocks of public companies in China, bonds, fund units and other securities and derivatives thereof recognised by the CSRC.

13.65 Private securities investment funds may not, however, invest in securities issued outside of China; except that in the future they may be allowed to participate in the sale and purchase of specified foreign stocks through stock connect programs and QDII[1] qualification and quota.

[1] See paras 13.71–13.73 below.

Registration procedures applicable to foreign-invested PFMs

13.66 On 5 January 2017, AMAC promulgated its Explanations on the Registration and Filing Requirements of Private Fund Managers as Wholly Owned and Jointly Owned Foreign Enterprises (the 'Explanations'). The Explanations elaborate on the requirements that foreign-invested enterprises will have to fulfil before being allowed to register with AMAC as a private fund manager trading securities in China.

13.67 The Explanations stipulate that, in addition to complying with general rules imposed on domestic private fund managers, foreign-invested PFMs will have to meet the following requirements:

- *Investment process*: Investment decisions must be made independently through a domestically installed system in China; remote orders via overseas institutions or systems are prohibited. The domestic system must make transaction paths transparent and traceable, and ensure that transaction data is completely stored and that the entire transaction process is adequately monitored. Foreign-invested PFMs should also designate persons responsible for making investment decisions and executing transactions respectively.
- *Personnel qualifications*: Senior management officers (including legal representatives, general managers, deputy general managers, investment managers, compliance or risk management officers, etc) must attain the fund practising qualification. Compliance or risk management officers of private funds should not carry out investments.
- *Corporate structure*: The foreign-invested PFM will have to disclose whether it owns any subsidiary (having 5% or more shareholding in a financial corporation or a listed company, or more than 20% shareholding in other types of companies), branch or related party (a financial corporation, asset management institution or organisation providing related services which is controlled by the same shareholder or beneficial owner as the foreign parent) in China, or an overseas related party which may have a substantive impact on the private fund business which the foreign-invested PFM intends to carry out in China.
- *Beneficial ownership*: The ownership of foreign-invested PFMs must be traced back to the ultimate beneficial owner. Documents relating to the ultimate owner's fitness and properness, such as business permits and licences issued by the home regulatory authority, as well as an

- *Qualified investors*: As stipulated in AMAC's regulations issued on 28 May 2014[1], a private fund should only be promoted and marketed to a qualified investor. If the investor in question is a non-legal entity, such as a partnership or an undertaking, whereby the funds of multiple investors are pooled to invest directly or indirectly in the private fund, the foreign-invested PFM should investigate whether the ultimate investor is qualified.

organisational chart illustrating the relationship between the ultimate owner and the foreign-invested PFMs, have to be submitted. Both the direct foreign shareholder and the ultimate owner must be a financial institution approved or licensed by the competent financial regulatory authorities in the country or region of its domicile. The securities regulatory authorities of the country or region of the financial institution's domicile should also have signed a memorandum of understanding on co-operation regarding securities regulation with the CSRC.

[1] AMAC's FAQs Regarding the Registration and Filing of Private Funds (No 3) (28 May 2014).

Marketing foreign hedge funds in China

General

13.68 Given that the Chinese currency (the Renminbi, 'RMB') is not fully convertible, it has presented some obstacles to foreign hedge funds accessing the Chinese market for potential investors. Under China's foreign exchange control regime administered by the State Administration of Foreign Exchange ('SAFE'), Chinese residents (both individuals and entities) need to seek governmental approval before they are allowed to convert their RMB funds into foreign currencies and remit them overseas for investment purposes. In particular, cross-border portfolio investment by Chinese residents in offshore securities and other financial assets is generally restricted by SAFE. This means that Chinese residents are generally restricted from converting their RMB funds into foreign currency or using their foreign currency funds within China to invest into foreign hedge funds, unless they can rely on certain cross-border schemes[1] or they are sovereign wealth funds in China.

[1] Such as the QDII and QDLP schemes, discussed at paras **13.71–13.73** and paras **13.74–13.78** respectively below.

13.69 However, to the extent that Chinese individuals and entities already hold legitimate foreign currency assets outside China (eg as a result of current account activities or permitted capital account activities), they may be able to invest such holdings in foreign hedge funds, subject to relevant Chinese laws and regulations pertaining to offshore investments.

13.70 As mentioned above[1], China has a series of requirements in terms of marketing a private fund domiciled in China, including marketing to qualified investors only, investors' suitability assessment, disclosure and acknowledgement of risks. On the other hand, the regulatory framework governing the marketing activities on a cross-border basis is still absent at present. A grey area therefore remains in terms of marketing and promotion of an overseas fund to a Chinese investor. Advice should be taken as to how to carry out those

13.70 Marketing – Selected Jurisdictions

promotion and marketing activities from a best practice point of view.

[1] See paras 13.50–13.53 above.

Qualified domestic institutional investors

13.71 As a partial lifting of the general restriction described above, China introduced the Qualified Domestic Institutional Investors ('QDII') Scheme in 2006. This scheme allows a number of approved domestic institutional investors (commercial banks, securities and fund management companies, trust companies and insurance companies) to raise RMB funds from Chinese residents for portfolio investments in certain offshore securities and financial products, subject to individual quotas approved by SAFE[1].

[1] Foreign Exchange Administrative Regulations on Offshore Securities Investments by Qualified Domestic Institutional Investors, effective 21 August 2013, replacing two previous SAFE regulations published in 2006 and 2009.

13.72 QDIIs consist of certain banks, trust companies, securities (including fund management) companies and insurance companies which have been granted QDII approval by their relevant regulators and which also have been granted a foreign exchange investment quota with which to make such investments. There is no single set of rules which apply to all QDIIs. The commercial bank (and trust company) QDIIs, securities (fund management) QDIIs and insurance companies QDIIs are subject to the rules issued by the CBRC, the CSRC and the CIRC, respectively. As a result, the scope of overseas investments which QDIIs are allowed to undertake is different depending on the respective regulator of the relevant QDII.

13.73 Interest in hedge funds does not fall into the permitted scope of QDII institutions unless the hedge fund itself is listed on a recognised exchange in a jurisdiction that has entered a memorandum of understanding with the CSRC. That said, certain types of QDII institutions are allowed to invest into structured investment products that are linked to the underlying assets such as hedge funds. Therefore, Chinese residents may be able to use the QDII channel to make indirect investments in foreign hedge funds. Under this approach, instead of the Chinese investors themselves, the relevant QDII institution will become the investor in the foreign hedge funds and manage such investments on behalf of the investors for a management fee.

Qualified domestic investment partnership

13.74 The Qualified Domestic Investment Partnership ('QDLP') Scheme is a pilot programme developed by local authorities, initially launched in Shanghai in 2013 then followed by Tianjin in 2014. It allows foreign asset managers to raise RMB funds from high net worth individuals and institutional investors in China to invest overseas.

13.75 Under the QDLP scheme, foreign asset managers can establish an investment entity in China as a general partner and set up a 'qualified domestic investment fund' (RMB Fund Enterprise, featuring as a feeder fund) to feed into the master fund managed by the management group overseas. This pilot programme requires the RMB Fund Enterprise to appoint a qualified commercial bank as custodian bank, which will operate the business of RMB and foreign exchange settlement, within the quota approved by SAFE.

13.76 The QDLP scheme is still a pilot programme and detailed regulations for its practical operation have not been officially promulgated. The municipal level Financial Services Office (the 'SFO') is the main local regulator of this pilot scheme and is said to have formed a cross-department QDLP committee with other local authorities in the municipality to oversee the approval, information disclosure and investment activities of the foreign hedge funds. According to press reports, the minimum capital of eligible foreign hedge funds should be no less than RMB 100 million and qualified individual investors will need to have more than RMB 5 million in cash assets[1].

[1] See http://m.weekly.caixin.com/zknews/2016-09-16/100988835.html (available in Chinese only).

13.77 No QDLP quotas were issued following an unofficial suspension in late 2015 when China tightened capital controls amid turmoil in its stock and currency markets. According to press reports in February 2018, following a two-year hiatus the SFO has resumed vetting QDLP applications and issued quotas in early 2018.

13.78 The QDLP scheme represents the latest development in the gradual liberalisation of China's capital account restrictions over the past decade. If the pilot program proves to be successful, foreign hedge funds can expect China to formulate a more established legal framework that allows them to market their products directly to Chinese investors.

Future trends

13.79 The legal landscape for hedge funds is changing at a fast pace in China.

13.80 As mentioned above, the segregation of supervision across different regulatory bodies (namely, the CSRC/AMAC, CBRC and CIRC) has sometimes led to ambiguity and regulatory arbitrage in practice. To address this issue, at the 19th National Congress of the Communist Party of China in Beijing in October 2017, the Chinese Government decided to create a new regulatory body. This new body will be led by the People's Bank of China (the 'PBOC') and will be responsible for co-ordinating financial supervision and enhancing regulation across the financial sector. It will oversee the activities of the CSRC, CBRC and CIRC to reduce the risk of conflicts and arbitrage.

13.81 On 17 November 2017, the PBOC, CSRC, CBRC, CIRC and SAFE jointly released a consultation paper setting out for public comment draft guidance on the regulation of asset management products[1], towards meeting the country's top agenda of curbing systemic risk in the financial system. One of the priorities set out in the consultation paper is to eliminate the channel businesses and ban guaranteed returns.

[1] Guiding Opinions on Regulating the Asset Management Business of Financial Institutions (17 November 2017).

13.82 After the proposals in this consultation paper take effect, foreign asset managers which have a strong investment management team and risk man-

13.82 *Marketing – Selected Jurisdictions*

agement capabilities will have an enhanced competitive edge in China against local market players.

13.83 These measures, coupled with the Chinese government's efforts towards internationalisation of the RMB and the gradual relaxation of its foreign exchange control, could lead to a more flexible and open Chinese hedge fund market. This creates more opportunities for foreign hedge fund managers operating in or based outside of China. Thus, it is critical that foreign hedge fund managers keep a close eye on the Chinese legal development in this field.

C FRANCE

Ian Rogers, Partner, Head of Asset Management, Simmons & Simmons, Paris

Introduction

13.84 The rules governing the creation and marketing of hedge funds are set out in the French Monetary and Financial Code and the General Regulations of the *Autorité des Marchés Financiers* (the 'AMF') (the French equivalent of the UK's Financial Conduct Authority).

13.85 Prior to the implementation of the Alternative Investment Fund Managers Directive[1] ('AIFMD') there was no rule that precisely defined a hedge fund. However, post-AIFMD, all non-UCITS collective investment schemes are subject to the French rules relating to alternative investment funds (hedge funds or 'AIFs').

[1] Directive 2011/61/EU of 8 June 2011.

13.86 Whilst AIFMD has greatly increased the breadth of funds available to French investors, the marketing of offshore (non-European) hedge funds in France is de facto impossible. In effect, it is only possible to actively market European UCITS, European AIFs and French fund structures to French based investors[1].

[1] See paras **13.97–13.102** below.

13.87 Nonetheless, it is ironic that a Directive that sought to restrain and limit hedge funds and their managers has led to more hedge funds being sold in France.

French fund structures

13.88 The AMF seized the opportunity presented by the implementation of AIFMD to simplify both the French fund range and some of the rules applicable to French funds. As a result, French funds are now:

- undertakings for collective investments in transferable securities ('UCITS');

- retail AIFs (including *fonds d'investissement à vocation générale*, private equity funds (*fonds commun de placement à risques*, venture capital funds and innovation funds), retail real estate funds and funds of funds); or
- professional investor funds – including *fonds professionnels à vocation générale*, professional real estate funds, specialised professional funds (formerly known as contractual funds), professional capital investment funds, employment funds and securitisation schemes.

13.89 With respect to the 'corporate' structure of French funds, these can be established either with a legal personality or as a contractual vehicle without legal personality. However, the vast majority of French funds are set up as *fonds commun de placement* ('FCPs') with no legal personality. This is because the structure allows the management company to concentrate on running the fund without undue paperwork (for example, there is no requirement to hold general meetings of unitholders). Moreover, since there is no board of directors, there is no requirement to set up quarterly board meetings at which the management company must be present. FCPs also have a number of tax benefits[1].

[1] See paras **13.110–13.113** below.

13.90 France has implemented the provisions of AIFMD in relation to the management passport without any gold-plating. Moreover, the passport has been sought and obtained by 150 European alternative investment fund managers ('AIFMs') out of the 217 European managers which have passported management services into France[1]. This is especially relevant in the current market as, in the context of large institutional mandates and requests for proposals by French institutional investors, there is a greatly increased demand by such investors to invest in French structures; as a result, the AIFMD management passport has proved to be extremely useful.

[1] As at 16 January 2018 (source: the AMF's GECO database).

Eligible investors in French structures

13.91 There is no longer any minimum investment for a retail AIF. Since French funds of funds are now retail AIFs, this means that any French investor can access a hedge fund portfolio via a French fund of funds.

13.92 The rules governing investments into professional investor funds have also been simplified. As a result, these funds are typically reserved for:

- professional clients (as defined by the recast Markets in Financial Instruments Directive[1]) or their foreign equivalent;
- persons investing at least €100,000; or
- any investor whose assets are managed pursuant to a managed account agreement.

[1] Directive 2014/65/EU of 15 May 2014.

13.93 *Marketing – Selected Jurisdictions*

13.93 For specialised professional funds and professional capital investment funds, additional categories of investors are also eligible, namely persons investing at least €30,000 and who meet at least one of the following criteria:

- they provide technical or financial assistance to unlisted companies covered by the fund's purpose to promote their creation or growth;
- they provide assistance to the management company of the fund in finding potential investors, or contribute towards the company's objectives in seeking, selecting, tracking and disposing of investments;
- they have acquired knowledge about venture capital by being a direct equity investor in unlisted companies or by subscribing to either (i) a private equity fund that is not advertised or promoted, or (ii) a specialised professional fund or an unlisted venture capital firm.

13.94 As a result of the EU Regulation on European long-term investment funds[1] (the 'ELTIF Regulation'), certain non-retail AIFs could also be eligible for investment by retail investors.

[1] Regulation (EU) 2015/760 of 29 April 2015.

Investment restrictions

13.95 The investment rules (including risk allocation ratios and financial instrument ratios) applying to French AIFs vary widely depending on the chosen structure.

13.96 On one side of the scale, retail AIFs (with the exception of French funds of funds) are subject to quite detailed investment rules. These rules are based on the UCITS restrictions and so would act as a limiting factor for most hedge fund strategies. On the other side of the scale are specialised professional funds. These funds (which do not need to be approved by the AMF and are only subject to a declaration a posteriori) are able effectively to write their own investment rules and restrictions, making them a very interesting French fund vehicle – particularly when coupled with the AIFMD management passport.

Active marketing of foreign hedge funds in France

Pre-AIFMD

13.97 As a reminder, in the halcyon days prior to the implementation of AIFMD, the AMF had to pre-authorise the marketing of any open-ended hedge fund in France and the distribution of unauthorised open-ended funds was prohibited. Nonetheless, the sale of closed-ended hedge funds was permissible on a private placement basis in certain circumstances; and so private equity strategies had a distinct advantage when marketing their funds in France.

Post-AIFMD

Marketing without a passport

13.98 In June 2014, the AMF published Instruction 2014-03[1]. This Instruction was very well received, as it set down the procedure for both the authorisation of offshore hedge funds managed by EU AIFMs (ie the 'Article 36 procedure') and the authorisation of offshore hedge funds managed by non-EU AIFMs (ie the 'Article 42 procedure').

[1] AMF Instruction – Procedure for marketing units or shares of AIFs (DOC-2014-03) (originally published on 30 June 2014 and last amended on 25 September 2017).

13.99 Whilst the conditions in Article 42(1)(a)–(c) of AIFMD were implemented without substantial change, in addition, it is necessary for the non-EU AIFM to respect the legal and regulatory rules applicable to French AIFMs (ie fully comply with the whole of AIFMD, with the exception of the depositary rules). The effect of these extra conditions makes it very unlikely that non-EU managers would seek to obtain approval for marketing. (To the author's knowledge, no non-EU manager has obtained an Article 42 authorisation.)

13.100 Other than the conditions of Article 36(1)(a)–(c), it is only necessary for an EU AIFM to appoint a French centralising agent in order to seek the authorisation for sale of a non-EU fund in France. This sparked a lot of interest amongst European AIFMs keen to enter the French market. Nonetheless, despite having received a number of applications, the AMF has, so far, refused to authorise the marketing of any Cayman funds under this new procedure. As a result, in reality, the AMF has maintained the *'ancien régime'* with respect to non-EU open-ended hedge funds and applied the same rules to closed-ended hedge funds.

Marketing with a passport

13.101 Noting the above, the AIFMD fund passport is currently the only way to actively market individual hedge funds in France. As a result, managers wishing to target the French market should consider establishing/adding a European AIF to their fund range.

13.102 Moreover, even though (initially) the AMF insisted that passported European AIFs put in place an agreement with a French centralising agent (mirroring the obligation imposed on European UCITS), this requirement has now been removed and so passporting a European AIF has become a very simple process.

Licensing issues

13.103 Whilst an AIF may be passported for sale in France, it will still be necessary to consider whether the marketing activities carried out by the AIFM would amount to the provision of an investment service (for instance, investment advice).

13.104 *Marketing – Selected Jurisdictions*

13.104 It is important to note that the AMF presumes that marketing activities necessarily involve the provision of either investment advice or the investment service of the reception and transmission of orders. As a result, to the extent that the relevant AIFM (or AIF) is domiciled in the UK, Brexit will have a huge impact on permitted marketing activities.

Passive marketing of foreign hedge funds in France

13.105 No law or regulation prohibits a French investor from investing in an unauthorised hedge fund provided that the investment is made on the basis of a genuine unsolicited approach by the French investor.

13.106 As a reminder, existing AMF rules specify that 'the act of marketing units or shares of a UCITS or AIF consists in presenting them in France by different means (advertising, direct marketing, advice) with a view to inciting an investor to subscribe or purchase them'[1].

[1] AMF Position – Guide to UCITS and AIF marketing regimes in France (DOC 2014-04) ('AMF Position 2014-04').

13.107 As a result, 'marketing' a fund would be comprised of the following elements:

- an activity in France;
- the presentation of a fund; and
- inciting an investment.

13.108 Pursuant to updated guidance[1], the AMF has specified five new situations which will not be considered to be fund marketing activities:

- The most important is the creation of a 'market sounding' regime for funds. This is a new safe harbour that was not possible to infer from the previous marketing rules. Pursuant to this regime, up to 50 professional investors could be contacted in advance of the launch of a fund (whether AIF or UCITS) to test local appetite. Note, however, that the information to be provided must not be accompanied by a subscription form and/or the finalised documentation for the fund.
  This safe harbour is extremely useful as it allows managers to 'test the waters' in France. However, those managers which do not wish to register their funds for sale in France will have to choose their contacts carefully. In effect, the AMF has specified that those persons contacted as part of the sounding can't invest in the fund on the basis of a reverse solicitation exemption – so managers will need to proceed with caution.
- Usefully, the AMF has also stated that participating in industry conferences or arranging investor meetings is permitted as long as comments are limited to market developments and trends and/or the investment manager's activities (ie a description of the manager's strategies, the manager's team, closed funds and any other general communication).
  To benefit from this safe harbour, all attendees must be professional investors and there can be no attempt to solicit investments or reference a fund open to investments.

This is a useful clarification of market practice as it is quite common for industry conferences and capital introduction events to be held in Paris. As a result, it will now be possible for managers to be more relaxed when speaking at such events.
- Replying to a request for proposal (an 'RFP') for the creation of a new AIF or UCITS, provided that the RFP was initiated by a legal entity qualifying as a professional investor, would not be considered as marketing.
- In certain circumstances, the secondary market transfer of fund shares would not be considered as an act of marketing.
- Finally, the subscription of fund shares pursuant to AIFMD or UCITS remuneration policies will not be deemed to be a marketing act.

[1] AMF Position 2014-04 was originally published on 30 June 2014 and has since been updated on 26 June 2015, 4 July 2016 and 15 March 2017.

13.109 These five new situations are to be read as an addition to the earlier reverse solicitation clarifications[1] provided in 2014, namely that the following fact patterns would not be viewed as marketing activities:

- the purchase, sale or subscription of shares or securities of a UCITS or an AIF in response to an investor's request, provided that (i) such response has not been solicited, (ii) the request relates to a specifically identified fund, and (iii) the investor is allowed to make such an investment;
- the purchase, sale or subscription of shares or securities of a UCITS or an AIF within the framework of an investment management mandate, provided that such financial instruments are eligible investments;
- the purchase, sale or subscription of shares or securities of a UCITS or an AIF within the framework of the management of a collective investment scheme, provided that such financial instruments are eligible investments.

[1] AMF Position – Guide to UCITS and AIF marketing regimes in France (DOC 2014-04).

Taxation

13.110 Finally, for a country with a reputation for being tax-unfriendly, France is actually surprisingly attractive for funds.

13.111 With respect to corporate taxes, there is no taxation on income or capital gains at the level of the SICAV[1], provided that the SICAV carries out its legal purpose. Similarly, there is no taxation at the level of an FCP on income or gains derived from its investments (provided that no individual holds 10% or more of the FCP units).

[1] *Société d'investissement à capital variable.*

13.112 In relation to the AIFM, management services supplied to either a SICAV or an FCP are VAT exempt unless the management company elects otherwise.

D GERMANY

Patrick Felcht, Senior Legal Counsel, Allianz Global Investors, Germany, Dr Harald Glander and Heiko Stoll, Partners, Simmons & Simmons, Germany

Regulatory framework

13.114 Since the introduction of the German Investment Act (*Investmentgesetz*, 'InvG') in 2004, hedge funds have been subject to regulation by the Federal Financial Supervisory Authority (*Bundesanstalt für Finanzdienstleistungsaufsicht*, 'BaFin'). On 22 July 2013, Germany adopted the German Capital Investment Code (*Kapitalanlagegesetzbuch*, 'KAGB'), implementing the Alternative Investment Fund Managers Directive[1] ('AIFMD') in Germany. Under the KAGB, non-German hedge funds distributed in Germany must comply with the KAGB's provisions for alternative investment funds ('AIFs') that have to be complied with for the registration of an AIF in Germany. Domestic hedge funds are required to comply with the KAGB's provisions and may only be established according to certain strict principles.

[1] Directive 2011/61/EU of 8 June 2011.

13.115 The following provides an introduction to the regulation of domestic hedge funds according to the requirements set out in the KAGB. The principles of distribution of non-German hedge funds to German investors are also explained.

Structure of German hedge funds

13.116 Authorised domestic AIF management companies (*Kapitalverwaltungsgesellschaften*, 'KVGs') may establish two categories of hedge funds in Germany: single hedge funds (*Hedgefonds*) and funds of hedge funds (*Dach-Hedgefonds*).

13.117 Single hedge funds are defined as general open-ended domestic AIFs that are only eligible for professional investors (*Spezial-AIFs*, 'special funds') and whose fund rules (*Anlagebedingungen*, ie the common regulations governing the legal relationship between the fund, the investment management company and the investor) provide for at least one of the following[1]:

- the use of leverage on a substantial basis; or
- the sale of assets which at the time of conclusion of the transaction do not belong to the fund (short sale).

[1] Section 283 of the KAGB.

13.118 If and when a hedge fund employs leverage on a substantial basis is to be determined according to Article 111 of the AIFMD Regulation[1].

[1] Commission Delegated Regulation (EU) No 231/2013 of 19 December 2012.

13.119 Funds of hedge funds, on the other hand, are defined as investment funds which invest in units of target funds[1]. The KAGB defines target funds as (i) single hedge funds, and (ii) EU-AIFs and non-EU AIFs comparable to single hedge funds, as described above, in their investment strategy[2].

[1] Section 225 of the KAGB.
[2] Section 225 of the KAGB. The definition of funds of hedge funds remained unchanged with the implementation of the KAGB.

Admittance and continuous surveillance

Legal form

13.120 Most German funds (including hedge funds and funds of hedge funds) are established using a contractual structure (*Sondervermögen*). This means that these funds do not have legal personality and therefore cannot legally act on their own. Previously, under the InvG, it was possible to issue German single hedge funds as mutual and special funds. In contrast to the regulation of German hedge funds under the InvG, the KAGB now specifies that German single hedge funds may only be established as a German special fund. This is why German single hedge funds (and not funds of hedge funds) are included in the section in the KAGB that deals with *Spezial-AIFs* (ie AIFs only eligible for professional and semi-professional investors). German funds of hedge funds, on the other hand, are included in the section in the KAGB that deals with mixed funds eligible for German retail investors.

13.121 Any German hedge fund (including a fund of hedge funds) must be managed by a KVG with a start-up capital of €300,000 in the case of an internally managed hedge fund, or must appoint an external KVG with a minimum start-up capital of €125,000. Additional capital requirements apply should the assets under management of the KVG exceed €250 million. However, the maximum capital requirement is capped at €10 million[1]. Under German law, neither category of German hedge funds is required to comply with the UCITS Directive. Instead, they qualify as an AIF and thus are subject to the AIFMD requirements (as implemented by the KAGB in Germany).

[1] Section 25 of the KAGB.

Prior notice to German authorities and ongoing obligations

13.122 As described above, single hedge funds established in Germany qualify as German special funds and are therefore subject to supervisory regulation of this type of fund. Pursuant to the provisions applicable to German special funds, the AIFM of the single hedge fund must provide BaFin with the fund rules of the hedge fund prior to launch[1].

[1] Section 273 of the KAGB.

13.123 The fund rules of a German fund of hedge funds must be provided to and approved by BaFin.

13.124 In accordance with the principles set out in AIFMD, German hedge funds must also comply with all reporting and disclosure requirements

13.124 Marketing – Selected Jurisdictions

applicable for AIFMs. This includes, in particular, disclosures to BaFin pursuant to Article 24 of AIFMD and the provision of information pursuant to Article 23 and Annex III of AIFMD to potential German professional or semi-professional investors[1] prior to their investment in the fund. Additional reporting requirements apply to German KVGs that manage such a hedge fund[2]. The disclosure requirements of Articles 23 and 24 of AIFMD also apply to non-EU and EU hedge funds which are registered for distribution in Germany.

[1] This is a new investor category introduced by the KAGB which sits between the retail and the professional investor categories.
[2] Section 34 of the KAGB.

13.125 In addition to the requirements set out above, the AIFM must comply with all trade-related disclosures such as, for example, the net short selling reporting obligations under the Short Selling Regulation[1]. The disclosures mentioned above do not replace the additional trade and product-related disclosure obligations that result from other product-specific EU legislation (including the Short Selling Regulation and the Transparency Directive[2]).

[1] Regulation (EU) No 236/2012 of 14 March 2012.
[2] Directive 2013/50/EU of 22 October 2013.

Fund rules

13.126 As noted above, the fund rules of a German single hedge fund must be disclosed to BaFin prior to the launch of the hedge fund, whereas the fund rules of a fund of hedge funds – like all fund rules of funds eligible for retail investors – have to be approved by BaFin. In addition, any changes to these fund rules must also be disclosed to BaFin. The fund rules of German hedge funds must contain information relating to[1]:

- whether the assets of the hedge fund are held by a prime broker or a custodian;
- in the case of a fund of hedge funds, the strategy according to which the target funds and the scale on which they, within the scope of investment strategies, may use (amongst other things) leverage and derivatives; and
- redemption procedures and requirements which, for German hedge funds, must be permitted at least once in every calendar quarter – redemption requests are to be announced well before the redemption date (100 calendar days in the case of a fund of hedge funds and 40 calendar days in the case of a single hedge fund).

[1] Section 227 of the KAGB.

Manager qualifications

13.127 The KAGB sets out the minimum standards for the manager of a fund. Previously, under the InvG – in addition to the general professional competence standards for fund managers – portfolio managers of funds with additional risks (ie a German hedge fund under the InvG) were required to have sufficient practical experience and knowledge in their field of practice[1], which was determined by BaFin on a case-by-case basis. The KAGB does not provide for this product-related concept for either category of domestic hedge funds. This is because AIFMD, a directive that only addresses fund managers, provides for a suitable regime for all KVGs, under which fund managers are required to have sufficient and experienced personnel and other mechanisms that are necessary for an adequate risk monitoring system. Therefore, there is no longer a need to apply special standards for KVGs which manage hedge funds because the same standards apply to a KVG regardless of what kind of fund the KVG manages.

[1] Section 120 of the InvG.

13.128 The KAGB permits the outsourcing of the functions of a KVG[1], including the portfolio management and risk management functions. The portfolio management function can only be outsourced to entities that are approved for the purposes of asset management and are subject to public supervision. It is possible to outsource the portfolio management function to entities located in non-EU countries provided that the co-operation between BaFin and the regulator of the non-EU country is secured and the entity carrying out the portfolio management function fulfils certain requirements.

[1] Section 36 of the KAGB.

Regulatory principles

Limitation of investment activities

13.129 Single hedge funds are subject to statutory restrictions. Subject to compliance with the risk diversification principle, a German single hedge fund may make investments in securities, money market instruments, derivatives or bank cash balances. In addition, a German single hedge fund must:

- mainly invest in financial instruments; and
- only invest in assets the value of which can be determined.

13.130 Furthermore, German single hedge funds are not allowed to take control over a company which is not listed on a stock exchange[1].

[1] Section 283 of the KAGB.

13.131 The regulatory situation differs for funds of hedge funds. Because these funds are eligible for retail investors the use of leverage is limited to a cash borrowing of a maximum of 10% of the fund's assets. The fund may not: (i) invest more than 49% of the fund's assets in liquid funds (such as money market instruments); (ii) invest more than 20% in any single target fund; (iii) execute short sale transactions; or (iv) invest in more than two target funds of the same issuer if, at the same time, it invests in more than two target funds of the same fund manager[1].

[1] Section 225(2) of the KAGB.

13.132 The fund may acquire foreign target funds provided that the assets of such foreign funds have been trusted to a depositary bank or a prime broker for safekeeping. There are detailed and restrictive requirements for German

13.132 *Marketing – Selected Jurisdictions*

banks when they fulfil this role[1].

[1] Section 225(3) of the KAGB.

Distribution restrictions

13.133 Because units of a German single hedge fund may only be held by professional or semi-professional investors, it is not possible to distribute German single hedge funds to retail investors or to accept retail investors that wish to invest into a German hedge fund.

13.134 German funds of hedge funds are not limited to the structure of special funds and thus it is possible for German funds of hedge funds to accept German retail investors. Therefore, German retail investors can only participate in the performance of a German single hedge fund through an investment in a German fund of hedge funds that invests in a German single hedge fund.

Transparency mechanisms

13.135 Only funds of hedge funds are required to publish a comprehensive prospectus in addition to their fund rules in order to be admitted to public distribution. Single hedge funds must disclose the information/documents pursuant to Article 23 of AIFMD to German professional and semi-professional investors prior to their investment into the fund.

13.136 Generally, comprehensive prospectuses are required to contain information such as the date of launch, summary of tax rules, conclusion of the fund's financial year, etc. A comprehensive prospectus of a fund of hedge funds must reveal additional information regarding[1]:

- the principles on which target funds are selected;
- the limitations on the purchase of units in foreign target funds not subject to supervision;
- the limitations on which the selected target funds may take up loans and execute short sales; and
- specific details and conditions for the redemption of units.

[1] Section 228 of the KAGB.

Taxation

13.137 From 1 January 2018, the new German Investment Tax Act (*Investmentsteuergesetz*, 'InvStG 2018') applies as a result of the German Investment Tax Reform Act (*Investmentsteuerreformgesetz*, 'InvStRefG'). The InvStG 2018 provides for a general opaque taxation regime for all types of investment funds.

13.138 The introduction of a general opaque taxation regime is a fundamental change in the German taxation of funds, considering that the regime will automatically apply for all types of German and foreign investment funds, including UCITS and AIFs.

Germany **13.143**

13.139 The following earnings may be taxed at a German corporation tax rate of 15% at investment fund level[1]:

- German source dividends and other dividend-like payments, including manufactured dividend payments paid under securities lending and repurchase transactions in relation to shares issued by German tax-resident corporations;
- income from real estate located in Germany; and
- certain other taxable German source income as defined in the German Income Tax Act (*Einkommensteuergesetz*, 'EStG') (but not capital gains from the disposal of shares in German tax-resident corporations).

[1] Sections 6 and 7 of the InvStG 2018.

13.140 The reduced rate of 15% only applies if the respective fund has applied for and received a specific 'fund status certificate'[1], issued by the Federal Tax Office (*Bundeszentralamt fur Steuern*, 'BZSt').

[1] Section 7(3) of the InvStG 2018.

13.141 The following earnings of an opaque investment fund will be taxable at the level of German investors ('investment income')[1]:

- distributions, including dividends and repayments of contributed capital, ie any payments which a German investor receives from the respective fund without a disposal (ie redemption or sale) of the fund units;
- the so-called 'lump sum taxation amount'; and
- capital gains from the disposal (ie redemption or sale) of the fund units.

[1] Section 16 of the InvStG 2018.

13.142 The 'lump sum taxation amount' will be attributed to German investors as deemed taxable income as of 2 January each year. The lump sum taxation amount is determined by calculating the minimum base income, as follows:

$$X \times Y \times Z$$

where:

X = the redemption price (or, alternatively, the stock exchange price or market price) per fund unit at the beginning of the previous year;
Y = the base interest rate (*Basiszins*) as determined on the basis of long-term return under public bonds (as published by the German Ministry of Finance; for 2018 this is 0.87% pa); and
Z = 70%.

13.143 However, the minimum base income will be capped by reference to the sum of (i) the actual increase of the redemption price (or stock exchange price or market price, as applicable) of a fund unit during the year, and (ii) the actual annual distributions (being the maximum base income). The lower positive value of the minimum base income and the maximum base income, as determined in the manner set out above, is then reduced by the actual annual

13.143 *Marketing – Selected Jurisdictions*

distributions of the investment fund and the (positive) result is the lump sum taxation amount.

13.144 Specific partial tax exemptions may apply at investor level in relation to the investment income if the respective investment fund continuously complies with certain investment restrictions (eg to always invest a certain ratio (25%/50%) of its total assets in specific equity participations (as defined under the InvStG 2018).

Marketing foreign hedge funds

13.145 The marketing of non-German hedge funds under the KAGB is very different from the previous requirements under the InvG. A foreign hedge fund generally qualifies as an AIF under the KAGB and thus must comply with the marketing principles and registration procedures applicable to non-German AIFs.

13.146 Generally speaking, any kind of marketing activity in Germany will qualify as distribution (the KAGB does not differentiate between 'public' and 'non-public' distribution like the InvG). This means that the private placement regime that was applicable under the InvG is no longer in existence (although transitional provisions were applicable until 21 July 2014 at the very latest).

13.147 Therefore, should an AIFM wish to distribute a non-German hedge fund in Germany (even to a limited number of potential investors), it is required to register the hedge fund with BaFin. Depending on the fund structure and home state of the AIFM/AIF, different registration procedures apply. Following is a brief summary of the German implementation of the procedures outlined in Articles 32, 36 and 42 of AIFMD. Although the distribution of non-German hedge funds to German retail investors is generally possible, the following procedures only apply for the distribution to German professional and semi-professional investors. The requirements for the distribution of foreign hedge funds to German retail investors are not covered.

Article 32 procedure

13.148 The Article 32[1] procedure applies to AIFMs located in the European Economic Area ('EEA') that wish to distribute EU-AIFs in Germany to professional and semi-professional investors. This is the simplest and most straightforward procedure. The reason for this is that it provides for a passporting procedure under which BaFin approval is not required.

[1] Implemented under section 323 of the KAGB.

13.149 The following must be provided to BaFin by the home state regulator of the AIFM:

- the information pursuant to Article 23 of AIFMD; and
- a certificate from the home state regulator confirming the AIFM's licence to manage certain types of AIF.

13.150 The AIF may begin to be distributed/marketed after the AIFM has been informed that the above information has been forwarded by the home state regulator. As stated above, approval by BaFin is not required. The information and documents may be provided in English.

Article 36 procedure

13.151 The procedure under Article 36[1] of AIFMD applies (amongst others) where an EU-AIFM wishes to distribute non-EU AIFs. Unlike the procedure under Article 32 of AIFMD, this procedure requires an application (ie distribution of the AIF is only permitted where BaFin has approved the application).

[1] Implemented under section 329 of the KAGB.

13.152 The following (amongst other documents/information) must be provided to BaFin:

- the information pursuant to Article 23/Annex III of AIFMD; and
- a certificate from the home state regulator of the AIFM confirming that the AIFM is properly licensed and the management of the non-EU AIF complies with AIFMD requirements.

13.153 In addition, the AIFM must have appointed one or more entities which carry out the functions of Article 21(7), (8) and (9) of AIFMD if the fund is distributed to professional investors only. This also applies to the master fund, should the non-EU AIF (that will be distributed into Germany) be a feeder fund. All information/documents may be provided in English. In addition, a memorandum of understanding ('MoU') must be in place between BaFin and the regulator of the country where the AIF is located.

13.154 Depending on the structure of the AIF, BaFin has a maximum review period of one to five months in which to approve the application. The review period is only triggered if the application is considered by BaFin to be complete.

Article 42 procedure

13.155 Article 42[1] of AIFMD provides for a registration procedure where both the AIFM and the AIF are located outside the EEA (amongst other applicable scenarios). Upon application, both the AIFM and the AIF are generally not subject to AIFMD. Therefore, all of the information pursuant to Article 23/Annex III of AIFMD is required to be submitted in relation to both the AIFM and the AIF (ie there is no certificate from a home state regulator that BaFin relies on). Also, the AIFM must have appointed one or more entities which carry out the functions of Article 21(7), (8) and (9) of AIFMD if the fund is distributed to professional investors only. This exceeds the requirements of Article 42 of AIFMD.

[1] Implemented under section 330 of the KAGB.

13.156 As with the Article 36 procedure, there must be an MoU in place between BaFin and the regulatory body where the AIF is located. In addition, an MoU must also be in place between BaFin and the regulator of the country where the AIFM is located. In June 2014, MoUs were in place with the most

13.156 *Marketing – Selected Jurisdictions*

common countries of hedge funds (eg the Cayman Islands, the US, Jersey and Hong Kong). However, some common offshore jurisdictions (eg the British Virgin Islands) have yet to enter into an MoU with BaFin. The registration of a foreign hedge fund is not possible unless such an MoU has been concluded.

13.157 Depending on the structure of the AIF, and whether the AIF will be distributed to professional investors only or also to semi-professional investors, BaFin has a review period of two to eight months in which to approve the application.

E   HONG KONG

Rolfe Hayden, Partner, Simmons & Simmons, Hong Kong and Gaven Cheong, Partner, Simmons & Simmons, Hong Kong

Introduction

13.158 When marketing hedge funds in Hong Kong, two issues need to be considered: (i) the category of person to whom investment advertisements concerning such funds may be issued; and (ii) whether or not a licensing requirement may be triggered by meeting in person prospective investors in Hong Kong. With regard to the former, there is a mismatch in the law and regulation as applicable to corporate funds and other entities used for fund vehicles.

13.159 A hedge fund structured as a limited partnership and interests in the fund, if not authorised by the Securities and Futures Commission (the 'SFC'), may only be offered (i) on a private placement basis or (ii) to an unlimited number of 'professional investors'. Documents may be sent to and meetings held with such persons in relation to such offerings. By contrast, hedge funds which are structured as corporates can be offered to a wider set of persons.

13.160 Financial institutions (such as banks, intermediaries, insurance companies and other funds) fall within the definition of 'professional investor'. No filing or notification is required in offering a hedge fund within an exemption. However, it is advisable to include a selling restriction on all written materials relating to a hedge fund.

13.161 There are two key pieces of legislation relating to marketing hedge funds in Hong Kong:

- the Securities and Futures Ordinance[1]; and
- the Companies (Winding Up and Miscellaneous Provisions) Ordinance[2].

[1] See paras **13.162–13.167** below.
[2] See paras **13.168–13.177** below.

The Securities and Futures Ordinance

13.162 The Securities and Futures Ordinance (the 'SFO') governs the offering of all types of securities including shares and any interests in funds of any type.

13.163 Under section 103(1) of the SFO, any 'advertisement' (which is very widely defined and includes oral communication) in connection with offering securities made to the public must either (i) be approved by the SFC or (ii) be within one of a number of exemptions set out in the SFO. Accordingly, the SFO prohibition applies to telephone calls and meetings in person as well as documentary communication (emails, letters, faxes and marketing materials, etc) directed at the public. A breach of the prohibition is a criminal offence.

13.164 The prohibition under section 103(1) of the SFO only applies to offers to the 'public' in Hong Kong. Accordingly, a private placement[1] could be made without falling within section 103(1). In addition, there are exemptions from the prohibition under section 103(2).

[1] See paras **13.178–13.182** below.

13.165 Pursuant to section 103(3)(k) of the SFO, any advertisement issued in respect of a fund which is only intended to be disposed of to 'professional investors' is also exempt from the prohibition. This exemption was confirmed in March 2015 by Hong Kong's Court of Final Appeal in the case of *Securities and Futures Commission v Pacific Sun Advisors Ltd and another*[1]. However, even though this exemption does not require the prospectus or any other marketing material relating to a fund to include such a statement, if section 103(3)(k) is being relied upon it is advisable to include a statement in the relevant document to the effect that the fund will only accept applications from investors in Hong Kong which are professional investors as defined in the SFO.

[1] [2015] HKCFA 27 – see http://www.hklii.hk/eng/hk/cases/hkcfa/2015/27.html.

13.166 The definition of 'professional investor' in Schedule 1 of the SFO essentially means financial institutions, whilst the definition under the subsidiary legislation – the Securities and Futures (Professional Investor) Rules (the 'PI Rules') – includes non-financial entities and high net worth individuals. High net worth individual professional investors for these purposes include individuals with net liquid assets of HK$8 million (approximately US$1 million) and non-financial institution operating companies with gross assets of at least HK$40 million (approximately US$7.8 million).

13.167 No notification to or filing with the SFC or other body is required in order to rely on an exemption under the SFO. Provided that the hedge fund is offered in Hong Kong only to 'professional investors' (as defined in the SFO and the PI Rules) or by way of an old fashioned private placement (hence not made to the public), no authorisation or regulatory approval of the hedge fund itself is necessary.

The Companies (Winding Up and Miscellaneous Provisions) Ordinance

13.168 The Companies (Winding Up and Miscellaneous Provisions) Ordinance ('C(WUMP)O') governs, amongst other things, the offer in writing of shares and debentures of both Hong Kong incorporated and non-Hong Kong companies to the public in Hong Kong. A document offering shares to the public may constitute a prospectus. The 'public' for this purpose includes any

13.168 *Marketing – Selected Jurisdictions*

section of the public. Accordingly, an offer limited to, say, only expatriates or Americans resident in Hong Kong would still constitute the public for these purposes (and under the SFO). Any 'prospectus' under the C(WUMP)O must (unless it relates to a fund authorised by the SFC) comply with the content requirements of the C(WUMP)O, be vetted by the SFC, and be registered with the Registrar of Companies in Hong Kong before any issuance of the document in Hong Kong. It would not be possible for a prospectus or private placement memorandum of a hedge fund to comply with the content requirements of the C(WUMP)O. In addition, the SFC requires all collective investment schemes offered to the public (unless within an exemption) in Hong Kong to be authorised under the SFO. This is onerous and it is unlikely that any existing hedge fund could satisfy the SFC's criteria for retail funds.

13.169 Where a document relates to an offer which falls within those listed in the Seventeenth Schedule to the C(WUMP)O (the 'safe harbours'), the document will not constitute a 'prospectus' for the purposes of the C(WUMP)O. As such, documents in respect of the Seventeenth Schedule offers fall outside the C(WUMP)O registration and content requirements applicable to prospectuses (ie they will not be required to be approved by the SFC under the C(WUMP)O or registered with the Registrar of Companies and there would be no other registration or filing requirement).

13.170 Three of the safe harbours are usually of assistance to an offer of shares in a corporate hedge fund. These are:

- the offers of shares of the same class are made to no more than 50 persons in a 12-month period;
- the offers of shares where the minimum investment per investor (numbers unlimited) equals or exceeds HK$500,000 (approximately US$64,100); or
- the offers of shares are only made to 'professional investors' (numbers unlimited) within the meaning of the SFO and the PI Rules.

13.171 Documents in respect of the first two safe harbours above must include the following prescribed warning statement in English (or Chinese, if appropriate) at the front of any document which might be considered to offer or advertise shares:

> 'WARNING
>
> The contents of this document have not been reviewed by any regulatory authority in Hong Kong. You are advised to exercise caution in relation to the offer. If you are in any doubt about any of the contents of this document, you should obtain independent professional advice.'

13.172 The inclusion of this statement is a condition of the ability to rely upon the relevant safe harbours. As well as including it in any prospectus, it would be advisable to include this statement in any document sent or provided to Hong Kong residents (existing or prospective investors).

13.173 In addition, although not a statutory requirement, it is advisable that, even where relying on a safe harbour, a selling restriction be inserted into each document in respect of such offers, including the relevant prospectus.

13.174 An offer (i) to professional investors in an unlimited number and (ii) to no more than 50 non-professional investors may be combined. However, an offer in reliance of the minimum investment per investor may not be combined. In other words, a fund could not be offered to, say, 1,000 persons in reliance of the minimum investment safe harbour and 49 persons for whom the minimum investment amount has been waived. A fund could be offered to an unlimited number of professional investors in Hong Kong as well as no more than 50 non-professional investors in Hong Kong.

13.175 Where a document is in respect of an offer not directed at the public, ie by way of a private placement, the C(WUMP)O prospectus requirements do not need to be considered. Such a document will not be a prospectus. A private placement of funds can therefore also be made outside the C(WUMP)O[1].

[1] See paras 13.178–13.182 below.

13.176 'Reverse solicitation' is not a concept recognised under C(WUMP)O, and there is no safe harbour under the Seventeenth Schedule for reverse solicitation. Moreover, the definition of 'prospectus' under C(WUMP)O covers not only a document offering shares to the public for subscription or purchase but also a document calculated to invite offers by the public to subscribe for or to purchase shares.

13.177 There is no requirement to notify or file with the SFC, the Registrar of Companies or other body in order to rely on a safe harbour.

Private placement

13.178 To the extent an offer of interests in a hedge fund is not made to the public, neither the C(WUMP)O nor the prohibition in the SFO applies. A private offer is therefore, by definition, not a public offer. Broadly speaking, a private placement has traditionally been taken by the market to mean no more than 50 offerees in Hong Kong in a 12-month period (although this market view has not been sanctioned officially by the SFC and there is no statutory basis for it – the first of the safe harbours referred to above is not a definition of a non-public offer, rather a form of statutory exemption from the consequences of a public offer as distinct from a private placement). However, a private placement depends on all the circumstances. The SFC has in the past agreed with the 50 offerees test but has also indicated that in certain circumstances it may consider an offer to a few offerees to be 'public'.

13.179 Accordingly, when relying on a private placement, it is advisable that each prospectus or private placement memorandum is:

- numbered;
- individually sent to a named offeree (who should be requested not to pass the prospectus to any other person); and
- not reissued in the event that it is returned by an offeree.

13.180 Although there is no written SFC guidance in respect of the class of offerees, to the extent such offerees are connected to the relevant hedge fund or hedge fund manager (for example, such offerees are existing investors) or are sophisticated, such as professional investors, then the argument that an offer is not made to the public would likely be more readily accepted by the SFC.

13.181 *Marketing – Selected Jurisdictions*

13.181 Subscriptions for the relevant fund should only be accepted from persons to whom the prospectus or private placement memorandum was sent. A record of offerees should be kept.

13.182 There is no requirement to notify or file with the SFC or other body in order to rely on a private placement.

Licensing

13.183 Aside from considering the categories of person to whom a hedge fund may be offered[1], the act of marketing in Hong Kong may trigger a licensing requirement for the person effecting the marketing activities.

[1] See paras **13.166** and **13.170** above.

Dealing in securities regulated activity

13.184 Where a person is carrying on a business in Hong Kong in a 'regulated activity', that person must be licensed by the SFC under the SFO. The most relevant regulated activity in respect of promotion of hedge funds, however indirect, is 'dealing in securities' (Type 1). What amounts to Type 1 regulated activity is widely drafted and includes offering to make an agreement with (or inducing or attempting to induce) another person to enter into, or offer to enter into, an agreement to, amongst other things, subscribe for securities. This captures promotion of funds. There are a number of 'carve outs' from an activity constituting Type 1 regulated activity.

13.185 Of relevance to any promotion of the fund is where a person as principal performs the act of dealing with a person who is a 'professional investor' under the SFO (excluding 'professional investors' under the PI Rules). This could apply where a director of the general partner of the fund performs the relevant 'dealing in securities', eg sends the prospectus, calls or meets prospective investors in Hong Kong in his capacity as a director.

13.186 The other useful 'carve out' is where the dealing is conducted through a Type 1 licensed dealer. Accordingly, the relevant manager of the hedge fund could appoint a distributor in Hong Kong provided the distributor holds a Type 1 licence. The distributor could accompany the representative of the manager to investor meetings.

13.187 Where a fund manager holds a Type 9 (asset management) licence in Hong Kong, the activity of marketing a hedge fund managed by that manager does not constitute Type 1 regulated activity. Accordingly, licensed fund managers in Hong Kong can market their own hedge funds without the more onerous Type 1 licence on the basis that it is incidental to their business.

Presentations or meetings in person in Hong Kong

13.188 Because the definition of advertisement under the SFO includes oral communications, the giving of a presentation or attendance at a meeting in person in Hong Kong is potentially subject to the SFO. In order to avoid any issues as to 'dealing in securities', any presentations or meetings should be limited in number so as to limit the risk that a business is considered by the SFC to be conducted in Hong Kong. The attendees at any such presentation or meeting should also be limited.

13.189 It is common for foreign managers to visit Hong Kong and to promote their services or hedge funds. Such intermediaries very often may be in breach of the SFO licensing requirements. The SFC has long recognised that such short visits occur and so has provided for an express temporary licensing regime in the SFO for visiting individual intermediaries. However, this is designed for foreign employees of overseas associated companies of a Hong Kong based, SFC licensed, company. It is not possible for an individual to obtain a licence as an individual without an SFC licensed company accepting responsibility for that individual's regulated activities in Hong Kong. It is possible for a foreign licensed entity to obtain a temporary licence in Hong Kong, in which case the individual visiting Hong Kong can be temporarily licensed. However, the required licensing process is time consuming (it takes at least two months) and the temporary licence only covers a period of three months.

Managed accounts

13.190 The marketing of discretionary managed accounts, even if following the same strategy as a hedge fund, is treated differently under Hong Kong law. Section 115 of the SFO provides that where a person from outside Hong Kong, directly or through an agent, actively markets to the public its services which, if performed in Hong Kong, would constitute a regulated activity, then that person is deemed to be carrying on a business in that regulated activity in Hong Kong. Accordingly, this places the person outside Hong Kong immediately in breach of the licensing requirements of the SFO. Unfortunately, there is no statutory definition of 'actively markets' and as a phrase it is unique to the SFO and to this section 115. In addition, unlike other sections in the SFO which prohibit behaviours to the public, there is no express exemption where the active marketing is directed at only professional investors. Section 115 'bites' on the offshore person whose services are promoted rather than the promoter. Any hedge fund manager promoting managed account services in Hong Kong from outside Hong Kong needs to take care it does not trigger a licensing requirement due to this provision.

Conduct requirements

13.191 As indicated above[1], a Type 9 licensed fund manager can market funds which it manages without the need for a Type 1 licence. However, in doing so, the manager or a distributor will, as a licensed corporation, need to comply with the SFC's Code of Conduct for Persons Licensed by or Registered with the Securities and Futures Commission[2] (the 'Code of Conduct').

[1] See para **13.187** above.
[2] Available on the SFC's website: see http://www.sfc.hk/web/EN/rules-and-standards/codes-and-guidelines/codes.

13.192 *Marketing – Selected Jurisdictions*

13.192 The Code of Conduct applies to all licensed persons in the carrying on of regulated activities for which such persons are licensed. The Code is not statute and does not have the force of law. Although a failure to comply with the Code will not, by itself, render a person liable to any judicial or other proceedings, in any proceedings under the SFO before any court, non-compliance with the Code is admissible in evidence. Further, a failure to comply with the Code may reflect adversely on the 'fitness and properness' of the relevant licensed person. Chapter 5 of the Code sets out 'know your client' requirements applicable to licensed persons. However, the need to establish a client's financial situation, investment experience and investment objectives as well as to ensure suitability may be waived for certain professional investors.

13.193 The term 'client' is not defined in the Code of Conduct. If interpreted narrowly, consistent with the SFO, the 'client' with respect to the marketing of funds would be the funds or group managers with whom the licensed corporation has a contractual arrangement pursuant to which the licensed corporation is engaged and remunerated (to market the funds to prospective investors). If the term 'client' is given a wider meaning, it may include a prospective investor in the funds. Accordingly, for the purposes of the Code, the licensed corporation may have two types of 'clients':

- the entity which appoints it; and
- the prospective investors in the funds, being persons to whom the funds are marketed by it.

13.194 Notwithstanding the likelihood that prospective investors may be considered 'clients' for the purposes of the Code of Conduct, context is important and must be taken into account. For example, a distributor marketing to an audience of invitees at a seminar as to the merits of a fund is undoubtedly 'dealing in securities' (ie engaging in a regulated activity), but he would not typically regard each attendee at the seminar as a 'client' for Code of Conduct purposes (although if he is promoting an unauthorised fund in order to comply with selling restrictions under the SFO, he should be satisfied that all members of the audience are professional investors, or at least make clear that the relevant fund is only available to professional investors).

13.195 Chapter 15 of the Code of Conduct provides a waiver regime applicable to licensed persons where the licensed person's clients are a certain type of professional investor. The type of professional investor under the Code of Conduct is effectively split into two classes:

- financial institutions under paragraphs (a)–(i) of the definition in Schedule 1 of the SFO ('institutional professional investors'); and
- either:
  - other non-individual categories under the PI Rules ('corporate professional investors'); or
  - individuals qualifying under the PI Rules ('individual professional investors').

13.196 The Code of Conduct makes a distinction between the treatment of professional investors which are (i) institutional professional investors, and (ii) corporate professional investors or individual professional investors. In respect of the former, the suitability and assessment and other requirements under the Code of Conduct are automatically disapplied. In respect of individual professional investors, the suitability assessment requirement under the Code of Conduct cannot be disapplied even with consent. For corporate professional investors, whether or not such professional investor can opt out of the 'client protections' under the Code of Conduct will depend on the following:

- the licensed person conducting a corporate professional investor experience assessment (a 'CPI assessment');
- whether or not the corporate professional investor passes the CPI assessment; and
- if it does pass, the corporate professional investor giving its consent.

F   ITALY

Agostino Papa, Partner, DLA Piper, Italy, Andrea Di Dio, Partner (taxation), DLA Piper, Italy, and Nicoletta Alfano, Lead Lawyer, DLA Piper, Italy

Introduction

13.197 The Italian legal framework which governs investment funds, including hedge funds, was revised in 2014/15 so as to implement the Alternative Investment Fund Managers Directive[1] ('AIFMD'). In particular, due to the implementation of AIFMD, the definition of 'hedge funds'[2] has been replaced by that of 'reserved alternative investment funds' ('RAIFs'). RAIFs are riskier than investment funds which are 'non-reserved alternative investment funds' ('non-RAIFs'), as RAIFs are allowed to derogate from the restrictions and prudential rules on risk containment and risk diversification which the Bank of Italy has laid down for non-RAIFs. For this reason, the marketing of, and the subscription for interests in, RAIFs is limited to certain categories of investors.

[1]   Directive 2011/61/EU of 8 June 2011.
[2]   The previous regulation concerning hedge funds was provided by the Bank of Italy Regulation of May 2012 (containing the Regulation on collective asset management) and by the Ministry of Finance Decree No 228 of 24 May 1999.

13.198 In this context, RAIFs can in principle be divided into two categories, depending on the extent to which they use leverage; but from a practical point of view, both of those categories are subject to the same regulatory framework established by the Italian regulatory authorities.

Regulatory framework

13.199 Following the amendment of Legislative Decree No 58 of 24 February 1998 (the 'Consolidated Law on Finance')[1], the Ministry of Finance issued Decree No 30 of 5 March 2015, setting out the general criteria with which undertakings in collective investments must comply ('Decree 30/15'). The Bank of Italy – the national central bank entrusted with the supervision of banks and financial entities – and *Commissione Nazionale per le Società e la Borsa*, known as 'CONSOB' – the authority entrusted with the supervision of public offerings, listed companies, investment companies and financial intermediaries and service providers – issued their respective implementing regulations, which entered into force at the same time as Decree 30/15, on 3 April

13.199 *Marketing – Selected Jurisdictions*

2015.

[1] By Legislative Decree No 44 of 4 March 2014, which implemented AIFMD in Italy.

13.200 Consequently, the Italian regulatory framework for alternative investment funds (including RAIFs) includes the following:

- the Consolidated Law on Finance;
- the Bank of Italy Regulation on collective asset management of 19 January 2015 (*Regolamento sulla gestione collettiva del risparmio*) (the 'Bank of Italy Regulation');
- Decree 30/15;
- the CONSOB Regulation No 11971 of 14 May 1999, containing the Regulation on issuers, as amended (*Regolamento emittenti*) (the 'CONSOB Regulation');
- the Bank of Italy and CONSOB Joint Regulation on the organisation and procedures to be adopted by intermediaries providing investment services or collective investment management services of 29 October 2007, as amended (*Regolamento congiunto Banca d'Italia e Consob in materia di organizzazione e procedure degli intermediari che prestano servizi di investimento o di gestione collettiva del risparmio*) (the 'Joint Regulation').

Regulatory bodies

13.201 The Bank of Italy and CONSOB are the two regulatory bodies responsible – with different tasks and powers – for supervising the entities which operate in the collective asset management market in Italy. Specifically, the Bank of Italy is entrusted with prudential supervision (risk limitation, financial stability, and sound and prudent management) whilst CONSOB is entrusted with the supervision of compliance with transparency and fair conduct standards.

Key characteristics of Italian RAIFs

Legal vehicles

13.202 Under the Italian regulatory framework, RAIFs may be established as closed-ended AIFs, in which the issue and redemption of shares or units can only be carried out in predefined terms[1], or as open-ended AIFs, which can issue and redeem shares or units at any time.

[1] In addition to the redemption upon expiry of the RAIF's duration, the AIF's management rules may provide for early redemption: (i) upon the initiative of the manager of the RAIF, on a pro-rata basis, in the event of divestments or excess available liquidity; and (ii) upon request of each unitholder/shareholder in an amount not exceeding the sums acquired through the issue of new units/shares.

13.203 Both open-ended and closed-ended RAIFs can be established by adopting (i) a contractual form (investment funds[1]), in which case the interests held by the investors are represented by units, or (ii) a company form, as investment companies with variable capital (*società di investimento a capital* *variabile*, 'SICAV') or investment companies with fixed capital (*società di investimento a capitale fisso*, 'SICAF'), in which case the interests held by the investors are represented by shares.

[1] An investment fund is a scheme established and managed by a manager as a segregated pool of assets divided into units belonging to a plurality of investors, managed as a whole in the best interests of the unitholders and independently from them.

Investment strategy

13.204 RAIFs can freely adopt/select their investment policies and objectives, provided that they comply with the basic principle of diversification in order to achieve portfolio optimisation. In particular, RAIFs can invest in any financial instrument regardless of the nature of the underlying assets and also in real estate assets[1]. Moreover, RAIFs may also grant loans. As anticipated, RAIFs can derogate from the restrictions and prudential rules on risk containment and risk diversification laid down by the Bank of Italy for non-RAIFs.

[1] Pursuant to article 12 of Decree 30/15, RAIFs which invest in real estate must be managed in accordance with a predetermined investment strategy and must abide by the following investment limits:
  (a) They are required to invest at least two thirds of their total value in: (i) real estate assets; (ii) rights in rem in respect of real estate assets, including those arising from leasing agreements with a transferal nature (*contratti di leasing immobiliare con natura traslativa*) and licence relationships (*rapporti concessori*); (iii) equity interests in real estate companies (*società immobiliari*); or (iv) other real estate alternative investments funds.
  (b) They can invest the remaining third of their total value in assets other than those in (a) above (eg listed or unlisted financial instruments).

13.205 The investment strategy of a RAIF is contained in the rules of management drafted and adopted by the fund manager of that RAIF (the 'AIFM'). The legal framework for RAIFs does not require the rules of management to be approved by the Bank of Italy nor fully to comply with the minimum criteria established by the Bank of Italy for retail funds which are available to the general public. Nevertheless, the AIFM must submit a notification of marketing to CONSOB, and within 20 working days following receipt of that notification, CONSOB is required to inform the AIFM of whether or not it may start marketing interests in the relevant RAIF in Italy.

Leverage

13.206 RAIFs are not subject to a maximum leverage. In this context, an exception is provided for credit funds (ie AIFs which grant and purchase loans), whose leverage ratio, calculated as the ratio between the exposure of the RAIF and its net asset value, cannot exceed the threshold of 1.5.

13.207 In addition, it is worth highlighting that if a RAIF consistently employs leverage (and specifically if the ratio between financial exposure and net asset value is equal to or higher than three), both the RAIF and its AIFM are subject to specific evaluations by the Bank of Italy regarding (i) the adequacy of the internal organisation and the risk management of that AIFM, and (ii) the potential effect of leverage on the financial stability of that RAIF.

13.208 *Marketing – Selected Jurisdictions*

Valuation and price

13.208 An AIFM must ensure that for each RAIF which it manages the net asset value per unit or share of that RAIF is calculated on the occasion of each issue, subscription, redemption or cancellation of units or shares and at least once a year.

Risk concentration limits

13.209 RAIFs are not subject to specific concentration limits. A specific concentration limit is stipulated for credit funds, which may invest in exposures to the same debtor no more than 10% of the greater of (i) the total value of the assets of that RAIFs, and (ii) the value of the assets of that RAIF (including investors' commitments). However, a de facto minimum level of risk diversification (based on the actual characteristics of the portfolio) must be ensured.

Governance of RAIFs

13.210 Although the management of a RAIF is the responsibility of the AIFM, which must manage in the best interests of the unitholders/shareholders and independently from them, the unitholders/shareholders can exercise certain rights, depending on the provisions set out in the rules of management/articles of association of that RAIF, through meetings of unitholders/shareholders and the advisory committee (if any) of that RAIF. Generally, such governance provisions are negotiated in accordance with market practice and are included in the rules of management/articles of association of that RAIF.

Number of investors

13.211 RAIFs, as well as other investment funds, have to raise capital from a plurality of investors. Under the Bank of Italy Regulation[1], this requirement is deemed to be satisfied where there is only one unitholder, provided that investment is made in the best interests of a number of underlying investors (as in the case of a master-feeder structure or a fund of funds). This provision is in line with the past market practice, whereby the requirement for a plurality of investors was deemed satisfied, on the basis of a 'look-through' approach, also where the investment was made by an investment scheme – which in turn represented a plurality of investors – through an intermediate vehicle.

[1] See para **13.200** above.

Management of RAIFs

13.212 A RAIF may be established and managed by an Italian asset management company (*società di gestione del risparmio*, 'SGR'[1]) which is authorised by the Bank of Italy, or by an authorised entity which has its registered office in an EU member state.

[1] See paras 13.220–13.232 below.

13.213 Moreover, it is possible for an asset management company which has its registered office in an EU member state other than Italy to establish and manage a RAIF either by using the European marketing passport or by establishing a branch in Italy, provided that it has been authorised to do so by the competent authority in its home jurisdiction in close co-ordination with the Bank of Italy and CONSOB.

Investors

13.214 RAIFs can be marketed to and invested in by the following:

- *Professional investors*, which are investors in possession of the experience, awareness and competence necessary to make their own informed decisions about investments and correctly evaluate the risks assumed. There are two categories of professional investors: professional investors by law and on request[1].
- *Non-professional investors* (including retail investors), provided that: (a) this is expressly provided for by the rules of management of the relevant RAIF; and (b) these investors are either (i) employees or directors of the AIFM of the relevant RAIF, or (ii) retail investors committing (on a continuous basis) a minimum amount equal to, or higher than, €500,000 each[2].

[1] The definition of 'professional investor' is contained in article 6 paras 2-quinquies and 2-sexies of the Consolidated Law on Finance.
[2] Pursuant to article 14 of Decree 30/15.

Marketing RAIFs

13.215 The marketing of RAIFs may only be carried out by the following:

- Italian investment firms (*società di intermediazione mobiliare*, 'SIMs').
- Italian asset management companies (*società di gestione del risparmio*, 'SGRs')[1], in relation to the marketing of funds managed by the SGR itself and/or by third parties.
- Open-ended retail funds constituted in company form ('SICAVs'), in relation to the shares of the SICAV itself.
- Closed-ended funds constituted in company form ('SICAFs'), in relation to the shares of the SICAF itself.
- Financial intermediaries entered in the register referred to in article 106 of the Legislative Decree No 385 of 1 September 1993 (the 'Consolidated Banking Law') which are authorised to provide placement services.
- Duly authorised banks.
- EU asset management companies and EU investment firms, either by establishing a branch in Italy or by using the European marketing passport. The establishment of a branch must be notified to the Bank of Italy and to CONSOB by the competent authority of the home

13.215 *Marketing – Selected Jurisdictions*

jurisdiction of the relevant company or firm. Furthermore, the provision of services under the European passport regime must be exercised in accordance with article 41-ter of the Consolidated Law on Finance by EU asset management companies and in accordance with article 27 of the Consolidated Law on Finance by EU investment firms.

- Non-EU investment firms, either with or without the establishment of a branch in Italy (which must be authorised by CONSOB pursuant to article 28 of the Consolidated Law on Finance).
- Non-EU banks, either with or without the establishment of a branch in Italy (which must be authorised by the Bank of Italy).

[1] See paras **13.220–13.232** below.

13.216 An Italian AIFM that wishes to market an Italian RAIF in Italy is required to notify CONSOB of its intention. Within 20 business days following receipt of the notification, CONSOB is required to inform the AIFM of whether or not it may start marketing interests in that RAIF in Italy.

13.217 In the case of an EU AIFM that wishes to market RAIFs in Italy, the so-called 'passport procedure' applies. Consequently, the competent authority of the home member state of the AIFM is required to notify CONSOB of the AIFM's intention to market the RAIF in Italy by submitting the relevant documentation, and to give notice to the AIFM of such notification. Once it receives this notice, the AIFM can start to market interests in the RAIF in Italy.

13.218 The notification to be submitted to CONSOB must include the documents listed in article 43 of the Consolidated Law on Finance[1] as well as the 'key information document' ('KID') under Regulation (EU) No 1286/2014 of 26 November 2014 concerning packaged retail and insurance-based investment products ('PRIIPs'). Indeed, CONSOB has specified that AIFMs must prepare KIDs in relation to RAIFs that are to be marketed in Italy to retail investors committing a minimum amount equal to, or higher than, €500,000 each.

[1] The notification must contain:
- the letter of notification accompanied by the business programme which identifies the RAIF to be marketed and the home state of the RAIF;
- the regulations and articles of association of the RAIF;
- the identity of the custodian of the RAIF;
- the description of the RAIF and the other information made available to investors under article 6 para 2(a) no 3-bis of the Consolidated Law on Finance;
- an indication of the home state of the master UCITS if the UCITS to be marketed is a feeder UCITS;
- if relevant, an indication of the EU member states other than Italy in which the relevant units or shares will be marketed;
- information about the procedures established to prevent the marketing of the RAIF's units or shares to retail investors – for this purpose, the regulations or the articles of association and the documentation made available to investors must stipulate that the shares or units in the RAIF may be marketed only to professional investors.

Should the marketing involve an offer of securities to the public pursuant to Directive 2003/71/EC of 4 November 2003 (the 'Prospectus Directive'), the additional requirements laid down by article 94 of the Consolidated Law on Finance will apply with reference to the drawing up, approval and distribution of a prospectus.

Italy 13.223

Reporting requirements

13.219 The AIFM is required to maintain the accounts of the RAIF. In addition to the records prescribed by the Italian Civil Code for business enterprises, the AIFM – in compliance with the same requirements provided by the Civil Code – must:

- maintain the RAIF's daily book which outlines on a day-by-day basis all the transactions relating to the management of the RAIF as well as appropriate details of any issue or redemption of shares or units;
- draft an annual management report of the RAIF which must be made available within six months following the end of any fiscal year or following the date of each interim distribution of proceeds made by the RAIF;
- draft a six-monthly management report of the RAIF which must be made available within two months following the end of the first half of each fiscal year; and
- prepare a prospectus which illustrates the value of each unit and the total value of the RAIF, with a frequency at least equal to the frequency of issue or redemption of units[1].

[1] In the case of RAIFs established by adopting a company form, the AIFM must prepare a prospectus which illustrates the value of the shares and the total value of the RAIF; such value is required to be calculated on the occasion of each issue, subscription, redemption or cancellation of shares and at least once a year.

Key characteristics of an SGR

13.220 The exercise of the collective portfolio management activity by an SGR is subject to authorisation, which is granted by the Bank of Italy if the business plan, the programme of activities and the structure of the SGR are such as to ensure sound and prudent management and if the persons performing administrative, management and control functions as well as shareholders and their representatives meet the requirements provided for in articles 13 and 14 of the Consolidated Law on Finance.

13.221 An SGR which proposes to exercise the collective portfolio management activity has to submit to the Bank of Italy documentation attesting that it has met the relevant requirements. The Bank of Italy will grant or deny the relevant authorisation within 90 days from receipt of the relevant documents (or later if the Bank of Italy requests further information).

13.222 SGRs are required to adopt the legal form of a joint-stock company (*società per azioni*) and have a minimum capital of not less than €1 million[1].

[1] If the SGR manages only RAIFs, the corporate capital may be reduced to €500,000; in addition, if the total assets under management of such RAIFs have a value below €500 million, or below €100 million in the case of RAIFs which use leverage, the corporate capital may be reduced to €50,000.

13.223 The costs in respect of the establishment and operation of an SGR are mainly related to the corporate capital of the SGR, management, personnel, controlling functions, board of statutory auditors, external auditors, as well as

13.223 *Marketing – Selected Jurisdictions*

other external service providers (if any). The amount of these costs may vary significantly depending on the number and size of the investment funds which that SGR manages[1].

[1] The Bank of Italy usually requires an SGR to be provided with working capital in order to meet the start-up costs without reducing the minimum corporate capital.

13.224 Once authorised by the Bank of Italy, an SGR is allowed to carry out the collective portfolio management activity. The exercise of such activity must be based on the independence and autonomy principle, ie apart from their governance rights[1], investors cannot interfere with the management of the RAIF or provide binding instruction to the SGR.

[1] See para **13.210** above.

13.225 In line with its specific objectives, investment policies and risk management, the SGR must seek to preserve and maximise the interests of shareholders and unitholders, implementing suitable measures to protect them and providing itself with the technical and human resources suitable to ensure the efficient conduct of its business.

13.226 Pursuant to the Consolidated Law on Finance, the Bank of Italy Regulation and the Joint Regulation, SGRs must adopt organisational measures and internal policies to ensure the sound and prudent management of the company and to conduct the relevant business in accordance with the principles of diligence, fair conduct and transparency.

13.227 Among other things, the SGR has to provide itself with an organisational structure designed to minimise the risk of conflicts of interest and adopt internal procedures and policies aimed at (i) identifying actual and potential conflicts of interest, and (ii) managing them in a fair manner.

13.228 Specific safeguards are provided with regard to the delegation of functions[1], which is permitted to the extent that the SGR does not become a 'letter box entity', that is, as long as the SGR remains the actual manager of the relevant RAIF[2].

[1] Such delegation of functions, however, does not have any consequence for the 'contractual' relationship between the SGR and the investors, since the SGR remains liable vis-à-vis the investors for the outsourced activity.
[2] According to the relevant European Level 2 Regulation (Commission Delegated Regulation (EU) No 231/2013 of 19 December 2012), the outsourcing/delegation will cause the SGR to be considered a 'letter box entity' when:
- the SGR no longer retains the necessary expertise and resources to supervise the delegated functions effectively and to manage the risks associated with the delegation;
- the SGR no longer has the power to take decisions in key areas which fall under the responsibility of senior management or to perform senior management functions;
- the SGR does not have or loses the right to inspect, obtain information from, have access or give instructions to its delegates; and
- the SGR delegates the performance of its investment management functions to an extent that exceeds, by a substantial margin, the investment management functions performed by the SGR itself.

13.229 With reference to the delegation of important or essential functions (mainly risk management and portfolio management[1]), the Joint Regulation provides for specific conditions to be met in the selection of service providers[2].

[1] As regards the precise identification of the 'important or essential operative functions', CONSOB has informally stated that property management activity should be considered as an important function, and therefore should be subject to the Joint Regulation, whereas, as regards the project management function doubts still remain. In any case, CONSOB has excluded due diligence activities, broker activities and agency activities from treatment as important or essential activities.

[2] In addition, the SGR must: (i) be able to demonstrate that the service provider is suitably qualified and able diligently to carry out the outsourced activity; and (ii) be able effectively to monitor the exercise of the outsourced activity by the service provider, to issue binding instructions and to revoke the mandate at any time, in order to safeguard the interests of unitholders/shareholders.

13.230 Therefore, an SGR that wishes to outsource important or essential functions usually invites several service providers (which may be affiliates of that SGR or of one or more investors) to tender for those services.

13.231 Furthermore, it is worth highlighting that the Joint Regulation states that an SGR that wishes to delegate important or essential functions must notify the Bank of Italy and CONSOB before doing so. Within 30 days following receipt of such notification, the Bank of Italy and CONSOB may start an administrative procedure aimed at prohibiting the outsourcing (otherwise the outsourcing will be treated as authorised).

13.232 SGRs are subject to applicable Italian anti-money laundering regulations and frequently outsource the anti-money laundering function to third parties (following the procedure described above).

Taxation

13.233 From a tax perspective, RAIFs are subject to the tax law framework provided for investment funds which invest in securities or real estate assets.

13.234 As far as Italian investment funds which invest in securities are concerned, according to article 73 of Presidential Decree No 917 of 22 December 1986 (the 'Income Tax Code'), such entities (unlike real estate investment funds) are in principle subject to Italian corporate income tax (*imposta sul reddito sulle società*, 'IRES').

13.235 However, the Income Tax Code provides that proceeds realised by such Italian investment funds are exempt from IRES. In addition, certain proceeds realised by such funds (eg dividends and capital gains in certain conditions) can be received free of any Italian withholding tax or substitute tax.

13.236 The tax treatment of proceeds arising in the hands of the investors of Italian investment funds which invest in securities depends on many factors including the type of proceeds (eg distributions made by the fund or capital gain realised as a consequence of a sale of shares or units), the nature of the investors and the investors' tax residence.

13.237 Marketing – Selected Jurisdictions

13.237 In general terms, in relation to investors which are resident in Italy for tax purposes, a provisional or a final withholding tax at a rate of 26% may apply.

13.238 Investors which are not resident in Italy for tax purposes may benefit from an exemption for proceeds distributed by a fund if, pursuant to the provisions of article 6 of Legislative Decree No 239 of 1 April 1996, they are:

- resident in a jurisdiction which allows for a satisfactory exchange of information with Italy;
- an international body or entity established in accordance with international agreements which have entered into force in Italy (so-called 'supranational entities and organisations');
- a central bank or an entity which is authorised to manage the official reserves of a state; or
- 'professional investors' (such as investment funds and pension funds) which are established and resident in a jurisdiction which allows for a satisfactory exchange of information with Italy.

13.239 Non-resident investors that do not qualify for this exemption are subject to a 26% withholding tax, potentially reduced by any applicable double tax treaty.

13.240 Pursuant to article 73 para 1(c) of the Income Tax Code, real estate investment funds are in principle liable to corporate income tax in Italy. However, if they satisfy the requirements provided by the regulatory framework in order to qualify as undertakings for collective investment, the income realised is not subject to IRES[1].

[1] See article 6 of Law Decree No 351 of 25 September 2001.

13.241 Whilst real estate investment funds are not subject to IRES in Italy, the profits arising from the investments of such a fund are taxed at the investor level upon distribution.

13.242 Proceeds distributed by a real estate investment fund whose units are held by institutional investors such as asset management companies or pension funds, or by non-institutional investors owning less than 5% of the interests in that fund, are subject to a 26% withholding tax. Such withholding is payable as a final withholding tax if the investor is an individual, or as an advance payment of tax if the investor is a corporate entity.

13.243 Conversely, in the case of a real estate investment fund held by non-qualified investors owning more than 5% of the interests in that fund, taxation applies on the basis of a 'transparency regime' pursuant to which the income generated by the fund is taxed directly vis-à-vis the unitholders irrespective of the distribution of the income.

13.244 As far as entities which are not resident in Italy for tax purposes are concerned, if the foreign investor is a specific qualified investor (such as an investment fund, pension fund or sovereign entity) which is resident in a 'white list' country[1], no withholding tax is due on the real estate investment fund's distributions. Otherwise, the relevant income is subject to a 26%

withholding tax, potentially reduced by any applicable double tax treaty.

[1] White list countries allow for an adequate exchange of information with Italy and are included in the so-called 'white list' provided for by the Ministerial Decree of 4 September 1996, as amended and supplemented.

13.245 In certain cases, Italian regional tax on productive activities (*imposta regionale sulle attività produttive*, 'IRAP') might be payable.

G MALTA

David Borg-Carbott, Senior Associate, GANADO Advocates, Malta

Regulatory framework

13.246 As noted in CHAPTER 4[1], collective investment schemes ('CIS'), including hedge funds, are regulated in Malta under the Investment Services Act (Cap 370, Laws of Malta) (the 'IS Act'). The IS Act regulates (and requires authorisation of) any CIS[2] which issues or creates any units or carries on any activity in or from within Malta. The 'issue or creation of units . . . in or from within Malta' limb is understood as applying to any CIS established in or operating from Malta[3], whilst the 'carry on any activity in or from within Malta' limb would apply to a CIS whether established in or outside Malta. There is no definition of 'carry on any activity' under Maltese law[4]. This is, however, generally considered by the Malta Financial Services Authority ('MFSA') as applying to the marketing, advertising or promotion of the CIS. Accordingly, any CIS, wherever established, which intends to market (including through intermediaries) its units or shares in Malta will, unless specifically exempted, require authorisation from the MFSA.

[1] See paras **4.324–4.437** in CHAPTER 4.
[2] See para **4.334** in CHAPTER 4 for the definition of a CIS under Maltese law.
[3] The place where the units or shares are issued would be the location of the register of members or similar register.
[4] Prior to 1 January 2014, the expression 'carry on any activity' was defined in the Investment Services Act (Licence and Other Fees) Regulations (SL 370.03, Laws of Malta) as 'includes but shall not be limited to marketing, advertising or otherwise promoting as may be further stipulated in the Guidelines issued by the competent authority . . . '. Regrettably, this definition was not included in the Investment Services Act (Fees) Regulations (SL 370.03, Laws of Malta) which repealed and replaced the Investment Services Act (Licence and Other Fees) Regulations with effect from 1 January 2014.

13.247 Following the transposition of AIFMD in Maltese law with effect from 22 July 2013, CIS in Malta can be categorised into two main types: (i) undertakings for collective investment in transferable securities ('UCITS') authorised under the UCITS Directive[1]; and (ii) alternative investment funds ('AIFs') as defined under AIFMD[2], which would apply to most hedge funds[3]. The Maltese regime which regulates the marketing of units or shares in CIS (including the MFSA's guidance on what constitutes marketing) differs according to whether the CIS is a UCITS or an AIF.

[1] Directive 2009/65/EC of 13 July 2009, as amended by Directive 2014/91/EU of 23 July 2014.
[2] Directive 2011/61/EU of 8 June 2011.
[3] There is, in theory, a third category which covers funds which although satisfying the definition of CIS under the IS Act are neither UCITS nor AIFs. This category would, however,

13.247 *Marketing – Selected Jurisdictions*

be limited to so-called 'funds of one' or single investor funds as well as family office vehicles restricted to pre-existing groups, each of which would not be permitted (without changing its regulatory status) to market its units or shares in Malta.

Maltese hedge funds

13.248 CIS established in Malta are, unless exempted, required under the IS Act to be authorised by the MFSA. Once the CIS is authorised by the MFSA, such authorisation will, unless restricted by the specific terms of its authorisation, permit the CIS to market its units or shares in Malta to eligible investors in Malta.

13.249 A detailed overview of the various regulatory regimes under the IS Act and their respective eligible investors is included in CHAPTER 4. The following table summarises this:

Fund type	Eligible investors	Minimum investment
UCITS	Any	None
Retail non-UCITS (being phased out)	Any	None
Retail alternative investment fund	Any	None
Alternative investment fund or notified alternative investment fund	Professional clients under MiFID[1]	None
Alternative investment fund or professional investor fund targeting experienced investors (being phased out)	Experienced investors including professional clients under MiFID	€10,000 (or equivalent)
Alternative investment fund, notified alternative investment fund or professional investor fund targeting qualifying investors	Qualifying investors	€100,000[2] (or equivalent)
Alternative investment fund or professional investor fund targeting extraordinary investors (being phased out)	Extraordinary investors	€750,000 (or equivalent)
Loan fund	Professional clients under MiFID	€100,000 (or equivalent)

[1] Directive 2014/65/EU of 15 May 2014.
[2] Funds established before 3 June 2016 may retain the previously applicable minimum investment of €75,000 or equivalent.

Marketing foreign hedge funds in Malta

Overview and definition of marketing

13.250 The incorporation of AIFMD into Maltese law resulted in dramatic changes to Malta's private placement regime for CIS. These changes included the introduction of a distinction between the meaning of what constitutes 'marketing' (which would give rise to the authorisation requirement under the IS Act) in relation to UCITS and that in relation to AIFs.

13.251 In relation to UCITS (which retain Malta's pre-AIFMD private placement regime), there is no comprehensive definition of what constitutes 'marketing' in Malta. Guidance issued by the MFSA, however, indicates that a UCITS would not be considered by the MFSA as marketing its units or shares in Malta (and consequently would not be required to passport its authorisation) if: (i) the units or shares were exclusively sold on a one-to-one basis in Malta by Maltese or EU authorised MiFID firms; (ii) the units or shares were not marketed in Malta in their own right but rather as available for linking to unit linked policies of insurance marketed in Malta; or (iii) without any prior solicitation, a Malta resident investor requests and is provided with information about that UCITS (reverse solicitation)[1].

[1] Investment Services Rules for Retail Collective Investment Schemes, Part A: The Application Process, Section 12 – see https://mfsa.com.mt/pages/viewcontent.aspx?id=265.

13.252 A UCITS which has exercised its right under the UCITS Directive and completed the relevant notification procedure (including payment of the relevant fee to the MFSA) is exempt from authorisation under the IS Act and may market its units or shares in Malta subject to compliance with local investment advertising rules (based on MiFID Level 2 rules).

13.253 In relation to AIFs, the definition of 'marketing' under AIFMD, which was incorporated into Maltese law by means of regulations issued under the IS Act[1], introduced a definition of marketing into Maltese law which is confined to AIFs.

[1] The AIFMD definition of 'marketing' was transposed word for word in (a) the Investment Services Act (Marketing of Alternative Investment Funds) Regulations (SL 370.21, Laws of Malta), and (b) the Investment Services Act (Alternative Investment Fund Manager) (Third Country) Regulations (SL 370.24, Laws of Malta).

13.254 Under AIFMD and the IS Act, 'marketing' is defined as 'a direct or indirect offering or placement at the initiative of the alternative investment fund manager ('AIFM') or on behalf of the AIFM of units or shares of an AIF it manages to or with investors domiciled or with a registered office in the European Union'. Whilst the MFSA has issued little additional guidance on that definition, it is, however, clear that (i) reverse solicitation remains excluded, and (ii) the MFSA considers that the 'domicile' test included in that definition may be assessed on the basis of the residence of the relevant individual[1].

[1] See Q103 of the MFSA's Alternative Investment Fund Managers Directive FAQs, which can be found on the MFSA's website – https://mfsa.com.mt/pages/viewcontent.aspx?id=510.

13.255 The incorporation of AIFMD into Maltese law altered the authorisation regime for foreign AIFs wishing to market their units or shares in Malta. With the exception of AIFs wishing to market their units or shares to 'retail investors' (equivalent to 'retail clients' as defined under MiFID) which remain subject to a prior authorisation requirement, foreign AIFs are now subject to a prior notification requirement.

13.256 Marketing – Selected Jurisdictions

13.256 This notification is intended to inform the MFSA how the relevant AIF and its AIFM satisfy the relevant requirements under Malta's post-AIFMD private placement regime. Accordingly, so long as the AIF and AIFM satisfy the requirements, make the notification and pay the relevant fee, units or shares in the AIF may be marketed in Malta to 'professional investors' (equivalent to 'professional clients' as defined under MiFID) upon receipt of the MFSA's confirmation of receipt[1]. AIFs whose AIFMs have been duly notified under this process are exempt from the authorisation requirement under the IS Act[2].

[1] The MFSA advocates awaiting confirmation of receipt of the notification before commencing marketing – MFSA Guidance Notes on the completion of the national private placement notification forms pursuant to the provisions of the Alternative Investment Fund Managers Directive (22 September 2014).
[2] Regulation 4(1) of the Investment Services Act (Marketing of Alternative Investment Funds) Regulations (SL 370.21, Laws of Malta), and regulations 8(1) and 22(1) of the Investment Services Act (Alternative Investment Fund Manager) (Third Country) Regulations (SL 370.24, Laws of Malta).

13.257 Responsibility for the making of the relevant notifications (or applying for authorisation in the case of retail investors) rests with the AIFM.

Prior notification or authorisation requirements

13.258 Mirroring the fund marketing requirements under AIFMD, Malta's fund marketing requirements differ according to:

- the type of investors targeted;
- the country where the AIFM is established as well as the country where the AIF is established; and
- whether the AIFM qualifies as a full AIFM (that is, it exceeds the AIFMD assets under management thresholds (the 'AIFMD AUM thresholds') or opts in to AIFMD) or a 'de minimis' AIFM (that is, it does not exceed the AIFMD AUM thresholds).

13.259 The following table summarises the fund marketing options presently available in Malta and their requirements:

Location of AIFM	Location of AIF	Type of investors	Requirements
EU AIFM	EU AIF (other than a feeder into non-EU AIF or EU AIF managed by a non-EU AIFM)	Professional clients	Exercise of marketing passport under Article 31 or 32 of AIFMD by AIFM Payment of the relevant fee (€2,500 plus €450 per sub-fund)
	Non-EU AIF (including an EU feeder into non-EU AIF or EU AIF with non-EU AIFM)	Professional clients	Compliance with Article 36 of AIFMD Prior notification to the MFSA Payment of the relevant fee (€2,500 plus €450 per sub-fund)

Location of AIFM	Location of AIF	Type of investors	Requirements
De minimis EU AIFM	EU or non-EU AIF	Professional clients	Must be permitted to privately place in other EU member states under the AIFM's home legislation Compliance with conditions akin to those in Article 36 of AIFMD Prior notification to the MFSA Payment of the relevant fee (€2,500 plus €450 per sub-fund)
Non-EU AIFM	EU or non-EU AIF	Professional clients	Compliance with Article 42 of AIFMD Prior notification to the MFSA Payment of the relevant fee (€2,500 plus €450 per sub-fund)
Any	Any	Retail clients	As above (as applicable according to the type and location of the AIFM and the AIF) Authorisation by the MFSA

13.260 The above will change once the AIFMD third country passport is introduced (Articles 35, 39 and 40 of AIFMD), with EU AIFMs intending to market non-EU AIFs and non-EU AIFMs being granted a 'passport' in addition to the private placement options. The EU has not yet introduced this passport.

EU AIFMs

13.261 Malta's fund marketing regime distinguishes between (i) EU AIFMs intending to market an EU AIF in Malta, (ii) EU AIFMs intending to market a non-EU AIF in Malta, and (iii) EU AIFMs that are below the AIFMD AUM Thresholds (that is, de minimis) intending to market an EU or non-EU AIF in Malta. In accordance with AIFMD and for the purposes of the marketing regime, an EU AIF which is a feeder fund[1] is only considered to be an EU AIF if its master fund is also an EU AIF managed by an EU AIFM.

[1] A feeder fund under AIFMD is an AIF which invests (or otherwise has an exposure of) at least 85% of its assets in another AIF (the master fund) or in multiple AIFs with identical investment strategies.

EU AIFMs – EU AIFs (AIFMD MARKETING PASSPORT)

13.262 AIFMD grants an EU AIFM authorised under the AIFM which manages an EU AIF a 'passport' to market that EU AIF in another EU member state (including its own home country if the EU AIF is in another member state) to professional investors. Under the Investment Services Act (Marketing of Alternative Investment Funds) Regulations (SL 370.21, Laws of Malta), where an EU AIFM completes the AIFMD passporting process to market units or shares in an EU AIF in Malta, that EU AIF will be exempt from the authorisation requirement under the IS Act. An EU AIFM intending to market an EU AIF may only market that EU AIF under the AIFMD marketing passport (that is, it is excluded from availing itself of any private placement options). As noted above, an EU AIFM managing an EU AIF which is a feeder

13.262 *Marketing – Selected Jurisdictions*

into a non-EU master AIF or an EU master AIF with a non-EU AIFM does not have an AIFMD marketing passport for that AIF (but can use the private placement regime).

13.263 In order to take advantage of the AIFMD marketing passport, the EU AIFM must notify its home competent authority (the regulator in the AIFM's country of establishment) of its intention to market the EU AIF in Malta. The notification, which will need to include the documentation and information listed in Annex III (for Maltese AIFMs) or Annex IV (for all other EU AIFMs) to AIFMD, would be in the format adopted by the home competent authority for such notifications. Provided the home competent authority is satisfied that the EU AIFM complies with AIFMD, the competent authority should transmit the notification file (together with a confirmation that the AIFM is appropriately authorised) to the MFSA within 20 working days of receipt.

13.264 Upon transmission, the home competent authority should without delay notify the EU AIFM that it has transmitted the notification file to the MFSA. The EU AIFM can commence marketing the relevant EU AIF to professional investors in Malta upon receipt of notification of transmission to the MFSA from its home competent authority.

13.265 The MFSA imposes a marketing fee of €2,500 (for each scheme) plus €450 per sub-fund (for umbrella funds) notified which becomes payable upon notification or commencement of marketing in Malta. Typically, EU AIFMs passporting in this manner would pay the relevant marketing fee in advance and enclose a copy of the receipt in the notification documents submitted to the home competent authority.

EU AIFMs – non-EU AIFs (Article 36 of AIFMD)

13.266 The Maltese authorities elected to implement Article 36 of AIFMD into Maltese law without imposing additional requirements other than prior notification and payment of a marketing fee. Under Article 36, the conditions that need to be satisfied by an EU AIFM wishing to privately place units or shares in a non-EU AIF (or an EU feeder AIF without a passport) with professional investors (the 'Article 36 conditions') are as follows:

- Ensure that the AIFM complies with all the requirements of AIFMD other than Article 21 (single depositary) subject to appointment of one or more third parties to provide the cash monitoring, safekeeping and oversight functions described in Article 21(7), (8) and (9) of AIFMD.
- Ensure that there is a co-operation agreement in the form approved by the European Securities and Markets Authority ('ESMA') for AIFMD between the EU AIFM's home competent authority and the competent authority of the non-EU AIF.
- Ensure that the country where the non-EU AIF is resident is not listed as a Non-Cooperative Country and Territory by the Financial Action Task Force ('FATF') on Money Laundering.

13.267 An EU AIFM wishing to privately place units or shares in a non-EU AIF will be required to submit a duly completed notification to the MFSA by email. The notification form (which can be downloaded from the

MFSA's website[1]) requires, in addition to information about the AIFM, the AIFs, and their service providers, confirmation that the Article 36 conditions have been satisfied (such as, the identity of the depositary-lite entities and an indication that the Article 23 disclosure to investors requirements have been satisfied). The notification form should be accompanied by a copy of the latest approved offering document(s) of each AIF notified.

[1] See https://www.mfsa.com.mt.

13.268 The MFSA imposes a marketing fee of €2,500 (for each scheme) plus €450 per sub-fund (for umbrella funds) notified which becomes payable upon notification. In order to avoid delays, a copy of the MFSA's receipt of payment should be enclosed with the notification documents submitted to the MFSA.

13.269 Marketing of the non-EU AIF to professional investors in Malta may commence upon notification to the MFSA although the MFSA recommends that AIFMs await confirmation of receipt of the notification before commencing marketing.

EU AIFMs (DE MINIMIS)

13.270 AIFMD applies to a limited extent to EU AIFMs below the thresholds in Article 3(2) of AIFMD which do not opt in to AIFMD ('de minimis EU AIFMs'); in particular, they are neither entitled to a marketing passport nor appropriately covered by Article 36 of AIFMD. Prior to 22 September 2014, this meant that de minimis EU AIFMs were, with effect from 22 July 2013, essentially prohibited from marketing units or shares in AIFs in Malta.

13.271 On 22 September 2014, the MFSA opted through an amendment to its AIFMD FAQs and publication of the relevant form to permit de minimis EU AIFMs to market units or shares in AIFs managed by them in Malta. This was made subject to: (i) the EU AIFM being permitted to privately place units or shares in AIFs in other EU member states under its home legislation; (ii) compliance with requirements akin to the Article 36 conditions[1]; (iii) prior notification to the MFSA; and (iv) payment of a marketing fee.

[1] See para **13.266** above.

13.272 The process for de minimis EU AIFMs wishing to notify the MFSA of their intention to market AIFs is similar to the process for EU AIFMs notifying their intention to market non-EU AIFs in Malta. A marketing fee of €2,500 (for each scheme) plus €450 per sub-fund (for umbrella funds) notified is also payable upon notification.

NON-EU AIFMs (ARTICLE 42 OF AIFMD)

13.273 Malta also elected to implement Article 42 of AIFMD into Maltese law without imposing additional requirements other than prior notification and payment of a marketing fee. Under Article 42 of AIFMD, the conditions that need to be satisfied by a non-EU AIFM wishing to privately place units or shares in an EU AIF or non-EU AIF with professional investors (the 'Article 42 conditions') are as follows:

13.273 Marketing – Selected Jurisdictions

- Ensure that the AIFM (and the relevant AIF) complies with the requirements of Articles 22 (annual report), 23 (disclosure to investors) and 24 (reporting to competent authorities) of AIFMD as well as Articles 26 to 30 of AIFMD (where the AIF acquires control of non-listed EU companies other than small to medium-sized enterprises ('SMEs') or special purpose vehicles ('SPVs')).
- Ensure that there is a co-operation agreement in the form approved by ESMA for AIFMD between the MFSA[1] and (i) the competent authority in the third country where the non-EU AIFM is established, and (ii) (if applicable) the competent authority in the third country where the non-EU AIF is established. If the AIF is an EU AIF there also needs to be a co-operation agreement in the form approved by ESMA for AIFMD between the competent authority in the EU AIF's home member state and the competent authority in the third country where the non-EU AIFM is established.
- Ensure that the country where the non-EU AIFM or the non-EU AIF is resident is not listed as a Non-Cooperative Country and Territory by the FATF.

[1] A list of AIFMD co-operation agreements signed by the MFSA can be found on the MFSA's website – see https://www.mfsa.com.mt/pages/viewcontent.aspx?id=506.

13.274 For the purposes of private placement, the MFSA does not distinguish between non-EU AIFMs that are above or below the AIFMD AUM thresholds[1].

[1] See Q107 of the MFSA's Alternative Investment Fund Managers Directive FAQs.

13.275 A non-EU AIFM wishing to privately place units or shares in an AIF will be required to submit to the MFSA a duly completed notification form, which can be downloaded from the MFSA's website. The notification form and a copy of the latest approved offering document(s) of each AIF notified should be submitted by email to the MFSA.

13.276 The MFSA again imposes a marketing fee of €2,500 (for each scheme) plus €450 per sub-fund (for umbrella funds) notified which becomes payable upon notification. In order to avoid delays, a copy of the MFSA's receipt of payment should be enclosed with the notification documents submitted to the MFSA. Marketing of the AIF so notified to professional investors in Malta may commence upon notification to the MFSA although the MFSA recommends that non-EU AIFMs await confirmation of receipt of the notification before commencing marketing.

Additional requirements for marketing to retail investors

13.277 AIFMD generally covers the marketing of AIFs to professional investors. Under Article 43 of AIFMD, EU member states were, however, granted the option to extend the relevant provisions to AIFs marketed to retail investors subject to such additional local requirements as may be required. In implementing AIFMD into Maltese law, Malta opted to permit AIFMs to market units or shares to retail investors provided that, besides complying with the relevant passporting and/or private placement requirements, they are authorised to do so by the MFSA.

13.278 Prior authorisation by the MFSA in order to market units or shares in the AIF to retail investors entails a formal application for authorisation, indicating how the relevant requirements are satisfied, as well as payment of the related application fee (presently €2,500 plus €450 per sub-fund). The requirements for authorisation to market units and/or shares in an AIF to retail investors are presently: (i) compliance with the relevant passporting or private placement requirements[1]; and (ii) the units or shares in the AIF must qualify as a 'non-complex' financial instrument under MiFID (including a requirement for a declaration from the directors of the AIFM to that effect). Given (a) the revisions to the definition of 'non-complex' financial instrument, following the coming into effect of MiFID II (the recast version of MiFID) on 3 January 2018 amending the definition of 'non-complex' financial instruments under that Directive, and (b) ESMA's Q&A[2] on the treatment of non-UCITS under MiFID II conclusively determining that non-UCITS will always qualify as 'complex' financial instruments under MiFID II, it is clear that the MFSA will, in the near future, need to revise this regime or will request compliance with bespoke alternative conditions.

[1] See para **13.259** above.
[2] Questions and Answers on MiFID II and MiFIR investor protection and intermediaries topics (ref ESMA35-43-349), Section 10 Appropriateness/Complex Financial Instruments' – available at https://www.esma.europa.eu.

13.279 Once the MFSA is satisfied that the requirements have been met it will issue an authorisation and the AIFM may commence to market the units or shares in the AIF to retail investors.

Ongoing marketing requirements

13.280 Ongoing requirements for AIFMs marketing non-Maltese AIFs in Malta or their AIFs differ according to the location of the AIFM, the location of the AIF as well as the type of prospective investors.

EU AIFMs marketing EU AIFs or non-EU AIFs

Regulatory reporting and transparency

13.281 Whether the EU AIFM is marketing an EU AIF (under the AIFMD marketing passport) or a non-EU AIF (under the Article 36 private placement regime) in Malta, the EU AIFM will not be subject to reporting in Malta and will instead be required to report information to its home competent authority under Article 24 of AIFMD. Similarly, Article 22 of AIFMD does not require the EU AIFM to make the annual report of the AIF available to the MFSA, but it requires the EU AIFM to make the annual report of each AIF which it markets in the EU available to its home competent authority and, where applicable, the home competent authority of the EU AIF.

13.282 Although the situation is unclear for de minimis EU AIFMs, particularly since provision needs to be made in the laws of the de minimis EU

13.282 *Marketing – Selected Jurisdictions*

AIFM's home member state to permit outward private placement, presumably the above would also apply with the necessary changes.

13.283 The MFSA is empowered, however, to request information from the EU AIFM or its home competent authority where it is deemed necessary for the supervision of the AIFM's compliance with AIFMD.

ANNUAL FEE

13.284 On each anniversary of notification of the intention to commence marketing an AIF in Malta the EU AIFM will be required to pay a supervisory fee of €3,000 (for each scheme) plus €500 per sub-fund (for umbrella funds). Where an EU AIFM is marketing more than 15 sub-funds of the same EU AIF in Malta using the AIFMD marketing passport no fee is payable for the 16th sub-fund or any additional sub-funds.

Non-EU AIFMs marketing EU AIFs or non-EU AIFs

REGULATORY REPORTING AND TRANSPARENCY

13.285 Non-EU AIFMs marketing AIFs in Malta are subject to the reporting obligation under Article 24 of AIFMD in respect of the AIFM as well as each AIF which it markets in Malta. Reporting frequency ranges from quarterly to annual depending on the assets under management of the non-EU AIFM concerned, whether or not the relevant AIF employs leverage, whether the AIF is open-ended or not, as well as the types of assets in which the AIF invests. The reporting templates to be used are those issued by ESMA[1], which also contain additional guidance on their completion[2]. AIFM reports need to be submitted through the MFSA's dedicated licence holder portal.

[1] Consolidated AIFMD reporting template (ref 2013/1359) – see https://www.esma.europa.eu/document/consolidated-aifmd-reporting-template-revised.
[2] AIFMD reporting IT technical guidance (rev 4) (ref 2013/1358) – see https://www.esma.europa.eu/document/aifmd-reporting-it-technical-guidance-rev-4-updated.

13.286 Non-EU AIFMs marketing AIFs in Malta are additionally required to: (i) make available to the MFSA the annual report of each AIF marketed in Malta; and (ii) where the AIF acquires control of non-listed EU companies other than SMEs or SPVs, make the disclosures required under Articles 26 to 30 of AIFMD.

13.287 The MFSA is empowered to request additional information from the non-EU AIFM where deemed necessary for the supervision of the AIFM's compliance with AIFMD.

ONGOING DISCLOSURE TO INVESTORS

13.288 The non-EU AIFM will, when marketing AIFs in Malta, be required to comply with the transparency requirements under Articles 22 and 23 of AIFMD.

Annual fee

13.289 On each anniversary of notification of the intention to commence marketing an AIF in Malta the non-EU AIFM will be required to pay a supervisory fee of €3,000 (for each scheme) plus €500 per sub-fund (for umbrella funds).

Additional requirements for AIFMs marketing to retail investors

13.290 AIFs authorised to market their units or shares to retail investors are, in addition to the reporting obligations imposed under the relevant passporting and/or private placement regime and annual fee, also required to ensure compliance with local rules on disclosures for retail investors and investment advertising rules (again, broadly based on MiFID Level 2 rules).

Taxation

13.291 CHAPTER 4 includes an overview of the Malta tax treatment of Maltese CIS and their investors[1] as well as the tax treatment of Malta resident investors in non-Maltese CIS[2].

[1] See paras 4.424–4.432 in CHAPTER 4.
[2] See paras 4.433–4.436 in CHAPTER 4.

H NETHERLANDS

Minke R Hoekstra, Counsel, Simmons & Simmons, Amsterdam

Introduction

13.292 In the Netherlands, funds, including hedge funds, are governed by both civil law and financial law provisions. Depending on the legal structure chosen, the Civil Code, general principles of Dutch contract law or the Dutch Code of Commerce (*Wetboek van Koophandel*) apply. In addition, the Dutch Financial Supervision Act (*Wet op het financieel toezicht*) regulates the governance and marketing of hedge funds. Finally, local conduct of business rules and guidance from the Netherlands Authority for the Financial Markets (*Autoriteit Financiële Markten*, 'AFM') and the Dutch Central Bank (*De Nederlandsche Bank*, 'DNB') should be adhered to when operating or marketing a hedge fund in the Netherlands.

13.293 The introduction of the Alternative Investment Fund Managers Directive[1] ('AIFMD') hugely changed the regulatory landscape for hedge fund managers. Since the implementation of AIFMD in the Netherlands, a fund qualifies as either a UCITS or a non-UCITS fund. The latter then by definition qualifies as an alternative investment fund (an 'AIF'). Hedge funds do not have a specific status in either civil or financial law and typically qualify as AIFs.

[1] Directive 2011/61/EU of 8 June 2011.

13.294 *Marketing – Selected Jurisdictions*

Dutch fund structures

13.294 In the Netherlands, commonly used vehicles to structure a private investment fund are as follows:

- mutual funds (*fonds voor gemene rekening*, 'FGRs')[1];
- limited partnerships (*commanditaire vennootschap*, 'CVs')[2];
- limited liability companies (*besloten vennootschap met beperkte aansprakelijkheid*, 'BVs', or *naamloze vennootschap*, 'NVs')[3]; and
- co-operatives (*cooperatie*)[4].

[1] See paras **13.296–13.299** below.
[2] See paras **13.300–13.302** below.
[3] See paras **13.303–13.304** below.
[4] See para **13.305** below.

13.295 FGRs and CVs are typical Dutch law concepts without legal personality. BVs and NVs as well as co-operatives are governed by Book 2 of the Dutch Civil Code and do have legal personality.

Mutual funds

13.296 An FGR is a contractual agreement (sui generis) governed by general principles of Dutch contract law. It has no legal existence and there are also no formal requirements as to the establishment of an FGR. Consequently, the parties to the FGR agreement are relatively free in determining the financial and governance structure of the FGR (within the boundaries of regulatory requirements described below). An FGR is generally structured as an agreement between a manager (*beheerder*), depositary (*bewaarder*) and the investors (participants) resulting in obligations between the manager and the depositary and between the manager and the depositary vis-a-vis the participants but (generally) not between the participants themselves.

13.297 The management entity of an FGR is generally a BV. Establishment of the manager BV entails a notarial deed whereby the provisions are governed by the requirements of Dutch corporate law. The manager is also registered with the Dutch Chamber of Commerce. The manager acts as the manager of the FGR, and its specific authorities, obligations and liabilities are set out in the FGR agreement. The depositary is a bankruptcy remote entity which usually takes the form of a foundation (*stichting*) with orphan characteristics. As the FGR is in essence an agreement and has no legal personality, the depositary holds the legal title to the assets and liabilities of the FGR. It will do so, however, on behalf of and for the account and risk of the (investors in the) FGR. In effect, the participants are the beneficial (economic) owners of the assets and liabilities of the FGR and consequently each participant has a share in the beneficial ownership of the assets held by the depositary. This share, however, does not represent an interest (and liability) in a specific asset but rather a share in the overall community of assets relative to the number of shares (and capital contributions made) in the FGR.

13.298 The role of the depositary is limited to being the legal owner of the assets and legal debtor of the liabilities of the FGR. The depositary generally has a very passive role and usually acts in conjunction with and on the instruction of the manager only. To express this (limited) authority, the terms and conditions of the FGR typically include a power of attorney from the depositary to the manager regarding acquisitions and disposals of assets. In theory a depositary can act as depositary to several FGRs; in practice, however, each FGR has its own depositary.

13.299 As the FGR is form free, parties are able to arrange for each agreement regarding set-up, governance and entitlements as they deem fit as long as they adhere to the AIFMD requirements set out below. The terms and conditions of the FGR typically arrange for: name, purpose and seat of the FGR; obligations of the manager; obligations of the participants (generally limited to the obligation to fulfil their capital contributions and possibly some administrative formalities); powers and authority of the depositary; conditions for issuance, redemption and transfers of participation rights; allocation of investment profits; costs and fees; responsibility for books and records; governance (meeting of participants, advisory board, resolutions etc); substitution of the manager and depositary; and dissolution and liquidation.

Limited partnerships

13.300 A CV is comparable to the Anglo-Saxon limited partnership. It is a special form of a partnership (*maatschap*), governed by Book 7A of the Dutch Civil Code and the Dutch Code of Commerce, generally focused on carrying on a business as opposed to a profession. A CV is a partnership for the purpose of a durable co-operation between one or more general partners (*beherend vennoten*) and one or more limited partners (*commanditaire* or *stille vennoten*). Only the general partners are able to represent the CV. The partners can take any legal form but can also be individuals. Generally, however, the general partner is a BV set up with the sole purpose of acting as the general partner to the CV. The CV is established by agreement either for a limited or an unlimited period of time. The general partners have unlimited liability and the liability of the limited partners (ie investors) is in principle limited to their capital contribution. If a limited partner is involved in management of the CV, directly or by proxy, its liability becomes unlimited similar to that of the general partners: the so-called 'management prohibition' (*beheersverbod*).

13.301 A CV has no legal personality but it has a separate legal estate (*afgescheiden vermogen*), resulting in private creditors of the general partners having no recourse against the estate of the CV and CV creditors having priority over private creditors in cases of bankruptcy or liquidation of the CV. A CV is registered in the Trade Register and annual accounts are required to be drawn up. The assets and liabilities of the CV are in principle the rights and obligations of the owners. So in principle, legal title to the assets (and liabilities) is held in (joint) ownership by the general partners and the limited partners. In practice, however, it is generally determined that the legal title to the assets (and liabilities) is held by the general partners (for and on behalf of the CV). For decades, the Dutch legislator has been contemplating the introduction of a CV with legal personality, but the codification proposals have time and again been put on hold and there is currently no noteworthy development on that front.

13.302 *Marketing – Selected Jurisdictions*

13.302 FGRs and CVs compared to entities with legal personality have the benefit of a limited set of legal requirements governing the incorporation and terms and conditions. Their lack of legal personality and hence the inability to own assets and liabilities, however, can also be perceived as a disadvantage. In addition to the AIFMD requirements which have been implemented in the Netherlands without any gold plating, the Financial Supervision Act distinguishes between investment funds with and without legal personality. For FGRs, the Act requires the appointment of a depositary, not being the AIFMD depositary, to hold legal title to the assets of the fund. This requirement fits in with the structure chosen for an FGR as described above and basically codifies the FGR absent any civil law recognition.

Limited liability companies

13.303 BVs and NVs have legal personality so are capable of owning their own assets and liabilities. The liability of shareholders/investors is limited to their capital contribution; distribution of capital is only possible when sufficient (freely distributable) reserves are available, and contributions can be made in cash or in kind (although the latter requires a statement of an accountant), all as further codified. The flip side of this codification is that there are formal formation requirements to be taken into account such as a notarial deed and trade registration requirements, minimum capital requirements and transfer restrictions. Book 2 of the Dutch Civil Code also contains governance requirements and provides for liability of managing and supervisory directors. The latter is generally relevant in advisory board context.

13.304 The main differences between BVs and NVs are that the shares of NVs can be transferred without restrictions and that they can be listed. In October 2012, the flex(ible) BV was introduced, taking away minimum initial capital requirements and providing for more flexibility in terms of the articles of association, the creation of non-voting and non-profit sharing shares, and abolishing the restrictions on transfer of shares. A flex BV can be an attractive fund structure for hedge funds. All in all, BVs and NVs are commonly used fund structures and therefore commercially attractive and perceived to be easier to market.

Co-operatives

13.305 A co-operative is a special form of association (*vereniging*) established with the intention to provide for the material needs of its members (*stoffelijke behoeften*). This notion encompasses all economic needs. Distinct from the association, a co-operative has the ability to distribute profits to its members, has legal personality and is registered in the Trade Register, but it is less regulated by Dutch corporate law requirements than BVs and NVs, for example. A co-operative is required to be established by at least two members by means of a notarial deed. There are no initial capital requirements and, unless determined otherwise (by the inclusion of 'UA' (*uitsluiting van aansprakelijkheid*) in the name of the co-operative), all members have equal liability. A co-operative therefore offers a certain amount of flexibility in terms of liability arrangements, governance and profit distributions, similar to an

FGR and a CV but with the generally perceived benefit of having legal personality and Civil Code protection.

Active marketing of foreign hedge funds in the Netherlands

13.306 Hedge funds can be offered to both institutional, ie qualified, investors and retail investors, and a licence requirement for alternative investment fund managers ('AIFMs') is triggered in three distinct situations:

- managing Dutch AIFs;
- offering EU and/or non-EU AIFs in the Netherlands to professional and/or retail investors; and
- Dutch based manager managing or offering AIFs.

13.307 In addition to the AIFMD requirements there is also a prospectus requirement for AIFMs offering AIFs unless:

- the fund units or shares are offered to qualified investors only;
- the fund units or shares are offered to fewer than 150 potential investors; and
- denomination or consideration of the fund units or shares is at least €100,000 each; or
- the public offering of the non-listed units or shares offered in aggregate does not exceed €5 million (as of 1 September 2017) calculated over a 12-month period.

13.308 If AIFs are offered to retail investors as well, specific local requirements need to be adhered to in addition to the AIFMD requirements. This so-called 'top-up retail' regime basically entails further transparency requirements, such as a website and prospectus, for the benefit and protection of the interests of retail investors.

13.309 Exemptions from the AIFMD requirements and the top-up retail regime are available for:

- exempted entities in accordance with AIFMD (ie limitative list of entities such as national central banks, municipalities, etc);
- fund size;
- passporting and equivalent supervision; and
- grandfathering in accordance with AIFMD.

13.310 The most important exemption in practice is the minimum threshold (de minimis) exemption which is available to Dutch based AIFMs only. If the aggregate of assets under management does not exceed €100 million when leverage is used and €500 million when no leverage is used and participations cannot be redeemed in the first five years following acquisition, the Financial Supervision Act caters for a simple registration regime. This so-called 'light regime' triggers a few registration and periodic reporting requirements only. Light AIFMs are registered in a special AFM register following a formal registration confirming its status as a light AIFM. Reporting requirements to DNB focus on type of assets, risk positions and concentration (risks).

13.311 *Marketing – Selected Jurisdictions*

13.311 If AIFs are offered to retail investors, the following requirements need to be met in addition to those mentioned above for the light regime to be applicable:

- the fund units or shares are offered to fewer than 150 potential investors; or
- denomination or aggregate consideration of the fund units or shares is at least €100,000 each.

13.312 When offering to non-professional investors on the basis of the de minimis exemption, a so-called 'wild west sign' has to be included in any marketing materials (stating that the AIFM operates outside of AFM supervision and that no prospectus is required).

13.313 AIFMs falling within the scope of the light regime can opt in to the AIFMD requirements, meaning that they voluntarily submit themselves to the AIFMD licence requirements. This is generally done for commercial reasons such as marketability as light regime AIFMs cannot market their AIFs outside the Netherlands since they are not within the scope of AIFMD. Another option to enable cross-border marketing for light regime AIFMs is qualification of the AIFs as either European venture capital funds ('EuVECA') or European social entrepreneurship funds ('EuSEF'). These regimes are only available when 70% of the investments are made in start-ups and innovative enterprises or with a social goal respectively.

13.314 An AIFM is allowed to market AIFs into other EU member states on the basis of an EU passport. This basically means that as soon as the home member state (the Netherlands) notifies the host member state (say, France), the AIFM can start marketing its AIFs in that particular country.

13.315 The same goes for MiFID services as AIFMs are also allowed to perform certain MiFID services, so-called 'MiFID top-up' or 'Super ManCo'. These services are: (i) reception and transmission of orders; (ii) individual portfolio management; and (iii) investment advice, but only and always in conjunction with managing AIFs. These MiFID services can, at least on the basis of current views of the AFM, be passported separately into other member states.

13.316 Apart from this AIFMD passport which allows AIFMs to market (specific) notified AIFs in EU member states, there are rules (Articles 32, 36 and 42 of AIFMD) for non-EU (third country) fund managers marketing (EU or non-EU) AIFs in the EU. For these managers an EU passport is to be developed. This passport should be designed and available in 2018 but its introduction might be postponed to 2019. Once introduced, non-EU AIFMs will be required to obtain a licence in an EU member state, basically bringing them in full scope of AIFMD. Until this time, non-AIFMD licensed, ie non-EU, AIFMs can make use of the national private placement regime ('NPPR') allowing them to manage EU funds and market EU and non-EU funds to EU investors. For the Netherlands the requirements which must be fulfilled for the NPPR are as follows:

- the fund units or shares are offered to professional (qualified) investors only;
- the fund units or shares are offered to fewer than 150 investors; and
- there is (nominal) participation value of at least €100,000.

13.317 A separate equivalent state regime, with similar requirements as set out above, is available for (investment) firms from the US, Guernsey and Jersey (*aangewezen staten regime*).

Investment restrictions and specific local rules

13.318 There are no investment restrictions for Dutch AIF structures.

13.319 Although the Netherlands did not gold plate AIFMD, local remuneration requirements do apply to AIFMs in addition to the AIFMD remuneration requirements (Annex II) and the European Securities and Markets Authority's sound remuneration principles. These remuneration rules contain clawback and adjustment of variable pay provisions as well as governance, transparency and information requirements regarding variable pay. A highly debated 20% bonus cap currently does not apply to AIFMs. When establishing an AIFM in the Netherlands or when providing (outsourced or insourced) services to a Dutch based AIFM, parties should take these local remuneration requirements into account.

Passive marketing of foreign funds in the Netherlands

13.320 In the Netherlands, marketing is understood to mean any direct or indirect offering or placement at the initiative of the AIFM or on behalf of the AIFM of units or shares of an AIF it manages to or with investors domiciled or with a registered office in an EU member state. An offer is understood to mean the provision of sufficient fund specific information to a potential investor which enables the investor to decide whether or not to invest in the AIF. Examples of such activities include one-to-one meetings, phone calls, investor presentations, and sending factsheets or other promotional documents containing (specific) information about the AIF(s). So there is a fine line between what constitutes marketing and what does not which should be taken into account. Avoiding this trigger point of marketing relies on the concept of reverse solicitation, ie at the initiative of the (potential) investor. This is a proven and recognised concept in the Netherlands but should be handled with care and properly documented.

Taxation

13.321 The Netherlands is generally perceived as being tax-friendly and attractive for hedge funds due to the availability of double taxation treaties with over 90 jurisdictions and flexibility in withholding and corporate income taxes, especially for institutional investors.

13.322 Provided some specific restrictions on transfer of participations are met, FGRs and CVs, for example, are tax transparent structures and consequently not subjected to corporate income tax, withholding tax, net wealth tax or subscription tax. Moreover, the Netherlands offers specific non-transparent regimes for the following providing certain specific distribution and transfer requirements are met:

13.322 Marketing – Selected Jurisdictions

- fiscal investment institutions (*fiscale beleggingsinstelling*, 'FBI'); and
- exempted investment institutions (*vrijgestelde beleggingsinstelling*, 'VBI').

13.323 An FBI can take the form of an NV, a BV or an FGR. A VBI can take the form of an NV or an FGR. The main advantages of the FBI regime include a reduction of or exemption from withholding tax on investments made by the fund under double taxation treaties, a 0% corporate income tax rate and a dividend withholding tax of 15% (to be off-set against other taxes of the fund). The VBI is also exempt from corporate income tax, dividend withholding tax, capital tax, net wealth tax and subscription tax.

13.324 Some institutional investors might also benefit from VAT discounts or exemptions in respect of AIFM management services.

I SINGAPORE

Danny Tan, Partner, Allen & Gledhill LLP

Regulatory framework

13.325 The regulatory framework which governs the marketing of hedge funds in Singapore is primarily found in the Securities and Futures Act, Chapter 289 of Singapore (the 'SFA'). The SFA regulates the offer of various types of securities, including shares or units of a collective investment scheme ('CIS securities').

13.326 Offers or invitations relating to interests in a hedge fund, being open-ended, to persons in Singapore for the subscription for or purchase of those interests would be regulated under the SFA as an offering of CIS securities.

13.327 Under the SFA, there is a requirement for an SFA-compliant prospectus to be registered with the Monetary Authority of Singapore (the 'MAS') for all offers of securities unless the offer is one which falls within specific exceptions under the SFA. Some commonly used exemptions from the prospectus registration requirements (described in further detail below) would include:

- the 'small offering exemption' (offers not exceeding S$5 million in any 12-month period)[1];
- the 'private placement exemption' (offers to no more than 50 persons in any 12-month period)[2];
- the 'institutional investor exemption' (offers only to institutional investors)[3]; and
- the 'section 305 exemption' (offers only to 'section 305 persons')[4].

[1] See paras 13.328–13.330 below.
[2] See paras 13.331–13.333 below.
[3] See paras 13.334–13.335 below.
[4] See paras 13.336–13.342 below.

Small offering exemption

13.328 The small offering exemption applies to offers of interests in a hedge fund made by any person where the total amount raised by the person from such offers does not exceed S$5 million (or its equivalent in any foreign currency) in any 12-month period.

13.329 There are conditions relating to advertisements and selling and promotional expenses that must also be complied with in order to take advantage of this exemption. Broadly, the offer must not be accompanied by an advertisement making an offer or calling attention to the offer or intended offer. Also, no selling or promotional expenses must be paid or incurred in connection with that offer, other than those incurred for administrative or professional services or incurred by way of commission or fees for services rendered by certain licensed or exempted persons.

13.330 Restrictions apply to the subsequent sale of interests in a hedge fund initially acquired under the small offering exemption.

Private placement exemption

13.331 If interests in a hedge fund are offered to no more than 50 persons in Singapore in any 12-month period, that offer may be made pursuant to the private placement exemption. No approval or registration formality is required to be complied with to take advantage of this exemption, although certain rules of aggregation would apply in determining the number of persons to which offers have been made.

13.332 There are conditions relating to advertisements and selling and promotional expenses similar to those described in para **13.329** above.

13.333 Restrictions apply to the subsequent sale of interests in a hedge fund initially acquired under the private placement exemption.

Institutional investor exemption

13.334 The institutional investor exemption provides that the prospectus registration requirements of the SFA will not apply in respect of an offer of CIS securities, whether or not those CIS securities have been previously issued, which is made only to institutional investors (as defined in the SFA)[1]. An offer of interests in a hedge fund pursuant to the institutional investor exemption may be made to an unlimited number of institutional investors.

---

[1] The Securities and Futures (Amendment) Act 2017 (A4/2017), which includes legislative amendments in relation to the definition of 'accredited investor' and 'institutional investor' was gazetted on 16 February 2017. However, the changes to the investor definitions have not yet come into effect.

13.335 Restrictions apply to the subsequent sale of interests in a hedge fund initially acquired under the institutional investor exemption.

13.336 *Marketing – Selected Jurisdictions*

Section 305 exemption

13.336 The section 305 exemption provides that the prospectus registration requirements of the SFA will not apply to offers made to the following persons ('section 305 persons'):

- a 'relevant person'; or
- a person who acquires the interests in the hedge fund as principal if the offer is on terms that these interests may only be acquired at a consideration of not less than S$200,000 (or its equivalent in a foreign currency) for each transaction, whether such amount is to be paid for in cash or by exchange of securities or other assets.

13.337 A 'relevant person' refers to:

- an accredited investor (as defined in the SFA)[1];
- a corporation the sole business of which is to hold investments and the entire share capital of which is owned by one or more individuals, each of whom is an accredited investor;
- a trustee of a trust the sole purpose of which is to hold investments and each beneficiary of which is an individual who is an accredited investor;
- an officer or equivalent person of the person making the offer (such person being an entity) or a spouse, parent, brother, sister, son or daughter of that officer or equivalent person; or
- a spouse, parent, brother, sister, son or daughter of the person making the offer (such person being an individual).

[1] The Securities and Futures (Amendment) Act 2017 (A4/2017), which includes legislative amendments in relation to the definition of 'accredited investor' and 'institutional investor' was gazetted on 16 February 2017. However, the changes to the investor definitions have not yet come into effect.

13.338 A notification of the offer to the MAS via an online platform, CISNet, must be made in order to rely on the section 305 exemption. Amongst other conditions, a copy of the information memorandum containing certain prescribed information must be submitted to the MAS.

13.339 Upon approval, the MAS will enter the collective investment scheme into the 'List of Restricted Schemes' which it maintains. A scheme will only be included on the list if the MAS is of the opinion that, inter alia, there is a manager for the scheme and that manager is:

- licensed or regulated to carry out fund management activities in the jurisdiction of its principal place of business; and
- a fit and proper person.

13.340 In determining whether a person is a 'fit and proper person', the MAS may take into account any matter relating to:

- any person who is or will be employed by or associated with the manager;
- any person exercising influence over the manager; or
- any person exercising influence over a related corporation of the manager.

13.341 The conditions relating to advertisements and selling and promotional expenses described in para **13.329** above must also be complied with for the purposes of the section 305 exemption.

13.342 Restrictions apply to the subsequent sale of interests in a hedge fund initially acquired under the section 305 exemption.

Marketing requirements

13.343 As the 'marketing of any collective investment scheme' is a financial advisory service regulated under the Financial Advisers Act, Chapter 110 of Singapore (the 'FAA'), the marketing of a hedge fund to persons in Singapore must be undertaken by a holder of a financial adviser's licence for the marketing of any collective investment scheme under the FAA, unless an exemption applies.

13.344 One exemption from the requirement to be licensed under the FAA is where a person provides financial advisory services only to institutional investors.

13.345 The licensing requirements under the FAA have extra-territorial effect. A person will be deemed to be acting as a financial adviser in Singapore if that person engages in any activity or conduct that is intended to or is likely to induce the public in Singapore or any section thereof to use any financial advisory service provided by that person, whether or not the activity or conduct is intended to or is likely to have that effect outside Singapore. Where a person does an act (such as the marketing of a collective investment scheme) partly in and partly outside Singapore which, if done wholly in Singapore, would constitute an offence under the FAA, that person will be guilty of that offence as if the act were carried out by that person wholly in Singapore, and may be dealt with as if the offence were committed wholly in Singapore.

13.346 As part of its continuing efforts to ensure the regulatory regime in Singapore remains current with market and international developments, the MAS has undertaken a comprehensive review of the SFA and issued a series of consultation papers seeking feedback on its proposed amendments. Some of the relevant proposals include the streamlining of the licensing requirements for the marketing of collective investment schemes and the introduction of a new licensing exemption for the marketing of funds managed by fund management companies which are registered or licensed in Singapore or their related corporations.

J   SPAIN

Ricardo Plasencia, Partner, DLA Piper, Spain

Legal and regulatory framework

13.347 The principal rules governing hedge funds in Spain are as follows:

- Law 35/2003 of 4 November 2003, regarding collective investment schemes ('CIS') (the 'CIS Law');

13.347 *Marketing – Selected Jurisdictions*

- Royal Decree 1082/2012 of 23 July 2012, which develops the CIS Law, and which has been partially modified by Royal Decree 83/2015 of 13 February 2015 (the 'CIS Regulations');
- Ministerial Order EHA/1199/2006 of 25 April 2006 from the Ministry of Economy and Finance (*Ministerio de Economia y Hacienda*), which develops the CIS Regulations; and
- Circular 1/2006 of 3 May 2006 of the National Securities Market Commission (*Comisión Nacional de Mercado de Valores*, the 'CNMV') about hedge funds.

Main features of Spanish hedge funds

13.348 The CIS Regulations established two types of hedge funds in Spain: (i) free investment CIS or 'hedge funds'[1], and (ii) CIS of hedge funds or 'funds of hedge funds'[2].

[1] Article 73 of the CIS Regulations.
[2] Article 74 of the CIS Regulations.

Free investment CIS/hedge funds

13.349 The main features of free investment CIS/hedge funds are as follows:

- *Investment strategy*: Spanish hedge funds can invest in any financial instrument regardless of the nature of the underlying assets, provided that their investment policy complies with the basic principles of liquidity, diversification and transparency.

  Additionally, and without being subject to the liquidity principle, Spanish hedge funds may also invest in invoices, loans, commercial effects commonly used in the field of commercial transactions, financial assets linked to investment strategies of more than a year and derivatives, provided that their settlement does not involve that a non-financial asset becomes an asset of any such hedge fund (a real estate asset as a result of a payment in lieu).

  Spanish hedge funds may also grant loans.
- *Leverage*: Spanish hedge funds are subject to a maximum leverage of five times their net asset value, provided that the leverage is consistent with the implementation of the investment policy of the relevant hedge fund. However, hedge funds whose investment policy involves the granting of loans cannot be leveraged. For the purposes of calculating that leverage limit, the temporary assignment of assets and financing received through stock loans or through derivatives are not taken into account (although this should be disclosed in the prospectus of the relevant hedge fund).
- *Calculation of net asset value*: Generally, the calculation of the net asset value of a Spanish hedge fund must be carried out at least on a quarterly basis. However, such period may be increased by up to a maximum of six months if the nature of the underlying assets requires a less frequent calculation. The investment manager may provide investors with preliminary estimates of net asset value, provided that the hedge fund's prospectus allows this.

- *Liquidity requirements*: Subscriptions and redemptions of shares or units in hedge funds must take place with the same frequency as the calculation of their net asset value. Hedge funds are not required to permit redemption on all the dates for calculation of the net asset value and may have lock-up periods for a maximum of one year, provided that this is authorised by the CNMV and it is disclosed in the prospectus (lock-up periods may be higher for hedge funds which invest in invoices, loans already granted by third parties or hedge funds which themselves grant loans). Hedge funds may establish a limit to the amount of redemptions on any given date. Pro rata rules may be applied where the redemption requests exceed that limit.

  Additionally, hedge funds may require notice periods with respect to subscriptions and redemptions, provided that such notice periods are disclosed in the hedge fund's prospectus.
- *Specific features for hedge funds granting or acquiring loans*: There are some specific requirements for hedge funds whose investment strategy involves granting or acquiring loans:
  - their prospectus must state the inherent risks of their investments as well as the procedure of analysis, assessment and granting of loans;
  - the portfolio of invoices, loans and other commercial bills must be sufficiently diversified and the prospectus must state the time period in which such diversification may be achieved;
  - the hedge funds may neither grant nor invest in loans granted to individuals, shareholders or unitholders of the relevant hedge fund, other CIS or related third party; and
  - hedge funds may only invest in loans granted at least three years before the investment by the hedge fund.

CIS of hedge funds/funds of hedge funds

13.350 The main features of CIS of hedge funds/funds of hedge funds are as follows:

- *Investment strategy*: Spanish funds of hedge funds must invest at least 60% of their assets in Spanish hedge funds and similar foreign hedge funds, provided that any such hedge fund is established in an EU member state or an OECD country, or is managed by a manager which is established in an EU member state or an OECD country subject to prudential supervision. Additionally, funds of hedge funds cannot invest in other Spanish or foreign funds of hedge funds.
- *Diversification*: Funds of hedge funds may not invest more than 10% of their net assets in a single hedge fund. If that 10% limit is exceeded, there is generally a period of one year within which such excess must be reduced. However, if the excess amounts to 35% or more, the fund of hedge funds must reduce this excess below 35% within six months. In any event, the total reduction must be effected within one year of the date on which that 10% limit was exceeded.
- *Leverage*: Funds of hedge funds are subject to the leverage limits which are applicable generally to CIS.

- *Calculation of net asset value*: Generally, the calculation of net asset value must be carried out at least on a quarterly basis. However, such period may be increased by up to a maximum of six months if the nature of the underlying assets requires a less frequent calculation. The investment manager may provide investors with preliminary estimates of net asset value, provided that the fund's prospectus allows this.
- *Liquidity requirements*: Subscriptions and redemptions of shares of funds of hedge funds must take place with the same frequency as the calculation of their net asset value. Funds of hedge funds are not required to permit redemption rights on all dates for calculation of the net asset value. Funds of hedge funds may have lock-up periods, provided that this is authorised by the CNMV, is required by the nature of the underlying assets and takes into account the marketing conditions, and is disclosed in the relevant prospectus.

    Additionally, subject to the CNMV's authorisation and according to their investment and marketing policy, funds of hedge funds may establish a limit to the amount of redemptions on any given date. Pro rata rules may be applied where the redemption requests exceed that limit. In addition, depending on the terms of the marketing policy of the fund and its investment strategy, the CNMV may authorise the application of notice periods with respect to subscriptions and redemptions of units or shares, provided that such notice periods (i) do not exceed the periods on which the net asset value must be calculated plus 15 days, and (ii) are disclosed in the fund's prospectus.

13.351 The investment policy of funds of hedge funds must comply with the basic principles of liquidity, transparency and diversification which are applicable generally to mutual CIS. The prospectus and the key investor information document (the 'KIID') must include, in addition to the standard information which is contained in the prospectus and the KIID of any mutual CIS, specific details about: (i) the fund's purpose; (ii) the investment policy of the hedge fund and the risks inherent in that investment policy; (iii) the risk profile of the hedge fund and of the prospective investors; (iv) the minimum prior notice period required for redemption of shares; and (v) the expenses and fees which will be directly or indirectly payable by the hedge fund. The particular risks inherent to the hedge fund must also be included in the prospectus, in the KIID and in any other marketing material of the fund of hedge funds.

Taxation

13.352 Spanish hedge funds and funds of hedge funds are subject to Spanish corporate income tax (*Impuesto de Sociedades*) at a 1% rate, provided that they have at least 25 and 100 investors respectively.

13.353 As regards the taxation of investors in hedge funds and funds of hedge funds, this will vary depending on, amongst other issues, the nature or type of the investor (eg corporations or individuals) and the jurisdiction in which they are resident for tax purposes.

Investors

13.354 In relation to investor profile and marketing restrictions, funds of hedge funds are subject to the general requirements for mutual CIS: there must be at least 100 investors but there is no minimum subscription amount per investor. By contrast, hedge funds must have at least 25 investors and the minimum subscription amount is €100,000, if the investor is not treated as a qualified investor.

13.355 Investors which are not qualified investors must, prior to subscribing for shares or units in a hedge fund or in a fund of hedge funds, make a statement in writing to the firm providing the investment services declaring that they are aware of the risks inherent in that investment.

13.356 Such statement would not be required if a retail client were to invest in such a fund through a portfolio management agreement in which investment in these kind of funds is authorised and which includes similar statements regarding risks.

Marketing hedge funds in Spain

Spanish hedge funds

13.357 Spanish hedge funds may be marketed in Spain to qualified investors. Marketing to retail investors in Spain is only permitted if they make an initial investment of €100,000 and they state in writing, prior to any subscription, that they are aware of the risks inherent in that investment.

13.358 However, as an exception to the general rule stated above, hedge funds which invest in invoices, loans, commercial effects commonly used in the field of commercial transactions, financial assets linked to investment strategies of more than a year and/or derivatives, provided that their settlement does not involve a non-financial asset becoming an asset of the hedge fund (eg real estate asset as a result of a payment in lieu), may only be marketed to qualified investors.

13.359 For these purposes, 'qualified investors' mean those investors that are deemed to have the experience, knowledge and qualification necessary to make their own investment choices and to assess their risks. In particular, the following will be considered as 'qualified investors':

(a) Financial institutions and other entities which are required to be authorised or regulated to operate in the financial markets by a state, irrespective of whether or not it is a member state of the EU, including credit institutions, investment firms, insurance and reinsurance companies, CIS and their management companies, private equity funds, closed-ended investment schemes and their management companies, pension funds and their management companies, securitisation funds and their management companies, commodity and commodity derivatives dealers, and other institutional investors.

13.359 *Marketing – Selected Jurisdictions*

(b) National and regional governments, public bodies that manage public debt, central banks, international and supranational institutions such as the World Bank, the International Monetary Fund, the European Central Bank, the European Investment Bank and other institutions of a similar nature.
(c) Companies which meet at least two of the following size requirements on an individual basis:
 (i) a total balance sheet equal to or greater than €20 million;
 (ii) annual net turnover equal to or greater than €40 million; and
 (iii) own funds equal to or greater than €2 million.
(d) Institutional investors (other than those specified in (a) above) whose main activity is to invest in securities and other financial instruments.
(e) Individuals and small and medium-sized companies which request in advance to their investment services provider to be treated as qualified investors and expressly waive their treatment as retail customers, and which are registered as such in the client registries of the entities providing investment services.

Spanish funds of hedge funds

13.360 Spanish funds of hedge funds are not subject to specific restrictions in connection with their marketing in Spain (and they may be marketed to different types of investors, including retail investors).

Foreign hedge funds

13.361 The CIS Law provides specific regimes for marketing shares or units in a foreign hedge fund in Spain depending on where that hedge fund and its manager are incorporated or authorised. In this regard, there are basically two different regimes as follows:

- *Passport system*: This only applies to the marketing of an EU hedge fund (managed by an authorised EU alternative investment fund manager ('EU AIFM')) to qualified investors where the manager of that hedge fund is authorised in a member state of the EU.
 The regulatory authority in the home jurisdiction of the manager must communicate to the manager that it has sent to the CNMV all the relevant documentation in order to enable it to market the hedge fund in Spain.
- *Prior authorisation by the CNMV*: This applies to the marketing in Spain of:
 – non-EU hedge funds managed by EU AIFMs to qualified investors;
 – non-EU hedge funds managed by non-EU AIFMs to qualified investors;
 – EU hedge funds managed by EU AIFMs to retail investors;
 – non-EU hedge funds managed by EU AIFMs to retail investors; and
 – non-EU hedge funds managed by non-EU AIFMs to retail investors.

In order to obtain authorisation from the CNMV, it is necessary to meet the relevant requirements. Whilst these requirements vary according to the type of foreign hedge fund which is to be marketed in Spain, they basically refer to the following:
- the existence of a similar category of hedge fund under Spanish law;
- the existence of co-operation agreements between the home competent authorities and the CNMV to ensure the effective exchange of information for supervisory purposes;
- the country where the hedge fund is domiciled is not listed as a Non-Cooperative Country and Territory by the FATF; and
- the jurisdiction in which the hedge fund is established and Spain have entered into a double taxation agreement which ensures an effective exchange of information in tax matters.

13.362 In relation to some types of hedge fund there are additional requirements. For instance, where a non-EU hedge fund managed by an EU manager is to be marketed in Spain, the CNMV may require a favourable report from the home state authority which is responsible for the supervision and inspection of the hedge fund or the manager acting on its behalf regarding its activities. Furthermore, where a hedge fund is to be marketed to retail investors in Spain, the CNMV may require a copy of that hedge fund's financial statements and relevant audit report prepared in accordance with the applicable law.

13.363 In all cases, in addition to prior authorisation by the CNMV, the hedge fund must be registered with the CNMV.

13.364 The CNMV is entitled to refuse to authorise a foreign hedge fund for a number of reasons, including: (i) prudential reasons; (ii) non-compliance with rules on organisation and discipline of the Spanish securities markets; and (iii) lack of protection of investors resident in Spain.

Investment managers

13.365 Investment managers of Spanish hedge funds and funds of hedge funds are subject to the general requirements applicable to mutual CIS managers and are also subject to certain additional requirements, as follows:

- With respect to capital requirements, management companies must have a share capital of at least €125,000 plus any increased asset-based requirements which are applicable depending on the level of funds under management and other criteria.
- Investment managers must have risk measurement and risk control systems appropriate for the specific investment strategies that they intend to implement. Additionally, they must periodically carry out stress tests and simulations of specific crisis scenarios in order to analyse their potential effect on the portfolio of the funds under management and on the proper management of liquidity. Effective internal communication systems with service providers are also required.

13.365 Marketing – Selected Jurisdictions

- Investment managers which have entered into prime brokerage agreements with a third party providing financing must be equipped with procedures that ensure the control of the asset positions which have been provided as collateral or over which such third party has exercised a right of disposition.

13.366 The management companies of hedge funds whose investment strategy is investing in invoices, loans, commercial effects commonly used in the field of commercial transactions, and granting loans must have a credit risk management procedure as well as a valuation and classification system for loans and for their borrowers.

K SWITZERLAND

Olivier Stahler, Partner, Lenz & Staehelin and Charlotte Gilliéron, Associate, Lenz & Staehelin

Legal and regulatory framework

13.367 The Swiss legal and regulatory framework which applies to the marketing of Swiss and foreign hedge funds is the Swiss Federal Act of 23 June 2006 on Collective Investment Schemes, as amended (the 'CISA'), and its implementing ordinance, the Swiss Federal Ordinance of 22 November 2006 on Collective Investment Schemes (the 'CISO').

13.368 On 28 September 2012, the Swiss Parliament enacted a major revision of the Swiss legal and regulatory framework for investment funds. The main purpose of this revision was to align the Swiss fund regulations with the Alternative Investment Fund Managers Directive[1] ('AIFMD'). The revision included significant changes to the rules about the distribution of interests in funds in Switzerland. In particular, the concept of 'public offering' was replaced by the concept of 'distribution'. The revised legal framework entered into force on 1 March 2013.

[1] Directive 2011/61/EU of 8 June 2011.

13.369 Following the CISA revision, the Swiss Financial Market Supervisory Authority ('FINMA') issued a revised Circular 2013/09 on the distribution of collective investment schemes ('Circular 13/09') on 10 September 2013. Circular 13/09 entered into force on 1 October 2013. The aim of Circular 2013/09 is to clarify the concept of distribution and the classification of investors.

13.370 Following the CISA revision, the Swiss Funds and Asset Management Association ('SFAMA') revised its guidelines on the distribution of collective investment schemes, which entered into force on 1 July 2014. These guidelines impose certain obligations upon the promoters and distributors of funds in Switzerland. They have been recognised by FINMA as a minimum standard.

Marketing foreign hedge funds in Switzerland

13.371 As stated in CHAPTER 4, Switzerland is not a jurisdiction in which hedge funds are established, but an important jurisdiction in which non-Swiss hedge funds are managed and distributed[1].

[1] See para **4.486** in CHAPTER 4.

Concept of distribution

13.372 The current Swiss legal framework is based on the concept of distribution. 'Distribution' is defined as any offer or advertisement for funds which is not exclusively directed at regulated qualified investors[1] with a view to obtaining subscription in a fund. As a consequence, marketing activities which are targeted at regulated qualified investors in Switzerland are not subject to any specific restrictions under Swiss law.

[1] See para **13.376** below.

13.373 According to the CISO and Circular 13/09, distribution activities encompass any proposal or marketing with a view of obtaining subscription for interests in any specific fund. The type or form of the distribution is irrelevant (whether by email, letter, cold-calling or road show).

13.374 The CISA provides for three situations where distribution is treated as not occurring. The provision of information about and the offer of interests in non-Swiss hedge funds fall outside the scope of the CISA in the following situations:

- At the instigation/own initiative of the investors. The reverse solicitation exemption under Swiss law is limited to situations where an investor requests information about, or acquires an interest in, a specific fund without any preliminary intervention or contact from the investment manager or a distributor of the fund. If the request does not refer to a specific fund, the information provided is deemed to be distribution.
- At the investor's request in the context of a long-term and remunerated advisory agreement entered into by the investor with a regulated financial intermediary (such as a bank, a securities dealer or a fund management company) or with an independent asset manager (subject to the conditions set out in the CISA and the CISO).
- Within the context of a written discretionary asset management agreement entered into by the investor with a regulated financial intermediary or with an independent asset manager (subject to the conditions set out in the CISA and the CISO).

Classification of investors

13.375 The requirements which apply to the distribution of foreign funds in Switzerland depend on the status of the target investors, specifically whether they are (i) regulated qualified investors, (ii) unregulated qualified investors, or (iii) non-qualified investors.

13.376 *Marketing – Selected Jurisdictions*

13.376 According to the CISA and the CISO, 'qualified investors' encompass the following[1]:

- *Regulated qualified investors*, which comprise:
  - regulated financial intermediaries such as banks, securities dealers, fund management companies and regulated investment managers of funds, as well as central banks; and
  - regulated insurance institutions.
- *Unregulated qualified investors*, which comprise:
  - public entities and retirement benefit institutions (pension funds) with professional treasury management;
  - companies with professional treasury management;
  - high net worth individuals: a high net worth individual is viewed as an unregulated qualified investor if he declares in writing his willingness to be considered as such (the 'opt-in' process) and if one of the following conditions is met:
    (i) he confirms in writing that he directly or indirectly holds assets which amount to at least CHF 5 million; or
    (ii) he confirms in writing that he directly or indirectly holds financial assets which amount to at least CHF 500,000 and demonstrates that he has sufficient knowledge to understand the risks of the investments based on his education and work experience or similar experience in the financial sector;
  - investors who have entered into a written discretionary asset management agreement, provided that (i) they do not exercise their right to 'opt-out' of qualified investor status, and (ii) the written discretionary asset management agreement is entered into with a regulated financial intermediary or with an independent asset manager (subject to the conditions set out in the CISA and the CISO).

[1] See article 10 paras 3, 3bis and 3ter of the CISA and articles 6 and 6a of the CISO.

13.377 Any investor who is not a regulated qualified investor or an unregulated qualified investor is a 'non-qualified investor'.

13.378 Independent asset managers are not qualified investors. According to Circular 13/09, distribution activities which are aimed at independent asset managers can, however, be regarded as distribution to unregulated qualified investors, provided that all of the four following requirements are met:

- the independent asset manager is subject, as a financial intermediary, to the Swiss Federal Act on Anti-Money Laundering of 10 October 1997;
- the independent asset manager is subject to the rules of conduct of a professional organisation which are recognised as a minimum standard by FINMA;
- the written discretionary investment management agreement entered into with the investor complies with the guidelines of a professional organisation which are recognised as a minimum standard by FINMA; and

- the independent asset manager has undertaken in writing to the distributor to use the fund related information exclusively with clients which are themselves qualified investors.

13.379 If one or more of these requirements is not fulfilled, the distribution activities which are aimed at the independent asset manager will be regarded as distribution to a non-qualified investor.

Distribution of non-Swiss hedge funds to investors in Switzerland

MARKETING ACTIVITIES TARGETED AT REGULATED QUALIFIED INVESTORS

13.380 Marketing activities which target regulated qualified investors fall outside the scope of the CISA. Therefore, marketing activities which target such investors exclusively are not subject to the requirements which apply at the foreign fund level and at the foreign distributor level referred to below.

DISTRIBUTION ACTIVITIES TARGETED AT UNREGULATED QUALIFIED INVESTORS

13.381 Distribution activities which target unregulated qualified investors are treated as distribution under Swiss law. Such distribution is subject to Swiss regulatory requirements at both the foreign fund level and the distributor level.

13.382 Non-Swiss hedge funds which are distributed to unregulated qualified investors are not subject to any registration or filing requirements with FINMA. Non-Swiss hedge funds which are distributed to unregulated qualified investors in Switzerland must appoint a Swiss representative and a Swiss paying agent. Further, the foreign fund documentation must include certain mandatory disclosures based on a document entitled 'Information for investors in Switzerland' issued by the SFAMA.

13.383 The distributor can be a Swiss or a non-Swiss institution provided that the following conditions are met:

- *Swiss distributor*: A Swiss institution is entitled to distribute interests in non-Swiss hedge funds to unregulated qualified investors provided that (i) it is authorised as a fund distributor by FINMA, or (ii) it benefits from the exemption from the requirement to obtain a separate Swiss distributor licence. Swiss law provides for a 'waterfall' licensing regime and, typically, higher level licences such as those for a bank, a securities dealer or an investment manager are deemed to cover distribution, so that no separate licence is required, for instance, for a Swiss investment manager to carry out fund distribution activities (provided, however, that the organisational regulations of that Swiss investment manager provide for distribution and it has adequate corporate governance to conduct such activity).
- *Non-Swiss distributor*: Non-Swiss distributors are entitled to distribute interests in non-Swiss hedge funds to unregulated qualified investors provided that they are authorised to distribute funds and are appropriately supervised in their home jurisdictions.

13.383 *Marketing – Selected Jurisdictions*

Swiss fund regulations and FINMA practice are silent as to the specific requirements that are to be met by a foreign distributor in its home jurisdiction in order to be considered as 'authorised to distribute funds'. The requirements that are applicable to a foreign distributor or investment manager in order to be authorised to distribute funds in and/or from its home jurisdiction are a matter of the domestic law of that home jurisdiction. As mentioned above, Swiss law provides for a 'waterfall' licensing approach and, typically, higher level licences such as those for a bank, a securities dealer or an investment manager are deemed by law to cover distribution. A similar approach should be applicable to foreign financial intermediaries, to the extent relevant.

There is no guidance on the concept of 'appropriate supervision' and FINMA has not issued any list of foreign regulatory authorities which apply 'appropriate supervision'. The supervision of AIFM by regulators in member states of the EU should be deemed appropriate for these purposes.

13.384 In addition, all (Swiss and non-Swiss) distributors which are involved in the distribution of non-Swiss hedge funds to unregulated qualified investors in Switzerland must enter into a distribution agreement, which is governed by Swiss law, with the Swiss representative of the relevant non-Swiss hedge funds.

DISTRIBUTION ACTIVITIES TARGETED AT NON-QUALIFIED INVESTORS

13.385 The distribution activities of non-Swiss funds which target non-qualified investors require the appointment of a Swiss representative and a Swiss paying agent, as well as the prior registration of the relevant foreign funds with FINMA, which is in practice currently available for funds which fall within the scope of the UCITS Directive. This means that hedge funds are only eligible for distribution in Switzerland to qualified investors.

Forthcoming amendments to the Swiss legal and regulatory framework

13.386 The Swiss Government submitted the Swiss Federal Financial Services Act (the 'FFSA') together with the Swiss Federal Act on Financial Institutions (the 'FAFI') to the Swiss Parliament on 4 November 2015[1].

[1] See paras 4.546–4.554 in CHAPTER 4 for further details.

13.387 The objective of the FFSA is to provide a new legal framework for the provision of financial services in Switzerland, including where such services are provided on a cross-border basis into Switzerland.

13.388 Notwithstanding that the FFSA is still under discussion, it is likely that the concept of the 'distribution of funds', which was introduced by the CISA in 2013, will be entirely abolished and replaced by the general concept of the offer of financial instruments under the FFSA. In this context, the specific authorisation regime for fund distributors under the CISA is likely to be abolished. Fund distributors, however, will be obliged, like any other financial services provider, to the extent that they are not prudentially supervised, to register their client advisers in a register that will be created in Switzerland. It is expected that that register will contain not only the name and address of those providers but also information about their corporate governance and their senior management.

13.389 Subject to final parliamentary debates, the current requirement to appoint a Swiss representative and paying agent should be suppressed where a placement of funds is made to unregulated qualified investors (such as pension funds, industrial enterprises or independent asset managers) other than 'opt-in' qualified investors (such as high net worth individuals).

Taxation

13.390 The main Swiss tax aspect of the distribution of funds within Switzerland arises out of the application of Swiss VAT to distributor fees.

13.391 Under the Swiss Value Added Tax Act of 12 June 2009, turnovers in connection with the distribution of funds are excluded from VAT. Swiss based distributors therefore do not charge VAT in respect of the activity of distribution provided that the services are provided to a qualifying fund. In accordance with the practice of the Swiss federal tax administration, this exclusion applies to Swiss funds and to foreign funds which are registered for distribution in Switzerland. For foreign funds which are not registered for distribution in Switzerland (such as hedge funds), a 0% rate of VAT would still typically apply since the Swiss provider exports its services.

Chapter 14

TAXATION OF HEDGE FUNDS – AN OVERVIEW

Martin Shah, Partner, Corporate Tax Group, Simmons & Simmons

A	Introduction	14.1
B	Structuring drivers	14.4
C	Typical hedge fund structures	14.14
D	UK taxation of the fund – tax residence considerations	14.24
E	UK taxation of the fund – 'trading in the UK' considerations	14.59
F	UK taxation of investors	14.89

A   INTRODUCTION

14.1 This chapter provides a background to the key tax drivers behind structuring a fund, with specific commentary in relation to the most common structures adopted for hedge funds.

14.2 It then considers in turn the principal UK direct tax issues relevant to the establishment and operation of an offshore corporate hedge fund managed by an investment manager in the UK.

14.3 The chapter concludes with a summary of the principal UK tax considerations relevant to UK investors investing in hedge funds.

B   STRUCTURING DRIVERS

Overview

14.4 When structuring a fund, tax considerations should be taken into account at three levels:

- the tax position of investors in the fund[1];
- the tax position of the fund itself[2]; and
- the tax position of the investments made by the fund[3].

[1] See paras **14.6–14.7** below.
[2] See paras **14.8–14.11** below.
[3] See paras **14.12–14.13** below.

14.5 Although tax considerations should not be considered in isolation, it will be important from a marketing perspective to seek to minimise unnecessary taxation for the fund and its investors. In addition to this being of benefit to the investors in the fund, by minimising taxation the fund's post-tax returns will be improved, which could result in increased fee revenues and/or other returns for the investment manager or investment adviser to the fund.

14.6 *Taxation of Hedge Funds – An Overview*

Tax position of investors in the fund

14.6 The starting point when structuring the fund is to seek so far as possible not to give rise to additional taxation liabilities that would not be suffered by investors were they to invest directly in the fund's underlying investments, ie to achieve tax neutrality. It is therefore important firstly to consider the tax position of the fund's investors so as to establish the base line from which to structure.

14.7 Although the tax profile of a particular investor cannot be anticipated when establishing a pooled fund, the following points should be considered:

- Are the investors in the fund subject to taxation in respect of their investment in the fund? If so, is their liability to taxation greater in respect of an investment in the fund than for a direct investment in the underlying investments of the fund?
- Do the investors qualify for any tax regime which could affect their tax treatment, eg are they dealers in securities, pension funds, sovereign wealth funds, insurance companies, charities, endowments or collective investment schemes?
- Will an investment in the fund be subject to anti-avoidance rules in the investors' home jurisdictions, eg anti-offshore fund rules, controlled foreign company rules or similar?
- What level of tax reporting will be required by, or is desirable for, investors to allow them to comply with their tax reporting obligations in their home jurisdictions? Is the extent and nature of any tax reporting relevant to the tax treatment of investors, for example to secure the application of a beneficial tax regime?
- Can distributions and redemption proceeds be paid to investors by the fund without any withholding or other taxes?
- Will any transfer or registration taxes arise on dealing by investors in their interests in the fund?
- Will the investors be happy to have tax filing and/or payment obligations in the jurisdiction of the fund or its investments?
- Will the investors present tax withholding and/or reporting challenges to the fund, for example under the US Foreign Account Tax Compliance Act ('FATCA') or the OECD's Common Reporting Standard (the 'CRS')? Generally, the fund should ensure that it is entitled to receive, process and disclose information on investors (and relevant related parties) in order to comply with its due diligence and reporting obligations under these and similar regimes, and may wish to seek indemnification or certain other protections in the event that investors trigger any liabilities or costs for the fund, for example where incorrect information is provided.

Tax position of the fund itself

14.8 There are two basic taxation models that can be used:

- *Structuring the fund as a tax transparent entity*: As noted above, it is important to seek so far as possible to avoid the creation of any additional layers of taxation when structuring the fund. The simplest means of achieving this objective, at least insofar as the fund itself is concerned, is to establish the fund as an entity that is transparent for tax purposes, so that the investors are treated as owning a share of their fund's investments for tax purposes. This may be beneficial where, for example, the underlying investments give rise to capital gains treatment that results in investors suffering a lower effective rate of taxation on their investment in the fund. It may also be useful in circumstances where investors are entitled to claim tax treaty benefits in respect of the fund's underlying investments, for example where the investors are pension funds. It should be noted that using a tax transparent structure could in some cases result in investors having tax filing and/or payment obligations in the jurisdictions in which the fund invests.

Potential structures for tax transparent funds will depend on the characterisation of the fund in the investors' jurisdictions and the jurisdictions in which the fund proposes to invest, but could include limited partnerships in the Cayman Islands, the Channel Islands or the US (typically established in the state of Delaware).

- *Structuring the fund as a tax-exempt entity*: The alternative model is to establish the fund as a tax-exempt entity, either on the basis that it benefits from a complete exemption from local taxation in the jurisdiction of its establishment or that it is effectively tax exempt insofar as it is entitled to deduct distributions etc to investors in computing its taxation liability. As noted[1], this may not be appropriate for investors if it means that their investment in the fund will be subject to anti-avoidance rules such as anti-offshore fund rules or controlled foreign company rules. In addition, using a tax-exempt structure may prevent the fund being treated as a resident of the jurisdiction in which it is established and thus make it ineligible for double tax treaty benefits.

  Potential structures for tax-exempt funds are varied but could include open-ended companies in the Cayman Islands or the Channel Islands, a *société d'investissement à capital variable* ('SICAV') in Luxembourg, or an investment company or Irish Collective Asset-management Vehicle ('ICAV') in Ireland.

[1] See para **14.7** above.

14.9 The manner in which the fund's investments are managed can affect the fund's liability to tax. For example, if the fund is treated as trading through the activities of its investment manager acting as the fund's agent, this may subject the fund to taxation in the jurisdiction in which the investment manager is located. It may be that there is a local exemption from taxation that could apply to the fund in these circumstances, such as the UK's investment manager exemption[1] or the US 'safe harbor' rules, which again will need to be addressed when structuring the fund. Alternatively, it may be that the fund should be self-managed through its board of directors or similar, with the role of the investment professionals being limited to acting as investment adviser to the fund.

[1] See para **14.67** et seq below.

14.10 *Taxation of Hedge Funds – An Overview*

14.10 As will be clear from the above, it may be that there is no perfect structure that meets both investor and investment requirements and this will require a cost-benefit analysis to be undertaken.

14.11 Although it is outside the scope of this chapter, the taxation position of the investment manager or investment adviser and its principals may also go to the model chosen when structuring the fund. For example, if there is a desire to have some form of carried interest in respect of which the principals are taxed at capital gains rather than income rates, this is generally easier to structure through a tax transparent fund such as a limited partnership.

Tax position of investments made by the fund

14.12 Again, this is a matter that requires analysis on a case-by-case basis, but the following are the principal considerations:

- Will the fund or its investors be subject to withholding taxes in respect of income and/or gains derived from investments made by the fund?
- Will the fund or its investors be directly assessable to tax in the jurisdiction of investment?
- Does the fund or its investors have any tax filing obligations in the jurisdiction of investment?
- Where the fund is a tax transparent entity, does the tax regime in the jurisdiction of investment look through the fund to its investors when assessing potential local liabilities to taxation? Can the investors rely on double tax treaty protection in such circumstances?
- Where the fund is a tax-exempt entity, does this expose the fund to higher taxation in the jurisdiction of investment, eg a higher rate of withholding taxes on payments to blacklisted tax haven entities? Does the fund benefit from double tax treaty protection if it is tax exempt?
- Is it necessary for the fund or its investors to register with the local taxation authorities and/or to hold investments in a particular way (eg through a local custodian) in order to benefit from a lower effective rate of taxation?
- Does the fund need to gather and hold particular information on its investors in order to minimise withholding or other taxes on the fund's investments? This may apply both domestically and on an international basis, in the latter case, for example, under FATCA and the CRS.
- Will the fund be subject to transfer or registration taxes in respect of its investments?

14.13 Again, a cost-benefit analysis should be undertaken to see whether it may be attractive to seek to mitigate local taxation in respect of the fund's investments. There are two principal means of achieving this:

- *Invest synthetically*: The fund does not hold the investment directly but instead takes a synthetic position in the investment, for example through a contract for differences or total return swap with a bank that then may separately decide to hedge by holding the physical investment concerned.

In these circumstances, it is necessary to analyse whether the payments to the fund in respect of its synthetic position are taxable, for example where the counterparty bank has to withhold on payments under a swap. In addition, the structuring may depend on the bank being treated as the beneficial owner of the physical position, which in some jurisdictions can be questionable where there is a back-to-back swap. Furthermore, tax developments (such as the US section 871(m) dividend equivalent payment rules[1]) may affect structures that have historically been adopted.

- *Invest indirectly*: The fund does not hold the investment directly but instead indirectly through an investment vehicle established in a suitable jurisdiction that (a) minimises taxation in the jurisdiction of investment but (b) does not create significant additional taxation in the jurisdiction of establishment of the investment vehicle. Jurisdictions commonly used for these purposes include Luxembourg, the Netherlands, Ireland, Cyprus and Mauritius.

In these circumstances, the argument runs that the local tax authorities are only entitled to consider the tax position of the investment vehicle and not look through to the fund, for example when considering whether double tax treaty protection is available. Again, back-to-back arrangements such as profit participating loans from the fund to the investment vehicle can prejudice this analysis. In addition, tax developments, such as those resulting from the OECD's Action Plan on Base Erosion and Profit Shifting ('BEPS'), may affect the use of such arrangements.

[1] In section 871(m) of the US Internal Revenue Code of 1986 (as amended) and related regulations.

C TYPICAL HEDGE FUND STRUCTURES

Background

14.14 Many of the complexities of a hedge fund structure result from the need to cater for the contrasting tax requirements of US tax-exempt investors and US taxable investors and the desire for managers to be able to tap the significant sources of capital available for allocation by such investors. This section provides a brief overview of the relevant tax and structuring issues. It should be noted that the US Tax Cuts and Jobs Act of 2017 has made a number of changes to US tax law, the effects of which may be relevant to US investors.

US tax-exempt investors v US taxable investors

14.15 As the name suggests, US tax-exempt investors are generally not subject to US tax on dividends, interest or capital gains. However, such investors are subject to US tax on certain types of income, in particular unrelated business taxable income ('UBTI'), which can arise, for example, where a hedge fund incurs debt to finance its investments.

14.16 *Taxation of Hedge Funds – An Overview*

14.16 Accordingly, US tax-exempt investors will generally wish to invest in a fund that is regarded as a corporate (ie tax opaque) entity for US tax purposes, since this avoids the need to report and suffer tax in respect of UBTI.

14.17 However, investment in such an entity that is established outside the US may be unattractive for US taxable investors for a number of reasons. For example, an offshore corporate fund is likely to be treated as a passive foreign investment company (a 'PFIC') for US tax purposes. This treatment can be materially disadvantageous for US taxable investors, unless those investors elect to have the PFIC treated as a 'qualified electing fund' (a 'QEF'). In order to be effective, such election is dependent upon the PFIC providing certain US tax and accounting information to each US investor who makes an election. Many offshore funds may not wish to commit to do so given the additional cost and administrative inconvenience involved in undertaking QEF reporting. Other issues may also arise for US taxable investors in a non-US corporate entity, for example under the US controlled foreign corporation ('CFC') rules.

14.18 As a result of these issues, US taxable investors are likely to wish to invest in a fund that is regarded as a transparent entity for US tax purposes, with the fund providing necessary tax reporting information annually to enable those investors to comply with their US tax filing and payment obligations.

Parallel v master-feeder structures

14.19 To cater for the differing requirements of US tax-exempt and US taxable investors, an offshore corporate fund is usually established for the US tax-exempt investors (into which non-US investors will also invest) and a separate offshore or US limited partnership is established for US taxable investors.

14.20 However, an equally important question, which always has to be considered, is whether these funds should be operated in parallel (or side-by-side) or through a 'master-feeder' structure and, if the latter, which fund should be the master fund.

14.21 The most frequently cited reasons for adopting a master-feeder structure are reduction of costs and greater administrative convenience, as all investments are made by a single master fund rather than needing to be split between two parallel funds. The use of a master-feeder structure may also achieve further commercial advantages, for example improved terms with market counterparties due to its greater size of portfolio.

14.22 Although there are various means of structuring a master-feeder arrangement, the most common is for the master fund to be an offshore corporate entity that 'checks the box' to be treated as a partnership for US tax purposes (note that certain 'per se' corporations cannot check the box, so this may influence the choice of entity). Two feeder funds, one an offshore corporate and the other either an offshore or US limited partnership, invest in shares in the master fund. From the perspective of US tax-exempt investors, the offshore corporate feeder fund acts as a 'blocker' in respect of UBTI. For US taxable investors, their preferred 'flow-through' treatment is achieved as both the limited partnership feeder and master fund are treated as partnerships for US tax purposes.

14.23 It can be a complex and costly exercise to restructure two existing parallel funds into a master-feeder structure, and if there is a possibility of raising capital from both US tax-exempt investors and US taxable investors, either at launch or in the future, it may be advisable to adopt a master-feeder structure from day one. Where it is not certain that US taxable investors will invest, it is possible to establish a 'one-legged' master-feeder structure involving an offshore corporate feeder fund and offshore corporate master fund (which would 'check the box') at day one, with a view to adding a second limited partnership feeder for US taxable investors in due course should sufficient capital be raised from them.

D UK TAXATION OF THE FUND – TAX RESIDENCE CONSIDERATIONS

Introduction

14.24 This section considers how an offshore fund which is a company incorporated outside the UK may be treated as resident in the UK for UK tax purposes, and the steps which should be taken to avoid this.

14.25 Where an offshore fund is treated as tax resident in the UK, it will be subject to UK corporation tax on all its profits, wheresoever and howsoever earned. It may also be liable to withhold UK income tax from any interest payments it makes. The consequences of residence should therefore be distinguished from other circumstances in which an offshore fund may be liable to UK tax, such as where it operates a permanent establishment such as a branch or agency in the UK and is liable to corporation tax on the profits of that branch or agency alone.

14.26 Subject to certain exceptions, any company incorporated in the UK is automatically UK tax resident, but any company incorporated elsewhere can become UK tax resident. It is possible for companies to be resident in more than one jurisdiction (for example, if they are incorporated in one jurisdiction but are managed in another), as the issue of residence in a jurisdiction is one of the domestic law in question. Where this is the case, if there is a double tax treaty in force between the jurisdictions in which the company is dual resident, the treaty may contain a 'tie-breaker' provision allocating residence, and therefore the primary right to tax the company, to one or other jurisdiction. If there is no treaty the company may be subject to tax in each jurisdiction.

How does an offshore fund become UK tax resident?

14.27 The following discussion assumes that there is no tax treaty in place between the UK and the place of incorporation of the offshore fund whose residence is in question. In practice, most offshore funds are incorporated in low tax jurisdictions with which there is no treaty that deals with these issues.

14.28 *Taxation of Hedge Funds – An Overview*

14.28 The basic rule is that a company will be resident in the UK if *central management and control* of the company is exercised in the UK.

14.29 Central management and control should be distinguished from the day-to-day running of the fund. Central management and control is the strategic decision-making process, and would generally include matters such as the setting and regular review of the investment policies and strategies of the fund and determining whether the fund should appoint a new investment manager. This contrasts with the day-to-day running which would include decisions such as whether or not to buy or sell a particular investment and which will usually be delegated to the investment manager.

14.30 Central management and control will normally be exercised by the board of directors of the fund, but could in appropriate circumstances be exercised by any other person (for example, the fund's investment manager).

14.31 UK tax residence is a question of fact and it will be necessary to show in each case that central management and control is genuinely exercised outside the UK.

Central management and control

Practical pointers

14.32 In identifying where the central management and control of a fund is exercised, the starting point will be its board of directors or equivalent. However, it will be necessary to take into account the system of company management under the law of the country of incorporation.

14.33 Normally the fund's constitution will give the board the relevant powers and, in considering the residence of the fund, the location of its board meetings is the best place to begin.

14.34 However, it is not automatic that residence will be in the jurisdiction in which board meetings are normally held, most obviously because the board may not in practice be exercising central management and control. Two questions in particular will be relevant:

- Does the board have any real discretion, or is it only allowed to take decisions within narrow parameters set down by (for example) the promoters of the fund? If its discretion is restricted, it may not be exercising central management and control.
- Is the board truly taking decisions when it meets? It may be merely rubber-stamping the decisions of those to whom it has delegated powers, or alternatively its members may take decisions in the UK before flying offshore for a meeting whose only purpose is presentational.

Restrictions on the discretion of the board

14.35 The question of restrictions which may be imposed on the board of a fund is a difficult one in the context of determining tax residence. It is obviously appropriate that investment objectives or other guidelines (eg

Tax residence considerations **14.41**

restrictions on borrowing) should exist. These will be incorporated into the prospectus or other document under which the fund's shares are offered to investors. These determine the parameters of the business which the fund is established to carry on, and which it is the directors' responsibility to manage.

14.36 HM Revenue and Customs ('HMRC') have issued guidance[1] on the general issue of influence by shareholders or other persons, which they acknowledge is a difficult matter.

[1] See HMRC Statement of Practice 1/90 and the guidance in HMRC's International Manual at INTM120000 et seq.

14.37 It seems safe to conclude that, in the case of a fund, the limits on the board's discretion imposed by the terms of the prospectus will not compromise the independence of the board. The non-UK residence status of the fund may, however, be called into doubt if the board is simply authorising actions already determined by the fund's promoters in the UK.

14.38 The manager, investment manager or administrator of the fund, as well as its UK promoters, may be considered to exercise the central management and control of the fund. The Court of Appeal decision in the case of *Wood and another v Holden (Inspector of Taxes)*[1] provides guidance on when the decision-making functions of the board of an offshore company may be 'usurped', in that case by the board of its UK parent, so that the central management and control of the company is exercised in the UK. The Court of Appeal drew a distinction between a third party merely influencing the decisions of the board, a third party dictating the decisions of the board, and a third party usurping central management and control.

[1] [2006] EWCA Civ 26, [2006] STC 443.

14.39 The case of *Laerstate BV v Revenue and Customs Commissioners*[1] provides an example of an individual usurping the management functions of the board to the extent that it was found that the individual exercised central management and control.

[1] [2009] UKFTT 209 (TC), [2009] SFTD 551.

14.40 The ruling in the *Holden* case makes it unlikely that the decision-making functions of the board of the fund could be said to have been usurped by the fund's UK promoters or investment manager (or others), even if it customarily acts in accordance with the wishes of any such person, provided that the board does not merely rubber-stamp the decisions of such persons. The board must, however, be provided with sufficient information to be able to decide whether to follow the advice of the fund's advisers such as its investment manager.

14.41 The *Holden* case also shows that, provided the taxpayer can provide evidence indicating that the company was not UK resident, such as proof that the company was incorporated offshore and board meetings were truly held, and minutes signed, outside the UK, the burden of proof will shift to HMRC to show that in reality central management and control was exercised in the UK.

14.42 *Taxation of Hedge Funds – An Overview*

Delegation of discretion

14.42 The constitution of a fund may permit the board to authorise individual directors or set up committees to take decisions on its behalf. This should be avoided unless the director is resident, and carries out his duties, outside the UK or the committee meets outside the UK and is not comprised of a majority of UK resident directors.

14.43 The appointment of a manager, investment manager or administrator of the fund does not contravene this principle provided that the duties delegated do not amount to central management and control. The board must retain the overall responsibility for the setting and regular review of the fund's investment policies and strategies and determining whether the fund should appoint new investment managers.

Location of real decision-making process

14.44 HMRC may be sceptical that board meetings are anything more than a rubber-stamping process if a majority of the board of directors are UK resident and are not themselves resident in the jurisdiction where board meetings regularly take place.

14.45 If, for example, a majority of the directors of a fund live and work in the UK but fly out to Jersey every three months for meetings, it will be difficult to convince HMRC, should they review the position, that the directors are not communicating with each other and discussing the business of the fund when in the UK, so that the board meetings are purely presentational. It is not sufficient for the board merely to meet in an offshore jurisdiction, it must also actually exercise central management and control there – in other words, the real strategic decisions must be taken offshore.

14.46 If the management of the fund is carried out outside board meetings, it is necessary to look at where and by whom the high level decisions are made, even if this is contrary to the fund's constitution.

14.47 The *Laerstate* case emphasised the need to look at the whole course of a company's business rather than identifying and considering specific instances of purported management. Mere physical acts such as signing resolutions and documents are not sufficient to constitute management and should be considered as part of a wider decision-making process.

14.48 HMRC may also be sceptical that board meetings are the real decision-making forum if many board members lack expertise and experience in investment management so that they are not in a position to reach reasoned and well-informed decisions on matters relating to the fund's investment policies and strategies. For example, if the board of a futures and options fund contains one UK resident derivatives specialist and four Cayman residents with no knowledge of the field, HMRC may contend that central management and control is being exercised by the UK resident individual.

14.49 The use of pre-drafted board minutes at board meetings will not necessarily affect the location of the fund's central management and control. However, care should be taken that such minutes are used merely as an agenda for discussion and that all of the issues and items contained in them are fully discussed at the meeting and documented. It is important that any such minutes are not merely 'rubber-stamped' by the directors, as this may cast doubt on where real control of the fund lies.

What to do in practice

14.50 Residence questions are rarely clear cut. There is invariably a great element of subjectivity and one's 'gut reaction' as to where a fund is actually run is often a good guide. However, by adopting the following guidelines the risk of a successful claim by HMRC that the fund has become UK tax resident can be substantially reduced:

- The board of directors should have sufficient expertise and experience in investment management among its members to be in a position to reach reasoned and well-informed decisions on matters relating to the fund's investment policies and strategies.
- The board of directors should have sufficient information to make strategic management decisions and should be kept fully informed of fund developments.
- The board of directors should hold board meetings regularly (ie at least quarterly) and should hold all meetings and make all decisions affecting the fund outside the UK.
- The majority of the board of directors and the majority of those directors attending board meetings should be resident outside the UK and no board meeting should be quorate without a non-UK majority being present.
- The meetings of the board of directors should be fully and accurately minuted, and board minutes should be sufficiently detailed to demonstrate the board's decision-making process, rather than showing the board rubber-stamping requests or advice from the UK.
- The fund should fully document all board decisions affecting policy, management or strategy to demonstrate that they have been duly considered.
- All fund documents and records (including minute books) should, as a matter of best practice, be kept outside the UK. If they are kept in the UK, they must be within the fund's control.
- All documents to which the fund is a party should be executed outside the UK. It is helpful if they can be prepared outside the UK as well, particularly in the case of board minutes, but this is often impractical (for example, if an agreement is governed by English law, the company will need English lawyers to draft it).
- Agreements and documents to effect board decisions should be executed by non-UK resident board members only outside the UK.
- The fund's constitution and/or code of governance should ideally prohibit:
  - the appointment of a majority of UK resident directors;
  - the appointment of UK resident individuals as alternates for directors who are non-UK resident;
  - the holding of any meetings of the directors (or any committee thereof) in the UK;

14.50 *Taxation of Hedge Funds – An Overview*

- any meeting of the directors (or any committee thereof) from being quorate if a majority of the directors (or their alternates) present in person or by telephone are resident in the UK;
- the holding of board meetings by telephone or video conferencing link (at least where a majority of the directors are telephoning from the UK) – however, see the guidance below if a fund wishes to retain the flexibility to have remote participation in board meetings;
- the exercise of any aspect of central management and control of the fund by any director resident in the UK other than at formal board meetings held outside the UK;
- the delegation of central management and control of the fund to persons resident in the UK; and
- the appointment of an agent or attorney of the fund in the UK whose powers extend beyond the implementation of the board's decisions without discretion.
• If the fund's directors act on the advice of UK advisers, the directors should consider all such advice objectively and should decline to follow that advice as they see fit. Any advice received should be reviewed, as appropriate, by local advisers.

Guidance on telephone and video conferencing

14.51 From a UK tax perspective alone, it may be preferable for a fund to ensure that its constitution does not permit board meetings to take place by telephone or video conferencing link or, at least, does not permit any director to attend board meetings by telephone or video conferencing from the UK. However, it is not always possible for an individual to travel to a board meeting and a director may wish to participate by telephone or video conferencing link.

14.52 Where unavoidable, remote participation in board meetings is possible from the UK as an occasional occurrence, provided that it is permitted under the law of the jurisdiction in which the fund is incorporated and under the provisions of the fund's articles of association or equivalent constitutional documents and it does not prejudice the location of the fund's central management and control. If there is any doubt as to whether it is appropriate for the director to participate, he should not do so. It may be possible for him to appoint an alternate director who is able to attend the meeting in person.

14.53 To ensure that the above requirements are complied with, the following rules should be considered:

• a director's participation by telephone or video conferencing link from the UK should be avoided unless the board meeting would be quorate without the participation of that director;
• the directors physically present at the board meeting should themselves have the necessary experience and abilities to make decisions on the fund's business affairs and the matters that are the subject of the meeting;
• the telephone call or video link should be initiated from the board meeting rather than by the individual; and

- written board minutes should be taken of each meeting and signed outside the UK by the meeting's chairman (who should therefore be outside the UK).

14.54 To some extent the application of the above rules will differ according to the type of business in question. Where a fund holds regular board meetings to discuss various issues from time to time, it may not be fatal if one meeting is held at which the director attending remotely is the most experienced in relation to the particular issue in question, although it is always desirable to avoid this where possible.

UK tax residence safe harbour

14.55 During the process for adoption of the Alternative Investment Fund Managers Directive[1] ('AIFMD'), concerns were expressed that the expanded duties of alternative investment fund managers ('AIFMs') could prejudice the location of a non-UK AIF's central management and control for UK tax purposes, resulting in such an AIF (where it is a corporate entity) being treated as resident in the UK for UK tax purposes should it appoint a UK AIFM.

[1] Directive 2011/61/EU of 8 June 2011.

14.56 To address this concern, the residence safe harbour in section 363A of the Taxation (International and Other Provisions) Act 2010 (that previously applied to corporate UCITS) was extended by the Finance Act 2014, with effect from 5 December 2013, to also apply to corporate AIFs, such that where a corporate offshore fund which constitutes a UCITS or an AIF established outside the UK would otherwise be treated as UK tax resident, that offshore fund will not generally be treated as UK tax resident (unless it falls within certain limited categories of 'excluded entity').

14.57 Although the extension of the safe harbour is helpful in clarifying the position where a UK AIFM has been appointed, the safe harbour goes wider than just this situation, and would in principle enable an AIF's board to take decisions in the UK without prejudicing the AIF's non-UK resident status. However, this is not typically viewed as advisable, given that other UK tax (such as VAT) and non-tax consequences may arise if relevant decisions are regularly taken in the UK.

14.58 To the extent that the UK AIFM's activities on behalf of the non-UK AIF amount to trading for UK tax purposes, notwithstanding the extension of the safe harbour, it will remain necessary to confirm that the provisions of the UK 'investment manager exemption' (or, in certain circumstances, a relevant double tax treaty) apply to avoid trading profits arising in the UK being subject to UK taxation.

14.59 *Taxation of Hedge Funds – An Overview*

E UK TAXATION OF THE FUND – 'TRADING IN THE UK' CONSIDERATIONS

Introduction

14.59 A company which is resident outside the UK is in principle liable to UK tax in respect of:

- UK source investment income (eg dividends on UK equities, interest paid on bonds issued by UK companies);
- profits from a trade, profession or vocation carried on within the UK; and
- capital gains realised on assets held for the purposes of a trade, profession or vocation carried on in the UK by the non-resident through a branch, agency or other permanent establishment in the UK.

14.60 Where a non-resident corporate fund has a permanent establishment in the UK, profits of the trade carried on through that permanent establishment will be subject to UK corporation tax. A company's 'permanent establishment' is a fixed place of business, such as a branch, through which the business of the company is carried on, or an agent acting on its behalf which has and habitually exercises authority to do business on behalf of the company, other than an agent of independent status. The permanent establishment is liable to the same extent as the non-resident company to file tax returns and pay any corporation tax due in respect of the non-resident company's profits arising through the permanent establishment.

14.61 A person providing only investment advice and not carrying out, or arranging to be carried out, investment transactions will not normally constitute a permanent establishment through whom a trade is being carried on.

14.62 Where a non-resident corporate fund does not have a UK permanent establishment, its profits, to the extent arising from a trade carried on within the UK, would instead be within the charge to income tax (at the basic rate only). However, where a non-resident company is not within the charge to corporation tax in respect of its trading profits, by reason of satisfying the conditions of the 'investment manager exemption'[1] in respect of such profits, those profits are also exempted from the charge to income tax. Accordingly, no further reference is made to the distinct charge to income tax on trading profits in this chapter.

[1] See para **14.67** below.

What amounts to 'trading'?

14.63 Whether a fund is carrying on a trade (as opposed to holding investments) will be a question of fact. A number of factors ('the badges of trade') are taken into account, such as the motive for the transaction, the subject matter of the transaction (in particular, whether it is an income producing asset), and the period for which it is held before disposal.

14.64 HMRC guidance[1] indicates that the active management of an investment portfolio of shares, bonds and money market instruments, such as bills, floating rate notes and commercial paper, does not constitute a trade, although each case should be considered on its facts.

[1] See HMRC Statement of Practice 1/01 (as amended), para 19.

14.65 Previously there was considerable uncertainty as to the tax treatment of transactions in derivatives such as futures and options, as well as short positions. Guidance has since clarified that HMRC view short positions as conceptually the same as long positions and synthetic positions as conceptually the same as real positions. In other words, a short or synthetic position will constitute investment and not trading to the extent that the equivalent long or real position, as applicable, would amount to investment.

14.66 Furthermore, to the extent that a financial future or option is used to hedge a transaction which itself constitutes investment, that hedging transaction should also amount to investment. Notwithstanding this guidance, the activities of many hedge funds are such that there may be at least some element that could risk being treated as trading, and it is therefore prudent to assume that this may be the case and structure accordingly.

The investment manager exemption

14.67 Where an offshore corporate fund is or may be trading for UK tax purposes, the principal exemption from charge that would be relevant is the 'investment manager exemption' ('IME'). An investment manager will not be assessable as a UK representative in respect of the trading income of the fund if that trading income derives from 'investment transactions' carried out in the course of the business of the investment manager as an investment manager and further requirements are met.

14.68 Until the enactment of the Finance Act 2008 ('FA 2008'), categories of qualifying investment transactions were defined in a combination of primary and secondary legislation, as expanded upon by guidance, and could not easily be updated (for example, to include new product types).

14.69 FA 2008 gave HMRC the power to make regulations designating certain transactions as investment transactions. The current regulations made under this power are the Investment Manager (Investment Transactions) Regulations 2014 (the 'Regulations'), which came into force on 8 April 2014. The Regulations in turn reference the consolidated 'white list' of permissible transactions now contained in the Investment Transactions (Tax) Regulations 2014[1], and replace the previous standalone Investment Manager (Specified Transactions) Regulations 2009.

[1] SI 2014/685.

14.70 Under the consolidated 'white list', most common transactions undertaken by hedge funds will be within the definition of a qualifying investment transaction. In particular, the following are covered:

(a)   Any transaction in stocks and shares.

14.70 *Taxation of Hedge Funds – An Overview*

- (b) Any transaction in a 'relevant contract', which covers a wide range of derivative transactions. A transaction which relates to land can only be a relevant contract where it uses an index that is publicly accessible, comprised of a significant number of properties and not maintained by the fund, the manager or connected persons. Where a contract provides for delivery of any property that is not a qualifying investment transaction (such as a physical commodity), that contract will not be a relevant contract where the property is delivered.
- (c) Any transaction which results in a fund becoming a party to a loan relationship or a related transaction in respect of a loan relationship. This includes transactions involving lending debts where the fund stands as debtor or creditor, or simple debts on which interest is payable to the fund or on which exchange gains or losses or discount arise to the fund (in the latter case, where the fund acts as creditor). A 'related transaction' in respect of a loan relationship is any disposal or acquisition (in whole or in part) of rights or liabilities under that loan relationship.
- (d) Any transaction in units in a collective investment scheme.
- (e) Any transaction in securities of any description not falling within (a)–(d) above.
- (f) Any transaction consisting in the buying and selling of any foreign currency.
- (g) Any transaction in a carbon emission trading product.
- (h) Any transaction in rights under a life insurance policy.

14.71 FA 2008 also removed the 'cliff edge' whereby previously if a fund entered into a trading transaction through its UK investment manager that was not a permitted investment transaction, this could result in the loss of the IME in respect of all trading transactions of the fund in the relevant accounting period, unless (by HMRC concession) the non-qualifying transaction was minor or made inadvertently and the profits from the transaction were charged to UK tax. The result was that a single non-qualifying trading transaction could have the effect of bringing the whole of a fund's UK trading profits for that accounting period into charge to UK tax. For accounting periods ending on or after 21 July 2008, only profits of non-qualifying trading transactions will be subject to UK tax, subject to satisfying the other requirements of the IME.

14.72 Notwithstanding these changes to the application of the IME, it is important that a UK-based investment manager analyses proposed transactions to see whether these fall within the scope of 'investment transactions', or whether steps should be taken to ringfence these from the activities of the wider fund, for example by undertaking them through a subsidiary of the fund. The latter approach may be particularly relevant if the investment manager is considering the problematic transaction types referred to above, such as spot transactions in physical commodities, transactions relating to land and insurance/reinsurance transactions.

14.73 The further requirements of the IME are:

- the transactions must be carried out in the ordinary course of the business of providing investment management services carried on by the investment manager;

'Trading in the UK' considerations **14.77**

- the investment manager must be remunerated at not less than the customary rate for that kind of business[1];
- the investment manager must be acting in an independent capacity[2]; and
- the investment manager must satisfy the 20% test[3].

[1] See paras **14.74–14.77** below.
[2] See paras **14.78–14.83** below.
[3] See paras **14.84–14.88** below.

Customary remuneration

14.74 There is no statutory definition of 'customary'. HMRC's basic approach is to treat 'customary' as if it means 'arm's length'. Consequently, HMRC will apply the OECD Transfer Pricing Guidelines in determining whether an investment manager is remunerated at the customary rate. HMRC will not only look at the gross remuneration structure between the fund and the investment manager in isolation for these purposes, they will also examine whether the net effect of arrangements between the investment manager and other persons is such that the investment manager receives remuneration which is below the arm's length rate. HMRC will treat amounts payable by the fund or the investment manager for services provided to or in connection with the fund as reducing the remuneration below the customary rate unless these amounts can be shown to be an arm's length rate.

14.75 The onus is on the investment manager to support its position with proper documentation evidencing a factual functional analysis and an acceptable transfer pricing methodology. Provided this documentation and methodology are in place, HMRC will, in the event that they successfully challenge a structure, permit an adjustment to the investment manager's tax return to be made without regarding there to be a failure to meet the customary rate test and the fund will continue to satisfy the IME. It is, therefore, important for the investment manager to review its fee structure and transfer pricing arrangements to ensure that it can demonstrate that the customary rate test is satisfied.

14.76 HMRC acknowledge that certain commonly encountered remuneration structures need not prejudice the customary rate test, provided these are otherwise properly treated for tax purposes, including:

- rebated, reduced or zero fees for unconnected investors, provided such arrangements are for genuine commercial reasons (eg to 'seed investors'); and
- deferral of management or performance fees, or reinvestment of such fees in the fund.

14.77 To meet the customary rate test, fees payable to the investment manager should be recognised for UK tax purposes when earned. This includes where payments of fees are deferred or reinvested in the fund.

14.78 *Taxation of Hedge Funds – An Overview*

Independent capacity

14.78 The investment manager must be acting in an 'independent capacity' in order for the IME to apply. HMRC guidance[1] indicates that this may be achieved in various ways.

[1] See HMRC Statement of Practice 1/01 (as amended), para 35 et seq.

14.79 For a non-resident fund, the independent capacity test will be met if either:

- it is a widely held collective fund (the 'widely held' test); or
- if not a widely held collective fund, the fund is being actively marketed with the intention of it becoming a widely held collective fund or it is being wound up or dissolved (the 'actively marketed' test).

14.80 A fund will be 'widely held' for these purposes if either no majority interest in the fund is ultimately held by five or fewer persons (with connected persons), or no single person (with connected persons) has an interest of more than 20%. In the case of a fund which is newly established (and so may, for example, need to create a track record), a period of 18 months is allowed for it to become 'widely held'. To be 'actively marketed' there must be evidence of ongoing genuine attempts to obtain third party investment and the subscription terms must not be prohibitive or discriminatory for that type of business. It is therefore important that the investment manager retains good records of the steps which it takes to obtain third party investment, for example records of meetings with all current and potential investors, and copies of placing or distribution agreements with third parties. The requirement for the fund to be actively marketed should not be taken to imply that the fund must be marketed in an uncommercial way.

14.81 Where neither the 'widely held' nor 'actively marketed' tests are met, the fund will need to establish that either:

- the services provided by the investment manager to the fund and its connected persons form less than 70% of the investment manager's business, either by reference to fees or some other measure where that would be more appropriate – if in the first 18 months from the start of a new investment management business the services provided to the fund exceed 70% of the investment manager's business, this requirement will still be met if the services are consistently below 70% in subsequent periods; or
- where such services represent more than 70% of the services provided to the non-resident and connected persons 18 months from the start of a new investment management business, this was for reasons outside of the investment manager's control and the investment manager had taken all reasonable steps to reduce this.

14.82 Where none of the above safe harbours are satisfied, it will be necessary to consider the overall circumstances of the relationship between the fund and the investment manager when assessing whether the independent capacity test is satisfied.

14.83 HMRC guidance[1] confirms that for master-feeder structures and umbrella funds it is the beneficial ownership of the feeder fund(s) or umbrella fund (as the case may be) that HMRC will look to in determining whether the independent capacity test is met.

[1] See HMRC Statement of Practice 1/01 (as amended), paras 42 and 43.

The 20% test

14.84 The '20% test' requires that the investment manager and persons connected with it should intend, in respect of a 'qualifying period', not to be entitled, directly or indirectly, to more than 20% of the income of the fund in respect of which exemption is sought which arises during this period. If the intention, although existing, is not fulfilled, the failure will be ignored if it arises due to matters outside the control of the investment manager, provided that the investment manager has taken all reasonable steps to fulfil that intention. This relaxation may enable the 20% test to be met in circumstances where it would otherwise be failed, such as:

- where the investment manager and/or connected persons have seeded the fund at launch, with the intention that their interest(s) would be redeemed or sufficiently diluted by third party investment within a short space of time, but due to market conditions, sufficient third party investment has not proved forthcoming; or
- where due to adverse market conditions, the fund suffers substantial third party redemptions.

14.85 The 'qualifying period' is either the accounting period of the fund in which the income arises or a period of not more than five years, including two or more complete accounting periods of the fund, provided that this five-year period also includes the accounting period in which the income arises.

14.86 The 20% test is concerned with entitlements arising through shareholdings, partnership interests and similar arrangements. Management and performance fees will normally be ignored, as they would be treated as deductible in computing the fund's taxable trading income. Profit or incentive allocations (for example, within a limited partnership feeder) are also treated in this way, provided they are recognised by the investment manager as fee income (or similarly treated where paid to an overseas affiliate).

14.87 If the 20% test is not met, exemption will be lost only for the proportion of the income of the fund to which the investment manager (or its connected persons) is entitled. This could, therefore, exclude the benefit of the exemption in respect of any investment transactions carried out to the extent that related entities, or certain participants in the investment manager or related entities, are investors in the fund and together are entitled to more than 20% of the fund's income.

14.88 The definition of a 'connected person' is wide and would include the fund itself if the investment manager and related entities or individuals have voting control of the fund. This would seem to have the consequence that the whole of the fund's income arising through the investment manager would not have the benefit of the IME. It is not certain that HMRC would take the point,

14.88 *Taxation of Hedge Funds – An Overview*

but best advice must be that the investment manager and related entities or individuals should have no more than blocking control in respect of certain limited matters at shareholders' meetings.

F UK TAXATION OF INVESTORS

Introduction

14.89 The regime for the taxation of investments in offshore funds is set out in the Offshore Funds (Tax) Regulations 2009[1]. The regime applies for periods of account of offshore funds that commence on or after 1 December 2009 (subject to transitional provisions).

[1] SI 2009/3001.

14.90 Given the increased interest from UK individual investors for investments that qualify for capital gains treatment (now generally taxed at up to 20%) rather than income treatment (taxed at up to 45%), the regime is of material importance to managers and promoters of offshore funds, including hedge funds. In order to achieve capital gains treatment, an offshore fund must qualify as a 'reporting fund' throughout an investor's relevant period of ownership (or qualify as a 'distributing fund' for periods of ownership before the 2009 regime took effect).

14.91 For UK corporate and tax-exempt investors, obtaining reporting fund status is less important although may still be relevant, for example, if a corporate investor has capital losses available against which only chargeable gains can be offset.

Definition of offshore fund

14.92 The definition of an offshore fund is a characteristics based definition, whereby a fund is an 'offshore fund' if it is a 'mutual fund' and is resident or established outside the UK. Funds structured as bodies corporate, unit trust schemes and contractual arrangements are within the rules.

14.93 The definition of a 'mutual fund' for these purposes almost entirely mirrors the UK regulatory definition of a collective investment scheme. To be a mutual fund, the purposes or effect of the arrangements constituting the fund must be to enable participants to participate in the acquisition, holding, management or disposal of property or to receive profits or income therefrom, and the participants must not have day-to-day control of management of the property. In addition, the 'reasonable investor' in the fund must expect to be able to realise its investment by reference to either the fund's net asset value or an index. Truly closed-ended funds may be within the scope of the definition of an offshore fund depending on the way in which they are structured. However, there are some exclusions from the definition of a mutual fund, which include companies with no fixed life and fixed-life companies where none of the assets of the fund are income producing.

14.94 It should be assumed that a typical open-ended offshore corporate hedge fund will be an offshore fund for these purposes.

14.95 A fund or sub-fund (in respect of an umbrella fund) if it has a single class of shares, or each class of shares where a fund or sub-fund has multiple share classes, is treated as a separate offshore fund if it falls within the definition. References to 'offshore fund' or 'fund' in this section should be read accordingly.

14.96 Where a fund is an offshore fund that falls to be treated as a 'bond fund' for relevant purposes (ie a fund that invests more than 60% of its assets in cash, debt securities or similar assets), distributions by that fund (including deemed distributions of reportable income where it is a reporting fund) will be taxed for UK purposes in the hands of UK individuals as interest and not dividend income. A similar position may apply to UK corporate investors[1].

[1] See the Corporation Tax Act 2009, Pt 6, Ch 3 and SI 2009/3001, reg 98.

Key aspects of the reporting fund regime

14.97 The reporting fund regime is an elective regime. The manager of an offshore fund may make a one-off application to HMRC for the fund to have reporting fund status, subject to meeting certain requirements, either in advance or, to facilitate the establishment of new funds, up to the later of (a) the end of the first accounting period in respect of which the fund wishes to be a reporting fund or (b) three months from the date the interests are first made available to UK investors. Reporting fund status can then be maintained, unless the reporting fund commits serious breaches of the reporting fund requirements. An offshore fund that does not elect to become a reporting fund is treated as a non-reporting fund.

14.98 UK investors that invest in reporting funds will be subject to UK income tax on actual and deemed distributions of income (reportable income) from the offshore fund but should benefit from capital gains treatment on a sale or redemption of their interests in that fund.

14.99 An offshore fund that elects to become a reporting fund will be required to report its income to its investors and to HMRC annually, but it will not be required to make actual distributions of income to investors, since the taxation of UK investors is based on the 'reportable income' of the offshore fund attributable to their shareholding, whether or not distributed. This avoids any need to have special distribution share classes to cater for UK investors, since they will be able to receive favourable capital gains treatment on the disposal of their shares without the offshore fund having to make actual distributions of income to investors. However, if a reporting fund makes no or insufficient distributions to investors for a period of account of the reporting fund, UK investors may have an unfunded liability to UK income tax in respect of their share of the reportable income of the offshore fund. In addition, some investors may wish to invest in distribution rather than accumulation shares for their own investment or other reasons.

14.100 'Reportable income' is to be calculated on the basis of accounts for the offshore fund prepared under International Accounting Standards ('IAS') or

14.100 *Taxation of Hedge Funds – An Overview*

another generally accepted accounting practice ('GAAP') acceptable to HMRC. The reportable income will need to be calculated on the basis of the 'total comprehensive income for the period' under IAS or an equivalent under a different GAAP, adjusted (amongst other things) for capital items that would be recognised in the statement of total return were the Investment Management Association's Statement of Recommended Practice for the financial statements of UK authorised funds to apply to the fund in question (ie profits and losses on investments).

14.101 Income from transactions that are trading in nature will typically give rise to reportable income. However, 'genuinely diversely owned' reporting funds that are 'equivalent' to diversely owned UK authorised investment funds can have certainty that gains realised on certain types of investments included on a 'white list' of investment assets are not treated as trading income and so are ignored in calculating the reportable income of the fund. A hedge fund will generally not be viewed as equivalent for these purposes. Even if the 'white list' does not apply, it may be open to a hedge fund, depending on its investment strategy, to take the position that its activities are not trading in nature, although this approach is not without risk.

14.102 The approach to the calculation of reportable income is intended to reduce the administrative burden for funds and their managers and administrators, but the rules that apply in relation to calculating the reportable income of a reporting fund that invests in other funds remain complex, for example in the context of multi-tier structures, and the obligation to report to investors and to HMRC presents administrative obligations and practical complexities.

Other tax considerations for UK investors

14.103 A number of other UK tax provisions may be relevant to UK investors in an offshore corporate hedge fund, including the following:

- *The 'transfer of assets abroad' rules*: Under these rules, undistributed income profits arising to the fund may be taxed on UK investors in limited circumstances.
- *The 'section 13' rules*: Where an offshore fund is closely held, capital gains (although not trading income) arising to the fund may be taxed on a UK investor who has a 25% or greater interest (together with connected persons) in the fund, although this should not apply in the case of a bona fide investment in an offshore hedge fund.
- *The 'controlled foreign company' rules*: Where a UK corporation tax paying investor has a 25% or greater interest (together with connected persons) in the fund, and the fund is controlled by UK residents, income arising to the fund may be apportioned to that investor and be subject to UK corporation tax, subject to the application of certain exceptions.
- *The 'bond fund' rules*: Where a UK corporation tax paying investor invests in a 'bond fund', ie a fund that invests more than 60% of its assets in cash, debt securities or similar assets, the investor's interest in the fund will be treated as a right under a creditor loan relationship and the investor will be taxed (or will be relieved from taxation) depending on fair value movements of the investment in the fund, which would result in tax liabilities arising in respect of unrealised gains. In addition, any distributions will be taxed as interest income.

14.104 For certain categories of UK investor, other tax considerations may be relevant, such as the annual deemed disposal rules that apply to an insurance company holding interests in an offshore fund.

Chapter 15

KEY FUND TERMS

Dale Gabbert, Partner, Simmons & Simmons and Andrew Wylie, Partner and Head of Investment Funds, DLA Piper

A	Introduction	15.1
B	Management and performance fees	15.2
C	Other common terms	15.26

A INTRODUCTION

15.1 As explained in earlier chapters, the term 'hedge fund' embraces a very broad range of structures, investment techniques and liquidity profiles. Accordingly, there are many fund-specific terms. Indeed, the only limits on the terms that can be imposed are the legal and regulatory parameters, the ingenuity of the sponsors (and, hopefully, their advisers) and, most importantly, what is acceptable to investors. There are, however, some terms that appear frequently and it is important to be familiar with them. Many of these terms are simply adaptations of common fund concepts and are not unique to hedge funds. This chapter explores these terms, starting with the management and performance fees, which are fairly specific to hedge funds, and then considers more generic terms, many of which are not unique to hedge funds and are merely relevant to many hedge funds.

B MANAGEMENT AND PERFORMANCE FEES

15.2 The primary motivation of a hedge fund is, of course, profit. Hedge funds have become known in the popular media not just because of the daring nature of the bets made by certain funds, such as George Soros's Quantum Fund betting against sterling on Black Wednesday (during the European Exchange Rate Mechanism crisis), but also for the fees paid to their managers. An understanding of the hedge fund industry starts with an understanding of the economics that have driven its establishment and growth.

15.3 Why do traders leave investment banks and start their own hedge funds? There are presumably a number of relevant factors, some of which motivate different people to different degrees. Nevertheless, a significant factor is financial rewards. Traders in banks and financial institutions are generally paid almost entirely by way of bonus, having a small (in City terms) annual salary and the expectation of making a multiple of that (and for senior traders, a very high multiple) at the end of their employer's financial year, once the firm's overall profits have been ascertained. As an employer, investment banks probably pay more of their profits to their workers than any other business. But before starting to think that this is some kind of socialist enterprise it is necessary to understand that this is not a utilitarian approach 'from each according to his

15.3 Key Fund Terms

ability, to each according to his needs' but rather according to perceived performance relative to one's peers. The methods of calculating and paying bonuses vary between institutions, but most start with an allocation to a business unit based upon its overall profitability and then divide that business unit's allocation amongst the employees who work in that business unit.

15.4 The highest paid traders in a bank are the ones who trade the bank's own capital for profit, which is known as proprietary trading. They are frequently responsible for generating a significant amount of a bank's profits. A proprietary trader's bonus will typically be calculated as a percentage of what he makes for the bank in the relevant financial year. If a trader does not generate any profit he will not be paid a bonus and may well be made redundant. During financial crises, the bonus system of remuneration is often criticised for allegedly promoting speculation because it creates a strong upside participation (because it is typically calculated by reference to profits generated by the relevant trader) with a limited downside – the trader doesn't participate in any losses which the bank may suffer, the trader simply risks the loss of his job. For a trader who is already financially secure because of past bonuses or whose services are likely to be in demand notwithstanding one poor year, the downside of making large bets is effectively quite limited. Of course, many banks make a large part of their bonuses payable in stock and use other devices to try to lock in key staff. Nevertheless, the City remains fundamentally driven by short-term performance. Whether the annual bonus system is a cause or an effect, or a bit of both, is an interesting debate which falls outside the scope of this book.

15.5 Coming back to the initial question posed: why does a successful trader leave the safety and security of a financial institution that pays him a considerable amount of money and offers him financial, intellectual and personnel resources and an infrastructure that dwarfs that of all but the largest hedge funds? Ignoring personal reasons such as the desire to make one's own mark, be a master of one's own destiny or have some sort of legacy (each of which is a potent driver in itself), one reason is money. By leaving a bank and establishing a hedge fund one becomes an owner of the investment manager and ceases to be an employee. If the fund is successful that investment manager will earn extremely large amounts of money and the fund may even become valuable in its own right, becoming capable of being sold to another financial institution, or if it is very successful, listed on a stock exchange.

15.6 Even if one ignores the potential value being created in the investment manager, the rewards are still enticing. A typical hedge fund will charge a management fee and a performance fee. Historically, the management fee has typically been 2% per annum[1] and is calculated by reference to the amount of assets which the fund manages. While the fund is small it will therefore do little more than cover the costs of operating the investment manager, paying rent, staff, regulatory costs and the fees of service providers. Once the fund becomes large, however, the management fee can become a profit centre in itself (particularly if a manager manages a number of hedge funds) provided that manager costs are kept under control.

---

[1] The hedge fund industry is also experiencing pressure like the rest of the fund management industry. Increasingly, hedge funds are agreeing to management fees of about 1% per annum.

15.7 The real profit element is the performance fee. The performance fee is normally paid at least annually and is commonly 20% of the increase in the net asset value per share during the relevant performance period. For instance, if the starting net asset value per share were US$100 and the closing net asset value per share were US$200, the performance fee would be US$20 (being an amount equal to 20% of the US$100 increase). Assuming that the management fee covers the costs of operating the investment manager and the fund employs a similar amount of money in its strategies as a proprietary trader is allowed to bet in a bank, it is likely that the principal of a hedge fund will earn more money in that role than as the employee of a bank. In addition, institutions frequently impose a complex series of position limits and risk controls that hamper a trader's ability to maximise returns. Accordingly, it is often the case that a trader will conclude that he will generate a better return pursuing his strategy within his own fund rather than working for an employer. This, coupled with the potential enterprise value of the investment manager and the freedom that comes with running one's own funds, has caused a large number of traders to leave employment and establish their own hedge funds.

15.8 The performance fee distinguishes hedge funds from a large number of securities funds, many of which (particularly 'long only' funds) only charge management fees calculated by reference to assets under management and not on performance. Because of their absolute return nature and the perception that they offer enhanced returns, traditionally very few hedge funds have a benchmark or hurdle that they need to reach before they get paid a performance fee[1]. This means that a hedge fund receives 20% of profits regardless of the size of the profit, the difficulty in generating that profit or the opportunity cost to the investor of the capital allocated by it to that hedge fund.

[1] This position is, however, increasingly being challenged by the introduction of at least cash rate based hurdles (and other forms of hurdle).

15.9 Two factors make performance fees more complicated in practice for hedge funds: (i) the fact that hedge funds are almost always 'open-ended' (that is, investors can subscribe for and redeem their shares at periodic intervals), and (ii) the price at which shares can be bought from and sold to, or 'redeemed', by the fund fluctuates over time and is calculated by reference to the value of the fund's assets and liabilities from time to time.

15.10 This creates a number of issues. The first and most basic is that a hedge fund may lose money. Obviously if an investor subscribes for shares at launch at US$100 and a year later those shares are only worth US$80, that investor will not be required to pay a performance fee (and may well wonder why it is required to pay a management fee). If, however, the hedge fund recovers and net asset value per share increases the following year to US$120, that investor does not want to pay the hedge fund for merely having recovered a prior loss. In this example, it would be unfair if an investor which subscribed US$100 were required to pay the manager a performance fee in year two based on the increase from US$80 to US$120 because half of the fee would relate to the recouping of the first year's loss of US$20. Accordingly, most hedge funds include a 'high-water mark' in the methodology for calculating performance fees. As the name implies, this sets the basis for calculation as the highest price

15.10 Key Fund Terms

achieved at which a performance fee was last paid (or, if no performance fee has been paid since the fund was launched, the launch price).

15.11 It is worth bearing in mind that the high-water mark is only determined at the end of each performance period, so that the share price may have been higher than the ultimate high-water mark at some time during that performance fee calculation period. The high-water mark is therefore not the highest price achieved for the shares (because if no performance fee were calculated at the time the highest price was achieved, the previous highest price will not be set as the high-water mark). In the prior example, if a high-water mark were imposed the manager would only be entitled to the difference between the launch price of US$100 and the highest subsequent closing price of US$120, meaning that no fee would be paid for recouping the loss made in year one. Obviously, where the net asset value of the relevant hedge fund has declined significantly there may be little incentive for a manager to seek to perform unless the high-water mark is reset.

15.12 The second and more complex problem is that investors subscribe at different prices and the performance fee is paid based on the same net asset value per share at the end of a performance fee period, as compared to the high-water mark (or if there is no high-water mark in operation, the share price at the start of the performance period), regardless of the price at which each investor actually subscribed for its shares. Obviously this can be inequitable between shareholders. Imagine that a hedge fund calculates performance fees annually as 20% of the increase in the net asset value per share between 1 January and 31 December in each year. It allows subscriptions to occur quarterly. During the year the price of shares in the hedge fund fluctuates. Accordingly, investors which subscribed for shares in different quarters are likely to have paid different prices for their shares. In the absence of any adjustment mechanism, some investors will pay higher performance fees than others as a proportion of the profits which they have actually made on their shares (because the performance fee is calculated for and borne by the class of shares as a whole by reference to the difference in price between the net asset value on 1 January and 31 December in each year and not on the difference in the price paid by subscribers for the specific shares they have bought and the net asset value per share of those shares on 31 December in each year).

Example 1

On 1 January in a year the opening price for that year is US$100 and Investor A has 1,000 shares. On 31 March in that year the price has increased to US$200 and Investor B subscribes for 1,000 shares. On 31 December in that year the closing price for the year is US$200 per share (see Table 1). There is no equalisation method in place and the calculation of performance fees occurs annually by comparing the opening price and the closing price. The opening price was US$100 and the closing price was US$200. The performance fee per share is therefore US$20 (being 20% of the difference between the closing price and the opening price per share during the course of the year where that yields a positive amount) (see Table 2).

Management and performance fees 15.13

Table 1

Date	Investor A			Investor B		
	No of shares	Price per share (US$)	Value of shares (US$)	No of shares	Price per share (US$)	Value of shares (US$)
1 January	1,000	100	100,000	–	100	–
31 March	1,000	200	200,000	1,000	200	200,000
31 December	1,000	200	200,000	1,000	200	200,000

Table 2

	Investor A		Investor B	
	During performance period (US$)	During period of ownership (US$)	During performance period (US$)	During period of ownership (US$)
Increase/decrease per share	100	100	100	0
20% performance fee per share	20	20	20	20
Number of shares	1,000	1,000	1,000	1,000
Performance fee of 20%	20,000	20,000	20,000	0

Clearly, it would be unfair to apply the performance fee to the investor which subscribed for shares on 31 March of that year because it has not made a gain over the period because the shares ended the year at the same price as that investor paid for those shares. Investor A, however, has doubled its money before the deduction of fees.

15.13 The following example considers the opposite scenario:

Example 2
As before, the opening price on 1 January in a year is US$100 per share and Investor A subscribes for 1,000 shares. This time, however, the price on 31 March in that year has fallen to US$50 per share and Investor B subscribes for 1,000 shares. On 31 December in that year the closing price is US$100 per share. Without any form of equalisation no performance fee would be payable because the opening price and the closing price are the same: US$100 per share. This is unfair for a different reason – Investor B has doubled its money without paying a penny in performance fees. This is clearly unfair to the manager of the hedge fund and it is also unfair to Investor A because Investor B benefits from the manager's performance without remunerating the manager by way of a performance fee payment – Investor B is getting a 'free ride' (see Tables 3 and 4).

483

15.13 Key Fund Terms

Table 3

| | Investor A ||| Investor B |||
Date	No of shares	Price per share (US$)	Value of shares (US$)	No of shares	Price per share (US$)	Value of shares (US$)
1 January	1,000	100	100,000	–	100	–
31 March	1,000	50	50,000	1,000	50	50,000
31 December	1,000	100	100,000	1,000	100	100,000

Table 4

| | Investor A || Investor B ||
	During performance period (US$)	During period of ownership (US$)	During performance period (US$)	During period of ownership (US$)
Increase/decrease per share	0	0	0	50
20% performance fee per share	20	20	20	20
Number of shares	1,000	1,000	1,000	1,000
Performance fee of 20%	0	0	0	10,000

Series method

15.14 There are basically two methods for addressing equitably the fact that investors subscribe for shares in a hedge fund at different times and prices. First, simply make each shareholder pay fees on its own shares. This could be done by contract if the fees are paid by the shareholder itself, but they are not, they are borne by the class of shares for which that investor subscribes and therefore reduce the value of that class as they accrue and are paid out of the assets attributable to that class. Accordingly, the simplest and one of the most popular methods of dealing with this issue is simply to create a new share class or 'series' on each subscription date. There can be no underpayment or overpayment because of the difference in subscription prices during a performance fee period. Unsurprisingly, this is known as the 'series' method. This has the advantage of being an elegant solution the fairness of which is easy to demonstrate, and the disadvantage from an operational perspective that the hedge fund ends up with a large number of share classes, which is not ideal from an investor relations, marketing or administrative perspective. Provided that the share prices of the various classes continue to increase in value, it is possible to consolidate the various series once a performance fee is paid, so that the number of series will not exceed the number of subscription dates in a performance fee period.

Management and performance fees **15.16**

15.15 Funds typically issue each series of shares within a class at the same offer price per share, to simplify administration and accounting. In the following example, the hedge fund will issue each series of Class A shares at US$100 per share.

Example 3
On 1 January in a year 1,000 Class A shares, denominated as 'Series 1', are issued to Investor A at US$100 per share. Investor A has 1,000 Class A shares – Series 1 with a gross value of US$100,000. On 31 March in that year Investor B also subscribes for 1,000 Class A shares, for an offer price of US$100 per share, and the hedge fund issues a new series, Class A shares – Series 2. During the first quarter, the assets attributable to Series 1 have increased by 10%. Accordingly, on 31 March in that year the Series 1 shares of Investor A are worth US$110,000. The combined value of Class A at any time is the combined value of each series of Class A shares in issue, and on 31 March in that year is therefore US$210,000 (which comprises US$110,000 of assets acquired with Investor A's subscription and the cash subscription just received from Investor B of US$100,000).

15.16 In order to ensure that a hedge fund does not have ever-increasing series of shares, it will, wherever possible, consolidate the series of shares which it has issued in any given year into one series (known as the 'Lead Series') at the end of the year after the relevant hedge fund has paid the performance fee in respect of each series. This is achieved by converting the series other than the Lead Series into shares of the Lead Series based upon the price per share of the Lead Series.

Example 4
There are no further subscribers in that year and at the end of the year the assets attributable to Class A have increased by a further 10%. In consequence, the assets attributable to Series 1 are now worth US$121,000 and the assets attributable to Series 2 are now worth US$110,000 (ignoring performance fee accruals) (see Table 5). Accordingly, the Series 1 shares will bear a performance fee based on the difference between the aggregate subscription price of US$100,000 paid by Investor A for its Series 1 shares and their closing value of US$121,000, namely US$4,200, which is an amount equal to 20% of US$21,000. After deducting this from the closing value one arrives at a net asset value of US$116,800 after payment of the performance fee, which one divides by the number of Series 1 shares in issue (1,000) to yield a net asset value per Series 1 share on 1 January of the following year of US$116.80.

The assets attributable to Series 2 have also increased, from US$100,000 to US$110,000. Accordingly, the Series 2 shares will bear a performance fee based on the difference between the aggregate subscription price paid by Investor B for its shares of US$100,000 and the closing value of those shares of US$110,000, namely US$2,000, which is an amount equal to 20% of US$10,000. This leaves the assets attributable to Series 2 as US$108,000. Series 2 is then consolidated into Series 1 by subscribing that US$108,000 for Series 1 shares at the prevailing net asset value of Series 1 (after payment of performance fee) of US$116.80, which leaves Investor B with 924.6575

15.16 Key Fund Terms

shares of Series 1 on 1 January of the following year (and Investor A with its original holding of 1,000 Series 1 shares).

In this example, Series 1 is the 'Lead Series' because it is the series into which the other series are converted at the end of the performance fee period.

Table 5

	Class A shares – Series 1 (US$)	Class A shares – Series 2 (US$)
1 January	100,000	100,000
31 December	121,000	110,000
Increase in value	21,000	10,000
Performance fee of 20%	4,200	2,000

15.17 Note that it will not always be possible to consolidate each series in issue into the Lead Series at the end of the relevant performance fee period. For example, if the net asset value of the Class A shares in a hedge fund declines after that hedge fund has issued Series 1 shares, it will not be possible to consolidate Series 2 with Series 1 at the end of the performance fee period because, if that were to occur, the investor which holds Series 2 shares would not be able to offset its loss against any subsequent performance fee that would otherwise be payable in respect of the class of which its series forms part.

15.18 To illustrate this, the previous example is revised slightly to provide that over the final two quarters of the relevant year the value of the assets attributable to the hedge fund declines by 5%.

Example 5
The assets which are attributable to Series 1 are now worth US$104,500, and the assets which are attributable to Series 2 have declined below the amount subscribed for them and are now worth US$95,000 (ignoring performance fee accruals) (see Table 6). Accordingly, the Series 1 shares will bear a performance fee based on the difference between their aggregate subscription price of US$100,000 and their aggregate closing value of US$104,500, namely US$900, which is an amount equal to 20% of US$4,500. After deducting this from the closing value one arrives at an aggregate net asset value for those Series 1 shares of US$103,600 after payment of the performance fee, which one divides by the number of Series 1 shares in issue (1,000) to yield a net asset value per Series 1 share of US$103.60.

The assets attributable to Series 2, however, have declined from US$100,000 to US$95,000. Accordingly, the Series 2 shares have actually suffered a loss of US$5 per share. If they were consolidated into Series 1 that loss would be crystallised (because the relevant shareholders would receive fewer Series 1 shares) so they will not be consolidated with the Series 1 shares until the loss is recovered.

Table 6

	Class A shares – Series 1 (US$)	Class A shares – Series 2 (US$)
1 January	100,000	100,000
31 December	104,500	95,000
Increase/decrease in value	4,500	5,000
Performance fee of 20%	900	0

15.19 This method, whilst simple in principle, is somewhat unwieldy in circumstances where a hedge fund has issued multiple share classes and each class itself has multiple series.

Liquidation

15.20 The alternative methods to the series method described above involve establishing debit or credit amounts which are then applied at the level of individual shareholders once the performance fee has been calculated, rather than issuing separate series of shares. These various methods are commonly referred to collectively as 'equalisation'.

15.21 Equalisation encompasses a number of different methods used to calculate performance fees at the individual shareholder level rather than at the level of the share class.

15.22 This is a complex and technical subject. The basic principles of equalisation are set out below. A presentation given by Dermot S L Butler of Custom House on 13 February 2002 contains a more detailed and yet highly readable explanation of equalisation[1].

[1] 'Equalisation – Why is it necessary?; how it works': a presentation given by Dermot S L Butler of Custom House at the 'Hedge Fund Administration and Prime Brokerage: Benefiting from Industry Expansion Workshop' (Ireland, 13 February 2002) – see http://www.customhouse group.com/speech/equalization-why-is-it-necessary-how-it-works.

Simple equalisation

15.23 The simple equalisation method is similar in some respects to the series method in that it attempts to resolve the issue of new shares. Under this method the net asset value per share is determined for each 'series' of shares which a hedge fund has issued on a subscription date and is revised, taking into account performance fee accruals. The fund only publishes one net asset value for the relevant class of shares, taking the lowest net asset value of each 'series'. At periodic intervals, those shareholders investing in a 'series' that has a higher net asset value are issued with extra shares at the published (and lowest) net asset value per share, so that their aggregate holding has the same value. The difference here is that there is no public acknowledgement of different series of shares – the hedge fund publishes a single net asset value for the class and investors are 'grossed up' to ensure that they have a number of shares which reflects their economic interest in that class of shares.

15.24 Key Fund Terms

Equalisation factor/depreciation deposit

15.24 The equalisation factor/depreciation deposit method uses an adjustment to the net asset value subscription price to take account of accrued performance fees. Where the net asset value has risen above a previous high-water mark and an investor subscribes for shares during a performance period at net asset value net of the performance fee accrual, that investor would pay for performance that had occurred prior to the date on which that investor subscribed for the relevant shares. It is desirable, however, that the new subscriber has the same amount of capital at risk and that there is a single net asset value for the share class, so the subscriber pays the full price without deducting for the performance fee accrual. Provided, however, that the performance does not decline, that investor will not bear the accrued performance fee element of the subscription price at year-end and the hedge fund will instead issue further shares equal in value to the accrued performance fee element of the subscription price to that investor. If the net asset value declines following the date on which that investor subscribed for the relevant shares, the equalisation payment will be lost until the fund's performance recovers.

Example: premium subscription
On 1 January in a year the net asset value of Class A shares is US$100. On 31 March in that year the value of those shares has increased to US$200 and there is an accrued performance fee of US$20 (20% of the increase of US$100 from 1 January in that year) which will be payable on 31 December in that year assuming that there is no decline in the net asset value of the Class A shares prior to that date. Investor A subscribes for 1,000 shares on 31 March at US$200 per share, so that the aggregate subscription price for those shares is US$200,000. In this scenario, the equalisation amount is US$20,000 (a US$20 accrual per share multiplied by the number of shares acquired). Assuming that the net asset value does not decline before the performance fee becomes due on 31 December in that year, Investor A will receive at the end of that performance period additional shares at the prevailing net asset value.

Example: deficit subscription
On 1 January in a year the net asset value of Class A shares is US$200, which is the high-water mark for those shares. On 31 March in that year the value of those shares has fallen to US$100. Accordingly, those shares need to increase by US$100 per share to regain the high-water mark. Investor A subscribes for 1,000 shares on 31 March in that year at US$100 per share, so that the aggregate subscription price of those shares is US$100,000. In this scenario, that investor must also subscribe an additional amount, the 'depreciation deposit' equal to the performance fee that would be payable if the net asset value were to regain the high-water mark. In this case the performance fee would be US$20 per share, which yields a depreciation deposit of US$20,000 and gives a total subscription price of US$120,000. If the shares recover the high-water mark, the depreciation deposit is paid to the manager as a performance fee. If the shares have not appreciated at

the time the investor redeems those shares, the depreciation deposit is returned to the investor.

Equalisation adjustment

15.25 The equalisation adjustment method operates on a similar basis to the equalisation factor/depreciation deposit method, but instead of a premium and deficit amount the adjustment on both the upside and the downside is made by adjustment of shares, by either the issue (credit) of additional shares or the redemption (debit) of some of the shares for which an investor initially subscribed (as opposed to forfeit of the depreciation deposit amount).

Example: premium subscription
On 1 January in a year the net asset value of Class A shares is US$100. On 31 March in that year the value of the Class A shares has increased to US$200 and there is an accrued performance fee of US$20 (20% of the increase of US$100 from 1 January in that year) which will be payable on 31 December in that year if there is no decline in the net asset value of the Class A shares prior to that date. Investor A subscribes for 1,000 shares on 31 March in that year at US$200 per share, so that the aggregate subscription price of those shares is US$200,000. In this scenario, the equalisation amount is US$20,000 (US$20 accrual per share multiplied by the number of shares acquired). Assuming that the net asset value does not decline before the performance fee becomes due on 31 December in that year, Investor A will at the end of the performance period receive additional shares at the prevailing net asset value by way of satisfaction of the equalisation credit.

Example: deficit subscription
On 1 January in a year the net asset value of Class A shares is US$100, which is the high-water mark for those shares. On 31 March in that year the value of those shares has risen to US$200. Investor A subscribes for 1,000 shares on 31 March in that year at US$200 per share, so that the aggregate subscription price of those shares is US$200,000, of which US$20 per share is accrued performance fee (and therefore US$20,000 in total of the subscription of Investor A is an equalisation credit in respect of the accrued performance fee that will be payable if the net asset value does not decline before 31 December in that year).

C OTHER COMMON TERMS

Subscription fees

15.26 In common with many managed funds, hedge funds typically reserve the right to charge subscription fees to investors which are frequently up to 5% of the subscription price of the relevant shares. In practice, hedge funds rarely levy subscription fees. Subscription fees serve two distinct purposes, however. First (and more importantly), they permit the incentivisation of distributors, in particular, independent financial advisers ('IFAs'), who may require an upfront

15.26 *Key Fund Terms*

sales commission (unlike larger institutions which are typically willing to receive trail commission on the management fee). Historically, the majority of investors in hedge funds were wealthy individuals, who may have subscribed through small IFAs. These IFAs may well have wished to receive an upfront fee taken from the application of a subscription charge which was then rebated to the IFA by the hedge fund (or its manager).

15.27 The second purpose of a subscription charge is to discourage potential investors which a manager does not wish to become investors in the hedge fund which it manages. This could be relevant, for instance, where a hedge fund maintains a listing of convenience (ie a non-dealing listing where the purpose is simply to enable the unit price to be published on an exchange and for investors to gain comfort that the fund must comply with the rules of the relevant stock exchange). In such circumstances, the existence of the hedge fund may come to the attention of potential investors which are not targeted or desired by the manager. Although the fund always has a discretion to refuse a subscription request, it may be embarrassing to do so for no reason, particularly where the potential investor may complain. In such circumstances, the ability to charge a subscription fee is a useful tool to dissuade would-be investors which are not welcome. Where subscription fees are imposed prior to the issue of shares in a fund, there is no prospect of any claim for differential treatment (unless there is a claim based upon misrepresentation) because at that time the person is not yet a shareholder. Accordingly, there can be no claim for breach of any supposed obligation to treat all shareholders or unitholders equally or fairly.

Redemption fees

15.28 Redemption fees serve two main purposes. The first is to recoup the cost to the hedge fund of providing liquidity to the redeeming investor (which in the absence of a redemption fee would be borne or shared by the remaining investors). This argument works best where the underlying portfolio is expensive or difficult to liquidate, for example distressed debt or certain bespoke derivatives. However, in a liquid portfolio such as an equity long-short strategy, it is arguable that such costs should be regarded as part of the normal trading expenses of the fund and should be payable out of the portfolio as a whole. After all, the investor is simply exercising a right granted to it (and the other investors) under the constitution of the hedge fund.

15.29 The second purpose of a redemption fee is to dissuade investors from redeeming their shares in a hedge fund. As has been seen, the industry is seeking to encourage medium to long-term investment. The purpose of this is to provide certainty of funding and avoid the expense involved in portfolio churn.

15.30 The argument for redemption fees works best where they are not discretionary (as most are) and where they are imposed for certain periods (rather than indefinitely, in which case the 'churn' argument is redundant since to avoid the imposition of the fee an investor would need to treat the hedge fund as closed-ended). Discretionary fees that are not limited in time have a less cogent rationale because the hedge fund has granted investors the right to redeem at certain intervals and it is difficult to see on what basis the discretion should be exercised.

15.31 One way of combating this criticism is to make the fee payable to the hedge fund itself (so that it will accrue to the remaining portfolio). Unless, however, the fee is a genuine pre-estimate of the costs of providing liquidity, it is difficult to argue for it from an investor perspective. Unlike the subscription fee, which is levied on the date on which an investor subscribes for shares in a hedge fund, the redemption fee is levied upon existing investors. Accordingly, where the application of the redemption fee (or the amount of that fee) is discretionary, care needs to be taken to ensure that there is a defensible basis for treating investors differently.

Lock-up

15.32 Hedge funds frequently wish to deter short-term investors, both to avoid the administrative and portfolio costs which are associated with investor churn and because hedge funds have a (somewhat logically indefensible) dislike of investors 'trading the fund'.

15.33 These concerns may be exacerbated where the underlying portfolio of a hedge fund is illiquid and/or hard to value, for example distressed debt or combination strategies which include private equity, real estate or real estate related assets. In such cases, there is an argument that investors which subscribe for and redeem shares quickly are taking advantage of 'genuine' investors which buy into the fund's strategy. This may be compounded by the fact that these investors are able to use information which they obtain from the fund together with their own information (where they are financial institutions) to take bets on the pricing of the portfolio and 'trade the fund'. Managers argue that this is not defensible because investors should essentially be passive adherents to the manager's strategy and not seek to trade the fund as if it were common stock.

15.34 Whatever one's views about the merits of this argument, it is fair to say that as an investor one would not want to pay higher costs because another investor was attempting to make short-term gains by 'trading the fund'. Aside from a redemption charge linked to the amount of time that has elapsed between the date of subscription for those shares and the redemption of those shares, there is also the more draconian route of imposing a prohibition on redemption altogether within a certain period of subscription. Such a provision effectively 'locks up' the subscription amount so that, although the fund allows redemptions by other investors, the subscriber which is still in the lock-up period (which may be anything from one to three years, depending on the strategy and the relative bargaining power of the manager and the investors) cannot exercise such rights (or may only do so on payment of a mandatory redemption penalty).

15.35 Lock-up offers a breathing space for managers, particularly where large capital inflows occur, and in practice is more appropriate than a discretionary redemption fee both because there is a known prohibition and because it is (or at least should be) applied to all investors in the same way. As an investor, it is therefore difficult to seek to resist a lock-up when it is part of the fund's constitution and applies to all investors. However, the negative liquidity impact of any lock-up should correlate to the nature of the underlying portfolio of the hedge fund. Liquid portfolios should not be subject to

15.35 Key Fund Terms

significant lock-up. There is an argument that even a liquid portfolio should be subject to lock-up where the hedge fund is recently established and small and therefore may be vulnerable to one or two large redemptions. This, however, can also be dealt with by the imposition of a 'gate', as described below.

The gate

15.36 A 'gate' is a provision that allows the directors of a hedge fund (typically on the advice of the manager of the hedge fund) to suspend redemptions in circumstances where the aggregate redemption requests received exceed a certain proportion of the assets of the hedge fund (or sometimes the relevant class of interests in the hedge fund). Gates are a common feature of hedge fund structures because they protect the hedge fund (and, by extension, investors) from a 'run on the fund'.

15.37 Unlike banks, which only have a proportion of their obligations in readily realisable assets and are therefore susceptible to collapse if more than a certain proportion of those obligations are called at any one time (a 'run on the bank'), hedge funds should, in theory, be able to meet all their obligations for the simple reason that shares in a hedge fund are priced at net asset value, reflecting the deduction by that hedge fund of all of its obligations from all of its assets. A 'run on a fund' is not therefore like a run on a bank. They have different issues. The concern for a hedge fund is not the excess of its obligations over its assets but the time required to realise its assets and the potential for unquantified or deferred liabilities which cannot be deducted from the net asset value at the time redemption requests are processed. The second issue can theoretically be dealt with by withholding a portion of the redemption proceeds until the completion of the audit for the financial year in which the redemption occurs (a withholding or 'hold back'). Likewise, in the context of a highly liquid portfolio, the necessity for a gate is harder to justify, particularly where there is a hold back. Nevertheless, it is common to provide the facility to operate a gate in most hedge funds, although it is rare that the gate will be put into operation in practice.

15.38 The existence of a gating mechanism gives the directors of a hedge fund the reassurance that they should not have to engage in forced liquidation of the assets of that hedge fund. In less liquid portfolios this is of real benefit to investors which are not redeeming as it prevents the liquidity being drained out of the portfolio due to the realisation of liquid assets by redeeming investors, thereby increasing the proportion of illiquid assets in the remaining portfolio (and decreasing the liquidity prospects for remaining investors). Likewise, in a situation where there is an unexpected market shock, it may not be possible to realise the portfolio on a pro-rata basis, meaning that a hedge fund has to realise its best assets to satisfy redemption requests, leaving the less attractive rump for remaining investors. This is not unique to hedge funds and has historically been a problem for open-ended funds which invest in emerging markets where there is limited liquidity during times of turbulence.

Withholding on redemption

15.39 Commonly, hedge funds seek a power to withhold up to 5% or 10% of redemption proceeds until completion of the audit for the financial year in which the redemption occurs. The justification for this is that net asset value figures are unaudited and therefore may be subject to correction due to the audit. The potential for a restatement of net asset value figures should depend on the robustness of the calculation of net asset value. This will be a function of the degree to which the administrator independently calculates net asset value.

15.40 As net asset value is assets minus liabilities, there are only two areas where this can go awry. The first is the calculation of the value of assets. The independence of the administrator of a hedge fund in determining the asset position will depend on the degree to which market prices are available in respect of the securities in the portfolio of that hedge fund. Where a hedge fund has invested primarily in exchange traded securities, the potential for pricing errors is low. Where, however, the investment strategy of a hedge fund involves investment in non-exchange traded securities such as bespoke derivatives, private equity, distressed debt undergoing restructuring or even real estate assets, it may be difficult to generate a genuine 'third party price', that is, a price determined independently of the manager. In such circumstances, the administrator may be forced to rely on the manager to assist it in determining the value of some or all of the assets of the portfolio of the relevant hedge fund. In these circumstances, there is more scope for an auditor to question the accuracy of the valuation of the underlying assets. One should bear in mind, however, that the auditor is likely to experience similar problems to the administrator.

15.41 The second area where valuation can go awry is in the determination of liabilities (and where there are multiple share classes, the allocation of those liabilities to those classes of share). Most liabilities will be non-exceptional, that is, they will arise in the normal course of the operation of the hedge fund and should be easy to allocate either on a class-specific basis (where the liability or expense is incurred in relation to a particular class) or on a fund basis (where it is not properly allocable to one or more classes of interest). The allocation of the liabilities of a hedge fund may be more difficult in the case of extraordinary expenses such as litigation expenses, but these are rare and it is likely that the manager or the directors of the hedge fund would seek advice as to their allocation if the proper method of allocation were unclear. Accordingly, widespread as this power is, investors should ask managers how often amounts which are withheld are retained post-audit and how any such withheld amounts are applied (that is, are they simply credited to the portfolio and what happens to investors which redeem their interests before the mistake is discovered). By contrast, funds rarely provide for the position where net asset value is understated – logically, investors which redeemed should receive their share of the shortfall amount. The withholding method, however, is widely accepted in the hedge fund industry and provided that it is applied consistently and with appropriate transparency is generally acceptable to investors.

15.42 *Key Fund Terms*

Suspension

15.42 Suspension can arise as an ability to suspend the calculation of the net asset value of a hedge fund and/or to suspend the right of redemption. The latter is obviously a more restricted version of the former concept, although in practice it is unlikely that a fund would seek to accept money in return for shares where the calculation of net asset value is suspended because it would not know how many shares to issue to the subscriber until net asset value per share could be determined.

15.43 The documentation which governs a hedge fund will typically give the directors of a hedge fund the right to suspend the calculation of the net asset value of that hedge fund in circumstances where it is difficult to determine the value of the portfolio. Typically, these will include circumstances where exchanges are closed due to force majeure events but may also include broader market disruption provisions and frequently also include a general power that is not referenced to any specific force majeure event. From a fund perspective it is important to consider both the nature of the assets in the portfolio of the hedge fund and the circumstances in which the administrator may be unwilling to calculate the net asset value of the hedge fund. Otherwise there is a risk that the fund may inadvertently be unable to suspend where the hedge fund administrator has the right to refuse to calculate net asset value. Accordingly, the most prudent course is to stipulate the circumstances in which the administrator is relieved from calculating net asset value (or simply to make a situation where the administrator is unable to calculate net asset value a suspension event).

15.44 From an investor perspective, one must consider whether the suspension powers are justified and, in particular, the nature of the triggers to start and end a suspension period. Whilst in practice it is unlikely that the directors of a hedge fund will abuse suspension powers, where the manager also controls the board of directors of a hedge fund, investors need to be confident that broad powers to suspend the calculation of net asset value (and thereby subscriptions and redemptions), for example 'for any reason', will not be abused. In practice, the manager's interests are usually aligned with those of shareholders because no manager wants a suspension of dealings in a fund which it manages. The fact remains, however, that a broad power of suspension can only be challenged on a narrow set of grounds (essentially by bringing a legal action against the hedge fund, which may be problematic and time consuming).

15.45 Finally, there is an argument that provided the calculation of the net asset value of a hedge fund is accurate, the fact that it is volatile should not prevent either suspensions or redemptions – investors should be able to exploit that volatility. These considerations militate against broadly defined market disruption or general powers and towards more tightly defined force majeure type events like the closing of exchanges on which the investments of a hedge fund are listed. From a manager's perspective this raises the issue of 'trading the fund', but investors would argue that the manager is itself entitled to exploit the volatility caused by the force majeure event.

15.46 An equally strong argument against overly broad powers of suspension is that in marginal cases a better response would be to raise the gate, preventing a situation where the manager of the hedge fund is overwhelmed by trying to deal with liquidity issues during a market crisis and preserving the sanctity of the calculation of the net asset value of the hedge fund.

Side pockets

15.47 Although hedge funds are typically open-ended and therefore typically invest in a portfolio that is fairly liquid, it has become increasingly common for hedge funds to take positions that are illiquid, for example in real estate assets, private equity or distressed securities that are subject to restructuring, bankruptcy or other procedures which make them difficult to sell and to value.

15.48 One of the problems of this approach is that where these interests are simply held at the level of the portfolio attributable to a particular class, the liquidity risk (that is, the risk that the class may not be able to satisfy redemption requests out of its assets) is increased. There are mechanisms to assist in this, including withholding a portion of the redemption proceeds and raising the gate, but these are not particularly designed with this end in mind. Allied to this is the fact that, unless the illiquidity is a feature of the strategy of the hedge fund (such as distressed debt, for example) some investors may be more reluctant to participate in illiquid investments than others.

15.49 Accordingly, a practice has developed of allowing the manager of a hedge fund to create a separate illiquid class of shares for illiquid investments. Shares of this class will have more restricted liquidity than shares of the class to which those assets would otherwise have been attributed – or even no liquidity, simply paying out as the relevant assets are realised. Such an approach is normally referred to as an 'illiquid side-pocket', for obvious reasons.

Chapter 16

INVESTING IN HEDGE FUNDS

Dale Gabbert, Partner, Simmons & Simmons and Andrew Wylie, Partner and Head of Investment Funds, DLA Piper

A	Why invest in hedge funds?	16.1
B	Mainstream funds	16.2
C	Hedge funds	16.9
D	Routes to investment in hedge funds	16.20
E	Fund of hedge funds	16.26
F	Key investment and due diligence issues	16.31
G	Side letters	16.34
H	Rights as an investor	16.42

A WHY INVEST IN HEDGE FUNDS?

16.1 Hedge funds now form part of the public imagination following two decades of colourful coverage by newspapers and Hollywood. Why have hedge funds grown so spectacularly and what motivates investors to participate in them? CHAPTER 1 defines what a hedge fund is and concludes that a key aspect of a hedge fund is that it is an 'absolute return' product, where the manager's success is determined by whether it has increased the value of the portfolio of the hedge fund over the course of a year, regardless of overall market conditions. There are a number of reasons why people invest in hedge funds. This chapter first examines the way in which mainstream funds generally operate and contrasts that with how hedge funds operate.

B MAINSTREAM FUNDS

Relative performance

16.2 To give investors back more money than they put in may sound like a generic description of investment itself rather than of a specific investment product. Most private investors wouldn't regard that 'mission statement' as anything other than self-evident. However, the surprising truth is that the investment management industry has been and largely remains inherently relative.

16.3 The managers of mainstream funds regard their performance as being properly measured by reference to a relevant benchmark. If those managers outperform that benchmark (what one might call 'relative performance') they will regard themselves as having been successful, regardless of whether they have made or lost money on an absolute basis. For example, a UK equity fund which focuses on large cap stocks might use the FTSE 100 as a benchmark. If the FTSE 100 were to rise in value by 10% and the fund were only to rise in

16.3 Investing in Hedge Funds

value by 8%, the manager would view itself as having underperformed even though the manager had generated a profit for investors. That is because one could have gained exposure to the FTSE 100 index passively and generated a return which exceeded that which the application of the manager's skill, research and experience generated. Conversely, if the FTSE 100 were to fall in value by 10% and the fund were only to fall in value by 8%, the manager would congratulate itself because it had outperformed the benchmark even though the investors had suffered a loss. What is probably even more surprising to the uninitiated is that most funds which invest in developed markets do not outperform their benchmarks on a consistent basis. Despite this, the fund management business has grown to an enormous size and manages assets for pension funds, governments, companies and individuals through a myriad of funds. There are now more funds which invest in the US stock market than there are quoted US companies.

16.4 The use of benchmarks has also led to what might be termed 'closet index-tracking'. Closet index-tracking occurs where a manager closely models its portfolio on the fund's benchmark. The manager will seek to outperform that benchmark by adjusting its allocation so that it is 'overweight' (that is, it has a larger proportion of its portfolio in a particular stock than the benchmark) or is 'underweight' (that is, it has less of its portfolio in a stock than the benchmark). For example, if the manager of a UK equity fund with a FTSE 100 benchmark does not favour oil stocks it might go underweight on British Petroleum, but in practice it is unlikely that it will not hold the stock at all because it is one of the largest constituents of the FTSE 100. That manager hopes by means of slight adjustments away from that benchmark to outperform that benchmark, but it is unlikely not to purchase, say, half of the stock in the FTSE 100 in this example. To do so would be to take a huge risk of underperformance by reference to that benchmark.

Fee structure is not sufficiently linked to performance

16.5 The fee structure of traditional investment funds is commonly calculated as a percentage of the value of assets under management, and does not have a performance-related element. The sanction for poor performance is simply that the investor redeems its shares and the value of the portfolio by reference to which the management fee is calculated falls. Provided the investors do not redeem their shares, the fund will continue to make money for the manager regardless of the performance of the fund (although the size of the portfolio by reference to which the fee is calculated will, of course, decline if the manager is losing money).

16.6 The incentive to engage in closet index-tracking is also increased where a manager perceives that its peer managers are engaging in that practice. In that situation, the risk of underperformance relative to the fund's peer group significantly increases if the manager does not adopt the same approach. Because of the fee structure and the fact that performance will be measured relative to other funds of the same type, it makes sense for a manager to converge its behaviour with that of its peer managers because the risk of underperformance, with investor redemptions and consequent loss of revenue, is greater than the reward for outperformance (because no performance fee is payable in respect of outperformance).

Long-only bias

16.7 Most funds only acquire shares or securities in the hope that they will appreciate in value, so-called 'long-only investing'. Betting that the price of a security will rise inherently is no more rational than betting that the price of a security will fall. Traditional funds are therefore hugely biased towards one view of the market – that it will rise. If traditional funds consider that the market will fall they are quite restricted as to what they can do (although with regulatory changes and the wider use of derivatives there is now scope for limited downside protection in a classic long-only fund). In practice, long-only funds can take some protective measures such as buying put options on their benchmark index and maintaining a larger proportion of their portfolio in cash, but long-only funds are not allowed to make an anticipated fall in the market their investment strategy. In other words, long-only funds cannot actively seek to profit from a market downturn.

Volatility

16.8 One of the most shocking facts about mainstream funds is that they can be highly volatile. Funds which track major indices such as the FTSE 100 are perceived to be low risk but even a developed market index such as the FTSE 100 is quite volatile. There is a perception that markets generally rise over the longer term. It is correct that the returns on the stock market since the Second World War have been undeniably positive. Nevertheless, there have been periods where the market has lost a large amount of its value including in the 1970s, 1980s and early 2000s and, indeed, during the financial crisis.

C HEDGE FUNDS

Absolute performance

16.9 Hedge funds are different to the long-only products which have comprised, and continue to comprise, the majority of funds available for investment. Hedge funds are absolute return products. In broad terms, they do not aim to beat an index nor do they judge their performance by reference to relative performance against a benchmark. Put simply, if an investor subscribes one million dollars for shares in a hedge fund it will not be a success unless at the end of that year that investor would be able to redeem its shares for more than one million dollars, regardless of whether the securities market as a whole has diminished in value over that period. If the value of a particular market appears likely to reduce in value, a hedge fund may generate profit by shorting that market (selling the market or individual securities through short sales or derivatives). If the value of a particular market appears likely to increase in value, a hedge fund may generate profit by going long (buying securities which that hedge fund considers will rise in value or get upside exposure through derivatives).

16.10 *Investing in Hedge Funds*

Investment freedom

16.10 Hedge funds are much less constrained by diversification rules than mainstream funds and can therefore make concentrated bets which are unregulated or at least lightly regulated. This is because, as investment funds which are unregulated or at least lightly regulated, they have complete freedom to set their own investment policy. Hedge funds can also borrow more and leverage the bets which they make. The effect of this is that the potential impediments to making money are far fewer. This also means that hedge funds may make bigger losses because of the effect of leverage on losing positions and the potential lack of diversification. Since 2008, a significant number of hedge funds have fallen prey to the financial crisis and its aftermath.

16.11 A consequence of this is that unlike mainstream managers, hedge fund managers are unlikely to engage in closet index-tracking because they are less likely to have a benchmark to track, have greater investment freedom and less ability to predict what strategies their competitors are pursuing.

16.12 Hedge funds have this freedom because the funds themselves are not regulated in the way that most publicly available funds are. In the UK and most onshore jurisdictions, if a sponsor wishes to market a fund to the public it must comply with a variety of diversification and risk control measures. In the EU these are contained in the UCITS Directives, a series of European directives which codify a common standard for European funds and allow European funds that meet this standard to be marketed in any member state of the EU, subject to certain registration formalities. In addition to UCITS there are also domestic funds in onshore jurisdictions that can be publicly marketed if they meet local criteria.

Fee structure

16.13 The fee structure of hedge funds is designed to generate the majority of the manager's income from the performance fee (assuming that performance is positive). As seen in CHAPTER 15, the performance fee is commonly 20% of qualifying profits[1]. Hedge funds also commonly charge a management fee (typically 1–2%) as a percentage of assets[2], in the same way as mainstream long-only funds. This is slightly at odds with their claim to be an absolute return product but the simple fact is that investors are willing to pay such fees.

[1] See para 15.7.
[2] See para 15.6.

16.14 Whatever its original rationale, the 'two and twenty' fee structure has become standard in the hedge fund industry. Whilst the payment of a management fee might seem contrary to their absolute return focus, for many smaller managers this is really just to cover costs and is not a source of significant profit. The performance fee does incentivise the manager to produce positive returns. It also replicates the reward system that investment banks themselves use to incentivise their proprietary traders.

Allocation and diversification

16.15 Hedge funds do not represent a uniform asset class but rather a variety of different management styles that offer differing return profiles. This enables investors to allocate capital to hedge funds that meet their particular investment and risk requirements. As has been seen, one of the attractions of hedge funds is their absolute return focus and low correlation to other asset classes. Many investors make hedge fund investments with a view to achieving an absolute return that is not correlated to the remainder of their portfolio.

Volatility of returns

16.16 A further advantage of hedge funds may, at first glance, appear counter-intuitive. Despite some high-profile failures, hedge funds are on average less volatile than mainstream long-only funds, which confounds the common perception that hedge funds are high risk products (bearing in mind that the performance of individual hedge funds varies considerably).

16.17 Consistency of returns and lack of correlation to the main securities market is very attractive, particularly to institutional investors such as pension funds which are managing various liabilities, some of which are current and some of which are deferred. Large fluctuations in the value of their assets are particularly problematic for pension funds.

16.18 Clearly, hedge funds have certain attractions both for individual and institutional investors. Pension funds, in particular US pension funds, have embraced the benefits of having a portion of their portfolio in alternative investments.

16.19 So, if hedge funds look like an attractive proposition, how does one go about investing in them?

D ROUTES TO INVESTMENT IN HEDGE FUNDS

16.20 Hedge fund investment has blossomed over the last two decades and was far more limited in earlier decades. Now there is a universe of thousands of hedge funds to choose from which offer a multiplicity of investment strategies, sizes and styles. There are also products that offer indirect access to, and/or blended returns from, a selection of hedge funds.

Direct investment

16.21 This is the simplest and most straightforward route but it presents a number of challenges. How does an investor select an appropriate hedge fund, gain access to it and manage the exposure which it provides? Unless an investor is particularly experienced or sophisticated this may be a daunting prospect, and even if an investor has selected a hedge fund, it may not be able to gain access to that hedge fund.

16.22 *Investing in Hedge Funds*

Advisory or discretionary investment

16.22 Direct investment by an investor in a hedge fund imposes a significant burden in terms of due diligence and the need to monitor that investment. It is therefore often attractive for an investor to access an investment in a hedge fund through an adviser or a discretionary manager which can give guidance on the selection and management of a hedge fund portfolio. Traditionally, private investors have gained access to hedge funds through introductions from private banks or investment managers that they have appointed to manage all or a portion of their portfolio. Pension funds almost invariably appoint an adviser to guide them through the process. This can be advisory, leaving the ultimate decision as to whether or not to invest with the client, or fully discretionary where the adviser will have discretion to manage the portfolio in accordance with agreed parameters.

Managed account

16.23 A managed account involves the manager of a hedge fund establishing a bespoke arrangement for one or more investors as an alternative to those investors investing in the hedge fund which it manages. An investor which gains access to a strategy in this way does not invest in the hedge fund itself; rather, the manager will invest the managed account portfolio broadly to reflect the trades the manager makes for the hedge fund whose strategy the investor wishes to replicate. The intention is that the performance of the managed account will broadly mirror that of the relevant hedge fund, although, of course, the performance will not be identical because of differences in economies of scale in trading the strategy and other factors. Typically, the minimum amount that a manager will accept to operate a managed account will be considerably greater than the minimum investment it will accept in the relevant fund which the managed account is intended to replicate. Managed accounts are generally less attractive from the point of view of the manager because the benefits of aggregating clients within a fund are forfeit. Nevertheless, it can be useful where the client is substantial and wants a slightly different exposure to that offered by the fund or where the client's particular needs cannot be met by way of a side letter.

Synthetic hedge fund platforms

16.24 A number of private banks and investment advisers offer hedge fund platforms. There are different ways in which such a platform can be created but one method is for the bank to have a series of managed accounts in place with the underlying hedge fund managers. It will then establish its own platform on top of this. This has the advantage that the investor benefits from the bargaining power of the bank and some conformity of terms and reporting across the system, together with access to a broad range of hedge funds. The private bank/investment adviser adds value by conducting ongoing due diligence and providing data about the hedge funds which it offers through its platform. The client will have access to online information relating to the platform funds which usually includes the latest published net asset value and may include more detailed information such as correlation and risk data. This clearly benefits investors which would not otherwise have the capacity to conduct legal and financial due diligence about numerous hedge funds before making an investment or would simply be unable to access such hedge funds. It also provides immediate diversified exposure, which may be difficult to achieve quickly by investing directly.

Structured products

16.25 Many European and US financial institutions have developed structured products or derivative instruments that give investors a return linked to the performance of a basket of hedge funds or hedge fund indices. Some investment banks issue certificates where the rate of interest or amount payable in respect of the certificate correlates to the performance of an underlying portfolio of hedge funds. In these cases the investor is not investing in a hedge fund but is rather investing in a certificate, note or derivative instrument that provides a similar exposure to investing in the specified basket of hedge funds. Some financial institutions offer capital guaranteed products.

E FUND OF HEDGE FUNDS

16.26 Instead of or in addition to investing in a number of single manager hedge funds, an investor may wish to invest in a single pooled investment vehicle which itself invests in a range of other hedge funds, commonly referred to as a 'fund of funds' or a 'multi-manager fund'.

Advantages

16.27 Investors may find a fund of hedge funds an attractive investment either instead of or as a complement to investment in single manager hedge for the following reasons:

- *Due diligence*: The fund of funds manager is responsible for conducting due diligence on the underlying hedge funds and their managers. This may represent a significant saving of time and cost for investors.
- *Manager's expertise*: The fund of funds manager is likely to have significant expertise in selecting the managers of single manager hedge funds.
- *Reduced financial risk*: The diversification of hedge fund investments and strategies within the fund of funds is likely to reduce financial risk if a single hedge fund collapses or makes a significant loss. It is, of course, possible that the excessive diversification of a fund of hedge funds portfolio could lead to lower returns.
- *A lower minimum investment amount*: Single manager hedge funds typically have minimum investment amounts from US$1 million to US$5 million and therefore smaller investors are unlikely to have sufficient capital available to invest in a diversified portfolio of single manager hedge funds.
- *Good liquidity*: Many funds of hedge funds give investors the opportunity to redeem their interests on a monthly or quarterly basis without being constrained by a significant lock-up period or redemption fee.

16.27 Investing in Hedge Funds

- *Transparency*: The underlying fund managers will often provide the fund of funds manager with enhanced transparency, thereby enabling it to monitor the overall portfolio more effectively.
- *Leverage*: Funds of funds do not typically employ high levels of leverage for investment purposes (although the underlying hedge funds in which they invest are likely to do so).

Disadvantages

16.28 The principal disadvantages of a fund of hedge funds are as follows:

- *The layering of fees and expenses*: Each single manager hedge fund in which the fund of hedge funds invests will typically charge a management fee of about 2% of net assets and a performance fee of 20%. The fund of hedge funds manager is likely to charge an additional management fee of about 1% of net assets and a performance fee of 5–10%. Some fund of hedge funds managers will seek to reduce this overall fee burden by negotiating a lower management fee or a rebate on the management fee with one or more of the underlying fund managers.
- *A blended return*: Since the fund of hedge funds invests in a portfolio of underlying hedge funds, its overall return will be lower than if the investor had simply invested directly in the higher performing underlying single manager hedge funds.
- *Strategy selection*: The manager will select the underlying funds and therefore the strategies to which the fund of hedge funds will be exposed. This contrasts with single manager hedge funds where the investor may select a hedge fund that meets its strategy requirements (or which it expects will offer high returns).

16.29 Investors in a fund of hedge funds will need to be satisfied that its manager has the experience and resources required to analyse and select appropriate underlying single manager funds.

16.30 The investor or the investor's agent will need to complete the subscription agreement of the fund of hedge funds and provide any additional documents required by the manager or the administrator of the fund of hedge funds. The subscription agreement will usually contain an anti-money laundering section or separate questionnaire which each prospective investor will need to complete.

F   KEY INVESTMENT AND DUE DILIGENCE ISSUES

16.31 The nature and sophistication of the investor, its goals, its investment approach and its legal and regulatory status will all affect the amount of due diligence that it will carry out before investing in a hedge fund. The trustees of UK pension schemes, for instance, must obtain advice when exercising their investment discretion, which means that they will often appoint external legal and financial advisers. Most individuals will not have the desire or resources to conduct extensive financial and legal due diligence on a manager, the fund or its service providers.

16.32 The due diligence about the manager may address some or all of the following:

- the establishment of the manager and its ownership structure;
- the biographies of the principals of the manager and its portfolio managers;
- references for the principals;
- disclosure of any legal or regulatory actions against the manager, its principals, directors and employees;
- the internal policies and procedures of the manager, with an emphasis on risk management and risk measurement;
- the manager's infrastructure – hardware, software and information service providers;
- trade execution and monitoring;
- disaster recovery/back-up procedures;
- professional indemnity insurance;
- the level of transparency and reporting which the manager will provide;
- the amount of investment by the principals and portfolio managers in the fund; and
- the use of side letters/preferential treatment given to other investors.

16.33 The due diligence relating to the fund will usually include:

- the establishment of the fund including copies of the constitutional documents and the latest offering memorandum of the fund;
- valuation of fund assets – how the assets are valued and the extent to which the valuation process is independent of the manager are key areas of investigation;
- fees and expenses;
- corporate governance, including the independence and experience of the directors of the fund;
- the latest and historic audited accounts of the fund;
- performance, volatility and risk data, including position limits/restrictions;
- the strategy of the fund and its implementation by the manager;
- the rights attaching to each class of interest in the fund;
- investment and liquidity terms;
- integrity, independence and competence of the service providers to the fund (some investors may require a separate due diligence report to be completed by the administrator and prime broker/custodian); and
- the use of leverage.

G SIDE LETTERS

General

16.34 A side letter is an agreement between a manager and/or a hedge fund and an investor which governs certain aspects of the investment by that investor in that hedge fund. In legal terms, a side letter is a collateral contract which supplements and amends the provisions in the subscription agreement of the fund. A side letter may, for example, contain a fee rebate agreement.

16.35 Historically, cornerstone investors have sought side letters in order to obtain preferential terms in return for the investment risk they take in seeding a new hedge fund. A broad range of investors now request side letters,

16.35 *Investing in Hedge Funds*

particularly institutional investors such as pension funds which have regulatory or constitutional concerns which must be addressed before they are able to invest in a fund. The ability of an investor to obtain a side letter depends on two main factors: (i) the policy of the manager and/or the fund in relation to side letters, and (ii) the amount of the proposed investment. Clearly, the larger the investment, the more likely it is that a manager will be amenable to granting a side letter.

Common side letter provisions

16.36 The following are common side letter provisions:

- a 'most favoured nations' or 'MFN' clause which entitles the investor to take the benefit of any terms which the hedge funds grants to other investors which are more favourable than the terms from which that investor benefits;
- a waiver or rebate on management and/or performance fees;
- preferential liquidity terms, including a waiver of the lock-up period, a shorter notice of redemption, more frequent redemption dealing days and/or the right to redeem upon the occurrence of specified events;
- notification of certain events, for instance changes in the personnel responsible for the management of the fund's portfolio;
- a 'key man' provision which entitles an investor to redeem its interests in the fund if certain employees of the manager are no longer responsible for managing the fund and/or leave the manager;
- enhanced disclosure of portfolio information;
- a limitation or prohibition on the ability of the manager or fund to distribute securities instead of cash (known as 'in specie' or 'in kind' distributions) to the investor on redemption or the dissolution of the fund;
- a right to make additional investments in the fund up to a specified monetary amount (known as a 'capacity right');
- the right to make a transfer to an affiliate or other group member; and
- additional representations and warranties to meet specific investor concerns.

16.37 An investor which subscribes for shares in a hedge fund may wish to know whether that hedge fund has granted preferential terms to other investors and in particular whether existing side letters contain enhanced liquidity or transparency terms. In both instances, investors which have the benefit of those terms may be able to redeem their interests in the fund before an event that may cause its net asset value to fall, either because they have a right to redeem their interests in circumstances where other investors do not or because they have access to information that will enable them to make a more informed decision about the merits of redeeming their interest in the fund. This could materially prejudice the ability of investors which do not have the benefit of the relevant side letter provisions to redeem their interests in the hedge fund. Although historically hedge fund managers have not disclosed side letter terms to their investors, managers are increasingly adopting a disclosure based approach because of increased pressure from both institutional investors and regulators.

Regulators and side letters

16.38 The US Securities and Exchange Commission (the 'SEC') and the UK Financial Conduct Authority (the 'FCA') do not regulate offshore hedge funds but rather the hedge fund managers, which are typically located onshore in either London or New York (in the case of the SEC, only those managers which are registered with the SEC). Their focus has been the potential unfairness to investors which do not have the benefit of side letter rights.

16.39 The FCA endorses industry guidance by the Alternative Investment Management Association ('AIMA') which requires the disclosure of material side letter terms to investors. Material side letter terms include liquidity preferences and greater portfolio transparency rights while non-material terms include fee rebates and MFN clauses. The AIMA guidance is expressed not to apply to fund of hedge fund managers.

16.40 Whilst the regulatory and legal ramifications of side letters on managers and funds is outside the scope of this book, it is important for investors to be aware of the existence of side letters and the potential effect which they may have on an investment in a hedge fund. Managers must also ensure that they are able to comply with their obligations under side letters to which they are a party and are able to demonstrate compliance with those obligations.

Negotiating side letters

16.41 The negotiation and monitoring of side letter terms is fairly onerous on managers because it requires substantial management time and often results in the manager instructing external lawyers. Bearing this in mind, the ability of an investor to negotiate a side letter with a manager will be influenced by:

- the policy of the manager in granting side letters to non-seed investors;
- the size of the prospective investment;
- the perception that the investor will be a long-term investor ('sticky money');
- the likelihood of further investments into the fund or other funds managed by the same manager or its affiliates; and
- the nature and reputation of the investor – the manager may attract new sources of capital by securing investment from a new category of institutional investor, for instance a large pension fund.

H   RIGHTS AS AN INVESTOR

16.42 The rights of an investor are those that attach to the interests in the hedge fund in which it has invested in and any statutory or common law rights which it has under the laws of the relevant jurisdiction. The rights of hedge fund investors will be entrenched in the constitutional documents of the fund and summarised in its offering documentation.

16.43 As mentioned in CHAPTER 5, it is common for the investment manager to hold all voting shares in a hedge fund and investors will usually only have the right to vote on a variation of class rights. Absent an express contractual provision in a side letter, investors will have no direct rights against the

16.43 Investing in Hedge Funds

investment manager and accordingly will rely on the fund's board of directors to enforce the rights which the fund has against the investment manager. The issues that this creates are as follows:

- What rights will investors have if the board of directors of a fund fails to enforce a contractual right of the fund (bearing in mind that the board is likely to include at least one director which the manager has appointed)?
- How can the investors enforce their constitutional rights where the manager holds all of the voting shares (which also permits the manager to amend the terms of the constitutional documentation)?

Enforcement of rights by a fund against its manager

16.44 Individual investors will seldom have a direct right of action against an investment manager and those rights will normally only arise where a side letter contains express covenants from the manager to operate the fund in a particular way. Accordingly, the normal position will be that the 'proper plaintiff' in any action against the manager will be the fund itself, which can only act through the board of directors of the fund.

16.45 If the board elects not to take any action against the investment manager, what options are open to the investors? Dismissing the board and taking action is unlikely to be possible since this power is usually vested in the holders of the voting shares. However, some relief may lie in the common law or a statutory derivative action (if the action can be adjudged to amount to fraud on the minority or where the directors have breached their fiduciary duties) or in remedies for unfair prejudice.

Enforcement of constitutional rights

16.46 The constitutional rights of investors will be set out in the fund's articles of association or the limited partnership agreement of the fund. Where the constitution has been breached it will be possible to bring an action. However, most hedge funds have extremely broad constitutional documents which give a wide source of discretion to the fund and limit shareholder rights to the minimum required by the law of the place of its establishment. The exercise of voting power is unlikely to be possible since subscribers normally hold non-voting shares.

Misrepresentation

16.47 Alternatively, investors may bring an action for misrepresentation where the fund is operated other than in accordance with the provisions of the offering documentation. Normally the offering document will have been drafted so as to ensure that the scope for such an action is limited. If the misrepresentation is sufficiently fundamental it may be possible to rescind the subscription agreement, but this will only be available where damages would not be an adequate remedy and bars to rescission, such as lapse of time, may apply.

Index

All references are to paragraph number.

A

Absolute performance
generally   16.9
Accountants
generally   6.4
Administered mutual funds
Cayman Islands   2.28, 2.31–2.32, 2.42, 2.44
Administrators
accepting investors   6.29–6.31
anti-money laundering obligations   6.30
British Virgin Islands   2.86–2.88, 2.123–2.125
calculating management fees   6.36
calculating net asset value   6.33–6.35
calculating performance fees   6.33, 6.36
company secretarial functions   6.42
generally   6.3, 6.22–6.25
Guernsey   3.104
Ireland   4.170–4.173
Jersey   3.14, 3.34–3.39, 3.54
Malta   4.405–4.407, 4.437
monitoring expenses   6.43
monitoring function   6.38–6.41
post-establishment activities   6.32–6.43
pre-establishment activities   6.26–6.28
registered office functions   6.42
reporting   6.37
stock exchange listings   6.43
trades, monitoring and settlement   6.38–6.41
Allocation
investment in hedge funds   6.39, 16.15
investors
    professional   10.123–10.127
    retail   10.123–10.127
Alternative investment funds (AIFs)
Alternative Investment Fund Managers Directive (AIFMD)
    Brexit   10.10, 10.269, 13.104
    exemptions   10.47–10.52
    generally   10.1–10.3
    impact   10.265
    implementation   10.1, 10.263, 10.264

Alternative investment funds (AIFs) – *cont.*
Alternative Investment Fund Managers Directive (AIFMD) – *cont.*
    MiFID and   10.45–10.46
    objective   10.2
    review   10.267
    text   10.4–10.6
alternative investment fund managers (AIFMs)
    authorisation   10.58–10.65, 10.81
    conflicts of interest   10.68
    definition   10.33–10.36
    EU AIFM managing an EU AIF   10.106–10.112
    external   10.43
    full scope UK   10.54, 10.61–10.63, 10.131, 10.148, 10.167
    internal   10.43
    non-EU, EU AIFM managing   10.113–10.114
    non-EU, marketing by   10.149–10.160
    non-EU, non-EU AIFM managing   10.117
    one only   10.44
    operational obligations   10.66–10.104
    registration of   10.51, 10.58–10.65
    role   10.37–10.40
    small authorised UK   10.54, 10.57, 10.61–10.63
    small registered UK   10.54, 10.56, 10.61–10.63
    small UK   10.54, 10.55, 10.61–10.63
    threshold requirements   10.47–10.52
    UK categorisation   10.53–10.57
    UK regulated activity   10.41–10.42
annual reports
    content requirements   10.164–10.166
    date of first   10.167
    generally   10.161–10.163, 10.184
assets under management (AUM)   10.49–10.50
British Virgin Islands   2.146–2.154
collective investment undertaking, as   10.14, 10.18

509

Index

Alternative investment funds (AIFs) – *cont.*
  defined investment policy   10.14, 10.25–10.27
  definition   2.147, 10.13–10.17, 10.28–10.29
  delegation of functions
    conditions generally   10.246–10.247
    duty to notify regulator   10.245
    instructing delegate   10.255
    liability and   10.259–10.262
    monitoring delegation   10.255
    non-EU delegates   10.250–10.251
    remuneration of delegates   10.258
    sub-delegation   10.256–10.257
    supervision   10.252
    who may be delegated to   10.248–10.250
    withdrawing delegation   10.255
  depositaries, provisions as to
    behavioural standards   10.213–10.215
    conflicts of interest   10.214–10.215, 10.242–10.244
    contractual arrangements and depositaries   10.231–10.235
    delegation of depositary function   10.216–10.223, 10.224, 10.230, 10.239–10.241
    depositary lite   10.196, 10.236–10.244
    duties, generally   10.201
    generally   10.195–10.197
    liability of depositary   10.224–10.232, 10.241
    location   10.198
    monitoring cash flows   10.201–10.203, 10.216
    oversight functions   10.201, 10.209–10.212, 10.216
    prime broker acting as depositary   10.200, 10.214
    safe-keeping of assets   10.201, 10.204–10.208, 10.218–10.239
    who may act as   10.198–10.200, 10.236–10.238
  disclosure to investors
    delegation of depositary function   10.222–10.223
    statements   10.170
  ESMA Guidelines   10.7–10.9, 10.16
    reporting guidelines   10.177, 10.180
  ESMA Opinion   10.180–10.183
  EU AIFs   10.106–10.112
  France   13.85–13.86, 13.88, 13.97–13.109
    non-retail funds   13.94
  Germany   13.114, 13.116–13.119, 13.122–13.125
  Guernsey   3.138–3.140, 3.144–3.145

Alternative investment funds (AIFs) – *cont.*
  income distribution, oversight   10.96
  investment compartments of undertaking   10.14, 10.19
  investment strategy, disclosure   10.171
  investors   10.14, 10.22–10.24, 10.48
    annual report to be available to   10.162
    disclosure of net asset value to   10.97–10.98
    disclosure to, generally   10.168–10.169
    domicile   10.118, 10.122
    periodic disclosures to   10.172–10.176
    pre-investment disclosure   10.171
  Ireland   4.88, 4.89, 4.93, 4.104–4.115
    management companies   4.150–4.157
    qualifying investor funds (QIAIFs)   4.104, 4.107–4.115
    retail investor funds (RIAIFs)   4.104, 4.105–4.106
  Italy, RAIFs *see* **Italy**
  Jersey   3.9, 3.21, 3.22
  joint ventures   10.30–10.32
  leverage
    assets acquired through   10.50
    calculation   10.90–10.92
    disclosure to investors   10.84–10.86
    disclosure to regulators   10.87–10.89
    generally   10.66, 10.80–10.81
    regular disclosures   10.175–10.176
    reporting requirements on   10.187–10.188
    setting maximum level   10.82–10.83
  liability
    delegation of functions, where   10.259–10.262
    depositary   10.224–10.232, 10.241
  Luxembourg *see* **Luxembourg**
  Malta *see* **Malta**
  marketing under AIFMD
    definition of marketing   10.118–10.121
    domicile of investors   10.118, 10.122
    EU AIFs   10.128–10.137
    European passport   10.154–10.160, 10.268, 13.90, 13.98–13.102, 13.217, 13.262–13.265
    national private placement regimes (NPPRs)   10.36, 10.144–10.153
    non-EU AIFMs   10.149–10.160
    non-EU AIFs   10.138–10.148
    passive or reverse enquiry/solicitation   10.119–10.120
    professional investors   10.123–10.127
    retail investors   10.123–10.127
    UK regulations   10.121
  master-feeder structure   10.24, 10.27, 10.60, 10.128, 10.129, 10.136, 10.146, 10.171, 10.182–10.183

Index

Alternative investment funds (AIFs) – *cont.*
  national competent authorities   10.2
  national private placement regimes
    (NPPRs)   2.146
  Netherlands   13.299, 13.302,
    13.307–13.316, 13.319
  non-EU, AIFM managing   10, 35,
    10.115–10.116
  non-EU, EU AIFM managing   10.113–10.114
  notified (NAIFs)   4.383–4.387, 13.249
  offering documents   10.69, 10.118,
    10.121, 10.170, 10.223
  periodic stress tests   10.179
  portfolio management   10.37–10.38,
    10.45
  prime brokers   7.3
  qualifying investor funds (QIAIFs)   4.104,
    4.107–4.115
  raising capital   10.14, 10.20–10.21
  redemptions, oversight   10.209
  regulation   10.4–10.10
  reporting requirements
    additional information requests   10.184–10.186
    annual reports   10.184
    ESMA guidelines   10.177, 10.189
    ESMA Opinion   10.180–10.183
    frequency and timeframes   10.189–10.193
    generally   10.177–10.179
    leverage, information on   10.187–10.188
  retail investor funds (RIAIFs)   4.104,
    4.105–4.106
  risk management
    disclosure to investors   10.173
    establishing risk limits   10.78–10.79
    functional and hierarchical separation   10.67–10.68, 10.200,
    10.214–10.215, 10.244
    generally   10.37–10.38, 10.66
    monitoring   10.75–10.77
    permanent risk management function   10.71–10.72
    reporting to regulators   10.179
    risk assessment   10.210
    systems for   10.69–10.77, 10.173
  Spain   13.361
  subscriptions, oversight   10.209
  Switzerland   4.484, 4.506
  timely settlement of transactions   10.209
  transparency
    additional information requests   10.184–10.186
    annual reports   10.161–10.167, 10.184
    disclosure to investors   10.168–10.176

Alternative investment funds (AIFs) – *cont.*
  transparency – *cont.*
    ESMA Opinion   10.180–10.183
    reporting to regulators   10.177–10.193
  United Kingdom
    AIFM categorisation   10.53–10.57
    FCA authorisation   9.25–9.29
    measures   10.11–10.12
    regulatory regime   9.17–9.18,
    10.41–10.42, 10.53–10.57
    safe harbour rules   14.55–14.58
  valuation obligations
    determining policies and methodologies   10.96
    disclosure of net asset value   10.97–10.98
    external valuers   10.100–10.103
    frequency of valuation   10.104
    generally   10.66, 10.93–10.95
    independence and staffing   10.99
    oversight   10.209
Alternative Investment Management Association
  generally   1.12
Anti-avoidance rules
  consideration, generally   14.7
Anti-money laundering
  administrators' function   6.30
  British Virgin Islands   2.155–2.156
  Cayman Islands   2.48–2.51
  funds of hedge funds   16.30
  Italy   13.232
  Jersey   3.34
  Malta   4.422–4.423
  Switzerland   4.430
Assets
  depositary's function
    delegation   10.216–10.223, 10.224,
    10.230, 10.239–10.241
    generally   10.201, 10.204–10.208
    sub-delegation   10.219
Auditors
  generally   6.4, 6.62
Australia
  Australian financial services licence
    (AFSL)   13.12, 13.14–13.18
  controlled foreign companies
    (CFCs)   13.20–13.25
  corporate CIVs   13.9
  definition of hedge fund   13.3
  disclosure and reporting obligations   13.2, 13.8
  fund operators   13.7
  hedge fund structure   13.4–13.9
  limited partnership CIVs   13.9
  managed investment schemes   13.4

Index

Australia – *cont.*
  marketing
    Australia 13.20–13.25
    email or telephone, by 13.13
    foreign hedge funds 13.10–13.18
    framework, generally 13.1–13.3
  promoter of foreign funds 13.12–13.18
  register of foreign funds 13.10–13.11
  taxation 13.19–13.25
    attributable taxpayers 13.22
    flow through 13.5
  unit trusts 13.5
  wholesale clients 13.11
Authorised funds
  United Kingdom 1.4

B

Back-to-back loans
  UCITS 12.137
Benchmarks
  market abuse 9.69, 9.119
Bermuda
  funds established in 1.4
Body corporate
  high net worth, promotion of hedge funds to 9.47–9.48
  sale, activities in connection with 9.21
Bond funds
  United Kingdom 14.96, 14.103
Borrowing
  British Virgin Islands 2.90
  Cayman Islands 2.39
  hedge funds' ability to use 1.4
  Stock borrowing 7.6
  UCITS 12.136–12.137
British Overseas Territory
  British Virgin Islands 2.58
  Cayman Islands 2.2
British Virgin Islands
  accounts and audit 2.95–2.99
  administrators 2.86–2.88, 2.123–2.125
  AIFMD 2.146–2.154
  anti-money laundering 2.155–2.156
  approved funds 2.65, 2.77, 2.83–2.85, 2.101
    accounts 2.99
    offering documents 2.94
  approved manager regime 2.128
  borrowing 2.90
  British Overseas Territory 2.58
  Business Companies Act 2.62–2.63, 2.111
  closed-ended funds 2.68, 2.147, 2.151

British Virgin Islands – *cont.*
  Common Reporting Standard (CRS) 2.133, 2.140–2.145
  corporate entities 2.109, 2.111
    approved manager regime 2.128
  custodians 2.86–2.88, 2.123–2.125
  EU Savings Directive 2.131–2.132
  exempted investors 2.70, 2.72
  finance industry 2.62–2.65
  fund incorporated, formed or organised outside the BVI 2.108
  fund interests 2.66–2.67
  fund ownership 2.102
  fund types, generally 2.66–2.76
  fund vehicles 2.109–2.122
    corporate entities 2.109, 2.111, 5.6
    generally 2.66–2.69
    limited partnerships 2.65, 2.66, 2.109, 2.116–2.119
    open-ended investment companies 2.110
    segregated portfolio companies 2.112–2.115
    unit trusts 2.66, 2.109, 2.120–2.122
  generally 1.4, 2.57–2.61
  Incubator and Approved Funds Regulations 2.65, 2.77–2.85
  incubator funds 2.65, 2.77–2.82, 2.101
    accounts 2.99
    offering documents 2.94
  Insolvency Act 2.63
  International Business Companies Act 2.62
  investment restrictions 2.89
  investors' rights 2.100
  judicial system 2.59
  jurisdiction
    finance industry 2.63–2.65
    generally 2.58–2.59
  Limited Partnership Act 2.116–2.118
  managers and administrators 2.86–2.88, 2.123–2.125
    approved 2.126–2.129
  master-feeder structure 2.65
  Money Laundering Reporting Officer (MLRO) 2.155
  mutual funds 2.65
    borrowing by 2.90
    definition 2.66
    in or from within the BVI 2.107
    fund interests 2.66–2.67
    incorporated, formed or organised outside the BVI 2.108
    investment restrictions 2.89
  Mutual Fund Annual Return (MFAR) 2.98
  offering documents 2.91–2.94, 2.104

Index

British Virgin Islands – *cont.*
  Mutual Funds Act   2.65
  Mutual Funds Regulations   2.65
  number of hedge funds   2.65
  offering documents   2.91–2.94, 2.104
  prospectus   2.91–2.94, 2.100
  open-ended funds   2.69, 2.151
  Partnership Act   2.117
  private funds   2.65, 2.69, 2.73–2.74, 2.101
    accounts and audit   2.95–2.98
    application for recognition   2.85
    functionaries   2.86–2.88
    offering documents   2.91
    recognition   2.105
    regulatory process   2.105
  Privy Council, appeal to   2.59
  professional funds   2.65, 2.69, 2.70–2.72, 2.88, 2.101
    accounts and audit   2.95–2.98
    application for recognition   2.85
    functionaries   2.86–2.88
    offering documents   2.91
    recognition   2.105
    regulatory process   2.105
  professional investors   2.70–2.71
  prospectus   2.91–2.94, 2.106
    misrepresentation in   2.100
  public funds   2.65, 2.69, 2.75, 2.100
    accounts and audit   2.95–2.98
    functionaries   2.86–2.88
    prospectus   2.92–2.93, 2.100, 2.106
    registration   2.106
    regulatory process   2.103–2.104
  recognised foreign funds   2.69, 2.76
  regulatory regime   2.66–2.76
    approved managers   2.126–2.129
    flexibility   2.62
    fund ownership   2.102
    fund types   2.66–2.76
    fund vehicles   2.109–2.122
    Incubator and Approved Funds Regulations   2.65, 2.77–2.85, 2.99
    mutual funds   2.65, 2.66
    process, generally   2.103–2.108
    Securities and Investment Business Act   2.66–2.76
  Securities and Investment Business Act   2.66–2.76
  segregated portfolio companies   2.112–2.115
  taxation   2.130
  trustees   2.123–2.125
  UK FATCA (UK CDOT)   2.132, 2.137–2.139
  unit trusts   2.66, 2.109, 2.120–2.122

British Virgin Islands – *cont.*
  US FATCA   2.132, 2.133–2.136

C

Capital introduction
  prime broker's role   7.6
Capital maintenance
  companies   5.10
Cash flow
  monitoring   10.201–10.203
Cayman Islands
  accounts   2.40, 2.43, 2.45
  administered mutual funds   2.28, 2.31–2.32, 2.42, 2.44
  AEOI Regulations   2.55–2.56
  AIFMD   10.3
  anti-money laundering   2.48–2.51
  borrowing   2.39
  British Overseas Territory   2.2
  Cayman Islands Monetary Authority (CIMA)   2.4
    registration and regulation by   2.28, 2.30, 2.32, 2.33, 2.35, 2.36, 2.40, 2.42–2.46
  closed-ended funds   2.11, 2.24
  Common Reporting Standard (CRS)   2.54–2.55
  companies   2.8, 5.6, 14.8
    exempted   2.12–2.16
    limited liability   2.22–2.24
    segregated portfolio   2.25, 4.5, 4.16
  directors *see* fund directors *below*
  exchange controls   2.53
  exempted companies   2.12–2.16
  exempted mutual funds   2.28, 2.36, 2.42
  finance industry   2.4–2.6
    infrastructure supporting   2.3
  fund directors
    breach of duty   8.64–8.67
    company insolvency   8.57
    conflicts of duty and interest   8.59, 8.63
    crisis management   8.81
    delegation of duties   8.54, 8.71, 8.76, 8.78, 8.79–8.80, 8.82
    documentation   8.88
    duty of care, diligence and skill   8.58, 8.85
    fees   8.83
    fiduciary duties   8.55, 8.59–8.63
    fund launch   8.76–8.78
    generally   8.53–8.56
    good faith   8.59–8.60
    liability   8.68–8.75

Index

Cayman Islands – *cont.*
  fund directors – *cont.*
    proper purpose principle   8.59, 8.61
    registration and licensing   8.89–8.90
    supervisory responsibilities   8.54,
         8.79–8.80, 8.82
    to whom duties owed   8.56
    unfettered discretion   8.59, 8.62
    Weavering case   8.53, 8.68–8.87
    wilful neglect or default   8.68–8.75,
         8.86
  fund ownership   2.41
  funds established in   1.4, 2.1–2.3
  funds with few investors   2.42
  fund vehicles
    choice of   2.13
    companies   2.12–2.16, 5.6, 14.8
    exempted companies   2.12–2.16
    limited liability companies   2.22–2.24
    limited partnerships   2.12, 2.17–2.21,
         2.52, 5.24, 14.8
    open-ended companies   14.8
    segregated portfolio companies   2.25,
         4.5, 4.16
    unit trusts   2.12, 2.26–2.27, 2.30, 2.52
  generally   1.4, 2.28–2.29
  Hong Kong, funds managed in   4.4–4.5,
     4.7
  investment managers and advisors   2.47
  investment restrictions   2.38
  judicial system   2.2
  jurisdiction generally   2.1–2.3
  licensed mutual funds   2.28, 2.30, 2.42,
     2.44
  limited liability companies   2.22–2.24
    Hong Kong, managed from   4.7
  limited partnerships   2.12, 2.17–2.21,
     2.52, 5.24, 14.8
  Money Laundering Reporting Officer
     (MLRO)   2.49–2.50
  mutual funds   2.8–2.11
    accounts   2.40, 2.43, 2.45
    administered   2.28, 2.31–2.32, 2.42,
         2.44
    borrowing by   2.39
    definition   2.8–2.10
    equity interests   2.8–2.9
    exclusions   2.10
    exempted   2.28, 2.36, 2.42
    exempted companies   2.14–2.16
    fees   2.43
    licensed   2.28, 2.30, 2.42, 2.44
    Mutual Funds Law   2.7
    offering documents   2.30, 2.37–2.38,
         2.43
    promoter   2.30, 2.31
    registered   2.28, 2.29, 2.33–2.35

Cayman Islands – *cont.*
    Mutual Funds Law   2.7
    number of hedge funds   2.4
    offering documents   2.30, 2.37–2.38, 2.43
    Privy Council, appeal to   2.2
    Proceeds of Crime Law   2.48
    registered mutual funds   2.28, 2.29,
         2.33–2.35
  regulatory regime
    flexibility   2.5–2.6, 2.14
    fund ownership   2.41
    fund types   2.42–2.46
    fund vehicles   2.11–2.21
    generally   2.4–2.7
    mutual funds   2.8–2.11
    Mutual Funds Law   2.7
    process, generally   2.35–2.38,
         2.42–2.46
  reporting financial institutions   2.56
  segregated portfolio companies   2.25, 4.5,
     4.16
  socio-political framework   2.3
  taxation   2.52–2.56
    tax-exempt funds   14.8
  UK IGA   2.54–2.55
  unit trusts   2.12, 2.26–2.27, 2.30, 2.52
  US FATCA   2.54
  US IGA   2.54–2.55
China
  background, generally   13.26–13.30
  collective asset management
     schemes   13.32
  collective investment trust schemes   13.32
  foreign exchange controls   13.68
  foreign hedge funds
    marketing, generally   13.68–13.70
    Qualified Domestic Institutional
       Investors (QDII)
       Scheme   13.71–13.73
    Qualified Domestic Investment
       Partnership (QDLP)
       Scheme   13.74–13.78
    qualified investors   13.70, 13.71–13.78
  fund managers, registration   13.33,
     13.41–13.43
  future trends   13.79–13.83
  investor qualification   13.46–13.49, 13.53
  private fund manager (PFM)
     funds   13.62–13.67
    beneficial ownership   13.67
    corporate structure   13.67
    investment process   13.67
    personnel qualifications   13.67
    PFM WFOE regime   13.62–13.67
    qualified investors   13.67
  private funds   13.27, 13.36, 13.50–13.61

Index

China – *cont.*
  private funds – *cont.*
    filing   13.33, 13.41, 13.44–13.45
    fund managers, registration   13.33, 13.41–13.43
    liability for illegal activities   13.61
    licensing for marketing   13.54–13.56
    marketing   13.50–13.61
    qualified investors   13.46–13.49, 13.53, 13.67
    regulatory framework   13.36–13.40
    restrictions on marketing   13.57–13.60
  public funds   13.36
  regulatory framework   13.36–13.40
  sunshine private funds   13.27–13.30
  supervising authorities   13.29
  wholly foreign-owned enterprises (WFOE)   13.62–13.67
Closed-ended companies
  generally   5.5
Closed-ended funds
  AIFMD   2.147, 2.151
  British Virgin Islands   2.68, 2.147, 2.151
  Cayman Islands   2.11, 2.24
  definition   2.11
  generally   5.5
  Guernsey   3.105–3.106
  Italy   13.202
  Jersey   3.20, 3.23, 3.36, 3.46, 3.47, 3.65, 3.77
  limited liability companies   2.24
  United Kingdom   14.93
Code of Market Conduct (CoMC)   9.59–9.60
Collective investment undertakings (CIUs)
  see also UCITS
  characteristics   10.18
Collective investment vehicles
  Australia   13.9
Commodity pools *see* United States
Common contractual funds (CCFs)
  Ireland   4.119, 4.136–4.139, 4.151, 4.180, 4.183
Common Reporting Standard (CRS)
  British Virgin Islands   2.133, 2.140–2.145
  Cayman Islands   2.54–2.55
  Guernsey   3.161
  Jersey   3.87
  tax considerations   14.7
Companies
  annual general meetings   5.11
  British Virgin Islands   2.66, 2.109–2.111, 5.6
    approved manager regime   2.128
    open-ended investment companies   2.110

Companies – *cont.*
  British Virgin Islands – *cont.*
    segregated portfolio companies   2.112–2.115
  capital maintenance   5.10
  Cayman Islands   2.8, 5.6, 14.8
    exempted companies   2.8, 2.14–2.16
    limited liability companies   2.22–2.24
    segregated portfolio companies   2.25, 4.5, 4.16
  class rights   5.9
  closed-ended   5.5
  dual share structure   5.7
  fund promoters   5.7
  funds of hedge funds   3.141–3.143
  generally   5.1–5.14
  group, promotion of hedge funds   9.44
  Guernsey   3.107, 3.108–3.113, 3.150, 3.151, 5.6
    taxation   3.150
  high net worth, promotion of hedge funds to   9.47–9.48
  investors' rights   5.9, 5.12–5.13
  Ireland   4.119, 4.126–4.133, 4.151
  Jersey   3.13, 3.16, 3.76, 3.78–3.79, 5.6
    incorporated cell companies (ICCs)   3.46, 3.51, 3.62, 3.76, 3.79
    protected cell companies (PCCs)   3.46, 3.51, 3.62, 3.76, 3.79
    regulated funds   3.24, 3.62
    unregulated funds   3.23
  legal personality   5.3
  limited liability
    Cayman Islands   2.22–2.24
    Malta   4.342
    Netherlands   13.294–13.295, 13.303–13.304
  limited partnerships compared   5.17, 5.22–5.25
  Malta   4.341–4.347
  master-feeder structure   5.1, 5.21, 5.31–5.37
  mutual funds   2.8
  offshore   5.2, 5.4, 5.6
  onshore   5.4
  redeemable shares   5.6, 5.7, 5.9
  shareholder liability   5.3, 5.6
  side letters   5.14
  Singapore   4.461, 4.464–4.468
  stock exchange listings   5.8
  structure   5.2
  Switzerland   4.489, 4.493–4.497, 4.502–4.505
  taxation   5.4
  treasury stock   5.5
  US investment companies   11.7–11.8

Index

Companies – *cont.*
  voting rights   5.7–5.9, 6.11
Company secretary functions
  generally   6.42
Contract for difference
  United UK regulatory regime   9.5
Contractual funds as fund vehicles
  Malta   4.359–4.360
  Switzerland   4.489, 4.490–4.492
Co-operatives
  Netherlands   13.294–13.295, 13.305
Creditors
  directors' duty to   8.6
Crisis management
  fund directors   8.81
Cross-product margining structure
  prime broker's role   7.25–7.26
Custodians
  British Virgin Islands   2.86–2.88,
                                   2.123–2.125
  Guernsey   3.142
  Hong Kong   4.82–4.84
  Jersey   3.14, 3.36, 3.54
  Malta   4.408–4.411, 4.437
  prime brokers as   6.45, 6.55, 7.6, 7.10,
                          7.11–7.14, 7.28
  segregation of assets   7.13, 7.28
Custody of assets
  prime brokers   6.45, 6.55, 7.6, 7.10,
                          7.11–7.14, 7.28
Cyprus
  indirect investment   14.13

D

Dealing in investments
  UK regulatory regime
    arranging deals   9.9–9.10
    overseas persons   9.22–9.24
    as principal or agent   9.6–9.8
Debt instruments
  UK regulatory regime   9.5
Delegation of functions
  AIFMD provisions
    conditions, generally   10.246–10.247
    duty to notify regulator   10.245
    instructing delegate   10.255
    letter box entities   10.253–10.254
    liability and   10.259–10.262
    monitoring delegation   10.255
    non-EU delegates   10.250–10.251
    remuneration of delegates   10.258
    sub-delegation   10.256–10.257
    supervision   10.252

Delegation of functions – *cont.*
  AIFMD provisions – *cont.*
    who may be delegated
      to   10.248–10.250
    withdrawing delegation   10.255
  directors, by   6.5, 8.1–8.4, 8.9, 8.22–8.24,
                      8.54, 8.79–8.80, 8.82
Depositaries
  AIFMD provisions
    behavioural standards   10.213–10.215
    conflicts of interest   10.214–10.215,
                          10.242–10.244
    contractual arrangements and depositar-
      ies   10.231–10.235
    delegation of depositary func-
      tion   10.216–10.223, 10.224,
                    10.230, 10.239–10.241
    depositary lite   10.196, 10.236–10.244
    duties generally   10.201
    generally   10.195–10.197
    liability of depositary   10.224–10.232,
                                10.241
    location   10.198
    monitoring cash flows   10.201–10.203,
                                10.216
    oversight functions   10.201,
                   10.209–10.212, 10.216
    prime broker acting as deposi-
      tary   10.200, 10.214
    safe-keeping of assets   10.201,
              10.204–10.208, 10.218–10.230
    who may act as   10.198–10.200,
                         10.236–10.238
  Ireland   4.174–4.177
  Luxembourg   4.268–4.271
  UCITS provisions
    behavioural standards   12.34
    delegation of depositary func-
      tion   12.37, 12.39–12.41
    duties, generally   12.33
    generally   12.11, 12.33–12.34
    liability of depositary   12.37–12.41
    reporting obligations   12.42
    re-use of assets held in custody   12.36
    who may act as   12.35–12.36
Depreciation deposit
  performance fees   15.24
Derivative contracts
  market manipulation   9.69
Derivative instruments
  hedge funds, generally   16.25
  market manipulation   9.69, 9.75
Derivatives, investment in
  generally   1.4
  UCITS *see* UCITS
Directors of the fund *see* Fund directors

Index

Disclosure and Transparency Rules
  (DTR)   9.59–9.60
Discretionary management
  investment managers' function   6.14–6.16
Distressed debt
  investment in   1.4
Distributing funds
  United Kingdom   14.90
Diversification
  investment in hedge funds   16.15
Dual-tiered structure *see* Master-feeder structure
Due diligence
  funds of hedge funds   16.27
  hedge funds   16.31–16.33

E

Employees
  directors' duty to   8.6
Equalisation
  equalisation adjustment
    deficit subscription   15.25
    generally   15.25
    premium subscription   15.25
  equalisation factor/depreciation deposit
    deficit subscription   15.24
    premium subscription   15.24
    generally   15.20–15.22
    simple method   15.23
Equity interests
  mutual funds   2.8–2.9
European Exchange Rate Mechanism crisis
  generally   15.2
European passport
  AIFMD marketing provisions   10.154–10.160, 10.268
  France   13.90, 13.98–13.102
  Ireland   4.88, 4.111, 4.154, 4.191
  Italy   13.217
  Malta   13.262–13.265
  Netherlands   13.309, 13.314–13.316
  Spain   13.361
European Union
  AIFMD *see* Alternative investment funds
  Code of Conduct on Business Taxation   3.156
  ELTIF Regulation   13.94
  Guernsey and   3.90, 3.144–3.145, 3.155–3.156, 3.163–3.165
  Ireland   4.88
  Jersey and   3.7–3.9, 3.12
  Lamfalussy process   9.57

European Union – *cont.*
  Market Abuse Directive (EU MAD)   9.56, 9.59, 9.81
  Market Abuse Regulation
    (EU MAR)   9.56–9.57, 9.59, 9.62–9.63, 9.69–9.75, 9.77–9.115
    extra-territorial dimension   9.73
    inside information   9.74–9.76
    insider dealing   9.77–9.81
    insider lists   9.104–9.108
    investment recommendations   9.109–9.112
    legitimate behaviour   9.86–9.92
    market manipulation   9.69, 9.99–9.103
    market soundings   9.93–9.98
    scope   9.68–9.73
    unlawful disclosure of inside information   9.82–9.85
  Markets in Financial Instruments Directive (MiFID/MiFID II)
    AIFMD and   10.45–10.46
    authorisation process   4.196–4.197
    EU MAR and   9.71
    Ireland   4.154, 4.189–4.200
    Malta   4.332, 4.365, 9.90, 13.249, 13.251, 13.252, 13.256, 13.279
    market abuse   9.71
    Netherlands   13.315
  Markets in Financial Instruments Regulation (MiFIR)   4.190, 10.46
  national private placement regimes (NPPRs)   2.146
  PRIIPs Regulation   12.149–12.150
  Savings Directive   2.131–2.132, 3.157, 3.163
  UCITS Directive *see* UCITS
  whistleblowing   9.113–9.114
Exchange controls
  Cayman Islands   2.53
Exempted mutual funds
  Cayman Islands   2.28, 2.36, 2.42
Expenses
  monitoring   6.43
Expert funds
  Jersey   3.20, 3.32, 3.36, 3.38, 3.58, 3.63–3.67

F

Fees
  administrators' function   6.33, 6.36
  funds of hedge funds   16.28
  investment managers
    management fee   6.18–6.19, 6.33, 6.36, 15.6–15.7

Index

Fees – *cont.*
  investment managers – *cont.*
    performance fee 6.18–6.20, 6.33, 6.36, 15.6–15.9
  mainstream funds 16.5–16.6
  management fees
    amount 1.4, 6.33, 6.36, 15.6–15.7
    generally 1.4, 6.18–6.20, 15.6–15.7
    purpose 6.19, 15.7
  performance fees
    amount 1.4, 6.33, 6.36, 15.6–15.25
    calculation 15.6–15.25
    equalisation 15.20–15.25
    generally 1.4, 6.18–6.20, 15.6–15.9
    high-water mark 15.10–15.12
    purpose 6.20
    series method 15.14–15.19
  prime brokers 6.61
  redemption fees
    gate 15.28–15.31
    generally 15.28–15.31
  structure generally 1.4, 16.13–16.14
  subscription fees 15.26–15.27

Financial Conduct Authority (FCA)
  authorisation by 1.4, 1.10, 9.3, 9.25–9.29
  Code of Conduct (COCON) 9.62, 9.131–9.133
  market abuse regulations 9.58–9.63
    disciplinary powers 9.64–9.67
  Part IV permission 9.25
  Principles for Businesses (PRIN) 9.62, 9.125–9.129
  regulation by 1.10–1.14
  Statements of Principle and Code of Practice for Approved Persons (APER) 9.62, 9.130

Financial statements
  reporting, generally 6.37

Financing provision
  prime broker's role 7.6, 7.10, 7.17–7.19

Fonds commun de placement **(FCP)**
  Luxembourg 4.225, 4.226–4.241

Foundation as fund vehicle
  Malta 3.357–3.358

France
  AIFMD 13.85–13.86, 13.97–13.109
    Brexit 13.104
    licensing issues 13.103–13.104
    passporting provisions 13.90, 13.98–13.102
  alternative investment funds (AIFs) 13.85, 13.88
    non-retail 13.94
  Autorité des Marchés Financiers (AMF) 13.84

France – *cont.*
  eligible investors 13.91–13.94
  ELTIF Regulation 13.94
  financial instrument ratios 13.95
  fonds commun de placement à risques 13.88
  fonds commun de placement (FCPs) 13.88
  fonds d'investissement à vocation générale 13.88
  fonds professionnels à vocation générale 13.88
  foreign hedge funds
    active marketing 13.97–13.104
    passive marketing 13.105–13.109
    unauthorised, investment in 13.105
  fund structures 13.88–13.90
  investment restrictions 13.95–13.96
  marketing, activities constituting 13.105–13.109
  regulatory framework 13.84–13.87
  risk allocation ratios 13.95
  taxation 13.110–13.113
  UCITS 13.86–13.88

Fund directors
  appointment 6.11
  attention to the business 8.20–8.21
  board 6.5–6.10
  company insolvency, duty on 8.8, 8.17, 8.57
  conflicts of interest 8.40–8.44, 8.59, 8.63
  crisis management 8.81
  declaration of interests 8.45–8.46, 8.54
  delegation by 6.5, 8.1–8.4, 8.9, 8.22–8.24, 8.54, 8.79–8.80, 8.82
  derivative actions against 8.50–8.52
  documentation 8.88
  duties 8.5–8.52
    breach 8.48–8.52, 8.64–8.67
    to whom owed 8.6, 8.56
    Weavering case 8.68–8.87
  duty of care 8.10, 8.14–8.15, 8.55, 8.58
  duty to act within powers 8.10, 8.12–8.13
  fettering of discretion 8.47, 8.59, 8.62
  fiduciary duty 8.5, 8.10, 8.25–8.26, 8.59–8.63
  fund launch 8.76–8.78
  generally 6.5–6.10, 8.1
  good faith 8.27–8.30, 8.59–8.60
  interests of company, duty to act in 8.27–8.30
  liability 8.68–8.75
  proper purpose, duty to act for 8.31–8.33, 8.59, 8.61
  role 6.7
  secret profits, making 8.34–8.39

Index

Fund directors – *cont.*
  skill, requirements as to   8.16–8.20
  supervisory responsibilities   8.54, 8.79–8.80, 8.82
  United States   6.9
Fund ownership
  British Virgin Islands   2.102
  Cayman Islands   2.41
Funds of hedge funds
  advantages   16.27
  disadvantages   16.28–16.30
  generally   1.4, 16.26
  Germany   1.4, 13.116, 13.119
  Guernsey   3.141–3.143
  Luxembourg   4.287, 4.300–4.301
Fund types
  administered mutual funds, Cayman Islands   2.28, 2.31–2.32, 2.42, 2.44
  alternative investment funds, Jersey   3.20, 3.27–3.29
  authorised funds, Guernsey   3.104–3.106, 3.122–3.130
  closed-ended funds
    Guernsey   3.105
    Jersey   3.20, 3.23, 3.36, 3.46, 3.47, 3.65, 3.77
  collective investment funds, Jersey   3.56–3.58
  exempted mutual funds, Cayman Islands   2.28, 2.36, 2.42
  expert funds, Jersey   3.20, 3.32, 3.36, 3.38, 3.58, 3.63–3.67
  funds of hedge funds, Guernsey   3.141–3.143
  Jersey eligible investor funds (JEIFs)   3.20–3.21, 3.32–3.33, 3.36, 3.38, 3.58, 3.70–3.71
  licensed mutual funds, Cayman Islands   2.28, 2.30, 2.42, 2.44
  listed funds, Jersey   3.38, 3.58, 3.68–3.69
  open-ended funds   5.5, 15.9
    Guernsey   3.105
    Jersey   3.77
  private funds
    British Virgin Islands   2.65, 2.69, 2.73–2.74, 2.101, 2.105
    Jersey   3.20, 3.22, 3.29, 3.36, 3.46, 3.57–3.58
  professional funds, British Virgin Islands   2.65, 2.69, 2.70–2.72, 2.88, 2.101, 2.105
  public funds, British Virgin Islands   2.65, 2.69, 2.75, 2.100, 2.103
  qualifying investor funds, Guernsey   3.128–3.131
  recognised funds, Jersey   3.58, 3.72

Fund types – *cont.*
  registered funds, Guernsey   3.104–3.106, 3.131
  registered mutual funds, Cayman Islands   2.28, 2.29, 2.33–2.35
  regulated funds, Jersey   3.24–3.29, 3.31–3.33, 3.37, 3.55–3.58
  unclassified funds, Jersey   3.58, 3.59–3.62
  unregulated funds, Jersey   3.20–3.21, 3.23, 3.30, 3.36–3.37, 3.47–3.54
Fund vehicles
  companies
    see also **Companies**
    British Virgin Islands   2.7, 2.109–2.111
    Cayman Islands   2.13–2.16
    funds of hedge funds   3.141–3.143
    generally   5.1–5.14
    Guernsey   3.107, 3.108–3.113, 3.150, 3.151
    Jersey   3.23–3.24, 3.78–3.79
    Malta   4.341–4.347
    master-feeder structure   5.1, 5.21, 5.31–5.37
    structure   5.2
  contractual funds, Malta   4.359–4.360
  corporate entities
    British Virgin Islands   2.109–2.111
    Cayman Islands   2.12, 2.13–2.16
  foundations, Malta   4.357–4.358
  limited liability companies
    Cayman Islands   2.22–2.24
    Netherlands   13.294–13.295, 13.303–13.304
  limited partnerships
    see also **Limited partnerships**
    British Virgin Islands   2.66, 2.116–2.119
    Cayman Islands   2.12, 2.17–2.21, 2.52
    generally   5.1, 5.15–5.24
    Guernsey   3.107, 3.114–3.117, 3.150, 3.152
    Jersey   3.16, 3.23–3.24, 3.46, 3.51–3.52, 3.80–3.82
    Malta   4.348–4.352
    master-feeder structure   5.1, 5.21, 5.31–5.37
    Netherlands   13.294–13.295, 13.300–13.302
  master-feeder structure   5.1, 5.21, 5.31–5.37
  segregated portfolio companies   2.112–2.115
    British Virgin Islands   2.112–2.115
    Cayman Islands   2.25, 4.5, 4.16
    definition   2.114
  unit trusts
    see also **Unit trusts**

519

Index

Fund vehicles – *cont.*
  unit trusts – *cont.*
    British Virgin Islands   2.66, 2.109, 2.120–2.122
    Cayman Islands   2.12, 2.26–2.27, 2.30, 2.52
    generally   5.1, 5.25–5.30
    Guernsey   3.107, 3.118–3.120, 3.150, 3.151
    Jersey   3.16, 3.23–3.24, 3.46, 3.51–3.52, 3.80–3.82, 3.83
    Malta   4.353–4.356
Futures
  UK regulatory regime   9.5

G

Gate
  meaning and purpose   15.36–15.38
Germany
  AIFMD   13.114
  Anlagebedingungen   13.117
  Bundesanstalt für Finanzdienstleistungsaufsicht (BaFin)   13.114
  contractual establishment   13.120
  Dach-Hedgefonds   13.116, 13.119
  distribution restrictions   13.133–13.134
  establishing funds   13.120–13.121
    prior notice to authorities   13.122–13.123, 13.126
  foreign hedge funds
    Article 32 procedure   13.148–13.150
    Article 36 procedure   13.151–13.154
    Article 42 procedure   13.155–13.157
    EEA-located AIFMs   13.148–13.150
    marketing   13.145–13.157
    non-EEA-located AIFMs   13.155–13.157
    non-EU AIFs   13.151–13.154
    registration   13.145, 13.147
  fund management   13.120
  fund rules   13.126
  generally   1.4
  Hedgefonds   13.116, 13.120
  hedge fund structure   13.116–13.119
  investor qualification   13.117
  Kapitalanlagegesetzbuch (KAGB)   13.114
  Kapitalverwaltungsgesellschaften (KVGs)   13.116
  limitation of investment activities   13.129–13.132
  manager qualifications   13.127–13.128
  regulatory framework   13.114–13.115

Germany – *cont.*
  reporting and disclosure requirements   13.124–13.125
  Spezial-AIFs   13.117, 13.120
  supervisory regulation   13.120–13.122
  taxation   13.137–13.144
  transparency mechanisms   13.135–13.136
  UCITS   13.121
Guernsey
  administrators   3.104
  AIFMD   3.138–3.140, 3.144–3.145
  authorised funds   3.104–3.106
    approval process   3.121–3.130
  closed-ended funds   3.105–3.106
  collective investment schemes   3.106
    Registered Collective Investment Scheme Rules   3.132–3.133
  Common Reporting Standard (CRS)   3.161
  companies   3.107, 3.108–3.113, 3.150, 3.151, 5.6
    fast-track incorporation   3.109
    hybrid   3.110
    incorporated cell (ICCs)   3.110, 3.113
    limited by guarantee   3.110
    limited liability   3.110
    multi-class   3.110
    protected cell (PCCs)   3.110–3.112
    single-class   3.110
    solvency test   3.109
    unlimited liability   3.110
  controlled investment business   3.102
  custodians   3.142
  customary law   3.92
  EU Savings Directive   3.157, 3.163
  European Union and   3.90, 3.144–3.145, 3.155–3.158, 3.163–3.165
  finance industry   3.95–3.98
  funds of hedge funds   3.141–3.143
  fund vehicles
    companies   3.107, 3.108–3.113, 3.150, 3.151, 5.6, 14.8
    limited partnerships   3.107, 3.114–3.117, 3.150, 3.152
    open-ended companies   14.9
    unit trusts   3.107, 3.118–3.120, 3.150, 3.151
  generally   1.4, 3.88–3.91
  Guernsey Financial Services Commission (GFSC)   3.98, 3.99–3.102
  historical background   3.91
  incorporated cell companies (ICCs)   3.110, 3.113
  investor protection   3.141–3.143
  legal system   3.91–3.94
  limited partnerships   3.107, 3.114–3.117, 3.150, 3.152, 14.8

Index

Guernsey – *cont.*
  limited partnerships – *cont.*
    legal personality 3.116
    manager led products (MLPs) 3.106, 3.138–3.140
  net asset value estimation 3.142
  number of hedge funds 3.97
  open-ended funds 3.105–3.106
  prime brokers 3.142
  private investment funds (PIFs) 3.106, 3.134–3.137
  protected cell companies (PCCs) 3.110–3.112
  Protection of Investors (Bailiwick of Guernsey) Law 3.100
  qualifying investor funds (QIFS) 3.122, 3.128–3.131
  registered funds 3.104–3.106
    approval process 3.121, 3.131–3.133
    Registered Collective Investment Scheme Rules 3.132–3.133
  regulatory regime
    controlled investment business 3.102
    fund authorisation 3.121–3.133
    generally 3.99–3.102, 3.141–3.143
    independent regulator 3.98, 3.99–3.102
    investment funds 3.104–3.107
    service providers 3.103
  service providers 3.103
  Stock Exchange (TISE) 3.146–3.148
  taxation
    companies 3.150, 14.8
    generally 3.149–3.150
    income tax 3.149, 3.151–3.154
    international tax initiatives 3.155–3.167
  The International Stock Exchange (TISE) 3.146–3.148
  trust instruments 3.118
  United Kingdom and 3.88
  unit trusts 3.107, 3.118–3.120, 3.150, 3.151
  US FATCA 3.159

H

Hedge funds
  absolute performance 16.9
  advantages for investors 16.1–16.47
  allocation and diversification 16.15
  characteristics 1.4–1.5
  fee structure 1.4, 16.13–16.14
    see also **Fees**
  historical background 1.3

Hedge funds – *cont.*
  investment
    see also **Investment**
    investment freedom 16.10–16.12
    parameters 1.2, 1.3, 1.4
  leverage or borrowing by 1.4
  losses 15.10
  mainstream funds compared 16.2–16.8
  market abuse *see* **Market abuse**
  meaning 1.1–1.2
    Australia 13.3
  offshore 1.4, 1.10
  overview 1.1–1.15
  portfolio liquidity 1.4
  private equity funds compared 1.5
  profits 15.6
  promotion *see* **Marketing and promotion**
  returns 16.16–16.19
  size of hedge fund industry 1.6
  structured products 16.25
  structuring *see* **Structuring hedge funds**
  synthetic platforms 16.24
  unregulated 1.4
Hedge Fund Standards Board (HFSB) 1.7
Hedge Fund Working Group (HFWG) 1.7
Hedging
  meaning 1.2
High net worth individuals
  promotion of hedge funds to 9.45–9.46
High value/low footprint businesses
  Jersey 3.19
Hong Kong
  asset management 4.28–4.31
    responsibility for funds 4.76–4.80
  audited accounts 4.66
  auditors 4.87
  changes that require SFC approval 4.69
  collateral valuation and management policy 4.81
  continuous professional training programmes 4.70–4.71
  corporate partnership hedge funds 13.158–13.159
  custodians, forthcoming changes 4.82–4.84
  C(WUMP)O 13.161, 13.168–13.177
  directors, changes of 4.68
  forthcoming regulatory changes 4.72–4.87
  fund managers
    accounts, submission 4.67
    Code of Conduct 4.72–4.75
    competence 4.40
    fees 4.67
    financial resource requirements 4.61–4.62

521

Index

Hong Kong – *cont.*
  fund managers – *cont.*
    fitness and properness   4.41–4.42, 4.66
    incorporation   4.39
    licensing *see* licensing *below*
    manager-in-charge regime   4.59–4.60
    notifications, duty to make   4.68–4.69
    obligations   4.66–4.71
    responsibility for funds   4.76–4.80
    Responsible Officers   4.43–4.57, 4.68
    securities lending and repos   4.81
  fund structures   4.4–4.5
  fund valuation   4.87
  growth of hedge fund industry   4.2–4.3
  haircut policy   4.81
  house accounts   4.87
  legal system   4.1
  leverage, forthcoming changes   4.86
  licensing
    application for   4.63–4.65
    continuous professional training programmes   4.70–4.71
    financial resource requirements   4.61–4.62
    key requirements   4.38–4.65
    over-the-counter (OTC) derivatives   4.32–4.37
    regulated activities   4.27–4.31
  limited partnership hedge funds   13.159
  liquidity risk, forthcoming changes   4.85
  litigation risk management   4.9, 4.13
  manager-in-charge regime   4.59–4.60
  marketing
    Code of Conduct   13.191–13.196
    dealing in securities   13.184–13.188
    emails   13.163
    licensing requirement   13.158, 13.183–13.189, 13.191–13.196
    managed accounts   13.190
    oral communication   13.163
    presentations or meetings in person in Hong Kong   13.158, 13.188–13.189
    private placement   13.159, 13.164, 13.167, 13.168, 13.175, 13.178–13.182
    professional investors   13.159–13.160, 13.165–13.167, 13.185
    regulated activities   13.184–13.187, 13.192
    reverse solicitation   13.176
    safe harbours   13.168–13.177
    share offers   13.168–13.177
    telephone calls   13.163
  master feeder funds   4.5, 4.10–4.13
  offshore funds   4.4–4.17

Hong Kong – *cont.*
  open-ended fund companies (OFCs), proposal for   4.17–4.26
  over-the-counter (OTC) derivatives licensing regime   4.32–4.37
  professional investors   13.159–13.160, 13.165–13.167
  reinvestment of cash collateral   4.81
  reporting to investors   4.81
  Responsible Officers
    ceasing to act   4.68
    qualifications required   4.46–4.57
    requirement for, generally   4.43–4.45
    transfer of accreditation   4.58
  securities
    advising on   4.28–4.31
    dealing in   4.28–4.31
    securities lending and repos   4.81
  Securities and Futures Commission (SFC)   4.1
    changes that require SFC approval   4.69
    reporting to   4.87
  Securities and Futures Ordinance (SFO)   13.161–13.167
  segregated portfolio companies (SPCs)   4.5, 4.16
  side pockets   4.87
  stand alone funds   4.5, 4.6–4.9
  taxation   4.4, 4.9
  umbrella funds   4.5, 4.14–4.16
  unit trusts   4.7
  US investors   4.13
Hurdle
  performance fees   1.4

I

Incorporated cell companies (ICCs)
  Guernsey   3.110, 3.113
  Jersey   3.46, 3.51, 3.62, 3.76, 3.79
Incubator funds
  British Virgin Islands   2.65, 2.77–2.82, 2.101
    accounts   2.99
    offering documents   2.94
Independent management companies (ManCos)
  Jersey   3.5–3.6, 3.20
  Super ManCos   4.147, 13.315
Inside information
  case law   9.143–9.151
  legitimate behaviour   9.86–9.92
  market abuse   9.74–9.76
  meaning   9.75

Index

Inside information – *cont.*
  unlawful disclosure 9.82–9.85
Insider dealing
  case law 9.134–9.142
  civil regime
    activities covered by 9.78–9.79
    legitimate behaviour 9.86–9.92
    prohibition 9.77–9.81
  criminal 9.116–9.117
Insider lists
  market abuse 9.104–9.108
Insolvency
  British Virgin Islands 2.63
  company, directors' duties 8.8, 8.17, 8.57
  prime brokers 6.48, 7.27–7.28
Investment
  absolute performance 16.9
  advisers *see* **Investment advisers**
  alternative investment funds 10.14, 10.25–10.27
    investment compartments 10.14, 10.19
    investment strategy, disclosure 10.171
  asset allocation 6.39, 16.15
  by hedge funds 1.4
  dealing in, UK regulatory regime
    arranging deals 9.9–9.10
    overseas persons 9.22–9.24
    as principal or agent 9.6–9.8
  diversification 16.15
  due diligence 16.27, 16.31–16.33
  fee structure 16.13–16.14
  funds of hedge funds
    advantages 16.27
    disadvantages 16.28–16.30
    generally 1.4, 16.26
  general public, by 1.4
  indirect 14.13
  investment freedom 16.10–16.12
  investment policy 6.38
  investor participation 1.4
  investor's rights, misrepresentation 11.50
  key issues 16.31–16.33
  listed funds 1.4
  mainstream funds
    fee structure 16.5–16.6
    long-only bias 16.7
    relative performance 16.2–16.4
    volatility 16.8
  managers *see* **Investment managers**
  promotion *see* **Marketing and promotion**
  reasons for 16.1–16.47
  recommendations, market abuse 9.109–9.112
  repurchase or reverse repurchase transactions 7.6
  returns, generally 16.16–16.19

Investment – *cont.*
  risks 1.12
  routes to
    advisory investment 16.22
    direct investment 16.21
    discretionary investment 16.22
    funds of hedge funds 1.4, 16.26
    generally 1.4, 1.12, 16.20–16.25
    managed accounts 16.23
    structured products 16.25
    synthetic platforms 14.13, 16.24
  side letters
    common provisions 16.36–16.37
    generally 16.34–16.35
    meaning 16.34
    negotiating 16.41
    regulators and 16.38–16.40
  synthetic platforms 14.13, 16.24
  trades
    clearing and settling 6.40, 6.45, 6.52–6.54, 7.6, 7.10, 7.15–7.16
    monitoring 6.38–6.41
  volatility of returns 16.8, 16.16–16.19
Investment advisers
  Cayman Islands 2.47
  independent financial advisers 12.26
  Malta 4.404
  taxation considerations 14.11
  trading in the United Kingdom 14.61
  United Kingdom
    regulatory regime 9.13–9.14
    tax residency and 14.50
  United States *see* **United States**
Investment companies with variable capital (SICAVs)
  Switzerland 4.489, 4.493–4.497
Investment company with fixed share capital (INVCO)
  Malta 4.342–4.343
Investment managers
  additional duties 6.17
  agents, delegation of duties to 6.21
  AIFMs *see* **Alternative investment funds**
  authorisation 1.4
  British Virgin Islands 2.86, 2.123–2.125
    approved Investment managers 2.126–2.129
  Cayman Islands 2.47
  companies 5.7
  discretionary management 6.14–6.16
  fees
    management fee 6.18–6.19, 6.33, 6.36, 15.6–15.7
    performance fee 6.18–6.20, 6.33, 6.36, 15.6–15.9
  generally 6.3, 6.5, 6.11–6.13, 15.6

Index

Investment managers – *cont.*
Germany, manager qualifications 13.127–13.128
Investment Management Agreement (IMA) 6.11–6.12, 6.15, 6.21
Ireland 4.168–4.169, 4.189–4.200
Jersey
  alternative investment fund managers (AIFMs) 3.27–3.29
  expert funds 3.66
  generally 3.21, 3.34–3.39
  independent management companies (ManCos) 3.5–3.6, 3.20
  listed funds 3.68
  local investment managers 3.5, 3.40–3.45
  regulation 3.34–3.39
  special purpose investment managers 3.41
  taxation 3.14, 3.86
Malta 4.399–4.403, 4.437
  offshore 6.13
  onshore 6.13
  regulated entity as investment manager 6.12
Singapore 4.455–4.459
Spain 13.365–13.366
Switzerland
  audit firm 4.515–4.517
  compliance 4.522–4.526
  corporate governance 4.519–4.521
  de minimis exemption 4.510
  financial guarantees 4.535–4.536
  foreign, Swiss branches 4.538–4.545
  governance structure 4.515
  internal control system 4.522–4.526
  internal regulations 4.527–4.529
  legal form 4.518
  licensing 4.508, 4.511–4.512
  regulation 4.507–4.509
  risk management 4.522–4.526
  rules of conduct 4.531–4.534
  taxation 4.560
taxation
  20% test 14.84–14.88
  UK investment manager exemption 14.9, 14.62, 14.67–14.73
United Kingdom 1.10
United States 1.10
Investment professionals
scheme promotion by 9.39–9.40
Investors
AIFMD provisions
  disclosure to investors 10.168–10.176
  domicile 10.118, 10.122
  professional investors 10.123–10.127

Investors – *cont.*
AIFMD provisions – *cont.*
  retail investors 10.123–10.127
alternative investment funds (AIFs) 10.14, 10.22–10.24, 10.48
placing agents/distributors 6.62
potential, introductions of hedge fund to 7.22
rights
  British Virgin Islands 2.100
  enforcement by fund 16.44–16.46
  generally 16.42–16.43
  misrepresentation 16.47
sophisticated, promotion of hedge funds to 9.49–9.52
tax position
  fund structuring 14.5, 14.6–14.7, 14.12
  reporting considerations 14.7
  United Kingdom 14.89–14.104
who may invest 1.4
Ireland
administrators 4.166, 4.170–4.173
AIFMD 4.89, 4.112–4.115
alternative investment funds (AIFs) 4.88, 4.93, 4.104–4.115
  management companies 4.150–4.157
  qualifying investor funds (QIAIFs) 4.104, 4.107–4.115
  retail investor funds (RIAIFs) 4.104, 4.105–4.106
Corporate Governance Code 4.118
depositaries 4.166, 4.174–4.177
double taxation treaties 4.90, 4.182, 4.189, 4.460
EU passporting provisions 4.88, 4.111, 4.154, 4.191
fitness and probity requirements 4.94, 4.116–4.117
fund authorisation 4.143–4.149
fund vehicles
  common contractual funds (CCFs) 4.119, 4.136–4.139, 4.151, 4.180, 4.183
  investment companies 4.119, 4.126–4.133, 4.151
  investment limited partnerships (ILPs) 4.119, 4.140–4.142, 4.151, 4.183
  Irish Collective Asset-management Vehicle (ICAV) 4.119, 4.121–4.125, 4.151, 4.179, 4.183, 14.8
  unit trusts 4.119, 4.134–4.135
growth of investment funds industry 4.91–4.92
indirect investment 14.13

Index

Ireland – cont.
  investment managers 4.166, 4.168–4.169, 4.189–4.200
  management companies (FMCs)
    AIFMs 4.150–4.157
    delegation of functions 4.154, 4.165
    designated persons 4.165
    directors 4.165
    establishing 4.159–4.165
    generally 4.150–4.158
    key requirements 4.165
    organisational effectiveness 4.165
    Super ManCos 4.157
    UCITS 4.150–4.157
  MiFID 4.155, 4.189–4.200
  portfolio management 4.153
  prime brokers 4.166
  regulatory authority 4.93
  regulatory framework 4.93–4.118
  risk management 4.153
  service providers 4.166–4.177
  Stock Exchange 1.4, 4.184–4.188
  taxation 4.90, 4.178–4.183
    VAT-exempt services 4.181
  UCITS 4.88, 4.93, 4.95–4.103, 4.150–4.157

Italy
  AIFMD 13.197
    passporting provisions 13.217, 13.361
  anti-money laundering regulations 13.232
  Commissione Nazionale per le Società e la Borsa (CONSOB) 13.199, 13.201
  fair conduct 13.201
  regulatory bodies 13.201
  regulatory framework 13.199–13.200
  reserved alternative investment funds (RAIFs) 13.197–13.198
    closed-ended 13.202, 13.215
    governance 13.210
    investment strategy 13.204–13.205
    investors 13.211, 13.214
    legal vehicles 13.202–13.203
    leverage 13.198, 13.206–13.207
    loans, power to grant 13.204
    management 13.212–13.213
    marketing 13.215–13.218
    non-professional investors 13.214
    number of investors 13.211
    open-ended 13.202, 13.215
    professional investors 13.214
    reporting requirements 13.219
    risk concentration limits 13.209
    risk containment 13.204, 13.225
    rules of management 13.205
    valuation and price 13.208

Italy – cont.
  società di gestione del risparmio (SGRs) 13.212, 13.215
    anti-money laundering regulations 13.232
    authorisation 13.220–13.221
    conflicts of interest 13.227
    delegation of functions 13.228–13.232
    independence and autonomy principle 13.224
    key requirements 13.220–13.232
    risk management 13.225
  società di intermediazione mobiliare (SIMs) 13.215
  taxation 13.233–13.245
  transparency 13.201, 13.226

J

Jersey
  administrators 3.14, 3.34–3.39, 3.54
  AIFMD provisions 3.7, 3.9, 3.21, 3.22
  alternative investment funds (AIFs) 3.20, 3.27–3.29
  AIF Code 3.27
  anti-money laundering 3.34
  closed-ended funds 3.20, 3.23, 3.36, 3.46, 3.47, 3.65, 3.77
  collective investment funds 3.56–3.58
  Common Reporting Standard (CRS) 3.87
  companies 3.13, 3.78–3.79, 5.6
  company law 3.16
  incorporated cell companies (ICCs) 3.46, 3.51, 3.62, 3.76, 3.79
  protected cell companies (PCCs) 3.46, 3.51, 3.62, 3.76, 3.79
  regulated funds 3.24, 3.62
  unregulated funds 3.23
  Control of Borrowing (Jersey) Order (COBO) 3.22, 3.46, 3.57
  custodians 3.14, 3.36, 3.54
  customary law 3.15
  European Union and 3.7–3.9, 3.12
  expert funds 3.20–3.21, 3.32, 3.36, 3.38, 3.58, 3.63–3.67
    fast-tracked 3.59–3.62, 3.64
    investors 3.67
    key requirements 3.66
  finance industry 3.3–3.9, 3.18–3.19
  Financial Services (Jersey) Law (FSJL) 3.22
  fund vehicles
    companies 3.16, 3.23–3.24, 3.76, 3.78–3.79, 5.6

525

Index

Jersey – *cont.*
  fund vehicles – *cont.*
    generally   8, 14, 3.23, 3.76–3.77
    limited partnerships   3.16, 3.23–3.24, 3.46, 3.51–3.52, 3.76, 3.80–3.82
    open-ended companies   14.8
    unit trusts   3.16, 3.23–3.24, 3.46, 3.51–3.52, 3.62, 3.76, 3.83
    unregulated funds   3.50–3.54
  generally   1.4, 3.1–3.9
  high value/low footprint businesses   3.19
  historical background   3.10–3.14
  incorporated cell companies (ICCs)   3.46, 3.51, 3.62, 3.76, 3.79
  investment managers
    alternative investment fund managers (AIFMs)   3.27–3.29
    expert funds   3.66
    generally   3.21
    independent management companies (ManCos)   3.5–3.6, 3.20
    listed funds   3.68
    local   3.5, 3.40–3.45
    regulation   3.34–3.39
    special purpose investment managers   3.41
    taxation   3.14
  investor protection   3.25
  Jersey eligible investor funds (JEIFs)   3.20–3.21, 3.32–3.33, 3.36, 3.38, 3.58, 3.70–3.71
    definition of eligible investor   3.48
    investor categories   3.71
    key requirements   3.70
  Jersey Financial Services Commission (JFSC)   3.20, 3.25, 3.27
  know your customer regulations   3.34
  legal system   3.10, 3.15–3.17
  limited liability partnerships   3.46
  limited partnerships   3.13, 3.16, 3.23–3.24, 3.46, 3.51, 3.76, 3.80–3.82, 14.8
    incorporated limited partnerships   3.16, 3.46, 3.82
    Jersey limited partnerships   3.16
    legislation   3.16
    regulated funds   3.24, 3.62
    separate limited partnerships   3.16, 3.46, 3.82
    unregulated funds   3.23, 3.51–3.52
  listed funds   3.20, 3.32–3.33, 3.38, 3.58, 3.59–3.62, 3.68–3.69
    fast-track   3.68
    investors   3.69
    key requirements   3.68
  local investment managers   3.5, 3.40–3.45
  open-ended funds   3.65, 3.77

Jersey – *cont.*
  partnership law   3.16
  prime brokers   3.36
  private funds   3.20, 3.22, 3.29, 3.36, 3.57–3.58
    key requirements   3.46
  Privy Council, appeal to   3.17
  promoters   3.39
  protected cell companies (PCCs)   3.46, 3.51, 3.62, 3.76, 3.79
  recognised funds   3.58, 3.72
  regulated investment funds
    annual fee   3.74
    collective investment funds   3.56–3.58
    Control of Borrowing (Jersey) Order (COBO)   3.22, 3.46, 3.57
    expert funds   3.20, 3.32, 3.36, 3.38, 3.58, 3.63–3.67
    generally   3.24–3.29, 3.37, 3.55–3.58, 3.62
    investment managers and service providers   3.37
    investment restrictions   3.73
    Jersey eligible investor funds (JEIFs)   3.20–3.21, 3.32–3.33, 3.36, 3.38, 3.58, 3.70–3.71
    listed funds   3.20, 3.32–3.33, 3.38, 3.58, 3.68–3.69
    private   3.57–3.58
    public   3.57
    recognised funds   3.58, 3.72
    regulatory regime   3.30–3.33, 3.73–3.75
    unclassified funds   3.58, 3.59–3.62
  regulatory regime
    fund vehicles   3.76–3.77
    generally   3.21, 3.25, 3.30–3.33
    investment managers   3.34–3.39
    regulated investment funds   3.30–3.33, 3.73–3.75
    service providers   3.34–3.39, 3.54
    unregulated funds   3.20–3.21, 3.23, 3.50
  safe harbour   3.20
  service providers   3.34–3.39, 3.54
  Stock Exchange (TISE)   3.84
  taxation   3.10, 3.13–3.14, 3.85–3.87, 14.8
  The International Stock Exchange (TISE)   3.84
  three-day approval process   3.20, 3.68
  trust law   3.16
  umbrella companies   3.76
  unclassified funds   3.58, 3.59–3.62
  United Kingdom and   3.8, 3.10
  unit trusts   3.13, 3.16, 3.23–3.24, 3.46, 3.51–3.52, 3.62, 3.76, 3.83

Index

Jersey – *cont.*
  unregulated funds
    eligible investor funds   3.20, 3.47–3.49
    establishing   3.47–3.49
    fund vehicles   3.23, 3.50–3.54
    generally   1.4, 3.20–3.21, 3.23, 3.30, 3.36–3.37, 3.50
    managers   3.36–3.37
    notification only requirement   3.47–3.49
    residence of functionaries   3.54
Joint ventures
  alternative investment funds (AIFs)   10.30–10.32

L

Legal advisers
  generally   6.4, 6.62
Letter box entity
  delegation of AIFM functions to   10.253–10.254
Leverage
  funds of hedge funds   16.27
  hedge funds' ability to use   1.4
  prime brokers   6.45, 6.58, 7.6, 7.10
Licensed mutual funds
  Cayman Islands   2.28, 2.30, 2.42, 2.44
Limited liability companies
  Cayman Islands   2.22–2.24, 4.7
  Malta   4.342
  Netherlands   13.294–13.295, 13.303–13.304
Limited partnerships
  British Virgin Islands   2.65, 2.66, 2.109, 2.116–2.119
    approved manager regime   2.128
  Cayman Islands   2.17–2.21, 2.52, 4.122.12, 5.24, 14.8
  companies compared   5.17, 5.22–5.25
  confidentiality   5.20
  creation   5.17
    by conduct   5.17
  England and Wales   5.24
  exempted   2.12, 2.17–2.21, 2.52
  fiduciary obligations   5.22–5.23
  generally   5.1, 5.15–5.24
  general partners   5.19, 5.23, 6.5, 6.6
  general partnerships compared   5.18
  Guernsey   3.107, 3.114–3.117, 3.150, 3.152, 14.8
    legal personality   3.116
  Hong Kong-managed funds   4.5, 4.8
  incorporated   5.17
  as investment vehicles   5.17

Limited partnerships – *cont.*
  Ireland   4.119, 4.140–4.142, 4.151
  Jersey   3.13, 3.16, 3.23–3.24, 3.46, 3.76, 3.80–3.82, 14.8
    incorporated limited partnerships   3.16, 3.46, 3.82
    Jersey limited partnerships   3.16
    regulated funds   3.24, 3.62
    separate limited partnerships   3.16, 3.46, 3.82
    unregulated funds   3.23, 3.51–3.52
  legal personality   5.24
  limited partners   5.19–5.20, 5.23
    taxation   5.21
  Malta   4.348–4.352
  master-feeder structure   5.1, 5.21, 5.31–5.37
  Netherlands   13.294–13.295, 13.300–13.302
  nominees, investment through   5.20
  offshore   5.15
  partnership agreements   5.17
  Scotland   5.24
  Singapore   4.461, 4.469–4.473
  structure   5.15
  Switzerland   4.489, 4.498–4.501
  taxation   5.21
  United States   5.24, 14.8
Liquidity
  funds of hedge funds   16.27
  hedge fund portfolios   1.4
  UCITS   12.145
Listed funds
  Jersey   3.20, 3.32–3.33, 3.38, 3.58, 3.68–3.69
Listing sponsors
  role   6.62
Lock-up
  meaning and purpose   15.32–15.35
Long position   1.3
Long-short technique   1.3
Luxembourg
  AIFMD   4.222, 4.265–4.267
  alternative investment funds (AIFs)   4.222, 4.230, 4.239, 4.266, 4.305–4.306
    generally   4.217–4.218
    unregulated special limited partnerships   4.305–4.306
  auditors   4.275–4.276
  central administration tasks   4.272–4.274
  definition of hedge funds   4.206–4.207
  depositaries   4.268–4.271
  fonds commun de placement (FCP)
    generally   4.225
    investors' rights   4.238–4.241
    legal concept   4.226–4.227

527

Index

Luxembourg – *cont.*
  fonds commun de placement (FCP) – *cont.*
    management company
      role   4.228–4.232
      rules of operation   4.233–4.237
  funds of hedge funds   4.287, 4.300–4.301
  indirect investment   14.13
  management companies   4.263–4.264
    fonds commun de placement
      (FCP)   4.228–4.232
    Newcits   4.277–4.280
  Part II funds
    borrowing   4.284, 4.286
    derivative financial instruments   4.277, 4.285–4.286
    generally   4.217–4.218, 4.265, 4.281
    investment in other UCIs   4.287
    risk diversification   4.281, 4.282
    short sales   4.283
  private equity   4.219–4.220
  real estate funds   4.217–4.218
  regulatory framework   4.215–4.224
    origin   4.208–4.214
  reserved alternative investment funds (RAIFs)
    eligible investors   4.288, 4.292
    generally   4.223, 4.265, 4.302–4.304
    taxation   4.317–4.318
  retail investors   4.277–4.287
  service providers   4.263–4.276
  size of hedge fund industry   4.201–4.205
  société d'investissement à capital fixe (SICAF)   4.225
  société d'investissement à capital variable (SICAV)   14.8
    available corporate types   4.244–4.248
    generally   4.225
    legal concept   4.242–4.243
    management   4.251–4.254
    variable share capital   4.249–4.250
  société d'investissement en capital à risque (SICAR)   4.219–4.220
  specialised investment funds (SIFs)
    borrowing   4.298
    derivative financial instruments   4.299
    eligible investors   4.288, 4.292
    generally   4.221, 4.293–4.295
    risk diversification   4.296
    short sales   4.297
    taxation   4.317–4.318
  taxation
    of investment funds   4.317–4.320
    of investors   4.321–4.323
  UCITS   4.215–4.216
    Newcits   4.277–4.280
  umbrella funds   4.255–4.262, 4.287

Luxembourg – *cont.*
  venture capital funds   4.217–4.218
  well-informed investors
    definition   4.288–4.292
    RAIFs   4.288, 4.292
    SIFs   4.288, 4.292

M

Mainstream funds
  fee structure   16.5–16.6
  hedge funds compared   16.2–16.8
  long-only bias   16.7
  relative performance   16.2–16.4
  volatility   16.8

Malta
  administrators   4.405–4.407, 4.437
  AIFMD   4.332, 4.371–4.376, 4.377–4.379, 13.247, 13.250–13.257
    passporting provisions   13.262–13.265
  anti-money laundering   4.422–4.423
  AUM thresholds   4.373
  collective investment schemes (CIS)
    alternative investment funds   4.335, 4.368–4.369, 4.370, 4.377–4.382, 13.249
    authorisation   4.361–4.398, 13.248
    definition   4.334–4.339
    disclosure to investors   13.267, 13.273, 13.288
    eligible investors   13.249
    foreign   13.250–13.290
    fund vehicles   4.340–4.360
    licensing requirement   4.337
    loan funds   13.249
    Maltese   13.248–13.249
    notified alternative investment funds (NAIFs)   4.383–4.387, 13.249
    private   4.337, 4.388
    professional investor funds (PIFs)   4.370–4.376, 4.386–4.387, 13.249
    regulatory regime   4.332–4.333, 13.246–13.247
    retail alternative investment funds   4.368–4.369, 13.249
    risk spreading   4.336
    UCITS   4.335, 4.361–4.367, 4.415, 13.247, 13.249–13.252
  corporate governance   4.413, 4.437
  custodians   4.408–4.411, 4.437
  experienced investors (ExpIFs)   4.374, 4.380
  extraordinary investors (ExtraIFs)   4.374, 4.380

Index

Malta – *cont.*
  fund authorisation   4.361–4.398
    fast track   4.371
  fund managers   4.399–4.402, 4.437
  fund vehicles
    companies   4.341–4.347
    contractual funds   4.359–4.360
    foundations   4.357–4.358
    generally   4.340
    investment company with fixed share capital (INVCO)   4.342–4.343
    limited partnerships   4.348–4.352
    société d'investissement à capital variable (SICAV)   4.342–4.346
    unit trusts   4.353–4.356
  generally   4.324–4.328
  growth of hedge fund industry   4.329–4.331
  high net worth individuals   4.370–4.387
  licensing requirement   4.332
  Malta Financial Services Authority (MFSA)   4.329, 13.246
  marketing
    definition   13.250–13.257
    EU AIFMs   4.414–4.418, 13.259, 13.261–13.272, 13.281–13.284
    foreign hedge funds   13.250–13.290
    generally   4.414–4.418
    non-EU AIFMs   13.259–13.260, 13.273–13.276, 13.285–13.289
    prior notification or authorisation   13.250, 13.258–13.260
    professional clients   13.259
    regulatory reporting and transparency   13.281–13.283, 13.285–13.287
    retail investors   13.259, 13.277–13.279, 13.290
    reverse solicitation   13.251, 13.254
  MiFID   4.332, 9.90, 13.249, 13.251, 13.252, 13.256, 13.279
  prime brokers   4.412
  professional investors
    marketing   13.259
    professional investor funds (PIFs)   4.370–4.376, 13.249
  qualifying investors (QIFs)   4.374–4.375, 4.380
  regulatory regime   4.332–4.333, 13.246–13.247
  retail investors   4.363–4.369, 13.259, 13.277–13.279, 13.290
  Stock Exchange   4.419–4.421
  taxation   4.424–4.437, 13.291
  trustees   4.408–4.411
  UCITS   4.335, 4.361–4.367, 4.415, 13.247, 13.249–13.252

Managed accounts   16.23
Management fees
  amount   1.4, 6.33, 6.36, 15.6–15.7
  calculation   6.36
  generally   1.4, 6.18–6.20, 15.6–15.7
  investment managers   6.18–6.19, 6.33, 6.36, 15.6–15.7
Manager led products (MLPs)
  Guernsey   3.106, 3.138–3.140
Managers *see* Investment managers
Manipulating devices
  market abuse   1.9
Manipulating transactions
  market abuse   1.9
Margin financing
  prime broker's role   7.6
Market abuse
  benchmarks   9.69, 9.119
  case law   9.134–9.151
  civil regime   9.68–9.115
  COBS 12.4   9.61
  Code of Market Conduct (CoMC)   9.59–9.60
  criminal regime   9.116–9.151
  disciplinary powers   9.64–9.67
  Disclosure and Transparency Rules (DTR)   9.59–9.60
  EU Directive (EU MAD)   9.56, 9.59, 9.81
  EU Market Abuse Regulation (EU MAR)   9.56–9.57, 9.59, 9.62–9.63, 9.69–9.115
  extra-territorial dimension   9.73
  false or misleading impressions   9.118–9.119
  false or misleading statements   9.118–9.119
  Financial Conduct Authority   9.58–9.63
    Code of Conduct (COCON)   9.62, 9.131–9.133
    Principles for Businesses (PRIN)   9.62, 9.125–9.129
    Statements of Principle and Code of Practice for Approved Persons (APER)   9.62, 9.130
  generally   1.9, 9.56–9.63
  inside information   9.74–9.76, 9.82–9.92
    case law   9.143–9.151
  insider dealing
    case law   9.134–9.142
    civil regime   9.77–9.92
    criminal   9.116–9.117
  insider lists   9.104–9.108
  investment recommendations   9.109–9.112
  liability, generally   1.9
  market manipulation
    civil regime   9.69, 9.99–9.103

Index

Market abuse – *cont.*
  market manipulation – *cont.*
    concealing facts   9.119–9.120
    criminal   9.118–9.124
    false or misleading impressions   9.118–9.119
    false or misleading statements   9.118–9.119
    manipulating devices   1.9
    manipulating transactions   1.9
  market soundings   9.93–9.98
  MiFID   9.71
  Model Code   9.59–9.60
  multilateral trading facilities (MTFs)   9.56, 9.68
  organised trading facilities (OTFs)   9.56
  regulation, generally   1.9
  SUP 15.10   9.61
  SYSC 18   9.61
  United States, concealing facts   9.119–9.120
  unlawful disclosure   9.82–9.85
  whistleblowing   9.113–9.115

Marketing and promotion
  see also Offering documents; Prospectus
  AIFMD provisions
    definition of marketing   10.118–10.121
    domicile of investors   10.118, 10.122
    EU AIFs   10.128–10.137
    European passport regime   10.154–10.160, 10.268
    national private placement regimes (NPPRs)   10.36, 10.144–10.153
    non-EU AIFs   10.138–10.148
    passive or reverse enquiry/solicitation   10.119–10.120
    professional investors   10.123–10.127
    retail investors   10.123–10.127
    United Kingdom   10.121
  Australia
    controlled foreign companies (CFCs)   13.20–13.25
    corporate CIVs   13.9
    disclosure and reporting obligations   13.2, 13.8
    foreign hedge funds   13.10–13.18
    framework, generally   13.1–13.3
    limited partnership CIVs   13.9
    promoters of foreign funds   13.12–13.18
    register of foreign funds   13.10–13.11
    taxation   13.19–13.25
  China
    background   13.26–13.30
    filing   13.33, 13.41, 13.44–13.45
    foreign hedge funds   13.68–13.83

Marketing and promotion – *cont.*
  China – *cont.*
    fund managers, registration   13.33, 13.41–13.43
    future trends   13.79–13.83
    liability for illegal activities   13.61
    licensing for marketing private funds   13.54–13.56
    PFM WFOE regime   13.62–13.67
    private fund manager (PFM) funds   13.62–13.67
    private funds   13.27–13.30, 13.36–13.40, 13.50–13.61
    QDII   13.71–13.73
    QDLP   13.74–13.78
    qualified investors   13.46–13.49, 13.53, 13.67, 13.70
    regulatory framework   13.36–13.40
    restrictions   13.57–13.60
    supervising authorities   13.29, 13.31–13.35
    wholly foreign-owned enterprises (WFOE)   13.62–13.67
  France
    eligible investors   13.91–13.94
    EU passporting provisions   13.90, 13.98–13.102
    foreign hedge funds   13.97–13.109
    fund structures   13.88–13.90
    investment restrictions   13.95–13.96
    regulatory framework   13.84–13.87
    tax issues   13.110–13.113
    what constitutes marketing   13.105–13.109
  Germany
    distribution restrictions   13.133–13.134
    establishing funds   13.120–13.125
    foreign hedge funds   13.145–13.157
    fund rules   13.126
    hedge fund structure   13.116–13.119
    investor qualification   13.117
    limitation of investment activities   13.129–13.132
    manager qualifications   13.127–13.128
    regulatory framework   13.114–13.115
    transparency mechanisms   13.135–13.136
  Hong Kong
    advertisements   13.158, 13.163
    Code of Conduct   13.191–13.196
    Companies (Winding Up and Miscellaneous Provisions) Ordinance (C(WUMP)O)   13.161, 13.168–13.177
    corporate partnership hedge funds   13.158–13.159
    dealing in securities   13.184–13.188

Index

Marketing and promotion – *cont.*
  Hong Kong – *cont.*
    emails   13.163
    licensing requirement   13.158,
         13.183–13.189, 13.191–13.196
    limited partnership hedge funds   13.159
    managed accounts   13.190
    oral communication   13.163
    presentations or meetings in person in Hong Kong   13.158, 13.188–13.189
    private placement   13.159, 13.164, 13.167, 13.168, 13.175, 13.178–13.182
    professional investors   13.159–13.160, 13.165–13.167, 13.185
    regulated activities   13.184–13.187, 13.192
    reverse solicitation   13.176
    safe harbours   13.168–13.177
    Securities and Futures Ordinance (SFO)   13.161–13.167
    share offers   13.168–13.177
    telephone calls   13.163
  Italy
    EU passporting provisions   13.217
    regulatory bodies   13.201
    regulatory framework   13.199–13.200
    reserved alternative investment funds (RAIFs)   13.197–13.198, 13.215–13.218
    società di gestione del risparmio (SGRs)   13.215
    società di intermediazione mobiliare (SIMs)   13.215
  Malta
    definition of marketing   13.250–13.257
    disclosure to investors   13.267, 13.273, 13.288
    EU AIFMs   4.414–4.418, 13.259, 13.261–13.272, 13.281–13.284
    EU passporting provisions   13.262–13.265
    foreign hedge funds   13.250–13.290
    generally   4.414–4.418
    Maltese hedge funds   13.248–13.249
    non-EU AIFMs   13.259–13.260, 13.273–13.276, 13.285–13.289
    prior notification or authorisation   13.250, 13.258–13.260
    professional clients   13.259
    regulatory framework   13.246–13.247
    regulatory reporting and transparency   13.281–13.283, 13.285–13.287
    retail investors   13.259, 13.277–13.279, 13.290

Marketing and promotion – *cont.*
  Malta – *cont.*
    reverse solicitation   13.251
  Netherlands
    aangewezen staten regime   13.317
    de minimis exemption   13.310, 13.312
    foreign hedge funds   13.306–13.317, 13.320
    generally   13.292–13.293
    investment restrictions   13.318
    licence requirement   13.306
    light AIFMs   13.310–13.313
    national private placement regime (NPPR)   13.316
    passive marketing   13.320
    prospectus requirement   13.307
    qualified investors   13.306–13.307
    retail investors   13.306, 13.308–13.309, 13.311
    Super ManCos   13.315
  Singapore
    extra-territorial effect   13.345
    licensing requirement   13.343–13.346
    marketing requirements   13.343–13.346
    regulatory framework   13.325–13.342
  Spain
    EU passporting provisions   13.361
    foreign hedge funds   13.361–13.364
    Spanish funds of hedge funds   13.360
    Spanish hedge funds   13.357–13.359
  Switzerland
    distribution, concept of   13.372–13.374, 13.380–13.385
    generally   13.371
  UCITS   12.47–12.48
  United Kingdom
    approved communications   9.31
    authorised persons   9.31
    CIS Exemptions Order, generally   9.38
    collective investment schemes   9.35–9.55
    documents   9.33
    exemptions   9.34–9.54
    Financial Promotion Order   9.53–9.54
    financial promotion restriction   9.30–9.34
    group companies   9.44
    high net worth companies, etc   9.47–9.48
    high net worth individuals   9.45–9.46
    investment professionals   9.39–9.40
    invitation or inducement   9.30, 9.33, 9.35
    non-real-time communications   9.41–9.43

Index

Marketing and promotion – *cont.*
  United Kingdom – *cont.*
    oral communications 9.33
    overseas, communications originating 9.31
    overseas marketing 9.55
    penalties for contravention 9.32
    promotion of collective investment schemes 9.35–9.37
    real-time communications 9.41–9.43
    sophisticated investors 9.49–9.51
    unregulated CIS 9.43
  United States
    accredited investors 11.93–11.94
    disqualified issuers 11.96
    Exchange Act 11.98, 11.101–11.104, 11.105–11.110
    foreign broker exemption 11.105–11.110
    issuer exemption 11.98, 11.99–11.100
    non-US managers 11.97–11.110
    private offering exemption 11.93, 11.95
    private placement 11.93, 11.97–11.98, 11.112
    SEC Regulation D 11.13, 11.66, 11.92–11.96, 11.97
    State 'blue sky' laws 11.111–11.112

Market soundings
  market abuse regulations 9.93–9.98

Master-feeder structure
  advantages 4.13, 14.21
  AIFMD provisions 10.24, 10.27, 10.60, 10.128, 10.129, 10.136, 10.146, 10.171, 10.182–10.183
  British Virgin Islands 2.65
  Cayman Islands registered mutual funds 2.35
  feeder fund 4.11, 5.32
    directors 5.36
  fees 4.11, 5.33
  flexibility 4.13, 5.36
  generally 5.1, 5.21, 5.31–5.37
  Hong Kong-managed funds 4.5, 4.10–4.13
  investment management agreement 5.35
  master fund 4.11, 5.32
    general partner 5.36
  parallel structure compared 14.19–14.23
  shareholder rights 5.34
  single-legged 4.11
  tax-transparent and tax-opaque vehicles 5.32
  UCITS 12.45, 12.49–12.50
  US tax-exempt investors 14.19–14.23

Master netting agreement
  generally 7.26

Mauritius
  indirect investment 14.13

Model Code 9.59–9.60

Money laundering *see* **Anti-money laundering**

Monitoring trades
  administrators' function 6.38–6.41

Multilateral trading facilities (MTFs)
  market abuse 9.56, 9.68

Multi-manager funds *see* **Funds of hedge funds**

Mutual funds
  British Virgin Islands 2.65
    borrowing 2.90
    definition 2.66
    in or from within the BVI 2.107
    incorporated, formed or organised outside the BVI 2.108
    investment restrictions 2.89
    Mutual Fund Annual Return (MFAR) 2.98
    offering documents 2.91–2.94, 2.104
  Cayman Islands 2.7–2.11
    accounts 2.40, 2.43, 2.45
    administered mutual funds 2.28, 2.31–2.32, 2.42, 2.44
    borrowing 2.39
    choice of vehicle 2.13
    equity interests 2.8–2.9
    exempted companies 2.14–2.16
    exempted mutual funds 2.28, 2.36, 2.42
    fees 2.43
    Hong Kong-managed funds 4.5
    licensed mutual funds 2.28, 2.30, 2.42, 2.44
    offering documents 2.30, 2.37–2.38, 2.43
    promoter 2.30, 2.31
    registered mutual funds 2.28, 2.29, 2.33–2.35
    types of fund vehicle 2.12–2.27
    unit trusts 2.12, 2.26–2.27, 2.30, 2.52
  definitions 2.8–2.10, 2.66
  equity interests 2.8–2.9
  exclusions 2.10
  Netherlands 13.294–13.299
  United Kingdom 14.92–14.93
  United States 1.4

N

National private placement regimes (NPPRs)
  EU regulation 2.146
  marketing AIFs 10.36, 10.144–10.153

Index

Net asset value (NAV)
  calculating   6.33–6.35
Netherlands
  AIFMD   13.299, 13.302, 13.307–13.316, 13.319
    passporting provisions   13.309, 13.314–13.316
  co-operatives   13.294–13.295, 13.305
  fund structures   13.294–13.295
  indirect investment   14.13
  light AIFMs   13.310–13.313
  limited liability companies (BVs)   13.294–13.295, 13.303–13.304
  limited partnerships (CVs)   13.294–13.295, 13.300–13.302
  marketing
    aangewezen staten regime   13.317
    de minimis exemption   13.310, 13.312
    foreign hedge funds   13.306–13.317, 13.320
    generally   13.292–13.293
    investment restrictions   13.318
    licence requirement   13.306
    national private placement regime (NPPR)   13.316
    passive   13.320
    prospectus requirement   13.307
    qualified investors   13.306–13.307
    retail investors   13.306, 13.308–13.309, 13.311
  MiFID   13.315
  mutual funds (FRGs)   13.294–13.299
  remuneration requirements   13.319
  Super ManCos   13.315
  taxation   13.321–13.324
  UCITS   13.293
Newcits
  Luxembourg   4.277–4.280
Notified alternative investment funds (NAIFs)
  Malta   4.383–4.387, 13.249

O

OECD
  Base Erosion and Profit Shifting (BEPS) project   3.5, 3.166–3.167, 14.13
  Common Reporting Standard (CRS)
    British Virgin Islands   2.133, 2.140–2.145
    Cayman Islands   2.54–2.55
    Guernsey   3.161
    Jersey   3.87
    tax considerations   14.7

OECD – *cont.*
  Multilateral Competent Authority Agreement   3.162
  Multilateral Convention on Mutual Administrative Assistance in Tax Matters   3.160
Offering documents
  AIFMD provisions   10.69, 10.118, 10.121, 10.170, 10.223
  asset allocations   6.39
  British Virgin Islands   2.91–2.94, 2.104
  Cayman Islands   2.30, 2.37–2.38, 2.43
  investment policy   6.39
Offshore companies
  generally   5.2, 5.4, 5.6
Offshore funds
  central management and control   14.28–14.49
  taxation   5.4
    UK *see* **United Kingdom**
  UK definition   14.92–14.96
  unregulated status   1.4, 1.10
Offshore limited partnerships   5.15
Open-ended investment companies (OEICs)
  generally   4.1
  Hong Kong-managed funds   4.12
Options
  UK regulatory regime   9.5
Organised trading facilities (OTFs)
  market abuse   9.56
Over the counter market
  Hong Kong licensing regime   4.32–4.37
  investment in   1.4
Overseas persons
  UK regulatory regime   9.22–9.24

P

Parallel structure
  master-feeder structure compared   14.19–14.23
Partnerships
  general partnerships   5.18
  limited *see* **Limited partnerships**
  mutual funds   2.8
Passive foreign investment company (PFIC)
  United States   14.17
Performance fees
  amount   5.6–5.13
  calculation   6.33, 6.36, 15.6–15.25
  equalisation
    adjustment   15.25
    deficit subscription   15.24, 15.25
    factor/depreciation deposit   15.24

Index

Performance fees – *cont.*
  equalisation – *cont.*
    generally   15.20–15.22
    premium subscription   15.24, 15.25
    simple method   15.23
  generally   15.6–15.9
  high-water mark   15.10–15.12
  investment managers' role   6.18, 6.20
  series method   15.14–15.19

Placing agents/distributors
  role   6.62

Prime brokers
  choice of   6.44, 6.50–6.51, 7.9, 7.33
  clearing and settling trades   6.40, 6.45, 6.52–6.54, 7.6, 7.10, 7.15–7.16
  consultancy services   7.22
  credit risk   7.13, 7.32
  cross-product margining' structure   7.25–7.26
  custody of assets   6.45, 6.55, 7.6, 7.10, 7.11–7.14, 7.28
  definition   7.3–7.10
  depositary, acting as   10.200, 10.214
  documentation terms and issues   7.27–7.33
  fees   6.61
  financing provision   7.6, 7.10, 7.17–7.19
  Guernsey   3.142
  insolvency and   6.48, 7.27–7.28
  Ireland   4.166
  Jersey   3.36
  leverage provision   6.45, 6.58, 7.6
  Malta   4.412
  number appointed   7.33
  regulation   1.10, 6.47, 6.49
  reporting   6.60, 7.21, 7.31
  role   6.3, 6.16, 6.31, 6.33, 6.38, 6.44–6.49, 7.1–7.2, 7.11–7.26
  securities lending   6.45, 6.56–6.57, 7.17–7.19
  security rehypothecation   7.13, 7.21, 7.29–7.30
  value add services   7.20–7.22

Private equity
  AIFMD   2.147

Private equity funds
  hedge funds compared   1.5

Private funds
  British Virgin Islands   2.65, 2.69, 2.73–2.74, 2.101
    accounts and audit   2.95–2.98
    application for recognition   2.85
    functionaries   2.86–2.88
    offering documents   2.91
    recognition   2.105
    regulatory process   2.105

Private funds – *cont.*
  Guernsey   3.106, 3.134–3.137
  Jersey   3.20, 3.22, 3.29, 3.36, 3.57–3.58
    key requirements   3.46
  Malta   4.337, 4.388

Professional funds
  British Virgin Islands   2.65, 2.69, 2.70–2.72, 2.88, 2.101
    accounts and audit   2.95–2.98
    application for recognition   2.85
    functionaries   2.86–2.88
    offering documents   2.91
    recognition   2.105
    regulatory process   2.105
  Malta   4.370–4.376, 13.249

Promoters
  Australia   13.12–13.18
  Cayman Islands mutual funds   2.30, 2.31
  Jersey   3.39

Promotion *see* **Marketing and promotion**

Proprietary trading
  meaning   15.4

Prospectus
  British Virgin Islands   2.91–2.94
    misrepresentation in   2.100
  UCITS   12.23

Protected cell companies (PCCs)
  Guernsey   3.110–3.112
  Jersey   3.46, 3.51, 3.62, 3.76, 3.79

Public funds
  British Virgin Islands   2.65, 2.69, 2.75, 2.100, 2.106
    accounts and audit   2.95–2.98
    functionaries   2.86–2.88
    prospectus   2.92–2.93, 2.100, 2.106
    registration   2.106
    regulatory process   2.103–2.104

Q

Qualified electing fund (QEF)
  United States   14.17

Qualifying investor alternative investment funds (QIAIFs)
  advantages   4.108–4.109
  Ireland   4.104, 4.107–4.115
  loan originating   4.110

R

Real estate funds
  Luxembourg   4.217–4.218

Index

Recognised foreign funds	
British Virgin Islands	2.69, 2.76
Recognised funds	
Jersey	3.58, 3.72
Redemption	
AIFMD provisions	10.209
fees	15.28–15.31
gate	15.36–15.38
lock-up	15.32–15.35
side pockets	15.47–15.49
suspension	15.42–15.46
withholding on	15.39–15.41
Registered mutual funds	
Cayman Islands	2.28, 2.29, 2.33–2.35
Registered office	
generally	6.42
Regulation	
generally	1.4, 1.6–1.15
offshore funds	1.4, 1.10
prime brokers	1.10, 6.47, 6.49
service providers	1.10
Reporting	
administrators	6.37
AIFMD provisions	10.161–10.167
prime brokers' role	6.60, 7.21, 7.31
Reporting funds	
United Kingdom	14.90, 14.97–14.102
Reserved alternative investment funds (RAIFs) *see* Italy; Luxembourg	
Retail investor alternative investment funds (RIAIFs)	
Ireland	4.104, 4.105–4.106
Reverse solicitation	
Hong Kong	13.176
Malta	13.251, 13.254

S

Safe harbour	
Hong Kong	13.168–13.177
Jersey	3.20
United Kingdom	14.55–14.58
United States	11.95, 11.101, 11.123, 14.9
Securities	
prime brokers's role	
custody of assets	6.45, 6.55, 7.6, 7.10, 7.11–7.14, 7.28
reporting	7.21
securities lending	6.45, 6.56–6.57, 7.17–7.19
rehypothecation	7.13, 7.21, 7.29–7.30
US definition	11.5

Securities and Exchange Commission (SEC) *see* United States	
Segregated portfolio companies (SPCs)	
British Virgin Islands	2.112–2.115
Cayman Islands	2.25, 4.5, 4.16
definition	2.114
Hong Kong-managed funds	4.5, 4.16
Series method	
performance fees	15.14–15.19
Service providers	
administrators	
accepting of investors	6.29–6.31
anti-money laundering obligations	6.30
calculating management fees	6.36
calculating net asset value	6.33–6.35
calculating performance fees	6.33, 6.36
company secretarial functions	6.42
generally	6.22–6.25
monitoring expenses	6.43
monitoring function	6.38–6.41
post-establishment activities	6.32–6.43
pre-establishment activities	6.26–6.28
registered office functions	6.42
reporting	6.37
stock exchange listings	6.43
trades, monitoring and settlement	6.38–6.41
auditors	6.62
brokers, separate	6.45
depositaries *see* Depositaries	
fund directors	6.5–6.10
generally	6.1–6.4
Guernsey	3.103
investment managers	
additional duties	6.17
agents, delegation of duties to	6.21
discretionary management	6.14–6.16
fees	6.18–6.20
generally	6.11–6.13
Investment Management Agreement (IMA)	6.11–6.12, 6.15, 6.21
offshore	6.13
onshore	6.13
regulated entity as investment manager	6.12
Ireland	4.166–4.177
Jersey	3.34–3.39, 3.54
lawyers	6.62
listing sponsors	6.62
Luxembourg	4.263–4.276
placing agents/distributors	6.62
prime brokers	
choice of	6.44, 6.50–6.51, 7.9, 7.33
clearing and settling trades	6.40, 6.45, 6.52–6.54, 7.6, 7.10, 7.15–7.16
consultancy services	7.22

535

Index

Service providers – *cont.*
  prime brokers – *cont.*
    credit risk   7.13, 7.32
    cross-product margining structure   7.25–7.26
    custody of assets   6.45, 6.55, 7.6, 7.10, 7.11–7.14, 7.28
    definition   7.3–7.10
    documentation terms and issues   7.27–7.33
    fees   6.61
    financing provision   7.6, 7.10, 7.17–7.19
    leverage provision   6.45, 6.58, 7.6, 7.10
    number appointed   7.33
    regulation   6.47, 6.49
    reporting   6.60, 7.21, 7.31
    role   6.3, 6.16, 6.31, 6.33, 6.38, 6.44–6.49, 7.1–7.2, 7.11–7.26
    securities lending   6.45, 6.56–6.57, 7.17–7.19
    security rehypothecation   7.13, 7.21, 7.29–7.30
    value add services   7.20–7.22
  regulation   1.10
Shares and stock
  UK regulatory regime   9.5, 9.7
Short selling
  generally   1.3, 1.14
  long-short technique   1.3
  Luxembourg   4.283
  prime brokers   6.56–6.57
  UCITS   12.139–12.144
Side letters
  common provisions   16.36–16.37
  companies   5.14
  generally   16.34–16.35
  meaning   16.34
  negotiating   16.41
  regulators and   16.38–16.40
Side pockets
  meaning and purpose   15.17–15.19
Singapore
  audits   4.458
  capital markets services (CMS) licence   4.456
  collective investment schemes (CIS)   4.452–4.454
  CIS Code   4.453–4.454
  conflicts of interest   4.459
  fund management companies (FMCs)   4.457
  fund vehicles
    companies   4.461, 4.464–4.468
    limited partnerships   4.461, 4.469–4.473
    unit trusts   4.461, 4.474–4.476

Singapore – *cont.*
  generally   4.438–4.441
  growth of finance industry   4.449–4.451
  hedge funds   4.452–4.454
    establishing   4.460–4.463
  institutional investor exemption   13.327, 13.334–13.335
  investment managers
    conduct and capital requirements   4.458
    establishing   4.458–4.460
    regulation   4.455–4.457
    taxation   4.480–4.483
  legal system   4.442–4.448
  marketing requirements   13.343–13.346
    extra-territorial effect   13.345
    licensing   13.343–13.346
    prospectus   13.327
  Monetary Authority of Singapore (MAS)   13.327
  private placement exemption   13.327, 13.331–13.333
  regulatory framework   4.455–4.457, 13.325–13.342
  risk management   4.458
  section 305 exemption   13.327, 13.336–13.342
  service providers   4.459
  Singapore variable capital companies (S-VACCs)   4.463
  small offering exemption   13.327, 13.328–13.330
  taxation
    double taxation agreements   4.478–4.479
    generally   4.477, 4.480–4.483
Société d'investissement à capital fixe (SICAF)
  Luxembourg   4.225
Société d'investissement à capital variable (SICAV)
  Luxembourg   4.242–4.254, 14.8
  Malta   4.342–4.346
Spain
  AIFMD   13.361
    passporting provisions   13.361
  CIS of hedge funds/funds of hedge funds   13.348, 13.350–13.351
    calculation of net asset value   13.350
    diversification   13.350
    investment managers   13.365–13.366
    investors   13.354–13.356, 13.360
    leverage   13.350
    liquidity requirements   13.350
    marketing   13.360
    prospectus and key investor information document   13.350–13.351

Index

Spain – *cont.*
  CIS of hedge funds/funds of hedge funds – *cont.*
    Spanish   13.360
    free investment CIS/hedge funds   13.348, 13.349
      calculation of net asset value   13.349
      investment managers   13.365–13.366
      investors   13.355
      leverage   13.349
      liquidity requirements   13.349
      loans, power to grant   13.349
      prospectus   13.349
    investment managers   13.365–13.366
    investors   13.354–13.356, 13.358–13.359
    legal and regulatory framework   13.347
    marketing
      foreign hedge funds   13.361–13.364
      qualified investors   13.358–13.359
      Spanish funds of hedge funds   13.360
      Spanish hedge funds   13.357–13.359
    taxation   13.352–13.353
Spot commodity contracts
  inside information   9.75
  market manipulation   9.69
Stock borrowing
  prime broker's role   7.6
Stock exchange listings
  administrators' function   6.43
  investor participation in hedge funds   1.4
  voting rights and   5.8
Stock lending
  prime broker's role   7.6
Structuring hedge funds
  drivers   14.4–14.13
  funds' tax position   14.5, 14.8–14.11
  generally   14.14
  investment's tax position   14.5, 14.12–14.13
  investors' tax position   14.5, 14.6–14.7, 14.12
  master-feeder *see* **Master-feeder structure**
Subscription fees
  generally   15.25–15.27
Super ManCos
  Ireland   4.147
  Netherlands   13.315
Suspension
  of calculation of net asset value   15.42
  of right of redemption   15.42–15.46
Switzerland
  alternative investment funds (AIFs)   4.484, 4.506
  anti-money laundering   4.430
  audit firm   4.515–4.517
  CISA   4.488

Switzerland – *cont.*
  CISO   4.488
  distribution
    concept of   13.372–13.374
    independent asset managers   13.378
    non-qualified investors   13.385
    of non-Swiss hedge funds   13.380–13.385
    regulated qualified investors   13.372, 13.380
    treated as not occurring   13.374
    unregulated qualified investors   13.381–13.384
  finance industry, generally   4.484–4.487
  Financial Market Supervisory Authority (FINMA)   4.488
  fund vehicles
    contractual funds   4.489, 4.490–4.492
    investment companies with fixed capital (SICAFs)   4.489, 4.502–4.505
    investment companies with variable capital (SICAVs)   4.489, 4.493–4.497
    limited partnerships   4.489, 4.498–4.501
  hedge funds, generally   4.486–4.487, 4.507
  investment managers
    audit firm   4.515–4.517
    compliance   4.522–4.526
    corporate governance   4.519–4.521
    de minimis exemption   4.510
    financial guarantees   4.535–4.536
    foreign, Swiss branches   4.538–4.545
    governance structure   4.515
    internal control system   4.522–4.526
    internal regulations   4.527–4.529
    legal form   4.518
    licensing   4.508, 4.511–4.512
    regulation   4.507–4.509
    risk management   4.522–4.526
    rules of conduct   4.531–4.534
    taxation   4.560
  investment restrictions   4.506
  legal and regulatory framework   4.487, 4.488, 13.367–13.370
  forthcoming amendments   4.546–4.554, 13.386–13.389
  marketing foreign hedge funds in
    distribution, concept of   13.372–13.374
    generally   13.371
    investor classification   13.375–13.379
    non-qualified investors   13.377, 13.385
    regulated qualified investors   13.372, 13.376, 13.380
  risk management   4.522–4.526
  shareholder regulation   4.513

Index

Switzerland – *cont.*
  taxation   4.555–4.558, 13.390–13.391
    investment managers   4.560
    investors   4.559
  UCITS   4.484, 13.385
  unregulated qualified investors   13.376, 13.381–13.384

T

Taxation
  anti-avoidance rules   14.7
  Australia   13.5, 13.19–13.25
  basic taxation models   14.8
  British Virgin Islands   2.130
  Cayman Islands   2.52–2.56
  companies   5.4
  double tax treaties   4.90, 4.182, 4.189, 4.460, 4.478–4.479, 14.12, 14.13
  filing obligations   14.12
  France   13.110–13.113
  fund management affecting   14.9
  general considerations   14.4–14.13
  Germany   13.137–13.144
  Guernsey
    companies   3.150, 3.151
    generally   3.141–3.150
    income tax   3.149, 3.151–3.154
    international tax initiatives   3.155–3.167
  Hong Kong   4.4, 4.9
  indirect investment   14.13
  investment advisers   14.11
  investment manager, of, generally   14.9, 14.11
  investment's tax position   14.5, 14.12–14.13
  investors' tax position   14.5, 14.6–14.7, 14.12
    reporting considerations   14.7
  Ireland   4.90, 4.178–4.183
  Italy   13.233–13.245
  Jersey   3.10, 3.13–3.14, 3.85–3.87, 14.8
  limited partnerships   5.21
  Luxembourg   4.317–4.323
  Malta   4.424–4.437, 13.291
  master-feeder structure   5.32
  minimising   14.5
  Netherlands   13.321–13.324
  offshore funds   5.4
  onshore companies   5.4
  parallel and master-feeder structures compared   14.19–14.23
  pooled funds   14.7

Taxation – *cont.*
  registration taxes   14.12
  Singapore   4.477–4.483
  Spain   13.352–13.353
  structuring drivers   14.4–14.13
  Switzerland   4.555–4.560, 13.390–13.391
  synthetic investment   14.13
  tax-exempt structuring   14.8
  tax opaque   5.4
    master-feeder structure   5.32
  transfer taxes   14.12
  transparency, tax   14.8, 14.12
  United Kingdom
    bond fund rules   14.103
    capital gains tax   14.59, 14.90, 14.99
    controlled foreign company rules   14.103
    corporation tax   14.62
    definition of offshore fund   14.92–14.96
    income tax   14.90
    insurance company, interests in offshore fund   14.104
    investors   14.89–14.104
    permanent establishment in UK   14.25, 14.60–14.62
    reportable income   14.99–14.102
    reporting funds   14.90
    section 13 rules   14.103
    tax residence *see* **United Kingdom**
    trading in UK   14.59–14.88
    transfer of assets abroad rules   14.103
    UK investment manager exemption   14.9, 14.62, 14.67–14.73
    UK source investment income   14.59
  United States
    passive foreign investment company (PFIC)   14.17
    qualified electing fund (QEF)   14.17
    tax-exempt and taxable investors   14.15–14.18, 14.19
    unrelated business taxable income (UBTI)   14.15–14.16
  unit trusts   5.26
  withholding taxes   14.8, 14.12

The International Stock Exchange (TISE)
  Guernsey   3.146–3.148
  Jersey   3.84

Trading the fund
  deterring   15.32–15.35

Transparency
  AIFMD provisions
    annual reports   10.161–10.167
    disclosure to investors   10.168–10.176
    reporting to regulators   10.177–10.193

Index

Transparency – *cont.*
  Disclosure and Transparency Rules
    (DTR) 9.59–9.60
  funds of hedge funds 16.27
  Germany 13.135–13.136
  Italy 13.201, 13.226
  Malta 13.281–13.283, 13.285–13.287
  structuring fund as tax transparent 14.8, 14.12
Treasury stock
  meaning 5.5
Trustees
  British Virgin Islands 2.123–2.125
  Malta 4.408–4.411
  United States 11.7, 11.11
  unit trusts 2.26–2.27, 5.27
Trusts
  Jersey 3.16
  unit trusts compared 5.29

U

UCITS
  administrative sanctions 12.43
  annual reports 12.24
  authorisation 12.44
  back-to-back loans 12.137
  borrowing by 12.136–12.137
    restrictions 4.97
  collateral 12.87–12.95, 12.134
  counterparty exposure to OTC derivatives 12.65, 12.72–12.74, 12.83–12.95
  cross-border distribution of funds 12.148
  dealing frequency 4.97
  depositaries
    behavioural standards 12.34
    delegation of depositary function 12.37, 12.39–12.41
    duties generally 12.33
    generally 12.11, 12.33–12.34, 12.44
    independent 12.44
    liability of depositary 12.37–12.41
    reporting obligations 12.42
    re-use of assets held in custody 12.36
    who may act as 12.35–12.36
  derivatives
    collateral 12.87–12.95, 12.134
    commitment conversion methodology 12.104–12.109
    commodities 12.58, 12.77
    cover rules for transactions 12.113
    credit 12.75–12.76
    diversification 12.79–12.81

UCITS – *cont.*
  derivatives – *cont.*
    embedded 12.124–12.129
    equivalent cash-settled instruments 12.71
    financial indices 12.78, 12.120–12.123
    global exposure 12.96–12.112, 12.124
    investment in, generally 12.52, 12.56, 12.66–12.67
    investment restrictions 12.82–12.119
    issuer concentration 12.84–12.85, 12.124
    long-short strategy 12.143–12.144
    netting agreements 12.86
    over-the-counter 12.65, 12.72–12.74, 12.83–12.95
    portfolio management techniques 12.130–12.135
    reporting requirements 12.119
    risk management 12.114–12.118
    rules generally 12.71
    total return swaps 12.79–12.81
    VaR calculation 12.110–12.112
  Directives 1.4, 4.98–4.99, 12.4–12.5
    UCITS II 12.6
    UCITS III 12.7–12.9
    UCITS IV 12.10
    UCITS V 12.11–12.43
    UCITS VI 12.146–12.147
  eligible assets 12.55–12.58
  France 13.86–13.88
  future legislative changes 12.146–12.150
  generally 12.1–12.2
  Germany 13.121
  global sale 4.96, 4.103
  historical background 12.3–12.5
  investments
    convertible bonds 12.128
    counterparty exposure to OTC derivatives 12.65, 12.72–12.74, 12.83–12.95
    credit-linked notes 12.128
    deposits with same body 12.64
    derivatives *see* derivatives *above*
    direct exposure to commodities 12.58, 12.77
    economically appropriate transactions 12.132
    eligible assets 12.54, 12.55–12.58, 12.128
    embedded derivatives 12.124–12.129
    exchangeable bonds 12.128
    financial indices 12.120–12.123
    issued by same body 12.60–12.63
    limits 12.59–12.69
    money market instruments 12.56, 12.60–12.63, 12.124–12.129

Index

UCITS – *cont.*
  investments – *cont.*
    not fully paid assets   12.138
    portfolio management tech-
      niques   12.130–12.135
    powers, generally   12.51–12.54
    restrictions   4.97, 12.44, 12.82–12.119
    total return swaps   12.79–12.81
    transferable securities   12.51, 12.56, 12.60–12.63, 12.124–12.129
    UCITS Equivalents   12.69
    units of non-UCITS   12.56
    units of UCITS   12.56, 12.69
  Ireland   4.88, 4.93, 4.95–4.103, 4.150–4.157
  lending   12.138
  leverage   12.134
  liquidity   12.145
  listed on stock exchange   12.45
  Luxembourg   4.215–4.216
    Newcits   4.277–4.280
  Malta   4.335, 4.361–4.367, 4.415, 13.247, 13.249–13.252
  Management Directive   12.7–12.8
  marketing   12.47–12.48
  master-feeder structure   12.45, 12.49–12.50
  meaning   12.3
  Netherlands   13.293
  object of the fund   12.44
  open-ended nature   12.4, 12.44
  passport   4.102, 12.10
  portfolio management tech-
    niques   12.130–12.135
  PRIIPs Regulation   12.149–12.150
  Product Directive   12.7, 12.9
  prospectus   12.23
  regulation   4.98–4.103
  remuneration
    deferral   12.15
    delegates   12.22
    disclosure   12.13, 12.23–12.25
    generally   12.11, 12.12–12.14
    guaranteed variable   12.19
    management companies   12.12–12.14
    material risk takers   12.13, 12.16, 12.20–12.21
    pay out process   12.14
    performance adjustment   12.18
    performance assessment   12.17
    proportionality   12.13, 12.30–12.32
    remuneration committee (RemCo)   12.23, 12.26–12.29
    risk management   12.12
    self-managed funds   12.12
    in UCITS units or equivalent instru-
      ments   12.16

UCITS – *cont.*
  remuneration – *cont.*
    variable   12.15, 12.16, 12.18–12.19
  repos   12.134
  requirements generally   12.44
  reverse repos   12.134
  risk-spreading   4.97, 12.44, 12.59–12.69
  securities lending   12.134
  short selling   4.283, 12.139–12.144
  structuring options   12.45–12.46, 12.49–12.50
  Switzerland   4.484, 13.385
  umbrella structure   12.45
  United Kingdom
    generally   1.4
    regulatory regime   9.15–9.16
UK CDOT *see* **UK FATCA**
UK FATCA (UK CDOT)
  British Virgin Islands   2.132, 2.137–2.139
Umbrella companies
  Jersey   3.76
Umbrella funds
  Hong Kong-managed funds   4.5, 4.14–4.16
  Luxembourg   4.255–4.262, 4.287
  United Kingdom   14.95
Unclassified funds
  Jersey   3.58, 3.59–3.62
Underwriters
  United States   11.7, 11.11
United Kingdom
  AIFMD   10.11–10.12
    Brexit   10.10, 10.269, 13.104
    implementation in UK   10.1
  Alternative Investment Fund Manager Or-
    der   10.11
  Alternative Investment Fund Manager
    Regulations   10.11
  authorised funds   1.4
  bond funds   14.96, 14.103
  Brexit   10.10, 10.269, 13.104
  Cayman Islands IGA   2.54–2.55
  closed-ended funds   14.93
  controlled foreign company rules   14.103
  Criminal Justice Act (CJA)   9.58
    insider dealing   9.116–9.117
  distributing funds   14.90
  Financial Conduct Authority (FCA)   1.1, 1.4, 1.10
  Financial Services Act (FSA)   9.59
    market manipulation   9.118–9.124
  Financial Services and Markets Act (FSMA)   9.3–9.4, 9.56
  Guernsey and   3.88
  Guernsey IGA   3.159

Index

United Kingdom – *cont.*
  insurance company, interests in offshore
    fund   14.104
  introduction   6.1–6.2
  Jersey and   3.8, 3.10
  Limited Partnerships Act   5.16, 5.18
  mutual funds   14.92–14.93
  offshore fund, definition   14.92–14.96
  Offshore Funds (Tax) Regulations   14.89
  Partnership Act   5.16, 5.18
  partnerships   5.24
  penalties for contravention   9.3
  promotion of hedge funds *see* **Marketing and promotion**
  registration of fund managers   1.4, 1.10
  regulatory regime
    administering investments   9.12
    AIFMs   10.41–10.42, 10.53–10.57
    alternative investment funds
      (AIFs)   9.17–9.18
    arranging deals   9.9–9.10
    arranging deals in investments   9.9–9.10
    CIS Exemptions Order   9.38–9.52
    collective investment schemes   9.5
    contracts for difference   9.5
    dealing in investments as principal or agent   9.6–9.8
    debt instruments   9.5
    establishing collective investment schemes   9.19
    exclusions   9.20–9.24
    exempt persons   9.3
    FCA authorisation   1.4, 1.10, 9.3, 9.25–9.29
    futures   9.5
    generally   1.10–1.15, 9.1–9.2
    general prohibition   9.3
    investment advice   9.13–9.14
    investment management   9.11
    managing investments   9.22
    market abuse *see* **Market abuse**
    offshore operators   1.10
    options   9.5
    overseas persons   9.22–9.24
    promotion of collective investment schemes   9.35–9.37
    promotion of hedge funds *see* **Marketing and promotion**
    regulated activities, generally   9.3–9.5
    safeguarding investments   9.12
    sale of body corporate   9.21
    Scope of Permission Notice   9.29
    shares and stock   9.5, 9.7
    specified activities   9.6–9.20
    specified investments   9.5

United Kingdom – *cont.*
  regulatory regime – *cont.*
    UCITS   9.15–9.16
    reporting funds   14.90, 14.97–14.102
    safe harbour rules   14.55–14.58
    section 13 rules   14.103
    service providers, regulation   1.10
    sub-funds   14.95
  taxation
    bond fund rules   14.103
    capital gains tax   14.59, 14.90, 14.99
    controlled foreign company rules   14.103
    corporation tax   14.62
    definition of offshore fund   14.92–14.96
    income tax   14.90
    investment manager exemption   14.9, 14.62, 14.67–14.73
    investors   14.89–14.104
    offshore funds   5.4, 14.24–14.104
    permanent establishment in UK   14.25, 14.60–14.62
    reportable income   14.99–14.102
    reporting funds   14.90
    safe harbour rules   14.55–14.58
    section 13 rules   14.103
    tax residence *see* tax residence *below*
    trading in the UK   14.59–14.88
    transfer of assets abroad rules   14.103
    UK source investment income   14.59
  tax residence
    alternative investment funds (AIFs)   14.55–14.58
    avoiding, guidelines   14.50
    board decisions   14.50
    board meetings   14.33, 14.41, 14.44–14.54
    central management and control   14.28–14.49
    corporation tax   14.25
    delegation of discretion   14.42–14.43
    dual resident companies   14.26
    exceptions   14.26
    execution of documents   14.50
    generally   14.24–14.27
    income tax   14.25
    location of decision-making process   14.44–14.49
    permanent establishment in UK   14.25, 14.60–14.62
    residence of board members   14.50
    restrictions on fund board   14.35–14.41
    telephone and video conferencing   14.50, 14.51–14.54
    trading in UK   14.59–14.88

Index

United Kingdom – *cont.*
  tax residence – *cont.*
    UK advisers   14.50
    withholding tax   14.25
  trading in the UK
    20% test   14.84–14.88
    badges of trade   14.63
    customary remuneration   14.74–14.77
    independent capacity   14.78–14.83
    investment advisors   14.61
    investment manager exemption   14.9, 14.62, 14.67–14.73
    investment transactions   14.61
    permanent establishment   14.61–14.62
    portfolio management   14.64
    tax liability of non-resident funds, generally   14.59–14.62
    what amounts to trading   14.63–14.66
    white list   14.69–14.70, 14.101
  transfer of assets abroad rules   14.103
  umbrella funds   14.95
  unit trusts   1.4

United States
  accredited investor requirements   11.13, 11.94
  Advisers Act   11.1, 11.4, 11.5–11.6, 11.19, 11.36
  associated persons   11.72–11.74
  beneficial owners   11.13–11.15
  Cayman Islands IGA   2.54–2.55
  chief compliance officers   11.37
  clearing houses   11.49
  commodities (CTFC) regulation
    associated persons   11.72–11.74
    CEA administration   11.47
    clearing houses   11.49
    commodity pools *see* commodity pools; commodity pools operators *below*
    commodity trading advisors *see* commodity trading advisors *below*
    derivatives exchanges   11.49
    disclosure regime   11.75–11.85
    futures commission merchants (FCMs)   11.51
    generally   11.46–11.52
    general partners   11.46
    introducing brokers (IBs)   11.51
    investment advisers   11.40, 11.46
    major swap participants (MSPs)   11.51
    managers   11.46
    NFA generally   11.49
    NFA registration   11.68–11.74
    principals   11.71
    promoters   11.46
    record-keeping   11.86

United States – *cont.*
  commodities (CTFC) regulation – *cont.*
    registration of derivatives intermediaries   11.51–11.67
    SEC regulation and   11.48
    swap dealers (SDs)   11.41
    swaps   11.47, 11.49, 14.13
  Commodity Exchange Act (CEA)   11.1, 11.4
    administration   11.47
  Commodity Futures Trading Commission (CFTC)   11.1
  commodity pools
    CEA regulation   11.49–11.50
    CTFC regulation   11.47
    definition   11.47
    generally   11.8–11.9, 11.40–11.41
    limited trading exemption   11.56–11.57
    non-US managers   11.58
    operators *see* commodity pools operators *below*
    primary business engagement test   11.9
  commodity pools operators (CPOs)   11.8, 11.40, 11.50
    annual questionnaire and review   11.85
    annual reports   11.83–11.84
    associated persons   11.72–11.74
    definition   11.54
    disclosure regime   11.75–11.78
    Form CPO-PQR   11.82
    limited trading exemption   11.56–11.57
    principals   11.71
    quarterly reports   11.80–11.81
    record-keeping   11.75, 11.86
    registration and exemptions   11.51, 11.53–11.58, 11.68–11.74
    reporting requirements   11.75, 11.79–11.85
    withdrawal from CFTC/NFA registration   11.87–11.91
  commodity trading advisors (CTAs)   11.40–11.41
    15 client de minimis exemption   11.63–11.66
    associated persons   11.72–11.74
    definitions   11.60
    disclosure regime   11.75–11.78
    principals   11.71
    record-keeping   11.75, 11.86
    registration and exemptions   11.51, 11.59–11.74
    reporting requirements   11.79
    withdrawal from CFTC/NFA registration   11.87–11.91
  Department of Labor (DOL)   11.1
  derivatives exchanges   11.49

Index

United States – *cont.*
  disclosure requirements
    commodity pools operators 11.75–11.78
    commodity trading advisors 11.75–11.78
    ERISA 11.121–11.122
  dividend equivalent payment rules 14.13
  Dodd-Frank Act 11.21, 11.22, 11.48
  Employee Retirement Income Security Act (ERISA)
    cross trades 11.123
    fiduciary duties 11.118
    generally 11.1, 11.4, 11.113–11.117, 11.123
    prohibited transaction rules 11.119–11.120
    reporting and disclosure 11.121–11.122
    soft dollar arrangements 11.123
  exceptions to Investment Company Act 11.7–11.18
  private investment companies 11.12
  Exchange Act 11.1, 11.4, 11.5–11.6
    marketing by non-US managers 11.97–11.110
    Rule 3a4-1 11.98, 11.101–11.104
    Rule 15a-6 11.98, 11.105–11.110
  exemptions, compliance 11.2
  exemptions from regulations, generally 11.2
  Financial Industry Regulatory Authority (FINRA)
    generally 11.124
    Rule 5130 11.125–11.126
    Rule 5131 11.127–11.129
  Foreign Account Tax Compliance Act (FATCA)
    British Virgin Islands 2.132, 2.133–2.136
    Cayman Islands 2.54
    consideration, generally 14.7
    Guernsey 3.159
  foreign private adviser exemption 11.23
  fund managers, regulation 1.10
  fund regulation 11.7–11.18
  futures commission merchants (FCMs) 11.51
  Guernsey IGA 3.159
  introducing brokers (IBs) 11.51
  investment advisers
    chief compliance officers 11.37
    compliance 11.35–11.42
    CTFC regulation 11.40, 11.46
    definition 11.19
    exemptions from registration 11.19–11.21

United States – *cont.*
  investment advisers – *cont.*
    non-US private funds 11.22, 11.23
    non-US SEC-registered 11.35–11.42
    private fund adviser exemptions 11.22, 11.25–11.27
    private fund assets 11.22
    qualifying private funds 11.22
    registration 1.10, 11.19–11.24, 11.28–11.34
    registration, withdrawal from 11.43–11.45
    regulatory regime, generally 11.19–11.21
    reporting advisers 11.21, 11.25–11.27
    US private fund advisers 11.22
    venture capital fund adviser exemption 11.24, 11.25–11.27
  investment companies
    definition 11.7–11.8
    registration 11.7, 11.11
    regulation, generally 11.7
  Investment Company Act (1940 Act) 11.1, 11.4, 11.5–11.6
    exceptions from 11.7–11.18
    registration under 11.7
  investors
    accredited 11.93–11.94
    regulated 11.94
    tax-exempt and taxable 14.15–14.18, 14.19
  issuer exemption 11.98, 11.99–11.100
  knowledgeable employees 11.15
  legislation 11.1, 11.4
  limited partnerships 5.24, 14.8
  managers
    CTFC regulation 11.46
    non-US, commodity pools 11.58
    non-US, marketing by 11.97–11.110
  marketing
    accredited investors 11.93–11.94
    disqualified issuers 11.96
    Exchange Act Rule 3a4-1 11.98, 11.101–11.104
    Exchange Act Rule 15a-6 11.98, 11.105–11.110
    foreign broker exemption 11.105–11.110
    issuer exemption 11.98, 11.99–11.100
    non-US managers 11.97–11.110
    private offering exemption 11.93, 11.95
    private placement 11.93, 11.97–11.98, 11.112
    SEC Regulation D 11.13, 11.66, 11.92–11.96, 11.97
    State blue sky laws 11.111–11.112

543

Index

United States – cont.
- mutual funds   1.4
- no-action letters   11.35
- non-US funds   11.11
- passive foreign investment company (PFIC)   14.17
- principals   11.71
- private fund adviser exemptions   11.22, 11.25–11.27
- private fund assets   11.22
- private investment companies   11.12
- promoters   11.46
- qualified electing fund (QEF)   14.17
- qualified purchasers   11.14, 11.17–11.18
- qualifying private funds   11.22
- regulators generally   11.1–11.4
- regulatory regime
  - compliance with exemptions   11.2
  - generally   11.2
  - investment advisers   11.19–11.21
  - securities generally   11.5–11.6
  - reporting requirements   11.75–11.85
  - ERISA   11.121–11.122
  - exempt reporting advisers   11.25–11.27
- safe harbour rules   11.95, 11.101, 11.123, 14.9
- securities, definition   11.5
- Securities Act   11.1, 11.4, 11.5–11.6
- Securities and Exchange Commission (SEC)   1.1, 1.4, 1.10, 11.1
- securities (SEC) regulation
  - accredited investor requirements   11.13, 11.94
  - beneficial owners   11.13–11.15
  - chief compliance officers   11.37
  - company registration   11.7, 11.11
  - CTFC regulation and   11.48
  - definition of investment company   11.7
  - exceptions from 1940 Act   11.7–11.18
  - generally   1.6, 11.5
  - investment adviser registration   11.19–11.24, 11.28–11.34, 11.43–11.45
  - issuer exemption   11.98, 11.99–11.100
  - knowledgeable employees   11.15
  - marketing regulations   11.92–11.96
  - no-action letters   11.35
  - non-US funds   11.11
  - non-US SEC-registered advisers   11.35–11.42
  - private offering exemption   11.93, 11.95
  - private placement   11.93, 11.97–11.98, 11.112
  - qualified purchasers   11.14, 11.17–11.18

United States – cont.
- securities (SEC) regulation – cont.
  - registration as investment adviser   1.10, 11.19–11.24, 11.28–11.34
  - reporting obligations   11.25–11.27
  - SEC Regulation D   1.10, 11.13, 11.66, 11.92–11.96, 11.97
  - service providers, regulation   1.10
- State blue sky laws   11.4, 11.111–11.112
- swaps
  - back-to-back   14.13
  - CTFC regulation   11.47, 11.49
  - major swap participants (MSPs)   11.51
  - meaning   11.47
  - swap dealers (SDs)   11.41
- taxation
  - parallel and master-feeder structures compared   14.19–14.23
  - passive foreign investment company (PFIC)   14.17
  - qualified electing fund (QEF)   14.17
  - tax-exempt and taxable investors   14.15–14.18
  - unrelated business taxable income (UBTI)   14.15–14.16
- trustees, registration   11.7, 11.11
- underwriters, registration   11.7, 11.11
- unrelated business taxable income (UBTI)   14.15–14.16
- venture capital fund adviser exemption   11.24, 11.25–11.27

Unit trusts
- Australia   13.5
- British Virgin Islands   2.66, 2.109, 2.120–2.122
- Cayman Islands   2.12, 2.26–2.27, 2.30, 2.52, 4.5
- fiduciary obligations   5.27, 5.30
- flexibility   5.27
- generally   5.1, 5.25–5.30
- Guernsey   3.107, 3.118–3.120, 3.150, 3.151
- Hong Kong   4.7
- Hong Kong-managed funds   4.5
- Ireland   4.119, 4.134–4.135
- Jersey   3.13, 3.16, 3.23–3.24, 3.46, 3.51–3.52, 3.62, 3.76, 3.83
- Malta   4.353–4.356
- managers   5.27–5.28, 5.30
- mutual funds   2.12
- private trusts compared   5.29
- rights of unitholders   5.27, 5.29
- Singapore   4.461, 4.474–4.476
- structure   5.25
- taxation   5.26
- trustees   5.27, 5.30
- United Kingdom   1.4

Index

Unregulated funds
  generally   1.4

Unregulated funds (Jersey)
  eligible investor funds   3.20, 3.47–3.49
    definition of eligible investor   3.48
  establishing   3.47–3.49
  fund vehicles   3.23, 3.50–3.54
  generally   1.4, 3.20–3.21, 3.23,
                                       3.36–3.37, 3.50
  managers   3.36–3.37
  notification only requirement   3.47–3.49
  residence of functionaries   3.54

Unrelated business taxable income (UBTI)
  United States   14.15–14.16

V

Venture capital funds
  Luxembourg   4.217–4.218

W

Whistleblowing
  EU MAR   9.113–9.114
  UK regime   9.115

Withholding on redemption
  meaning and purpose   15.39–15.41